W9-CBM-864

Law and the
Life Insurance
Contract

The Irwin Series in
Insurance and Economic Security

DAVIS W. GREGG   Consulting Editor

Law and the Life Insurance Contract

JANICE E. GREIDER, LL.B., F.L.M.I., C.L.U.

Counsel, State Farm Insurance Companies

and

WILLIAM T. BEADLES, D.B.A., C.L.U.

Professor of Insurance, Emeritus
Illinois Wesleyan University
National Insurance Education Adviser
State Farm Insurance Companies

 Third Edition · 1974

RICHARD D. IRWIN, INC.   Homewood, Illinois   60430

Irwin-Dorsey International, London, England   WC2H 9NJ
Irwin-Dorsey Limited, Georgetown, Ontario   L7G 4B3

Third Edition

First Printing, August 1974
Second Printing, November 1974
Third Printing, April 1975

ISBN 0-256-01613-5
Library of Congress Catalog Card No. 74–78156
Printed in the United States of America

To
Morris G. Fuller, C.L.U.

Preface

This book originated as an attempt to present and discuss the major principles of life insurance contract law in terms that would be meaningful to students who do not have a legal background. To that end, we made a definite effort to explain legal concepts in simple, everyday English. In spite of our best efforts, however, we found that some legal terms were indispensable. These we have tried to define as they are introduced, and many have been incorporated parenthetically for the sake of precision—as well as to acquaint the reader with the language of the law.

Some legal terms and phrases have been used again and again. This is because words such as waiver and estoppel, consideration, constructive delivery, and so forth, have an integral place in life insurance as well as in the law. Thus, a person contemplating a career in life insurance will need to make them a part of his working vocabulary even though he does not intend to become a lawyer, just as he must have a working acquaintance with such concepts as reserves, net premiums, and loadings, although he does not intend to become an actuary.

In this third edition, we have added two chapters on group life insurance and one chapter on health insurance law. We have included many new illustrations from recent cases, and hardly a page has escaped some revision. Nevertheless, we have retained the original organization for the main part of the book, beginning with the processes of application and issue, continuing through the many aspects of administration—premium payment, assignments, beneficiary changes, and so forth—and concluding with the settlement of claims. This involves some repetition that might have been avoided with a different approach, but it permits a more realistic handling of the problems that can arise under the contract. Legal solutions differ by reason of the way a problem arises, when it arises, and, often, the jurisdiction in which it arises. It is hoped that some of this ever-changing, evolving pattern is suggested by our combination of explanation, illustration, and repetition, as the life insurance contract is formed and tested, as it operates during the lifetime of the insured, and, finally, as the benefit is paid.

Illustrations in this revised volume, as were those in the previous editions, have been taken from the law itself—the court cases. Recent cases have been used as much as possible. New cases are being decided every day in most of the areas discussed, and it is hoped that the use of relatively current cases will help to convey the present day realities of the subject matter that are sometimes obscured by the many historical references that remain necessary.

We have continued in this edition to use "illustrative cases" at the end of many chapters. It is hoped that this feature of the text will provide the student with a firsthand introduction to legal thinking and legal tradition.

As was true of the earlier editions, we have had the generous cooperation of many people. We particularly want to thank Louis A. Maier, Jr., of Maier and Styles, Ltd., Milwaukee, Wisconsin, who reviewed the revised manuscript in its entirety and made many valuable suggestions. We are indebted also to Margaret Walsh, Manager, Curriculum Development, and other members of the Life Office Management Association Staff, and to George King, FLMI, Claims Consultant, The Prudential Insurance Company of America, Western Home Office.

July 1974   Janice E. Greider
                                               William T. Beadles

Contents

PART III
The Contract in Operation

PART IV
The File Is Closed

Establishing the Proper Payee, 541
The Amount to Be Paid, 547

**PART V
Group Life Insurance**

**PART VI
Health Insurance Contracts**

APPENDIXES

PART I

Introduction

This introductory section consists of three chapters. Chapter 1 gives a general overview of the various sources of law, briefly reviews the major steps in the trial of a case, and outlines the legal framework within which insurance is regulated. Chapter 2 brings together the most basic principles of contract law, and Chapter 3 serves essentially the same purpose in the area of agency law. Together, these three chapters are intended to furnish a general framework which will help in understanding the following, more specific, discussions concerning legal principles that apply to life and health insurance contracts.

Chapter Outline

Chapter 1

Insurance and the Law

IN ITS broadest sense, law may be defined as a system of rules and principles, in the nature of commandments, that comprise a definite and enforceable standard of human conduct. This book is concerned primarily with legal principles that relate to life and health insurance contracts, and thus its major emphasis is on principles of contract law. Anything but the most superficial consideration of this subject, however, leads almost inevitably to many other areas of the law. As an introduction, therefore, this chapter will give a brief overview of the nature and purpose of insurance and the reasons for its regulation, the sources of law, the major steps in the trial of a case, and a brief summary of the legal framework within which insurance is regulated.

A. THE NATURE AND PURPOSE OF INSURANCE

1.1 Risk and Insurance

In simple terms and in its clearest role, insurance is a way of dealing with the risk of economic loss resulting from the happening of a future possible but uncertain (contingent) event. In fire insurance, the risk is the possibility that one's property may be destroyed by fire; in life insurance, the risk is that of economic loss resulting from premature death. A policy from a fire insurance company in the one case, or a life insurance company in the other, affords insurance protection to the policyowner by assuring that if the loss insured against occurs, the insurer will pay a stated or ascertainable amount of money to the insured or (in life in-

5

surance) to someone the policyowner has designated to receive it. An insurance contract, therefore, is sometimes defined as an agreement under which an individual transfers to the insurance company his (the individual's) risk of loss by reason of a specified peril—for example, loss by fire, loss by theft, or loss by early death.

Although the individual transfers to the insurer a true risk of loss, the insurance company is in a different position. The insurer assumes the risk, it is true; but using the science of probability and the law of large numbers, the insurance company can predict, with a considerable degree of reliability, the number (though not, of course, the identities) of the insureds who will suffer losses of a given kind during any specified period. Predictable, also, with considerable accuracy, is the extent of such losses. As a result, premium rates can be developed that will provide the funds necessary to meet expected losses and the expenses of conducting an insurance business over a period of many years. For the insurance company, therefore, uncertainty, or risk, is reduced to a minimum.

1.2 Insurance in Practice

Even though adequate premium rates can be developed within reasonable limits, there will always be some risk in the operation of an insurance plan. Thus, there will be fluctuations in the number of claims actually experienced, by contrast with those that are planned for. There will always be some years in which investment earnings will be higher than estimated and some in which they will be lower. Inflation may increase expenses beyond those estimated, and economic recessions may reduce them below predicted levels. Possible catastrophic losses—as the result of epidemics and wars—must be anticipated and planned for. Providing an effective and solvent insurance service of any kind, therefore, requires a significant degree of technical knowledge and experience, sound business judgment, and contracts of a highly specialized nature. Unfortunately, these requirements have not always been met by organizations formed to provide such services; and the results in losses to the insuring public, as well as damage to the insurance industry itself, have been responsible for the enactment of an unusually extensive body of regulatory insurance law.

B. INSURANCE REGULATION

Insurance is regulated primarily because of the size and importance of the industry. For example, more than $1 trillion of life insurance has been in force on the lives of residents of the United States since 1967; and this figure has been steadily increasing in every year since then. Two out of every three people in this country have some insurance on their lives, and many billions of dollars in life insurance premiums are paid every year. The combined assets of United States life insurance companies are well over $200 billion; and the investments of such companies comprise a significant factor in the economy generally. A business of such size, with personal significance for so many people, obviously constitutes one of the most important private financial institutions in the country.

For these reasons, courts and legislatures speak of insurance as a business "affected with a public interest." This means that it is so significant and of such importance to so many people that it is in the public interest to enact whatever laws are necessary to assure that the great trust vested in insurance companies is not abused.

1.3 The Police Power

Regulatory statutes are said to be enacted under the police power of the state. This is a basic term, and like many basic terms, it is not easy to define. The police power is an essential attribute of the power to govern (that is, sovereignty). By virtue of the police power, the conduct of individuals and the ways in which property may be used are always subject to reasonable regulation by the government if such regulation seems necessary for the public good.

Because insurance is affected with the public interest, it is a proper subject for regulation and control under the police power. As a result, it is strictly regulated by a system of insurance laws that apply to every major phase of the business. The safekeeping of accumulated funds; company solvency; qualified, ethical agents; adequate margins of safety; contracts that safeguard the rights of policyowners and beneficiaries—all these and almost every other aspect of the insurance business have been acknowledged as proper subjects for regulation. To this end, new insurance measures are introduced into state legislatures every year and enacted into law in an almost steady stream.

1.4 Life and Health Insurance Contract Law

State laws specifically concerned with life and health insurance contracts account for an important, though by no means major, part of insurance regulatory law. They also comprise an important part of the law of life and health insurance contracts, but not, in any sense, all of it. Furthermore, statutes must always be read and interpreted in the light of a broad base of general law; and, in this instance, the most important basic law is the general law of contracts.

Fundamentally, the law of life and health insurance contracts rests upon principles that were developed in connection with contracts in general, long before insurance contracts as we know them today had their beginnings. In many respects, insurance contract law follows the same paths and is governed by the same general rules and principles that apply to any other contracts. In other words, a life or health insurance contract is first and primarily a legal agreement.

Insuring agreements, however, may, and often do, provide economic benefits that are far in excess of the premium or premiums paid. Without some special legal safeguards, therefore, it would be quite possible for unscrupulous insurers to issue policies and collect premiums over an extensive period of time without making adequate financial preparation for paying benefits when claims arose. Alternatively, it would be possible for unscrupulous policyowners to use such policies for wagering purposes. To guard against these and other undesirable possibilities, a large body of special insurance law has been developed in which general principles of contract law have been modified—tempered in some instances, strengthened in others—to apply to the special problems of insurance contracts and to make sure that such contracts are written and administered in the best interests of the policyowners and beneficiaries.

1.5 Related Legal Areas

A study of life and health insurance contracts would be extremely limited if it were confined entirely to contract and insurance law. Insurance companies are corporate organizations, and thus transact their business through agents. For this reason, the law of insurance contracts is strongly affected by the law of agency.

Ownership rights under a life insurance contract and the values such a contract represents constitute a unique and highly valuable kind of property. Therefore, the law of property is often involved. Life insurance contracts may be owned by minors and incompetents; they may become a part of the property involved in a divorce action; they may represent a significant part of a decedent's estate. Principles of property law are often as significant or more so than insurance law in resolving problems' in areas such as these.

Finally, forming the life insurance contract is an intricate and important business, and the minds of many people have been busy devising new approaches to it. For this reason, the law of the life insurance contract has traveled at times and for short distances also with the law of torts. (The law of torts is that field of law, exclusive of contract law, that is concerned with actionable civil wrongs, compensable in damages—for instance, legal actions based on negligence.)

In a beginning study, it is enough to have some acquaintance with the major areas of law with which the life insurance contract may be concerned: the law of contracts, agency, property law, and torts. One also needs some understanding of the meaning of law itself—the objectives sought, the methods used, and some notion of how our courts are organized and the way they operate.

C. LAW AND WHERE IT IS FOUND

1.6 What Law Is

In a very general sense, insurance law may be divided into two parts—statutory and case law. Statutory law consists of the enactments of the various legislatures; and, as it applies to insurance, it is primarily concerned with general principles. Thus, statutory law defines, in general terms, the requirements that must be met by people who conduct an insurance business. Case law, by contrast, is made up of the decisions of the courts and is more concerned with whether a particular transaction before the court at a given time satisfies the requirements set out in the statutory law and prior court decisions. Courts consider specific questions that arise, while statutes deal with broad general issues and are intended to govern many different individual activities.

When people speak of a law, they usually mean a specific rule or requirement (a statute, in legal terms) laid down by a legislative body. In the general sense, however, law is a great deal more than just a collection, or even a system, of individual statutes. In addition to state statutes and congressional enactments, it also embraces the broad general philosophies and principles of constitutional law, specific agreements embodied in treaties between nations, decisions of state and federal courts, rules and regulations of innumerable administrative departments of the government, and many general principles of custom and public policy dating back so far that no one can say accurately when they had their origins.

1.7 How Law Is Classified

Public and Private Law. For purposes of discussion or study, law has been variously classified. Thus, it is sometimes divided into public and private law, to distinguish between law that deals with the state in its political or sovereign capacity (public law) and the law that relates to the rights and duties of one individual with respect to another (private law). In this sense, constitutional law, administrative law, and criminal law would be classified as public law. Contract law, the law of torts, and the law of domestic relations are examples of private law.[1]

---

[1] Legislatures often pass laws that are designated as private laws because they relate to some specific matter, such as a claim by a resident against the jurisdiction concerned. Laws such as these may be published in the session laws (that is, the laws enacted during that particular session of the legislature) but they are not included in the general statutes.

Substantive and Adjective Law. Another common classification divides the law into substantive and adjective law. Substantive law goes to the substance of a question and thus defines and regulates rights and obligations. Adjective or procedural law, on the other hand, describes the ways in which these rights and obligations can be enforced. For example, laws defining the obligations and responsibilities of a life insurer are substantive laws. Laws describing legal remedies available to the insurer are adjective or procedural laws. Thus, adjective law is the law of procedure—the way one proceeds to enforce his rights by judicial process.

1.8 Where to Find the Law

It is often necessary to consult a number of sources before all the applicable law on any given subject may be determined. Constitutions must be examined, as well as pertinent statutes, rules and regulations of administrative bodies, reports of court decisions. Sometimes treaties between nations and executive orders and proclamations have an important bearing on the question under consideration.

The constitutions and legislative enactments of the federal and state governments are separately compiled and published, as are the reports of many courts. In fact, the latter occupy many shelves in any law library, and detailed systems have been devised for indexing them. In that connection, it is important to understand the standard form of reference for court cases. The title of the case is given, thus: *Smith* v. *Jones.* Then follow the volume number, the abbreviation for the court or reporter system referred to, and the page on which the case is reported. Thus, the case of *United States* v. *South-Eastern Underwriters Association,* 64 Sup. Ct. 1162, will be found in Volume 64 of the United States Supreme Court decisions, on page 1162.

Other examples may help in understanding this. For instance, one of the famous life insurance cases is that of *Metropolitan Life Insurance Co.* v. *Conway,* 252 N.Y. 449, 169 N.E. 642 (1930). This means that this case is reported in Volume 252 of the Court of Appeals of New York reports on page 449, and in Volume 169 of the North Eastern Reporter on page 642. The case was decided in 1930. Similarly, the case of *Monahan* v. *Metropolitan Life Insurance Co.,* 283 Ill. 136, 119 N.E. 68 (1918) is reported in Volume 283 of the Illinois Supreme Court reports on page 136, and in Volume 119 of the North Eastern Reporter on page 68. It was decided in 1918.

Lawyers also make frequent use of various treatises on the law, such as *Williston on Contracts, Vance on Insurance, Bogert on Trusts,* and "Restatements of the Law," prepared by the American Law Institute, to name only a very few of the general references available. A study of any part of the law requires some acquaintance with these different sources and a knowledge of the significance of each with respect to the others.

D. THE CONSTITUTIONS

In any discussion of law in this country, two kinds of constitutions must be considered—the constitutions of the various states and the Constitution of the federal government. Because of this dual system, it is not enough to know the specific constitutional question that may be concerned in any given question. It is also necessary to bear in mind the basic relationships of the state and federal constitutions to each other.

1.9 What a Constitution Is

General in Nature. A constitution, as we think of it in this country, is a written instrument setting forth in broad, general terms the basic principles that form the legal foundation of a government. Because of its great importance as an instrument of government, the most serious consideration is given to the drafting and adoption of a constitution. In addition, extensive safeguards are incorporated to guard against frequent or ill-considered amendment. As a result, a constitution tends to be permanent in nature, as contrasted with statutes. It is general in language also, rather than specific; and the deliberations involved in the amendment process tend to provide a basic stability to the government that would not otherwise exist.

A Twofold Purpose. A constitution has a twofold purpose. Fundamentally, it describes the structure of the government, defining the extent of its powers and outlining the principles on which it is to operate. Thus, it is customary to provide for three branches of government—legislative, judicial, and administrative—and to establish a system of checks and balances to guard against the supremacy of any one.

In addition, a constitution establishes a system of safeguards and guarantees of basic human rights such as freedom of speech, freedom of worship, and the other great freedoms enumerated, in their most familiar form, in the Bill of Rights of the federal Constitution. A government such as this is said to be a constitutional government, a government of laws and not of men.

1.10 The Federal Constitution

Delegated Powers. Historically, the governing power in this country was exercised individually and separately by the original 13 colonies, which had well-defined existences as political units before there was a federal government of any kind. When representatives of these colonies met together to frame a constitution for a proposed central government, therefore, the authority of the government so formed was delegated to it by the colonies. This idea is summarized in Article X (of the Bill of Rights) of the federal Constitution, as follows: "The powers not delegated to the United States by the Constitution, nor prohibited by it to the States, are reserved to the States respectively, or to the people."

Nevertheless, the federal Constitution was adopted by the people, not the colonies. Thus, the federal government is more than a mere confederation of sovereign states; and it has direct authority over the people themselves within those areas of the governing power delegated to it.

The fact that federal powers are delegated has meaning primarily in areas of legal interpretation, that is, the judicial consideration of the meaning of the federal Constitution, the laws adopted by Congress, and the actions taken by elected and appointed officials. Once it has been established that a power is properly exercisable by the federal government, any acts of that government in that particular area take precedence over the acts of any state or subdivision of a state in the same area.

The "Supreme Law of the Land."   The federal Constitution, the laws of the United States which are enacted under its provisions, and all treaties made under the authority of the United States are declared by the federal Constitution to be the "supreme law of the land." A law, whether federal or state, which violates a provision of the federal Constitution is unconstitutional and void. A court decision, whether federal or state, which violates a right guaranteed by the federal Constitution will be overruled. The act of an administrative officer will be ineffective if it is unconstitutional. A provision of a state constitution will be ineffective if it is in conflict with the Constitution of the United States. Nevertheless, there are many areas in which the state constitutions are supreme.

1.11 State Constitutions

Limitation of Powers.   In one sense, a state constitution performs the same functions for the state that the federal Constitution performs for the United States. That is to say, it outlines the broad general framework of the government and spells out the guarantees of fundamental human rights. It is basic in constitutional law, however, that a state constitution does not grant the power to govern; instead, it functions as a limitation of the power that it recognizes as already existing. The governing power is considered to exist whether there is a constitution or not. Thus, the state constitution has been called the "mandate of a sovereign people to its servants and representatives."

While the federal Constitution enumerates delegated powers, therefore, a state constitution limits powers already acknowledged to exist, powers which in all other respects are unlimited. The practical effects of this concept are enormously significant. For instance, if an act of the state legislature is challenged, it will be considered to be constitutional unless the state constitution (or the Constitution of the federal government) prohibits it. By contrast, an act of Congress must be based upon some affirmative provision of the federal Constitution.

The Supreme Law of the State. Under the federal Constitution, some of the powers that would otherwise be exercisable by the states were given up and delegated to the federal government, as previously pointed out. In all other areas, however, the state constitution constitutes the supreme law of the state. Thus, the Constitution of the United States and the constitutions of the various states—each operative in its respective sphere—taken together provide the broad, fundamental principles on which our government is based.

E. STATUTES

A statute has been defined as "an act of the legislature declaring, commanding, or prohibiting something; a particular law enacted and established by the will of the legislative department of government; the written will of the legislature, solemnly expressed according to the form necessary to constitute it the law of the states."[2]

Collections of compiled laws are often referred to as "revised statutes," and a collection of laws systematically arranged, indexed, revised, and reenacted by the legislature in that form is often referred to as a "code." Thus, an insurance code is a collection of the insurance laws of a given state; the criminal code is a collection of laws relating to crimes; and so on.

Within their respective jurisdictions, both the federal Congress and the state legislatures enact statutes. Statutes are more temporary in nature than provisions found in constitutions; and they are ordinarily expressed in more specific terms, as rules and standards of conduct. In areas of powers granted to the federal government, the Congress of the United States enacts the necessary laws. In areas that are primarily the concern of the individual states, the legislatures of the respective states enact the legislation. If it is not clear whether Congress or the state legislatures have the power to legislate in a given area, the question may be referred to an appropriate court for the necessary decision. This is true also of questions regarding the interpretation of statutes. If there is a question, it is decided by a court.

---

[2] *Black's Law Dictionary* (4th ed.; St. Paul: West Publishing Co., 1951), p. 1581.

F. ADMINISTRATIVE RULES AND REGULATIONS

1.12 The Rule-Making Power

Theoretically our governments, both state and federal, are based upon a clear-cut separation of powers. Under this theory, laws are made only by the legislative branches of the government. A rule set down by an administrative officer purporting to have the effect of law would not ordinarily be effective.

The increasing complexities of modern business, however, have brought about a relaxation of this strict separation-of-powers approach. Highly technical businesses require technical knowledge for the preparation of regulatory legislation. Obviously, legislators cannot have a technical knowledge of every business that must be regulated. For this reason, in many instances they have adopted the practice of enacting regulatory laws in general terms only. They then authorize the administrative officer or agency having the duty of administering the law to "fill in the details" by means of administrative rules and regulations that have the force and effect of law. This delegation of rule-making power to administrative officers has been consistently upheld by the courts as constitutional so long as the rules so made are subject to judicial review, are within the scope of the delegated power, and are surrounded by other similar safeguards.

1.13 Insurance Rules and Regulations

Today, most state legislatures have authorized the commissioners or directors of insurance to implement the provisions of the insurance laws of their particular states by rules and regulations. Often such rules and regulations constitute a major part of the regulatory law with which the life insurance business is concerned.

G. THE COURTS

Because of the dual nature of our state and federal governments, we have two general court systems. Each of the individual states has its own system of state courts, and there is an overall system of federal courts. In matters over which they have complete authority—i.e., in areas where the governing powers have not been delegated to the federal government—the decisions of the state courts are final. In other areas, appeals may be taken to the United States Supreme Court. Many questions can be tried in either a state or federal court as the parties may prefer.[3]

---

[3] See further discussion of this point in Sec. 1.16.

1.14 The Federal Courts

Established by Federal Law. The federal courts are provided for in the federal Constitution and established by laws enacted by Congress under its authority. They have been established on three levels—district courts on the first level, appellate courts on the intermediate level, and the United States Supreme Court at the top of the hierarchy. Most cases involving subjects over which federal courts have jurisdiction are brought first in the United States district courts. Next they may be appealed to one of the 11 Circuit Courts of Appeal. Lastly, they may be appealed to the United States Supreme Court for a final decision.

The United States Supreme Court. The Supreme Court of the United States consists of nine judges and is basically an appellate court. This means that most of the cases it hears come to it on appeal from a lower court. Some cases, however, may be taken directly to the Supreme Court. These include certain cases arising under the United States Constitution, federal laws, or treaties; cases affecting foreign ambassadors, ministers, and consuls; and controversies between two or more states.

Special Federal Courts. In addition to the district courts, courts of appeal, and the United States Supreme Court, there are several special federal courts. These include the Court of Claims, the Court of Military Appeals, the Tax Court of the United States, and the Court of Customs and Patent Appeals.

1.15 The State Courts

Courts of Original Jurisdiction. The courts of some of the states reflect the same type of three-level organization which is followed in the federal courts. Other states do not have courts on the intermediate appellate level. However, every state has one or more courts of original jurisdiction in which suits may be brought. Some of these courts, such as justice of the peace courts, municipal courts, county courts, probate courts, and the like, are termed courts of limited jurisdiction because the kinds of cases they are authorized to decide are limited. For example, probate courts handle questions relating to wills and estates exclusively. Other courts, known variously as chancery courts, circuit courts, district courts, and sometimes superior courts, are major trial courts—courts of original jurisdiction, it is true, but handling all kinds of civil and criminal cases.

Appellate and Supreme Courts. Intermediate courts, often termed appellate courts, are available in about half the states for appeals from the decisions of the courts of original jurisdiction. Lastly, each state has a supreme court, whose decision is final with respect to interpretations of the state constitution and cases brought under state and local laws.

Appeals may be taken from the state supreme courts to the United States Supreme Court, however, on any question involving the federal Constitution or federal laws and treaties.

1.16 Courts and Their Jurisdictions

In a system involving so many different courts, it is obvious that there must be some rules for determining which cases are properly handled by each of the various courts. These rules are called rules of jurisdiction.

Jurisdiction in General. A court has jurisdiction in a given case if the constitutional or statutory provisions which establish the court give it the right or power to decide cases involving that particular subject matter, disputes between parties of that particular description, or both. In those areas the court has the power to hear cases and to make decisions which can be enforced. In other words, it has jurisdiction.

Ordinarily, cases in which a court has jurisdiction are defined as those involving certain types of subjects or persons or questions arising in a certain geographical area; but often the amount in controversy will be a governing factor also. For example, justice of the peace courts do not ordinarily have jurisdiction in cases involving more than a very limited amount of money. On the other hand, the United States district courts do not have jurisdiction in some kinds of cases unless the amount involved is in excess of $10,000.

Jurisdiction over the Person. It is not enough that the statute or constitution provide that the court has jurisdiction over a certain type of case. Jurisdiction over the person being sued must also be obtained by compliance with certain constitutional requirements. Legal papers (summons) must be issued by the court and must be served upon the defendant, usually personally, although in some cases publication is sufficient. In any case, jurisdiction must be obtained in such a manner that the court actually has asserted its power over the person being sued, regularly and by "due process of law."

Where Jurisdictions Overlap. Often more than one court may have jurisdiction in a given kind of case. This is particularly true in insurance cases, which frequently involve citizens of different states and thus present what is known as "diversity of citizenship." Since United States district courts are expressly given jurisdiction in cases involving diversity of citizenship, many cases involving life or health insurance contracts can be brought either in a local state court or in a U.S. district court. Often a case is brought in the state court and then removed to the U.S. district court. In either case, a summons will be served on the defendant in the regular manner and by due process of law.

1.17 The Applicable Law

Conflict of Laws. The discussion thus far might seem to imply that state courts apply the law of their respective states and the federal courts apply the law of the federal government. Obviously, however, there are many cases where the laws of more than one jurisdiction are involved. This is especially true with respect to cases involving the life insurance contract. A life insurance contract must meet all the requirements of the state where the insured has legal residence (his "domicile," in legal terminology) at the time it is issued and delivered. Often the insured will have lived in one state when he received the policy and another state at the time of death, while the beneficiary may bring a court action in still another state. In such cases, the laws of several jurisdictions may be involved in questions of rights and obligations, as well as questions of interpretation and of procedure.

This type of conflict was interestingly illustrated in one case[4] where there had been an attempted beneficiary change under two policies. The insured had been attending college in North Carolina at the time she made application and took the medical examinations for the life insurance. The policies were issued in Massachusetts and New Jersey respectively; and they were delivered and the first premiums paid in Florida, her domicile.

At the insured's death, both the original beneficiaries and the beneficiary to whom she had wished to change made claim for the proceeds. Two of the claimants were residents of Mississippi, another was a Florida corporation, and still another was a California corporation. The case was brought in the United States District Court for the Southern District of California (which had jurisdiction because of diversity of citizenship); and the court held that the rights of the parties should be determined in accordance with Florida law. This decision was reached by applying principles of law developed for the purpose of deciding just such complicated questions. Brought together, these principles constitute a study known as the "conflict of laws," presenting still another field of law that is involved in the law of the life insurance contract.

Common Law and the Federal Courts. As pointed out earlier, if there is no statute or constitutional provision on a given question, the court will ordinarily apply previous case law on the subject. As a general rule, this means the case law as developed by state courts. This practice is followed by the federal courts because of a specific provision in the statute which created them. There it was provided that in cases involving diversity of citizenship, the federal court would apply the law of the state in which

[4] *New England Mutual Life Insurance Co.* v. *Lauffer*, 215 F. Supp. 91 (S.D. Ca., 1963).

the court was sitting. This was clear as far as it went, but "law" is a word susceptible of many meanings. The question of exactly what law to apply soon became important.

Swift v. Tyson. In 1842, in the case of *Swift* v. *Tyson*,[5] the United States Supreme Court decided that the word "law" as used in the statute creating the courts meant statutory and not case law. For almost a hundred years thereafter, the federal courts conscientiously applied the statutory law of the state in which they were sitting; but if there were no applicable statutory laws, they applied their own version of the common law. In this way there was built up a federal common law which was often advantageous to insurance companies.

Erie Railroad Company v. Tompkins. The *Swift* v. *Tyson* decision was followed in the federal courts until 1938. Then, in the case of *Erie Railroad Company* v. *Tompkins*,[6] the United States Supreme Court overruled the former decision on this point and held that both the statutory and case law of the state in question must be applied by the federal courts.

H. HOW A CASE IS TRIED

The rules for bringing a court action are a part of what is known as procedural law. Requirements vary as to jurisdictions and the different kinds of courts. They are very simple in some courts and for some types of actions, and very technical in others. The following discussion is in general terms because of the wide variations in terminology and practices from one jurisdiction to another.

1.18 The Case Begins

A Complaint Is Filed. Ordinarily a case begins when the person suing (the plaintiff) files a complaint, or declaration. This is a formal statement of his cause of action. For example, in a contract case, the plaintiff will set forth the provisions of the contract, state (allege) those respects in which the person he is suing (the defendant) has failed to perform his promise, and state the amount of damages he seeks.

When a complaint has been filed, the court issues a summons, which is served on the defendant by the sheriff or other designated officer. The summons is a notice to the defendant that an action has been filed against him and that judgment will be granted against him unless he answers within the specified time.

The Defendant Answers. The defendant answers the complaint in a formal statement, usually termed an answer, in which he sets forth a denial or an excuse or otherwise explains the facts alleged by the plaintiff.

---

[5] 16 Pet. 1 (1842).
[6] 304 U.S. 64 (1938).

He may admit what the plaintiff says but contend on his part that his actions still do not constitute an actionable wrong. He may deny the contentions of the plaintiff. He may admit the facts but show that his own actions are excusable under the law. Regardless of the nature of his defense, however, he files an answer.

An Issue Is Reached. If the defendant denies that the plaintiff has a case or if he denies that the facts are as stated, an issue is presented as to the truth or falsity of the various statements. The case is then ready for trial. If the defendant admits the contentions and pleads an excuse that would be sufficient as a matter of law if proved, then the plaintiff must file a reply denying the facts on which the defendant seeks to be excused or denying that it is, as a matter of law, a valid excuse. In either case, an issue will have been presented, and the case will be ready for the court.

1.19 How Cases Are Decided

In a Court of Law. In a court of law, questions of fact are submitted to a jury for decision; questions of law are decided by the judge. However, in arriving at its decision, the jury will be instructed by the judge, who is guided by the applicable statutory, constitutional, and case law. This entire process will be governed by rules of procedure which are also the result of many years of legal development. One cannot begin to list or even to indicate all the many concepts which have their application in this process. A few of them, however, are mentioned again and again in cases one may study in connection with any area of the law; and some idea of what they mean and how they are used is essential to any understanding of the law. Three of these concepts will be described in the following paragraphs.

Presumptions. One of the most useful devices in the development of the law has been the concept of presumptions. In deciding a case at law, as in any other question, there must be some place to start. In law, the place to start is with a presumption. In a general sense, a presumption may be defined as a conclusion that the law draws from a given set of facts, which conclusion will stand until evidence is presented to the contrary.

For example, every person is presumed to be capable of making a valid, binding contract. In any case involving a question with respect to the contractual capacity of one of the parties, therefore, the law starts with the presumption that he has the capacity. The person challenging this always has the privilege of showing that the person whose capacity is challenged does not have contractual capacity by reason of age, mental incompetence, etc. But the presumption with respect to any individual is that he does have contractual capacity and, in the absence of evidence to the contrary, the presumption will stand.

The Prima Facie Case. Another important concept in trying a case is that of the prima facie case. A prima facie case is a set of facts that in the absence of evidence to dispute them entitles one to the relief he is asking. For example, the person who sets forth the provisions of a contract and alleges failure on the part of the defendant to carry out the terms of the contract has presented a prima facie case of breach of contract. It is then the defendant's responsibility to show that it was not a valid contract, that he was excused from performing, that the plaintiff made it impossible for him to perform, or any of a number of other acceptable excuses for nonperformance. But if the defendant does not show an excuse or deny the facts as stated by the plaintiff, the latter has set out a prima facie case and the decision will be in his favor.

Burden of Proof. A third concept of importance in this area is referred to as the burden of proof. In every case, one party or the other has the responsibility of establishing the truth of the statements he has made or the position he has taken; he is said to have the burden of proof. There are two schools of thought on this question, and it becomes highly technical almost as soon as it is introduced. In its simplest form, however, it means that if you have two people making opposing contentions, one will have the burden of proving the truth of his statements; if he fails, he loses the case. The other person does not have to prove anything. The fact is that most legal questions involve some evidence on both sides. In order to establish a reasonably orderly way of deciding such questions, the burden of proof idea has been developed.

One of the clearest illustrations of the way the burden of proof concept operates in life insurance is found in connection with the denial of a claim on the basis of suicide during the suicide period. A person is generally presumed to wish to continue living. When an insurer denies a claim on the basis that the insured took his own life, therefore, the burden is on the insurance company to prove its contention. In one illustrative case,[7] the court summarized this rule as follows: "It is the established jurisprudence in this state that, where a defense of suicide is interposed by an insurance company to a suit on a life insurance policy, the insurer must establish the suicide to the exclusion of every other reasonable hypothesis."

In this case, the insured had been shot several times, but there was no evidence to support the insurer's contention that she had shot herself, and there had been ample opportunity for someone else to have shot her. The court held, therefore, that the insurance company had not sustained its burden of proof and that the death benefit was payable.

---

[7] *Willie J. Brooks* v. *Louisiana and Southern Life Insurance Company,* La. App., 246 So. (2d) 270 (1971).

I. COURT DECISIONS

1.20 Case Law

When a question reaches a court for decision, the statutory or constitutional law will be applied if there is any such law on the subject. If there is no applicable law in those areas, the courts that follow the common-law system (which includes most of the courts of the United States) search previous court decisions for what are called *precedents*.[8] A precedent is any previous decision by that same court (or an appellate court of the same jurisdiction) on the same question and involving the same general set of facts. If there is such a decision, it will be followed unless there is strong reason to depart from it; and when a court does depart from a previous line of decisions with respect to a given question, it is said to have reversed itself.

In deciding a question in this way—that is, in accordance with precedent—the court is applying what is known as the doctrine of *stare decisis*. This means the practice of following previous decisions on the same questions unless, as previously noted, there is strong reason to depart from such reasoning. This does not mean that every time a question arises it will be decided in exactly the same way it was before. If that were true, no progress would ever be made. It does, however, mean that the court will not lightly depart from previous approaches and will bear in mind the importance of consistency, so that it can be relied upon not to reverse itself except for serious and compelling reasons.

1.21 Principles of Common Law

Sometimes there is no applicable statutory law and there have been no previous court decisions (case law) on the question. In such instances, the court will decide the question before it in accordance with what is called the common law. This is a term that is variously defined, as will be noted later; but in this sense it means a body of general rules, principles, and maxims that have been developed or followed by courts in English-speaking countries over many hundreds of years.

Authorities differ as to whether there is a common law for every jurisdiction or one general, all-enveloping concept that takes in all the common-law jurisdictions. It is rather generally agreed, however, that the meaning of the common law for any particular jurisdiction is defined by

---

[8] This is possible because all appellate courts and some trial courts support their decisions with written opinions that are printed, published, and made available to the public. By and large, court decisions are of interest primarily to lawyers and judges; but they are available to anyone who is interested, and they form a continuous record of the opinions and decisions of the court.

the courts of that jurisdiction. In deciding a case in accordance with the common law, therefore, the court is making case law and establishing a new precedent that will in turn be followed in later cases involving essentially the same set of facts.

J. LAW AND EQUITY

1.22 What the Common Law Means

As a System of Law. It is extremely difficult to define the term "common law" because it means so many different things. In one sense, it distinguishes the system of law followed by English-speaking nations from that followed in other parts of the world. The term is especially used in this sense to contrast with legal systems based upon and developed from the Roman law. England, Canada (except Quebec), and most of the states in the United States are common-law jurisdictions in this sense of the term. By contrast, France, Spain, Italy, Quebec, and a few states in the United States (notably Louisiana and the states of the Southwest) derive their legal systems in part at least from the Roman law. These countries and states are said to be civil-law jurisdictions.

Perhaps the most important distinguishing characteristic of the civil law is that it attempts to bring together all the general principles of law and to organize them into a relatively complete code. Court decisions then are made only with reference to principles that have been made a part of that code. In common-law jurisdictions, there is no attempt to write down all the principles that may be used, although such principles are often enacted into statutes or expressed as case law.

As Case Law. In another sense, the term "common law" is sometimes used to distinguish case law from statutory law or legislative law. In that sense, the common law of a jurisdiction is said to be made up of the decisions of the courts, as contrasted with legislative enactments or written constitutions.

As General Principles. In its broadest meaning, the common law is a kind of heritage of general principles and concepts involving customs, public policy, and basic ideas of justice that are followed as a matter of legal philosophy by courts of common-law jurisdictions. The traditions of the common law were brought to this country by the early settlers from England. Its origins were in such an early period that its beginning cannot be definitely established. Local courts were in existence, however, in the days of the early Saxons.

After the Norman conquest of England in the year 1066, the Norman kings began to send their personal delegates through the country to represent them locally in various matters, and in the 12th century this practice developed into a regular system of itinerant courts. Eventually, these courts replaced the local courts, and the law of the "King's Courts" became law common to everyone, nobleman or commoner, and hence the "common" law.

1.23 The Courts of Equity

In the early days of the common law, the person seeking justice applied for a royal order (writ) which authorized the judge to hear his case. During the 13th century, these writs became highly formalized and would apply only to certain kinds of cases. In order to take a problem to court, however, one still had to fit his case into one of the writs that were available. Often this was not possible, and as a result, there was no remedy at law. In those situations, special appeals were often made to the king himself. He, in turn, would refer the question to his special advisor, the chancellor. By the 15th century, in cases where the remedy at law was not adequate, or where there was none, the chancellor was issuing special decrees. The remedies thus sought were said to be obtained "in chancery" and were known as equitable remedies.

Equitable Remedies. Since equity courts arose out of the inadequacy of the ordinary legal remedies, remedies available in equity have, as a matter of history, been considered extraordinary in nature. For instance, the legal remedy for breach of contract (failure to perform) is money damages. In situations where money does not adequately compensate the injured person, a remedy known as specific performance may be sought in equity. If granted, this remedy will require that the contract be carried out as promised.

Among other remedies available in equity are those of reformation and rescission of contracts. When an equity court grants reformation—for instance, if an error has been made in drafting the contract—the court decides what the parties actually intended and then decrees that the contract shall be construed and carried out as if the error had not been made. Rescission is the cancellation of a contract in certain instances—as where there has been fraud or material misrepresentation in its formation. The remedies of reformation and rescission are frequently used in connection with problems arising under life insurance contracts.

Trial by Jury. Ordinarily, in a court of law, questions of fact are decided by a jury, as previously noted, and questions of law by the judge. Thus, if a case involves a dispute as to what actually happened or what was, in fact, said or done by either of the parties, the jury will hear the evidence and decide what the facts are. This is called a "finding of fact." The judge, however, makes the rulings with respect to the legal effect of the facts so decided.

In a court of equity, the procedure is different. There the judge has the power to decide every question, whether of law or fact, which comes before the court. The constitutionally guaranteed right to a jury trial, therefore, does not apply in courts of equity. The judge in an equity court may submit a question of fact to a jury for a decision, if it seems advisable; but, as a general rule, the finding of the jury will be advisory only.

1.24 Law and Equity Today

The distinction between courts of law and equity was preserved in the court systems of the United States for many years. At the present time, however, it has been abolished by statute in most of the states. A single system of law with a single court and a single system of procedure (pleading is the technical word) is now ordinarily the rule. Equitable remedies, however, continue to be distinguished from those available at law, and there has been no change in the basic principles of equity. Both legal and equitable remedies are often available in the same suit; and, where there is a conflict, the principles of equity will govern.

This is illustrated with respect to the right to a jury trial in a 1949 case[9] brought in the United States District Court for the District of Maryland. In that case, the insurance company brought an action to cancel (rescind) two policies of life insurance on the grounds that the insured had misrepresented material facts in the applications. The defendants requested a jury trial, but the court held that the issues were equitable rather than legal and that there was no right to a jury trial. The opinion reads in part as follows:

> . . . It is very well known that the Federal rules of civil procedure, while generally merging law and equity cases for procedural matters, *were not intended to destroy the distinction between law and equity with respect to the matter of jury trials.* In a typical case for equitable relief, such as the instant case, there was no right to a jury trial. On the contrary it is well established both by Federal and Maryland law and judicial decision that in equity cases, where there is no adequate remedy at law, there is no right to a jury trial at common law or by statute. [Emphasis added.]

K. REGULATION OF INSURANCE

1.25 The Early Years

In the early days, the states regulated insurance companies just as they did other corporations. Very little was involved in either case except the details of incorporation and some taxation, and no very serious challenge as to the right of the states to "regulate" insurance arose for a number of

---

[9] *Connecticut General Life Insurance Company* v. *Candimat Company,* 83 F. Supp. 1 (D.C. Md., 1949).

years. As the insurance companies began operating in states other than those in which they were organized, however, the question arose as to whether the transaction of an insurance business across state lines should not subject the business to federal regulation as interstate commerce.

The federal government has the power to regulate interstate commerce by reason of what is referred to as the "commerce clause" in the federal Constitution. This is found in Article I, Section 8, which reads in part as follows: "Section 8. The Congress shall have Power . . . To regulate Commerce with foreign Nations, and among the several States, and with the Indian Tribes, . . ."

As the result of this provision, there is no question but that Congress has the sole power to regulate commerce among the several states. Exactly what constitutes commerce, however, and when it is transacted among rather than within the several states, have not always been simple questions. This has been especially true of the business of insurance, which presented a basic question in this area, at intervals, for many years. Until 1944, however, the question was consistently resolved in favor of state regulation.

In 1868, the question of whether insurance was properly regulated by the states reached the United States Supreme Court in the case of *Paul* v. *Virginia*.[10] This case arose when an insurance agent named Paul refused to comply with certain statutory requirements imposed by the state of Virginia. In reaching its decision that Virginia had the right to regulate the business of insurance, the court stated quite simply that

> . . . Issuing a policy of insurance is not a transaction of Commerce . . . in any proper meaning of the word. . . . They (insurance policies) are governed by the local law. They do not constitute a part of the commerce between the States.

This view—that issuing contracts of insurance is not "commerce" and thus cannot constitute a part of the "commerce among the several states"—prevailed in the area of insurance regulation for the next 75 years. Other insurance cases followed, but in each of them the court made it clear that insurance was not commerce. Obviously, then, it could not be interstate commerce, and obviously also it was not subject to federal regulation. The last important case following this reasoning was *New York Life Insurance Co.* v. *Deer Lodge County*,[11] decided in 1913. After the Deer Lodge case, there seemed little reason to question the regulation of insurance by the several states.

As a result of this unbroken line of decisions, every state developed an extensive system of laws to regulate the business of insurance and provided for the supervision of insurance companies operating within

---

[10] 8 Wall. 168 (1868).
[11] 231 U.S. 495 (1913).

their respective jurisdictions by a special administrative department. In some instances this was a separate insurance department; in others, it was a department combining insurance regulation with supervision over other related businesses, such as banking. This was the situation in 1944, when the *South-Eastern Underwriters* decision was handed down by the United States Supreme Court.

1.26 The South-Eastern Underwriters Decision

The facts of the South-Eastern Underwriters case[12] were these: a group of fire insurance agents were accused of violating a federal antitrust statute, and their defense was that the federal statute did not apply because insurance was not commerce and thus not a proper subject for regulation by the federal government. In this case, therefore, the United States Supreme Court considered the question of insurance as commerce in connection with a different set of circumstances—the effect of an act of Congress with respect to insurance transactions conducted across state lines.

The South-Eastern Underwriters Association and its nearly 200 private stock fire insurance company members had been indicted for alleged violations of the Sherman Antitrust Act. The court pointed out that prior cases had concerned the power of the individual states "to regulate and tax specific activities of foreign insurance companies which sell policies within their territories." Stating the difference clearly and distinctly, the court continued:

> Not one of all these cases, however, has involved an Act of Congress which required the Court to decide the issue of whether the Commerce Clause grants to Congress the power to regulate insurance transactions stretching across state lines. Today for the first time in the history of the Court that issue is squarely presented and must be decided.

The District Court had held, in effect, that "even though an insurance company conducts a substantial part of its business transactions across state lines, it is not engaged in 'commerce among the states' within the meaning of either the Commerce Clause or the Sherman Antitrust Act"; but the Supreme Court took a different view.

It was a four-to-three decision, with a strong dissenting opinion by Justice Stone; but the conclusion of the majority was that insurance is commerce. There had been no question that it was a business conducted across state lines. The court concluded, therefore, that when so conducted, it is interstate commerce and thus subject to regulation by the federal government. The gist of the decision is found in the following passage:

---

[12] *United States* v. *South-Eastern Underwriters Association,* 64 Sup. Ct. 1162, 322 U.S. 533, 88 L. Ed. 1440 (1944).

Our basic responsibility in interpreting the Commerce Clause is to make certain that the power to govern intercourse among the states remains where the Constitution placed it. That power, as held by this court from the beginning, is vested in the Congress, available to be exercised for the national welfare as Congress shall deem necessary. No commercial enterprise of any kind which conducts its activities across state lines has been held to be wholly beyond the regulatory power of Congress under the Commerce Clause. We cannot make an exception of the business of insurance.

1.27 The McCarran Act

The *South-Eastern Underwriters* decision presented a serious problem for the insurance industry. For 75 years it had been assumed that the question of federal regulation was settled. Insurance was regulated by the states exclusively and there were no applicable federal statutes. Because the situation could have become chaotic, Congress almost immediately enacted Public Law 15—the McCarran Act—to clarify the situation.

In very general terms, the McCarran Act declared that continued regulation and taxation of the insurance business by the states was in the public interest. It stated that the business should continue to be regulated and taxed by the states, regardless of federal laws, and that no federal law that did not specifically relate to insurance should supersede or affect the validity of any state law in this area. Finally, it provided that for a limited period, insurance companies would not be subject to the federal antimonopoly laws (the Sherman Act, the Clayton Act, and the Federal Trade Commission Act) except as to special provisions of the Sherman Act concerning boycott, coercion, or intimidation. After the expiration of this period, insurance would be subject to these laws "to the extent that such business is not regulated by state law."

1.28 Federal Regulation

Immediately after the enactment of the McCarran Act, an "All-Industry Committee" made up of representatives of various kinds of insurance companies—fire, casualty, and so on—began the work of drafting model laws designed to strengthen the state laws so that the federal antimonopoly laws would not apply. Rate-making laws were among the first to be developed and adopted, but a model Unfair Trade Practices Law was also enacted by all the states, and most of the states have enacted antitrust laws that apply to insurance companies.

In spite of the enactment of these laws by the various states, some federal laws have been held to apply to insurance companies. In 1954, the Federal Trade Commission took action against 41 insurers on the grounds that the health insurance advertising of these companies violated the Federal Trade Commission Act. Since the states cannot regulate advertising beyond their individual borders, the Commission contended that an area existed that could not be governed effectively by state laws. The cases against two of the insurers were rejected by the Supreme Court in 1958, on the grounds that F.T.C. jurisdiction was limited to states having no laws regulating advertising. However, the Commission maintained that it had jurisdiction over mail order companies, and that position was upheld by the Supreme Court in 1960.[13]

In 1956, the Securities and Exchange Commission brought an action against two variable annuity companies, contending that their variable annuities must be registered with the Securities and Exchange Commission. This action was based on the premise that the variable annuity does not resemble a fixed-dollar annuity (which is exempt from S.E.C. jurisdiction) as closely as it does a security, which is subject to regulation by the S.E.C. In *S.E.C.* v. *Variable Annuity Life Ins. Co. et al*[14] the United States Supreme Court upheld this position, conceding that variable annuity contracts contain some insurance features, but pointing out that they also contain "to a very substantial degree" characteristics of investment contracts issued by equity investment trusts. The court felt, therefore, that the contracts presented regulatory problems of exactly the kind the Securities Acts of 1933 and 1940 were enacted to resolve; and it held that the exemptions of insurance policies and annuity contracts from the operation of the Acts did not include variable annuities.

1.29 Variable Life Insurance Contracts

When a similar question arose in connection with variable life insurance, the decision of the Securities and Exchange Commission (in 1973) was somewhat different. The insurance companies sought a ruling that would have exempted variable life insurance contracts meeting certain specified requirements from the Securities Act, the Securities Exchange Act, the Investment Company Act, and the Investment Advisers Act. The decision was that "the investment characteristics" of variable life insurance contracts would require that any public offering of such contracts be registered under the Securities Act, and that anyone wishing to sell them must register as a broker-dealer under the Securities Exchange Act.

With respect to the other acts, however, the Commission ruled that although the separate account of a life insurance company offering vari-

---

[13] *F.T.C.* v. *National Casualty Co.* and *F.T.C.* v. *American Life Ins. Co.*, 357 U.S. 560, affirming 263 F. (2d) 719 and 246 F. (2d) 883.
[14] 359 U.S. 65, 79 S. Ct. 618, 3 L. Ed. (2d) 640 (1959).

able life insurance was an investment company as defined in the Investment Company Act, such accounts would be exempt from the regulatory requirements of that act; and insurance companies would be exempt from the Investment Advisers Act. These exemptions were granted in deference "to the established congressional policy of preserving state regulation of insurance." The statement continued:

> In particular, the commission is persuaded by the active participation of the National Association of Insurance Commissioners in the hearing and in the Model Variable Contract Law and Regulations adopted by them, which the commission views as the beginning of the development of a uniform state regulatory structure designed specifically to meet the requirements of variable life insurance and the needs of variable life insurance contract holders beyond the disclosure which the Securities Act would provide.

The announcement ended with a statement that the Commission would "closely monitor" the development of state regulatory law with respect to variable life insurance and, if there seemed to be "substantial deficiencies," the Commission would consider modifying or rescinding the exemptions.

1.30 The Applicable Law

At the present time, most of the statutes specifically regulating life and health insurance contracts are state statutes. However, variable life insurance contracts must be registered under the Securities Act; and the Sherman, Clayton, and Federal Trade Commission acts are all applicable to insurance to the extent that the business is not regulated by state law. Insurance activities are also subject to the National Labor Relations Act and the Fair Labor Standards Act of the federal government.

SUMMARY

Insurance

Insurance is a plan for dealing with the risk of economic loss resulting from the happening of a future contingent event. The individual reduces his risk by transferring it to an insurer by means of an insuring agreement. The insurer reduces the risk it thus assumes by a scientific application of the mathematics of probability and the law of large numbers. An insurance service requires a high degree of technical skill, financial acumen, and integrity; and to assure that these standards are met, a large body of insurance regulatory law has been enacted in this country.

Insurance Regulation

Insurance is said to be a business "affected with a public interest," and for that reason it is subject to regulation under the police power. This regulation is accomplished in part by legal requirements concerning the insurance contract. Such requirements are found to a large extent in the statutory law of the various states. Nevertheless, these statutes must be read in the light of general contract law; and other areas of the law are also involved, including the law of agency, property law, and the law of torts. As a result, the law of the life insurance contract is found in many different places.

Law and Where It Is Found.   Statutory law consists of the legislative enactments of the various jurisdictions concerned. Case law is made up of the decisions of the courts. Law is variously classified—for instance, as public and private law, as substantive and adjective law. It is found in constitutions, statutes, the rules and regulations of administrative bodies, and court decisions, as well as treaties and executive orders and proclamations.

Constitutions

A constitution sets forth the broad general principles that form the legal foundation of a government and, in addition, establishes a system of guarantees of basic human rights. The federal Constitution sets forth the powers delegated by the individual states, while state constitutions define and limit governing powers that are recognized as already existing.

Statutes and Administrative Rules

Ordinarily it is the function of legislatures to make the laws and the function of administrative agencies to carry them out. However, the rule-making power may be delegated to administrative agencies charged with administration in technical areas. In these situations, the agencies are empowered to fill in the details of general regulatory laws by issuing rules and regulations that have the effect of law. Administrative rules and regulations constitute an important part of insurance regulatory law.

The Courts

Because of our dual system of government, each state has its own system of courts, while there is a separate system of federal courts, each having jurisdiction in its own area. At one time, in deciding cases based on diversity of citizenship, the federal courts applied the statutory but not the common law of the state in which the court was sitting. In 1938, however, in the case of *Erie Railroad Company* v. *Tompkins,* it was held that the common law as well as the statutory law of the state in which the court was sitting must be applied.

How a Case Is Tried

Law cases begin with the filing of a complaint by the plaintiff. A summons is then issued. The defendant answers, and each party replies to the other until an issue is reached. At that point, the case is ready for the court.

Court Decisions

In deciding cases that are brought before them, courts ordinarily apply statutory law. If there is no statutory law on the subject in question, courts in common-law jurisdictions ordinarily follow previous decisions, if any, concerning the same set of facts. Such decisions are called precedents; and the practice of following precedents unless there is strong reason to depart from them is known as the doctrine of *stare decisis.* In the absence of an applicable statute or precedent, the court may base its decision on general principles of common law.

Law and Equity

The term "common law" has a number of different meanings, according to its use. It may mean a system of law followed by English-speaking nations, as contrasted with legal systems based originally on the Roman law and known as civil-law systems. The civil law differs from the common law basically in the fact that it attempts to bring together and record all the principles of law that will be used in the jurisdiction concerned.

In another sense, the common law may mean case law as distinguished from statutory law; and in still another sense, the common law is a heritage of general principles, maxims, and concepts that have been developed by the courts of common-law countries over many centuries.

Law courts were known in England from a very early time. By the 13th century, however, the court systems had become so highly formalized that it was sometimes impossible to fit one's case into the necessary legal forms. As a result, appeals were sometimes made to the king himself, who referred the question to the chancellor. Remedies granted by the chancellor were obtained "in chancery" and were known as equitable remedies. This terminology has been brought down to the present day, and such remedies as reformation and rescission of a contract are still known as equitable remedies. The distinction between legal and equitable actions is also preserved in the fact that the right to a trial by jury applies only to legal actions.

Regulation of Insurance

Prior to 1944, insurance was regulated by the states on the theory, consistently upheld by the courts, that insurance was not commerce. Thus, it could not be interstate commerce, which is subject to federal regulation. In 1944, the Supreme Court of the United States considered the question again—this time viewing the effect of an act of Congress with respect to insurance transactions conducted across state lines—and decided that insurance is commerce. Where insurance is conducted across state lines, therefore, it is interstate commerce and subject to regulation by the federal government. However, Public Law 15 was enacted by the Congress almost immediately, suspending the exercise of the regulatory power of Congress in this area so long as regulation by the states remains effective.

In 1954, the Federal Trade Commission brought an action against a number of health insurers alleging that their health insurance advertising violated the Federal Trade Commission Act. This contention was upheld with respect to mail order companies in 1960. In 1959, variable annuities were held not to be exempt from (and thus to be subject to) regulation by the Securities and Exchange Commission; and in 1973, the Commission held that variable life insurance was subject to the provisions of the Securities Act and the Securities Exchange Act. However, life insurance companies were held to be exempt from the Investment Company Act and the Investment Advisers Act, provided the various states enacted satisfactory regulatory laws in these areas.

ILLUSTRATIVE CASE

The following case[15] is included in this introductory chapter because it illustrates in a relatively simple way the use of presumptions and prima facie evidence to arrive at a decision in a difficult, but not unusual, kind of situation. Explanatory footnotes have been added where the legal terminology may not be clear.

Robinson, as executor of the Creighton estate, brought the suit against the life insurance company. In the lower court, therefore, Robinson was the plaintiff and the insurance company was the defendant. The decision was in favor of Robinson, and the company appealed. In the court of appeals, therefore, the insurance company was the appellant and Robinson was the appellee. This information is conveyed in the title of the case

---

[15] 490 Pac. 2d. 81 (1971).

by referring to Robinson as "plaintiff-appellee" and the insurance company as "defendant-appellant."

WM. HEDGES ROBINSON, JR., EXECUTOR OF THE ESTATE OF J. R. CREIGHTON, DECEASED, Plaintiff-Appelee v. NEW YORK LIFE INSURANCE COMPANY, Defendant-Appellant

Colorado Court of Appeals, Div. II, Sept. 21, 1971
Rehearing Denied, Oct. 13, 1971

COYTE, Judge.

This is an action on the double-indemnity clause of an insurance contract which provides for double recovery of benefits in case of death by accident. However, double recovery is not provided in the policy where death occurs because of suicide. The company claimed the insured committed suicide, whereas the estate maintained that his death was accidental, thereby entitling it to recover under the double-indemnity clause. From a jury verdict favoring the estate, the company appeals.

The alleged error is that the verdict is unsupported by the evidence, and that the trial court should have directed a verdict in the company's favor or granted it a new trial.[16]

The insured in this case was a man in his fifties, suffering from a variety of ailments, including a blood disorder, congestive heart failure and partial paralysis which affected his speech. He was under medication and was being cared for by a private nurse.

The decedent, together with his wife and nurse, went to Hawaii for a vacation. While there, they rented a suite of rooms on the twentieth floor of a hotel. Adjacent to the suite was an outside balcony, the outer perimeter of which was surrounded by a wall and railing. There was a wooden platform in one corner of the balcony upon which the decedent had stood on occasion to view the scenery.

The following evidence was given concerning the death of decedent. On the night of his death, the decedent and his wife had dinner in the hotel restaurant. Both consumed alcoholic beverages and had been quarreling during dinner. The nurse helped both back to their rooms after dinner. She helped the decedent to bed after giving him his medication and a sleeping pill. Some time after 3:00 A.M., the wife awoke and found her husband had left the bed. She went to the balcony and saw him just before he plunged to his death, but had no other recollection of the event.

The police investigated the occurrence but did not question the wife upon their arrival because she was unresponsive and appeared to be in deep, heavy sleep.

Later in the day, in the afternoon, the wife was questioned concerning her husband's death. The police investigator testified that at that time she stated

---

[16] Appeals are generally permitted from any decision of a lower court if an error or errors can be shown. In this case the error alleged is that the evidence did not support the verdict. The court is said to "direct the verdict" when it makes the decision for the jury because the evidence is so clear that there is no fact question to be decided by the jury.

to him that she went to the balcony and found her husband standing there; that she asked him if he wanted a drink; that he apparently became angry and pushed her away and then went to the platform and began to climb over the wall and railing; that she went to him and attempted to hold him, but again he pushed her away, and went over the side to his death.

This testimony of the officer as to the statement given to him by decedent's wife was the only evidence presented to the jury concerning the precise manner in which the decedent met his death. Whether he accidentally fell or deliberately jumped was the question to be answered by the jury, which found that death was the result of an accident.

The certificate of death, duly authenticated and admitted into evidence, listed death as being "accidental." The certificate showing death to be accidental was prima facie evidence of "accidental death." C.R.S. 1963 [Citations given.][17]

Defendant maintains that the notation on the death certificate was placed there as a routine matter by the medical officer who signed the certificate and that he had no basis for placing the words "accidental death" on the certificate. The certificate would still be prima facie evidence of its contents, but its weight depends upon the information upon which it is based, the source of that information, and the manner in which it is obtained. [Citation given.]

In any event, there is no dispute that defendant met his death as a result of a fall from the balcony. Death by suicide is not a natural occurrence, and is never presumed. The burden is on the company to prove by a preponderance of the evidence that the insured committed suicide. [Citation.]

It is the contention of the insurance company that the statement made by the wife to the investigator is direct evidence as to how and why the fall occurred and is conclusive proof of the fact the decedent took his own life, and that the court erred in refusing to direct a verdict in the company's favor. We disagree.

After the death certificate was introduced into evidence showing the fact of death to be "accidental," the plaintiff had established a prima facie case and the defendant company then had the burden of proving that death occurred because of suicide. It was for the jury to determine whether the defendant had sustained this burden by producing evidence which outweighed the presumption that decedent had met his death by accident. The presumption was sufficient evidential weight to support the jury verdict. [Citations.]

The only witness to the death of the husband was the wife. There is a conflict between her testimony at the trial, when she testified that she did not remember the details of her husband's death, and the facts relating to decedent's death as testified to by the investigator, which testimony was received without objections. It was for the jury to hear and weigh the testimony and determine the credibility of the witnesses.

The question as to whether defendant insurance company had sustained the burden of proof as to the manner in which decedent met his death was

---

[17] This reference is to a statute which declares that a death certificate shall be prima facie evidence of the cause of death. Following the statutory reference, a list of cases was cited to support or explain the point just given. In order to simplify this report, such cases will be omitted and only the note "citations given" will be used.)

properly left to the jury. Based on proper instructions, it resolved the matter in favor of the estate.

Judgment affirmed.[18]

QUESTIONS FOR REVIEW

1. In general terms, what is meant by the statement that insurance is a business affected with a public interest?

2. List three sources of law.

3. Which of the following statements describes the federal Constitution? Explain.
   a. It establishes a government of delegated powers.
   b. It imposes limitations on the power of the government.

4. What important constitutional question relating to insurance was considered in each of the following cases?
   a. *Paul* v. *Virginia.*
   b. The Deer Lodge case.
   c. The *South-Eastern Underwriters* decision.
   What was the decision in each case? What effect did each decision have on the regulation of insurance?

5. Briefly summarize the principal provisions of Public Law 15.

6. Why are administrative rules and regulations considered necessary? What is the legal significance of such rules and regulations?

7. Explain and illustrate the doctrine of *stare decisis.*

8. In general terms, outline some of the principal differences between law and equity:
   a. As to origin.
   b. As to formality.
   c. As to remedies available.

9. List two remedies available in equity that are frequently utilized in connection with the life insurance contract.

10. What legal question was considered in each of the following cases?
    a. *Swift* v. *Tyson.*
    b. *Erie Railroad Co.* v. *Tompkins.*

---

[18] That is, the decision in the lower court in favor of the estate was upheld.

Chapter Outline

Chapter 2

What a Contract Is

IN BROAD general terms, a life or health insurance contract is simply a legally enforceable agreement between an applicant and an insurance company. Ordinarily, an insurance agreement is set forth in a policy, but this is not essential. If the actions of the parties and the documents involved otherwise satisfy the legal requirements for the formation of a contract, an insurance contract may be held to be effective even though no policy has been issued. Conversely, if any of the basic legal requirements for the formation of a contract have not been met, or if there has been material misrepresentation or fraud in the application, the insurer may not be legally obligated even though a policy has been issued and delivered.

Under these circumstances, it is necessary to have some acquaintance with the basic principles of general contract law before the specialized legal principles applicable to life and health insurance contracts can have much meaning. The purpose of this chapter is to discuss the more important of these general principles, with an emphasis on those with which life and health insurance contracts are most frequently concerned.

A. CONTRACTS ARE "MANY AND VARIOUS"

2.1 A Contract Is a Promise

A contract has been defined as a "promise or set of promises, for breach of which the law gives a remedy, or the performance of which the law in some way recognizes as a duty."[1] It is fundamental that there

---

[1] *Williston on Contracts* (New York: Baker, Voorhis & Co., Inc., 1957), Vol. 1, p. 1.

must be a promise or, in some cases, several promises, of such a nature as to create a legal duty of performance on the part of the person or persons making the promise.

Life and health insurance contracts illustrate this definition clearly. One after another, life insurance policies read, "The A.B.C. Life Insurance Company agrees to pay . . ."; "The X.Y.Z. Life Insurance Company agrees to pay . . ."; and so on. Health insurance contracts follow a similar pattern.

"Agrees to pay" are promissory words, which, when other requirements are met, create a legal duty of performance on the part of the insurance company. This duty has been affirmed and enforced by court decisions again and again.

2.2 By One or Both Parties

A person who makes a promise or promises under a contract is called a promisor. A person to whom a promise is made is a promisee. Promises may be made by either or both parties to a contract.

Contracts under which promises are made by both parties are said to be bilateral contracts (having promises on both sides); contracts which consist of a promise or promises by only one party are called unilateral contracts (having promises on one side only).

2.3 The Life Insurance Contract Is Unilateral

Unilateral contracts were recognized and given legal effect at a much earlier date than bilateral contracts; and they continue to be of greater interest to the student of life insurance. Neither the policyowner nor the beneficiary actually promises to do or to pay anything under today's life insurance contract. The contract can be kept in force only if premiums are paid as they become due, but the policyowner does not promise to pay them. If they are not paid, certain clearly defined results will follow; but the policyowner cannot be sued by the insurer for failure to perform the contract.

By contrast, the life insurance company makes a legally enforceable promise to pay the amount of insurance specified, upon receipt of proof of the death of the insured. Other promises are also included in most life insurance contracts; and when any required conditions have been met, the insurer must perform its promise or promises or the policyowner or beneficiary will have a legal action for breach of contract. In other words, the life insurance contract contains legally enforceable promises on the part of the insurance company but none on the part of the policyowner. Thus, it is an important modern-day example of a unilateral contract.

B. FORMAL AND INFORMAL CONTRACTS

The mere fact that one has promised something does not, of course, mean that the promise will be legally enforceable. However, if a contract is intended, there are two main ways in which a promise can be made contractually binding. One method concerns the form of the instrument in which the promise is expressed. Promises under seal and negotiable instruments have legal effect as binding contracts if they comply with special requirements as to form. A deed, for instance, is a written instrument "signed, sealed, and delivered," although the seal is no longer required in many jurisdictions. Negotiable instruments must comply with similar special requirements. Agreements of this kind are said to be binding because of their form, and for this reason they are called formal contracts.

Other contracts—and the life insurance policy is an excellent example—create legal duties because the parties have met requirements that relate more to the nature than to the form of the transaction. Contracts of this kind are called "informal"—that is, not formal contracts. Sometimes they are referred to as "simple" contracts.

C. THE CONTRACT AS AN AGREEMENT

In terms of legal requirements, an informal contract is, first of all, an agreement. In fact, a contract is often defined as "an agreement enforceable at law," and that is the way the life insurance contract was defined at the outset of this chapter. To say that it must be enforceable at law implies that there may be other agreements that are not so enforceable; and that is true. "Agreement" is a broad term, which includes such things as executed sales and gifts, as well as many kinds of promises of such a nature that they cannot be enforced by court action. A contract, therefore, is a special kind of agreement: one that the law will enforce.

Lawyers sometimes say that there must be a "manifestation of mutual assent" to express this idea of agreement and to make it clear that the law does not try to ascertain the actual state of the minds of the parties. It concerns itself only with their discernible words and actions. This idea is sometimes obscured by language to the effect that a contract requires a "meeting of the minds." In many instances, it would be impossible to determine the state of mind of any contracting party. The state of mind that actually controls, therefore, is that which is evidenced by the words and actions of the persons concerned. As a general and basic rule, mutual assent (agreement) is evidenced by the making of an offer or proposal by one party and the acceptance of it by another.

In legal terms, therefore, two basic elements of an informal contract are (1) an offer and (2) an acceptance. In addition, if the agreement is

to be enforceable at law, there must be (3) a legally adequate consideration; (4) a form required by law, if one is required; and (5) no statute or
rule of law declaring a contract of that kind void (that is, of no legal
effect).

A large body of law has been developed in connection with each of
these requirements, and much of it applies to life and health insurance
contracts. Before such contracts become enforceable, therefore, they must
meet these basic requirements of any informal contract, which will be
considered in the following discussion.

D. THE OFFER

Defined in its simplest form, an offer is a proposal which, if accepted
by another according to its terms, will create a binding contract. The
person who makes an offer is the offeror, and the person to whom the
offer is made is the offeree.

Generally, an offer is made in the form of a promise to do or refrain
from doing something. For instance, it may be a promise to pay a sum of
money, on condition that the offeree performs an act or makes a promise
or promises requested by the offeror. If the offeror requests the performance of an act in exchange for his promise, the contract, when completed,
will be a unilateral contract, since it will involve a promise or promises by
the offeror only. If the offeror requests and receives a promise from the
offeree, the resulting contract is bilateral.

An offer is always conditional in the sense that acceptance in accordance with its terms is a condition that must be met before the offer will
become a binding obligation. However, an offer may also be so expressed
as to remain subject to further conditions after acceptance. This is true,
for instance, of life and health insurance contracts. The promises expressed in such contracts are enforceable only if conditions set forth in
the policy are met.

The requirements of offer and acceptance apply to life and health
insurance contracts just as they do to any other informal contract. Traditionally, the applicant has been considered as making the offer when he
completes an application for life or health insurance and pays the
premium. That is, he is making a proposal which, if accepted according
to its terms, will result in a legally enforceable agreement between him
and the insurance company. The insurer is said to accept this offer when
it issues and delivers the policy applied for.

The extensive use of conditional and binding premium receipts has
introduced enough complexities into this traditional offer and acceptance
analysis that a considerable part of Chapter 4 will be devoted to a
discussion of such receipts as they are used in life and health insurance.
In the meanwhile, however, it should be borne in mind that the life or

health insurance contract, like any other informal contract, is formed by the making of an offer by one party and its acceptance by the other.

2.4 Requirements of a Valid Offer

It Must Be Definite. One of the most basic requirements of a legally· sufficient offer is that it must be definite. When accepted, it must create a contract that if necessary can be given exact meaning by a court of law. As a general rule, if an offer is so indefinite that the promise cannot be clearly ascertained, it is not a legally sufficient offer.

It Must Be Communicated. Equally important is the requirement that an offer must be communicated. Clearly, the offer must come to the attention of the offeree before it can be accepted. However, it is not enough that knowledge of the offer be obtained by accident. Basic in the law of contracts is the principle that one may choose the person or persons with whom he is willing to contract. For this reason, communication of an offer for contractual purposes requires that the offeror intentionally and actually bring the offer to the notice of a person or persons with whom he wishes or would be willing to contract. Thus, if the offer is sent by mail, it must be received by the offeree. If it is published, as in the offer of a reward, the person who performs the act requested and claims the reward must actually have seen the offer and must have performed the act in reliance upon it.

2.5 Duration of the Offer

Duration May Be Specified. The offeror may, if he wishes, specify the length of time he will hold the offer open. The offer will then terminate automatically at the expiration of the stated period without further action on the offeror's part. Any attempt to accept after the offer has expired will be ineffective, since one of the conditions stated in the offer—that it be accepted within the time specified—will not have been met.

If the offer contains no mention of an expiration date, it is presumed to remain open for a reasonable length of time. What constitutes a "reasonable length of time" is a question of fact[2] that depends on many different things—the type of contract, the customs of the business, the nature of the subject matter, etc. It may be a very short time in contracts where circumstances change rapidly or a much longer time—in offers of rewards, for example.

Offer May Be Withdrawn. Unless the offer has been made under seal or for a consideration,[3] the offeror has the privilege of withdrawing it at any time he wishes, so long as it has not been accepted. However, it is

---

[2] If the question reaches a court of law, this, like all questions of fact, will ordinarily be decided by the jury.

[3] In which case, it is an option.

generally considered to be necessary to notify the offeree of the withdrawal. At one time, notice was not thought legally necessary if the offeree knew of actions on the part of the offeror which reasonably implied withdrawal. Today, however, notice of withdrawal is considered necessary, or acceptance within a reasonable length of time will be legally effective. After an offer has been accepted, of course, it cannot be withdrawn.

Offers Are Terminated by Death or Insanity of the Offeror. An offer may be terminated for reasons other than withdrawal or revocation by the offeror. For example, the death of the offeror prior to acceptance by the offeree terminates the offer; and death of the offeree, assuming that there was only one, ordinarily precludes the possibility of acceptance.

At one time, the insanity of either the offeror or offeree was considered to have the same legal effect as death. More recently, however, the legal capacity of insane persons to create binding contracts under some circumstances has been increasingly recognized. The judicially established insanity of either the offeror or offeree is still generally held to terminate an offer, but if the insanity has not been established, the person's legal capacity to complete the contract is a question of fact to be decided in the light of all the pertinent circumstances of the particular case.

2.6 The Offeree

It is legally impossible for anyone to make a binding contract with himself, even though he may act in different representative capacities. The concept of offer and acceptance, therefore, assumes that in addition to an offeror who makes the offer or proposal, there must also be an offeree, to whom the offer is made and who, on his part, evidences his assent by accepting the offer.

In considering an offer, the offeree has several choices. He may, of course, ignore the offer, unless his silence could be misunderstood by the offeror. If he wishes to reply, he has three choices. First, he may reject the offer. If he does this, the offer terminates immediately; and that particular offer cannot be revived by the offeree, even if he later wishes to accept it in absolute accordance with its original terms.

Second, if he is unwilling to accept the offer as it stands but would be willing to contract on different terms, the offeree may reject the original offer and make a counteroffer. In fact, under such circumstances, he need not state specifically that he rejects the offer. Words or actions that are not in themselves definite rejections but which reasonably imply that the offeree does not intend to accept will be given their reasonable effect and considered to be rejections. Any attempt to substitute new terms or modify the original offer, for instance, will be considered a rejection of the old offer and the making of a counteroffer. This is especially applicable in the case of an answer purporting to accept the offer "on condition that. . . ." In legal effect, this is a rejection. The offeree has clearly indicated that he is not willing to contract on the terms set forth in the offer. In any of these situations, therefore, the original offer lapses and the original offeror becomes, in effect, an offeree. The counteroffer is then subject to acceptance or rejection by the original offeror.

As a third choice, the offeree may accept the offer in accordance with its terms and thus complete the agreement.

E. ACCEPTANCE

Any words or actions on the part of the offeree indicating assent to the offer as made by the offeror will constitute acceptance. The simple statement "I accept" is sufficient if made with reference to the offer and if the offer is of such a nature as to request a promise in return. Performance of the act requested in an offer for a unilateral contract is a legally sufficient acceptance. It is highly important, however, that the action be taken or the promise made with reference to the offer. A manifestation of mutual assent is basic. Thus, if each of two persons were to send identical offers to the other and if the offers were to be received simultaneously, no agreement would result. Each promise must be made with reference to the other or the assent will not be mutual.

Only the person or persons to whom the offer is made can accept it in the legal sense of the word. An offer need not be directed only to one person, however. It may be made to any member of a large group as, for example, in the case of an offer of a reward. Regardless of the number of persons who may be eligible to accept, however, some one person must manifest assent to the offer in accordance with its terms or there will be no agreement. For this reason, as a general rule, silence on the part of an offeree will not be construed to be an acceptance. However, in some instances, prior conduct may make it clear that silence is to be so interpreted.

2.7 Acceptance Must Be . . .

. . . *Positive.* The general rule is that an acceptance must be sufficiently positive to indicate a clear assent to the exact terms proposed by the offeror. If an act is requested, that act must be performed. If a promise is asked, then that promise and no other must be given.[4]

. . . *Unconditional.* Acceptance must be unconditional. As previously pointed out, any attempt to impose new conditions in a purported acceptance will be construed as the making of a counteroffer.

---

[4] However, the Uniform Commercial Code has modified some of the more technical aspects of the law of offer and acceptance as it relates to the sale of goods.

. . . *Intentional.* Although it is sometimes said that the offeree must have an intent to accept, the actual intent of the parties is ordinarily not important if there is an adequate manifestation of assent. A secret intent not to be bound, for example, is of no significance if the person's actions or words are such as to justify a reasonable person in believing that the other person has seriously promised to do or refrain from doing something for a valuable consideration.

Nevertheless, a person's subjective state of mind is important if it is ascertainable from his overt acts. For example, if an offer is obviously made as a joke, one cannot accept it and complete a binding agreement. The offer is ineffective not so much because there was no "meeting of the minds" as because there was no manifestation of assent in the sense that a reasonable person would take action in reliance upon such an offer.

2.8 Communication of the Acceptance

Unilateral Contracts. It would seem that a manifestation of mutual assent would require that acceptance, like the offer, be communicated. However, this is not always true. There are some instances in which acceptance does not have to be brought to the knowledge of the offeror. For example, an offer for a unilateral contract usually contemplates the performance of an act as acceptance. In such cases, unless the offeror specifically requests notification, performance of the act is generally held sufficient to complete a binding agreement. In those instances where the offer is the performance of an act, however, it is necessary that acceptance in the form of a promise be communicated.

Bilateral Contracts. An offer for a bilateral contract contemplates acceptance in the form of a return promise. This, of course, implies that the promise shall be communicated. However, acceptance does not have to be communicated in the literal sense of the word if the offeree uses a means of communication designated by the offeror. The legal theory is that if the offeror requests acceptance by mail, he is, in effect, making the mail service his agent for this purpose. When the offeree mails his letter of acceptance, therefore, a contract is completed even though the letter is never received by the offeror. By mailing the acceptance, the offeree is, in legal effect, delivering it to the agent of the offeror.

A similar result is achieved with respect to any other designated means of communication. If an answer by telegram is requested, delivery of the message to the telegraph company will be sufficient. However, if the requested means of communication is not used, the situation is quite different. In that case, the means of communication selected by the offeree is considered to be his agent, and actual delivery of the acceptance to the offeror is required. Thus, if a telegram is requested, and the offeree decides to reply by mail, the mail service is considered to be the agent of the offeree, and the letter must actually reach the offeror in order for the acceptance to have been communicated.

If the offeror does not specify any particular means of communication, he is presumed to expect the offeree to reply by the same method that was used in communicating the offer. If the offeror writes a letter, the offeree may accept by letter, and the acceptance is considered to have been communicated, in the legal sense of the word, the instant the letter is mailed. In any event, however, if the offeree actually makes his acceptance known to the offeror, it will have been effectively communicated.

F. WHEN THE AGREEMENT BECOMES EFFECTIVE

Assuming that the other requirements are satisfied, the agreement is generally considered to be complete and to become effective at the moment there is an overt act manifesting assent to the offer. Nevertheless, there are many exceptions to this rule. For instance, in some cases, the parties may plan to reduce their agreement to writing at a later date and not to be bound until this has been done and the contract signed. Alternatively, they may enter into a binding oral agreement to execute a written contract.

Finally, there may be a binding oral agreement even though the parties planned to put their contract into writing later. If they have, in fact, made the necessary promises to each other orally, the fact that they plan to reduce the contract to writing does not change the legal effect of their mutual promises. Unless the contract is one required by law to be in writing, the oral promises of the parties may be held to have constituted an effective contract.

G. WHAT CONSIDERATION MEANS

Promises under seal (i.e., formal contracts) were recognized and enforced at common law long before the law of the informal contract and the accompanying concept of consideration were developed. Later it was sometimes said (and it is occasionally so suggested even now) that with respect to formal contracts, the seal "imports consideration." As a matter of fact, long before the idea of consideration was born, the formal contract was effective by reason of its form alone. Historically, therefore, the doctrine of consideration was not applicable to formal contracts.

With respect to the informal contract, it is fundamental that there must be a legally sufficient consideration for the promise or promises sought to be enforced. This means that the person who seeks to enforce the promise of another must have given something of value for it. He may have given another promise, a sum of money, or something else of value. He may have performed an act or refrained from doing something he was legally entitled to do. In some way, however, he must have promised or given something the promisor requested. In brief, consideration is the price requested and given for a promise.

2.9 When Is Consideration "Legally Sufficient"?

The Question of Adequacy. As a general principle, the law does not inquire into the monetary adequacy of the consideration agreed upon and given in exchange for a promise. If there was consideration and if it was what the promisor requested, the courts will not substitute their own judgment as to its value for that of the parties to the contract. The classic statement is to the effect that under such circumstances "even a peppercorn" will be considered legally sufficient. After all, adequacy and value are subjective concepts. Something that may have great value to one person may have little or no value to another. In the absence of fraud, therefore, the courts take the position that the parties knew what they were doing and that the promisor knew what he wanted in return for his promise.

One exception to this general rule is found in cases which involve a promise to pay in money a larger sum for a smaller sum. If the smaller sum represents more than its nominal value, as with a rare or otherwise valuable coin, for instance, a promise to pay it will be sufficient consideration for a promise to pay a larger sum at the same time and place. If there is no such unique value, however, a promise to pay a small sum in money will not be a legally sufficient consideration for a promise to pay a larger sum at the same time and place.

The Legal Tests. There are two generally accepted approaches that may be used in determining the sufficiency of consideration. One approach, and perhaps the one more frequently used by the courts, is that consideration is any act or promise requested and received by the promisor in exchange for his promise. This, it will be noted, is the definition previously given. Thus if A requests an act on the part of B in exchange for A's promise to pay a specified sum of money, and if B performs the act, the performance of that act is sufficient consideration for A's promise. That is what A requested and received in return for his promise.

As a second approach to the question, consideration is sometimes defined as "any benefit to the promisor or detriment to the promisee." However, these words are not necessarily interpreted literally. For example, a detriment, in the legal sense of the word, need not operate to the promisee's actual disadvantage. The classic illustration of this point concerns an uncle who promises his nephew a sum of money on the latter's

21st birthday if the nephew refrains from smoking until that date. Here the consideration for the uncle's promise, abstention from smoking on the part of the nephew, is not physically detrimental to the nephew. However, in legal theory, the voluntary forgoing of an undeniable right is a detriment. In this sense, there is a detriment to the nephew and thus a legally sufficient consideration for the promise of the uncle. It should be noted that abstention from smoking is also the action requested and received in exchange for the promise by the uncle. This example meets both tests with respect to consideration.

A Promise for a Promise. Generally speaking, mutual promises constitute sufficient consideration for each other. In other words, in a bilateral contract, each promise is consideration for the other, since each is "the thing requested and received in exchange" for the promise of the other party to the contract.

Conditional Promises. Even a conditional promise will be sufficient consideration for another promise or an act if it otherwise meets the tests outlined above. It will be recalled, for example, that an offer is always conditional in that it specifies the conditions of acceptance. The promise in an offer may, however, continue to be conditional even after acceptance. That is, it may bind the promisor to act or to refrain from acting only if a certain thing shall or shall not happen. Thus a promise to pay an insurance benefit, even after the promise becomes binding in a contractual sense, continues to be conditional in the sense that payment will be made only if the loss insured against occurs. Many term life insurance policies are issued and expire without the payment of a claim. The insurer promised to pay a death benefit, but only if the insured died during the term of the policy. The fact that the insured did not die during that term does not mean that the contract was not valid or that the promise was not binding. It only means that the specified condition did not occur.

H. COMPETENT PARTIES

2.10 Void and Voidable Agreements

Consideration, as a requirement in connection with the informal contract, is absolute. Without it, there is said to be a "failure of consideration" and no contract. The requirement that the agreement be between competent parties is somewhat less definite. For example, in some instances, the incompetency of one or both parties to an agreement will result in what is known, not too logically, as a "void" contract—that is, no contract at all. A void contract is, by its own terms, an impossibility, since a contract is defined as an enforceable agreement. A void agreement, therefore, is the better term.

In other instances, a contract made by an incompetent person is held to be "voidable." A voidable contract is an agreement which, because of some imperfection, may be disaffirmed by one or more parties, but in the absence of such disaffirmance will remain enforceable according to its terms.

Under still a third set of circumstances, a person of limited contractual capacity may be bound by a contract he has made if it was fair and reasonable and the other contracting party had no knowledge of the incapacity.

2.11 Who Is Competent?

Generally speaking, any person is presumed to be capable of entering into a valid and binding contract. Minors, married women, insane persons, intoxicated persons, convicts, and aliens, however, all either have or at some time in the past have had limited contractual capacity. At the present time, the incapacity of most of these persons is evidenced more by their freedom to disaffirm an otherwise valid contract into which they have entered than by an incapacity to make a contract in the first place.

Nevertheless, the fact that some people have the power to disaffirm (*avoid*) a contract, after having made it, is of the utmost importance to anyone who contemplates making a contract with a person of limited contractual capacity. In practical effect, the competent party to the contract will be bound, while the other party has the privilege of deciding whether to carry out the contract or disaffirm it.

2.12 Married Women

At common law, a married woman was legally incapable of entering into a binding contract. A purported contract with her was void, not voidable. This rule has been almost completely modified or removed in most states today, but it is still important as historical background. Statutes that remove this disability must be read with the knowledge of the common-law rule they change before they become very intelligible.

2.13 Insane Persons

If a party to a contract is insane, the validity of his contract varies with the circumstances. If he has been declared legally insane and a conservator or guardian has been appointed, any contract he makes thereafter in his own name will be legally ineffective. If no conservator or guardian has been appointed, the courts generally take the view that the insane person may affirm or disaffirm the contract upon regaining his sanity. After his death, his personal representative or his heirs may exercise the right to disaffirm.

2.14 Minors

At common law, a minor, sometimes referred to as an infant, was any person under the age of 21. This rule has been modified by statute in most of the states to provide that anyone age 18 or over will have contractual capacity as an adult. The laws vary, however; and as a result, the contractual capacity of a person 20 years of age, for example, will depend entirely upon the law of the state in which the question arises.

At one time, contracts entered into by a minor were classified as void, voidable, or valid, depending upon whether they were harmful, uncertain, or beneficial in their effect upon the minor. This made the courts responsible for determining whether the contract was in fact harmful or beneficial. As a general rule today, a few kinds of contracts made by a minor are valid; all others are voidable but not void. This means that with respect to most of his contracts, the minor himself can decide whether it is beneficial to him and thus whether he wishes to be bound. The other party, however, (if his own contractual capacity is unimpaired), is bound by the agreement unless and until the minor decides to disaffirm it.

When a minor disaffirms a contract, he simply declares that thereafter he will not be bound by its terms. He is free to disaffirm most of his contracts at any time during his minority and within a reasonable time after he has attained the age of majority. However, he cannot disaffirm a contract conveying real property until he has reached the age of majority, and then he must disaffirm it within a reasonable time. If he has not disaffirmed a contract after the expiration of a reasonable time after he has reached the age of majority, he will be held to be bound by its terms.

As a general rule, disaffirmance of a contract on the grounds of infancy requires that the minor return any consideration he has received if he still has it in his possession. However, if he no longer has the consideration, he can still avoid the contract and recover what he parted with, without restoring the other party to the status he had prior to the making of the contract. There is conflicting law on this point, and the applications of the basic principles have varied widely from jurisdiction to jurisdiction.

2.15 Some Special Contracts of Minors

The minor's privilege of avoiding a contract he thinks detrimental to his interests is accorded him as a protection from unscrupulous persons who might otherwise seek to take advantage of him. For this reason, if there is no statute to the contrary, the privilege is almost absolute. It applies to anyone who has not yet attained the age of majority, regardless of how nearly of age he may be and regardless also of the fact that he may be engaging in business for himself or otherwise have assumed the responsibilities of adulthood.

Even at common law, however, there are some kinds of contracts that a minor may not disaffirm. Agreements in fulfillment of a legal duty, for example, will be held to be binding. Thus, if the obligation has been legally satisfied, the execution by a minor of a release of a mortgage cannot afterwards be disaffirmed by him. Similarly, such agreements as marriage, enlistment, and apprenticeship are held to be binding on a minor.

Contracts for "Necessaries."   It is sometimes said that a minor is liable under his contracts for "necessaries," but this is not entirely true. A minor is liable for the reasonable value of necessaries furnished him or his family, but this is not always the contract price. The term "necessaries" also requires elaboration.

Section 2 of the Uniform Sales Act defines necessaries as "goods suitable to the condition in life of the infant and to his actual requirements at the time of delivery." As suggested in this definition, the term necessaries is much broader than the word "necessity," for it includes not only necessities but also other things which may be reasonably necessary for the minor's maintenance, with proper regard for his social position and financial status. Luxury articles are not usually included, but the fact that an article is expensive does not keep it from being a "necessary" if the minor is in actual need of it.

Significantly, for our present purposes, life insurance has been held not to be a "necessary." Thus, special statutory authorization is required before a minor can enter into a contract for life insurance under which he may execute binding releases and otherwise exercise all his rights as a policyowner on the same basis as if he were an adult.

Life Insurance Contracts.   In the absence of a special statute, a minor may disaffirm a contract of life insurance just as he may avoid any other contract he has made. In fact, the majority rule is that upon such disaffirmance, he may recover all of the premiums that he has paid for the insurance and thus be in the position of having had the insurance protection during the period of minority without cost. Many states, however, have statutes that permit minors of a certain age and over to enter into life insurance contracts which bind them as well as the insurer. A typical statute of this kind reads as follows:

> Any minor of the age of fifteen years or more may, notwithstanding such minority, contract for life, health and accident insurance on his own life for his own benefit or for the benefit of his father, mother, husband,

wife, child, brother or sister, and may exercise all such contractual rights and powers with respect to any such contract of insurance as might be exercised by a person of full legal age, and may exercise with like effect all rights and privileges under such contract, including the surrender of his interest therein and the giving of a valid discharge for any benefit accruing or money payable thereunder. Such minor shall not, by reason of his minority, be entitled to rescind, avoid, or repudiate such contract, or any exercise of a right or privilege thereunder.[5]

This statute permits a minor 15 years of age or older to insure his own life on the same basis as if he were an adult. Note, however, that the beneficiary must be his estate (as indicated by the words "for his own benefit") or a person or persons closely related to him. Statutes of this general nature also sometimes permit the minor to insure the life of a child or spouse, as well as his own life.

2.16 Corporations

The contractual capacity of a corporation is determined by the provisions of its charter and the statutes of the state under whose laws it was organized (its domiciliary state). A corporation has no express powers except those granted in its charter or the laws under which it was created. A corporation does, however, have implied and incidental powers when and if they are necessary in the exercise of the powers specifically granted.

The charter or certificate of authority of a life insurance company ordinarily sets forth in general terms that the company is authorized to transact a life or life and health insurance business. Implied is the power to issue contracts of life or health insurance as well as the other contracts incident to the conduct of a life and health insurance business. However, this authority applies only to the state in which the insurer was chartered. In order to qualify to do business elsewhere, therefore, the company must formally apply to the proper official of the jurisdiction in question for permission to do an insurance business there. If the company meets the necessary requirements, it will be granted a certificate of authority to do business in that jurisdiction.

The contractual capacity of an insurance company, therefore, depends upon two things. First, under its charter and the laws under which it was formed, the company must have been empowered to issue contracts of insurance in the desired area—i.e., life, fire, etc. Second, it must have been authorized (licensed) to do an insurance business—i.e., issue contracts of insurance—in the state where the contract becomes effective.

The legal effect of a contract of insurance made by a nonlicensed

---

[5] Illinois Revised Statutes, Chap. 73, Art. XIV, Sec. 854 (1971).

insurer varies with the laws of the different states. Some statutes declare such contracts to be void, creating no rights. Others specify that the contracts will be enforceable by the policyowners according to their terms. In other states, there are no applicable statutes. In the absence of an applicable statute, the tendency of the courts is to uphold the rights of the policyowner who has entered into the contract in good faith and without knowledge of the legal incompetency of the insurer. In still a fourth group of states, the laws provide only for a penalty upon the insurer that does business in the state without being licensed. The prevailing opinion in these states is that a contract made with an unlicensed company is valid and enforceable by the policyowner.

I. A FORM REQUIRED BY LAW

2.17 Contracts in Writing

There are a number of practical reasons for expressing contracts in writing. For one thing, it is more convenient for the parties to the contract; and memories are not infallible. It is also usually easier to prove the terms of a written agreement in the event of the death or incompetency of one or more of the parties. As a matter of law, however, an informal contract need not be in writing to be valid. This principle applies to life insurance contracts as well as to any other informal contract. In the absence of a special statute to the contrary, therefore, the life insurance contract does not have to be in writing.

At least one state, Georgia, has a statute requiring insurance contracts to be in writing. However, laws that merely specify provisions that must be included in a life insurance contract do not necessarily mean that a written contract is essential. They merely require that oral contracts be interpreted as if they included the provisions set forth in the law. It is doubtful that oral life insurance contracts would be upheld as a matter of practice under the laws of most of the states, but there are many individual instances where an oral contract of life insurance has been held to be effective.

Some contracts are required by law to be in writing. Conveyances of land and negotiable instruments are examples. Special laws may require other kinds of contracts to be written in certain instances. The most important general groups of contracts requiring writings of some kind are listed in what is known as the Statute of Frauds. This statute, in its most common form, does not apply to the life insurance contract, but some understanding of its relationship to the life insurance contract is necessary for a reasonably complete understanding of life and health insurance law.

2.18 The Statute of Frauds

The Statute of Frauds was originally enacted in England in 1677, expressing as its stated purpose the "prevention of many fraudulent practices." Some form of this statute has since been enacted in most of the states of the United States. In its most usual form, the statute enumerates five classes of contracts[6] as follows:

1. A promise by an executor or administrator to pay a claim against the estate out of his own funds.
2. A promise to be legally responsible for the debt or default of another.
3. A promise made in consideration of marriage.
4. An agreement to sell or a sale of any interest in real property.
5. An agreement that cannot be performed within one year after the contract is made.

As enacted in most states, the statute lists these five classes of contracts and provides that any oral agreement falling in any one of them will be unenforceable unless it is evidenced by some note or memorandum signed by the party to be charged. This means that a person who sues another for breach of any agreement falling in one of these categories can prove the existence of the agreement only if it is in writing or if he has some note or memorandum signed by the other party to the agreement—that is, the party charged with performance. Note that the contract itself does not have to be writing. A written note or memorandum evidencing the promise is all that is required. The statute, therefore, usually concerns the matter of proof rather than the validity of the contract.

The fifth class of agreement listed in this statute is of greatest significance in a discussion of life insurance contract law: an agreement that cannot be performed within one year after the contract is made. Since many life insurance contracts remain in force for many years, the contention has sometimes been made that life insurance contracts are within the Statute of Frauds and that oral contracts of life insurance cannot be proved except by a written note or memorandum. This contention is not supportable under the statute as it has been enacted in most states, however, since any life insurance contract may become a claim and thus be performed "within one year after the contract is made." In fact, many life insurance contracts are performed within the first year; and an agreement that *can* be performed within one year from the date it is made, whether or not it *is* performed, is not usually within the Statute of

---

[6] The English Statute of Frauds also included a section dealing with the sale of "goods, wares, or merchandises" for a price in excess of a specified sum. This provision was included in the Statute of Frauds as it was originally adopted by many of the states, but it has since been replaced in many states by appropriate provisions of the Uniform Commercial Code.

Frauds. Thus, an oral contract of life insurance does not ordinarily have to be proved by a written note or memorandum.

A special exception to this general rule is found in the statute as it is enacted in New York in the New York Personal Property Law, Article 3, Section 31, which reads in part as follows:

> Section 31. Agreements required to be in writing.
>
> Every agreement, promise or undertaking is void, unless it or some note or memorandum thereof be in writing, and subscribed by the party to be charged therewith, or by his lawful agent, if such agreement, promise or undertaking;
>
> 1. By its terms is not to be performed within one year from the making thereof *or the performance of which is not to be completed before the end of a lifetime.* . . . [Emphasis added.]

Since this statute includes any contract "the performance of which is not to be completed before the end of a lifetime," this New York Statute specifically includes life insurance contracts.

2.19 The Parol Evidence Rule

The parol evidence rule, as its name suggests, is a rule of evidence. This means that it becomes important only when a dispute arises and the parties to the contract take their question to a court of law.

As generally stated, the parol evidence rule provides that if a contract has been reduced to writing, it will be assumed that any preceding oral agreements that have been made were merged into the written contract. Thereafter parol (oral) testimony will not be admitted to modify or contradict the terms of the written agreement.

Life insurance contracts, as written contracts, are subject to the parol evidence rule. Thus, oral testimony cannot ordinarily be admitted to contradict the provisions of a life insurance contract.

Exceptions to the Rule. As is true of most legal rules, there are a number of exceptions to the parol evidence rule. Thus, oral evidence can be introduced in the following situations:

1. Where No Contract Was Ever Made. The parol evidence rule does not prohibit oral testimony for the purpose of showing that no contract was ever formed.

In this connection, parol testimony was admitted in one life insurance case to show that someone other than the insured made application for the insurance. The court noted the general rule, that parol testimony cannot be introduced "for the purpose of contradicting, changing or adding to the terms incorporated into and made a part of a written contract." But it pointed out that this was not the purpose of oral testimony in this case, saying:

In a case such as the instant one, where the defense of fraud is invoked, in that the named insured never knowingly made application for insurance and where a person other than the named insured was substituted for the medical examination, we are of the opinion that the Parol Evidence Rule can not be invoked to preclude the medical examiner from giving testimony as to the facts and circumstances connected with and surrounding the parties at the time of such examination. The purpose of such testimony is not to vary or contradict a contract, but to show that the alleged contract never came into existence.[7]

2. *Where the Contract Is Incomplete.*   If the face of the written agreement shows that something remained to be done or another provision was to be incorporated, parol evidence can be used to show those provisions on which the parties had orally agreed but which they failed to incorporate into the written agreement.

3. *Where There Is Fraud, Accident, or Mistake.*   If by reason of fraud, accident, or mistake, some portion of the instrument was omitted, oral testimony may be used to show the provision or provisions so omitted.

4. *Where There Is Ambiguity.*   Oral evidence is also permitted in cases of ambiguity, if the ambiguity is evident on the face of the contract. This exception is sometimes stated in terms of *patent* as contrasted with *latent* ambiguities. A patent ambiguity is one that is evident on the face of the instrument; a latent ambiguity is not. For example, if a word were used in two obviously contradictory meanings, it would be a patent ambiguity, while if oral testimony is necessary to prove that an ambiguity exists, it is a latent ambiguity. At one time, oral testimony was permitted in the case of patent but not latent ambiguities. This rule is not followed nearly so strictly today, however, and oral testimony is frequently admitted to clarify any ambiguity, whether it is patent or not.

5. *Where the Terms or Expressions Used Have Technical Meanings.* Where words used in a contract have a special trade meaning or a specialized meaning by reason of the locality in which the contract was drawn up, parol evidence can be used to explain that meaning.

J. NOT AGAINST PUBLIC POLICY

It will be recalled that the last-named requirement for a valid contract was that it not be illegal and that there be no statute or rule of common law declaring it void or against public policy. The term "public policy" is frequently used in a discussion of contract law, but it is difficult to define. One rather standard definition summarizes it thus:

---

[7] *Obartuch* v. *Security Mutual Life Insurance Company,* 114 F. (2d) 873 (C.C.A. Ill., 1940).

. . . "Public policy" is the community common sense and common conscience extended and applied throughout the state to matters of public morals, public health, public safety, public welfare, and the like; it is that general and well-settled public opinion relating to man's plain, palpable duty to his fellow men having due regard to all the circumstances of each particular relation and situation.[8]

2.20 Illegal Contracts

If the formation or performance of the contract constitutes a crime or an actionable civil wrong (a *tort*), or if it is against public policy, the contract is said to be illegal. Contracts to use bribery or other unlawful means to influence the legislative or judicial processes of the government, for example, are illegal.

Ordinarily, the law will not aid either party to an illegal contract. If the contract has not been performed, neither party can compel performance or obtain damages. If the contract has been performed, neither can sue the other for damages.

Sometimes a particular type of contract will be declared against public policy as a means of protecting one of the parties to such a contract. Thus, statutes concerning the validity of life insurance contracts issued by nonlicensed insurers have as their purpose the protection of the citizens of the state. For this reason, they often do not declare such contracts void and unenforceable but instead permit the owner to bring suit against the company at fault.

2.21 Wagering Agreements

Wagering agreements comprise one of the important classes of contracts that are generally held to be illegal as against public policy. In the earliest days of the common law, they were not prohibited, but laws were later enacted declaring certain kinds of wagers to be against public policy. Statutes to this effect are now in force in most of the states.

Wagering agreements are of particular interest in any consideration of insurance contracts, since insurance contracts as well as wagers are classified as aleatory contracts. This distinguishes them from commutative contracts, which involve the exchange of more or less equivalent values. By far, the majority of contracts in the noninsurance world are commutative contracts.

An aleatory contract, by contrast, is an agreement under which one of the parties may recover a great deal more in value than he has parted with, depending upon the happening of a future contingent event. By

---

[8] *Black's Law Dictionary* (4th ed.; St. Paul: West Publishing Co., 1951), p. 1318.

definition, therefore, both wagers and insurance contracts are aleatory agreements.

It is commonly accepted today that insurance contracts are in the interests of society. If issued with proper safeguards, there is no question of their validity. However, this question has not always been so clearly settled, for reasons that are not difficult to understand. In its basic outline, a life insurance contract obligates one party to pay another a specific sum of money on the happening of an event that is presumably not within the control of either. Such an agreement bears more than a passing resemblance to a wager. It is obvious also that an unscrupulous person standing to gain from the destruction of an insured piece of property or an insured life might feel a strong temptation, under some circumstances, to implement the whims of chance in his own favor. If life insurance contracts were issued indiscriminately, therefore, they could pose a double threat to the public welfare. To the evils attendant on gambling would be added the possibility of creating a motive for murder in the minds of the unscrupulous. These problems are avoided by one legal requirement—the requirement of an insurable interest on the part of the person who will benefit from a life insurance contract. This is such an essential concept in life and health insurance law that it will be discussed at some length in Chapter 4.

SUMMARY

Definitions

A contract is a "promise or set of promises, for breach of which the law gives a remedy, or the performance of which the law in some way recognizes as a duty." If promises are made by both parties, the contract is a bilateral contract; if only one party makes a promise, the contract is unilateral. The life insurance contract is a unilateral contract.

The life insurance contract is also an informal contract. This means that it is enforceable because it meets legal requirements relating to the nature of the agreement rather than the form. An informal contract is an agreement between competent parties expressing definite assent to the terms of a promise or promises and supported by legally adequate consideration. If a special form (such as writing) is required, the contract must be completed in that form; and there must not be a special statute or rule of law declaring such contracts invalid.

Elements of a Contract

The assent of competent parties is ordinarily evidenced when one party makes an offer and the other accepts. In contract law, an offer is a proposal which if accepted according to its terms will create a binding contract. An offer must be definite, and it must be communicated to the offeree. An offer remains open for a reasonable length of time if the time is not otherwise specified, and it is terminated by the death or established insanity of the offeree.

An offer may be accepted or rejected by the offeree, or ignored by him unless a previous course of dealing would cause his silence or inaction to be given a different meaning. However, any attempt to accept an offer but impose different terms is, in legal effect, a rejection and a counter-offer; and a counteroffer must, in turn, be accepted by the original offeror or no contract will result.

Acceptance must always be made with reference to the offer itself or it will not be legally effective. Acceptance must be positive, unconditional, intentional and ordinarily it must be communicated. As a general rule, if performance of an act is contemplated by the offer, the offeror does not need to be notified that the act has been performed. If acceptance is in the form of a return promise or promises, however, communication is usually required.

An acceptance is generally held to have been communicated when the offeree delivers his answer to the communication medium chosen by the offeror. Thus, if the offeror has requested an answer by mail, acceptance is complete when the letter of acceptance is mailed. If no mode of communication is specified, acceptance is communicated in the legal sense when the offeree delivers a message to the same agency used by the offeror. In any event, if the offeree actually brings his acceptance to the notice of the offeror before the offer terminates or is withdrawn, it does not matter what mode of communication he uses.

The general rule is that the agreement becomes effective as a contract the moment there is an overt act manifesting assent to the offer, as, for example, when the offeree mails a letter of acceptance if that mode of reply is requested—but there are exceptions to this rule. The parties may plan to reduce their agreement to writing and not to be bound until this has been done, or they may enter into an oral agreement to execute a written contract. However, they may also have a binding oral agreement even though they plan later to reduce the agreement to writing. In each case, the facts determine the legal effect.

Consideration

Informal contracts are not binding unless there is consideration for the promise sought to be enforced. However, in the absence of fraud, the courts will not substitute their judgment as to the adequacy of the con-sideration for that of the parties to the contract. Consideration is any act or promise requested and received by the promisor in exchange for his promise. Another view considers that any requested benefit to the promisor or detriment to the promisee will be sufficient consideration to support a promise. Generally speaking, a promise is sufficient consideration for another promise.

Competent Parties

As a general rule, every person is presumed to be capable of entering into a valid and binding contract, but minors, married women, insane persons, intoxicated persons, convicts, and aliens either have or at some time in the past have had limited contractual capacity.

For the most part, today, statutes have removed the incapacity of married women to contract; but at common law a married woman was legally incapable of entering into a binding contract.

If a person has been declared legally insane and a conservator or guardian has been appointed, any contract he purports to make will be legally ineffective. If no conservator or guardian has been appointed, the insane person may, upon regaining his sanity, affirm or disaffirm a contract he made while insane.

At common law, any person under the age of 21 was a minor, but this has been changed to 18 in many states today. Unless there is a statute to the contrary, almost any contract a minor makes may be disaffirmed by him. He may disaffirm most contracts at any time before attaining his majority or within a reasonable time thereafter, but contracts conveying real property may not be disaffirmed until the minor reaches his majority and then they must be disaffirmed within a reasonable time. When he disaffirms a contract, the minor must return any consideration he has received if he still has it.

Some contracts made by a minor, such as marriage and enlistment, are legally binding; and a minor is also liable for the reasonable value of necessaries furnished him or his family. Life insurance has been held not to be a necessary; so there must be statutory authority before a minor can enter into a contract for life insurance that he cannot later disaffirm.

The contractual capacity of a life insurance company depends upon its charter and the statutes of the state under which it was formed, as well as whether it has qualified to do business in any other state in which it wishes to operate as an insurance company.

Form

It is always advisable to express a contract in writing, but not always required. Conveyances of land and negotiable instruments must be in writing, but the largest group of contracts in which a writing is required is listed in what is known as the Statute of Frauds. This statute, which has been enacted in most of the states, specifically requires that a number of contracts either be in writing or that a writing or memorandum shall be required to prove them. It has sometimes been contended that the life insurance contract is within the Statute of Frauds, as an agreement that cannot be performed within one year after the agreement has been made. Since the life insurance contract *could* be performed within one year, however, it is generally held not to be within the Statute of Frauds.

New York has enacted this statute with special wording that refers to an agreement that "by its terms is not to be performed within one year from the making thereof or the performance of which is not to be completed before the end of a lifetime." Because of this special wording, the Statute of Frauds as enacted in New York does apply to contracts of life insurance.

The Parol Evidence Rule

The parol evidence rule provides that if a contract has been reduced to writing it will be assumed that the preceding oral agreement, if there was one, was merged into the written contract. Oral testimony will not then be admitted to modify or contradict the terms of the written contract. As written contracts, life insurance contracts are subject to this rule. The rule, however, does not prohibit oral testimony to show that no contract was ever formed or that, if completed, the contract has been performed. Oral testimony will be admitted if the contract is incomplete; if by reason of fraud, accident, or mistake, some part of the contract was omitted; where there is an ambiguity; and where the terms or expressions used have technical meanings.

Not against Public Policy

A contract that is against public policy is said to be illegal, and in most of the states today wagering contracts are so considered. Although insurance contracts are aleatory contracts just as wagering agreements are—both providing for the receipt, under some circumstances, of a great deal more money than one has parted from—insurance contracts are generally considered to be in the interests of society if issued with proper safeguards. The principal safeguard in this respect is the requirement of an insurable interest.

ILLUSTRATIVE CASE

The discussion in this chapter has, of necessity, been in general terms. The principles so discussed, however, all apply to the life insurance contract. The following case has been selected because it illustrates the most basic of these principles, the operation of offer and acceptance, in connection with the life insurance contract.

JOHN HANCOCK MUTUAL LIFE INSURANCE COMPANY v. DONALD H. DIETLIN et al.[9]

Supreme Court of Rhode Island, April 6, 1964

This is a bill in equity[10] to declare null and void a policy of life insurance issued by the complainant[11] insuring the lives of Donald H. and Charlotte R. Dietlin, husband and wife, and their minor children, Donna J., Paula R., and Patricia A. Dietlin, all of whom are respondents,[12] as well as the life of Kathleen B. Dietlin, deceased. After appointment of a guardian ad litem[13] to represent the interests of the minor respondents, the cause was heard on bill, answer and proof[14] by a justice of the superior court who entered a decree declaring the policy to be null and void, ordering the respondents to surrender it to the complainant for cancellation, and granting the complainant other incidental relief. In addition the complainant was directed by the decree to refund to the respondents the sum of $14.60, being the amount of the premium paid at the time of the execution of the application for the policy. From that decree the respondents have appealed to this court.

The material facts are not in dispute. The application for the policy was made by Donald H. Dietlin, hereinafter sometimes referred to as the "insured," and is dated February 28, 1959. Listed therein for inclusion as insured lives in the policy were all of respondents as well as Kathleen, and in reference to the latter the application states that "About 2 months ago Kathleen had pneumonia after which her heart was impaired & has been treated at St. Josephs Hosp. Prov., R.I. since then." In the course of the preparation of the application, James R. Lockett, complainant's soliciting agent, questioned whether in the light of her condition Kathleen would be covered in the policy. He told the insured and his wife that Kathleen's name and those of the other minor children were required to be listed on the application, but that he could not assure them that the company would include her as an insured family member.

In the course of the processing of the application by complainant, there was stapled to it a company form designated "Underwriting Data Sheet" on which, under a heading entitled "Company's Action On Application," appear the notations "3–16 Delete Kathleen" and "Deleted Kathleen," the latter having been approved on March 24, 1959.

---

[9] 199 A. (2d) 311.

[10] A written complaint addressed to a court of equity; the remedy sought is an equitable one—rescission (cancellation) of the policy.

[11] The insurance company.

[12] Literally, those who respond.

[13] A guardian appointed by the court to represent a minor or minors who are parties to the proceedings.

[14] "The cause was heard on bill, answer and proof" means that the case was heard on a basis of the bill in equity filed by the insurer, the answer that was filed by the respondents, and the proof presented in support of the various contentions. Here the decree or decision in the lower court was in favor of the insurance company, and the Dietlins appealed.

Thereafter a life insurance policy designating the insured, his wife, and all of their minor children as insured family members was received by Lockett from complainant. Attached to it was a copy of the application and a document designated "Amendment To Application," the former document having been affixed apparently pursuant to clause 19 of the policy which provided in part that "The entire contract between the Company and the applicant consists of the policy and the written application, a copy of which is attached at issue." That amendment, which required the signature of the insured, provided that Kathleen be deleted from the list of the proposed family members on the application and that no coverage should be provided under the policy for her.

Not being able to contact the insured who was not at home when he called, Lockett left the policy and attached documents with the insured's wife, and requested that she have her husband execute the amendment. Although the version given by Mrs. Dietlin on this phase of the cause differed slightly from that of Lockett, respondents make no contention that the acceptance by the trial justice of the Lockett version was either clearly wrong or that in accrediting that account he overlooked or misconceived any evidence. In those circumstances in accordance with our well-settled rule his finding on that issue is conclusive. . . .

The amendment had not been signed by the insured when Kathleen died on April 2, 1959 and subsequent refusals so to do resulted in the instant suit being brought.

The only question is whether the insurance policy is in effect.

In the formation of a contract of insurance as in other contracts there must be a manifestation of mutual assent in the form of an offer or proposal by one party and an acceptance thereof by the other. . . . Ordinarily, the application for a policy is the offer . . . and before a contractual relationship can come into being the offer must be unconditionally accepted. . . . An acceptance which is equivocal or upon condition or with a limitation is a counteroffer and requires acceptance by the original offeror before a contractual relationship can exist. . . .

In this case the application or original offer was for a policy insuring the lives of all respondents as well as of Kathleen. The complainant was not required to nor did it accept that offer. Instead it attached the amendment to the contract of insurance, thereby proposing to the insured that there be deleted from the policy one of the lives included in the original application. This constituted a counteroffer and required the unequivocal assent of the insured as a prerequisite to a completed contract. By the terms of such offer that assent could be manifested only by the insured affixing his signature to the amendment. Because that signature was not obtained the counteroffer was not accepted and the policy did not take effect as a contract of insurance. *McDonald* v. *Mutual Life Ins. Co.*, 6 Cir., 108 F. 2d 32.

The respondents' appeal is denied and dismissed, the decree appealed from is affirmed, and the cause is remanded to the superior court for further proceedings.[15]

---

[15] The case was sent back (remanded) to the superior court for the procedures necessary to carry out the original decision.

QUESTIONS FOR REVIEW

1. Tell what a contract is.

2. Differentiate between a bilateral and a unilateral contract. Explain why the life insurance contract is a unilateral contract.

3. What is meant by the phrase "meeting of the minds" in connection with the formation of contracts? Must there always be a meeting of the minds?

4. Define an offer. What are the important requirements of a valid offer? How may an offer be terminated?

5. What is meant by a counteroffer? What is the legal effect of making a counteroffer?

6. Define and briefly discuss the meaning of consideration as it applies to informal contracts. Would a contract to sell a very valuable painting for approximately half its actual worth be supported by a legally adequate consideration?

7. List three classes of people who may or may not be competent to enter into a contract. If an insane person makes a contract, what are the possible legal effects?

8. What is meant by the legal term "minor"? What is the common-law rule concerning minority and the capacity to contract? If a minor disaffirms a contract, what is the legal effect of his action?

9. Must a life insurance contract always be in writing? Is a life insurance contract an agreement "that cannot be performed within one year after the contract is made"?

10. Briefly summarize the parol evidence rule. Why is this rule important in connection with the life insurance contract? What are some of the exceptions to the parol evidence rule?

Chapter Outline

Chapter 3

The Meaning
of Agency

A CORPORATION is an artificial being, formed by one or more persons, and authorized by law to transact a business of a specified kind under its corporate name. The corporation itself is an abstract legal concept—a *legal entity*, the lawyer says; and its existence and operation are separate and distinct from its owner or owners. The business of a corporation is always transacted by a natural person or persons, acting for the corporation, an idea which is sometimes summarized by the statement that, by their very nature, corporations must transact all their business through agents.

Since the modern life insurance company is corporate in its form of organization, it too must transact its business through agents, sometimes field underwriters,[1] sometimes the officers in the home or other administrative office. From the company's point of view, therefore, the story of a life or health insurance contract, from the first step in the application process to the final closing of the file, is a story of actions taken and words spoken by many different persons, all acting for and on behalf of the corporation and, thus, agents in the legal sense of the word. The purpose of this chapter is to discuss the more significant principles of agency law as they apply to life and health insurance contracts.

[1] "Field underwriter" is used here to distinguish the life insurance soliciting agent from other persons who represent the insurance company in an agency capacity. To avoid monotony, the terms "field underwriter," "soliciting agent," "life underwriter," and sometimes "insurance agent" will be used interchangeably to refer to the person who represents the insurer in the field and solicits applications for life insurance from the general public.

65

A. DEFINITION AND NATURE OF AGENCY

3.1 What Agency Is

Agency is a relationship in which one person is authorized to represent and act for another person, or for a corporation, in the creation or modification of contracts between the person or corporation represented and others. The person representing and acting for the other is an agent; the person represented is the principal.

With few exceptions, an agent may be appointed to perform any act which the principal himself could do. This excludes crimes or acts contrary to public policy. There are also a few perfectly lawful acts, such as voting or making a will, which must be done personally or not at all. Nevertheless, as a general rule, anything that one can do for himself he can do through an agent.

In most instances, if a person is acting for another as an agent, he is called an agent. However, principles of agency law often apply in situations where no one is either referred to or thought of as an agent. One of the most difficult aspects of agency law is the fact that it often applies in situations which, on the surface, do not seem to involve any agent-principal relationship whatsoever.

For example, in the case of *Morrison* v. *The Mutual Life Insurance Company of New York,*[2] the beneficiary of a life insurance contract visited the San Francisco office of the insurer and, according to her testimony, discussed her problem with two of the "head men." In a subsequent lawsuit involving the policy, the company maintained that the men she talked to did not have the power to modify a company contract. Nevertheless, on the facts as developed in the trial, the court held that the men concerned were "in responsible charge" of the office and had apparent, if not actual, authority to clarify her rights under the contract and bind the company. Thus the general principles of agency law were applied even though the company maintained that the persons the woman talked to were not its agents.

The point of the Morrison case is that in an agency question, it is the facts that govern, not the terminology the parties use. This is illustrated, in an opposite way, in the situation where a life insurance agent writes an application for insurance on his own life. Here he is called an agent—that is, he does not terminate his agency relationship, but in this particular transaction, he does not act in an agency capacity. He cannot represent the company[3] in this transaction with himself for, as previously noted, there must be two parties in any contract situation. When an agent

---

[2] 15 Cal. (2d) 579, 103 P. (2d) 963 (1940).

[3] See William R. Vance, *Handbook on the Law of Insurance* (3d ed., by Buist M. Anderson, St. Paul: West Publishing Co., 1951), p. 116.

completes an application for insurance on his own life, therefore, he is actually contracting as an individual directly with the insurer.

Agents and Employees. It is not necessary that the agent be authorized to negotiate and complete a binding contract. Indeed, in its broadest sense, the law of agency applies to persons acting in a strictly employee capacity, who have no contractual authority whatever. In a truer sense, however, and in the sense in which the word will be used here, agency means a relationship in which contracts are created or modified by one person in the name of, and for, another whom he is authorized and entitled to represent.

In this sense the relationship of an agent and the person he represents differs from that of an employee and his employer in both nature and scope. An agent represents his principal and acts not only for him but in his place. The employee merely works for the employer. The employee performs his duties according to the employer's directions and instructions, but he cannot commit the employer in any contractual way.

For example, assume that the beneficiary in the Morrison case had talked to a secretary instead of the "head men." The secretary would have been an employee but would not have had authority to change or modify company contracts in any way. No words or actions on the secretary's part could have changed the company's liability under the contract in question. What the "head men" said, however, was binding on the company.

Agents and Independent Contractors. So far as instructions are concerned, the independent contractor is at the other end of the scale from the employee. Nevertheless, the independent contractor's situation, too, is different from that of the agent. An independent contractor is a person who contracts with another to perform a service, but with almost complete freedom as to methods and details of the work to be performed. The independent contractor, as such, therefore, does not represent the person he is performing the service for in any agency sense.

Since the same person may be an agent with respect to some actions and an independent contractor with respect to others, it is often difficult to say as a matter of law whether a specific action on the part of an independent contractor was taken in his capacity as an independent contractor or as an agent. A principal, however, is responsible for the acts of his agent within the scope of the latter's authority. The independent contractor is responsible for his own acts. For many reasons, therefore, it is often highly important to distinguish between the independent contractor and an agent.

Perhaps the most important single factor to be considered in distinguishing between the acts of an independent contractor and those of an agent is the matter of control. Ordinarily the independent contractor is responsible only for the end result of his work. By contrast, the principal has complete and continuing control over the agent even though he may not always choose to exercise it. Thus it is reasonable for a person to be held responsible as a matter of law for the actions of his agent and not for those of an independent contractor who may happen to be performing work for him.

3.2 Nature of the Agency Relationship

The essence of the agency relationship is power. An agent has the power to bring about or modify contractual relationships between his principal, whom he represents, and third persons with whom the contracts are made. In legal effect, the agent is substituted for the principal in these transactions. Any action he takes in connection with the business of his principal has exactly the same legal effect as if it had been done by the principal.

No one is an agent unless he has this power to affect the contractual relations of his principal. Also, if he has this power he is an agent, so far as the law is concerned, regardless of the title he may have. For example, the field underwriter of the life insurance company is an agent of the company as a matter of law. However, the officer or the employee in the home office who approves risks also has the power to affect the legal relationships of the company and represents it in many ways. He, too, is an agent in the legal sense of the word.

Although power is sometimes confused with authority, it is a far broader term. An agent is authorized by his principal, expressly or by implication, to do certain things. However, by reason of circumstances, he may have the power to bind the principal in many other ways. For this reason, agency law is not at all limited to situations where the agent actually has been authorized to do what he did. It encompasses all the many situations where he may reasonably seem to have the authority he professes to exercise. In these latter cases the agent is said to have the power, though not the authority, to bind his principal.

3.3 Other Characteristics

A Fiduciary Relationship.   Certain people, such as trustees, guardians, executors, etc., have positions involving such a high degree of trust and confidence that the law exacts of them a higher standard of conduct than is required in the usual course of business. These people are said to be fiduciaries, that is, persons who bear toward others a special relationship of trust and confidence. An agent is a fiduciary with respect to his principal and the business with which he is concerned. He has a duty to act primarily for the benefit of the principal and to deal fairly with him in every way.

Control. Another characteristic of the agency relationship is the right of the principal to control the conduct of the agent. This right of control is continuous as far as the duties of the agency are concerned, and its presence or absence often determines whether a given relationship is or is not that of agency.

B. BASIC PRINCIPLES OF AGENCY LAW

3.4 The Acts of the Agent

It is basic in agency law that the actions of the agent within the scope of his authority are the actions of the principal. (In this connection, one often sees a Latin phrase which means "he who acts through others, acts through himself.") By virtue of the agency relationship, the principal can be in many places at the same time, perform many different actions, complete many contracts. At times the agent can do things for the principal that the principal does not have the skill to do for himself. The attorney, for example, represents his client as the latter's agent and uses his legal skills in the client's behalf.

3.5 The Contract

When an agent completes a contract on behalf of his principal, it is exactly the same as if the principal had completed it by and for himself. In the eyes of the law, the contract is the contract of the principal. He is entitled to all the benefits and is charged with all the duties and responsibilities connected with it.

In the typical agency transaction where the life underwriter solicits applications for life insurance, accepts the first premium, and often arranges for the medical examination, he initiates a series of actions which culminate in an effective and binding contract of life insurance. That contract is a contract between the applicant on the one hand and the company on the other, and the actions of the various company agents have, in legal effect, been the actions of the company.

3.6 Payment to the Agent

Another significant legal concept in agency law concerns payments made to the agent on behalf of the principal. If it is within the agent's authority to accept such payments, payment to the agent on the principal's behalf has exactly the same effect as if the payment had been made to the principal. Here, the phrase "within his authority" is of the utmost importance. For example, it is customary for the life underwriter to have the authority to collect the first premium in connection with the application for a life insurance policy but not subsequent premiums, and a notice to that effect is usually included in the policy. Ordinarily, subsequent premiums must be paid direct to the home office or other designated location and not to the soliciting agent.

Suppose that under a policy including this limitation, a renewal premium is paid to and accepted by the agent. Suppose further that this takes place immediately prior to the expiration of the grace period but that the payment does not reach the administrative office shown on the premium notice until after the grace period has expired. Meanwhile the insured has died. Under these circumstances, is the insurance company bound by this payment, assuming that it was made to a soliciting but not a general agent of the company?

It is situations of this kind that make the principles of agency so important, not only in the origin of the contract of insurance but throughout its life. In fact the "life" of the contract often literally depends upon the authority of the agent whose actions are concerned. In the situation outlined above, if the insurance company was bound by payment to its agent—that is, if payment to the agent was payment to the principal—the insurance policy was in effect at the date of the insured's death. If the company was not so bound, the policy was not in effect.

In a case[4] presenting this precise question, the court noted the applicable provisions in the policy, as follows:

> The first premium only may be paid to agent. All subsequent premiums are due and payable in advance at the Home Office of the Company without notice. However, they may be paid to an authorized agent of the Company on or before the date when due, but only in exchange for a receipt signed by the President, Vice-President, Secretary or Assistant Secretary, and countersigned by such agent.

The purpose of this policy provision was to make it clear that only the first premium was properly payable to the soliciting agent. Subsequent (renewal) premiums were payable at the home office of the company, without notice, except that they could be paid to an "authorized" agent (that is, an agent authorized to accept renewal premiums) in exchange for an official receipt. Thus, acceptance of any premium after the first was beyond the scope of the soliciting agent's authority. If the policyowner entrusted subsequent premiums to the soliciting agent, therefore, the latter would be the policyowner's agent for that purpose, not the agent of the insurer; and the premium would not be considered paid until it reached the company's home office. The court concluded as follows:

> . . . but when she made said Pope her agent to remit it to the defendant, she assumed the risk of his failure to send it in and, while this may be what is termed "a hard case," we must heed the admonition of the great

[4] *Kansas City Life Insurance Co.* v. *Root*, 238 Ala. 412, 191 So. 219 (1939).

and lamented Chief Justice Stone, "Let not hard cases make shipwreck of the law."

3.7 Knowledge of the Agent

Generally speaking, the knowledge of the agent concerning matters related to the business of his principal is presumed to be the knowledge of the principal. This general principle is illustrated in the case of *Mickle* v. *Dixie Security Life Insurance Co.,*[5] a South Carolina case decided in 1949. In this case, the insurer's defense (against a suit brought after a death claim was denied) was based on the contention that the answers to the questions in the application were fraudulent and that the insured was not in sound health on the date the policy was issued. The principal question related to alcoholism on the part of the insured and the fact that the soliciting agent, an old friend, was personally acquainted with the habits of the insured. The question, then, was whether the agent's knowledge of the habits of the insured must be presumed to be the knowledge of the company.

The court noted that no questions concerning alcoholism were included in the application and said that it was "for the jury to pass upon the question of fraud and materiality." The opinion continued:

> However, aside from this, it can reasonably be inferred that the appellant's local insurance agent, Mr. Anderson, was, through close association, fully aware that the insured sometimes drank to excess. He drank with him, knew he had been treated several times for alcoholism, and knew its probable effect upon the state of his health.
>
> It has been uniformly held in this State that the knowledge of an agent acquired within the scope of his agency is imputable to his principal, and, if an insurance company, at the inception of the contract of insurance, has knowledge of facts which render the policy void at its option, and the company delivers the policy as a valid policy, it is estopped to assert such grounds of forfeiture. . . .
>
> Upon a consideration of the evidence in this record, it may reasonably be inferred that if alcoholism be a disease, and that it adversely affected the health of the insured, then appellant's local agent was fully conversant with the situation, and such knowledge is imputable to his principal.

In other words, the agent was well acquainted with the drinking habits of the insured at the time the contract was made. This knowledge was imputable to the company—that is, the company was presumed to have the same knowledge. Thus, when it issued the policy, the company had knowledge that would have permitted it to avoid the policy. Since it issued the policy with that knowledge, it could not use those facts to avoid the policy at the time of claim.

---

[5] 57 S.E. (2d) 73 (S. Car., 1949).

C. WHO MAY BE AN AGENT?

3.8 Qualifications Generally

Contractual Capacity. Since the act of an agent is considered to be the act of his principal, it is not necessary that the agent himself have contractual capacity. It is the principal's capacity that governs. Thus a contract completed by an agent who is a minor, for a principal of legal age, cannot be avoided at a later date on the ground that the agent was a minor.

The modern life insurance company and its officers clearly illustrate the fact that an agent does not have to have contractual capacity in his own right to complete contracts of a specified kind. Under presently existing laws, few individuals could or would care to qualify to issue legal reserve life insurance contracts as insurers. However, such contracts are completed every day by individual officers acting as agents for corporate insurers.

Partnerships and Corporations. It is customary to think and speak of agents as individuals. However, partnerships and corporations may also act as agents. The general rules of agency law apply whether the agent is an individual, a partnership, or a corporation.

Statutory Requirements. In the case of real estate agents, brokers, insurance agents, and others whose activities involve the general public, the various states have imposed certain statutory restrictions in the public interest. Before they may be appointed to represent others in such capacities, agents must meet these special statutory requirements.

D. WHO MAY BE A PRINCIPAL?

As a general rule, any person who has the capacity to make a contract may appoint an agent to make one for him. It will be remembered that every person is presumed to have contractual capacity, in the absence of a contrary showing. However, persons who do not have the capacity to make a contract cannot cure that incapacity by appointing someone with contractual capacity to act as their agent and make a contract for them.

Thus an adult appointed by a minor cannot make a binding contract for the minor. Similarly, if a life insurance company is not authorized to do a life insurance business in a given state, the qualifications of its field underwriters are ineffective to make up for that lack of authority.

E. AGENCY IN LIFE AND HEALTH INSURANCE

3.9 Agents

Insurance agents are among those agents whose activities involve the general public, and for that reason they must meet statutory requirements in almost every state. Usually the agent takes an examination given by the department of insurance of the state where he will represent the company, and he must otherwise satisfy the department that he is generally fitted for such a position of public trust. The agent also completes a contract with the insurance company he will represent. This contract defines the soliciting agent's authority and responsibility and sets forth the agreement of the parties with respect to commissions and other details of the agency relationship.

In most instances, there is little question but that the life agent represents the insurer, although the latter has the right to limit and define the agent's authority. Still, one of the most important chapters in the history of life insurance law deals with the question of whom the agent represents in completing the application for insurance.

The Life Agent Represents the Insurer. Today the law is almost completely settled that when the life insurance agent fills out an application for the signature of the applicant, he is representing the insurance company, not the applicant; but this has not always been true.

The relationship of principal and agent carries with it some very definite legal responsibilities as well as privileges, and the insurer may be held responsible for any fraud or mistakes made by its agents in carrying out their duties. In an early effort to avoid some of these consequences, some insurance companies included in their policies provisions to the effect that the agent, in completing the application, should be considered the agent of the applicant and not the agent of the company. In considering the legal effect of such policy provisions, however, the courts consistently held that they were ineffective to change the fact that the insurance agent was really representing the insurer in completing the application. For example, in one case involving such a policy provision, the court said:

> It would be a stretch of legal principles to hold that a person dealing with an agent, apparently clothed with authority to act for his principal in the matter in hand, could be affected by notice, given after the negotiations were completed, that the party with whom he had dealt should be deemed transformed from the agent of one party into the agent of the other.[6]

Some insurers then began inserting a provision in the application to the effect that in completing the form, the agent was acting as the agent of the applicant. This served as notice to the applicant prior to issuance of the policy (which a provision in the policy did not do). Nevertheless the majority of courts held that provisions of this kind were also ineffective. One court summarized the situation in this way:

---

[6] *Kausal* v. *Minnesota Farmers' Mut. Insurance Association,* 31 Minn. 17 (1883).

This is but a form of words to attempt to create on paper an agency which in fact never existed. It is an attempt of the company, not to restrict the powers of its own agent, but an effort to do away with that relationship altogether by mere words, and to make him in the same manner the agent of the assured, when in fact such relation never existed.[7]

Although case law differs from state to state, the majority of decisions on the subject hold that the agency relationship between the insurer and the life underwriter cannot be changed by statements to the contrary in either the application or the policy.

Agency Is a Matter of Fact. It is important to keep in mind that what the parties say they meant is not important if what they did shows a different intent. Thus, an insurance company cannot make the life underwriter the agent of the applicant simply by saying he is, if the facts show that he represents no one but the company. However, there is nothing to keep the applicant himself from authorizing the life underwriter to represent him for certain purposes. If he does this, the underwriter for those purposes will be the agent of the applicant and subsequent policyowner.

In one case,[8] for example, a beneficiary sued for the $5,000 death benefit under a life insurance policy issued to her son. The contestable period had not elapsed, and the company defended on the grounds that material facts concerning the applicant's health were misrepresented in the application for the policy. The beneficiary maintained that the false statements were not made by the applicant but were inserted in the application by the field underwriter.

The evidence showed that at the time of application the applicant told the doctor that the field underwriter knew all the details and he, the doctor, could get the information he needed from him. On this evidence and the other facts of the case, the court held that, in legal effect, the insured had made the field underwriter his agent for the purpose of giving this medical history. The misrepresentations of the agent were the misrepresentations of the principal, but in this case the principal was the applicant. Again, the facts of the case governed; and the false statements were held to have been made by the applicant, since he had made the insurer's soliciting agent his agent for the purpose of answering those questions.

3.10 Insurance Brokers

In the legal sense of the term, an insurance broker is a person who is in business to obtain insurance for anyone who requests him to do so. For this reason, the insurance broker represents and, in the legal sense of the

---

[7] *Continental Insurance Co.* v. *Pearce*, 39 Kan. 396 (1888).

[8] *Indovina* v. *Metropolitan Life Insurance Company*, 334 Pa. 167, 5 A (2d) 556 (1939).

word, is the agent of the applicant for the purpose of obtaining the insurance. Life insurance presents a special problem in terminology, however. In life insurance, the term "brokerage business" is often used to describe any policies issued upon applications submitted by persons who are not regular members of the insurer's agency force (although they may be appointed agents for this purpose).

Even a regular member of the agency force of a particular company may also have a broker's license and submit an occasional application to another insurer, perhaps through a general agent of that insurer. This is sometimes done when coverage is available through the second insurer that is not offered by the first. For example, the proposed insured may require a highly rated policy which is not available from the agent's regular company.

Because state licensing laws and the practices of the various companies differ so widely, it is impossible to discuss this subject briefly in any but the most general terms. Nevertheless, any life insurance agent may represent the insurer for some purposes and the applicant for others; and in brokerage business, this is especially likely to be true. The important thing, therefore, is to analyze the situation and determine whom the agent is really representing. After that, most questions can be answered by the application of general principles of agency law.

3.11 Principals and Life Insurance

The life insurance company, as a corporate entity, must transact all of its business through agents. As a general rule, the applicant is an individual acting for himself alone. Nevertheless, there is nothing to prevent the applicant from authorizing another person to act for him; and if the applicant is itself a corporation (as is true in many business insurance situations), it must be represented by an agent. Thus, many life insurance transactions involve agency situations on both sides. The agent for the insurer deals with the agent for the applicant; and the basic rules of agency law apply in either case.

F. HOW AGENCY IS CREATED

3.12 Between Principal and Agent

There are at least three parties in any agency relationship: the principal, the agent, and a third person with whom the contract is made. Between the principal and the agent, the agency relationship is created by mutual consent and not otherwise. It may be established by express agreement, as in the case of an agency contract, or it may be implied from a prior course of dealing. If there is consideration for the agreement, it is contractual. However, consideration is not necessary. An agreement may be sufficient to establish an agency relationship, even though it is not a binding contract.

The principal's consent need not precede the transaction or transactions in question. Instead, he may adopt the actions as his own after they have been performed. In that case, there is said to be an agency by ratification.

3.13 Agency by Ratification

Sometimes an agent who is authorized to represent his principal in one line of business makes a contract in the name of the principal in an entirely different business. Sometimes, also, a person who has no agency authority whatever purports to make a contract for another, as his principal. In situations such as these, the contracts so made will not ordinarily have any binding effect upon the purported principal. However, if the contract proves advantageous, the person in whose name (but without whose consent) it was made—the purported principal—may adopt it as his own by ratifying it.

Ratification may be defined as the intentional adoption on the part of one person of the acts of another, taken purportedly as his agent but without authority. The relationship established in this way is called agency by ratification.

When one person, as principal, ratifies the acts of another, as agent, the ratification reverts back to and becomes effective as of the date of the act or actions that are ratified. For this reason, there can be no agency by ratification if the principal could not have authorized the act at the time it took place. For example, a corporation cannot ratify the contracts its promoters made before the date of incorporation, because the corporation was not in existence at the time the contracts were made. Thus, the corporation could not have authorized the acts of its promoters at the time they were taken. Similarly, the purported principal must have had the capacity to perform the act at the time it was performed. In other words, ratification cannot make a transaction valid if it was invalid at the time it took place.

Requirements for Ratification. Several requirements must be met before the act of a purported agent will be held to have been ratified. They are:

1. *There must have been a purported agency relationship of some kind.* One of the first requirements for ratification is that the agent must have assumed to act on behalf of the principal. The agent must have represented himself as an agent, and the third party must have thought

he was dealing with an agent. Without a purported agency relationship, ratification is impossible. Generally speaking, any acts which may be authorized beforehand may be ratified afterwards.

2. *The intended principal must ratify.* No one except the person intended as principal may ratify the act. Thus if agent Jones makes a contract in the name of Harold Brown, John Smith cannot ratify the action for his own benefit. The contract can be ratified by Brown and then assigned to Smith if the parties wish to do this, but it is legally impossible for Smith to become a party to the contract by ratification.

3. *The principal must have full knowledge.* The principal must have full knowledge of all the facts surrounding the transaction at the time he ratifies it. If this is not true—that is, if he did not know all the facts—he may later, upon learning the truth, cancel ("avoid" is the legal term) the ratification.

4. *He must ratify the act in its entirety.* The principal must intend to ratify the act, have the power to do so, and ratify it in its entirety. He cannot select the parts of the transaction that he likes, ratify them, and deny responsibility for the others. In fact, if he ratifies any part of the transaction, as a matter of law he ratifies it all.

Form of Ratification. If a special kind of authorization (in writing, for example) would have been required to authorize the act in the first place, ratification must be effected in that form also. In the absence of such a requirement, any conduct indicating approval of the act is sufficient to constitute an effective ratification. Thus, ratification may consist of express words, spoken or written, or it may be implied from conduct on the part of the principal that clearly indicates that he ratifies the actions of the purported agent and accepts them as his own.

Even if the purported principal does not intend to ratify the actions of an agent, he may be held to have done so if he accepts or retains the benefits or proceeds of the agent's activities. For example, acceptance by a life insurer of the premium for a life insurance contract, with full knowledge of an agent's misconduct in accepting the application and premium, may constitute ratification of the agent's action. The underlying principle is that one may not accept the benefits of a transaction while refusing to assume the responsibility it entails.

Silence alone does not indicate ratification. However, a principal will ordinarily be held to have ratified the agent's act if, with full knowledge of the facts, he fails to repudiate it within a reasonable length of time.

Ratification in Life Insurance. Like every other aspect of agency, ratification operates with respect to either party to a contract. Thus in the life insurance field it applies to the insured as well as the insurer. In fact, some agency principles, especially those which operate without the volition of the parties, can be illustrated more clearly in connection with the insured than with the insurer. In one case,[9] for example, a licensed broker named Kantoff obtained a $50,000 policy for Sedlak Motor Sales, Inc., on the life of Sedlak and later paid a premium in the amount of $1,529 during the grace period in order to keep the policy from lapsing. Sedlak had not authorized this payment and refused to reimburse the broker on the grounds that the latter was an agent for the insurance company. Sedlak contended that under accepted rules of agency law Kantoff could not act for him and also for the company without the consent of both parties. In other words, Sedlak took the position that Kantoff was not his agent, and the latter brought suit for the amount of premium he had paid. The court decided the case as follows:

> . . . Defendants [Sedlak Motor Sales, Inc.] urge that plaintiff [Kantoff] could not be their agent since he was also the agent for the insurance company, and this they claim violated the rule of law that an agent's duty of loyalty prevents him from acting for adverse parties without the consent of both. We think, however, that this rule is not applicable because, as the court properly found, defendants, with knowledge of plaintiff's agency with the insurance company, authorized him to represent them in obtaining insurance. *Adams* v. *Larson*, 279 Ill. 268, 277–8.
>
> We think, further, that, even if we assume that payment of the premium was beyond the scope of the authorized agency, defendants ratified this act and thereby incurred liability for the amount paid on their behalf. The reasons for this conclusion are as follows: Sedlak's acceptance of the policy made him liable for the premium. *Equitable Life Assurance Society* v. *Mueller*, 99 Ill. App. 460. After several unsuccessful attempts to see Sedlak with respect to the premium, plaintiff paid the premium during the grace period in order to protect his principal by preventing the policy from lapsing. Defendants knew plaintiff paid the premium because they received no premium notice from the company but they did receive a bill from plaintiff on his own stationery. With this knowledge they retained the policy even until the trial. They therefore had the protection of the policy (*Nalty* v. *Federal Casualty Co.*, 245 Ill. App. 180, 183) and the inference is they intended to have that benefit, for the earlier policy which Sedlak rejected was returned at once. Furthermore, they at no time disclaimed plaintiff's authority to pay the premium. Under these circumstances we conclude that payment, even if unauthorized, was ratified and bound defendants, who accepted the benefits, to reimburse. *Cobb* v. *Sparr*, 153 Ill. App. 92, 99. As between principal and agent the conduct of the principal will be liberally interpreted in favor of ratification. *Holmes* v. *Morris*, 341 Ill. 351, 358.

Note first that the decision is based on the principle of agency by ratification. The motor company contended that Kantoff could not be the agent of both parties to the contract without the consent of both. However, the court said that the motor company had authorized Kantoff to

---

[9] *Kantoff* v. *Sedlak Motor Sales, Inc.*, 130 N.E. (2d) 289 (Ill. App., 1955).

represent it in obtaining the insurance; and even if payment of the renewal premium might be assumed to be beyond the agent's authority, the motor company had ratified the action in two ways. First, knowing of the payment, it retained the policy—that is, it retained the benefits of the transaction. And, second, with full knowledge of the facts, it did not dispute Kantoff's authority to pay the premium, presumably not until the trial.

3.14 Agency by Estoppel

So far as principal and agent are concerned, the agency relationship cannot be created except with the consent of the principal. With respect to third parties, however, there are some circumstances under which, for technical reasons, the purported principal may be legally prohibited from denying that an agency relationship existed even though it did not in fact exist and, indeed, may have been contrary to his intentions. In such situations, the principal is said to be *estopped* to deny that there was an agency relationship; and the result is agency by estoppel. The legal effect is no different from that of a genuine agency relationship so far as the third person is concerned, but the situation of the purported agent is different. For example, he may not be entitled to any compensation.

Agency by estoppel requires an appearance of agency. The principal must have permitted this appearance to continue and must have conducted himself in such a way that a reasonable person would be justified in believing that an agency relationship actually existed. Agency by estoppel also requires a third person who relies on that appearance of agency and who would experience a loss if the principal were permitted to deny the existence of the agency.

As an illustration, assume that Bill Smith is an agent of the Jones Company for the sale of Jones Company products. The company makes a small store available for his use; and the Evans Service Company provides the janitorial services. Bill pays all bills for these and other services and is reimbursed by the Jones Company.

After a few months, Bill learns that the Evans company will supply the service for a lower price if the user contracts to use the services for not less than a year. Even though he is not authorized to make contracts of this kind, Bill enters into such a contract with the Evans Service Company as an agent for and in the name of the Jones Company; and the services are supplied as agreed upon for several months. Then the Jones Company learns that it can obtain similar services from another company at a lower price and notifies the Evans company that its services will no longer be needed. Evans objects, saying that it has a contract with the Jones Company, completed by Smith, its agent, to furnish the service for the remainder of the year.

The Jones Company replies that although Smith was and is its agent for the purpose of selling its products, he was never authorized to complete contracts for services in the name of the company. Therefore, the contract he made in the name of the Jones Company is not binding.

The Jones Company is right about Smith's authority, but the situation may not be quite as simple as it seems. If the Evans Service Company sues the Jones Company, the latter may find, under the circumstances outlined, that it is estopped to deny that Smith had the authority he appeared to have to make the contract in question.

First, there was an appearance of agency. Certainly Smith represented the Jones Company for the sale of its products, and he appeared to be in charge of the shop. The Jones Company permitted that situation to continue and allowed Smith to pay the bills as they were presented. The Evans company relied upon the appearance of agency and had no reason to believe that Smith did not have the authority to complete the contract in question. In situations of this kind, a company in the position of the Jones Company may be estopped (forbidden as a matter of law) to deny that Smith had the authority he appeared to have. The Jones Company would then be in the position of having to honor the contract or be liable in damages for its breach.

An estoppel always operates against the wishes of the principal. For this reason it is essential that, by his own conduct, the principal shall have been responsible for misleading the person who seeks to establish the agency. Nothing the agent does or says will be sufficient, and there is no presumption of agency. The fact that John Doe tells you that he is an agent for the White Company does not justify you in believing that he is. There must be evidence of some kind to support his statement—some identification furnished by the company, an established place of business with the company name displayed, or a course of dealing with him as an agent of the company. A third party cannot merely assume that an agency relationship exists. It is also necessary that the third party shall in fact have relied upon the appearance of agency which the principal has permitted to exist.

Estoppel in Life Insurance. Agency by estoppel situations frequently occur in connection with the formation and operation of the life insurance contract. One court states it thus:

> As in the case of other agencies, an insurance company will be estopped to deny that a certain person is its agent or possesses the authority he assumes to exercise where the insurance company knowingly causes or permits him so to act as to justify a third person of ordinarily careful and prudent business habits to believe that he possesses the authority exercised.[10]

---

[10] *Pagni* v. *New York Life Insurance Co.*, 173 Wash. 322, 23 P. (2d) 6, 93 A.L.R. 1325 (1933).

Thus a life insurance company might terminate an agency and yet permit the agent to retain some or all of the credentials, documents, and the like, that he had been using. If John Jones has been the duly authorized soliciting agent of the X.Y.Z. Life Insurance Company and still retains a supply of life insurance application forms and a rate book, there is no very compelling reason for a third party to doubt that he continues to be an agent of that company. For this reason, life insurance companies are usually very strict about requiring the surrender of all such insignia of agency at the termination of an agency contract.

3.15 Estoppel Distinguished from Ratification

An estoppel operates only for the benefit of the third person, who has dealt with a person who appeared to be but was not an agent. An estoppel does not create an agency relationship; it only prevents the third person from suffering a loss that would result if the agency were successfully denied. Ratification, by contrast, does establish the agency relationship. Thus, it guarantees the agent his compensation and any other benefits to which he may be entitled.

In either instance—agency by estoppel or agency by ratification—the third party will have an enforceable contract with the principal. In agency by ratification, however, the principal is usually liable under the contract because he wanted to perform the contract; in estoppel situations, he must perform or be held liable in damages in spite of what he may actually have wished.

G. AUTHORITY

3.16 Power and Authority

In a general sense, the word "power" denotes all the things that an agent might do to obligate his principal in the contractual sense. The term "authority," by contrast, encompasses only what he is authorized to do. In a basic sense, the power of an agent to create or modify the contracts of his principal arises out of the authority the principal gives. As a practical matter, however, his power may be considerably broader than his authority.

3.17 Express, Implied, and Apparent Authority

The power of the agent to bind the principal combines three general kinds of authority—express, implied, and apparent. *Express* authority is the authority the principal intends to give the agent and does give him, either orally or in writing. Incidental or *implied* authority is authority which is not expressly granted but which must be exercised if, as a practical matter, the express authority is to have any real meaning. An agent is said to have implied authority to transact the business of the principal in accordance with the general customs of the business. The fact that the principal may not actually be acquainted with such customs does not alter the rule.

Apparent authority is the authority the actions of the principal may lead innocent third parties to believe the agent has. Thus it is the basis for agency by estoppel. Apparent authority includes all the authority that a person of ordinary prudence, acquainted with the customs and nature of the business, would be justified in assuming that the agent had. Apparent authority is quite apart from and often in conflict with the principal's actual intentions.

Although apparent authority must rest upon and grow out of the words or actions of the principal, third persons are generally justified in relying upon a course of dealing with the agent in which the principal has seemed to acquiesce. This principle is frequently met in life insurance situations where agents who are not authorized to collect renewal premiums may nevertheless receive such premiums over a period of time and remit them to the company without objection from the company. After such a course of conduct, if the agent later neglects to forward a premium so collected, the insurer may declare the policy lapsed for non-payment of premiums. In such cases, the insurer is usually held to be estopped to deny that the agent had the authority to collect the premium he did not remit since the insurer's own conduct helped to create the appearance of such authority.

To illustrate, assume that a policy lapses without nonforfeiture values and the insured dies a few days later. The insurer denies the death claim and the beneficiary sues, claiming that the premium was paid to the soliciting agent before the end of the grace period. The insurer answers that the agent had no authority to accept renewal premiums. Therefore, the premium was not paid until it reached the home office. If the beneficiary can show a course of conduct in which other premiums had been paid to the soliciting agent, forwarded to the home office, and accepted without objection by the insurer, the insurer will usually be held to be estopped to deny that the agent had the authority he appeared to have. The claim then will be payable because the premium was paid, in the legal sense, within the grace period.

A third person cannot maintain that he relied on the agent's apparent authority if, in fact, he knew of limitations of that authority. Neither can he disregard irregularities in the agent's behavior that should arouse suspicions in the mind of a reasonable person. In other words, the situation must have been such that a reasonable person would actually have been misled, and the party attempting to establish the estoppel has the responsibility of proving that the facts were such as to justify him in believing that the agent was acting within his authority.

3.18 Authority to Contract

Since agency in its purest sense concerns the formation or modification of contractual relationships, it might be supposed that an agent always has the power to complete a binding contract on behalf of his principal, but this is not true. The agent always has the power to affect the contractual relationships of his principal, but he does not necessarily have the power to complete a contract. For instance, the life insurance field underwriter works in some of the most crucial stages of the development of the life insurance contract, but most agents do not have the express authority to complete contracts of life insurance except in a limited way. For instance, they are usually authorized to issue a conditional or a binding receipt and they may complete contracts by delivering policies and collecting the initial premiums. In either situation, however, their authority is usually strictly defined.

Unless the principal and agent agree otherwise, authority to make a contract is implied if the agent has the authority to carry out a particular transaction and making a contract is incidental to that transaction. Similarly, the authority is implied if making contracts is reasonably necessary in order to perform the main duty of the agency. Authority to make contracts may be implied from a custom of the business, and there may be apparent authority if the principal has permitted the agent to seem to possess that authority.

Customs of the Insurance Business. Since the authority to make a contract may be implied from a custom of the business, it is of special importance to note the respects in which the customs of the life insurance business differ from the customs in other lines of insurance. For example, the fire insurance agent usually has the authority to complete a binding contract of fire insurance. After underwriting review by the company, the contract can be canceled, if necessary.

In life insurance, the contract is not cancelable, and the agent is not usually authorized to complete the contract. Thus the customs of the life insurance business differ markedly from the customs in other lines of the insurance business with which most people are familiar. It is highly important that this difference be made clear to any persons with whom the life agent may deal; otherwise situations of apparent authority to complete a life insurance contract can easily develop. In this day of growing companion line businesses, where one agent may handle several lines of insurance for associated companies, such a distinction is of even greater importance. The same person may have considerably broader authority as an agent of a fire insurance company, for example, than he has as the agent of the companion life insurance company.

3.19 Authority to Receive Payments

If the agent has the express authority to receive payments, payment to him is, in legal effect, payment to the principal. The full significance of this statement is not apparent until one realizes that although the agent has a duty to deal with his principal in good faith, there is no effective guarantee that he will do so. Thus, if receiving payments is within the scope of the agent's authority, a third person who pays the agent will be protected even though the principal never receives the money.

Authority to receive payments will be implied if the collection or receipt of money is incidental to the agency transaction or is ordinarily considered necessary in carrying out the main authority expressly conferred. An agent authorized to receive payment of a principal sum, for example, has the implied authority to receive interest payments on it.

3.20 Limitations of Authority

The principal has the right to limit the extent of the authority he is willing to grant to the agent. Even if secret, such limitations will govern the conduct of the agent and the principal. Secret limitations, however, are not binding on a third party who does not know of their existence. Thus limitations of the agent's authority must be communicated to the persons who may rely on the agency or they will not be effective as far as those persons are concerned. In spite of these general rules, however, if the violation of secret limitations is so flagrant as to arouse the suspicion of a reasonable person, a third party is not entitled to rely upon the fact that he was not actually informed of the limitations. In such cases, he is put on notice by the unreasonable aspects of the situation and must ascertain the facts before dealing with the agent.

Limitations and the Life Insurance Agent. A life insurance company has the same right to limit the authority of its field underwriters that any other principal has to limit the authority of its agents. The limitations must be made known to the persons with whom the field underwriters deal and must not be in conflict with any settled rule of law. Generally speaking, if these limitations are set forth in the policy, they will be considered to have been communicated to the insured whether he actually learns of them or not. He is presumed to read the contract even if he does not actually do so. However, limitations communicated in this manner are binding upon the insured only with respect to transactions that take place after the delivery of the policy.

To make such limitations effective with respect to transactions which take place prior to the delivery of the policy, they are often included in the application form. It is generally held that the insured is charged with notice of any valid limitations set forth in the application even though he may not actually have read them. It is his duty to read the application.

3.21 Unenforceable Limitations

Making the Agent the Agent of the Insured. As previously mentioned, a number of companies attempted in the early days to make the life underwriter the agent of the applicant by including an appropriate provision, first in the policy, and then later in the application. By the great weight of authority, the courts have held that provisions of this kind are unenforceable.

Notice to the Agent. One limitation frequently included in applications for life insurance concerns two basic principles of agency law: that notice to the agent is notice to the principal and that the knowledge of the agent is the knowledge of the principal. It is quite generally held that these principles cannot be completely circumvented. Life insurance companies frequently include in their applications a provision to the effect that notice to or knowledge of any agent or medical examiner of the company shall not be deemed to be notice to or knowledge of the company unless the information is recorded in the application. One company includes the following paragraph in its application:

> *Authority of Agent.* It is agreed that no agent or medical examiner is authorized to make any contract for the company or to determine insurability or to waive or alter any conditions of the application, contract or receipt; and that notice to or knowledge of any such agent or examiner, as to any facts whenever given, shall not be deemed notice to the company unless recorded in this application.

The court decisions are in conflict as to whether this type of provision is valid. For instance, one landmark case,[11] decided in 1886, held that provisions of this general type are valid. The leading case holding that such provisions are not valid is the case of *Sternaman* v. *Metropolitan Life Insurance Company*,[12] a New York Court of Appeals case decided in 1902. There the application had included a provision that the answers and statements contained in the application and those made to the medical examiner would become a part of the contract of insurance, that the answers were "full, true and correctly recorded," and continued in part as follows:

---

[11] *New York Life Insurance Company* v. *Fletcher*, 117 U.S. 519, 6 S.Ct. 837, 29 L. Ed. 934 (1886).
[12] 170 N.Y. 13, 62 N.E. 763, 57 L.R.A. 318, 88 Am. St. Rep. 625 (1902).

. . . and that no information or statement not contained in the application and in the statements made to the medical examiner, received or acquired at any time by any person, shall be binding upon the company, or shall modify or alter the declaration and warranties made therein; that the persons who wrote in the answers and statements were and are our agents for the purpose, and not the agents of the company. . . .

Note that the insurer had attempted to make this an agreement that no information or statements not contained in the application would be binding on the company and, in addition, that the "persons who wrote in the answers and statements" were the agents of the applicant and not the agents of the insurer.

The insurer introduced evidence to show that the answers to some of the more than 100 medical questions were not true. The attorney for the beneficiary wished to show by oral testimony that true answers were given and that the medical examiner said that they were unimportant. This testimony was excluded on the grounds that it was "incompetent, immaterial, and in violation of the contract."

The court said that regardless of the wording of the contract, the medical examiner was the agent of the insurer and not the applicant. In other words, the agency relationship was a matter of fact that could not be changed simply by a declaration to the contrary. The decision continued:

Sound public policy prohibits the company from stipulating for immunity from the consequences of its own negligence, or, what is the same thing, the negligence of its agent. . . .

The court then quoted the agreement concerning information or statements not contained in the application and continued as follows:

The facts sought to be proved were contained in the oral statements made to the medical examiner, but assuming that recorded statements only were meant, the result would be an agreement that the company might perpetrate a fraud upon the insured by issuing a policy and accepting premiums thereon, knowing all the time that the contract was void, or voidable at its election. The law does not permit this, for it declares that the company is estopped from taking advantage of such a contract, because it would be against equity and opposed to public policy.

Cases on this question are so various that it is difficult to say that one line or the other represents the majority opinion. The numerical weight of authority, however, seems to be on the side of the case that upheld the limitation preventing the knowledge of the agent from being the knowledge of the principal unless the information in question is contained in the application.

H. DUTIES AND LIABILITIES

For obvious reasons, much of the law of agency has developed out of instances in which the agency relationship has either not existed or where it has been misunderstood in its nature and scope by one or another of the parties concerned. As a result, the emphasis in a discussion of the law of agency is very often on the responsibility of the principal in cases in which he did not want responsibility, on liabilities that were his when he wanted only the benefits, on the disadvantages of the agency relationship to the virtual exclusion of the benefits. As with most human relationships, if things go smoothly the question of legal rights and responsibilities rarely arises. It is only when something goes wrong that the parties go to court for a clarification of their respective rights, duties, and responsibilities.

The following discussion relates primarily to those principles that govern when questions as to legal rights and responsibilities arise among the principal, the agent, and third parties who may be involved. However, it should be borne in mind that by far the majority of agency transactions operate to the mutual advantage of principal and agent, and even when problems arise, the majority are resolved without court action.

3.22 Of the Agent

The agent has the duty of proper conduct, the duty to act with reasonable care, and the duty to act within his authority. It will be remembered that he is a fiduciary and bound to exercise the utmost good faith and loyalty towards his principal. He must not act adversely to the interests of the principal, either to his own advantage or by serving as agent for another third party whose interests are adverse to those of the principal. Because of this duty of loyalty and good faith, he may not obtain any secret profit or advantage from the agency relationship or furnish anyone else with information that might result in actions adverse to the interests of the principal.

The agent who has violated any of his duties to his principal may be sued by the latter for damages. The agent is also personally liable to other persons for any damages resulting from his fraudulent, malicious, or negligent acts. Even though he is acting as an agent, he is as responsible for any damages resulting from his own misconduct as if the agency did not exist.

3.23 Of the Principal

It is a general rule of law that every person has a duty to conduct his affairs, whether through his own efforts or those of his agents, in such a way as not to injure others. If he does not do this and if injury results to others, he may be responsible in damages. Thus the principal is liable for all statements made by the agent in the course of transacting his business, even though they may be wrongful and even though he (the principal) has not authorized or even known of the misconduct. The principal is liable for the frauds and misrepresentations of the agent within the scope of the latter's authority and is chargeable with, and bound by, any knowledge or notice acquired by the agent within the scope of his authority.

I. HOW AGENTS ARE CLASSIFIED

Traditionally, agents have been classified according to the extent of their authority. Thus, a special agent is one who has the authority to complete one special business transaction and nothing more. A general agent has the authority to transact all the business of the principal in connection with a specific subject matter, or all the business at a certain location. Those persons who are authorized to transact all the business of a principal, of whatever kind, are said to be universal agents.

3.24 Classifications in Insurance

In the field of insurance, the same terms are used as in other agency areas, but sometimes with quite different meanings. As a result, the terminology is often confusing. Not only do the meanings differ from those of the traditional agency terminology, but they also vary from one kind of insurance to another. Special agents for fire insurance companies, for example, usually have power that would make them general agents as that term is used in the traditional sense.

3.25 The General Agent

In life insurance, a general agent is ordinarily a person who represents his company within a certain geographical area. Regardless of his title, however, a general agent in life insurance is only a special agent in the usual sense of the term, since he does not have the authority, except in a very limited sense, to complete a life insurance contract with the applicant.

Officers. The executive officers of a life insurance company are often said to be special agents, since they have only the authority granted them by the charter or articles of association and the bylaws of the corporation. However, in the general conduct of the business the officers exercise all the powers of the corporation, by authorization of the board of directors. Thus, they should be considered general agents as that term is ordinarily used.

3.26 Special Agents

A special agent is an agent who has the authority to perform some special act or acts. Solicitors, attorneys, and medical examiners are all special agents of the life insurance company which they represent. The local agent is also a special agent because of the limitations on his authority. Nevertheless, it should not be assumed that limited authority means limited effectiveness. For example, the medical examiner's authority is narrowly restricted, but within this special area he has the power to bind the company by his acts and by his knowledge concerning one of the most important factors of insurability—the physical condition of the applicant. Knowledge of the medical examiner with respect to diseases or prior treatment of the applicant not disclosed on the application is often imputed to the company and may effectively prevent it, by estoppel, from asserting an otherwise valid defense based on misrepresentation of material facts.

J. TERMINATION OF THE AGENCY RELATIONSHIP

3.27 How Agency Is Terminated

Once an agency is proved to have existed, it will be presumed to have continued unless there is clear evidence of its termination. The general rule is that an agency can be terminated only by action or agreement of the principal and the agent or by operation of law. The principal ways in which such termination can be effected are:

1. By action of the parties. An agency is terminated if the principal discharges the agent or if the agent renounces the agency. Even though the agent's actions are wrongful he may still abandon the agency, but he will be responsible to the principal in damages.

2. In accordance with the parties' agreement. The agency contract may give either the principal or the agent, or both of them, the right to cancel the agency relationship at will. It may also provide that the agency shall continue for a certain length of time and then terminate automatically, or that it shall continue until a specified objective has been accomplished. In either of these latter situations, the agency will terminate at the completion of the period specified or on attainment of the designated objective.

3. By operation of law. At common law, except in special circumstances, the death of the principal automatically terminated the agency, even though the third party or parties were ignorant of his death; and this rule is followed by most courts today. Death of the agent also terminates the agency, as will loss of a license or failure to qualify for one.

Bankruptcy of the principal terminates the authority of the agent, but insolvency alone does not. Bankruptcy of the agent has the same effect if his financial condition affects the interest of the principal to such an extent that, with knowledge of the facts, the principal would have revoked the agent's authority.

The outbreak of war does not necessarily terminate the agency relationship, but if it makes the agent an enemy alien of the country of the principal's residence, the agency will be terminated automatically.

3.28 Effect of Termination

Generally. When the authority of the agent is terminated, he loses all right to act for the principal. He has then only the duty to account to the principal.

Notice. If the agency is revoked by the principal, the revocation is not effective until the agent is notified. Notice must also be given to third persons with whom the agent has had previous dealings. Otherwise the agent's power to bind his principal continues until they do receive notice of the termination, although he no longer has the authority to do so.

SUMMARY

Definition of Agency

In any situation where one person is authorized to represent and act for another in the creation or modification of contracts, the relationship that exists between the person having the power and the person he represents is known as agency. As a general rule, anything that one can do for himself he can appoint an agent to do for him. This excludes committing a crime or such personal actions as making a will or voting.

The agency relationship depends upon the facts of a situation, not the terminology used; and it differs from the employer-employee relationship, in which one person works for another but does not have the authority or power to commit him contractually. Different also is the role of the independent contractor, who performs services for another but is not under the latter's control.

Nature of Agency

The basic characteristic of the agency relationship is the power on the part of the agent to bring about or modify the contractual relationships between his principal and third parties. There are, however, other important characteristics of the relationship. Thus, it is a fiduciary relationship, which means that the agent has a duty to act primarily for the benefit of the principal. A second characteristic is the fact that the principal has a continuous right of control so far as the duties of the agency are concerned.

Basic Principles of Agency Law

Among the most important general principles of agency law are the following:

1. The acts of the agent within the scope of his authority are the acts of the principal; and the acts of the agent within the apparent scope of the agent's authority may be held to be binding on the principal as the result of estoppel.
2. The contract, once made, is the contract of the principal.
3. Payment to the agent, within the scope of his authority, is payment to the principal.
4. Knowledge of the agent is the knowledge of the principal.

Qualifications

Of Agents. It is not necessary that an agent have contractual capacity in his own right, but in the case of insurance agents, as well as other kinds of agents whose activities involve the general public, there are often statutory requirements that must be met before an agent is qualified for appointment.

Of Principals. Anyone who has contractual capacity may appoint an agent to represent him; and everyone is presumed, as a matter of law, to have such capacity. However, one who does not have the capacity to contract cannot remedy that lack by appointing an agent who has it.

Life Insurance Agents

Life and health insurance agents must qualify under the laws of the state in which they are to act, and the agent's authority is usually defined in his contract with the insurer. Insurance brokers are persons who are in business to obtain insurance for anyone who requests them to do so. They thus represent the applicant rather than the insurer.

Creation of Agency

By Mutual Consent. Between principal and agent, the relationship of agency is created only by mutual consent. However, it is not essential that the consent of the principal precede the action or actions taken by the agent.

By Ratification. If the consent of the principal is given after the agent has acted on his behalf, the agency relationship is established by ratification. In such cases, there must have been a purported agency relationship to begin with; the intended principal (not a stranger to the transaction) must ratify the action; he must ratify it with full knowledge of the circumstances of the transaction in question; and he must ratify the transaction in its entirety. Ordinarily, no particular form of ratification is required.

Estoppel

If the purported principal has permitted another person to appear to be his agent and a third party has entered a contract with that person in the belief that the latter was authorized to take the action he took, the principal may be estopped to deny that the agent had the authority he appeared to have. Such situations are said to create an agency by estoppel. This is true only with respect to the principal and the third party, however. Estoppel benefits the third person. Ratification benefits the agent as well. In either case, however, the purported principal is bound by the contract.

Power and Authority

The power of the agent to create or modify the contractual relationships of his principal is based upon the authority granted him by the principal. This consists of express authority, incidental or implied authority, and apparent authority. Express authority is that which the principal gives the agent, either orally or in writing. Implied authority is that which is not specifically granted but which the agent must have in order to exercise the express authority he has been given. Apparent authority, as the term implies, is authority which the agent only appears to have.

The authority to make a contract is implied if the agent has other duties that reasonably require making contracts. Implied also is the authority to receive payments if such collection is necessary in carrying out the agent's major duties.

Scope of the Agent's Authority

Generally speaking, the principal has the right to limit the extent of the agent's authority in any way he wishes. However, if these limitations are not communicated to others, the latter may rely on the agency and deal with the agent as if there were no limitations. An insurance company has the same right to limit the authority of its agents as does any other principal; and one relatively common limitation concerns the rule that notice to or knowledge of the agent is notice to or knowledge of the principal. In their applications, insurers frequently include provisions to the effect that knowledge of the agent will not be imputed to the principal unless it is reduced to writing and included in the application. Although not uniformly upheld, such provisions are considered valid in many jurisdictions.

Agents Classified

Terminology concerning agents in life insurance differs from that used in general agency law. Thus a general agent in life insurance is usually a person who represents his company within a certain geographic area. However, he is a special agent as that term is customarily used, since he does not usually have the authority to complete a life insurance contract with the applicant.

Duties and Liabilities

The agent has several duties toward his principal and must not act adversely toward him. He may not obtain any secret profit; and, if he violates any of his duties, he may be sued by his principal for damages. The agent is also personally liable to third persons for damages resulting from his own wrongful conduct.

The principal is liable to third parties for all statements made by the agent in the course of transacting the principal's business; and he is liable for the frauds and misrepresentations of the agent within the scope of the latter's authority.

Termination of the Agency Relationship

The agency relationship may be terminated in any of the following ways:

1. By action of the parties.
2. In accordance with the parties' agreement.
3. By operation of law; this includes the death of the principal or of the agent, loss of a license, or failure to qualify for one. Bankruptcy of the principal and, under some circumstances, bankruptcy of the agent will terminate the agency, as will the outbreak of war if it makes the agent an enemy alien of the principal's country of residence.

ILLUSTRATIVE CASE

The following case has been selected because it illustrates many of the principles discussed in this chapter. It is printed here almost in its entirety in order that the student may follow the reasoning of the court in applying these principles of agency law.

WELDON THOMAS FRUGÉ, *Plaintiff-Appellee*, v. WOODMEN OF THE WORLD LIFE INSURANCE SOCIETY, *Defendant-Appellant*[13]

Weldon Thomas Frugé instituted this suit against Woodmen of the World Life Insurance Society to recover benefits alleged to be due plaintiff under a life insurance contract issued by defendant. Under this contract defendant insured the life of plaintiff's minor son, Ronald Anthony Frugé, now deceased, and plaintiff is named as the beneficiary. Defendant denies coverage and liability on the ground that in answer to questions contained in the application for this insurance coverage plaintiff made material misrepresentations relating to the health of his minor son, who was the insured.

After trial on the merits, judgment was rendered by the trial court in favor of plaintiff for the sum of $1,000.00, being the full amount of benefits provided in the policy, subject to a credit of $43.23, the last mentioned sum having been deposited by defendant in the registry of the court representing a refund of the premiums which had been paid on the policy plus the court costs which had accrued up to the time the deposit was made. Defendant has appealed.

The sole issue presented is whether plaintiff misrepresented facts relating to the health of his minor son in the application submitted to defendant for this insurance coverage, and, if he did, whether the misstatements were of such a nature as to vitiate the certificate of insurance.

The record shows that plaintiff's son was born on October 14, 1949, with a congenital heart defect known as a leaking heart, and that he continued to have this heart condition up to the time of his death. Within a few weeks after the child was born, however, the defendant issued a life insurance contract or certificate insuring the boy's life, and plaintiff kept that certificate in effect by the regular payment of premiums until the insured was seven or eight years of age, at which time plaintiff voluntarily surrendered the policy for its cash surrender value. The evidence does not show whether the defendant knew of the insured's heart condition at the time the first policy was issued or while it was in effect.

Sometime during the month of October, 1962, which was several years after the first insurance certificate had been surrendered, plaintiff discussed with Norbert L. Miller, sales representative for the defendant insurer, the question of whether defendant would issue another life insurance certificate covering the life of plaintiff's son, who was then thirteen years of age. Plaintiff and Miller differ somewhat in their recollection of what was said about the boy's health at that time. They agree, however, that in that discussion Miller expressed the opinion that the defendant would issue a certificate insuring the

---

[13] 170 So. (2d) 539 (CA La. 3d Cir., 1965). Here, again, "plaintiff-appellee" shows that this person brought the action in the lower court, but the other party appealed the decision.

life of the boy, especially since the company had previously insured him, and Miller at that time informed plaintiff that he would check into the matter and would let plaintiff know.

On November 6, 1962, Miller called on plaintiff at the latter's home and informed him that the defendant company was willing to issue a certificate of insurance on the life of plaintiff's son. Miller then produced a form of application for a life insurance certificate, and he proceeded to ask plaintiff the questions which were on this form, and Miller wrote the answers on this form as they were given to him by plaintiff. After Miller had completed the form of application he handed it to plaintiff for his signature, and plaintiff proceeded to sign the completed application without reading it.

Pursuant to that application a certificate was issued by the defendant Society on December 1, 1962, insuring the life of plaintiff's minor son, and plaintiff was named as the beneficiary under that insurance contract. The insured died of a heart disease on July 8, 1963, which was less than eight months after the policy was issued.

      ❋ ❋ ❋ ❋ ❋

Plaintiff testified that he became aware of his son's heart condition a few weeks after the birth of the child, and that he knew that his son still had that condition in November, 1962, when he submitted to defendant a formal application for the aforementioned insurance coverage. He further stated, however, that while discussing this matter with Miller a few weeks before the formal application was completed, he informed Miller, "that the boy still had the heart condition, and that whenever he exerted too much or exercised too much . . . that his body would turn blue, and that he could not participate in any sports, rugged sports. . . ." He further testified that while the application was being filled out on November 6, 1962 . . . plaintiff then again informed Miller fully of his son's existing heart condition. He stated that when Miller finished writing answers to the questions contained in the form, he handed the completed application to plaintiff, and that plaintiff signed the application without reading it over. Plaintiff testified that he did not know what answers had been written in response to the abovementioned questions until after defendant had refused payment of the benefits allegedly due under the contract following his son's death.

Defendant's agent, Miller, acknowledges that while discussing the matter with plaintiff in October, 1962, plaintiff told him that his son "was born with a leaking heart," but he does not recall plaintiff telling him that the heart condition still existed. He states that it was his understanding that the boy had not had any more trouble with his heart and that he was then in good health, although he admits that he does not remember plaintiff making any statement to that effect. Miller further testified that in asking plaintiff questions 4, 5 and 7 appearing on the application he purposely omitted asking him anything about the boy's heart condition, because he explained, "I thought the Woodmen of the World had a record of that particular statement before." Miller concedes that the boy's heart condition was mentioned while the application was being completed, but he says he stated to plaintiff at that time that "The Woodmen of The World evidently has a record of that already, so that's nothing to worry about." He does not recall whether plaintiff read the application before signing it, but he states that plaintiff could have read it if he had asked to do so.

(1) We think the evidence establishes that plaintiff fully and correctly informed defendant's agent, Miller, of the existing heart condition of the insured before the application was submitted, and that he informed Miller again of that condition while the application was being completed. Miller, although being fully aware of the boy's condition, nevertheless wrote answers to questions in the application which indicated that the boy did not have and had never had a heart disease. The answers to questions 4, 5 and 7 in the application are false insofar as they relate to the boy's heart condition, and in our opinion the nature of the insured's heart ailment was such that it materially affected the hazard assumed by the insurer.

Plaintiff, however, carefully gave true and correct answers relating to the health of the insured at the time Miller filled out the application form, and he previously had informed defendant's agent fully of the boy's heart condition. Miller, nevertheless, being fully aware of this condition, inserted false answers in the application. Plaintiff then signed the application without reading it, and he was unaware of the fact that false answers had been given in it. We think the evidence establishes clearly that plaintiff answered the questions propounded to him by defendant's agent truthfully and correctly, that plaintiff was in good faith, that he is not chargeable with fraud, and that he clearly had no intent to deceive defendant or its agent.

✿   ✿   ✿   ✿   ✿

(2, 3) We think it is settled, therefore, that in view of the provisions of LSA-R.S. 22:619 an insurer cannot succeed in avoiding liability on a life insurance policy on the ground that false statements were made in the application, unless the insurer establishes: (1) That the false statements were made with actual intent to deceive; *and* (2) that the facts allegedly misstated were material. The law also is clear that where the insurer asserts a special defense of this sort the burden of proof rests on the insurer to establish both the materiality and an actual intent to deceive. . . .[14]

(4) The rule also prevails in this state that when the agent of an insurer, acting within the scope of his authority, proceeds to fill out the blanks in an application for a policy of insurance, the acts, representations and mistakes of that agent are considered to be those of the insurance company. In such a case if the agent by mistake, fraud or negligence inserts erroneous or untrue answers to the questions contained in the application, these representations bind the *insurer* but are not binding upon the *insured,* provided that the insured was justifiably ignorant of the erroneous answers, had no actual or implied knowledge thereof, was guilty of no bad faith or fraud, and had no intent to deceive the insurer. [Citations.][15]

---

[14] The court is stating here the provisions and requirements of the Louisiana statutory law. The exact requirements for supporting the denial of a claim on the basis of material misrepresentation differ somewhat from state to state, as will be discussed in Chapter 8.

[15] Here a list of citations summarizes rules of law developed in court decisions.

These rules are applicable when the agent of the insurer deals with the beneficiary in regard to the insurance, as well as when the agent deals with the insured himself. *Harris* v. *Guaranty Income Life Insurance Company,* supra.

(5) In the instant suit the plaintiff was justifiably ignorant of the fact that incorrect answers had been written by defendant's agent to some of the questions contained in the application. Plaintiff had no actual or implied knowledge of the fact that these incorrect answers had been given. He was guilty of no bad faith or fraud, and clearly he had no intent to deceive the defendant. Under those circumstances we think the trial court correctly held that defendant is not entitled to avoid liability on the ground that plaintiff had misrepresented facts which materially affected the risk.

Defendant contends, however, that it is immaterial whether plaintiff was in good faith, and that it is entitled to be relieved of liability on the sole ground that the false representations in the application were material to the risk. In support of that argument it relies on *Flint* v. *Prudential Ins. Co. of America,* La. App. 1 Cir., 70 So. 2d 161; *Karno* v. *Metropolitan Life Ins. Co.,* D.C., 137 F. Supp. 893 (affirmed 5 Cir., at 242 F. 2d 141); and *Radosta* v. *Prudential Life Ins. Co. of America,* 163 So. 2d 177, La. App. 4 Cir.

The Flint and Karno cases were decided prior to the time the decision was rendered by our Supreme Court in *Gay* v. *United Benefit Life Insurance Company,* supra. If those cases are in conflict with the decision rendered in *Gay* v. *United Benefit Life Insurance Company,* then we feel that we must apply the rule stated in the last mentioned case.[16] The Radosta case, supra, is inapplicable because there the court found that the false statements relating to matters material to the risk were made by the insured at the time the application was submitted, and that such statements were made with actual intent to deceive the insurer.

(6) Defendant also contends that plaintiff is presumed to know the contents of the application because he signed it and thereafter he held the certificate (to which a copy of the application had been attached) in his possession for several months immediately before the death of the insured. It takes the position that since plaintiff made no "objection" to the contents of the application during that period of several months he must be held to have adopted the answers in that application as his own.. We find no merit to that argument. Under the circumstances presented here, where defendant's agent filled out the application and assured plaintiff that the insurer "evidently has a record of that already," we think plaintiff would have been justified in not calling the incorrect answers to defendant's attention after the issuance of the policy, even if plaintiff had read the application and had then become aware of the answers. See *National Life & Accident Ins. Co.* v. *Vaughan,* La. App. 1 Cir., 32 So. 2d 490.

For the reasons herein assigned, therefore, the judgment appealed from is affirmed. The costs of this appeal are assessed to defendant-appellant.

---

[16] Here the court is following the decision in the most recent case. Two of the cases cited by the defendant in support of its position were decided prior to that case and thus were not applicable. The Radosta case was not persuasive because the facts were different.

QUESTIONS FOR REVIEW

1. Define agency. What is the difference between an agent and an employee? An agent and an independent contractor?
2. Distinguish between the power and the authority of an agent. Why is this difference important?
3. In completing the life insurance application, whom does the agent represent? Does he ever represent the other party?
4. What is "brokerage business" in life insurance terminology?
5. List two ways in which the agency relationship may be established.
6. What are the principal requirements for agency by ratification?
7. What is meant by agency by estoppel? Which party—company, agent, or insured—is most likely to be benefited by this concept?
8. List and describe briefly three kinds of authority the agent is said to possess.
9. In what ways may the agency relationship be terminated?

PART II

Formation, Interpretation, and Validity of the Life Insurance Contract

Chapter Outline

Chapter **4**

The Life Insurance Contract Is Formed

THE STUDY of life insurance contract law brings together two highly specialized subjects: contract law and insurance itself. The combination is especially complex in the case of the life insurance contract, because the business of life insurance is complex. Without discussing life insurance in any exhaustive sense, it is the purpose of this chapter to show how basic principles of general contract law are utilized in the formation of the life insurance contract in such a way as to meet essential insurance requirements.

A. INSURANCE AND THE CONTRACT

4.1 The Role of the Contract

The life insurance contract performs a dual role. Individually, each contract defines the rights of the policyowner on the one hand and the commitments of the insurance company on the other. Collectively, however, the contracts must operate in such a way that the mortality experience developed under them will be reasonably comparable to the statistics on which the premium rates were based. In other words, the contracts, when considered on a group basis, must operate in such a way that a successful insurance business is possible.

For this reason, the life insurance contract is more than just a "promise or set of promises" on the part of the life insurance company; it is a vital part of the very structure of the business. Thus it is not enough that the individual contract meet the requirements for the formation of a valid, enforceable agreement. These requirements must be met within the technical requirements of the insurance operation itself; and this means that every life to be insured under an individual life insurance contract must be insurable according to the underwriting rules and practices of the insurer.

4.2 The Importance of Risk Selection

Strictly speaking, the idea of insurability has little to do with contract law. However, it is fundamental in the law of contracts that one has the right to choose both the subject of a proposed contract and the person or persons with whom he is willing to do business. In legal effect, the selection of risks by a life insurance company is nothing more than a way to accomplish these objectives. In third-party ownership cases (where the applicant and the insured are different persons), the selection of risks relates only to the subject of the insurance—that is, the life to be insured—because the company is not at any time doing business with that person. In the more typical case, where the proposed insured is also the applicant, risk selection relates not only to the subject matter of the contract but also to the person with whom the company is willing to do business.

Risk appraisal, or underwriting, is common to all lines of insurance. However, in the formation of the life insurance contract, it presents a special complication that does not characterize the application process in other lines of insurance. The reason is that in the absence of fraud or misrepresentation of material facts, the life insurance contract, once completed, is not cancelable by the company. This is not true in most other lines of insurance, where the insurer can cancel a contract if the risk is later found not to be acceptable according to the company's standards of risk selection. In other words, in most other lines of insurance, it is not essential that underwriting be completed before a contract is made. In life insurance, it is; and this introduces some special complexities into the life insurance application process.

It also explains why the authority of the life insurance agent is customarily more limited than the authority of agents in other lines of insurance. The life insurance agent, unlike most agents—even agents in other fields of insurance—does not ordinarily have the authority to complete a contract on behalf of the insurance company or to pass upon the insurability of an applicant. He has the authority to solicit applications, to deliver policies, and to collect the initial premium; but he is rarely, if ever, authorized to complete an unconditionally binding contract of insurance with anyone. (As previously noted, however, there is sometimes a wide difference between what an agent is authorized to do and what he may have the power to accomplish.)

B. OFFER AND ACCEPTANCE IN LIFE INSURANCE

Life insurance contracts are completed, as are other informal contracts, by the making of an offer by one party and its acceptance by the other. Depending upon the individual circumstances of the transaction, the offer in life insurance may be made either by the applicant or by the life insurance company.

4.3 When the Insurer Makes the Offer

It is often said that an application for life insurance is an offer. This is not always true, however, since acceptance of the application by the insurer does not always complete a contract. If nothing but the application is submitted to the company, it is only part of the preliminary negotiations that often precede the making of a contract. It is an invitation for the insurer to make an offer, but it is not an actual offer. Under these circumstances, the insurance company makes the offer when it issues a policy and sends it to the agent for delivery to the applicant.

In this situation, if the policy cannot be delivered and the premium collected during the lifetime and continued insurability of the insured, the agent must return the policy to the issuing office. Even if delivery can be made, the applicant is free to accept or reject the offer. He accepts by performing the act requested: paying the initial premium; and an enforceable contract is completed. He rejects the offer by simply saying that he does not want the policy or by any actions that clearly convey that meaning.

4.4 When the Applicant Makes the Offer

If No Receipt Is Given. Almost invariably today, if the agent collects the initial premium amount at the time the application is completed, he will issue either a conditional or a binding receipt, which specifies the conditions under which and the date when the insurance will become effective. In those cases, the terms and conditions of the receipt govern the completion of the contract. In the absence of such a conditional or binding receipt,[1] if the initial premium is paid when the application is submitted, an effective offer is made by the applicant.

By submitting the premium with his application, the applicant makes it clear that he intends to enter into a contractual relationship with the insurer. If the insurer issues a policy in exact accordance with the terms of that application, the company accepts the applicant's offer and a

---

[1] Although it is customary for the agent to give a conditional or a binding receipt when the initial premium is paid at the time of application, this is not always done.

binding insurance agreement is completed. This does not necessarily mean that the insurance becomes effective immediately, for the effective date of coverage may be specified in the policy. However, if the company issues a policy in exact accord with the terms of the application, an effective contract results; and in cases of this kind, it is generally held that manual delivery of the policy is not essential to the completion of the contract.

If the company cannot issue the policy applied for, or issues that kind of policy at a higher than standard premium (a rated policy), it is rejecting the applicant's offer and making a counteroffer. In accordance with general contract law, this counteroffer must be accepted by the applicant (the offeror) before it will have any contractual effect. As a consequence, the death of the proposed insured prior to such acceptance will not ordinarily be covered. The law in counteroffer situations is clearly summarized in one case[2] as follows:

> The company reserved the right to accept or reject the proposition contained in the application.
> "The application being a mere proposal to the company, it can either accept the proposal, decline it altogether or impose such conditions as to the making of the contract, as it may choose." *McCully's Admr.* v. *Phoenix Mutual Life Ins. Co.*, 18 W. Va. 782.
> See also *Mutual Life Ins. Co.* v. *Young*, 23 Wall 85, 23 L. Ed., 152.
> In this case the insurance company's reply to the application was the sending of a policy, differing in essential terms from that applied for, to the Wheeling Branch Office. This amounted to a counter-proposition and there was no contract, no meeting of the minds of the parties on the new terms, without acceptance thereof by Kronjaeger.

4.5 When a Premium Receipt Is Given

A conditional premium receipt is a receipt for the initial premium (or a portion of it) paid to the life insurance agent in connection with an application for life insurance. The special significance of such receipts in the formation of the life insurance contract arises out of their wording, which, in general terms, provides that insurance will become effective as of a date specified in the receipt (but always earlier than the effective date of the policy, if a policy is issued), subject to conditions that are specified in the receipt.

The individual facts differ from case to case; but, in general, any premium receipt gives the agent the opportunity to persuade the applicant to pay the initial premium at the time the application is completed.

----

[2] *Kronjaeger* v. *The Travelers Insurance Company et al.*, 124 W. Va. 730, 22 S.E. (2d) 689 (1942).

In effect, therefore, the agent is authorized to extend an offer on the part of the company to make insurance effective as of a date earlier than would ordinarily be true, subject to conditions that are specified in the receipt. The applicant accepts this conditional offer by performing the act requested—paying the premium at the time the application is submitted—and thereby transforms the offer into a binding agreement.

C. THE USE OF CONDITIONAL RECEIPTS

4.6 Why They Are Used

Regardless of whether the applicant pays the initial premium for his insurance at the time the application is submitted or when the policy is issued and delivered to him, there is always some delay between the date of the application and the date the insurance takes effect under the policy. During this period, if a premium receipt were not used, the death of the proposed insured would not be covered.

From an early date, therefore, it was apparent that it would be to the advantage of the applicant (or his beneficiary) to provide some coverage, if at all possible, during the period in which the underwriting procedures were being completed. It was just as clearly to the advantage of the agent and the insurance company to provide such coverage. Without it, there was no very compelling reason for the applicant to pay the initial premium before the policy was delivered; and if the premium was not prepaid, the agent often found himself in the position of having to "sell" the applicant twice—once when the application was completed and again when he delivered the policy. Often it was more difficult, and sometimes it was impossible, to make the sale the second time.

Nevertheless, if the applicant paid the initial premium when he submitted the application and the proposed insured died before the policy was issued, the situation was even more difficult. There the agent was in the position of explaining that although the company had had the premium during the intervening period, the applicant had not had any insurance coverage.

For these reasons, life insurers began at an early date to experiment with ways to provide some insurance coverage during the period while an application was being considered. This would bring life insurance practices more nearly in line with practices followed in other lines of insurance, where coverage is often made effective immediately, subject to the company's right to cancel later if the application is found not to be acceptable. To provide similar coverage in life insurance, however, some way had to be devised under which the agent could offer earlier coverage conditionally (subject to a final underwriting decision in the issuing office) if the initial premium was paid with the application. This problem was met, with varying degrees of success, by the use of what have come to be known as "conditional receipts" or "conditional binding receipts."

4.7 The Problem of Conditions

Because of the significance of conditions in this area of life insurance law, it is important to distinguish between promises and conditions, as well as to differentiate between a condition precedent and a condition subsequent.

A promise, in general terms, is an undertaking that one will take or refrain from taking a certain action in the future. However, it does not have to be absolute. It may be a commitment to take or not to take the action in the future if something else shall happen or not happen. In this case, the promise is said to be subject to a condition. The promise will not become binding unless the condition happens. A condition, therefore, is an event or happening which determines whether a promisor will or will not be required to carry out his promise.

There are two major kinds of conditions: conditions precedent and conditions subsequent. If the condition must happen or be performed before the promise becomes binding, it is called a condition precedent, since it precedes the duty to perform. If the event or happening, if it occurs, terminates rights already established, it is a condition subsequent. For example, if A owes B a sum of money, B's right to repayment is an established right. If A promises to repay the indebtedness as of a specified date on condition that the indebtedness be canceled if he should die prior to that date, his death prior to the specified date is a condition subsequent.

In the conditional receipt situation, most life insurers intend that the insurance provided by their conditional receipts will become effective only if the conditions expressed in the receipt are met. Thus the conditions are intended to be conditions precedent. This reserves to the company the right to determine insurability before it becomes liable under any life insurance contract it issues.

If a conditional receipt is interpreted by the courts as establishing a condition subsequent rather than a condition precedent, the result is very different. In that case, the insurance is held to be effective immediately, subject to termination by the insurer if the proposed insured is found not to be insurable. Thus, under this interpretation, the insurance is held to be effective during the interim between the date of the receipt and the date the applicant is notified that the condition was not met. Such interpretations are said to establish interim insurance, and, contrary to the intent of the insurers, this means liability in some instances even though the proposed insured was not, in fact, insurable.

D. MAJOR KINDS OF PREMIUM RECEIPTS

4.8 The Binding Receipt

Some companies use what is correctly termed a "binding" receipt. Under it insurance becomes effective, with some limitations as to maximum amount, on the date of the receipt and continues for a specified period of time or until the company disapproves the application, if earlier. This type of receipt has not presented any significant legal problems. The customary practice, however, is to use some type of conditional receipt rather than a binding receipt.

4.9 "Approval" Type of Conditional Receipts

At one time, the intent of the insurer under probably the majority of conditional receipts was to make insurance effective as of a specified date (always prior to the date a policy was issued) on condition that the application was approved. Since there was no coverage until the approval was given, a receipt of this kind gave the applicant only a little more in the way of protection than he would have had if he had merely completed an application and waited until delivery of the policy before he paid the premium. Nevertheless most of the early court decisions upheld this requirement as a valid condition precedent. In such cases, when the death of the proposed insured occurred after the application date but before approval, he was not covered.

Other courts took the position that under this type of receipt the applicant was in effect paying for coverage for a period in which he actually had no insurance. It seemed inequitable to these courts to permit a life insurance company to collect the premium and then give very little more coverage than if no premium had been paid. Hence the tendency of the courts, when a proposed insured died before the application had been approved, was to decide, if at all possible, that coverage had been in effect under the receipt on the date of death. One very common way of reaching this conclusion was to consider that the language of the receipt was ambiguous and thus should be interpreted in favor of the beneficiary.

Illustrative of this approach is the leading case of *Gaunt* v. *John Hancock Mutual Life Insurance Company*,[3] in which the court said:

> . . . An underwriter might so understand the phrase, when read in its context, but the application was not to be submitted to underwriters; it was to go to persons utterly unacquainted with the niceties of life insurance, who would read it colloquially. It is the understanding of such persons that counts; and not one in a hundred would suppose that he

[3] 160 F. (2d) 599 (C.C.A. Conn., 1947).

would be covered, not "as of the date of completion of Part B," as the defendant promised, but only as of the date of approval. Had that been what the defendant meant, certainly it was easy to say so; and had it in addition meant to make the policy retroactive for some purposes, certainly it was easy to say that too. To demand that persons wholly unfamiliar with insurance shall spell all this out in the very teeth of the language used, is unpardonable. It does indeed some violence to the words not to make actual "approval" always a condition, and to substitute a prospective approval, however inevitable, when the insured has died before approval. But it does greater violence to make the insurance "in force" only from the date of "approval"; for the ordinary applicant who has paid his first premium and has successfully passed his physical examination, would not by the remotest chance understand the clause as leaving him uncovered until the insurer at its leisure approved the risk; he would assume that he was getting immediate coverage for his money. . . . A man must indeed read what he signs, and he is charged, if he does not; but insurers who seek to impose upon words of common speech an esoteric significance intelligible only to their craft, must bear the burden of any resulting confusion.

As illustrated by this case, a number of courts reached the conclusion that conditional receipts of the approval type really expressed a condition subsequent and thus established insurance as of the date of the receipt, subject to a later determination of insurability. For this reason, and because insurability of the proposed insured is the only condition essential to the insurer's purpose, the present prevailing practice is to use conditional receipts of the insurability type.

4.10 "Insurability" Receipts

A typical conditional receipt of the insurability type provides that insurance will become effective as of the date of the receipt (or of the medical examination, if later) on condition that the proposed insured is found to have been insurable on the date of the receipt for the plan, the amount, and the premium rate of the insurance applied for. Illustrative of this type of receipt is the example shown on page 111.

The majority of life insurance companies today use the insurability type of conditional receipt. Under it, even though insurance is not effective unless the proposed insured is found to be insurable, his insurability as of the specified date can still be determined after his death. The result is that the proposed insured does have significantly more coverage than he would have had in the absence of the receipt.

To illustrate, assume that John M. Jones completes and signs an application for a $50,000 policy with the Ajax Life Insurance Company and submits the initial premium in cash. James Brown, the agent, issues a conditional receipt (of the insurability type), forwards the application to

THE FACE OF THE RECEIPT

CONDITIONAL RECEIPT

RECEIVED FROM _____, Applicant,
Name of Proposed Insured
if other than Applicant _____
(Amount of cash)
(settlement received) $....................in connection with the initial
premium for the proposed insurance for which an application is this day made
to the Ajax Life Insurance Company.

Life Insurance and any additional benefits in the amount applied for (but
not exceeding a maximum liability of $50,000, including all additional benefits
on all pending applications to the company combined) shall be deemed to take
effect as of the date of this receipt, subject to the terms and conditions printed
on the reverse side hereof.

The amount of settlement received shall be refunded if the application is
declined or if a policy is issued other than as applied for and is not accepted.
Any check, draft, or money order is received subject to collection.

Date of Receipt   Signature of Agent

PROVISIONS ON THE BACK OF THE RECEIPT

Subject to the limitations of this receipt and the terms and conditions of the
policy that may be issued by the company on the basis of the application, the
life insurance and any additional benefits applied for shall not be deemed to
take effect unless the company, after investigation and such medical examination, if any, as it may require, shall be satisfied that on the date of this receipt
each person proposed for insurance was insurable for the *amount* of life insurance and any additional benefits applied for according to the company's rules
and practice of selection; provided, however, that approval by the company
of the insurability of the Proposed Insured for a plan of insurance other than
that applied for, or the denial of any particular additional benefit applied for,
shall not invalidate the terms and conditions of this receipt relating to life
insurance and any other additional benefit applied for.

(Not to be detached unless issued under the requirements for using Conditional Receipt)

---

the issuing office, makes arrangements for a medical examination, and
orders an inspection report.

From the previous review we know that by completing the application
and paying the initial premium, Jones has accepted the conditional offer
of the Ajax Life Insurance Company made by agent Brown, and that
insurance will become effective prior to delivery of the policy if Jones is
found to be insurable. Assume further that the wording of the receipt is

completely clear and the condition—that the proposed insured be found to be insurable—is a true condition precedent, which must be fulfilled before insurance becomes effective.

Where the Condition Is Fulfilled. First, take the simple case where the condition is fulfilled. Personnel in the issuing office of the company review the application, the medical examiner's report, and the inspection report, and find that Jones does, in fact, meet their risk appraisal requirements. An authorized officer then approves the issuance of a policy on the exact plan and in the same amount that Jones applied for. Assume that he has just approved and initialed the application when the telephone rings.

It is Brown calling long distance to say that Jones was struck by a hit-and-run driver while crossing the street. Jones died in the ambulance on his way to the hospital. Was he insured?

The answer can be given only after all the facts have been ascertained and considered, and the underwriting department may want to consult the legal counsel[4] of the company because of the many delicate questions that may be involved. However, once the facts have been ascertained, the answer will be relatively simple. For example, the conditional receipt may provide that insurance will take effect as of the date of the receipt if the applicant is found to be insurable as of that date. In that case, the determination of Jones's insurability and the decision on the part of the appropriate officer (even after the death of the insured) that a policy can be issued will put the insurance into effect. The condition has been fulfilled, and Jones was insured as of a date prior to his death.

Where the Condition Is Not Fulfilled. Going back to the same set of original facts, consider a different set of subsequent events. Assume that agent Brown mails the application and the premium check to the company, arranges for a medical examination, and orders an inspection. Assume also that the risk appraiser reviews the documents and finds that Jones does not meet the company's requirements in accordance with its standard practices of risk selection. He has just made that notation on the application file when the telephone rings, as in the first illustration, and Brown reports the same fatal accident to Jones.

It seems clear that in this instance Jones is not insured. The condition of insurability specified in the conditional receipt has not been met. Even though no actual notice of disapproval has been sent, this can follow the death of the applicant. However, as a practical matter, the company should be adequately prepared to support its decision with respect to the applicant's lack of insurability and to set forth the controlling wording of

---

[4] It has been suggested that the legal aspects of this type of situation are not always the most significant. In situations where the facts are very uncertain, the insurer may prefer, as a matter of good public relations, to pay the claim, even though as a strictly legal matter it might not be required to do so.

the conditional receipt in a court of law if necessary. Even then, the liability of the company may depend entirely upon the jurisdiction in which the question arises, as indicated in the following discussion.

E. CONDITIONAL RECEIPTS IN THE COURTS

4.11 The Majority Rule

The majority of the courts that have considered questions involving conditional receipts have upheld the conditions intended by the insurer. Thus, unless the wording is definitely ambiguous, it will be held to express a condition precedent. The result is that no insurance will be held to have been effective until the condition has been met. Usually, then, the receipt provides that the insurance relates back to—that is, becomes effective on a retroactive basis on—the date of the receipt or the date of any required medical examination.

Illustrative of this line of decisions is the case of *Mofrad* v. *New York Life Insurance Company*,[5] decided by the United States Court of Appeals for the 10th Circuit in May, 1953. There, the beneficiary contended that the receipt established interim insurance (that is, that the insurance was effective until the insurer terminated it) or that it was ambiguous; but the court said, in part:

> But, "a contract of insurance rests upon and is controlled by the same principles of law applicable to any other contract. What the contracting parties intended, mutually agreed to, and their minds met upon, is the measure of their obligations." *Bowen* v. *Prudential Life Ins. Co.*, 178 Mich. 63, 144 N.W. 543, 51 L.R.A. (N.S.) 587, as cited in *New York Life Ins. Co.* v. *Gist*, 63 F. 2d 732. And if the intentions of the parties are clear from an examination of the contractual documents, this court will not rewrite the contract. *Bennett* v. *The Preferred Acc. Ins. Co. of New York*, 192 F. 2d 748 (10 Cir., 1951); *New York Life Ins. Co.* v. *Gist, supra.*
>
> The language of the application and of the receipt is definite and clear; the application bears the signature of the Applicant and it must be presumed that he read the agreement and was aware of its contractual import. Certainly there is nothing in the evidence to indicate that he was misled.
>
> And there are no provisions in the agreement which would lead to a conclusion that an interim contract was intended by the parties. There are other clearly prescribed conditions within the agreement than the payment of the premium and delivery of the receipt to the applicant, which lead only to the conclusion that the applicant was merely applying for a contract of insurance which could be consummated only upon the fulfillment of the conditions set out in the application. And where a policy application contains such conditions precedent, performance thereof is a

---

[5] 206 F. (2d) 491 (C.A. Utah, 1953).

prerequisite to the taking effect of insurance coverage. *Hurt* v. *New York Life Ins. Co.*, 51 F. 2d 936 (10 Cir., 1931).

      o   o   o   o   o

We must conclude that the applicant failed to meet the required conditions precedent to the consummation of an insurance contract, and the judgment of the trial court is affirmed.

Since most conditional receipts provide that the insurance will become effective as of the date of the receipt or of the medical examination, if later, a question sometimes arises if two medical examinations are necessary and only one has been made when the proposed insured dies. At least two courts have held that if more than one medical examination was required and only one was made, the language of the receipt on this issue was ambiguous. In accordance with the general rule of interpretation, this ambiguity will be resolved in favor of the insured or beneficiary; and the coverage, therefore, will become effective as of the date the first examination was completed. Court decisions differ as to the situation where a medical examination is requested later by the underwriter but was not required at the time of application and had not been made at the time of the death of the proposed insured. In some such cases, the courts have held that the medical examination was a condition precedent that was not met and the coverage therefore did not become effective. In other instances, the requirement has been held not to be a condition precedent; and the insurance coverage was therefore effective.

Generally, if the insurability of the proposed insured has not been evaluated at the time of his death, the company is required to evaluate it afterwards. This evaluation must be made in good faith and in accordance with the company's own insurability rules. If the company does not make such a decision, the jury must decide what underwriting decision the company should reasonably have made.

4.12 The Minority View

Decisions holding that conditional receipts actually establish interim insurance are in the decided minority so far as numbers are concerned. A recent tabulation shows only a few states falling in this group. Nevertheless, such decisions are highly significant, representing as they do a strong trend toward interpreting these agreements contrary to the intention of the insurers. Illustrative of this view is the much-cited case of *Ransom* v. *Penn. Mutual Life Insurance Co.*,[6] decided in 1954, which reads in part as follows:

We must determine whether a contract of insurance arose immediately upon receipt by defendant of the completed application with the premium

---

[6] 274 P. (2d) 633 (Cal., 1954).

payment, subject to the right of defendant to terminate the agreement if it subsequently concluded that Ransom was not acceptable, or whether, as defendant contends, its satisfaction as to Ransom's acceptability for insurance was a condition precedent to the existence of any contract.

The courts in several jurisdictions have construed clauses similar to the one involved here. A number of decisions have held, in accordance with defendant's view, that no contract of insurance exists until the insurer has been satisfied as to an applicant's acceptability, and that the provision that the insurance shall be in force from the date of the application means that, if and when the company is satisfied, the contract shall be considered to relate back and take effect as of that date. . . .

On the other hand a number of courts have held that the provision to the effect that the insurance shall be in force from the date of the application if the premium is paid gives rise to a contract of insurance immediately upon receipt of the application and payment of the premium, and that the proviso that the company shall be satisfied that the insured was acceptable at the date of the application creates only a right to terminate the contract if the company becomes dissatisfied with the risk before a policy is issued. . . .

We are of the view that a contract of insurance arose upon defendant's receipt of the completed application and the first premium payment. The clause quoted above is subject to the interpretation that the applicant is offered a choice of either paying his first premium when he signs the application, in which event "the insurance shall be in force . . . from the date . . . of the application," or of paying upon receipt of the policy, in which event "no insurance shall be in force until . . . the policy is delivered."

A more recent illustration of the minority view is the case of *Allen* v. *Metropolitan Life Insurance Company*,[7] decided by the Supreme Court of New Jersey on March 29, 1965. There the receipt provided that if the full first premium was paid with the application and if the application was approved "either before or after the death of the Life Proposed," the policy would be issued effective as of the date of the receipt. There was testimony that the agent told the proposed insured that there would be immediate coverage if the premium was paid in advance. Noting that there was no mention of "insurability or good health" in the receipt, the judge in the trial court asked: "If there were no immediate coverages, why would the company take the advance premium and of what benefit could a thing of this sort be to a person who applies for insurance?" It was his conclusion that the proposed insured was covered by interim insurance without regard to insurability.

The appellate court reversed the decision of the trial court and decided in favor of the insurer, but the Supreme Court granted leave to appeal and then decided in favor of the beneficiary, saying, in part:

[7] 208 A. (2d) 638 (1965).

It appears to us that when confronted with conditional receipts in the form used by the defendant or in comparable form, recognition of interim coverage pending the company's approval or disapproval would be the just and equitable course and would fulfill the applicant's reasonable expectations while avoiding the serious impracticalities which would result from acceptance of the company's position that liability should turn on its good faith determination of insurability; these impracticalities are particularly evident where, as here, the company's Impairment Guide is not dispositive, no industrywide standards of insurability appear, and the company places its reliance on a judgment determination of uninsurability first made by its own medical director after he had knowledge of the applicant's death.

Two general courses have been followed in reaching a holding that conditional receipts establish immediate coverage, subject to the finding of insurability necessary to terminate it. One approach is to hold that, as a matter of public policy, the receipt should be interpreted as providing immediate coverage. The second and more widely followed course is to find the language of the receipt ambiguous. This course is illustrated in the Gaunt case quoted in Section 4.9 above and in other New Jersey holdings.

It is also important to note the significance of the agent's statement concerning coverage. This is mentioned in the Allen case and has been an important contention in a number of cases. Generally, the application form contains a statement that no one but the president, a vice president, or a secretary of the company has the authority to make or modify a contract or to waive any of the company's requirements. When this provision is clear, the agent is held not to have had the authority to bind the insurer. However, this is not true of a general agent in the legal sense of the term, since such an agent is generally considered to have that power. This point was given an interesting treatment in one case[8] where the appellate court ruled in favor of a new trial to determine whether the sales manager had trained the agent to tell the client that he had immediate coverage. If this was found to be true, the court said, the actions of the sales manager could have the effect of waiving the terms of the conditional receipt and establishing immediate coverage.

Finally, the "reasonable expectations" of the applicant are also considered to be important. In the Allen case, for instance, the court mentioned fulfilling "the applicant's reasonable expectations." In an effort to accomplish this, the statements of the agent as well as other circumstances involved in the application process may be examined. This is illustrated in the case of *Van Koevering* v. *Manufacturers Life Insurance*

---

[8] *Colontuono* v. *State Farm Insurance Company*, 289 N.E. (2d) 235 (Ill. App., 1972).

Company,[9] which involved the question of coverage under a conditional receipt prior to the issuance and delivery of a policy. The court held that insurance was in force, saying:

> Under the circumstances of this case, it would be grossly unfair to deny insurance coverage. The applicant for life insurance, untutored in the practices of the insurance trade, must be protected against the ambiguous and the unfamiliar in insurance policies when such are used as a basis for escaping liability.

❖   ❖   ❖   ❖   ❖

> It may be well for us to reconsider the concise statement made by Mr. Justice Holmes in *Coppage* v. *Kansas* (1915) 236 U.S. 1:
> "If that belief, whether right or wrong, be held by a reasonable man, it seems to me that it may be enforced by law in order to establish the equality of position between the parties in which liberty of contract begins."
> These insurance contracts are in altogether too many instances a totally unilateral proposition and in interpreting them courts should look to the mind of the applicant and the impressions and representations which have been conveyed to the applicant by the agent, the activities and the circumstances involved.

4.13 The Statutory Approach

At least one state (California) has sought to reduce the number of problems in the conditional receipt area by requiring by statute[10] that claims be paid in any situation where the proposed insured dies prior to approval of the application if he was insurable and the premium was paid at the time of the application. (It does not matter whether a receipt was or was not issued.) This statute permits the insurer to limit the amount for which it may be liable prior to issuance and delivery of a policy to an amount "not less than its maximum retention" or $50,000 if the application contains a statement to that effect.

F. DELAY IN ACTING ON THE APPLICATION

So far in this discussion of the formation of the life insurance contract, it has been assumed that the activities of the various people involved have been carried out with reasonable promptness. At this point, however, suppose that after completing the application and collecting the initial premium, the agent does not issue a conditional receipt and in fact takes no further action, perhaps not even sending in the application.

---

[9] D.C. Mich., 234 F. Supp. 786 (1964).
[10] Deering's California Codes, Ins. C. A., Sec. 10115.

Suppose also that it is a nonmedical case and that although the applicant is in excellent health and is otherwise insurable when the application is completed, he is accidentally killed some five or six weeks later. Does the company have any liability in a situation of this kind?

Clearly these facts point up the advantages of the conditional receipt, both to the company on the one hand and the applicant (or beneficiary) on the other. For if a conditional receipt of the insurability type is issued, the liability of the company can be clearly established. Thus, in the illustration given, if the applicant was found to have been insurable on the date of the receipt, the company would have been on the risk on the date of the accident. If he was not insurable, the company would not have been liable. In the absence of a conditional receipt, however, it is understandable that a somewhat unique approach has been developed in a few jurisdictions, an approach which seeks to establish liability in tort where there was admittedly no liability in the contractual sense.

4.14 Unreasonable Delay and Tort Liability

Simply stated, a tort is any wrongful act (or failure to act) on the part of one person which does not arise out of a contractual relationship and which gives another person a right to sue for damages. A suit of this kind is called an "action in tort" and is based on a duty on the part of the person sued, a violation of that duty (usually through negligence), and resulting damages to the person bringing suit.

In the formation of the life insurance contract, the tort liability theory has been based on the premise that when a life insurance company receives an application, it has a duty to act on it with reasonable promptness. Those persons who have taken this position concede that most business organizations have no comparable duty, but they maintain that because insurance is affected with a public interest and insurers operate under a franchise from the state, there is a public duty on their part to act promptly in considering an application, either accepting or rejecting it within a reasonable length of time. Failing to do this, if the applicant has submitted the initial premium and would have been an acceptable risk except for his death prior to issuance of the policy, the company is liable in damages to the amount that would have been recoverable under the policy if it had been promptly issued and in effect at the date of death.

This idea is ably set forth in a 1940 case, *Bekken Adm'x v. The Equitable Life Assurance Society of the United States*,[11] decided by the North Dakota Supreme Court. The applicable portions of that decision read as follows:

---

[11] 70 N.D. 122, 283 N.W. 200 (1940).

Insurance is a contract, which, like other contracts, results only from an offer and an acceptance of the offer. There is a conflict in the authorities as to whether legal obligations arise only after a contract of insurance has been made, or whether in certain circumstances a legal duty arises, from the relationship created during the negotiations between an applicant for insurance and the insurance company, to act promptly upon the application, and to inform the applicant whether the offer is accepted or rejected. Generally speaking, there are two main lines of decisions dealing with these questions. According to one view, the legal relations between an applicant and the insurance company "are fundamentally the same as those between parties negotiating any other contract, and are 'purely contractual' "; that "mere delay, mere inaction by an insurance company in passing on an application does not constitute an acceptance or establish the relationship of insurer and insured," and that such delay or inaction does not constitute any breach of duty by the insurance company. *Thornton* v. *Natl. Council,* 110 W. Va. 412, 158 S.E. 507. According to this view, no duty arises unless, and until, a contract has been created; if there is no contract, there is no duty, and consequently there is no liability on the part of the insurer because of any delay or inaction on its part in passing upon the application, or in issuing or delivering the policy.

*   *   *   *   *

The other line of decisions holds that an insurance company that has solicited and received a completed application for insurance is under a legal duty to take prompt action on the application, and give prompt notice to the applicant of its action; and that consequently such insurance company is liable in tort for negligent delay in acting upon the application, and notifying the applicant in case the application is rejected. . . .

In our opinion this latter line of decisions announces the correct principle.

As noted in this case, many courts hold that there is no duty on the part of the insurer that is violated by delay in acting on the application. In fact, this is the majority view, and it is supported by several arguments. Probably the most significant, is the argument, upheld by many courts, that insurers are not public utilities and must be permitted freedom to choose the persons with whom they are willing to contract.

One of the earliest and most definite rejections of the tort liability doctrine was voiced in 1929 by the Supreme Court of Mississippi in the case of *Savage* v. *Prudential Life Insurance Company.*[12] There the court said:

The fact that the insurance companies are granted a franchise to do business in this state does not and should not impose upon them the duty to consider promptly all who offer to them the risk of insuring their lives, no more than would be required of a bank to lend money promptly to all

---

[12] 154 Miss. 89, 121 So. 487 (1929).

who should make application and suffer loss while the bank was negligent in determining whether or not it would accept the offer and enter into a contract.

4.15 Unreasonable Delay and Contract Law

As noted in Chapter 2, mere silence on the part of the offeree does not constitute acceptance of an offer as a matter of general contract law. By the almost overwhelming weight of authority, this principle applies just as clearly in the case of offers for life insurance contracts. Nevertheless, a few courts have held that where the premium is paid at the time of the application, unreasonable delay in acting on the application in effect amounts to an acceptance. The theory is that retention of the premium is inconsistent with rejection.

Illustrative of this point of view is the discussion of the Michigan Supreme Court in the case of *Wadsworth* v. *New York Life Insurance Co.*[13] That case dealt with an application for ordinary life insurance on the part of a captain in the United States air force who paid the first full premium in cash at the time of application and received a conditional receipt. He was lost in action in the Korean war before the application was approved. In one section of the decision, the court discusses the effect of delay in considering the application as follows:

> Appellant contends in her second issue that a contract arose as a matter of law through defendant's unreasonable delay in acceptance or rejection of the application filed by the deceased.
>
> Michigan, it appears, is among the minority of States in holding that there is a duty on the part of the insurance company to act with reasonable promptness. In *Robinson* v. *United States Benevolent Society,* 132 Mich. 695, p. 699, this Court stated:
>
> "In insurance contracts of this character it is the duty of the company to act with reasonable promptness. Failing to reject within reasonable time, the law implies an acceptance."
>
> See, also, Mich. L. Rev. 484.
>
> We do not know what other facts may be shown on retrial but where, as currently shown in the record before us, substantial delay in accepting or rejecting is coupled with retention of the first and succeeding premiums, the question of whether or not there was such unreasonable delay on the part of the defendant or its agent as to imply acceptance would be a question of fact for the jury.

Although this discussion is phrased primarily in terms of offer and implied acceptance, the idea that there is a duty on the part of the company to act upon an application with reasonable promptness brings it very close to a true tort liability philosophy.

---

[13] 84 N.W. (2d) 513 (Mich., 1957).

Summary. The tort liability theory has never been widely approved by the courts, and it has been severely criticized by many life insurance spokesmen and lawyers. Although it became rather popular in the 1920s, this popularity seemed to diminish in the 1930s, and in the past several years there has been little change in the number of states in which the doctrine has been adopted or definitely rejected. The use of a liberal conditional receipt that establishes obligation, as a matter of contract, from the earliest possible date, on condition that the applicant is found to be insurable, has no doubt played an important part in this slowing of what once appeared to be a popular trend. Cases where liability once seemed morally if not legally indicated are ordinarily within this type of conditional receipt and are therefore covered as a matter of contract. Thus, there is no need for attempting to establish liability in tort. Nevertheless, the opportunities for litigation on this basis remain in every situation where there is delay and the applicant is found not to be insurable. For this reason the tort liability theory, based on negligent delay in handling life insurance applications, can never safely be disregarded, particularly in those jurisdictions where it has been followed in the past.

G. OTHER ELEMENTS OF THE CONTRACT

The informal contract, it will be recalled, has been defined as "an agreement between competent parties expressing definite assent to the terms of a promise or promises supported by legally adequate consideration." The agreement must be in a form required by law and must not be declared ineffective by any special statute or rule of common law.

The offer and acceptance process presents special problems in connection with the formation of the life insurance contract, and for that reason, it has been discussed at some length. There remain for discussion the requirements of "legally adequate" consideration, competent parties, a form required by law, and any special statutes or rules of common law which might declare a life insurance contract void.

H. CONSIDERATION

4.17 A Legal Concept

Under the informal contract, the promise or promises to be enforced must always be supported by a legally sufficient consideration. As noted, in life insurance, except in rare cases, the promises are all made by the company. What, then, is the nature of this consideration, which makes an enforceable contract of what would otherwise be a mere set of promises?

In the law of contracts, consideration takes a number of different forms. It may consist of positive actions on the part of the promisee, or it may be another promise or other promises on his part, as it is in the bilateral contract. In legal terms, it is a "benefit to the promisor or detriment to the promisee" or, alternatively, the "value requested and given in exchange for the promise or promises sought to be enforced."

4.18 In Life Insurance

Life insurance policies typically contain language such as this: "In consideration of the application and the initial premium, the Ajax Life Insurance Company agrees to pay. . . ." By the terms of the contract, therefore, the consideration for the promises of the company consists of the application and the initial premium. The premium is of basic importance, but an application is also required.

Most life insurance policies specifically state that the insurance shall not be effective until the first premium is paid, and the validity of this stipulation has uniformly been upheld. By clear implication, therefore, payment of the first premium is the "value requested and given in exchange for the promise or promises sought to be enforced." Together with the application, this payment constitutes the consideration which makes those promises on the part of the company enforceable.

I. COMPETENT CONTRACTING PARTIES

4.19 Who Is a Party?

The informal contract is "an agreement between competent parties," and the life insurance contract is an informal contract. However, in discussing the competency of the parties it is perhaps advisable to clarify at the outset exactly who the "parties to the contract" are.

The Beneficiary. In some ways the life insurance contract involves three parties—the applicant (who becomes the policyowner), the life insurance company, and the beneficiary. However, in the legal sense of the term, the beneficiary is not a party to the contract—that is, he is not a person with whom the contract is made. In fact, in the most usual life insurance situation, it is not necessary that the beneficiary even know that an application has been completed or a policy issued. The fact that a beneficiary designation can usually be revoked without the beneficiary's knowledge or consent is even further evidence that the beneficiary is not a contracting party.

The Insured. If one bears in mind that the applicant is the only person other than the insurance company who is a party to the contract in the legal sense of the term, a great deal of possible confusion may be avoided. This definition automatically excludes the beneficiary. It also excludes the insured in situations where he is not the applicant (third-party ownership cases).

For example, a partner may apply for and be issued a policy of life insurance on the life of another partner. In this situation we have partner A, the applicant, who is ordinarily, though not necessarily, also the beneficiary; partner B, who is the insured; and the life insurance company, with whom the contract is made. Partner A and the life insurance company are parties to the contract; partner B is not.

A similar example is presented where the A.B.C. Corporation applies for and is the beneficiary of a policy on the life of M, an officer or key employee. In this case the A.B.C. Corporation is a party to the contract; the officer or key employee is not.

To use a nonbusiness illustration, a wife may apply for life insurance on the life of her husband. In that case we would have the wife, who applies and is beneficiary; the husband, who is the insured; and the life insurance company, with whom the contract is made. Here the wife and the life insurance company are parties to the contract; the husband is not.

Each of these three situations involves a contract under which the insured is not a party. The contract insures his life but it is not made with him in any sense of the word; he is merely the "vehicle for the insurance" as it is sometimes expressed. In insurance terms these are "third-party ownership cases." However, the same basic rule obtains as with any other life insurance contract. The applicant or applicants are parties to the contract on the one hand; the life insurance company is a party on the other.

Consent of the Insured. On analysis, all third-party ownership cases reduce themselves to a situation where one or more persons having an insurable interest in another have applied for and been issued a policy of insurance on the life of that person. The insurance company is one party to the contract; one or more applicants are also parties. The insured is not a party to the contract and signs the application only to signify his consent that someone else shall be issued a policy promising the payment of money, sometimes a great deal of money, at his death. The implications of such a promise are so serious that as a matter of public policy, the insured's consent is required in every case where he is not also the applicant, unless there is a statute expressly providing otherwise.

This requirement is statutory in some states, as, for example, in New York. There the Insurance Law provides as follows:

> No contract of insurance upon the person, except a policy of group life insurance or of group or blanket accident or health insurance as defined in this chapter or family insurance, shall be made or effectuated unless at or before the making of such contract the person insured, being of lawful

age or competent to contract therefor, applies therefor or consents in writing to the making thereof, except in the following cases:

(a) A wife or a husband may effectuate such insurance upon the person of the other.

(b) Any person having an insurable interest in the life of a minor under the age, as determined by nearest birthday, of fifteen years, or any person upon whom such minor is dependent for support and maintenance, may effectuate a contract of insurance upon the life of such minor, in an amount which shall not exceed the limits specified in section one hundred forty-seven which are applicable to such contract.[14]

Note that this statute expressly requires the consent of the person whose life is to be insured in any situation where that person is not the applicant, except in two situations. One is where a husband or wife applies for insurance on the life of his or her spouse, and the other is where insurance is applied for on the life of a minor by someone having an insurable interest in that minor's life.

Assured and Insured. In the past, efforts have been made in third-party ownership cases to distinguish between the person whose life is insured and the person or persons to whom the policy is issued, by speaking of the former as the insured, the latter as the assured or assureds. This distinction was never widely adopted in this country and, in fact, the terms "insured" and "assured" are considered by many to be synonymous. It is more customary, therefore, to refer to the person to whom the policy is issued as the owner and the person whose life is insured as the insured. If the insured is also the owner, that fact is pointed out in the policy wording.

4.20 Competency of the Contracting Parties

The Insurer. A life insurance company is considered competent to issue contracts of life insurance if (1) it has been authorized to do so by the terms of its charter or articles of incorporation, and (2) it has a certificate of authority issued by the state in which the contract is completed. In this sense of the word, the competency of the company is ordinarily certified to each year by the various individual states in which it does an insurance business.

The Applicant. Only those persons who are parties to the contract need to have contractual capacity. Other than the company, therefore, it is only the applicant or applicants who are concerned in any discussion of contractual capacity. Insurability and the presence or absence of an insurable interest are significant factors, but neither is involved in the basic question of contractual capacity.

In the absence of evidence to the contrary, every person is presumed

---

[14] New York Insurance Law, Sec. 146, 3.

to be competent to make a valid contract. Of course, there are exceptions, and some of them are more significant than others in the life insurance situation. For instance, the possible lack of contractual capacity on the part of a possibly insane applicant will not generally present a problem in connection with a life insurance application because of the investigation and medical aspects of determining insurability. (The question of contractual capacity may be more significant in connection with applications for annuities, since the insurability of an annuitant is not so carefully evaluated; and some method of verifying contractual capacity may be advisable. Otherwise, the contract, once issued, could be disaffirmed if the annuitant lacked contractual capacity.) Probably the most commonly recurring problem in the area of contractual capacity concerns the contractual capacity of minors.

The Minor Applicant.   As noted earlier, the contracts of an infant (minor) are binding only as long as he wishes them to be, and at common law any person is an infant until he is 21 years of age. This has been modified downward by statute in most states, but 21 still remains the age of majority unless there is a statute to the contrary.

As previously noted, the general rule is that a minor has the right to disaffirm at any time most contracts he has made except contracts for the sale of land, and he may disaffirm a contract for the sale of land upon reaching his majority. (Ordinarily he will be held responsible for the reasonable value of necessaries, but life insurance has been uniformly held not to be a necessary.) Generally, if the minor has in his possession the consideration he has received, he must return it when he avoids the contract. Then he may demand and receive back whatever he has parted with, so that the situation is again as nearly as possible what it was prior to the making of the contract. If the minor no longer has the consideration he has received or if the property has been damaged, he may still demand and receive back whatever he himself has given.

Applied to the avoidance of a life insurance contract, this rule presents some difficulties. Obviously the minor cannot return the "protection" he has received. May he then receive back all the premiums he has paid, or should he reasonably be charged for the pure insurance coverage he has had?

The decided cases on this point are in conflict. There is a minority line of cases that hold that when a life insurance contract is disaffirmed by a minor, the insurer may deduct the cost (on a term insurance basis) of the insurance protection the insured minor has had during the period the policy was in force. The majority rule, however, is that when a minor repudiates a life insurance contract on his life, he is entitled to receive back all the premiums he paid during his minority.

Most of these cases arose and were decided in a very different economic atmosphere from that of the present day. They involved different contracts, different practices, and different laws as to the ages of majority. They are significant, however, as background for understanding present-day statutes, such as those discussed in Sec. 2.15, which have as their objective the removal or modification of the contractual incapacity of minors. In one case,[15] for example, the plaintiff, aged 19, applied for $25,000 of life insurance in December, 1931. Beneficiaries were his mother and sister. One month earlier, the insured's father (president of a bank) had died, leaving a will making the insured, his mother, and his sister beneficiaries of a $100,000 trust fund. The insured received a salary of $80 from the bank.

In the next few months, the father's estate was found to be insolvent; there was no trust fund, the bank closed, and the insured lost his job. In December, 1932, he repudiated his life insurance contract and asked for his premiums back. The insurer refused, and suit was filed. The court held that he was entitled to have the premiums returned, saying:

> In the District of Columbia an infant's contracts which appear upon their face to be to his prejudice are void, while his other contracts are voidable, except for necessaries furnished to him at fair prices.
> ´ And his inability to return the consideration and restore the status quo does not deprive him of his right to repudiate. . . .
> Without intimating that a policy of insurance can never be a necessary for any infant, we think the facts here clearly show that this insurance was not a necessary for this infant.
> Even if the carrying charges to the company had been shown here, to allow them would be to hold that an infant is liable not only for necessaries, but for the cost price of purchases not necessary, so that an adult could knowingly sell anything to an infant, secure in the doctrine that if he fails to gain a profit, at least he cannot lose.
> For the reasons stated, the judgment is affirmed with costs.

This case illustrates the majority opinion concerning a minor's right, in the absence of a statute to the contrary, to disaffirm a contract of life insurance and receive back the premiums paid during his minority. As previously noted, many states have special statutes today which remove life insurance contracts from the group of contracts which the minor has the right to disaffirm. These statutes have the effect of placing minors of a specified age on the same status as adults with respect to life insurance contracts, within the limitations specified by the statutes.

J. INSURABLE INTEREST

The requirement of an insurable interest is imposed by reasons of public policy and goes back to the early 18th century in England. At that

---

[15] *Mutual Life Insurance Company of New York* v. *Harry Schiavone*, 63 App. D.C. 257, 71 F. (2d) 980, 94 A.L.R. 962 (1934).

time life insurance policies were not applied for and issued to the persons whose lives were to be insured. Instead they were applied for and issued to third persons, and the insureds were concerned only as the subjects of the insurance. Often the insured did not know the person who obtained the insurance or even that insurance had been effected on his life.

The abuses to which this arrangement might be subjected are apparent. At one time it was almost a sport to wager that public figures would or would not live for even such a short period of time as a few days. Persons in public life were thus made the subjects of so-called life insurance contracts by people who were not even acquainted with them. Obviously this was wagering of a peculiarly vicious nature, so vicious indeed that it shocked the conscience of an 18th-century public not too highly noted for its squeamishness.

In 1774, Parliament finally took action and enacted a law to put an end to such "a mischievous kind of gaming." The law so enacted provided in part as follows:

> That, from and after the passing of this Act, no insurance shall be made by any person or persons, bodies politic or corporate, on the life or lives of any person or persons, or on any other event or events whatsoever, wherein the person or persons for whose use, benefit, or on whose account such policy or policies shall be made, shall have no interest, or by way of gaming or wagering; and that every assurance contrary to the true intent and meaning hereof shall be null and void to all intents and purposes whatsoever.[16]

This statute has not been made a part of the common law of any of the states in the United States, as many of the early English statutes have. Nevertheless, the requirement of an insurable interest as a safeguard against the possible misuse of life insurance was early adopted, independently, in the United States. Sometimes it was enacted into statutory law; sometimes it was expressed as case law, as a matter of public policy. For instance, one of the early definitions of the term was made by the United States Supreme Court in 1881 in the case of *Warnock v. Davis*,[17] as follows:

> It is not easy to define with precision what will in all cases constitute an insurable interest, so as to take the contract out of the class of wager policies. It may be stated generally, however, to be such an interest, arising from the relation of the party obtaining the insurance, either as creditor of or surety for the assured, or from ties of blood or marriage to him, as will justify a reasonable expectation of advantage or benefit from the continuance of his life. It is not necessary that the expectation of advantage or benefit should always be capable of pecuniary estimation; for a parent has an insurable interest in the life of his child, and a child

---

[16] 14 Geo. III, Chap. 48.
[17] 104 U.S. 775 (1882).

in the life of his parent, a husband in the life of his wife, and a wife in the life of her husband. The natural affection in cases of this kind is considered as more powerful—as operating more efficaciously—to protect the life of the insured than any other consideration. But in all cases there must be a reasonable ground, founded upon the relations of the parties to each other, either pecuniary or of blood or affinity, to expect some benefit or advantage from the continuance of the life of the assured. Otherwise the contract is a mere wager, by which the party taking the policy is directly interested in the early death of the assured. Such policies have a tendency to create a desire for the event. They are, therefore, independently of any statute on the subject, condemned, as being against public policy.

This statement constitutes a relatively complete summary of the law of insurable interest as it applies to life insurance. In essence, the objective is to prevent people from profiting from insurance on the lives of others. Thus, there are two basic rules. One concerns the situation where the proposed insured applies for insurance on his own life; the other relates to third-party applicants.

Where the Insured Is the Applicant. In general, the insured who applies for insurance on his own life does not need to be concerned with the question of insurable interest. This rule is sometimes summarized in the statement that every person has an unlimited insurable interest in his own life. It is also sometimes said that an insurable interest is unnecessary if the insured himself makes the contract of insurance. Neither statement is completely true. For if it is shown that the application was completed by the proposed insured with the intention then to assign the contract to another who had no insurable interest, the contract may be declared void. That situation is simply a ruse to permit one who has no insurable interest to obtain the benefit of insurance on the life of another, and this is against public policy. It seems more nearly correct, then, to say that in any case where a person applies for insurance on his own life in good faith, the question of insurable interest will not be involved, and he may designate anyone he wishes as beneficiary.

This rule is illustrated in a somewhat unusual way in a case decided by the Louisiana Court of Appeals in July, 1954.[18] There the insured, as a joke, offered to apply for a policy on his own life on condition that the beneficiary pay the premiums. The background of facts and the insurable interest question are best presented in the words of the court, as follows:

> The only serious question which appears to be involved in this case concerns the contention that this plaintiff was without any insurable interest. In this connection the circumstances surrounding the making of the application for insurance are somewhat pertinent.
> On the date of the making of the application, that is, March 24, 1952,

---

[18] *Nora v. Unity Life Insurance Co.,* 73 So. (2d) 486 (La. App., 1954).

Balthazar and an agent of defendant, one E. B. Joseph, were in a saloon owned and operated by plaintiff. It appears that Joseph was complaining of the fact that he was not doing much business in the way of writing insurance, whereupon Balthazar volunteered an offer to take out a policy if Nora would pay the premium, asserting that he would "will" the policy to Nora. The offer, which may perhaps have been initiated in jest, was taken up and acted upon by all parties; the application was filled out, signed by Balthazar, certified by Joseph and the initial premium paid by plaintiff, Nora. Nora continued to pay the premiums on the policy until the death of Balthazar, which occurred something less than four months later.

Examination of the authorities convinces us that the defense of lack of insurable interest is unsound for it appears that the use of this phrase is interpreted as having application only in those instances where the insurance is procured by a party who is designated as beneficiary, without the application or the knowledge and consent of the insured.

We find the general rule to have been definitely stated in *Dolan* v. *Metropolitan Life Ins. Co.*, 123 So. 379, in which case the court declared:

"There is nothing in the law of [or] public policy which would prevent an insured from taking out a life insurance policy and designating a stranger as the beneficiary, and, upon his inability to pay the premiums, permitting the beneficiary to pay them."

        ✻   ✻   ✻   ✻   ✻

In the instant case there is no showing of any fraud, conspiracy, nor any act in contravention of public policy nor of good morals on the part of this plaintiff. It is obvious under the facts that the insured at any time was at liberty to make a change of beneficiary without notice to plaintiff.

The court thus held that the beneficiary did not have to have an insurable interest because the insured had applied for the insurance on his own life, and could, at any time, have changed the beneficiary.

Third-Party Applicants. It is customary to say that in third-party ownership situations, the applicant must have an insurable interest in the life to be insured. This is because in such cases, for the most part, the insurance is applied for by the applicant for his own benefit. Thus, he is both applicant and beneficiary. In modern practice, however, this is not always true; and in the past decade or so, several states have enacted statutes on this subject that make it clear that in such situations it is the beneficiary—the person to be benefited—who must have the insurable interest in the life to be insured. The New York Insurance Law states the requirement as follows:

Any person of lawful age may on his own initiative procure or effect a contract of insurance upon his own person for the benefit of any person, firm, association or corporation, but no person shall procure or cause to be procured, directly or by assignment or otherwise any contract of insurance upon the person of another unless the benefits under such contract are payable to the person insured or his personal representatives, or to a person having, at the time when such contract is made, an insurable interest in the person insured.[19]

4.21 What Constitutes an Insurable Interest?

In general terms, one person has an insurable interest in the life of another if they are related by blood or marriage or if they have a business relationship of such a nature that the person to be benefited by the contract may reasonably expect to benefit from the continuance of the life insured or to suffer a loss upon its premature termination.

Relationships by Blood or Marriage. There is no question but that the relationship of husband and wife is sufficient to meet the requirement of insurable interest. In fact, the technical validity of the marriage has been held not actually essential if there was a good faith belief in its validity.

It is also generally considered that blood relationship of a fairly close degree is adequate to constitute an insurable interest. The relationships between parent and child. grandparent and grandchild, brother and brother, sister and brother have been considered sufficiently close to meet the requirement as far as the law is concerned. Aunt or uncle and niece or nephew, and cousins, do not qualify by reason of the relationship alone.

Business Relationships. There are many relationships in the business world which if severed by the sudden death of one of the parties could mean serious financial loss to the survivor. In any situation of this kind, the person who would lose by the death of the other has an insurable interest in the life of the other and a right to insure the other's life in his favor. Thus the employer has an insurable interest in the life of the key employee, an unsecured creditor in the life of his debtor, one partner in the life of another. In one such case[20] the court said:

> Certainly Luchs had a pecuniary interest in the life of Dillenberg on two grounds: Because he was his creditor and because he was his partner. The continuance of the partnership, and, of course, a continuance of Dillenberg's life, furnished a reasonable expectation of advantage to himself. It was in the expectation of such advantage that the partnership was formed, and, of course, for the like expectation, was continued.

An especially interesting application of this principle is found in the case of *Theatre Guild Productions, Inc., v. Insurance Corporation of Ireland,*[21] where the Theatre Guild had procured five policies providing that the insurer would pay $1,500 for each performance that the star

---

[19] New York Insurance Law, Sec. 146.
[20] *Connecticut Mut. Life Ins. Co.* v. *Luchs,* 108 U.S. 498 (1883).
[21] 25 A.D. (2d) 109, 267 N.Y.S. (2d) 297 (1966).

missed by reason of accident, illness, death, or total disability. The play was "Dear Me, The Sky Is Falling," and the star was Gertrude Berg. The show opened on March 2, 1963. On July 11, 1963, Miss Berg became ill, and the show closed on July 22, 1963. The question related to the total indemnity owed by the insurer, but on the question of insurable interest the court said:

> Plaintiff's insurable interest derived from its employment of Gertrude Berg as the star of its production. (Insurance Law, Sec. 146, Subd. 2.) The economic success of the production depended on the effective appearance and performance of Gertrude Berg.

Debtor-Creditor Relationships. In only one instance is the life insurance contract treated primarily as an indemnity agreement. That is the case of the creditor who insures the life of his debtor for the purpose of indemnifying himself if the insured should die before repaying the loan. Here the principles of indemnity and of life insurance meet in a somewhat conflicting situation. The problem has been resolved in several different ways.

There is no question but that the unsecured creditor has an insurable interest in the life of the debtor. Certainly he stands to lose if the debtor should die before the debt is paid and leave no property out of which the debt could be satisfied. The principal question is whether his interest is limited to the actual amount of the indebtedness. In a true indemnity contract it would be so limited, but as we have seen, limitation is not in accord with the view usually taken in connection with the life insurance contract.

Although each case is ordinarily decided on its own merits, a general rule has been evolved in cases where the creditor himself has applied for and paid the premiums on the policy on the life of the debtor. In such cases, if the amount of the insurance and the amount of the indebtedness are not widely disproportionate, there is no reason to deny the creditor the benefits of the insurance he had the foresight to procure. Consequently the courts ordinarily hold him entitled to the proceeds in full. However, if the insurance is unreasonably high in relation to the amount of the debt, the facts themselves suggest that the transaction is in reality a wager. In these cases, the courts generally hold that the policy is void on grounds of public policy.

Parenthetically, it should be noted that when the insured himself is the applicant and policyowner and the creditor is a collateral assignee, the creditor is entitled only to recover the amount of his indebtedness out of the proceeds.

The basic rules concerning the insurable interest requirement are always subject to exceptions, especially in situations where the facts show an other than good faith application for the insurance. For instance, it is often stated that partners have an insurable interest in the lives of each other, and ordinarily that would be borne out by the facts. Nevertheless, a number of court decisions indicate that this is not necessarily true. For example, in one case[22] two partners were involved in a hunting accident. The victim was insured for $25,000 in favor of the other partner, and the question of insurable interest was presented. The court said in part:

> While it is true that partners usually, and perhaps in most cases, have an insurable interest in the life of a copartner, it is the existence of circumstances which arise out of or by reason of the partnership, and not the mere existence of the partnership itself, that give rise to an insurable interest. The legal relationship of one partner to the other does not, and should not, necessarily create an insurable interest as does the relationship of husband and wife.
>
> ☼   ☼   ☼   ☼   ☼
>
> The better rule, and the one based on sound reasoning, is that an insurable interest does not necessarily arise by virtue of the mere partner relationship alone. Therefore, the showing by appellant that he and Hankinson were partners did not of itself establish the existence in him of an insurable interest in the life of Hankinson. We must therefore look to the circumstances arising out of or by reason of the partnership to determine whether an insurable interest existed in this case.
>
> Appellant's evidence conclusively establishes that Hankinson made absolutely no financial or capital contribution whatever to the alleged partnership, and that he did not in any way obligate himself to do so; that he had no technical knowledge, skill or ability as a worker or manager to add to the partnership; that he did not have any experience in the type of work he was to do or in the business of the alleged partnership; that appellant had no legal claim for his continued services; and that Hankinson did not purchase or acquire an interest in the business or the tools and equipment used in the business. Also there is nothing to indicate that Hankinson brought or could be expected to bring any business to the partnership, or that his presence as a partner increased or favorably affected the partnership good will.
>
> ☼   ☼   ☼   ☼   ☼
>
> Therefore, we are constrained to and do conclude that appellant's evidence affirmatively establishes that as a matter of law he had no insurable interest in the life of Hankinson.

Because of the careful risk appraisal practices of life companies today, it is sometimes said that the matter of insurable interest, in the legal sense of the word, is largely academic. It is true that risk appraisal automatically eliminates most cases where insurable interest might present a question, and no policies are issued on such applications. However, if risk appraisal practices are not conscientiously followed, or if an apparent

---

[22] *Lakin v. Postal Life and Casualty Co.,* 316 S.W. (2d) 542 (Mo., 1958).

insurable interest at the date of application is not borne out by facts as they may later develop, the question is ultimately decided by legal principles rather than risk appraisal requirements.

4.22 Effect of Lack of Insurable Interest

The matter of insurable interest became of considerably more than academic interest in the mid-1950s, when three life insurers were sued for damages as the result of issuing life insurance to an applicant who had no insurable interest in the life to be insured. The case, *Liberty National Life Insurance Company* v. *Weldon*,[23] involved a very unusual application of the law of torts and concerned the issuance of policies on the life of a small child on the application of the child's aunt-in-law.

The applicant in question was a registered nurse working in a small town in Alabama. One summer afternoon in 1952, she visited her brother-in-law and his family in a neighboring town and during her visit gave her two-year-old niece a soft drink in a cup. The child died before evening. An autopsy showed arsenic in the cup, in the child's body in sufficient quantities to cause her death, and in the clothes both of the child and the aunt. The woman was charged with murder, convicted, and executed.

In the course of the murder trial it was brought out that three life insurance companies had issued policies on the applications of the aunt, insuring in her favor the life of the two-year-old niece. One policy, a $500 endowment at age 17, was issued December 1, 1951. Another, a $5,000 policy, was issued in March, 1952. A third, for $1,000, was in the hands of the agent, though not delivered, at the time the child died. The child's parents had not given their consent to the issuance of the insurance in any of these cases.

The parents brought suit against the life insurance companies under what is called a wrongful death statute. This is a special kind of law permitting certain persons to sue and recover damages from any person whose negligence has caused the death of a person. The theory of the suit in this instance was that the companies were under a duty to use reasonable care not to issue a life insurance policy in favor of a beneficiary who had no interest in the continuation of the life of the insured, and that issuing such policies was a breach of that duty, resulting in the death of the child by murder. A verdict in the parents' favor was appealed to the Supreme Court of Alabama, which quoted a prior decision in part as follows:

> . . . there are forcible reasons why a mere stranger should not be permitted to speculate upon the life of one whose continued existence would bring to him no expectation of possible profit or advantage . . . wager policies, or such as are procured by a person who has no interest in

---

[23] 100 So. (2d) 696 (Ala., 1957).

the subject of the insurance, are undoubtedly most pernicious in their tendencies, because in the nature of premiums upon the clandestine taking of human life. . . .

The reason of the law which vitiates wager policies is the pecuniary interest which the holder has in procuring the death of the subject of insurance, thus opening a wide door by which a constant temptation is created to commit for profit the most atrocious of crimes. . . .

The court quoted a basic rule of torts, that there is a duty upon everyone to exercise reasonable care not to injure another. It then said that a life insurance company has a duty to use reasonable care not to issue a life insurance policy to someone who has no interest in the continuation of the life of the insured.

"Policies in violation of the insurable interest rule are not dangerous because they are illegal," the court said; "they are illegal because they are dangerous." The opinion continued:

We cannot agree with the defendants in their assertion that we should hold as a matter of law that the murder of the young girl was not reasonably foreseeable. This created a situation of a kind which this court and others have consistently said affords temptation to a recognizable percentage of humanity to commit murder. . . .

The jury had held that the issuance of the policies was the proximate cause of the murder of the child and awarded damages in the amount of $100,000. The reviewing court reduced this to $75,000, but even so it remained the largest wrongful death verdict ever to come before that particular court. This case, decided in 1957, illustrates perhaps more clearly than any other argument the importance of the insurable interest requirement as a matter of public policy.

K. WHEN THE POLICY BECOMES EFFECTIVE

4.23 Required Legal Form

If there is no statute to the contrary, an oral contract of life insurance is valid. However, life insurance contracts are so comprehensive and of such importance that it is the invariable understanding that, after approval of the application, the contract itself will be expressed in a written policy issued by the company and delivered to the policyowner. The next important question, therefore, is what constitutes delivery.

4.24 Delivery of the Policy

Most life insurance applications expressly provide that the insurance shall not become effective until approval of the application, issuance of a policy, and delivery of the policy and payment of the initial premium during the continued good health of the proposed insured. If there is no agreement to the contrary, each of these conditions must be fulfilled before the insurance becomes effective, and thus they are all conditions precedent.

Conditional Receipt Cases. Typically, the terms of most conditional receipts modify these basic requirements concerning delivery and make insurance effective if the condition expressed in the receipt is met. Where there is a conditional receipt, therefore, issuance and delivery of the policy are not conditions precedent to the effectiveness of insurance, although they may be applicable to the policy itself, by contrast with insurance under the terms of the receipt. For instance, if the receipt limits its effectiveness to a specified amount of insurance and the policy is issued for an amount greater than that provided by the receipt, the conditions under which insurance becomes effective under the policy must be met.

No Conditional Receipt. If the initial premium is not paid at the time the application is completed, the insurer makes the offer by issuing a policy and sending it to the agent for delivery. The contract is completed when the agent delivers the policy and collects the initial premium; but even in this situation, delivery does not necessarily mean that the policy must be placed in the hands of the applicant. It is important, therefore, to know the legal meaning of "delivery."

4.25 What Does "Delivery" Mean?

Generally speaking, a policy has been delivered, in the legal sense of the word, any time the company has parted with legal control of the policy with the intention to be bound by it as a completed instrument. If a policy has in fact been placed in the hands of the applicant, the requirement of delivery has, of course, been met. However, delivery may be accomplished the moment the company relinquishes possession of the policy by mailing it to the agent, if nothing further remains to be done but the ministerial act (that is, an act that involves no discretion) of seeing that the applicant receives the policy. Under these circumstances, mailing the policy to the agent for delivery is construed to be delivery to the applicant. This is said to be "delivery by construction" and thus "constructive delivery." In the terms of the general definition, there has been a parting of possession or control, accompanied by an intention on the part of the insurer to be bound by the policy as a completed instrument.

A policy left at the residence of the applicant or at his regular place of business is also said to be constructively delivered. Delivery to an agent of the applicant is, in legal effect, delivery to the applicant.

4.26 Delivery for Inspection

Occasionally an applicant is permitted to keep a policy for a few days for inspection, but without legal obligation on the part either of the insurer or the applicant. This, of course, is not delivery in the legal sense of the word, for there is no intention to be bound. Nevertheless, if the insured dies while the policy is in his possession, it is sometimes difficult for the insurer to establish that no binding obligation was intended. For this reason, it is customary to have the applicant sign an "inspection receipt" in such cases, specifying the conditions under which the policy was left with him and making it clear that the policy has not been "delivered" in the legal meaning of the word.

4.27 Effective Date of the Policy

In the light of the foregoing discussion of conditional receipts and delivery, it is perhaps obvious that the date the policy is issued is not necessarily the date the insurance becomes effective. Policies may also be dated back (though generally not more than six months) at the request of the applicant, to obtain a lower premium rate because of a lower age.

In many cases, policies are given an issue date as well as a policy date, so that the date on which the policy was actually issued can readily be established. As a general rule, if a policy bears a policy date, the insurance will be effective as of that date and it will be given effect in any later consideration of questions relating to the payment of premiums. However, the suicide and contestable periods may be held to run from the earlier of the two dates.

SUMMARY

Insurance and the Contract

Individually, the life insurance contract defines the rights of the policyowner on the one hand and the commitments of the insurer on the other. Collectively, however, the life insurance contracts of every life insurer must operate in such a way that the mortality experience developed under them will be within expected limits. This means that the special requirements of insurance must be blended with legal requirements in the formation of every individual life insurance contract.

Insurability. Risk appraisal, though involved in every line of insurance, is especially critical in life insurance because once the contract is formed, there is no contractual right of cancellation by the company.

Since risks must be appraised before the contract is completed, the life insurance agent's authority is more strictly limited than that of agents in other lines of insurance. As a general rule, therefore, the life insurance agent rarely has the authority to complete a binding contract.

Offer and Acceptance in Life Insurance

A life insurance contract is completed when an offer is made by one party and accepted by the other. Traditionally, the application is said to be an offer, but this is true only if it is accompanied by the initial premium. Then the application constitutes an offer in the legal sense of the term; and if it is accepted, a contract will have been completed.

If the initial premium is not paid at the time the application is completed, the applicant is, in effect, inviting the company to make an offer to him. The offer is made when the company issues a policy and sends it to the agent for delivery. The applicant accepts this offer by paying the initial premium, and a contract is completed.

In most instances, if the applicant pays the initial premium when he completes the application, either a conditional receipt or a binding receipt is issued, and the terms and conditions of the receipt govern the operation of offer and acceptance. In a general sense, however, the insurer, in using a conditional receipt, is making a conditional offer to establish insurance at an earlier date than would otherwise be the case; and the applicant accepts that offer by payment of the initial premium.

If the initial premium accompanies the application and the insurer issues a different kind of contract from that applied for, it is making a counteroffer. This counteroffer may, in turn, be accepted or rejected by the applicant (the original offeror).

Premium Receipts

In the absence of either a conditional or a binding receipt, the insurance applied for may not become effective until several days, sometimes weeks, have elapsed. If the proposed insured dies during this period, he is not covered even though he has paid the premium. It may also be necessary for the agent to resell the policy when he delivers it. For these reasons, life insurance companies customarily authorize their agents to issue either a conditional or a binding premium receipt if the applicant pays the initial premium at the time he applies.

A binding receipt establishes insurance as of the date of the receipt, subject to the right of the insurer to terminate the insurance if the proposed insured is found not to be insurable. (In other words, it provides coverage, subject to a condition subsequent.)

Conditional receipts (which are far more widely used than binding receipts) provide that insurance will become effective if conditions that are specified in the receipt are met. Typically, such receipts provide that if the initial premium is paid, insurance will become effective as of a date specified in the receipt—usually the later of the date of the receipt or of the medical examination, if one is required—on condition that the insured is found to be insurable as of the specified date. Conditional receipts of this kind are generally referred to as insurability receipts. If the insurance will become effective only if the application is approved, the receipt is referred to as an approval type of receipt.

Conditional Receipts and the Courts

In a minority of the states there are court decisions holding that conditional receipts actually establish interim insurance. This result is reached by interpreting the conditions expressed in the receipt as conditions subsequent instead of conditions precedent. The majority view, however, is that such receipts, unless clearly ambiguous, establish a condition precedent and that no insurance is effective unless the condition is met.

Delay in Acting on the Application

If an application for life insurance is not handled promptly, the insurer may, in a minority of the states, find itself being held liable on one of two theories based on what is termed unreasonable delay. One of these theories—a theory of liability in tort—assumes that there is a duty on the part of the insurer to act with reasonable promptness on an application. Failing that duty, it is liable in damages if the insured dies during the interim. The beneficiary can, therefore, recover the amount of the insurance that would have been payable if the application had been accepted promptly.

Those who oppose this approach take the position that mere silence on the part of the offeree has no contractual significance and that the insurance company has no duty to the public that can be violated even though there is unreasonable delay in acting on an application. It is their contention that insurers are not public utilities and thus are free to choose the persons with whom to contract.

Related to the theory of tort liability, but based in contract law, is the theory that unreasonable delay in considering an offer is an implied acceptance. This theory has been applied in a few cases to hold the insurer liable for the amount of insurance that would have been in force if the application had been acted upon with reasonable promptness and accepted.

Other Elements of the Contract

Consideration. In the legal sense of the word, the requirement of consideration for the promises of the insurer is met by payment of the initial premium and completion of the application.

Competent Contracting Parties. Not every person who has an interest in the life insurance contract is a contracting party. Thus, the beneficiary is not a contracting party, nor is the insured in third-party ownership cases. The insured's consent is required, however, in such third-party cases, as a matter of public policy.

An insurer is competent to issue contracts of insurance if it has been authorized to do so by its charter or articles of incorporation and if it has a certificate of authority issued by the state in which the contract is completed. Other than the insurer, only the applicant must have contractual capacity.

In the absence of evidence to the contrary, every individual is presumed competent to make a valid contract. There are several exceptions, but one of the most important single exceptions involves the contractual capacity of minors. A minor may disaffirm most contracts he makes during his minority except one for the sale of land, and he may disaffirm that upon reaching his majority. (He is generally held liable for the actual value of necessaries, but life insurance is not a "necessary.") When a minor disaffirms a contract, he must return any consideration he has received if he still has it. However, the fact that he no longer has the consideration does not preclude him from disaffirming the contract. This rule has been applied differently in the case of the life insurance contract, some courts holding that a minor is liable for the actual cost of the protection he has received if he disaffirms. The better decisions, however, hold that a minor may disaffirm a life insurance contract and receive back all the premiums he has paid.

Insurable Interest. A person is said to have an insurable interest if he has an expectation of gain from the continued existence of the object or person insured, or an expectation of injury from its loss.

Generally speaking, a person is said to have an unlimited insurable interest in his own life. Therefore, he may apply for life insurance on his own life and name anyone he wishes as beneficiary, so long as the application is made in good faith. If one applies for and receives a policy of insurance on the life of another, the insurance must be payable to someone who has an insurable interest in the life to be insured. The New York insurance law forbids such contracts to be issued unless "the benefits are payable to the person insured or his personal representatives, or to a person having at the time when the contract is made an insurable interest in the person insured."

A fairly close relationship by blood or marriage is said to constitute an insurable interest. In business relationships, anyone who would stand to lose by the death of another may be said to have an insurable interest in that person's life. Thus the employer has an insurable interest in the life of a key employee, the creditor in the life of his debtor, and one partner in the life of another. In every case, however, the facts must bear out the actual possibility of loss.

Although a creditor has an insurable interest in the life of his unsecured debtor, the rule concerning the amount recoverable is different if the creditor himself applies for the insurance than if the applicant is the insured. If the creditor is the applicant, he is generally held to be entitled to the proceeds in full unless the difference between the amount of the debt and the amount of the proceeds is so large as to suggest a wagering agreement. If the policy is applied for by the insured and assigned to the creditor as security, the creditor's recovery is limited to the amount of the debt.

If the insurance is to be payable to someone who has no insurable interest at the time the contract is completed, the contract will be void. The insurer is not generally responsible in damages, but the Supreme Court of Alabama, in 1957, held that an insurer has a duty to use reasonable care not to issue a life insurance policy in favor of a beneficiary who has no insurable interest in the life to be insured. Issuing such a contract was a breach of that duty, the court held, and the insurer was responsible in damages.

When the Policy Becomes Effective. It is common practice to provide that a life insurance contract will not become effective until a policy has been issued and delivered and the premium paid during the continued good health of the proposed insured. Conditional receipts and binding receipts modify this requirement, and delivery is not always required in the sense that the policy must actually be put into the hands of the applicant.

Delivery in the legal sense of the term has been accomplished any time the insurer has parted with legal control of the policy with the intention to be bound by it as a completed instrument. Whenever circumstances indicate that this has been done, the actions of the parties will be construed to mean that delivery has been made. This is termed constructive delivery. Thus if the policy has been mailed to the agent with instructions to deliver it to the applicant but with no further discretion on the agent's part, it will be construed to have been delivered. Delivery to the place of residence of the applicant or to his regular place of business is constructive delivery. Ordinarily, if the agent leaves the policy with the applicant for the purpose of inspection only, he should obtain the applicant's signature on an inspection receipt specifying that the policy has not been delivered for any other purpose.

QUESTIONS FOR REVIEW

1. Why do most insurers believe that the process of risk selection in life insurance must be completed before the contract is made?

2. Who makes the offer and who accepts in each of the following situations?
   a. The applicant does not prepay the initial premium.
   b. The applicant pays the initial premium when the application is completed but does not receive a conditional or binding receipt.
   c. The first premium is paid at the time the application is completed and a conditional or binding receipt is given.

3. Differentiate between the insurability and the approval types of conditional receipts. How does a conditional receipt differ from a binding receipt?

4. In general terms, what is the responsibility of a life insurance company for acting promptly on a pending application? Upon what reasoning does a court rely when it holds that the insurer is liable because of unreasonable delay in acting on an application? What is the reasoning if the decision is against such a contention?

5. Which of the following persons become parties to the contract when a life insurance policy is issued?
   a. The applicant.
   b. The proposed insured.
   c. The beneficiary.
   d. The life insurance company.

6. What constitutes an insurable interest?

7. In approving a claim by a creditor under a policy of insurance on the life of a debtor, how would settlement be made in each of the following situations?
   a. The creditor applied for and owned the policy and was the beneficiary.
   b. The debtor applied for and owned the policy but had executed a collateral assignment in favor of the creditor.

8. Explain the basis for the decision in the case of *Liberty National Life Insurance Company* v. *Weldon* (the case where the aunt-in-law obtained insurance on the life of her niece and later caused her death).

9. Under what circumstances would a life insurance policy become effective on the date the application was approved?

10. Indicate the significance of the word "delivery" as a requirement in connection with the effectiveness of a life insurance contract. What is meant by "constructive delivery"?

Chapter Outline

A. Rights of an Applicant

B. The Beneficiary's Rights

C. The Beneficiary Designation
   5.1 Insurable Interest
   5.2 Beneficiaries in the Order of Their Rights
   5.3 The Mechanics of the Designation
   5.4 Who May Be Named
   5.5 Designating Minor Children
   5.6 Business Life Insurance

D. The Optional Modes of Settlement
   5.7 The Settlement Agreement
   5.8 Contingent Payees under Settlement Options

E. Life Insurance and Trusts
   5.9 The *Inter Vivos* Trust
   5.10 The Testamentary Trust
   5.11 The Trustee as Beneficiary

F. Trusts and the Optional Modes Compared

G. Some Special Legal Problems
   5.12 The "Common Disaster" Problem

H. Some Incidental Rules of Law
   5.13 The Rule against Perpetuities
   5.14 The Rule against Accumulations

Chapter 5

The Applicant Names the Beneficiary

THE PURPOSE of this chapter is to discuss the major legal principles that are or may be concerned in connection with the designation of beneficiaries and the election of optional methods of settlement under life insurance policies.

A. RIGHTS OF AN APPLICANT

The beneficiary is the person named in a life insurance policy to receive the benefit payable on the death of the insured. Designating the beneficiary, therefore, is one of the most important actions the applicant takes; and his rights as a policyowner with respect to later beneficiary changes are among the most significant rights he acquires under the contract.

In the typical life insurance situation, a person applies for insurance on his or her own life and designates wife or husband as beneficiary. Most present-day life insurance policies provide that unless a beneficiary is designated irrevocably, the policyowner may change the designation from time to time merely by complying with the procedure described in the policy. In other words, unless the applicant or policyowner limits his right to make later changes, he may change the beneficiary designation whenever he wishes, without the beneficiary's consent. Under these circumstances, the owner is also free to exercise any of the other ownership rights under the policy without the consent of the beneficiary. Thus he may request and receive policy loans, change the dividend option election, or surrender the policy for cash. In most jurisdictions, the policyowner may also transfer his ownership rights under the policy (assign the policy) to someone other than the beneficiary if he wishes, without the beneficiary's consent.

B. THE BENEFICIARY'S RIGHTS

The rights of the beneficiary under present-day life insurance policies depend, in most instances, upon the rights the policyowner reserves to himself. For historical reasons, however, there are some variations in a limited number of jurisdictions, and a brief history of the rights of the beneficiary may help to clarify some of these differences.

The earliest life insurance contracts were what we now think of as third-party contracts. They were applied for and owned by the beneficiary, and the insured was concerned only as the subject of the insurance. Even when the insured was a party to the contract—that is, when he was the applicant and policyowner—the beneficiary was considered to have the ownership rights; and the insured had no power to alter the interest of the beneficiary.

About 1900, however, some life insurers began to include in their policies a provision permitting the applicant who applied for the insurance on his own life to reserve the right to change the beneficiary later, if he wished. At first there was some doubt about the legality of this kind of provision, but the question was settled affirmatively when the standard policy provisions law, enacted in New York following the Armstrong investigation, included a change of beneficiary provision. Once the right to change the beneficiary was reserved, the beneficiary had no rights under the policy that could not be terminated by the policyowner if he wished.

Nevertheless, there followed a period during which the revocable beneficiary was generally considered to have what was called a qualified interest in the policy. (The lawyer said it was a "vested right, subject to being divested.") Clearly, the policyowner could terminate the beneficiary's right if he revoked the designation; but until he did so, the beneficiary's consent was considered necessary before any ownership rights under the policy could be exercised. This view is still held in a very few jurisdictions, but the generally accepted rules in most of the states of the United States today may be summarized as follows:

The Revocable Beneficiary. A beneficiary designation that can be changed whenever the policyowner wishes is said to be a revocable designation. Since the rights of this kind of beneficiary can be terminated any time the policyowner wishes, the revocable beneficiary is said to have a "mere expectancy" so far as his rights under the policy are concerned. He can "expect" to receive the proceeds at the insured's death, but he has no guarantee that this will be true.

The Irrevocable Beneficiary. An applicant or policyowner may name a beneficiary irrevocably if he wishes. If he does this, the person so named has what the law terms a vested right to the benefit payable at the death of the insured. This means a right of such a nature that it cannot be reduced or destroyed without the beneficiary's consent. Nevertheless, an irrevocable beneficiary's vested right is subject to other possibilities of termination. For instance, the policy must be in force at the death of the insured or there will be no benefit to which anyone will have a right. Also, most present-day policies terminate the rights of a beneficiary, whether revocable or irrevocable, if he or she dies prior to the death of the insured.

At one time, it was customary for creditors to request that they be designated as irrevocable beneficiaries of life insurance intended for credit protection, but by and large this type of designation is not used nearly as frequently now as was once the case. The whole life insurance contract today includes a significant cash value during the lifetime of the insured. A right to share only in the proceeds at the time of death, therefore, is a limited kind of protection compared to the right of an assignee, who ordinarily has that right as well as the right to surrender the contract for its cash value. Consequently, the person who once requested designation as an irrevocable beneficiary under his debtor's life insurance policy now usually prefers an assignment in his favor as a more extensive and straightforward means of protecting himself against death or defaults of the debtor. In present-day financial transactions, therefore, the policyowner is more likely to treat his policy as property and assign it than to designate the creditor as an irrevocable beneficiary.

C. THE BENEFICIARY DESIGNATION

5.1 Insurable Interest

The question of insurable interest is closely related to the subject of beneficiary designations. However, as a legal matter, the insurable interest question is involved only when the policy is applied for by someone other than the person whose life is insured.

As a matter of practice, a company's issuing office will probably inquire fully into the reasons for naming as beneficiary a person who appears to have little insurable connection with the proposed insured, even if that person is the applicant. Insurers follow this practice as a matter of routine in order to avoid any possibility that the insurance is applied for for speculative purposes. Generally speaking, however, there are no legal restrictions concerning insurable interest if the policy is applied for by the person whose life is to be insured, and he designates the beneficiary. In order to concentrate on the problems of beneficiary designations, therefore, it will be presumed in the rest of this chapter that the person whose life is to be insured has applied for the insurance.

5.2 Beneficiaries in the Order of Their Rights

The Primary Beneficiary. The applicant designates the beneficiary by stating in the application the name or names of the persons to whom he wishes the company to pay the benefit that will become payable at the death of the insured. He may specify that the benefit be paid to one person or that it is to be shared by several persons in proportions as he may indicate. Regardless of the number or the proportions in which these people are to share the proceeds, the person or persons who are designated to receive the proceeds of a life insurance policy, if they are living at the insured's death, are called primary beneficiaries, or sometimes "first" or "direct" beneficiaries.

Contingent Beneficiaries. In the days when the policy was applied for and owned by the beneficiary, the beneficiary's rights were of such a nature that they became an asset in his estate if he died prior to the death of the insured. This created practical problems, particularly where the insured survived the beneficiary by many years. In such situations, the estate of the beneficiary might have been closed long before the insurance became payable, yet the proceeds would still be payable to that estate. Even when the estate could be reopened, tracing the heirs and otherwise satisfying the necessary legal requirements could become very complex.

This problem was resolved about the beginning of this century, when insurers began providing in their policies that if the designated beneficiary died before the death of the insured, the benefit would be payable to the estate of the insured. This eliminated the possibility that the death benefit could become payable to an estate that had been closed many years before, and it permitted the policyowner to designate another beneficiary following the death of the first one. It also created a new contingency that might be provided against when the policy was applied for—the possibility that the first-named beneficiary might die before the insured and the death benefit become payable to the estate of the insured. Now it became possible for the applicant or policyowner to name a contingent beneficiary, who would have the right to receive the death benefit if the primary beneficiary did not survive the insured. And since the contingent beneficiary might also predecease the insured, most companies today permit the insured to name a second contingent beneficiary. Settlement will be made to this person if there is no surviving primary or first contingent beneficiary at the death of the insured.

The rights of each class of beneficiaries are usually determined as of the date of death of the insured. If, at that time, the first-named (primary) beneficiary is living, the rights of the contingent and final beneficiaries are automatically extinguished. The primary beneficiary takes all. If that person dies immediately thereafter, payment will be made to his or her personal representatives; but neither the contingent nor the final beneficiaries will have any rights to any of the proceeds.

On the other hand, if the primary beneficiary is not living at the insured's death, the contingent beneficiary becomes entitled to the proceeds. If the contingent beneficiary dies after the insured but prior to receiving the money, it will be paid to his or her estate. Often this sequence is specifically outlined in a policy provision.

5.3 The Mechanics of the Designation

The beneficiary designation is as important to the life insurance company as it is to the applicant, although perhaps in a different way. Payment to the beneficiary fulfills the basic promise under the insurance policy and a release discharges the company from any further obligations under the contract. If the provisions of the beneficiary designation are clear and unambiguous, settlement is simple. If the provisions are not clear, court procedures may be required. Often they are expensive; always they are time consuming. For this reason, it is as much to the advantage of the company as to the policyowner that the beneficiary and settlement specifications be clear and unequivocal at the outset. It is important also that they be reviewed frequently in order that they may continue to reflect the changing needs and circumstances of the policyowner throughout the lifetime of the insured.

In practice, most beneficiary designations are simple. The application blank contains a special section in which the names of the various beneficiaries are to be written, and many present-day policies contain a provision such as the following:

> The beneficiary is as designated in the application for this policy unless otherwise provided by endorsement at issue or unless subsequently changed as provided in this policy.

When this practice is followed, the policy itself specifies the order in which the beneficiaries become entitled to the proceeds, but their names are not generally set forth in the policy itself.

Nevertheless, many companies still endorse the beneficiary designation on the policy when it is issued, incorporating the names of the beneficiaries and the details of the applicant's request in the endorsement.

The exact wording of this beneficiary designation endorsement is something over which the applicant himself has little control except to make his wishes as clear as possible. The company is responsible for drafting the endorsement in such a way that the designation will not be ambiguous and the wishes of the applicant will be carried out. It must always be borne in mind that the beneficiary designation written in 1974 may very well not be acted upon until the year 2000, or later. At that time, no person concerned in phrasing the original designation may be living. It is highly important, therefore, that every effort be made to express the wishes of the applicant as clearly and as simply as possible in the beneficiary provision.

In the typical case, where the applicant names his wife as primary beneficiary and his children as contingent beneficiaries, the policy might be endorsed to provide that the proceeds would be payable to:

> Mary Jones, wife of the insured, if living, otherwise to those among the children of the insured by the said wife who survive, if any; otherwise to the executors, administrators, or assigns of the insured.

Under this designation, if Mary is living at the death of the insured, the death benefit will be payable to her. If she is not living but any child or children of the insured and Mary survive, settlement will be made to them equally. If neither wife nor any child survives, settlement will be made to the estate of the insured.

5.4 Who May Be Named

In situations where a life insurance policy is applied for and issued to the proposed insured, the major legal problems relate to the matter of identity and the exact circumstances in which a given beneficiary becomes entitled to the policy proceeds. A beneficiary designation is essentially personal in nature. Thus, the person who is to receive the benefit should either be named or described in enough detail that he or she can be readily identified.

For instance, if the applicant wishes to name his estate as beneficiary, the policy should provide that the beneficiary will be:

> The executors, administrators, or assigns of the insured.

Today, the executors or administrators of the insured are frequently referred to as his "personal representatives" and the beneficiary designation may be so phrased. In either case, the designation does not name the person to whom the proceeds are to be paid, since the personal representative of the insured cannot be known until after the insured's death. However, it describes the person with sufficient clarity that he can readily be identified. Payment made to the person so described will discharge the company of its obligations under the policy.

Wife of the Insured. When the applicant designates his wife as beneficiary, she is usually so described. The wife should be designated by her given name—"Mary Jones, wife of the insured," not "Mrs. John Jones."

Ordinarily this type of designation will carry out the wishes of the applicant, and it indicates with certainty the person to whom the proceeds are to be paid. The courts have almost unanimously held that in the absence of a controlling statute, the words "wife of the insured" are descriptive only. Thus, with this type of designation, except in a few jurisdictions, the policy proceeds would be paid to "Mary Jones" at the insured's death, regardless of whether she were then the wife of Jones or not.

Similar reasoning was applied in connection with the word "fiancée" in one illustrative case[1] which involved a beneficiary designation such as the following:

> Mary Doe, fiancée, if living; otherwise to William George Roe, father.

The insured in this case was killed while in military service. About six months before his death, his fiancée wrote to him saying that she was going to marry another man. The insured did not change the beneficiary designation of the policy; the fiancée was married as she had said she planned; and at the insured's death both the father and the former fiancée claimed the proceeds. The company, therefore, paid the money into court, asking a decision as to the person rightfully entitled to it. The court said:

> In *Simmons* v. *Simmons*, 272 S.W. 2d 913, we held that where a beneficiary is named or can otherwise be definitely identified, her designation as wife is descriptive only. The rule applies in this case to appellee. Her name as beneficiary is followed in the policy by the word "Fiancée," and it may well be that insured would not have named her beneficiary except for his engagement to her, yet the fact remains that from February, when the engagement was broken, until July 13, when he was killed, he did not change the beneficiary nor did he do all he could have reasonably done to change the beneficiary.

Thus the court held that the proceeds should be paid to the former fiancée, although it was admitted that the claim of the father (the contingent beneficiary) appealed strongly to one's sympathies. "Our function, however," the court concluded, "is to determine the legal rights of the parties, not to sit in judgment on appellee's conscience."

5.5 Designating Children

Applicants often wish to designate their children by name as beneficiaries of their insurance. This may present a problem if additional children are born later and the beneficiary designation is not suitably revised to include them. One way to avoid such oversights is to designate the children as a class.

---

[1] *Scherer et ux.* v. *Wahlstrom,* Texas Court of Civil Appeals, 318 S.W. (2d) 456 (1958).

Class Designations. A class beneficiary designation is a designation that names several people as a group, without listing them individually. Life insurers do not generally favor such designations because of the practical as well as legal problems that may be encountered in ascertaining the identities and locating the various members of the group who are living at the time settlement is to be made. Often life insurance proceeds do not become payable until many years after the designation is made, and frequently the members of the group are widely dispersed by that time. If any have died, their deaths must be verified, and all must be located or accounted for; for each, if living, has a valid claim to a share of the proceeds.

In spite of these possible problems, most insurers will permit the designation of "children of the insured" as a class or the "brothers and sisters" of an insured child, especially as successor or contingent beneficiaries. In such situations, the possible additional problems of settlement are considered to be outweighed by the convenience to the applicant and policyowner. Since the designation takes effect as of the date of death of the insured, it includes all children then in existence, as well as those in being but not yet born. Thus, such designations automatically include later-born children, even though the beneficiary designation is not revised. If the applicant wishes to name the children he then has, a modified class designation such as the following may be used:

> Children of the insured, including Michael, Anne, and James, equally or to survivor.

If a designation of this kind is used, the policy proceeds will be payable to all the children of the insured who are living at his death, just as would be true under a class designation. However, it is a little more personal than a class designation, since it names the children who are in existence when the designation is requested.[2]

Nevertheless, class designations of children present some special legal problems in addition to the usual ones involved in class designations generally. This is especially true if the word "children" is used without further explanation. For instance, does the term include illegitimate children of the insured? Does it include stepchildren?

Some courts have held that the term "children" includes illegitimate children; other courts have held that it does not. Generally they will be included if the intent to include them is clear; but it is ordinarily quite difficult to determine intent, and no company willingly endorses a policy with a beneficiary designation that can be clarified only by court action.

---

[2] Many life insurance agents are able to get the attention of a prospect by asking him if he has "disinherited his grandchildren" by a beneficiary designation such as this. They then point out that this inequity can be avoided by a *per stirpes* or "right of representation" designation. This is discussed later.

Stepchildren are not ordinarily included in the term "children," but adopted children are. The term also includes legitimated children (that is, children born out of wedlock whose parents subsequently marry). To be sure that persons in these special groups are included, if that is the policyowner's wish—or excluded, if that is what he intends—the language of the designation must be clear and precise.

Generally speaking, if the applicant wishes to designate his children as a class, the term "children" should be used and not the term "issue" or "heirs." The word "issue" definitely should be avoided since in its true legal sense it includes all lineal descendants, regardless of how remote the relationship. The word "heirs" also presents problems. Originally the term denoted those persons who by law succeeded to the real property of the person who died without a will. By statute and otherwise, its meaning has been extended to include persons entitled to take the personal property also. When used in life insurance, however, the word "heirs" has no generally established meaning and therefore should be avoided.

The prompt settlement of life insurance claims is in the best interests of the insured, the beneficiaries, and the insurance company. Class designations, therefore, although sometimes justified by the circumstances of the individual case, should always be worded in such a way as to make possible the identification of the members of the group at a very early date following the death of the insured, and thus insure the prompt settlement of the sum payable under the policy.

Irrevocable Designations of Children. As a general rule, it is not advisable to designate a minor child or children as irrevocable beneficiaries. Even when the irrevocable beneficiary is an adult, the policyowner can exercise his ownership rights only with the consent of the beneficiary. A minor, however, cannot give consent, and consent cannot be given for him. As a consequence, the owner who names a minor child as irrevocable beneficiary will be unable to surrender the policy, effect a policy loan, make an assignment, or exercise any other ownership right until the child reaches his majority and can and does give his consent.

Per Stirpes and Per Capita Designations. Occasionally an insured will want to designate his wife as primary beneficiary, and name his children *per stirpes* as successor beneficiaries. The term *"per stirpes"* or "by right of representation" means "by the branch," as contrasted with the term *"per capita,"* which means "by the person," or individually. Most beneficiary designations are on a *per capita* basis, so the persons are entitled to share in the policy proceeds on an individual basis; that is, if three primary beneficiaries are named, each will receive one third of the proceeds. If only two survive the insured, each will receive one-half. A *per stirpes* designation modifies this to provide that the proceeds are to be divided among the members of a group of persons, such as the children of the insured, with the share of any deceased member of the group going to that person's surviving children, if any.

To illustrate, assume that Robert Black wishes to name his wife Sara as primary beneficiary of his policy and their children as successor beneficiaries. Their children are grown, and several have children of their own. Mr. Black wants his insurance distributed equitably, and he fully realizes that he himself may survive one or more of his children. If he does, he would like the orphaned grandchildren to take the share their father or mother would have taken if he or she had lived. By requesting a designation of the children *per stirpes*, or by right of representation, he achieves that result.

Assume, then, that the Blacks have four children: Robert, Jr., John, Sally, and Diane. Each of them is married and has one or more children at the time Mr. Black effects the beneficiary designation. One type of *per stirpes* designation in a situation of this kind would read as follows:

> To Sara Black, wife of the insured, if living; otherwise in equal shares to the children of the insured by said wife who are living and *per stirpes* to the lawful children who are living of any children of the insured by said wife who shall have died.

If at Mr. Black's death, Mrs. Black is not living but the four children are, the benefit will be shared by the four of them equally. However, suppose that only Robert, Jr., John, and Sally are living. In that case, assuming that Diane left two children, Jane and Roger, the benefit will still be divided into four shares, and the fourth share, Diane's, will be paid to Jane and Roger, in equal shares, or to their legally appointed guardians if they are minors.

Guardians as Beneficiaries. Parents sometimes wish to name as beneficiaries persons whom they wish to be, or have designated under their wills as, guardians of their minor children in the event of the parents' deaths during the children's minority. Even when a parent has named a guardian in his will, however, there is no certainty that that person will be living at the time of the parent's death or, if living, that he will be appointed as guardian or be able to qualify. In addition, there is also the possibility that when the proceeds become payable the children will be grown and fully competent to receive the proceeds on their own account.

For all these reasons, if the applicant wishes his children to receive the proceeds of his life insurance, the best solution is just to designate the children as beneficiaries. (Alternatively, a trust may be established for their benefit during their minority, as will be discussed later.) Life insurance companies are not usually willing to pay benefits in any significant amounts directly to minor beneficiaries, since a minor can always disaffirm a release he has given. If there is a need for a guardian at the time of settlement, therefore, the insurer will require such an appointment before settlement will be made.

5.6 Business Life Insurance

Life insurance is frequently purchased by business firms for business purposes. In such instances, the applicant and policyowner will usually also be designated as the beneficiary. For example, a corporation may apply for, own, and be the beneficiary of a policy on the life of a key employee. Here the basic principles of beneficiary designations generally apply, but in addition a few special problems arise out of the particular form of organization under which the firm is conducting its business.

For instance, it is not unusual for a man to be conducting his business under a trade name such as the John Smith Company even though it has never been incorporated. In that case, the man and the company are one and the same. If, therefore, a policy of life insurance on the life of John Smith is endorsed with a beneficiary designation naming the firm as beneficiary, the legal effect will be exactly the same as if he had directed that the benefit be paid to his estate.

A similar situation exists in a partnership. There, it is the partners who have legal significance and not the name under which they may be doing business. Thus, if the business is to be named as beneficiary of a life insurance policy, the names of the partners themselves should usually be used. Assume that the partnership does business as Smith and Company. If it is in fact a partnership, and if Smith and Jones are the partners, the designation will ordinarily read as follows:

> Smith and Company, a partnership composed of John Smith and Thomas Jones.

By contrast, a corporation is a legal entity, authorized by law to carry on a business of a specified nature and permitted to sue and be sued in its corporate name. For this reason it can and should be designated as the beneficiary of a life insurance policy by its corporate name. One form of such a designation would read as follows:

> The A.B.C. Company of Chicago, Illinois, an Illinois corporation, its successors or assigns.

It should be noted that this designation contains its own contingent beneficiary—the corporation's successors or assigns. For this reason, when a designation of this kind is used, no other contingent beneficiary should be named.

D. THE OPTIONAL MODES OF SETTLEMENT

5.7 The Settlement Agreement

If the applicant wishes to provide an income settlement to the beneficiary, he may elect one or more of the optional modes provided by the policy. In that case, his wishes are set forth in a special agreement, often called a "settlement agreement," which will usually be included in the policy at issue. Regardless of what they are called, these settlement specifications are, in effect, only elaborate beneficiary designations. As in the one-sum designation, the applicant states the persons who are to receive the benefit payable under the policy at the death of the insured. However, in the settlement agreement he also stipulates which optional settlement methods are elected and how they are to be applied.

The optional modes of settlement are different methods of settlement provided by the contract. The first statute expressly permitting such provisions was enacted by the New York legislature in 1906; but for some time prior to that date, individual companies had issued some policies providing for settlement in instalments. Other states have enacted statutes similar to the New York statute; and today it is the rule, rather than the exception, to include optional modes of settlement in a life insurance policy.

Typically, the applicant may elect one or more optional modes for each of the beneficiaries[3] he designates; and if no optional mode election is in effect at the insured's death, a beneficiary for a one-sum settlement may elect to receive the money under one of the optional modes.

Briefly stated, there are only four basic types of optional settlements, and two of these are very similar. One is the interest option, under which the company retains the sum payable, paying interest on it at a guaranteed rate to a designated person, who may or may not be given the right of withdrawal or the right to change to another option or options. Two other modes—the fixed amount and the fixed period options—involve payments of sums over a period of time until the proceeds are exhausted; and a fourth mode—the life income option—provides for payment to a designated payee for that person's lifetime.

The following discussion summarizes the provisions of typical options offered under present-day life insurance policies. The word "payee" is used instead of beneficiary to reflect the fact that the person to whom payments are made under a settlement option will not necessarily have been a beneficiary under the policy. For example, the beneficiary for a one-sum settlement may elect to receive the proceeds under an optional settlement mode and name additional persons to receive any benefits that may remain payable at his (the beneficiary's) death.

The Interest Option. Under the interest option, the policyowner may elect to have the sum payable held by the company at interest at not less than a stipulated rate. Interest will be paid at regular intervals to the named primary payee during the latter's lifetime; and at the payee's death, the principal will be paid to a successor payee or payees. The

---

[3] Except that if a trust or estate is the beneficiary, the optional methods may be available only with the consent of the insurer.

owner may give the primary payee a limited or unlimited right to withdraw any part or all of the principal, or no withdrawal rights at all. He may also give the payee the right to change to another option or options if he wishes. Usually a successor payee or payees are named to receive any amount remaining at the death of the primary payee.

An illustrative interest option policy provision reads as follows:

> *Option 1—Interest.* Retained by the company as a fund with payment of interest at an effective rate not less than three and one-half percent per annum, the amount so retained to be withdrawable by the payee, unless otherwise provided, in sums of $100 or multiples thereof. Payment of interest will be made annually or, if requested, in semiannual, quarterly, or monthly instalments.

It will be noted that interest is specified at a rate not less than 3½ percent per year. As a matter of fact, most companies pay interest in excess of the guaranteed amount, if earned, though this may be called a dividend or surplus interest.

The Fixed Period Option. Under the fixed period option, the company agrees to retain the proceeds and make regular payments in equal amounts for a period of time decided upon by the policyowner. An illustrative provision reads as follows:

> *Option 2—Fixed Years Instalments.* Payment in equal monthly instalments at the beginning of monthly payment intervals for a fixed number of years according to the Fixed Years Instalments Table.

FIXED YEARS INSTALMENTS TABLE

MONTHLY INSTALMENTS THAT $1,000 WILL OBTAIN
FOR NUMBER OF YEARS ELECTED

No. of Years Elected	Monthly Instalments	No. of Years Elected	Monthly Instalments	No. of Years Elected	Monthly Instalments
1	$84.65	11	$9.09	21	$5.56
2	43.05	12	8.46	22	5.39
3	29.19	13	7.94	23	5.24
4	22.27	14	7.49	24	5.09
5	18.12	15	7.10	25	4.96
6	15.35	16	6.76	26	4.84
7	13.38	17	6.47	27	4.73
8	11.90	18	6.20	28	4.63
9	10.75	19	5.97	29	4.53
10	9.83	20	5.75	30	4.45

Under this option, dividends or extra interest will increase the amount of income but have no effect on the period during which it will be paid.

The Fixed Amount Option. The fixed amount option is one of the simplest of the options. Under this provision, the company retains the proceeds and pays them out in regular payments of a specified (fixed) amount until the fund is exhausted. Under this option, dividends and extra interest extend the period but do not change the amount. An illustrative provision follows:

> *Option 4—Fixed Amount Instalments.* Payment of equal fixed amounts at the beginning of annual, semiannual, quarterly, or monthly payment intervals until the fund, together with interest on the unpaid balance at a rate equivalent to not less than three and one-half percent per annum, is exhausted, the final payment being the balance remaining with the company. The fixed amount payable each year shall not be less than five percent of the initial amount applied under this option.

Life Income.   Under the life income option, the insurer retains the proceeds and pays them out to the named payee in an income of a guaranteed amount for the lifetime of that payee. This privilege is almost unique with respect to life insurance—the privilege of having payments made for the remainder of the payee's lifetime on a guaranteed amount basis, no matter how long the payee may live. It is customary also to guarantee payments for a specified minimum period if the policyowner wishes. This is called a life income with a period certain; and guarantees of 5, 10, and 20 years are ordinarily available.

Often a variation of the life income option is available under which payments are made to two people for as long as they both live, and with payments continued to the survivor for his lifetime as well. This is called a joint and last survivor annuity. Payments may be reduced at the first death or, in some cases, they will be continued to the survivor in the original amount. Either of these options is a highly valuable privilege if an income for more than one person's life is important.

Limitations in the Settlement Section.   Most companies establish some limitations concerning the methods of payments to beneficiaries, in the interests of efficiency and economy of operation. Among the more important are limitations on amounts held and limitations on withdrawal.

Limitations on Amounts Held.   Because it is highly inefficient to make payments of small amounts over long periods of time and because such payments are of limited value to the recipient, most insurers will not make payments of amounts less than a stated minimum—often $20. Thus, the company may reserve the right to make immediate settlement of the entire amount left at interest, if interest on a monthly basis would be less than $20. Also, as indicated in the quoted policy provision, the amount to be paid out under the fixed amount option each year is often required to be at least 5 percent of the amount placed under this option.

Limitations on Withdrawal.   Sometimes withdrawal of part of the proceeds is not permitted although the payee may be permitted to withdraw all the proceeds remaining unpaid. This limitation is frequently found in the fixed period option. As a general rule, no withdrawal is permitted under the life income option, since this would make completion of the company's promise (to make payments of a fixed amount for the payee's lifetime) impossible of fulfillment.

5.8 Contingent Payees under Settlement Options

As a general rule, the rights of a primary beneficiary will be the same whether the insurance proceeds are payable in one sum or under a settlement agreement. If the primary beneficiary survives the insured, he becomes entitled to the insurance proceeds. By contrast, although the contingent beneficiary for a one-sum settlement has no right to the proceeds if the primary beneficiary is living at the insured's death, the contingent payee's rights under a settlement agreement are not necessarily extinguished under those circumstances. On the contrary, settlement agreements are customarily drafted in such a way that the contingent payee will still be entitled to receive any amounts or instalments remaining unpaid at the death of the primary payee, even though the latter survives the insured and receives some payments.

Suppose John Jones wishes the death benefit under his policy paid to his wife, Mary, if she is living at his death. If she does not survive him, he wants the money to go to their children, Mike, Anne, and Jimmy, in equal shares. Assume further that although he realizes the value of the optional methods of settlement, he knows that Mary can elect an optional mode of settlement if she wishes after his death. He decides, therefore, to have payment made to Mary in one sum and permit her to elect an appropriate method of settlement at the time the benefit becomes payable if she wishes. This would mean a one-sum beneficiary designation as follows:

> To Mary Jones, wife of the insured, if living; otherwise to the children of the insured by said wife, including Michael, Anne, and James, equally or to survivor.

In this case Mary will receive the proceeds if she is living at the date of John's death. She may elect an optional mode of settlement if she wishes, but this will have no effect upon the rights of the children. Those rights were completely contingent and were terminated by the fact that at the death of the insured the primary beneficiary, Mary, survived. (If she wishes, she may name them as contingent payees under the supplementary contract she will receive, which defines the agreement of the company to retain the policy proceeds and pay them under a settlement option. But she is free to name anyone she wishes, or no one, to receive any guaranteed payments remaining unpaid at her death.)

Alternatively, John could himself elect an optional method of settlement and provide that the benefit be paid to Mary in instalments or held at interest, with interest payments made at regular intervals to her. By naming the children as contingent or successor payees, he could make it possible for any remaining payments, or any undistributed balance at Mary's death, to be continued or paid in one sum to the children.

E. LIFE INSURANCE AND TRUSTS

The optional modes of settlement represent a very valuable financial service to a beneficiary who has had little, if any, experience in handling large sums of money. They make the investment facilities of the life insurer available, at no additional cost, to every policyowner or beneficiary who wishes to take advantage of the service. However, insureds with unusually large amounts of life insurance, or persons who have extensive financial interests in addition to their life insurance, often prefer to provide an integrated financial plan for their dependents by establishing a trust or, in some instances, more than one trust. In such situations, the applicant may request that the proceeds of his life insurance be paid to a trustee or trustees. Before discussing trustee beneficiary designations, however, a few words of explanation concerning trusts seem appropriate.

5.9 The *Inter Vivos* Trust

A trust may be defined as a legal arrangement under which one person (called a grantor or trustor) transfers property to another person (called a trustee) on condition that the trustee hold and use the property for the benefit of the grantor or a third person called a beneficiary. The wishes of the grantor concerning the administration of the trust, how the funds are to be invested, how the income is to be paid and to whom, and how the property is to be disposed of eventually are set forth in the legal instrument that creates the trust—the trust agreement or deed of trust.

If an arrangement of this kind takes effect during the lifetime of the grantor, it is called an *inter vivos* or living trust. For example, assume that Robert Black, Sr., at the time of his retirement has an estate (in addition to his life insurance) in excess of half a million dollars. If capably managed, this property could produce a comfortable income; without skilled management, it can rapidly depreciate in value. At the time of his retirement, therefore, he decides to convey it to the Allen National Bank and Trust Company, to be held in trust for his own benefit and that of Mrs. Black. Accordingly, he asks his attorney to prepare a trust agreement for his execution, reciting that he, Black, is conveying certain described property to the bank in trust and setting forth the purposes of the trust, the persons to be benefited, how the trust is to be administered, and how the property is to be distributed following the death of the last surviving beneficiary.

Exactly this same arrangement can be made with respect to insurance if Mr. Black has a sufficient insurance program and wishes to create an insurance trust. In that case he would also execute an appropriate trust agreement, but he would make the trustee the beneficiary of the insurance and deliver the policies to him instead of deeds, bonds, and stock certificates. If only the life insurance policies are conveyed to the trustee, it is said to be an unfunded insurance trust. If Mr. Black also conveys money or property out of which premiums on the life insurance are to be paid, it it said to be a funded insurance trust. In either case, if the trust is created by a trust agreement intended to take effect during the lifetime of the grantor, it is an *inter vivos* insurance trust.

5.10 The Testamentary Trust

It is also possible to create a trust which is not to take effect until the grantor's death. In that case the instrument by which the trust is created is a will, regardless of its form; and it must be executed in accordance with the requirements relating to wills or it will not be given legal effect. A trust of this kind is called a testamentary trust, that is, a trust created by the last will and testament of the insured.

From one point of view, a life insurance trust will not ordinarily become effective in any practical sense until the death of the insured, since the proceeds will not be payable until that time. Thus it was a perfectly natural development for an *inter vivos* life insurance trust to be challenged as an attempt to dispose of property after one's death (an attempted testamentary disposition) which must be executed as a will or be held to be inoperative.

This point is hardly open to serious question today. The weight of opinion is clearly to the effect that an *inter vivos* life insurance trust is not a testamentary trust. The reasons for this holding are set forth in the case of *Bose* v. *Meury*.[4] There the insured named the Montclair Trust Company beneficiary under several policies of insurance on his own life and deposited them with the trust company under a trust agreement which authorized the trustee to pay the income from the proceeds to the grantor's wife for life, with the remainder to be paid to the children at the death of their mother. He reserved the right to add policies to or withdraw them from the trust and to revoke the trust. At his death, his estate was insolvent, and the trust was challenged on the grounds (1) that the gift in trust was incomplete because of the reserved right to withdraw policies and to revoke the trust; and (2) that the trust was testamentary. The discussion of the court is an excellent summary of the role of insurance in a trust situation, and it is quoted here in part. Incidentally, the word *res* simply means the trust property.

---

[4] 112 N.J. Eq. 62, 163 Atl. 276 (1932).

. . . Whatever merit there may be to the points, were the *res* in trust the property of the trustor, they are beside the question where, as here, the *res* is the proceeds of insurance on the life of the trustor which never were his property. The proceeds are the fulfillment of promises by the insurance company to the Montclair Trust Company, trustee, to pay the stipulated sums, upon the death of the insured. The insured paid the consideration for the promises and he had the right, under the terms of the policies, to change the promises at will, but when the day came—the insured's death—the obligations of the insurance company were due to the Montclair Trust Company, trustee. Its source of title was the promise in the policies, not the trust agreement. The trust agreement is no more than a declaration of trust by the trustee that it would hold the proceeds of the policies for the benefit of the insured's wife and children, and whether it had physical possession of the policies or whether there was a stripping[5] of interest by the "donor" or that the trust deed was testamentary, is wholly immaterial. . . .

5.11 The Trustee as Beneficiary

Trusts and the Life Insurance Company. Neither the *inter vivos* nor the testamentary trust actually concerns the life insurance company. The company is not a party to the trust and has no responsibility for determining its validity. The insurer does, however, have a basic responsibility not to endorse an insurance policy or record a beneficiary designation that it cannot carry out. When the applicant specifies that he wishes the proceeds paid to a trustee, therefore, the company's first duty is to find out whether a trust agreement is in existence.

Most companies do not object to the naming of a trustee as beneficiary of a life insurance policy if the trust in question is an *inter vivos* trust and a trust instrument is in existence at the time the beneficiary endorsement is made. A company will usually request the date of the trust and the names of the parties to the trust agreement. There is a question as to whether the company may be charged with some of the trust responsibilities if it has had a copy of the trust agreement itself for review. For this reason company practices differ as to requests for the actual trust instrument. Nevertheless, the company will usually request facts that verify that a trust agreement is in existence. All too often the person who intends to create a trust at the time he applies for life insurance never quite gets around to doing it. (If no trust were ever created, settlement would be made in accordance with the policy provision for settlement in the absence of a beneficiary designation. However, establishing that no trust was ever, in fact, created would not only delay settlement but it might also be quite difficult to accomplish, as a practical matter.)

The second part of the insurer's problem is that the trust agreement,

---

[5] Giving up.

although in effect at the time the policy is endorsed, may have been terminated long before the death of the insured. With the usual beneficiary designation, if the beneficiary dies before the insured, the problem is taken care of by a policy provision making the benefit payable to the estate of the insured. With the discontinuance of a trust agreement, however, the situation is different. Here the designated beneficiary is not dead. He just isn't qualified. That eventuality must be considered, therefore, and is taken care of by the italicized portion of the following wording:

> John Doe, as Trustee, or his successor or successors in trust, under trust agreement between Robert Black and John Doe, dated November 30, 1974 and supplements or amendments thereto, *if said agreement shall then be in force* and, if not, to the executors, administrators, or assigns (personal representatives) of the insured.

From the insurer's point of view, it is highly advisable to add a second paragraph in such a designation, absolving the company of any responsibility if the proceeds are not disposed of according to the provisions of the trust, thus:

> In no event shall the Ajax Life Insurance Company be responsible for the application or disposition by the Trustee of the sum payable. The payment to and receipt by the Trustee shall be a full discharge of the liability of the Ajax Life Insurance Company for any amount paid to such Trustee.

Corporate Trustees. The designation of a corporate trustee does not generally present as many problems as when an individual trustee is designated. The continued existence and qualification of the corporation is ordinarily more fully assured, and a trust agreement with such a trustee will ordinarily have been prepared with the advice of legal counsel. However, there are possible pitfalls in the designation of a corporate trustee also, and the beneficiary designation should be worded somewhat as follows:

> The A.B.C. Bank and Trust Company of Chicago, Illinois, an Illinois corporation, as trustee, or its successors in trust, under trust agreement between Robert Black and the A.B.C. Bank and Trust Company dated November 30, 1974 and supplements or amendments thereto, if said agreement shall then be in force and, if not, to the executors, administrators, or assigns (personal representatives) of the insured.

The Testamentary Trustee. The testamentary trust presents a number of problems that are not present in the *inter vivos* trust situation. First, since it is created by will, it is subject to all the uncertainties that surround the will itself. A will is called "ambulatory" by lawyers. This means that it continues to be subject to change until the very moment of the maker's death. No will, therefore, may be said to be effective until the date of the testator's death. Even then it may be found to have been superseded or amended, or its validity may be successfully attacked on any of a number of grounds—incapacity of the testator, undue influence, or failure to comply with all the statutory requirements, to name only a few of the hazards in the successful probate of a will.

A trust purportedly created by an instrument subject to so many hazards is at best uncertain, and a trustee named under such a trust is a very uncertain person to designate as beneficiary under a life insurance policy. The insurer that permits the applicant to designate a testamentary trustee as beneficiary of his life insurance, therefore, must take great care to word the endorsement in such a way that these eventualities are foreseen and provided for. A beneficiary designation of the following type is thought to protect the company, though it will delay settlement at a time when the beneficiaries' need for ready money is ordinarily greatest.

The beneficiary shall be:

> The trustee named in the Last Will of the insured; PROVIDED, HOWEVER, that if no will of the insured has been admitted to probate within ninety (90) days after the date of death of the insured, or if the will admitted to probate within such ninety (90) days fails to name a trustee, or if the will admitted to probate within such ninety (90) days names a trustee but no trustee shall have qualified within one (1) year after the date of death of the insured, payment of said sum payable shall be made in one sum to the executors, administrators, or assigns of the insured.
>
> The Ajax Life Insurance Company shall not be obliged to inquire into the terms of any trust affecting this policy or its sum payable and shall not be chargeable with knowledge of the terms thereof. Payment to and receipt by the trustee or payment to and receipt by the insured's executors, administrators, or assigns, as hereinabove provided, shall fully discharge all liability of the company to the extent of such payment.

F. TRUSTS AND THE OPTIONAL MODES COMPARED

From this discussion, it is apparent that the applicant who does not wish to place on his beneficiary or beneficiaries the responsibility of investing and managing his life insurance proceeds may choose between electing an optional mode of settlement under the policy or establishing a trust and having the insurance money paid to the trustee. Either method has some advantages and some disadvantages. In making such a decision, therefore, a few especially significant factors should be considered, particularly the following.

1. How Much Discretion Is Advisable. One of the most significant considerations in deciding between the optional settlement modes and a trust is the fact that a trustee may exercise a considerable amount of discretion in carrying out the terms of a trust if the grantor wishes him to do so. The optional settlements, by contrast, will be administered strictly in accordance with the provisions of the contract and the settlement agreement. The life insurer will not assume any responsibility for exercising discretion in connection with any payment or payments it makes. If the possible needs of one's beneficiaries seem difficult to anticipate, therefore, or if they may fluctuate widely among the various beneficiaries, a trust would seem to be much the preferable way to provide for the handling of the insurance proceeds. For instance, a trustee may be given the power to increase or decrease the payments made to designated beneficiaries of the trust in accordance with their needs. The life insurance company cannot assume or carry out such discretionary powers.

2. *The Degree of Flexibility Desired.* Generally speaking, if frequent changes seem indicated, a trust is probably preferable. However, a certain amount of flexibility is also possible under the settlement options. The applicant may elect to have the insurance proceeds retained at interest and give the beneficiary full rights of withdrawal, as well as the right to elect one or more different options if and when that seems desirable. In putting proceeds under the fixed amount option, provision may be made to have payments increased or decreased for various specified periods. The basic difference is that these variations must be specified in advance and cannot be determined solely on the basis of the beneficiary's needs as of any given date in the future.

3. *The Importance of Guarantees.* If guarantees are of basic importance, the applicant will favor the optional settlements rather than a trust. In keeping with the basic philosophy of life insurance, the safety of the insurance proceeds is guaranteed under the optional settlements. In addition, a minimum rate of interest is also guaranteed, as well as a share of any excess interest that may be earned by the insurer. A trust, on the other hand, offers no guarantees whatsoever, either as to principal or income. This is not altogether a disadvantage. If he wishes, the trustor may free the trustee from many restrictions otherwise imposed on the investment of trust funds and provide that the trust property may be invested in common stocks or other types of equities. Under these circumstances, the prospects of gain (as well as loss) may be considerably enhanced, as compared with the more limited, and therefore more conservative, investment possibilities available to the life insurer.

4. *The Matter of Expense.* A corporate trustee charges a fee for the administration of a trust, while the settlement option services of the life insurance company are offered at no additional cost. Since the trust also offers no guarantees, it might, at first glance, seem strange that any applicant would prefer a trust unless the needs for discretion and flexibility were compelling. This is not necessarily true, since the trustee also

acts as a personal counselor. The decision to establish a trust may, therefore, be based on many considerations, including the beneficiary's ability or interest in managing his property.

A trust may not be advisable if the insurance proceeds are relatively limited. Even with a relatively large insurance estate, the optional modes of settlement may be adequate for the needs and wishes of many beneficiaries. If the general estate is large, however, and if it is made up of considerable property in addition to the life insurance, the owner may want to establish a trust for the unified administration of all his property; and, in that case, he would make the trustee the beneficiary of his life insurance.

5. The Availability of a Life Income.   The final and perhaps most significant difference between trusts and settlement options lies in the availability of a life income under the settlement options. An income for life can, of course, be provided under a trust, but it would not be guaranteed. Under the life income settlement option, principal and income are together distributed to named payees in such a manner that both will be exhausted and yet payments of a guaranteed amount will be made during the entire lifetime of the payee or payees. An income of this kind is available commercially only through the facilities of a life insurance company. In addition, up to $1,000 a year representing the interest portion of annuity-type options (not interest only) may be received income tax-free by the spouse of the insured; no similar privilege is available with respect to income from a trust.

Other Considerations.   Generally speaking, there are similarities between a life insurance trust and a settlement agreement under which the life insurance proceeds are retained by the life insurance company and paid out to designated payees in specified instalments. The beneficiary does not have possession or control of the property in either situation; but in both cases, the benefits are payable to him. One of the basic differences is the fact that a trustee has the legal title to the property under a trust, while the life insurance company holds the funds under a debtor-creditor relationship with the beneficiary.

Several states have statutes that permit a life insurance company to act as a trustee with respect to the policy proceeds which it retains. In those states, the similarity of the options and the trust situation may appear to be particularly significant. However, even in this situation, the settlement option arrangement differs from a trust in several essential ways. First, there is the matter of guarantees, previously mentioned. Secondly, the property of an individual trust is usually segregated from the property of other trusts and invested and managed separately. This means separate investment and separate accounting, although the enactment of so-called common trust fund laws in some of the states permits the commingling of the funds of small trusts for investment purposes. Proceeds of insurance retained by a life insurance company under an optional settlement are not segregated, however. On the contrary, they are commingled for investment purposes with all the other funds of the company; and income and losses can thus be shared by the smallest unit on exactly the same terms as the largest.

G. SOME SPECIAL LEGAL PROBLEMS

5.12 The "Common Disaster" Problem

A "common disaster" is any disaster common to several people in which they lose their lives. The term has no implication that it commonly occurs or that there is anything commonplace about it. Any disaster that takes the lives of several people more or less instantly is a common disaster. If those persons include both owners and possible heirs, special problems are frequently presented concerning the inheritance of any property involved.

Problems of this kind are especially significant in the life insurance situation. There, even the fact of the insurer's liability to pay turns on the question of death; and the amount payable often is determined by how the death occurred. Questions about the fact or manner of death, therefore, not only relate to the persons having a right to receive payment; they may also determine how much, if anything, is actually payable.

As previously noted, at one time the rights of the beneficiary were considered vested from the date of the contract. In such cases, the right to receive the death proceeds was not terminated by the beneficiary's death prior to that of the insured, and was thus enforceable by the beneficiary's personal representatives regardless of how much later the insured's death may have occurred. This situation changed, however, when the companies began using a policy provision providing that the rights of any beneficiary who predeceased the insured would revert to the estate of the insured. Survival of the beneficiary then became essential to the perfection of his right to the death benefit; and establishing that survival in common disaster situations brought the law of the life insurance contract face to face with the problem that had faced executors and administrators for many years.

How Survivorship Is Established.   At common law (which ordinarily means in the absence of a statute),[6] there was no presumption with respect to survivorship in a common disaster. In situations where the insured and beneficiary were killed in the same accident, the question as

---

[6] Except in those states which derive their systems of law from France and Spain, as explained in Chapter 16, section A.

to which one survived the other became very important and was decided on various bases, depending primarily on whether the rights of the beneficiary were or were not vested.

In jurisdictions where the beneficiary's interest was considered to be vested subject to being divested, the beneficiary was presumed to have survived unless the person seeking to prove otherwise could present sufficient evidence to support his contention. That is, the person seeking to prove that the insured survived the beneficiary had the burden of introducing evidence to that effect. If he failed, the proceeds would be paid to the personal representatives of the beneficiary on the presumption that the beneficiary had survived the insured.

In jurisdictions where the beneficiary's interest was considered to be a mere expectancy, the personal representative of the beneficiary had the burden of introducing evidence to show that the beneficiary survived the insured. If he failed, the proceeds would be paid to the personal representative of the insured. Thus, in cases where there was no evidence as to survivorship, the results, so far as the payment of the life insurance proceeds was concerned, depended entirely on whether the beneficiary's rights were considered to be vested subject to being divested or a mere expectancy. Thus the same set of facts would be decided differently in different states.

For some time, however, a general movement has been in progress toward bringing uniformity into the various state laws. In keeping with this trend, an act known as the Uniform Simultaneous Death Act was introduced into the legislatures of many of the states during the 1940s and enacted into law. This or similar legislation is now the law in all the states.

The Uniform Simultaneous Death Act.   As it applies to life insurance, this law reads, generally, as follows:

> Where the insured and the beneficiary in a policy of life or accident insurance have died and there is no sufficient evidence that they have died otherwise than simultaneously the proceeds of the policy shall be distributed as if the insured had survived the beneficiary.[7]

This act provides a reasonably satisfactory solution in any case where the beneficiary and the insured die under circumstances which make it impossible to tell who survived the other. Assume, for instance, that Jim Bennett and his wife, driving home one night, fail to see or hear a fast train at an unguarded crossing and lose their lives when the train strikes their car. Assume further that each is the primary beneficiary of insurance on the life of the other.

If there is no reason to believe that they were killed other than instantly, under the Uniform Simultaneous Death Act the insurance on the

---

[7] Illinois Revised Statutes, Chap. 3, Sec. 192.4 (1965).

life of each will be distributed as if the other had died first. If there are contingent or successor beneficiaries, therefore, the insurance proceeds will be paid to them in accordance with the provisions of the beneficiary designation or settlement agreement and this settlement presumably will be in accordance with the insured's wishes. If there are no contingent or successor beneficiaries, the proceeds will be paid to the insured's estate and distributed as directed in his or her will or the appropriate law if there is no will.

Short-Term Survivorship. In many instances, however, the facts are more complicated. For instance, assume that Alice was Bennett's second wife and that he had three grown children from his first marriage and no children of the second marriage. Most of his property was tied up in business interests, and his insurance was payable to "Alice Bennett, wife of the insured, if living; otherwise to the children of the insured, equally or to survivor." In other words, he wanted Alice to have the insurance if she survived him; but if she did not, the proceeds were to be paid to his children.

Again, if there is no evidence to prove that the Bennetts were killed other than simultaneously, under the Uniform Simultaneous Death Act the insurance on Bennett's life will go to his children in equal shares (since he will be presumed to have survived his wife).

But assume now that the Bennetts were not killed simultaneously. Assume that Jim was killed instantly but that Alice lived to recognize and talk to the first people on the scene, although she was dead on arrival at the hospital. Assume also that she had no will. Because of the accidental death, a significant amount of life insurance was payable under her husband's life insurance policies in a lump sum. (Note that the simultaneous death act does not apply, since she survived him, even momentarily.) By the mere fact of her survival, the proceeds are payable to her and not to the contingent beneficiaries—Bennett's children. Because she survived even for a short while, his children's rights were terminated. The proceeds, therefore, would be paid to her personal representative for final distribution, after payment of her debts, to members of her family under the applicable state law.

Few people would criticize this disposition if the wife had lived a longer time—as much, for example, as a year or two. However, the fact that any survival, however brief, makes payment possible to her brothers and sisters rather than to the insured's children is difficult for many people to accept. Yet this may be the legal effect, for the Uniform Simultaneous Death Act does not apply in any way if the beneficiary can be proved to have survived the insured.

In the illustrative situation, the beneficiary designation showed that Jim wanted his own children to receive the proceeds if Alice was not alive to use them, and it is highly probable that Alice would have made different arrangements herself if she had survived long enough to make a will. Thus, the Uniform Simultaneous Death Act often does not provide a satisfactory solution in situations where there is evidence to show that one party survived the other.

For this reason and because the beneficiary in many common disaster situations survives the insured for a very brief period only, special provisions are sometimes included in the beneficiary designation to assure, in such instances, that the proceeds will be distributed in accordance with the insured's wishes. One approach is to include a time clause in the beneficiary designation.

The Time Clause.   A time clause is a provision included in the beneficiary designation which requires that the beneficiary survive the insured for a specified length of time, usually 30 or 60 days, before becoming entitled to the insurance proceeds.

A beneficiary designation of this type reads something like the following:

> Alice Bennett, wife of the insured, if living on the thirtieth day after the death of the insured; otherwise equally to the children of the insured who are living on the thirtieth day after the death of the insured, if any; otherwise to the executors, administrators, or assigns (personal representatives) of the insured.

A beneficiary designation like this effectively takes care of most short-term survivorship problems. However, if the beneficiary dies on the 31st or the 61st day without having made different arrangements, the situation is no better than if the time clause had been omitted. An optional settlement, therefore, provides a better solution.

Optional Settlements.   As a practical matter, the use of any interest or instalment settlement option for the primary beneficiary, if a successor or contingent payee is designated, accomplishes the same purpose as the time clause without the disadvantage of a time limit. Under these circumstances, no matter when the primary payee dies, if any proceeds or instalments remain to be paid under an option, the successor payees will receive them.

In the Bennett case, for example, a settlement agreement could have been used, naming Alice Bennett as the primary payee, if living, and the children of the insured as successor payees. Then their rights, unlike those they had under the one-sum beneficiary designation, would not have terminated at the insured's death. Instead, they would have been entitled to receive any guaranteed payments that had not been paid at the primary payee's (Mrs. Bennett's) death.

In that situation, therefore, the insured's wishes would have been carried out regardless of the order of his and the primary beneficiary's deaths. Thus a settlement agreement is a plan of settlement that can provide different arrangements as circumstances change, even after the death of the insured.

H. SOME INCIDENTAL RULES OF LAW

5.13 The Rule against Perpetuities

Property interests which may extend into the future present a number of possible legal problems for which special rules have been devised. For instance, it is perfectly possible to draft an instrument creating successive interests in property to continue for many, many years without vesting—that is, without the property becoming definitely and wholly owned by anyone. One of the easiest ways to do this would be to establish a trust for the benefit of one's children, grandchildren, great-grandchildren, etc., in succession, so that the title to the trust property would never vest so long as there were additional descendants of the original owner. As a matter of public policy, however, the law tries to keep property in the channels of commerce. To this end there has long been a rule known as the "rule against perpetuities" that limits the time during which such successive nonvested interests can continue.

Statement of the Rule. The rule against perpetuities is most commonly stated as follows: "No interest is good unless it must vest, if at all, not later than 21 years after the death of some life or lives in being at the creation of the interest." In general terms, this means that one cannot create an interest in property which will postpone the vesting of ownership beyond a period equal to the remaining lifetime of someone living at the time the interest was created, plus 21 years. If the attempt is made, the interest is void, and vesting is immediate in the person or persons otherwise entitled to take.

How the Rule Applies. It has been said that the rule against perpetuities is easy to state but difficult to apply. Certainly it is a highly technical rule in a highly technical field of law. Fortunately, it is rarely applicable in life insurance itself. It applies to life insurance trusts, just as it applies to any other kind of trust. The policyowner who elects to have the insurance benefit paid to a trustee, therefore, should be concerned with the rule against perpetuities in connection with the trust agreement. The interest created by the trust must be capable of vesting within the prescribed time under any circumstances, or it is void. If there is any possibility that it will not so vest, the interest is ineffective. It is no argument that it actually does vest within the prescribed time.

In every case the period is measured from the time the interest is created—the date of the *inter vivos* trust if that is used, the death of the testator if a testamentary trust is the instrument in question.

How the rule against perpetuities applies to life insurance settlement agreements is quite a different matter. A leading case on the subject is *Holmes* v. *John Hancock Mutual Life Insurance Co.,*[8] where the rule was held not to apply, since the proceeds of the insurance constituted a debt and not a trust. There the court said:

> Each of the policies contained provisions permitting the insured to nominate and change the beneficiary to whom the proceeds of the policies should be paid and also offering to the insured "optional methods of settlement." Before his death the insured nominated his wife, the defendant Marie F. Holmes and his nephews, the defendants William R. Holmes and Morgan Dwight Holmes, as beneficiaries under each of said policies, and directed that the proceeds of the policies be left on deposit with the company, and that the interest be paid quarterly to his wife during her lifetime and after her death to his nephews "until the elder or survivor of said nephews attains the age of thirty-five," and that thereafter the principal be paid to the nephews or to the survivor. The plaintiff challenges the validity of these directions on the ground that they constitute an unlawful suspension of the power of alienation.[9]

The court said that the provision would be void under the New York law if it applied, but added:

> The insurance company does not, however, hold the proceeds of the policy as a trust fund. By the terms of the policy it has contracted to pay stipulated amounts, at stipulated times and in stipulated manner. "The obligation of the insurance company constitutes a debt from the company to . . . the beneficiary, under the policy." The stipulated payments "are not income on personal property. They constitute deferred payments which the company agreed to make to the beneficiary. . . . (*Crossman Co.* v. *Rauch,* 263 N.Y. 264, 273.)" The provisions of section 11 of the Personal Property Law have no application to such an obligation.

It is notable that New York and a few other states have special statutes that modify the common law rule. As the above quotation shows, such statutes have been held not to be applicable in the case of insurance proceeds held under optional modes of settlement. A contrary opinion has been expressed in at least one case,[10] however, and the general philosophy of the law favors limitations on any devices which tend to keep property out of the channels of commerce for any extensive period of time. For this reason, life insurance companies usually follow practices which limit settlement plans under life insurance contracts to a period which accords with that of the rule against perpetuities, even though as a technical matter the rule does not apply. A settlement agreement naming the wife as primary beneficiary and the children as contingent benefi-

---

[8] 288 N.Y. 106, 41 N.E. (2d) 909 (1942).

[9] This means that the trust provision is alleged to have violated the rule against perpetuities.

[10] *First National Bank & Trust Co.* v. *Purcell,* 244 S.W. (2d) 458 (Ky., 1951).

ciaries ordinarily fulfills the wishes of the policyowner and yet runs no risk with respect to violation of the underlying philosophy of the rule.

5.14 The Rule against Accumulations

As a general rule, if property is left by one person to another in such a way that it is to accumulate interest for the latter for a period extending too far into the future, it is held to be an illegal accumulation. One of the most famous laws defining the periods that would be permissible was the Thellusson Act, an English law passed in 1800. The Thellusson Act specified a number of alternative methods by which the permissible period could be measured. One of these methods was the minority of any infant living at the death of a testator or at the time the interest was created. In other words, it was permissible to leave property at interest to be accumulated for a minor beneficiary until he became 21 years of age.

Because this is a simple and practical rule, many life insurance companies, as a matter of practice, do not permit interest on proceeds left under the interest option to be accumulated except during the minority of a beneficiary. However, many states today permit interest to be accumulated for the full period specified in the rule against perpetuities—that is, the lifetime of a life or lives in being and 21 years thereafter. These laws are generally believed to apply to life insurance companies. Some companies, therefore, permit interest to be accumulated, in special situations, for periods not limited to the minority of a beneficiary.

SUMMARY

Rights of an Applicant

The typical applicant applies for insurance on his own life and designates his spouse as the beneficiary. Unless he himself gives up or limits his right to change the beneficiary designation at a later date, he may make such changes when and as he wishes, by following the change of beneficiary procedure provided in the policy. So long as he has not relinquished his right to change the beneficiary, he is also free to exercise all ownership rights and assign the policy, if he wishes, without the beneficiary's consent.

The Beneficiary's Rights

Under the earliest life insurance policies, the beneficiary was also the owner. Thus the insured had no power to alter or diminish the beneficiary's rights. Later, as contracts were applied for and owned by the insured, provisions were introduced permitting the applicant to reserve the right to make later beneficiary changes, and today the majority rules are as follows:

1. A revocable beneficiary is said to have a "mere expectancy" under the policy.
2. An irrevocable beneficiary has a vested right to the proceeds of the policy, although most present-day policies provide that his interest, like that of the revocable beneficiary, will terminate if he is not living at the death of the insured.

The Beneficiary Designation

The person or persons who will be entitled to the proceeds of the policy if they are living at the death of the insured are primary beneficiaries (although other similar terms such as "first" or "direct" beneficiaries are sometimes used).

The person or persons who are named to receive the proceeds if no primary beneficiary survives the insured are contingent or successor beneficiaries.

Many companies provide in their policies that the beneficiaries are as designated in the application unless otherwise provided by endorsement when the policy is issued or subsequently changed. As suggested by this language, beneficiary designations may be endorsed on the policy in some instances.

Who May Be Named

So far as legal requirements are concerned, if a life insurance contract is applied for by the insured, he may name anyone he wishes as beneficiary (although the insurer may refuse to issue a policy if the designated beneficiary does not have an insurable interest in the life of the insured). In the absence of a controlling statute, divorce does not terminate the interest of a wife, and the courts have rather consistently held that the words "wife of the insured" are descriptive only.

When children are designated, the designation should be so worded as to include after-born children. One of the simplest ways to do this is to designate the children of the insured as a class.

Class designations include all the members of the class who are living at the death of the insured. If children are designated as a class, a question may be presented concerning the inclusion of illegitimate children, stepchildren, etc. Class designations may cause delays in settlement in situations where locating all members of the class may be difficult. Nevertheless, class designations of children are rather generally permitted by life insurers.

As a general rule, it is not wise to designate children as irrevocable beneficiaries, since this limits the owner's later exercise of ownership rights. Ordinarily, such rights cannot be exercised without the consent of an irrevocable beneficiary, and minor children cannot give a legally effective consent.

Most beneficiary designations entitle the beneficiaries to share in the proceeds on an individual basis and thus involve a *per capita* designation—that is, "by the person." If the children of a deceased beneficiary are to be included in any settlement, however, a *per stirpes* designation should be requested. A *per stirpes* designation means that the proceeds are to be divided among the members of a class, such as the children of the insured, with the share of any predeceased member of the class going to that person's surviving children, if any.

An individual should never be named beneficiary under a life insurance contract on the assumption that the named person will be the guardian of minor children. A guardian is always appointed by a court of law; and as a general rule, if minor children are to be benefited by the insurance, it is better practice just to name the children as beneficiaries, since a guardian will be appointed if necessary. Payment can then be made to the person so appointed, in his capacity as guardian.

Business Designations.   A sole proprietorship has no legal significance in and of itself. If the owner of such a firm designates his business as beneficiary, the legal effect is the same as if he had designated his executors, administrators or assigns.

A partnership is usually designated by using the names of the persons who comprise it, and a corporation should be identified by corporate name, including the state under whose laws it was incorporated.

Settlement Agreements and the Optional Modes

If one or more of the optional modes of settlement are elected, the wishes of the applicant with respect to beneficiaries and the methods of settlement are often set out in a special section of the policy that is termed a settlement agreement.

A settlement agreement is more elaborate than a one-sum beneficiary designation, since the applicant also states (in addition to the beneficiaries) the optional settlement method or methods he elects and the way or ways in which they are to be applied.

There are four basic types of optional settlements. They are:

1. The interest option, under which the policy proceeds will be retained by the insurer at interest, which will be paid at regular intervals, as elected. Withdrawal rights may be limited or unlimited as the policyowner directs, and usually a successor payee may be named to receive any sum remaining with the company at the death of the primary payee.

2. A fixed period option, under which the proceeds, with interest, will be paid out in equal instalments over any of several specified periods. Dividends or extra interest will increase the amount of income but not extend the period.

3. The fixed amount option, under which the proceeds and interest will be paid out in instalments of a specified amount. Under this option, dividends or additional interest will extend the period over which payments are made but will not increase the amount of individual payments.

4. The life income option, under which payments will be made to a named payee for the remainder of his or her lifetime. If these payments are to be made for not less than a specified period regardless of the date of death of the primary payee, and thereafter for that person's remaining lifetime (if longer), the arrangement is said to be a life income with period certain.

Limitations are frequently imposed by the insurer concerning minimum amounts that will be retained under an option, and the right of withdrawal may be restricted or denied in connection with some options.

Contingent Payees under Settlement Options

The rights of contingent or successor payees are usually more extensive under a settlement agreement than under a one-sum beneficiary designation. The contingent beneficiary under a one-sum designation will become entitled to share in the policy proceeds only if the primary beneficiary does not survive the insured. Under a settlement agreement, however, the contingent or successor payee may be given the right to receive any unpaid instalments or amounts remaining with the company at the primary payee's death, even though the latter may have survived the insured and received some of the payments or may have withdrawn some of the proceeds held at interest.

Life Insurance and Trusts

The optional modes of settlement provide a valuable financial service with respect to the proceeds of the policy after the death of the insured. However, the insured may prefer to provide such services through the use of a trust. In that case he may request that the proceeds be paid to a trustee.

A trust is an agreement under which one person transfers money or other property to another person, called a trustee, to be held and managed for the benefit of the transferor or others. If this agreement is effective during the lifetime of the grantor (the person establishing the trust), it is called an *inter vivos* trust. If it is intended to become effective after the death of the grantor, it is called a testamentary trust and must be executed in accordance with the laws governing wills.

The Trustee as Beneficiary

If a trustee is named as beneficiary of the life insurance contract, the insurer will have no further responsibility after making payment to the person designated. If the trust is an *inter vivos* trust, the company may request the date of the trust and the persons who are parties to the agreement before permitting the designation. Practices differ as to whether the insurer will want a copy of the trust agreement itself.

Naming as beneficiary the trustee under a testamentary trust may present more problems than naming an *inter vivos* trustee. For that reason, the insurer may want to protect itself against the possibility that no will may be admitted to probate at the insured's death; or if one is admitted, that no trust will be established by it; and other similar problems. As a general rule, however, with some safeguards, the designation of a testamentary trustee will accomplish the objective of the applicant without special hazards to the insurer.

Trusts and Optional Settlements Compared

In choosing between the optional modes of settlement and a trust, the applicant or policyowner will generally consider the need for the use of discretion, the degree of flexibility that is desired, the importance of guarantees, the matter of expense, and the availability of a life income to the beneficiary.

Generally, if there is a very significant need for the exercise of discretion, or a need for a flexible program of financial services, a trust will be indicated. If guarantees are important—either of principal or income—the optional modes of settlement will be preferable. The matter of expense is significant also, since a fee is charged for the trustee's services while the optional modes of settlement are provided at no extra charge. Finally, if a life income is indicated, the choice will be the life income option, since an income of a fixed amount for life cannot be guaranteed under a trust.

Some Special Legal Problems

The "Common Disaster" Problem. A common disaster is any disaster in which several people lose their lives. This presents a problem in connection with property and is especially frequent in life insurance. A number of rules have been followed in establishing survivorship, and a Uniform Simultaneous Death Act has been enacted in all of the states in an effort to provide a uniform rule. However, this act has no application if there is any evidence to prove that the beneficiary actually did or did not survive the insured.

A time clause is sometimes used to meet the problem of short-term survivorship, but if the beneficiary survives beyond the time established—30 or 60 days, usually—the situation is no different than if a time limit had not been used.

Electing an optional settlement for the primary beneficiary and naming contingent payees to receive any proceeds or instalments remaining unpaid at the primary payee's death is a more satisfactory solution than the use of the time clause. The optional settlement accomplishes the same purpose and is effective no matter how much or how little time elapses between the death of the insured and that of the beneficiary. (The use of a trust also provides a solution.)

Incidental Rules of Law

Two rather basic rules of property law have had some influence upon company practices concerning settlement options. One is the rule against perpetuities, which may be stated as follows: No interest is good unless it must vest, if at all, not later than 21 years after the death of some life in being at the creation of the interest. This rule is not generally thought to apply to insurance proceeds held under the optional modes of settlement, but there has been at least one opinion to the contrary, and life insurers usually follow this rule as a matter of practice.

A second rule is the rule against accumulations, which varies among the states. However, in most states property may be left at interest to accumulate for a minor beneficiary until he reaches 21 years of age. This rule is generally held to apply to life insurance settlement agreements.

ILLUSTRATIVE CASE

The following case illustrates one of the many different possible problems that must be considered in phrasing a beneficiary designation.

FLACK v. PRUDENTIAL INSURANCE COMPANY OF AMERICA[11]

The defendant, Prudential Insurance Company of America, moves this Court to permit it to pay into Court the sum of $3120.00, the amount which it claims to hold as a stakeholder subject to the conflicting claims of the plaintiffs herein. The defendant also moves for an order appointing a special guardian to represent the interest of unknown persons who may be beneficially entitled under the designation of "Henry E. Flack, trustee under agreement dated September

---

[11] 248 N.Y.S. (2d) 323 (1964).

3, 1935" as the beneficiary under the insurance certificate, the proceeds of which are the subject herein. The plaintiff, Flack, opposes both motions of the defendant and cross-moves for the reference of all matters to an official referee, for an accounting by the defendant of the proceeds of the policy in question and for summary judgment. The plaintiff, Griswold, appeared at the oral argument of the motion, but submitted no opposing affidavits. The attorneys for both plaintiffs, Flack and Griswold, entered into a Stipulation of Facts dated January 11, 1964.[12]

The Prudential Insurance Company of America issued a group life insurance policy to the St. Lawrence County Utilities, Inc. George A. Lawyer, an employee, was covered by the participation certificate issued to the Utility Company by the defendant, Prudential, on September 3, 1935. He designated as the beneficiary in the policy "Henry E. Flack, trustee, under an agreement dated September 3, 1935." Mr. Lawyer died on September 22, 1944, at which time the proceeds due on the policy were in the amount of $3120.00. Emma L. Cleveland and Elizabeth M. Griswold are the residuary legatees under Mr. Lawyer's last will. Henry E. Flack died February 25, 1945, leaving him surviving [sic] a wife, Amy B. Flack. George A. Lawyer and Henry E. Flack were personal friends for a great number of years. They entered into a trust agreement on November 22, 1944, which trust agreement has been fully executed and performed by the parties. The trust agreement referred to under date of September 3, 1935, has never been found. Amy B. Flack claims the proceeds of the policy as executrix of the Last Will and Testament of Henry E. Flack. Elizabeth M. Griswold and Emma L. Cleveland claim the proceeds both as next of kin and heirs at law as well as residuary legatees of the last will of George A. Lawyer. Actions were commenced by these claimants in Supreme Court during the year 1948.[13]

The defendant, Prudential, made an application for interpleader of the Flack Estate at a Special Term held in the Supreme Court of Lewis County on September 20, 1948, in the Lawyer action against it, and moved that the defendant be discharged by paying into Court the amount of the policy. The Court (Malpass, J.) granted an order on September 20, 1948, consolidating the two actions. The Prudential Insurance Company remained as a nominal

---

[12] Here the insurance company did not deny that it owed the insurance money to someone. However, several people claimed it. Therefore the company requested permission to pay the insurance money into court and have the court decide who among the claimants was entitled to payment. Amy Flack had sued the company for payment and now opposed the request of the insurance company. She requested instead that the question be submitted to a referee for an accounting by the company and an immediate judgment in her (Flack's) favor. (A stipulation of facts means facts that are mutually agreed upon.)

[13] This paragraph gives the full background. A group certificate insuring George Lawyer was issued on September 3, 1935, with Henry Flack designated as beneficiary. His name was followed by the words "trustee under an agreement dated September 3, 1935." The insured died in September, 1944, and Flack died in February, 1945. No trust agreement dated September 3, 1935 was ever found. Flack's wife, however, claimed the proceeds of the insurance as executrix of Flack's will; and Elizabeth M. Griswold and Emma L. Cleveland also claimed the proceeds, as next of kin, heirs at law, and recipients under the insured's will.

defendant "subject to the further order of this Court in respect to the payment of the sum of $3120.00, plus any interest to the date of this order for which it may be legally liable and for which it is and remains ready to pay as soon as the rightful recipient thereof can be determined."[14] No appeal was ever taken from the order of Justice Malpass.

*   *   *   *   *

The question to be resolved here is whether the words, "Henry E. Flack, trustee under agreement dated September 3, 1935" are merely *descriptio personnae*. The plaintiff, Flack, contends that the absence of the word "as" is significant and that the inclusion of "as" directly preceding the word, Trustee, would have made it clear that Henry E. Flack was taking the proceeds of the life insurance policy in question in a representative capacity. The plaintiff, Flack, further contends that the absence of "as" compels a construction that the words quoted above were merely descriptive and served only to identify Mr. Flack. This Court reaches no such conclusion. The word "as" is not governing.[15]

It is well settled that where a proceeding is brought against a person and a question is raised as to whether the action is against that person as an individual or in a representative capacity, the whole record is inspected to ascertain the true nature of the action, and the action will be treated as an individual or representative one as disclosed by this total examination. [Citations.] Where the word "trustee" is employed, the frame and scope of the averments must be carefully analyzed, to derive the intent of the settlor. From them such character may be fixed upon the trustee as falls within the scope of these intentions. (*Beers* v. *Shannon*, 73 N.Y. 292 [1878]; *Bennett* v. *Whitney*, 94 N.Y. 302 [1884]). Even where the word "as" directly precedes the word, trustee, title may be vested in the trustee in the absence of any other evidence. (*Pratt* v. *Prentice*, 166 App. Div. 906, 151 N.Y.S. 259 [Fourth Dep't. 1914]).

Similarly, in the construction of wills, where there is equivocal language used, the will in its entirety must be read to disclose the primary intent of a testator. [Citations.]

Here, there is more than just the word "trustee," there are, in addition, the words, "under agreement dated September 3, 1935." It seems clear to this Court that this was no mere means of identification. In 1944 Mr. Lawyer appointed Mr. and Mrs. Flack as trustees of an inter-vivos trust for the distribution of certain personal property to named individuals. Commissions were provided for the payment to the trustees for services. It would have been a simple matter for Mr. Lawyer to have designated Henry E. Flack as an individual beneficiary of the proceeds of this life insurance policy.

---

14 The insurance company asked permission to pay the money into court and be dismissed from the action. Judge Malpass combined the two cases, but the insurance company was retained as a defendant in the sense that it was to pay the proceeds plus interest as soon as a decision was made.

15 Here the court summarizes the basic question. Are the words "trustee under agreement dated September 3, 1935" merely descriptive of the person who is to take the proceeds—that is, Flack—or do they specify the capacity—as trustee—in which he was to take the money?

From a reading of this record in its entirety, this Court cannot fairly and justly conclude that Mr. Lawyer intended Mr. Flack to keep the proceeds of the insurance in question for himself. (Matter of Falvey's Will, supra.)

Under the circumstances, this Court concludes that it was Mr. Lawyer's intention to create a trust. The trust agreement, dated September 3, 1935, has never been found, however. Its absence leaves unanswered the name of the designated beneficiary of these funds. Without it, there is no valid trust created but merely a "dry" trust. [Citations.] Where there is a trust void for uncertainty of beneficiaries, the proceeds descend to and become vested in the heirs of law and next of kin entitled thereto. (Levy v. Levy, 33 N.Y. 97 [1865].)

The application of Prudential to be discharged by the payment of the face amount of the policy into Court (Civ. Prac. Law and Rules, Sect. 1006) does not need to be determined. The decision of Justice Malpass of September 20, 1948, is the law of the case. No appeal was taken from that order, and, of course, the time within which to do so has long since expired. Interest is payable from the date of receipt of proofs of death by Prudential to September 20, 1948. (Insurance Law, Sec. 166).

A direction in a Court decree which specifically provides that money is to be held "until the further order of this Court," clearly shows that the Court intended the money to be held readily available for disposition. (Matter of Schmidt v. Chamberlain of the City of New York, 266 N.Y. 225, 194 N.E. 685 [1935].) Prudential does not have to account for its use of the proceeds of this policy to claimants. The moving papers before this Court reveal that the delay of eighteen years was not occasioned by the defendant Prudential but by the claimants themselves. It appears that Prudential urged the parties to proceed to a trial in order to dispose of their conflicting claims.

The defendant's motion for the appointment of a special guardian is denied. The Report of George E. Reed, Special Guardian appointed by the Court, is sufficient. It clearly indicates that there are no unknown or incompetent persons' property interests to be protected. The plaintiff's cross-motion to refer this matter to an Official Referee is similarly denied. The plaintiff's cross-motion for an accounting is denied for the reasons stated in this opinion. The motion of the plaintiff, Flack, for summary judgment, is denied. Summary judgment is granted to plaintiffs Griswold and Cleveland. No costs, expenses or disbursements shall be allowed to any of the parties.[16]

QUESTIONS FOR REVIEW

1. Define the word "beneficiary."
2. Distinguish between a revocable and an irrevocable beneficiary.

---

[16] The court decided that the insured had intended to create a trust and that Flack was designated beneficiary as a trustee and not in his own right. No record was found of the trust. Therefore, the trust failed; and in such cases, the money would go to the heirs at law and next of kin—Griswold and Cleveland. The fact that it took 18 years to reach a solution in the case gives some indication of the reasons insurance companies exercise a great deal of care in phrasing beneficiary designations involving trusts and trustees.

3. What are the rights of a contingent beneficiary if—
   a. The primary beneficiary survives the insured?
   b. The primary beneficiary does not survive the insured?

4. Briefly summarize some of the possible problems that may result from—
   a. Designating minor children as beneficiaries irrevocably.
   b. Class beneficiary designations.

5. Explain what is meant by a *per stirpes* beneficiary designation.

6. Why is it not advisable to designate a guardian by name as a beneficiary under a life insurance policy?

7. Define each of the following terms as they apply to trusts:
   a. Grantor.
   b. Trustee.

8. Distinguish between an *inter vivos* and a testamentary trust.

9. Describe the so-called common disaster problem. Briefly summarize the Uniform Simultaneous Death Act as it applies to life insurance settlements.

10. What two common devices are used to meet the problem of short-term survivorship? Which is preferable? Why?

Chapter Outline

Chapter 6

The Policy
Is Reviewed

THE LIFE underwriter will usually review the life insurance policy when he first receives it to see that the settlement provisions are in accordance with the request of the applicant and that the policy is of the form and in the amount applied for. When he delivers the policy he should also spend some time with the policyowner reviewing the outstanding features of the policy.

As a matter of fact, of all the policyowner's personal papers none is more closely related to his daily living than his life insurance policy. As his family grows, as his finances change, as his business needs vary, the values of his insurance program can and should keep pace. If he is as familiar with the various provisions of the policy as he should be, he will always be in a position to utilize it to its best advantage.

The purpose of this chapter is to give a rapid, general review of an illustrative whole life insurance policy so that the policy can be viewed in its entirety and, as a result, be better understood and utilized as the flexible, adaptable instrument it really is.

A. THE POLICY AS A CONTRACT

In the language of general contract law, the policy is the written expression of the insuring agreement between the applicant and the company. Pending the issuance of the policy, a contract may be evidenced by a conditional or a binding receipt; and in the absence of a statute to the contrary, an oral agreement may be effective. Because of the comprehensive nature of the life insurance contract, however, and the length of time it often remains in force, it is almost universal practice to issue a printed policy in which the agreement is completely expressed.

These considerations no doubt have prompted the enactment of legal requirements in some jurisdictions that the life insurance contract be in writing. Georgia, for example, has a statute that specifically declares that the life insurance contract shall be in writing, and New York accomplishes the same objective through special wording of its Statute of Frauds.

In any event, the issuance of a policy is so much the custom that one can safely say that the applicant and the insurance company from the first "contemplate that their negotiations shall be reduced to writing." Thus, the life insurance contract falls squarely within the requirements of the parol evidence rule. Once the policy has been issued and delivered, oral evidence will not be permitted to vary or contradict its terms.[1]

6.1 The Meaning of the Contract

In legal terms, the life insurance contract may be described in a number of different ways. It is informal rather than formal; aleatory rather than commutative; unilateral rather than bilateral. In interpreting the provisions of the policy, however, the most important descriptive phrase terms it a contract of *adhesion,* as contrasted with a bargaining contract. A contract of adhesion is a contract that is drafted by one party and accepted or rejected by the other, with no opportunity to bargain in any way with respect to its terms.

This concept is most important when it becomes necessary for a court to determine the meaning of terms or provisions of a policy that is the basis for a lawsuit. As a general rule, the words of a life or health insurance contract, like those of any other contract, will be given their usual and ordinary meanings in such situations. However, if there is any reasonable conflict as to the meaning of any terms or provisions, the contract is said to be ambiguous. In that case, it may be necessary for the court to determine the meaning in order to decide a legal question. In such situations, the court is said to interpret, or construe, the contract; and the rules by which it is guided in making this interpretation are called rules of construction.

One of the basic rules of construction in general contract law is the rule that ambiguities in a contract of adhesion will be construed against the party who drafted the contract and thus in favor of the other party. As this rule applies to the life insurance contract, it means that any ambiguities will be interpreted against the life insurance company and in favor of the policyowner or beneficiary.

---

[1] See discussion at Sec. 2.19.

This rule is based on the assumption that the party drafting the instrument has had the opportunity to select his own terms and wording and that it can be assumed that he would adequately have protected his own interests. As a matter of fact, however, the insurer's freedom to choose such policy provisions as it may wish is materially limited by statutes and insurance department rulings, and a few courts have recognized this fact. Thus, when the provision in question is required by statute and is worded in such a way as to have been approved by the insurance commissioner of the state in question, some courts have held that the general rule—that an ambiguity will be resolved in favor of the policyowner or beneficiary—does not apply. By and large, however, the life insurance contract is generally interpreted in accordance with this basic rule, even though it is a contract of adhesion only in the sense that it is not the result of negotiation between the parties with respect to its terms.

6.2 State Regulation of the Contract

Most states include as a part of their insurance legislation some laws concerning provisions that may or may not be included in the life insurance contract. Such provisions usually fall into one or more of the following groups:

1. Provisions that must be included in the contract, though not, as a general rule, in the exact words of the statute;
2. Provisions that may, but do not have to, be included in the contract; and
3. Provisions that must not be included in the contract.

The Standard Policy Provisions Laws. The insurance laws enacted in New York in 1906, as the result of the Armstrong investigation, prescribed uniform policy forms for ordinary, limited pay, endowment, and term life insurance policies; and life insurers were required to issue policies in exactly those forms. When this legislation proved too rigid, it was replaced in 1910 by a law that specified provisions that must be included in life insurance policies—grace period, misstatement of age, incontestability, and so on—but permitted the insurance companies to use different wording so long as the substance of the provision was essentially the same as that prescribed in the law and the language used was not less liberal to the policyowner and beneficiary. The Uniform Standard Policy Provisions Law, subsequently enacted by many of the other states, was so worded from the first as to permit compliance in substance instead of requiring the precise words of the statute.

Approval of the Commissioner. To assure compliance with the policy provisions laws, every insurance commissioner is given some responsibility concerning policy forms, although the nature of this responsibility varies, as do the laws themselves, from state to state. In one group of states, for example, insurers are prohibited from issuing or delivering a policy until the form has been approved by the commissioner. In some of these states, the commissioner is required to notify the company within a stated period, usually 30 days, if the policy form does not comply with the statutory requirements. If notice is not received, therefore, the insurer can assume approval. Other states require that policy forms be filed but do not specify the length of time within which notice of disapproval must be given. In these states, the insurer must wait until actual approval is received before the form can be used.

If a policy is issued without the approval of the commissioner if approval is required, or without filing if that is the requirement, it is generally held to be a valid contract, enforceable by the insured. In other words, the statutory requirements are for the benefit of the policyowners. For this reason, such contracts are usually considered binding on the insurer. However, they are construed as if they included any required provisions that might be more favorable than those actually included in the policy. Usually, also, there is a penalty for issuing a policy that has not been filed with or approved by the commissioner as required by the statute. This penalty may be a fine or, in some instances, even the revocation of the insurer's license to do business in that state.

B. THE POLICY IN GENERAL

Ordinarily, a life insurance policy is intended to remain effective over many years and to be an important part of the policyowner's financial planning. Thus, it is important that its provisions be clearly expressed. For this reason many life insurance companies wage a kind of continuing battle against overly technical and obscure policy language. As a result, the language of most present-day policy forms is surprisingly simple when compared to the wide assortment of benefits and protections the policy affords.

By and large, most of the provisions of a life insurance contract are relatively easy to understand. When the contract is considered as a whole, however, it is helpful to break it down into several basic sections. For example, one important section of any policy will be devoted to the beneficiary provisions and settlement options. This section provides for designating and changing the beneficiary, describes the optional modes of settlement, and in general includes all the provisions relating to the rights and privileges of the owner and the beneficiary or beneficiaries, as well as the obligations of the insurer, with respect to settlement of the proceeds of the policy. For ease of reference, this will be called the settlement section.

A second important section of a whole life or endowment policy is generally referred to as the nonforfeiture section. It consists of the options available to the policyowner in case he finds it necessary (or simply prefers) to cease paying premiums before the policy has become paid up. In that event, if he has paid premiums for a specified minimum length of time, he is entitled to a cash value on surrendering the policy, or, alternatively, this value may be applied to extend his coverage under options set forth in the policy. This nonforfeiture section of the policy is made up of tables and policy provisions that are required by law to be included in every whole life and endowment policy, as well as level term life insurance policies for terms longer than 15 years.

In addition to the settlement and the nonforfeiture sections, there are always a number of general provisions, including standard provisions required by law and provisions that may be included at the option of the company. Often these will be found in a section titled "general provisions."

The provisions of a typical ordinary life insurance contract can be discussed under these three subheadings; but in addition, there is a face page, and additional coverages may be added by special sections or riders. This discussion will begin with the face page.

C. THE FACE PAGE

The face page of an illustrative life insurance policy is reproduced in Appendix B. Note that it states the name of the company, the name of the insured, the amount of insurance, the premium amount, and the effective date of the policy. Usually, as shown here, there is a simple statement that "in consideration of the application and the payment of premiums as they become due," the company promises to pay the face amount (or the amount of insurance, or in some instances, the sum insured) to the beneficiary immediately on receipt of "due proof" of the death of the insured. The face page thus expresses the basic promise of the life insurance company and the most important condition—premium payment—related to it. (In that connection, however, it should be remembered that the application and payment of the initial premium—not renewal premiums—constitute the consideration for the contract, in the strict legal sense of consideration.)

The remainder of the policy defines this basic promise more precisely and explains the various privileges and other benefits available to the policyowner. These provisions and specifications are often referred to in the wording used on the face page, such as the following:

. . . subject to the provisions and specifications on this and the following pages of this policy.

The execution paragraph, including the signatures of the company officers—usually the president and secretary—completes this statement of the basic promise in the policy and constitutes the testimonium or attestation clause. This clause evidences the execution of the document by authorized company officers and, in effect, transforms a policy form into a statement of the contract.

At the bottom of the face page will be found a brief policy description. One of the basic objectives of legislation concerning life insurance policy provisions is to assure that the policyowner understands the coverage he has under his policy. For that reason, a very common statutory provision requires that a brief description of the coverage be included on the face page of every policy. For example, one company describes its whole life policy as follows:

> Whole Life Policy with Waiver of Premium for Disability.
> Premiums payable for life. Insurance payable on death.

A number of the states have this kind of statutory requirement, the purpose of which is to make it clear to the policyowner, at least in general terms, the kind of coverage his policy provides.

D. THE STANDARD PROVISIONS

The standard provisions law, which was enacted in New York after the standard policy law proved too restrictive, has been adopted with some modifications by considerably more than half the states, including most of the states which have the largest insurance companies. Most life insurance policies now being issued, therefore, comply with this legislation and include the provisions it requires. The following discussion is intended merely as a brief review of these provisions in order that attention may be kept upon the policy as a whole.

6.3 The Introductory Language

The standard policy provisions law is usually introduced with a general paragraph similar to the following:

> No policy of life insurance, except as stated in subsection three, shall be delivered or issued for delivery in this state unless it contains in substance the following provision or provisions which in the opinion of the superintendent are more favorable to policyholders. . . .[2]

Note first that the law applies to all policies delivered in the state in question or issued for delivery in that state. Thus it automatically applies to all domiciliary companies and the policies of any out-of-state company

---

[2] New York Insurance Law, Sec. 155, 1.

that are actually delivered in the state. Second, the phrase "in substance" makes it clear that the policy provision need not be stated in the exact words of the statute. Finally, whether the policy provisions actually used are "more favorable to policyholders" than the provisions outlined in the statute is left to the opinion of the superintendent.

"Superintendent" is a title given to the head of the New York Insurance Department. In other states, this same official is variously referred to as "director" or "commissioner." It might be noted that subsection 3 of the New York law (referred to in the quoted passage) excepts from the requirements listed such policies as single-premium policies, nonparticipating policies, and term policies to the extent that any of the listed required provisions may not be applicable. Thus, a nonparticipating policy would not be required to include dividend provisions, for example; and a single-premium policy would not be required to contain provisions relating to the payment of renewal premiums.

6.4 The "Entire Contract" Provision

Probably one of the most basic provisions required to be included in a life insurance policy is one that specifies the documents that may be considered part of the contract. This requirement grows out of a standard rule of contract law that permits contracting parties to incorporate into a written contract any document or documents they wish, simply by referring to them in the contract itself. Any document so incorporated must be in existence at the time the contract is made, and the reference must be expressly made and in such a way that the document can be clearly identified. When this has been done, the document referred to is an integral part of the agreement, and its terms are part of the terms of the contract. This practice is called "incorporation by reference," and it greatly simplifies contract drafting in many instances.

As applied to the life insurance contract, however, incorporation by reference can be subject to distinct abuse. Provisions of the insurer's charter and bylaws, for example, could be made an effective part of every life insurance contract a company issued simply by adequate reference to them in the contract, and the privileges and benefits under the contract could be significantly modified or limited in that way. Yet the policy-owner would never see the charter or bylaws themselves, and in many if not most instances he would be completely unaware of their provisions.

This practice, with its potential for abuse, was effectively terminated by the standard provisions law, which, in the present wording of the New York Law, requires the inclusion of:

> A provision that the policy shall constitute the entire contract between the parties, or, if a copy of the application is endorsed upon or attached

to the policy when issued, a provision that the policy and the application therefor shall constitute the entire contract between the parties.[3]

A typical policy provision in compliance with this requirement reads as follows:

> This policy and application, a copy of which is attached when issued, constitute the entire contract.[4]

This provision is so universally used in life insurance policies today that the need for it is little more than historical. The purpose is to assure the owner of the contract that he has in his possession every document that relates to the privileges and benefits—as well as the duties and conditions—the policy provides. Nevertheless, it should be borne in mind that if any legally required provision has been omitted, the contract will be construed as if it were included. The policy and the application (if attached) constitute the entire contract, therefore, unless there is a statutory provision that is required to be included and has been omitted. In that case, the statutory provision is considered to be a part of the contract. The result is that no document may be included by reference only, but no essential statutory provision may be effectively omitted, either.

6.5 The Incontestable Clause

Most standard provisions laws require a provision making the life insurance policy incontestable after it has been in force during the lifetime of the insured for a specified length of time not longer than two years from the policy date. In the absence of this provision, the life insurance contract, like any other contractual agreement, could be avoided by the insurer if it had entered the contract in reliance on fraudulent misstatements or even when the misstatements were not fraudulent but were material to the agreement.

The incontestable clause was first introduced by life insurance companies on a voluntary basis in the latter half of the 1800s in an effort to counteract a growing attitude of distrust toward the life insurance business. This feeling was due largely to the practices of some insurers of taking full advantage of their right to disaffirm a contract if any statement, even a relatively unimportant one, in the application were not literally true.

Often premiums had been paid over a long period of time, and the

---

[3] Except where otherwise noted, all statutory quotations in connection with this discussion of "The Standard Provisions" are from the New York Insurance Law, Sec. 155, 1 (a) through (i).

[4] This and all other policy provisions used in this chapter are quoted from *The Spectator Handy Guide* (Philadelphia, Pa.: Chilton Co.).

misstatements concerned were relatively trivial, yet the company would disaffirm the contract at the death of the insured, leaving the beneficiary in the difficult position of either having no insurance or suing the company and defending against an alleged misstatement made many years earlier in the application and about which he knew little or nothing. As a matter of fact, the early life insurers had a considerable amount of success in disaffirming their policies in circumstances of this kind, but this success, as one commentator has put it, rapidly gained for them a reputation as "the great repudiators." In an effort to counteract this growing reputation and to assure the insureds and beneficiaries that such purely technical grounds would not be used to disaffirm their contracts, the incontestable clause was introduced in the latter half of the 19th century by the companies themselves.

The first American insurance company to use an incontestable clause was the Manhattan Life Insurance Company. In 1864, this company included in its policies a provision making the policy incontestable after five years "for or on account of error, omissions and misstatements in the application except as to age."

In 1879, the Equitable Life Assurance Society announced that its policies were being made incontestable after three years, with a provision as follows:

> And the said Society does hereby further promise and agree that after three years from the date hereof, the only conditions which shall be binding upon the holder of this policy are that he shall pay the premiums at the times and place, and in the manner herein stipulated, and that the regulations of the society as to age, residence, travel, occupation and employments shall be observed, and that in all other respects, after the expiration of said three years, the liability of the said society under this policy shall not be disputed.

By the time of the Armstrong Investigation in 1905, the incontestable clause was being widely used, and it was made mandatory by the Standard Policy Provisions Law. Today, the policy provisions laws in a number of states require such a clause, and a typical policy provision reads as follows:

> Incontestable Clause. After this policy has been in force during the lifetime of the Insured for a period of two years from the date of issue it shall be incontestable except for nonpayment of premiums, and except as to provisions and conditions relating to benefits in the event of total and permanent disability, and those granting additional insurance specifically against death by accidental means, contained in any supplemental agreement attached to, and made a part of, this policy.

The incontestable clause has no effect on the validity or invalidity of a life insurance contract per se. It only says that after the contract has been in effect for a specified length of time, the insurer cannot have it declared invalid for any of the previously noted reasons. Thus, in effect, it establishes a period of two years during which the policy can be contested on the same basis and for the same reasons as any other contract. After the expiration of this "contestable period," the life insurance contract is incontestable.

In a general sense, the incontestable clause resembles what are called statutes of limitation. These are statutes establishing a specified period within which one may file certain kinds of lawsuits and declaring that after the expiration of that period, such actions cannot be begun. Such statutes are sometimes termed statutes of repose, also, which just means that they reduce the number of lawsuits that may be brought in the area of the law to which they apply.

6.6 The Grace Period Provision

A grace period provision is usually required in statutory language such as the following:

> A provision that the insured is entitled to a grace period either of thirty days or of one month within which the payment of any premium after the first may be made, during which period of grace the policy shall continue in full force, but if a claim arises under the policy during such period of grace before the overdue premiums or the deferred premiums of the current policy year, if any, are paid, the amount of such premiums, together with interest, not in excess of six per cent per annum, on any overdue premium, may be deducted from any amount payable under the policy in settlement.

An illustrative grace period provision from a typical life insurance policy reads as follows:

> *Grace Period.* A grace period of thirty-one days shall be allowed for payment of a premium in default. This policy shall continue in full force during the grace period. If the Insured dies during such period, the premium in default shall be paid from the proceeds of this policy.

Like many of the other standard provisions, the grace period provision was first included in life insurance policies by insurers on a voluntary basis. By the time of the Armstrong Investigation, such provisions were widely being used. Thus, the legislation only required all insurers to follow a practice already adopted by the better companies.

The grace period provision simply gives the policyowner an additional period of time in which to pay the premium after it has become due. During that period, the policy continues in force and the premium continues to be payable. If the insured dies during the grace period and prior to payment of the premium, therefore, the premium will be deducted from the proceeds of the policy. If the insured does not die during the grace period and if the premium is not paid by the end of the period, the policy lapses, but the policyowner owes nothing for the additional 31 days of protection.

Length of the Period. Most ordinary life insurance policies provide a grace period of 31 days, and if the last day of grace falls on Sunday or a holiday the premium is ordinarily payable on the following business day.

Occasionally when a premium is past due, a premium-extension agreement may be used for temporary accommodation. (This is an agreement to extend the premium due date for that particular premium.) In these circumstances the weight of authority is that the grace period may not be added to the time stipulated in the extension agreement. The extension period dates from the day the premium was due, not from the end of the grace period.

Interest Charge. Interest earnings play a large part in the business of insurance, and if premiums are paid at the end instead of the beginning of the grace period, the insurer will have lost the investment value of the premium for one month. For this reason, the statute permits the insurer to charge interest on the overdue payments. For competitive reasons, however, as well as the fact that such losses are not generally too significant, most companies do not contemplate making an interest charge as indicated in the provision quoted above. It is of some interest to note, however, that in many instances interest is charged under group policies in similar situations.

6.7 Misstatement of Age

The age of the proposed insured is of such great importance with respect to the degree of risk assumed that a misstatement of age may make a significant difference in the amount of premiums that should have been paid. Yet errors, honest and otherwise, in stating the age of the proposed insured were common from the outset of the life insurance business. Thus some equitable method of adjusting the amount of premium paid or the amount of insurance payable has been necessary from a very early date. The problem was resolved in the standard policy provisions law by a requirement stated in the New York Insurance Law as follows:

> A provision that if the age of the person insured has been misstated, any amount payable or benefit accruing under the policy shall be such as the premium would have purchased at the correct age.

Most life insurers follow the language of this statute rather closely in their policies, as shown in a typical policy provision:

Age. This policy is issued at the age shown on page one, which is the insured's age at last birthday on the Policy Date, according to the date of birth given in the application.

If the age of the insured has been misstated, the amount payable and every benefit accruing under this policy shall be such as the premiums paid would have purchased at the correct age.

This provision assures the policyowner that all cases involving misstatements of age will be decided uniformly and equitably. In the absence of a statute, the problem could be resolved by adjusting the amount of insurance or by refunding or paying the difference in premium. The statute requires that the policy state that the amount of insurance will be adjusted. Thus, if the age of the insured has been understated, the beneficiary is precluded from paying the difference in premium after the death of the insured and in effect "buying" more insurance than would have been provided by the premium actually paid. However, if the age has been overstated, a larger amount of insurance will be payable.

This provision is sometimes modified slightly to include a reference to sex in policies for which different, and lower, premium rates are charged for women. In such instances, the second paragraph of the above quoted provision refers to both the age and sex of the insured.

6.8 Divisible Surplus

One of the problems inquired into by the Armstrong Investigation concerned the dividend practices of some of the large life insurance companies at that time. Instead of paying dividends each year, as is done today, it was customary for insurers to set aside a portion of the surplus each year and accumulate it for long periods of time—often 20 years or more. Only those policyowners who survived to the end of the period shared in the funds so accumulated. Those who died or withdrew during the period, therefore, forfeited their share.[5] Recommended legislation growing out of the investigation made it mandatory under participating policies for insurers to ascertain and apportion divisible surplus to the various policies and policyowners at frequent intervals and required this to be expressed as a policy provision. Accordingly, the present New York Insurance Law requires:

A provision that the insurer shall annually ascertain and apportion any divisible surplus accruing on the policy.

An illustrative policy provision reads as follows:

Dividends. Annual dividends such as the company may apportion shall be payable while this policy is in force, other than as extended term in-

---

[5] The Tontine System, so-called because originally devised by Lorenzo Tonti, a Neapolitan.

surance, without condition as to the payment of any subsequent premium. . . .

The meaning of this provision is scarcely open to question. A few states also specify the optional methods of applying these dividends and require that these options be included in the contract.

6.9 The Nonforfeiture Provisions

Nonforfeiture provisions had been required by the laws of several of the states prior to the Armstrong Investigation. Consequently, it is not surprising that one of the standard required provisions deals with this subject directly and requires:

> A provision specifying the cash surrender values and nonforfeiture options available under the policy in the event of default in a premium payment after premiums have been paid for a specified period, together with a table showing, in figures, the options so available, and also the loan values, if any, available during each of the first twenty years after the issuance of the policy. Such options shall include a cash surrender value, and shall conform with the requirements of subsection one of section two hundred eight or two hundred eight-a.

The specific reference to subsection 1 of section 208 or 208–a is a reference to the sections that set out the details and technical requirements for the nonforfeiture benefits that must be included in the policy. Today this standard nonforfeiture law has been enacted or adopted by most of the states in this country; and in compliance with this law, life insurance contracts, other than relatively short-term contracts, include detailed nonforfeiture sections.

Nonforfeiture provisions are the direct result of the level premium system. Because of it, every owner of a whole life or endowment policy is in the position of having contributed more in premium payments in the early years than would have been required to meet his proportionate share of the current mortality cost to the company. If he keeps the policy in force, this apparent inequity will be remedied in later years when he will be paying less than his proportionate share. However, if he permits the policy to lapse, he will have contributed more than the value of his protection; and in the absence of nonforfeiture benefits, that difference is forfeited. In the early days of life insurance, this is exactly what happened to the policyowner whose policy lapsed for nonpayment of premiums; and as recently as 1875, this was not considered particularly unfair.

Among those persons who did not share this view was Elizur Wright, the first insurance commissioner of Massachusetts. Largely by reason of his efforts, in 1861 Massachusetts enacted the first nonforfeiture law. It required that whenever any policy lapsed, four fifths of its "net value" must be used to purchase extended term insurance. Similar laws were passed in other states in the next few decades, but this type of legislation received its first real impetus in connection with the standard provision laws.

The standard policy provisions legislation required that in the case of lapse of a whole life insurance contract that had been in effect for a minimum stated period (usually three years), the insurer must provide a cash surrender value. Alternatively, either paid-up insurance for a reduced amount or extended term insurance for the net face amount, or both, must be offered in whatever amounts could be purchased by the net cash surrender value. One of these alternative benefits must be automatic— that is, it must become operative immediately upon the lapse of the policy if the policyowner did not make an election.

As a general rule, these early nonforfeiture benefits were computed on the American Experience Table of Mortality at a rate of interest not to exceed that stated in the law. This mortality table became more and more out of date in the 1930s, however, and the rate of interest earnings of all life insurance companies declined. In 1937, therefore, a committee, under the chairmanship of Alfred N. Guertin, was appointed to study the nonforfeiture situation. This committee's recommendations led to the adoption by the National Association of Insurance Commissioners of two model statutes referred to as the "Guertin legislation."

The Guertin Laws.   The model nonforfeiture legislation recommended by the Guertin Committee included up-to-date mortality tables (the Commissioners' 1941 Mortality Table) and otherwise modernized the nonforfeiture requirements. One of the most important innovations was the complete separation of the idea of nonforfeiture benefits from policy reserves. Prior to this time, nonforfeiture values had been computed by subtracting from the reserve a declining and ultimately vanishing "surrender charge." Thus the nonforfeiture values were tied very closely to the reserve. Under the Guertin legislation, the nonforfeiture benefits were to be calculated as specified in the law, without reference to the amount of the policy reserve.

Under the Guertin laws, a paid-up nonforfeiture benefit is required to be provided for every whole life policy in case of lapse for nonpayment of premiums if and when the specified formula produces a positive value. A cash surrender value must be provided if the policy has been in force for three years. The company must include tables of benefits in the policy and a statement of the methods used in calculating the benefits. The nonforfeiture section of the policy is thus somewhat complicated, but it assures the policyowner that if the policy lapses, equities will be available to him in the form of a cash surrender value or other nonforfeiture benefit.

By January 1, 1948, the Guertin nonforfeiture laws had either been enacted or otherwise made effective in every state. It is important to note, however, that these laws related only to policies issued after the effective date of the laws themselves. It is basic constitutional law that legislation cannot impair contracts already in effect. Life insurance policies issued prior to that date, therefore, continued with their nonforfeiture sections effective as written. Only those issued thereafter were required to conform to the Guertin legislation.

1958 C.S.O. Mortality Tables. As the years passed, the 1941 C.S.O. Mortality Tables, like their predecessors, became out of date. To remedy this, new mortality tables were developed. These tables are referred to as the 1958 Commissioners' Standard Ordinary Mortality Tables (the 1958 C.S.O. Mortality Tables). Legislation adopting these tables as the standard for minimum nonforfeiture values had been enacted or otherwise made effective in every state by January 1, 1966, which was the mandatory operative date.

As a result of these changing requirements, policies now outstanding may have nonforfeiture benefits in accordance with laws which were effective prior to 1948; others, with benefits based on laws effective between 1948 and 1966; and still others, with nonforfeiture benefits based on the 1958 C.S.O. Mortality Tables. Each policy is lawful; each is valid; each is different from those with nonforfeiture benefits based on a different set of laws. By reason of the detailed legislative requirements on the subject, however, each policy is self-determining, since it includes in its own printed provisions an explanation of the nonforfeiture benefits it provides and how they are calculated; and tables of the benefits are required to be included. An illustrative nonforfeiture section will be found in the specimen policy included in Appendix B.

6.10 The Policy Loan Provision

The policy loan provision, like the nonforfeiture provisions, grew out of the legal reserve, level premium system. The nonforfeiture benefits guarantee to the policyowner an equitable share of the values he has helped to accumulate, but only if he surrenders the policy for cash or permits it to lapse. The policy loan provision benefits the policyowner who does not wish to lapse his policy and yet has a temporary need for cash. Policy loans were first made available on a voluntary basis, later by statutory requirement. The New York statute is lengthy and is quoted here only in part. It requires:

> A provision that after three full years' premiums have been paid, the insurer issuing the same will, at any time while the policy is in force, advance, on proper assignment or pledge of the policy and on the sole security thereof, at a specified rate of interest, not exceeding four and

eight-tenths per centum per annum if payable in advance or the equivalent effective rate of interest if otherwise payable, a sum equal to, or at the option of the person entitled thereto less than the amount required by section two hundred eight-b under the conditions specified thereby. . . .[6]

An illustrative policy provision reads in part as follows:

LOAN PROVISIONS

(1) *Policy Loan.* At any time while this policy is in force, other than as extended term insurance, the company, upon satisfactory assignment of this policy, will advance to the owner on the sole security of this policy any amount which shall be within the limit of the then maximum loan value, if any, less any existing indebtedness to the company secured by this policy. The policy need not be presented for endorsement unless required by the company.

The company reserves the right to defer the granting of any loan, other than to pay premiums on policies in this company, for a period not exceeding six months from the date the request for such loan was received.

(2) *Loan Value.* The maximum loan value shall be that amount which, with interest at the rate of five per cent per annum to the date on which the next premium is due or, if no further premiums are payable, to the next anniversary of the Policy Date, equals the cash value as of such date.

(3) *Loan Interest.* Interest on loans shall accrue from day to day at the rate of five per cent per annum and shall constitute an indebtedness to the company against this policy as and when it accrues. Interest shall be payable on each anniversary of the Policy Date subsequent to the date of loan until the loan is repaid. Any interest unpaid when due shall be added to and form a part of the loan and bear interest at the same rate. If at any time the total indebtedness to the company on this policy, including accrued interest, exceeds the then maximum loan value, the accrued interest shall become due and this policy shall be void thirty-one days after the company has mailed notice to the last known address of the owner and the assignee of record, if any.

(4) *Loan Repayment.* All or any part of a loan may be repaid, with accrued interest on the amount so repaid, at any time while this policy is in force other than as extended term insurance. Any existing indebtedness to the company secured by this policy shall be deducted from the sum payable at the time of any settlement.

Although this provision refers to a "policy loan," a legal analysis establishes that these are not actually loans but rather advances. That is to say, there is no debtor and creditor relationship between the policyowner and the company.[7]

The Automatic Premium Loan. A special application of the policy loan is found in the automatic premium loan. In the past, various states

---

[6] Section 208–b refers to the cash surrender values required in policies issued before and after the effective date of this law.

[7] This analysis is discussed at considerably greater length in Chapter 13.

enacted laws requiring insurers to include in their policies a provision for an automatic premium loan in the event of default in the payment of premiums. Such a provision requires the insurer, in the event of a default in premium payment, and if there is a sufficient loan value for the purpose, to establish a loan against the policy for the purpose of paying the premium then due. Such laws are no longer found except in Rhode Island. However, most companies include an automatic premium loan provision in their policies on a purely optional basis. That is to say, it is not operative unless the applicant or policyowner requests it. Illustrative of this type of policy provision is the following:

> *Automatic Premium Loan.* If this provision is elected in the application or otherwise in writing before the end of the grace period, a loan shall be automatically granted on this policy to pay a premium in default. The owner may revoke such election as to its subsequent application by giving written notice to the company.
>
> No such loan will be granted if the loan value, less any existing indebtedness, is not sufficient to pay the premium then due under this policy.

6.11 The Reinstatement Clause

Reinstatement clauses came into general use in life insurance policies in this country during the final decade of the last century. Until 1905, however, there were no laws requiring them. At the present time, more than half the states have laws requiring that any policy issued or issued for delivery in their jurisdiction must include a reinstatement provision.

The New York statute requires:

> A provision that the policy will be reinstated at any time within three years from the date of default, unless the cash surrender value has been exhausted by payment or unless the period of extended insurance has expired, upon the application of the insured and the production of evidence of insurability, including good health, satisfactory to the insurer and the payment of all overdue premiums and the payment or reinstatement of any other indebtedness to the insurer upon said policy with interest at a rate not exceeding six per centum per annum compounded annually.

This may be contrasted with the Illinois statute, which requires:

> A provision that if in event of default in premium payments the value of the policy shall have been applied to the purchase of other insurance as provided for in this section, and if such insurance shall be in force and the original policy shall not have been surrendered to the company and cancelled, the policy may be reinstated within three years from such default, upon evidence of insurability satisfactory to the company and payment of arrears of premiums and the payment or reinstatement of any

other indebtedness to the company upon the policy, with interest on the premiums and indebtedness at the rate of not exceeding 6% per annum payable annually.[8]

A literal reading of the Illinois statute would suggest that reinstatement does not have to be granted unless the policy has been in force long enough to acquire nonforfeiture values. Nor is it required after the cash value has been paid or any extended term insurance has expired. As a general rule, however, insurers do not usually take advantage of this right to deny reinstatement after a period of extended term insurance has expired. Reinstatement is usually to the companies' advantage, and they do not place many stumbling blocks in the way. Nevertheless, the statutory requirement that the policy shall not have been surrendered for cash is usually a part of the policy wording. The surrender of a policy is a deliberate act on the part of the policyowner, and it is not unreasonable to consider the contractual relationship terminated by it.

An illustrative reinstatement policy provision reads as follows:

> *Reinstatement.* This policy may be reinstated at any time within three years from the due date of the first unpaid premium, if a cash surrender value has not been paid. Such reinstatement shall be subject to:
> (1) Evidence of insurability, including good health, of the insured satisfactory to the company;
> (2) Payment of all premiums in default, with interest at the rate of five per cent per annum;
> (3) Payment or reinstatement of any loan secured by this policy on the date of premium default, with interest at the rate of five per cent per annum from that date.

It will be noted that under this policy provision, reinstatement would not be permitted if the policy had been surrendered for its cash value. However, the fact that the policy might have gone on extended term insurance and the period of such insurance had expired would not prevent the policyowner from reinstating the policy if the specified requirements were met. The statute permitted the insurer to phrase its reinstatement provision to deny reinstatement in that instance, but the insurer chose to make the policy provision more liberal.

In the absence of a statute, the reinstatement of a lapsed policy would not require a special policy provision. Contracting parties are always free to modify their agreement, discontinue it, and put it back into effect as they might agree. In the absence of either a statute or policy provision, the insurer and the policyowner, therefore, could reinstate a lapsed policy on whatever conditions they might wish. Including this right as a provision in the policy itself, however, clarifies the right, guarantees its availability to the policyowner, makes it unnecessary to negotiate con-

---

[8] Illinois Revised Statutes, Chap. 73, Sec. 836(i) (1973).

cerning the terms of reinstatement when a request is made, and helps to assure that all policyowners will be treated uniformly.

E. PROHIBITED PROVISIONS

The freedom to make contracts without unreasonable restriction is one of the great basic freedoms. However, this freedom may be limited if restriction seems necessary for the public good. In addition to specifying certain required provisions, therefore, the insurance laws of most of the states also specify some policy provisions that may not be included in life insurance contracts because they are considered adverse to the public interest.

The Illinois Insurance Law, for example, lists a number of prohibited provisions, introduced as follows:

> After the effective date of this Code no policy of life insurance shall be issued or delivered in this State if it contains any of the following provisions. . . .[9]

The first prohibited provision under the Illinois law is:

> (a) A provision limiting the time within which any action at law or in equity may be commenced to less than three years after the cause of action shall accrue.

In the absence of a specific statute, a contractual limitation with respect to the time within which suit must be brought will generally be upheld. If there is no such limitation, the question will be governed by the general statutes of limitations which have been enacted by most of the states and which apply to various kinds of legal actions. Usually, these statutes are not too restrictive. Illinois, for example, requires an action on any written contract to be brought within 10 years of the date the cause of action arose.

However, a delay of this length of time in bringing an action under a life insurance contract could mean a decided and unnecessary hardship to life insurance companies. Typically, the burden of proof is on the insurer (to defend a claim denial, for instance). In the course of several years, key witnesses could die or disappear and other circumstances change so much that it would be difficult or impossible for the insurer to support its position with convincing proof. For this reason, the special statutory provision quoted above permits the period to be considerably shortened with respect to insurance, by specific provision in the contract, but not to less than three years. A number of other states have similar laws, specifying periods ranging from one to six years. Most frequently specified are periods of two and three years.

---

[9] Illinois Revised Statutes, Chap. 73, Sec. 837 (1).

6.12 Dating Back

Occasionally an applicant wishes the policy dated back to "save age," which simply means that he wants the benefit of a lower premium because of a lower age and therefore asks that his policy be dated back to accomplish this. Within reason, there should be no objection to this procedure. However, any date-back means that a premium will be payable for a period in which the policyowner has had no coverage. In addition, the contestable and suicide periods would, in practical effect, be shortened by the period for which the policy has been dated back. That is, if the two-year contestable and suicide periods begin on the policy date, a policy issued on July 1 but dated January 1 would be contestable for 18 months only; and the insured's suicide 19 months later would be beyond the suicide period. In order to prevent these results, therefore, many of the states have enacted statutes making it unlawful for companies to date back policies beyond a stipulated period, usually six months prior to the date of the original application for the insurance.

The Illinois Insurance Law accomplishes this by prohibiting:

> A provision by which the policy shall purport to be issued or take effect more than six months before the original application for the insurance was made.

The New York version of this prohibition forbids dating any policy more than six months before the application was made if that reduces the premium below the premium that would be payable as determined by the nearest birthday of the insured on the application date. However, it specifically excepts original date conversions or the exercise of any conversion right provided for in the contract.

6.13 "Less Value" Statutes

The "less value" statutes, enacted by several of the states, have presented a number of legal questions because of their apparent conflict with other provisions of the policy, particularly with restrictions concerning aviation activities. The Illinois law meets this problem by prohibiting:

> A provision for any mode of settlement at maturity after the expiration of the contestable period of the policy of less value than the amount insured on the face of the policy plus dividend additions, if any, less any indebtedness to the company on or secured by the policy, and less any premium that may by the terms of the policy be deducted, except as permitted by clause (c) of subsection (1) of section 224.

A statute of this kind is obviously intended to prevent the company from promising benefits on the face of the policy that are later curtailed or extinguished in the body of the policy. The practices of most companies of excluding the hazards of war and aviation under some circumstances have created a direct conflict with this type of statute. The above quotation, however, specifically provides for such exceptions in its reference to clause (c) of subsection (1) of section 224. The latter clause specifically permits aviation and war hazard restrictions.

6.14 Forfeiture and Policy Loans

The Illinois Insurance Law also forbids:

> A provision for forfeiture of the policy for failure to repay any loan on the policy, or to pay interest on such loan, while the total indebtedness on the policy, including interest, is less than the loan value thereof.

The latter portion of this statute points up the type of abuse the law is directed toward preventing. It should also be noted that it thus implements the required standard provision with respect to policy loans.

6.15 Agent of the Insured

It will be recalled that courts have generally held legally ineffective any attempt on the part of an insurer to make the insurer's agent, by policy provision, the agent of the insured for the purpose of taking the application. The Illinois Insurance Law specifically enacts this into statutory law by prohibiting:

> A provision to the effect that the agent soliciting the insurance is the agent of the person insured under said policy, or making the acts or representations of such agent binding upon the person so insured under said policy.

F. OPTIONAL POLICY PROVISIONS

In addition to those policy provisions that are specifically required by law, a number of provisions such as the assignment and suicide provisions (and the automatic premium loan in most states) are permitted but not required. Other optional provisions simply make the policy more understandable, more easily administered, or more favorable to the insured.

6.16 Ownership Provisions

There is no general pattern or practice with respect to ownership provisions in the usual life insurance policy. Most policies are issued on the application of the insured who names a revocable beneficiary and thus has full ownership and control over the policy throughout its existence. Most companies also have what are called "ownership," or third-party, policies, which are applied for and issued to persons other than the insured so that the insured has no ownership rights under the contract. It is customary today, therefore, to name the owner if other than the insured, but to specify that the insured is the owner where that is true. It is also customary to specify the rights of the owner, as illustrated in the following policy provision:

> *Ownership.* Every right, benefit, and privilege available under this policy while the insured is living, prior to the Maturity Date, is vested in the owner and may be exercised without the consent of any revocable beneficiary. However, all rights of the owner are subject to the rights of any assignee of record and of any irrevocable beneficiary.
>
> The owner may transfer ownership of this policy to a successor owner by written request. The company reserves the right to require the policy for endorsement of any change of ownership.

Policies owned by someone other than the insured are not new. The first policy issued by the Mutual Life of New York was applied for by a woman on the life of her husband, and she was both the owner and the beneficiary. However, the most frequent use of ownership policies today is found in business situations. Personal insurance is more usually issued on the application of the proposed insured. In either case, however, an ownership provision is helpful to clarify the rights and privileges granted by the policy. The title status of the policy is then readily ascertainable at all times.

6.17 The Assignment Provision

No Provision Required. Unless otherwise specifically stated, the owner of a life insurance policy has the right to assign it as a matter of law, and a policy provision to that effect is not required. For this reason, policy provisions do not generally "grant" the right to assign the policy; they merely define the company's responsibilities in case the owner elects to exercise his right to make an assignment. One illustrative policy provision reads as follows:

> *Assignment.* The company assumes no responsibility for the validity or effect of any assignment of this policy, and no assignment will be recognized until it has been duly filed with the company. An assignment of this policy shall operate to the extent thereof to transfer to the assignee the interest of any beneficiary whom the assignor has the right to change. Any amount payable to the assignee shall be payable in one sum, notwithstanding any settlement agreement in effect at the time the assignment was executed.

6.18 The Suicide Provision

If the policy does not include a provision specifically declaring that suicide is a risk not assumed under the policy, the death of the insured by suicide is generally considered to be covered. Some states specifically limit the period of time during which suicide can be excluded; and one state, Missouri, permits the company to deny a claim on the grounds that the insured took his own life only if the insurer can prove that at the time of application the insured "contemplated" that action.

In many ways, the risk of suicide presents a difficult problem in life insurance. The law recognizes the possibility that life insurance may be obtained by persons who at the time of application are planning to take their own lives. In that case, the insured is not a truly insurable risk, since the risk is within his control. On the other hand, the protection of the dependents of persons who die prematurely is one of the basic objectives of life insurance, and the reason for the death is decidedly secondary so far as his dependents are concerned. The most typical suicide provision, therefore, establishes a compromise between the requirements of an insurable risk and public policy on the one hand and the social needs of a suicide's dependents on the other. This is accomplished by providing a two-year period during which suicide will not be covered and eliminating all restrictions thereafter.

An illustrative policy provision reads as follows:

> *Suicide.* The suicide of the insured within two years from the Policy Date or the Issue Date, whichever is the earlier, is a risk not assumed under this policy. In such event, however, there shall be a death benefit of an amount equal to the premiums received, without interest.

6.19 Change of Plan

The parties to any contract may by mutual consent change their agreement to incorporate new terms or even to effect an entirely new contract. This is true with respect to the life insurance contract, as well as any other; and a "change of plan" provision is often used to make this clear. An illustrative provision of this type reads as follows:

> *Change of Plan.* The plan or Amount of Insurance, or both, may be changed by mutual agreement with the company.

G. THE SETTLEMENT SECTION

The policy as issued will include beneficiary specifications in accordance with the applicant's instructions in the application. This will usually be a simple beneficiary designation if settlement is to be in one sum; but more elaborate provisions, often called settlement agreements, may be used if settlement is to be made under one or more of the optional modes. The settlement section of the contract, therefore, includes these specifications as well as a change of beneficiary provision and a description of the various optional modes of settlement available. These options have been discussed in Chapter 5 and will not be repeated here.

SUMMARY

The Policy as a Contract

The life insurance policy is the written expression of the insuring agreement between the applicant and the company; and as a written contract, it is subject to the parol evidence rule. In legal terms, the life insurance contract is informal, not formal; aleatory, not commutative; unilateral, not bilateral; and a contract of adhesion, not a bargaining contract. Since it is a contract of adhesion, if there is an ambiguity, it will be resolved in favor of the policyowner or beneficiary and against the party who drafted it, the insurer.

Insurance laws regulating the life insurance contract to some extent are found in every state. Many of these laws specify some provisions that must be included, some provisions that may but do not have to be included, and others that are forbidden to be included in the contract. The best known and most commonly required provisions are those specified by the uniform standard policy provisions law enacted in New York in 1910 and by a number of other states since that time.

Life insurance contract forms are ordinarily required to be approved by the commissioner or superintendent of insurance of the state in which the policy is to be issued or delivered. However, as a general rule, if the policy form has not been approved prior to issuance of the policy, the contract will be held to be valid but a penalty will be imposed upon the insurer.

The Policy in General

For ease of discussion, it is helpful to break down the life insurance policy into several general sections. Thus, the section dealing with beneficiary designations may be termed the settlement section; the nonforfeiture section specifies rights and privileges available if the policyowner discontinues premium payment before the policy becomes paid up; and a number of general provisions may be grouped in a third section. In addition, there is a face page; and other provisions, including additional benefits, may be provided by additional sections or riders.

The Face Page

The face page of a life insurance policy typically includes a statement of the company's promise to pay the face amount to the beneficiary on receipt of due proof of the death of the insured, and a statement of the premium payable. The testimonium or attestation clause consists of the execution paragraph and includes the signatures of company officers—usually the president and secretary. The remainder of the policy defines this basic promise' in more detail and explains the various rights and privileges of the owner.

A common statutory provision also requires a brief description of the coverage provided by the policy to be included on the face page of the life insurance contract.

The Standard Provisions

The standard policy provisions law lists a number of provisions that must be included in a life insurance policy form before it will be approved, but the company is not required to include these provisions in the exact words of the statute. It is sufficient if they comply with the statutory provisions "in substance."

The "Entire Contract" Provision. One of the simplest of the required provisions specifies that the policy or the policy and the application, if a copy of the latter is attached, constitute the entire contract between the parties. This precludes the insurer from incorporating other documents, such as the company charter or bylaws, as a part of the policy merely by referring to them in the contract. The latter practice, known as incorporation by reference, was relatively common at one time and permitted insurers to include as legally effective parts of the insurance contract documents to which the policyowner might have no access whatever.

The Incontestable Clause. Most standard provisions laws require a provision making the policy incontestable after it has been in force for a specified period of time, not longer than two years. During this period, the life insurance contract, like any other contract, can be avoided for material misrepresentation or fraud in the application. After the expiration of this contestable period, however, the contract cannot be avoided in this way, and the contract is said to be incontestable.

The incontestable clause was first introduced on a voluntary basis by the insurers themselves because a number of companies had carried to an extreme their right to contest the validity of a contract on the basis of any misrepresentation, no matter how slight the misstatement may have been nor how long the policy had been in effect. The clause, therefore, was in the nature of an affirmation of good faith on the part of the insurers who adopted it. After the Armstrong Investigation, legislation was enacted making it compulsory for all insurers to follow the practice already adopted by the more progressive companies.

The Grace Period Provision. As was true of the incontestable clause, the grace period provision was first adopted by many insurers on a voluntary basis and only later required by law. In ordinary policies, this provision gives the policyowner a period of 30 or 31 days following the due date of any premium after the first during which he may pay the past-due premium without penalty. If the insured dies during the grace period while the premium remains unpaid, the policy remains in force but the insurer may deduct the unpaid premium from the proceeds. The statutory provisions usually provide that the insurer may charge interest on the overdue premium, but as a matter of practice, this is not usually done.

The Misstatement of Age Provision. Another commonly required provision specifies the adjustment that will be made in computing any benefits if the age of the insured has been misstated. In such cases, the policy must provide that the benefit will be such as the premium actually paid would have purchased at the correct age.

Divisible Surplus. It is also relatively common practice to require participating policies to include a provision for the annual apportionment of surplus, and some states specify the dividend options that must be provided.

The Nonforfeiture Provisions. The uniform standard provisions law requires a provision specifying the cash surrender values and nonforfeiture benefits available under certain policies after they have been in force for a specified period. A number of nonforfeiture laws have been enacted in the various states since 1861, when the first such law became effective in Massachusetts. At the present time, a uniform nonforfeiture law has been enacted or adopted in every state, based on the 1958 C.S.O. Mortality Tables. This law guarantees a cash surrender value whenever a positive value is produced by a formula set forth in the law. The option of taking extended term insurance or reduced paid-up insurance must also be granted, and one option must go into effect automatically if no election is made.

The Policy Loan Provision. A policy loan provision must be included in any but short term insurance contracts, permitting the policyowner to borrow up to the amount of the cash surrender value of the policy, using the policy itself as security. A variation of this is the automatic premium loan provision, under which the company initiates a loan for the purpose of paying any premium not otherwise paid at the end of the grace period. The automatic premium loan privilege is available under the policies of most companies, although it is not required except by the laws of Rhode Island.

The Reinstatement Clause. The majority of states require the inclusion of a policy provision for reinstating the policy in case of lapse if request is made within a stated period of time, usually three to five years. Satisfactory evidence of insurability must be furnished, all back premiums paid, and any indebtedness at the date of lapse either paid or reinstated.

Prohibited Provisions

Companies are specifically prohibited from including some kinds of provisions in their policies as against public policy. Illustrative of such prohibited provisions are:

1. A provision limiting to less than 3 years the time in which an action on the policy can be brought.
2. A provision which purports to make the policy effective more than a specified period (typically, six months) prior to the date of the application.
3. A provision for a mode of settlement at maturity after the expiration of the contestable period providing payment of a lesser amount than the amount stated on the face of the policy, adjusted for dividends, indebtedness, and any unpaid premiums.
4. A provision for forfeiture of the policy for failure to repay any policy loan or loan interest while the total amount of the policy loan and interest is less than the loan value.
5. A provision purporting to make the soliciting agent an agent of the person insured under the policy.

Optional Policy Provisions

Among those policy provisions that are not required but are often included are the following:

1. Ownership provisions, which specify the person who may exercise the ownership rights, benefits, and privileges under the policy.
2. An assignment provision, which clarifies the responsibilities of the insurer if the policy is assigned.
3. The suicide clause—a clause that limits the liability of the company to a return of premiums paid if the insured's death occurs within a specified period, usually two years, as a result of suicide.
4. A change of plan provision—which provides that the amount or plan of insurance may be changed by mutual agreement with the company.

The Settlement Section

The settlement section of a life insurance policy includes beneficiary specifications and the details of the optional modes of settlement provided.

ILLUSTRATIVE CASE

The following case illustrates the need to construe the provisions of a life insurance policy and the way in which such problems are considered by a court.

SUGGS v. THE LIFE INSURANCE COMPANY OF VIRGINIA[10]

These are the material facts: On July 1, 1955 the Company issued its policy insuring the life of William Durwood Suggs, III, who was born on February 16, 1942, became twenty-one years of age on February 16, 1963, and died on April 16, 1963. The plaintiff was named as beneficiary in the policy and at the time of the death of the insured all of the premiums had been paid.

Under the terms of the policy the Company contracted to pay $3,000 as "Initial Insurance" "in the event of the death of the Insured during the initial insurance period," or to pay $15,000 as "Ultimate Insurance" "in the event of the death of the Insured after the initial insurance period." The policy defined the "Initial Insurance Period" as "the period between the policy date and the policy anniversary nearest the Insured's 21st birthday excluding such policy anniversary."

On the back of the policy and at the bottom of the first page the following was printed:

JUNIOR ESTATE BUILDER
Insurance Payable at Death of Insured—Increased After Age 21
Premiums Payable to Age 65 or Until Prior Death
—Non-Participating—

It is agreed that these notations are printed on the policy pursuant to Code, Section 38.1–403 (Repl. V. 1953), which provides:

> On the face and on the back of each such policy there shall be placed a title which shall briefly and accurately describe the nature and form of the policy.

The question presented is whether the plaintiff is entitled to the initial insurance of $3,000, payable during the initial insurance period as defined in the policy, or the ultimate insurance of $15,000 payable after the initial insurance period.

The plaintiff does not question that under the policy definition of the initial insurance period, standing alone, she is entitled to recover only $3,000. It is clear that the death of the insured on April 16, 1963, occurred within

---

[10] 147 S. E. (2d) 707 (April 25, 1966).

the initial insurance period which is defined as "the period between the policy date (July 1, 1955) and the policy anniversary nearest the Insured's 21st birthday (February 16, 1963)." But she contends that the Junior Estate Builder endorsement is a part of the insurance contract; that since the death of the insured occurred after he had reached 21 years of age, under the provision in the endorsement—"Insurance payable at Death of Insured"—"Increased After Age 21"—she became entitled to the increased amount of insurance, or $15,000. She further contends that there is an inconsistency as to when the ultimate insurance is payable under the language in the endorsement and that in the body of the policy, and that this inconsistency creates an ambiguity which under familiar principles should be resolved against the Company and in her favor.

The lower court held that the Junior Estate Builder endorsement, which it characterized as a "Title" description, is not a part of the insurance contract, nor is it the purpose and intent of the statute . . . to make it a part of the contract. It further held that if such endorsement be deemed a part of the insurance contract, the language therein is not inconsistent with the provisions in the policy fixing the time for the payment of the initial insurance and the ultimate insurance, respectively, and that the plaintiff was entitled to recover the initial insurance of $3,000.

There is a conflict of authority as to whether an endorsement on an insurance policy, designating its kind and type, is a part of the insurance contract. [Citations; brief discussion of two cases, both of which differ from the case in question.]

The obvious purpose of Section 38.1–403 is to require an insurance company to display on the face and on the back of a policy a description of its nature and form in order that a prospective purchaser may know what type of insurance he is purchasing. Such requirement is for the benefit of the prospective purchaser and he is entitled to rely on it. While it may not be strictly accurate to say that such an endorsement is a part of the contract of insurance, in construing the contract the policy must be considered as a whole and the endorsement read in connection with the remainder thereof, as an aid in arriving at the intention of the policies. [Citations.]

The contention of the plaintiff that she is entitled to increased amount of insurance under the language of the endorsement is based upon the premise that the word "After" in the phrase "Increased After Age 21" means "immediately after," "upon," or "as soon as." She argues that as soon as such event occurred she became entitled to the increased amount of the insurance— $15,000. We do not agree with this contention.

When the contractual terms and the provisions of the policy including those in the endorsement, are read in their entirety it is clear that the word "After" as used in the phrase "Increased After Age 21" means "subsequent in point of time" to, or "later in time" than, the insured's attainment of his 21st birthday. This is in accord with the commonly accepted definition of the word after.[11]

---

[11] *Webster's Third New International Dictionary,* 1961 ed.,"later than a particular time or period of time." *Black's Law Dictionary* (4th ed.; St. Paul: West Publishing Co., 1951), "later, succeeding, subsequent to, inferior in point of time or of priority or preference."

The language indicating that the amount of insurance payable at the death of the insured is "Increased After Age 21" obviously refers to the provision in the policy that upon the happening of that event the amount of the insurance is increased as therein provided.

Such interpretation removes any question as to the inconsistency between the language of the endorsement and that of the other provisions of the policy and brings them into complete harmony. It accords with the principle that all of the provisions of a contract of insurance should be considered and construed together and seemingly conflicting provisions harmonized when that can be reasonably done, so as to effectuate the intention of the parties as expressed therein. . . . Thus, while the insured's death was "After Age 21," it was also within the initial insurance period.

We agree with the holding of the lower court that there is no inconsistency or ambiguity in the provisions of the policy and that since the insured died "After Age 21" but within the initial insurance period the plaintiff was entitled to recover the amount of the initial insurance—$3,000.

The judgment is affirmed.

QUESTIONS FOR REVIEW

1. What is meant by the statement that the life insurance contract is a contract of adhesion? Why is this important in interpreting ambiguities in the contract?

2. What is meant by "compliance in substance" with a statute setting forth required policy provisions?

3. What is the general rule concerning the legal effect of issuing a life insurance policy on a policy form that has not been approved as required by the proper state official?

4. What provisions are typically included in the settlement section of a life insurance policy?

5. Briefly discuss the significance and development of the Guertin legislation.

6. List and briefly discuss five standard provisions specifically required by the standard provisions laws. What other provisions, although not required, are often included in a life insurance policy?

7. Briefly discuss the requirements set forth in a typical reinstatement provision.

8. List three policy provisions that are frequently prohibited by state law.

9. Summarize a typical suicide provision in a life insurance policy.

Chapter Outline

Chapter **7**

Added Benefits
and Limitations

THE TRADITIONAL life insurance contract provided one benefit, payable at the death of the insured. Today, it is common practice to make additional benefits available, sometimes as an integral part of the basic policy and sometimes by means of separate, additional sections called riders. The practice of adding benefits by appropriate riders permits a great deal of flexibility in adapting basic general plans to individual needs.

Two benefits commonly added by riders are the accidental (or accidental means) death benefit and the waiver of premium for disability coverage. Other benefits are often added, however; and sometimes riders are used to limit coverages otherwise provided. This chapter will describe the more common of these additional benefits and limitations and discuss the more important legal problems that have been associated with their use.

A. ACCIDENTAL MEANS AND ACCIDENTAL DEATH

The accidental means or accidental death benefit is one of the most common additional benefits offered by life insurers in connection with the life insurance policy. This benefit is made an integral part of some policies, and, in fact, one company currently includes it automatically at no extra charge in all policies it issues under $10,000 at standard rates. (This only means that the premium is included in the regular premium rates for the policy; there is no separate, extra charge.) As a general rule, however, the accidental death benefit is available only for an additional, stated premium; it must be applied for; and the proposed insured must meet some underwriting requirements.

215

Typically, the accidental death benefit is provided in an amount equal to the amount of insurance provided by the policy. Thus, if the policy provides $10,000 of insurance, the accidental death benefit will be an additional $10,000. This benefit may be doubled, however, under some policies, in the event the accidental death occurs while the insured is a passenger on a common carrier.

Today the benefit is more frequently offered as an accidental death benefit than as a "benefit in the event of death by accidental means." In fact, a recent review of representative policies of more than 100 life insurance companies disclosed that more than half of them (70 out of 120) no longer use the term "accidental means." Instead, the majority of policies now being issued refer to death resulting from "accidental bodily injury," as illustrated in the following policy provision:

> The Company agrees to pay an Accidental Death Benefit upon receipt at its Home Office of due proof that the death of the Insured resulted, directly and independently of all other causes, from accidental bodily injury, provided that death occurred within ninety days after such injury and while this benefit is in effect.

Nevertheless, many life insurers continue to offer an "accidental means" death benefit, under which the company promises to pay the specified amount:

> . . . upon receipt of due proof that: (1) death of the insured resulted independently of all other causes . . . from bodily injury effected directly and independently of all other causes by violent, external and accidental means and evidenced by some mark or contusion visible on the exterior of the body or by internal injury visibly manifest on an autopsy; and (2) such death occurred within ninety days after such injury was sustained.

The distinction between the terms "accidental death" and "death by accidental means" has occupied an extensive and not very clear chapter in the history of life insurance law, as the following discussion may indicate.

7.1 "Accidental Means"

Accidental means is a technical term, readily and clearly defined by insurance people and insurance lawyers, particularly company counsel, as death resulting from causes that are themselves accidental. In other words, both the cause and the result must have been accidental. Many deaths qualify under this definition and thus present no problem. For instance, if a painter working on a scaffolding should slip, lose his balance, and fall to his death, both the cause—his slipping—and the result—his death—are accidental. The death, therefore, would qualify as death by accidental means.

Many deaths that are popularly and properly termed "accidental," however, are only the accidental results of actions that were themselves intentional and performed in the usual and generally accepted way. Thus, if the painter had intentionally jumped and been killed, it would have been an accidental death but not death by accidental means. That is, the result would have been accidental but the means would not.

This distinction—between accidental means and accidental death—is, in many ways, difficult to explain or to apply; and no matter how the benefit is defined, it is popularly known as "double indemnity"[1] or accidental death. The concept of "accidental means," therefore, often seems unduly technical, not only to beneficiaries and their lawyers but also to the courts. The result is that while some courts interpret the words literally, others have been less technical, and still others have stated flatly that the distinction between accidental means and accidental results will not be followed in their jurisdictions. Often, however, a court will modify a position previously taken, on the basis of the special facts of a case before it, so that it is not possible to make any very definite list of the states where court decisions fall into these various categories.

7.2 When the Distinction Is Upheld

It is a basic legal rule that a court will not "construe" contractual language if that language is plain and unambiguous. The problem with respect to accidental means is that while the term may seem plain and unambiguous to some courts, it seems anything but clear to others. Illustrative of court decisions where the term "accidental means" is given effect in accordance with its generally intended meaning—that is where the benefit is payable only if death resulted from a cause or causes which were themselves accidental—is a case decided in 1954 by the Supreme Court of Tennessee. In that case,[2] the insured was receiving treatment for a stiff neck. The treatment was administered while the patient lay on a table and consisted mainly of manipulating the insured's head and neck. At the conclusion of such a treatment late in 1951, the insured was unable to move. Subsequent surgery revealed a chipped bone in his neck, and he died 36 hours later.

The insurance company took the position that death was the result of a voluntary and intended act and thus was not caused by accidental means as required by the policy. On behalf of the beneficiary, it was contended that "excessive force and pressure was unintentionally and accidentally applied . . . and, as a result, a bone in the neck was accidentally broken." The court held that the benefit was not payable, saying:

---

[1] Although life insurance is not an indemnity contract and therefore this language is not appropriate.

[2] *Avent* v. *National Life and Accident Insurance Company,* Commerce Clearing House Life Cases (2d) 662 (Tenn., 1954).

. . . It is not sufficient that the injury be unusual and unexpected, but the cause itself must have been unexpected and accidental. . . .

The cause of the injury which resulted in the death of Avent was the aforesaid manipulation of his neck. That manipulation was not unexpected or accidental. It was intended by both Avent and the doctor. The means, therefore, producing the injury were not accidental under the rule followed in this State. That being so, the action of the court . . . was correct.

The student's own probably mixed reaction with respect to whether this death should come within the coverage intended under this section of the policy will illustrate the basic problem before the courts. Does one apply the policy language with strict logic, as was done in this case; or should one take a less technical and thus more liberal approach to the question?

7.3 Where the Distinction Has Been Abolished

In the past several years, there has been a definite trend toward modifying the application of the accidental means test even though the policy wording uses this terminology. (Of course, when the policy provides an "accidental death" benefit, the question of accidental means does not arise.) However, even when the additional benefit is provided "in the event of death by accidental means," a number of courts have reached the conclusion that the concepts of accidental means and accidental death are so difficult to distinguish that they will be treated as essentially the same in their jurisdictions. This position is illustrated in the case of *Burr* v. *Commercial Travelers Mut. Acc. Ass'n.,*[3] as follows:

> In this State there is no longer any distinction made between accidental death and death by accidental means, nor between accidental means and accidental results. As was said by Chief Judge Crane in *Mansbacher* v. *Prudential Ins. Co. of America,* 273 N.Y. 140, 143, 144, 7 N.E. 2d 18, 20, 111 A.L.R. 618: "Accidental death means death by accident, and excludes suicide; death occurring through 'accidental means' in this case and under these circumstances is the same as death occurring 'by means of an accident.'" We cited with approval, Richards on the Law of Insurance (3d ed., Sect. 385) to the effect that accidental means are those which produce effects which are not their natural and probable consequences. . . . We pointed out that insurance policies upon which the public relies for security in case of accident should be plainly written in understandable English "free from fine distinctions which few can understand until pointed out by lawyers and judges." A distinction between "accidental means" and "accidental results" is certainly not understood by the average man and he is the one for whom the policy is written.

---

[3] 67 N.E. (2d) 248 (1946).

Thus, in states where the courts follow this reasoning, even though the insurer has used the accidental means language in its policies, the court will treat it no differently from accidental death. This, of course, is the most liberal interpretation from the point of view of the insured.

7.4 Modifications

Many of the courts that continue to give effect to the accidental means terminology if used in a policy have modified its basic meaning, particularly in situations where a voluntary act on the part of the insured results in his injury and death. In fact, the distinction between accidental means and accidental death is so often qualified in its application to specific sets of facts that it is considerably easier to follow in theory than in practice. A brief reference to two often-cited cases may illustrate this point.

1. United States Mutual Accident Association v. Barry. This case,[4] referred to with special frequency, was decided in 1889 by the United States Supreme Court. In it, the insured, a doctor, died from internal injuries after jumping from a platform four feet high. Another doctor, who had made the same jump, testified that the insured made a heavy, inert sound when he landed. The Supreme Court upheld, as correct, the following instructions given by the trial court to the jury:

> In other words if a result is such as follows from ordinary means, voluntarily employed, in a not unusual or unexpected way, then, I suppose it cannot be called a result effected by accidental means . . . you must go further and inquire . . . was there or not any unexpected or unforeseen or involuntary movement of the body, from the time Dr. Barry left the platform, until he reached the ground, or in the act of alighting? . . . Did he accomplish just what he intended to do, in the way he intended to do?

Then the court went further and said:

> . . . if, in the act which precedes the injury, something unforeseen, unexpected, unusual occurs which produces the injury, then the injury has resulted through accidental means.

This case is particularly notable since it has been cited as supporting authority both by courts adhering to a strict interpretation of the term "accidental means" and by those approaching the problem less technically.

2. Landress v. Phoenix Mutual Life Insurance Company. This case[5] was decided in 1934 and concerned the death of a golfer by sunstroke. The court held that it was not a death by accidental means, a decision definitely contrary to the weight of authority today. The case is notable,

---

[4] 131 U.S. 100, 9 Sup. Ct. 755, 33 L. Ed. 60 (1889).
[5] 291 U.S. 401, 54 S. Ct. 461, 78 L. Ed. 934, 90 A.L.R. 1882 (1934).

however, because of the dissenting opinion by Mr. Justice Cardozo in which he said: "The attempted distinction between accidental results and accidental means will plunge this branch of the law into a Serbonian Bog."[6]

Many scholars and jurists have quoted Mr. Justice Cardozo's words approvingly; and the consensus, as well as the trend of decisions today, is away from an overly technical interpretation even in jurisdictions where the distinction has not, in specific language, been abolished. The following are some of the areas in which this trend away from the technical interpretation is apparent.

7.5 Intentional Acts with Unintended Results

In any case where the insured's death resulted from doing exactly what he intended to do in the way he intended to do it, the courts in states where the term accidental means is recognized and given effect will usually hold that the accidental result is not enough to meet the accidental means requirements of the policy. This was the holding in a Missouri case[7] where the insured took an overdose of a prescription drug (paraldehyde) and died. There the court said:

> In poison cases, where the poison is mistaken for a harmless substance, there is lack of knowledge of, and intent to take, poison. There is thus unexpectedness with reference to the means. But in the instant case the insured knew he was taking paraldehyde, and the only thing unexpected was the result.

The court, therefore, held that the means were not accidental. (The insured had done exactly what he intended to do.) However, the opinion continued:

> . . . If it had been shown that when insured was in the act of drinking from the bottle of paraldehyde, intending to take the dose prescribed, his foot slipped causing him to gulp down an excessive amount, the requirement of accidental means would have been satisfied. . . .

In other words, the court said that if there is a·slip or mishap in the action causing the injury, the cause would be accidental as required by the accidental means provision. In this case, however, the court held that taking an overdose of the prescription drug was not such a "slip or mishap" as to make the means accidental.

By contrast, however, a Kansas court has held that taking an overdose of barbiturates was accidental means and the insured's death, therefore,

---

[6] Referring to Lake Serbonis in Egypt in which, according to Herodotus, whole armies were engulfed.

[7] *Murphy v. Western and Southern Life Insurance Company*, 262 S.W. (2d) 340 (Mo. App., 1953).

was death by accidental means within the meaning of that phrase. The court said:

> There is no evidence that the insured was aware of what amount of the drug would produce death. Without repeating all the evidence as to dosages taken by the insured, we think it such the jury could properly infer that insured was in ignorance that the amount she took was a lethal dose and that her death was by accidental means.[8]

It would seem, therefore, that taking an overdose of a prescription drug may or may not constitute accidental means, depending largely on the jurisdiction in which the question is presented. However, where there is a genuine mistake as to the preparation taken, the means seem clearly accidental, as is illustrated in a case[9] where the insured took an arsenic preparation thinking it was a vitamin tonic. There the court held that because of the mistake, the means were accidental, saying: "When death or injury results from taking poison by mistake, the injury or death results from external, violent or accidental means within the terms of a policy of insurance."

An Unknown Factor.   The presence of a factor unknown to the insured has been the deciding point in some cases involving the question of accidental means. Thus, in a New Jersey case[10] where the death of the insured resulted from a smallpox vaccination, the court said: "It is common knowledge that people do not normally react in such a manner to such a common medical practice. . . ." Therefore, there was "something unforeseen, unexpected, and unusual" in the action which caused the death.

It is in accordance with this theory that the majority of courts today hold that death by sunstroke is death by accidental means.

7.6 Intentional Injury Inflicted by Another

As a general rule, if the insured dies as the result of a blow struck by another, without his consent, the death is considered death from accidental means. However, if the insured is the assailant, this may not be true. Some of the borderline problems in this area are suggested in an Illinois case, *Yates v. Bankers Life and Casualty Company*,[11] decided by the Illinois Supreme Court in March, 1953.

In that case, the insured, Yates, who had been physically impaired since the age of eight, limped into the home of the Richardson family, apparently completely by mistake and with no evident intention of doing any harm. He walked into the living room, hands extended and open,

---

[8] *Hawkins v. New York Life Ins. Co.*, 176 Kan. 24, 269 P. (2d) 389 (1954).

[9] *National Life and Accident Insurance Co. v. Karasek*, 240 Ala. 660, 200 So. 873 (1941).

[10] *Bernard v. Union Central Life Insurance Co.*, 117 F. Supp. 456 (1954).

[11] 111 N.E. (2d) 516 (Ill., 1953).

carrying no weapon, making no threats or menacing gestures. He did not answer when spoken to, but the testimony showed that he had been hard of hearing as well as partially paralyzed since childhood. Richardson pushed him by the shoulders, out the front door, where he stumbled, fell backwards, and struck the back of his head. Yates died as the result of a skull fracture.

The court held that death resulted from accidental means, explaining:

> It is evident, therefore, that decedent's bewildered conduct can in no way be analogized to the type of aggressive action involved in the *Cory* and *Hutton* cases, hence, those decisions may not properly be deemed determinative. Moreover, irrespective of those cases, the death of the decedent as a result of a fall under the circumstances presented in this record cannot be deemed to be the natural and probable consequence of his confused conduct in walking into Richardson's house in full view of the occupants without manifesting an evil or aggressive intention. We do not know his purpose in limping into that household, but can only surmise from the nature of his conduct therein that he did not enter pursuant to a malevolent design which could conceivably have led to his death. As in the *Barry* case, the injuries and death of Yates were caused by something unforeseen and unexpected occurring in the course of an intentional act, i.e., the backward fall from the living room to the lower level of the porch and down the step onto the cement sidewalk, where he hit the back of his head and fractured his skull. Therefore, under the concept of "accidental means," adopted and reiterated by the Illinois court, the jury could properly have found that the death of the insured Oliver Yates was caused by accidental means, and that plaintiff, as beneficiary of the policy issued by defendant upon Yates's life, was entitled to recover thereunder.

7.7 Voluntary Assumption of a Known Risk

Generally speaking, if injury or death is the natural and probable result of the insured's voluntary act, there is neither an accident nor accidental means. It is a basic legal principle that a person is presumed to have intended the natural and probable consequences of his own actions. Thus, if the insured deliberately exposes himself to what he knows are dangerous circumstances, it cannot be maintained that his death, if that is the result, was death from accidental means or that it was even an accidental death.

In one case,[12] for instance, the insured, a fireman, was overcome by smoke in the course of fighting a fire. He died as the result. His death was held not to be the result of accidental means because he voluntarily went into the burning building.

Foreseeability. Many cases which deal with situations in which the insured voluntarily undertook to do something dangerous or voluntarily

---

12 *Henderson* v. *Hartford Accident and Indemnity Co.*, 150 S.E. (2d) 17 (1966).

entered a situation he should have known could result in injury or death turn on the question of whether death or serious injury was reasonably foreseeable. This approach is suggested in the Barry case, previously discussed, where the court said that if, in the act that preceded the injury, something unforeseen, unexpected, and unusual occurred to produce the injury, the injury would be the result of accidental means. In other words, "something unforeseen, unexpected, and unusual" could transform an intentional act, performed in the intended way, into an accidental means situation. The test of foreseeability is derived from this reasoning, since a result that is foreseeable is not an accident. As is true of accidental means definitions generally, it is not difficult to follow the reasoning, and the rule is easy to state: if a person performs an act voluntarily and intentionally which, as a reasonable man, would cause him to foresee that death or injury would probably result, the death or injury is not an accident. The difficulty arises in applying the rule to a specific set of facts.

Some courts follow a strict line of reasoning with respect to the meaning of accidental means, and therefore apply this rule with little, if any, modification. This is illustrated in one case[13] where the insured went into his burning home several times in order to retrieve his personal belongings and then collapsed and died. The court held that death was not the result of accidental means as required by the policy, saying:

> . . . (1) it is not enough that the result was unusual, unexpected or unforeseen, but it must appear that the means were accidental; and (2) accident is never present when a deliberate act is performed, unless some additional, unexpected, independent, and unforeseen happening occurs which produces or brings about the result of injury or death.

If death or injury is not the natural or probable result of the act—or where something unforeseen occurs in the doing of the act—it is an accident under the terms of a policy insuring against death or injury from an accident; and, in jurisdictions that no longer recognize a distinction between accident and accidental means, it is also death or injury under accidental means policy provisions.

The significance of whether the result is foreseeable or not is brought out in the case of *Terry* v. *National Farmers Union Life Insurance Company*,[14] a Montana case decided in 1960. There the insured became involved in a fist fight in connection with a card game. The fight was very short and only a few blows were struck, but the insured died shortly afterwards. The beneficiary brought suit for the accidental means death

---

[13] *Johnson* v. *Business Men's Assurance Company of America*, 228 P. (2d) 760 (Wash., 1951).

[14] 138 Mont. 333, 1356 P. (2d) 975.

benefit after her claim for it was denied. It was her contention that death resulting from a fist fight in which no other weapon was used was death from accidental means as required by the policy provision.

The insurer, on the other hand, contended that death as the result of a fist fight, though unexpected and unintended, is nevertheless foreseeable and when the means preceding and producing a result of this kind are voluntary and intentionally committed, death is not the result of accidental means.

The court summarized the general approach to this question, saying that the mere fact that one person assaults another does not necessarily mean that his death cannot be accidental under any circumstances. On the contrary, "such injuries may be regarded as accidental unless they were a natural or probable result of the insured's actions, reasonably foreseeable by him or by a reasonably prudent man in his position."[15]

"If foreseeability is the test," the court continued, "the question of foreseeability in the particular situation is a question of fact to be decided by the jury."

In the trial court, the jury had decided that the result was not foreseeable under the circumstances of this case, and the trial court's verdict was in favor of the beneficiary. The insurance company appealed, and the supreme court affirmed the judgment of the trial court.

Russian Roulette Cases.   Some of the most vivid illustrations of the difficulties involved in interpreting the term "accidental means" are found in cases where the insured was playing Russian Roulette—the "game" where a person places one cartridge in a revolver, spins the cylinder, and then pulls the trigger. As one commentator put it, "If you live, you win."

In one such case,[16] the Georgia Supreme Court considered a situation where the insured picked up his father's revolver "removed all of the cartridges from the cylinder except one, spun the cylinder around, placed the end of the gun barrel to his head, and pulled the trigger. . . ." He had demonstrated this several times before, and the gun had not discharged. In this particular demonstration, however, the remaining cartridge fired and he was killed instantly.

The court said that considerations of the "literally hundreds of cases where the courts have sought to construe such provisions in policies of insurance and interpret the term 'accidental means' brings one to the sharp realization of the great truth in Justice Cardozo's warning 'that trying to distinguish between accidental means and accidental results would plunge this area of the law into a Serbonian Bog.' The cases," the court said, "are in irreconcilable conflict."

---

[15] Quoted from 26 A.L.R. (2d) 399 in *Terry* v. *National Farmers Union Life Insurance Co.*, ibid.

[16] *Thompson* v. *Prudential Ins. Co.*, 84 Ga. App. 214, 66 S.E. (2d) 119 (1951).

Nevertheless, the court in this case quoted from another case[17] a helpful overview of the law in this area, as follows:

> There can be no doubt that there is much confusion in these decisions. Analyses can be of no assistance in harmonizing them or formulating a body of criteria by which all of them can be justified. Most of them rely upon *United States Mutual Accident Ass'n v. Barry*, 131 U.S. 100 (9 S. Ct. 755, 33 L. Ed. 60). Some of the courts relying upon this case seem to have construed "accidental means" as including an intentional act effecting an unusual or unexpected consequence or result. Among the earliest of these decisions, often cited, is *Western Commercial Traveler's Ass'n. v. Smith* (C.C.A.), 85 F. 401, 40 L.R.A. 653. Other courts have drawn a distinction between accidental injury or death and injury or death resulting from accidental means, by looking in the former case to the result, and in the latter to the means. *Landress v. Phoenix Ins. Co.*, 291 U.S. 491, 54 S. Ct. 461, 78 L. Ed. 934, 90 A.L.R. 1382, affirming the decision of this court, 65 F. (2d) 232, is an authoritative and conclusive approval of this distinction. The courts accepting it have generally held that where an injury is the result of a voluntary act, in the performance of which there was a "slip or mishap," it is to be regarded as having been caused by accidental means. . . . Many courts have held, too, that the means are accidental if the doer of the voluntary act was ignorant of a material fact or circumstance which would have caused him, had he known it, to do the act differently or not do it at all. . . . It has been said, though, that the doer of a voluntary act is chargeable with knowledge of the obvious and that which is usual or to be expected, and although he was ignorant of a material fact or circumstance, if he might have known of it by the exercise of ordinary care it cannot be relied upon to effect accidental means. . . . In their application there will be cases, no doubt, in which the courts will feel that the facts and circumstances require a finding that the unknown element was so clearly without the realm of reasonable anticipation as to exclude an hypothesis for accidental means.
>
> "An effect which is the natural and probable consequence of an act or course of action is not an accident, nor is it produced by accidental means. It is either the result of actual design, or it falls under the maxim that every man must be held to intend the natural and probable consequence of his deeds." *Western Commercial Traveler's Ass'n. v. Smith, supra*.

The court said this latter rule was the rule that had been applied in Georgia. It then reviewed the facts in the case under consideration and held that the insured's death was not death by accidental means, saying:

> The insured, so far as the evidence showed, was not "play-acting" or engaging in a pseudo game of Russian Roulette. The cartridges were not blanks. He placed a "live" cartridge in the cylinder of the revolver and made no effort to ascertain the position in which the cartridge stopped in relation to the firing mechanism, before pulling the trigger. Such reck-

---

[17] *Aetna Life Insurance Co. v. Kent*, 73 Fed. (2d) 685 (C.C.A., 1934).

less abandon and exposure to a known and obvious danger can not be said to have been accidental, nor can it be said that his death was effected by accidental means. The most that can be said for such a participant is that he hoped the cartridge would not stop in the firing position when his turn to pull the trigger came. Under these circumstances we think the plaintiff failed to establish that the insured's death was effected by accidental means within the meaning of that term in the policies of insurance and it follows that the trial court did not err in directing a verdict for the defendant, nor in overruling the motion for a new trial.

In another case[18] involving similar facts, the two witnesses who testified in the case seemed to believe that the insured had unloaded the pistol before he raised it to his head and fired. As a matter of fact, the patrolman who investigated the case found that the .38 caliber pistol had two cartridges in it. One had been discharged and the other had not.

The question in this, or in the other case, was whether the death of the insured was the result of accidental means. However, the court did not grant the insurer's motion for a directed verdict in its favor and instead allowed the question to be submitted to the jury, which found in favor of the beneficiary (that it was accidental means). The insurer filed a motion for a new trial and in that trial the judge granted the motion for a directed verdict in favor of the insurer (that it was not accidental means). The Tennessee Court of Appeals reviewed the case to determine if there was sufficient evidence to support the jury's verdict (in favor of the beneficiary) and thus to make the directed verdict an error. It summarized the applicable rule as follows:

> Thus, it appears that where the insured commits a voluntary or intentional act, which because of the exercise of certain safety precautions, would not be expected to result in injury, but there is some mishap or mischance or slip in the doing of the act itself, and as a result of such mishap, mischance or slip, an injury results, such injury is accidental within the meaning of an ordinary accident policy.

In this case, the court continued, there is evidence that the insured attempted to unload the pistol before placing it against his head.

> Therefore, the jury could have concluded from this evidence that the cause of injury was the fact that the decedent accidentally overlooked the presence of two cartridges in the pistol and was not, therefore, such a result as could be expected to occur from the voluntary movements of the decedent in placing the pistol in a position where the falling of its hammer would naturally result in injury or death.

The case, therefore, was sent back for a new trial consistent with the opinion of the appeals court that the jury could have been correct in holding that the means were accidental.

---

[18] *Holmes* v. *Interstate Life and Accident Insurance Co.,* 197 S.W. 2d 551 (C. A. Tenn., 1946).

Perhaps the only reasonable conclusion that can be drawn from these two cases (and from many others) is that cases that seem to present similar sets of facts may differ markedly when examined more closely. Thus even in jurisdictions taking the same general interpretation of the term "accidental means," the decisions may differ widely.

7.8 Other Requirements

The 90-Day Requirement. In a further attempt to clarify the kind of injury referred to, policies providing either the accidental means or the accidental death type of benefit also customarily include a requirement that death must occur within 90 days after the injury. This requirement is intended primarily to reduce problems that may arise when the intervening time lapse might make it difficult if not impossible to prove that the injury was the true cause of the death. Nevertheless, this time limit sometimes raises other questions.

For instance, it is not uncommon for an insured to be injured in an automobile accident or otherwise and lie in a coma for more than 90 days before dying. Is a 90-day limit realistic, then, in this day of medical skill in prolonging life? Current policies of several companies indicate that some thought has been given to this question, and different lengths of time are beginning to be specified. For instance, one company uses a limitation of 120 days, and another uses 180 days.

Second, when it is clear from the circumstances, as in the example given, that death resulted from the accident and that only medical skill prolonged the insured's life beyond the limit specified, is it within the intent of the coverage to deny the benefit simply because death did not occur within the time limit specified? Most court cases on the subject indicate that if a time limit is specified, it will be enforced. In one case,[19] however, the Pennsylvania supreme court held that the 90-day limitation is against public policy.

In that case, the facts were these: On January 10, 1959, the insured was struck by an automobile while crossing a street. After extensive brain surgery, he was kept alive for four and a half years, although he was, in the words of the court opinion, "a complete and hopeless invalid, unable to speak, subject to surgeries, and requiring constant nursing and medical care." The trial court's judgment was for the insurance company, and the beneficiary appealed.

Although there was a strong minority opinion to the contrary, the supreme court held that the 90-day limitation was against public policy, saying:

---

[19] *Burne* v. *Franklin Life Insurance Company,* Pa. Sup. Ct. 301 A. 2d 799 (Pa., 1973).

There are strong public policy reasons which militate against the enforceability of the ninety day limitation. The provision has its origins at a much earlier stage of medicine. Accordingly, the leading case construing the provision predates three decades of progress in the field of curative medicine. Advancements made during that period have enabled the medical profession to become startlingly adept at delaying death for indeterminate periods. Physicians and surgeons now stand at the very citadel of death, possessing the awesome responsibility of sometimes deciding whether and what measure should be used to prolong, even though momentarily, an individual's life. The legal and ethical issues attending such deliberations are gravely complex.

After additional consideration of the legal and ethical issues, the court held that the 90-day exclusion was unenforceable as against public policy. The basic issues are placed more clearly in perspective, however, if the minority opinion is considered, especially the following paragraphs:

It is obvious that the Court is here determining the validity of a contract by means of hindsight. In so doing it fails to observe the fundamental principle that the judicial function in determining the validity of contractual terms must be limited to examination of circumstances known to the parties at the time of contracting. Thus the American Law Institute, in its section dealing with unconscionable contracts or terms, provides:

"If a contract or term thereof is unconscionable *at the time the contract is made* a court may refuse to enforce the contract, or may enforce the remainder of the contract without the unconscionable term, or may limit the application of any unconscionable term as to avoid any unconscionable result." Restatement (Second) of Contracts §234 (Tent. Draft No. 5, March 31, 1970) (emphasis added).

Contrary to what the Court apprently holds, it is my view that we must allow persons to make contracts which are reasonable in the light of circumstances known to them at the time of contracting. More we cannot ask; more we should not impose. Absent a violation of some external rule limiting freedom of contract, a court should not presume to intervene and redraft contracts which were reasonable at the time they were entered into.

Although the majority of life insurance policies continue to require that death result within 90 days of the accident before the accidental death (or accidental means death) benefit will be payable, an informal survey suggests that if a difference of only a few days is involved, some insurers consider waiving the requirement. As a result of this Pennsylvania case, such action may be taken more frequently than has been true in the past.

"External and Violent Means." Although many companies have simplified their requirements in connection with the additional death benefit payable in the event of accidental death, many still continue to state that the benefit will be paid:

". . . upon receipt of due proof that the death of the insured resulted directly and independently of all other causes from bodily injuries effected solely through external, violent and accidental means evidenced by a visible contusion on the exterior of the body, except in the case of drowning or of internal injuries revealed by an autopsy. . . ."

Generally speaking, the courts have been rather liberal in interpreting these requirements. For example, the word "violent" is generally held to contemplate an act that is unusual, but a very slight force is usually held to satisfy this policy requirement.

Decisions have been equally liberal in connection with the requirement that the injury be evidenced by external and visible marks. Any objective symptoms that are discernible or perceptible usually will be held sufficient.

7.9 Risks Not Assumed

At one time or another, insurers have included in their policies a relatively extensive list of situations in which the accidental death benefit will not be paid. Often listed under the heading "Risks Not Assumed," these situations include the following:

* Suicide or self-destruction.
* Self-inflicted injuries.
  Gunshot wounds inflicted by insured.
  Taking poison.
* Inhaling gas or fumes.
* Illness or disease.
* Bodily or mental infirmity.
  Insanity.
  Drugs.
* Committing or attempting to commit assault or felony.
  Violation of law.
  Insurrection or any act attributable thereto.
  Homicide or intentional injuries inflicted by another.
  Police duty.
* Travel or flight in any kind of aircraft except as a fare-paying passenger in a licensed plane operated by a licensed pilot.
* War or any act attributable thereto.
  Military or naval services in time of war.

A current life insurance reference source[20] lists 50 exclusions of this kind currently being used, but most insurers do not use more than a small fraction of them. Probably the most representative exclusions are those

---

[20] 1973 *Life Rates and Data* (National Underwriter).

marked with an asterisk in the above list. Of these, probably the largest number of questions have arisen in connection with whether the death resulted from an accident or bodily infirmity or disease.

7.10 Injury and Disease

As a general rule, if an injury causes a disease and death results, the accident will be considered to be the cause of death. The fact that the insured had a bad heart or other physical infirmities at the time of the injury will not relieve the insurance company of liability under the accidental means death section of its policy if the accident was the direct cause of the death. However, if the injuries were relatively slight and the preexisting condition serious, the result will be different. The fact that a slight injury preceded a heart attack, for instance, will not convert the resulting death into an accidental means death. The test is the actual cause of death.

Proximate Cause. In legal terminology, the test in any of the instances mentioned is expressed in terms of the proximate cause of the death. "Proximate cause" is a term borrowed from the law of torts and means a cause that is either directly responsible for the death or that initiates an unbroken chain of events, each causing the next, which leads to and logically brings about the result alleged. Thus if the means were accidental and the accident was the proximate cause of the death in this sense, the death is generally considered to result from accidental means. If the insured's diseased condition is the proximate cause, the death does not meet the accidental means test, nor is it accidental. The question is a question of fact and will ordinarily be considered and decided by a jury, with appropriate instructions from the judge as to the law.

B. DISABILITY BENEFITS

Disability benefits were first offered in connection with the life insurance contract shortly before the beginning of the present century, in the form of a waiver of premium for disability. A disability income benefit was added not long afterward and provided at first for payment of the face amount of the policy in annual instalments. Later, instalment payments were made in addition to the face amount, which was left intact. It was customary to provide these instalments in the amount of $10 per month for each $1,000 of amount of insurance and, in addition, to waive the premiums on the contract as long as the disability continued.

In offering disability benefits, life insurers were embarking on uncharted seas, for disability does not involve the clear-cut and ascertainable set of facts that death ordinarily presents. On the contrary, it is a highly subjective risk, and the only statistics available to the early life insurers were derived from the experience of the fraternal orders. The latter had been providing disability benefits for some time, but their business was conducted in a very different way from that of the commercial insurers. To complicate the situation further, competition soon caused the companies to increase the benefits they offered, although they had no assurance that their rates were adequate.

By the middle 1920s, it was generally recognized that the premiums for disability income coverages were inadequate; but before any very definite steps could be taken to correct the situation, the depression of the 1930s had struck. With it came some of the most unfavorable experience ever suffered in this or any other field by the life insurance industry. So disastrous was the period that the majority of the larger life insurance companies ceased issuing disability income coverages entirely. After the close of World War II, a number of life insurers resumed offering the coverage, but their rates were based on much more adequate statistics.

Disability income benefits are offered by many life insurance companies in riders that may be attached to a basic life insurance policy. Generally, such benefits are offered in the form of a monthly income payable in the event the insured becomes totally disabled as defined in the policy. Such coverages are customarily classified as either long- or short-term coverages. Typically, a long-term disability income benefit will be payable during the continuance of total disability, as defined in the policy, until the insured's attainment of age 70. Under short-term coverages, income benefits are payable for not more than two to five years, depending upon the provisions of the policy.

Waiver of premium benefits are much more extensively offered and purchased. Briefly, this coverage provides that if the insured becomes totally disabled, as defined in the policy, the company will waive the payment of premiums becoming due during the continuance of the disability. Once the waiver has begun, there is usually no termination date for the benefit except termination of the disability, although the benefit is not usually granted for disability beginning after the insured has reached a specified age, such as 60 or 65.

Both the disability income and disability waiver of premium coverages involve the same basic concepts, as the following discussion will show; and probably the most important is the definition of total disability.

7.11 Definition of the Risk

Exactly what constitutes a disabling condition is a subjective question. A relatively minor physical problem can be disabling to one person; an extensive impairment little more than a challenge to another. Clearly, disability, in the sense of an insurable risk, cannot be defined in terms of physical limitations. As an insurance term, also, the concept must include the idea of economic loss. Disability insurance, therefore, is defined as insurance against loss by reason of disability; and loss in this case is defined in terms of the insured's inability to work.

7.12 Total and Permanent Disability

At one time, it was customary to provide a waiver of premium for disability benefit in language similar to the following:

> Upon receipt at its home office of due proof that the insured has become totally and permanently disabled as hereinafter defined, and subject to all the terms and conditions of this section, the company shall waive the payment of each premium becoming due during the continuance of such disability commencing with the premium on or next following the date of commencement of such disability.

This provision established two major requirements. The disability must be total and it must be permanent. Exactly what constituted total and permanent disability was presumably made clear in a definition that was worded somewhat as follows:

> Total and permanent disability is disability as the result of bodily injury or disease originating after the insurance under the policy and this section took effect so that the insured is and will be thereby wholly prevented from performing any work, following any occupation, or engaging in any business for remuneration or profit, and which disability has continued uninterruptedly for a period of at least six months (such disability of such duration being deemed to be permanent only for the purpose of determining the commencement of waiver of premiums hereunder).

7.13 Total Disability

Exactly when an insured is totally disabled so as to be eligible for benefits under a policy defining total disability in this way is not a simple question, as a multitude of court decisions indicate. Interpretation seemed necessary from an early date; and, since ambiguous policy language will be construed in a way most favorable to the insured or beneficiary, the interpretations have generally relaxed the apparent rigidity of the definition.

Exactly how much interpretation can be justified, however, becomes a question. For instance, if the insured can qualify for benefits only by being so disabled as not to be able to perform "any work," is the C.P.A. who can no longer practice accounting still not totally disabled if he can perform any menial task? On the other hand, is it enough that the insured be only sufficiently disabled to be unable to resume his usual and ordinary occupation? If so, the surgeon with a slight hand impairment would qualify as totally disabled even though he might turn to other fields of medicine, with equal or even greater financial rewards.

Whether an insured is totally disabled within the meaning of the definition is a question of fact to be determined by the jury, but the court instructs the jury as to the law. In clarifying this general definition, therefore, the courts have generally followed one of three interpretations.

The literal view—that if the insured is able to work at anything, he is not totally disabled—has been taken by some courts, though not many. By far the majority of court decisions today take the position that total disability does not mean a state of absolute helplessness, as would be true under the literal interpretation. The reasoning is that benefits payable only if the insured is "wholly prevented from performing any work, following any occupation, or engaging in any business for remuneration or profit" would actually be of limited value. Under this interpretation, an almost complete paralysis would not be disabling, since a person with sufficient gifts and spirit could presumably work at something even under those circumstances.

On the basis that a reasonable interpretation is intended, therefore, the great majority of courts have taken the position that the insurers could not have intended to require a state of complete helplessness, as would be true if the definition were literally applied. Instead, the definition is interpreted by the majority of courts to mean a disability of such a nature as to prevent the insured from working at his customary occupation or any other occupation for which his education and training might reasonably fit him. This is the interpretation followed by most insurers, also.

There have been holdings more liberal to the insured, where the position is taken that if the insured is unable to work at his customary occupation, he is totally disabled within the meaning of this definition. In effect, this rewrites the policy provision. However, most courts do not go this far in their interpretations.

An excellent summary of these views is given in the case of *Anair* v. *The Mutual Life Insurance Company of New York*,[21] where the court said:

> . . . The decisions may be divided into three groups. In the first it is held that disability exists within the meaning of the provision if the insured is unable to work in his usual occupation, thus, in effect, changing the provision to an occupational disability provision. In the second group the test is declared to be inability to work in any occupation. In the third group an intermediate position is taken. The cases in this group recognize that "total disability" is a relative and not an absolute term or concept. For this reason the cases in this latter group make total disability depend on

---

[21] 114 Vt. 217, 42 Atl. (2d) 423, 159 A.L.R. 547 (1945).

whether it is shown that the insured is unable to work at or follow an employment or occupation for which he is qualified, mentally or physically, by age, experience, education, or training. Under this construction the occupation or work of the insured is included and others similar thereto.

7.14 Other Definitions

Many companies today use a policy definition of total disability that incorporates the interpretation followed by the majority of the courts. Illustrative of this type of definition is the following:

> Total disability is disability of the insured as a result of bodily injury or disease which causes the insured to be wholly and continuously prevented thereby from engaging in any gainful occupation for which he is reasonably fitted by reason of his education, training, and experience.

A smaller number of companies use a definition that combines the very liberal interpretation relating to the insured's own occupation with the majority interpretation, as in the following provision:

> Total disability is incapacity, as the result of bodily injury or disease, to engage in an occupation for remuneration or profit. During the first twenty-four months of disability, occupation means the occupation of the insured at the time such disability began; thereafter it means any occupation for which he is or becomes reasonably fitted by education, training, or experience.

Still another approach is occasionally taken, in which a completely objective test is included as an alternative, so that the insured will be considered totally disabled if he is unable to work at any occupation for which he is fitted by training and experience or if the income he is able to earn is reduced to a specified fraction of the income he earned before the disability began. Illustrative of this approach is the following policy definition:

> The insured will be deemed to become totally disabled on the Total Disability Date which is the day when for a period of four consecutive months, because of accidental bodily injury or sickness, either (a) he has been unable to engage in his former occupation or in any other occupation for which he is suited by education, training, or experience, or (b) his average monthly Earned Income has been reduced to one-fourth or less of his former monthly income.

Variations such as these in the definition used by many of the life insurance companies today indicate a considerable willingness to modify the traditional approach in order to resolve an admitted problem. Even so, many life insurers still define total disability as inability to "perform any work, follow any occupation, or engage in any business," and the majority either use this definition or refer to "any occupation for which he is fitted by education, training, or experience." Regardless of the exact wording, however, most insurers interpret their definitions as if they used the latter approach unless specific language referring to the occupation of the insured is used.

An additional and separate concept of total disability is also commonly provided for. This concept defines total disability as the total loss of the use of both legs, or both arms, or one leg and one arm, or the total loss of the sight of both eyes. Usually, this definition has no reference to whether the insured is able to work. The following provision is typical of this approach:

> The total and irrecoverable loss of the sight of both eyes, or of the use of both hands, or of both feet, or of one hand and one foot shall be considered total disability even if the insured shall engage in an occupation.

7.15 When Is "Total" Disability "Permanent"?

If the courts have been somewhat uncertain as to the interpretation of the term "total disability," they have been only slightly less divided with respect to the meaning of a permanent disability. The vagaries of human existence being what they are, the only truly permanent disability obviously is one that continues until the death of the insured. However, this is scarcely what the insurers meant. They have long included in their policies provisions relating to the cessation of benefits upon recovery of the insured. Obviously, under these circumstances, they cannot have contemplated only disability that continues until the death of the insured. Again, therefore, there is the entering wedge of ambiguity and the necessity of interpretation by the courts.

It seems relatively certain that in the early days the insurance companies intended, by a permanent disability, to indicate a disability of long-term duration. How long, however, is a different question; and what of the disability from which the insured has already recovered at the time suit is brought for the disability benefits?

A majority of the courts have held that a permanent disability is a disability lasting for an indefinitely continuous period of time. Often, therefore, if the insured had recovered at the time the suit was brought, his disability was considered not to have been permanent and he was not entitled to the benefit. Even during the continuance of disability, some courts have given the words "permanent disability" their ordinary meaning, that the disability shall continue until the end of the insured's lifetime. However, the more reasonable point of view seems to be the view that is summarized in *Kramer* v. *Metropolitan Life Insurance Company,*[22] where the court quoted from a prior Ohio case as follows:

> The term "permanent disability," as used in a disability insurance policy providing for payments to one who "has become totally and permanently disabled so as to be unable at any time to perform any work or engage in any business for compensation or profit" does not mean that such disability must necessarily continue for the remainder of the life of the insured, but that it shall, with reasonable probability, continue for some indefinite period of time.

For a long time, most life insurers used the words "total and permanent" to describe the disability of the insured that would entitle him to disability insurance benefits. It was also customary, as it is today, to require that the total disability must have continued for at least six months before benefits would become payable. Efforts were sometimes made, therefore, to have this six-month period construed to mean that any total disability that had continued for the period named would be presumed to be permanent in the literal sense of the word. Benefits would then be payable without further question. As a general rule, however, the courts have interpreted the six-month (sometimes four-month) period to be a mere waiting period, included in the policy for the purpose of relieving the insurer of the expense of having to consider and investigate numerous premature claims.

If the words "total and permanent" are used together, it is customary to emphasize that the six-month waiting period is not to be interpreted to indicate permanence in the literal sense, by using language such as the following:

> If, and only if, total disability as herein defined has existed uninterruptedly during the lifetime of the Insured for at least six months, it shall be deemed to have been and to be permanent, but only for the purpose of determining the commencement of liability hereunder.

Many insurers no longer refer to a "permanent" disability in any sense. Instead, they provide disability benefits if total disability has continued "uninterruptedly" for at least a specified length of time, as illustrated in the following policy provision:

> If the insured becomes totally disabled as defined below, the company will waive the payment of each premium becoming due under this policy during the continuance of such disability, commencing with the premium due on or next following the date of commencement of such disability, subject to the terms and conditions of this Disability Section.
>
> Waiver of premiums shall be allowed only for total disability which shall have commenced prior to the insured's attainment of age sixty and

---

[22] 144 Ohio St. 13, 56 N.E. (2d) 248 (1944).

which shall have continued uninterruptedly for a period of at least six months during the lifetime of the insured.

This is a more realistic approach, since it establishes six months only as a measurable period after which the benefits will become available.

7.16 Risks Not Assumed

As is true of the accidental death benefit provision, insurers usually specify some risks not assumed with respect to the total disability of the insured. One illustrative provision lists such risks, as follows:

> *Risks Not Assumed.* The Company shall in no event incur any liability under this agreement if total disability shall result directly or indirectly, wholly or partly, from any of the following: (a) intentionally self-inflicted injury; (b) war, declared or undeclared; or (c) service in the military, naval or air forces of any country at war, declared or undeclared.

Often the only exclusions are disability resulting from intentionally self-inflicted injury and that resulting from war. Occasionally, other causes are listed, such as "committing or attempting to commit a felony" or "participation in parachute jumping, sky diving, or skin or scuba diving"; but most companies use only two or three exclusions, and intentionally self-inflicted injury and war are the most common.

C. RIDERS THAT LIMIT COVERAGE

Riders are frequently used to limit the insurance otherwise provided by the life insurance contract, and, as a result, they sometimes create conflicts or raise other legal problems. As a general rule, however, such questions are not so much the result of the form in which the limitation is introduced as the nature of the limitation itself. The use of riders is relatively commonplace, and their effectiveness as a part of the contract is not usually questioned. The effect of the provisions they introduce into the contract, therefore, is ordinarily no different than if the provisions were a part of the basic contract in the beginning.

7.17 The War Limitation Rider

The hazard of war is generally acknowledged not to be capable of prediction. Obviously it is impossible to predict wars in the first place, and it is equally impossible to predict the death toll after a war has begun. Thus statistical studies on which life insurance rates are based do not generally include war deaths; and some underwriting limitations are, therefore, generally thought necessary with respect to such hazards.

Acceptable solutions have not been easy. To refuse to insure persons who are subject to the hazard is one possible solution; and some insurers have followed this practice to some extent. Limiting the amount of coverage that will be offered to such persons constitutes a second possible approach. The third approach is to issue life insurance as applied for but with what is generally called a war hazard limitation rider.

In general terms, a war limitation rider is a special section of a life insurance policy that limits the liability of the insurer in the event that the insured loses his life as the result of war. It is used only during periods when young people are rather widely subject to call to military duty and when the proposed insured is in an age group that makes him particularly subject to such call. The use of the rider, therefore, varies according to the company's risk selection practices, and these practices vary according to the existence or imminence of a state of war. Since 1940, however, there have been so few periods in which military action has not at least been a possibility that the use of this rider has been a relatively constant consideration with most insurers during that period.

It should be remembered, however, that the use of this rider is not as negative as it might seem. As a matter of fact, it does not represent so much a limitation on coverage in the broad sense as a practical way of issuing coverage that would not otherwise be made available to a large number of young persons in time of war or when war is imminent. In other words, the use of a war limitation rider permits the issuance of insurance that would not otherwise be provided, so that the insured does have coverage for all risks except those relating to war, whereas without the rider he might not obtain any coverage at all.

The "Result" Clause.   Although war clauses are worded differently, a typical clause reads as follows:

> It is agreed that notwithstanding any contrary provisions, the following are risks not assumed under this policy:
>
> (1) Death as the result of war or an act of war or as the result of the special hazards incident to military service for any country at war, if the cause of death occurs or has its inception while the insured is outside the home area and in military service for any country, provided such death occurs while the insured is outside the home area and in military service for any country or within six months after (a) the insured's return to the home area or (b) termination of military service, whichever occurs first; and
>
> (2) Death within two years from the Policy Date, or the Issue Date, whichever is the earlier, as the result of war or an act of war or as the result of the special hazards incident to any civilian noncombatant occupation associated with the military, naval, or air forces of any country at war, if the cause of death occurs or has its inception while the insured is outside the home area and engaged in such occupation, provided such death occurs while the insured is outside the home area and engaged in such

occupation or within six months after (a) the insured's return to the home area or (b) termination of such occupation, whichever occurs first. . . .

Briefly, paragraph (1) of this provision means that if the insured is in the military service, his death as the result of war or an act of war will not be covered if the cause of death occurs while he is outside the home area and he either dies there or dies within six months after he returns home or leaves the military service, if earlier. Paragraph (2) applies to the insured who is not in the military service but is engaged in a civilian noncombatant occupation "associated with the military, naval, or air forces of any country at war." If this person dies as the result of war, his death, too, will be a risk not assumed, if the cause of death occurs outside the home area and his death occurs either outside the home area or within six months after he returns to the home area or termination of his occupation, if earlier. "Home area" must be defined, according to the New York Insurance Law, as the states of the United States, the District of Columbia, the Canal Zone, the Virgin Islands, Puerto Rico, and Canada.

This provision illustrates the prevailing approach taken today—the use of the so-called result clause. When this approach is taken, death that occurs as a result of military activities is a risk not assumed under the policy. If death results from some cause unrelated to such service, even though the insured is in military service at the time, it will be covered in the same way it would have been if no war clause had been included in the policy. In contrast to this "result" approach, a different wording has been used in what are called "status" clauses.

The "Status" Clause. The status war clause, not widely used today, simply exempted from coverage any death that occurred while the insured was in military service, regardless of its cause. With this type of clause, the insured had no life insurance protection during the period of his military service.

Use of the status clause had the double disadvantage of creating poor public relations and going much farther than necessary to compensate for the added risk created by the insured's military service. When the result type of war clause is used, the risk assumed by the company is limited only with respect to the extra risk due to war. This makes the insurance effective for the man in military service on the same basis as for anyone else unless he is killed in battle or as the result of an act peculiar to war.

With the status clause, the effect is quite different. Assume, for instance, that two young men, aged 22, are involved in an automobile accident near their homes and both are killed. One is on leave from the army; the other is a civilian. Both have life insurance contracts with the same insurer, and both contracts have a war limitation rider. Under the result type of wording, both contracts would be effective, and the beneficiaries of the insureds would receive the face amount of the policies. Under the status type of wording, however, only the beneficiary of the civilian would receive the full proceeds. The soldier's beneficiary would ordinarily receive only the amount of premiums paid or the reserve, whichever was the greater.

The payment only of premiums or the reserve in this type of situation is difficult to explain, and for that reason, among others, the majority of companies today use the result type of wording. As a practical matter, every company that does business in New York uses this type of wording because of a provision in the New York Insurance Law, as follows:

> In permitting war exclusions it is the legislative intent that such exclusions are not to be construed or interpreted as exclusions because of the status of the insured as a member of such forces or units or because of the presence of the insured as a civilian in a combat area or area adjacent thereto. Such permissible exclusions shall be construed and interpreted according to the fair import of their terms so as not to exclude deaths due to diseases or accidents which are common to the civilian population and are not attributable to special hazards to which a person serving in such forces or units is exposed in the line of duty.[23]

What Is War?   Since the majority of companies use the result type of war clause rather than the status type today, the major legal problem that is involved is the question of what constitutes war. This question was raised on a significant scale at the outset of World War II in connection with the deaths at Pearl Harbor. Some three thousand military and naval personnel were killed there on December 7, 1941, but in four different cases on the subject it was held that a state of war, as that word was used in the war clause of life insurance policies, did not exist until war was officially declared by Congress on December 8, 1941. The Korean and Vietnam conflicts presented an even more difficult question, for in those instances war was never officially declared.

Court decisions on the subject have varied, depending primarily on whether the court has taken a technical or more general approach. For instance, in the case of *Beley* v. *Pennsylvania Mutual Life Insurance Company*[24] the court held that the word "war" must be given its strict constitutional meaning. War was not actually declared by Congress; therefore, the activity in Korea was not war. A New Jersey court, considering the same question shortly afterward, held that the words must be given their "ordinary and generally accepted meaning" rather than their technical or legal meaning, and held that the Korean hostilities constituted war in the practical or ordinarily accepted meaning of the

---

[23] New York Insurance Law, Section 155, subsection 2.
[24] 373 Pa. 231, 95 A. (2d) 202 (Pa., 1953).

word. This latter point of view has been followed by the majority of the appellate courts and the federal district courts, and some of the philosophy of these decisions is summarized in one case[25] as follows:

(1) For this court to hold that the so-called "Korean Action" was not a war would be closing our eyes to the events of our times and to the world in which we live. The world of chivalry in conflict between nations ended abruptly with the infamous attack on Pearl Harbor. The progress of science in the art of war has so far advanced that any thought we may entertain that our nation would be allowed an opportunity to formally declare war is certainly burying our heads in the sand to reality.

Not only has the machinery of attacking another nation been refined to a point that has virtually disposed of warning, but the weapons of attack and their destructive power are so devastating as to be nearly incomprehensible. In this world of restlessness in every country, with our resources, both material and human, being used in every corner of the earth, and possibly in the near future into outer space, the law must recognize what we know as individuals. To say that the attack on Pearl Harbor, the action in Korea, the activities in Viet Nam are not wars, and that those killed were not killed by war, is saying, in effect, that war is not war.

Attacks without warning, so-called police actions throughout the world, American service men on every continent, are a fact of life and a part of our way of life, whether we approve or not. Freedom for mankind is challenged every minute of every day and its enemies are unconcerned with the formalities of yesterday and will resort to any means they feel necessary to accomplish their desired goal.

The parties here agreed, as stated in the written contract of insurance entered into between them, that "war" means "war, declared or undeclared." We must give effect to what the parties expressly agreed upon and we fail to find any authority, and none has been called to our attention which authorizes us to disregard the express language of the parties, or place a strained interpretation thereon contrary to the intent of the parties expressed in words of common understanding and acceptation.

According to this judicial reasoning, the Korean action was held to be war for the purpose of determining the applicability of the war exclusion rider, even though war had not been declared by Congress.

Later decisions involving the conflict in Vietnam raise essentially the same basic questions as those relating to the Korean conflict. One case[26] in which these questions were discussed summarized the decisions of other courts as follows:

. . . So we must decide whether, in the context of the insurance policy, the United States is engaged in war in Vietnam.

---

[25] *Stucker* v. *College Life Insurance Co. of America,* 208 N.E. (2d) 731 (Ind., 1965).

[26] *Jackson* v. *North America Assurance Society of Virginia, Inc.,* 212 Va. 177, 183 S.E. 2d 160 (Va., 1971).

"There is war in the legal sense, and in the material sense. Legal war exists when there is an interruption of all pacific relations between nations and an authorized contestation of armed forces by the constitutional authority of the nations, while material war is evidenced by the use of armed forces by the parties." *New York Life Ins. Co. v. Bennion,* 158 F. 2d 260, 266 (10th Cir. 1946). [Dissenting opinion.]

Our use of armed forces in Vietnam does not constitute war in the legal sense because Congress has not declared war against North Vietnam. U.S. Const. art. I, §8. For the purposes of this opinion, we may assume that our use of armed forces there does constitute war in the material sense.

The authorities differ sharply in construing the word war as used in exclusionary clauses of insurance policies. Some assign the legal meaning, while others assign the material meaning. See *Hammond* v. *National Life & Acc. Ins. Co.,* 243 So. 2d 902 (La. App. 1971). . . . We construe "war" in the exclusionary clause before us to mean war in its legal sense. . . .

In this case, the action in Vietnam was held not to be war because Congress had not declared war.

7.18 The Aviation Limitation Rider

The risk of death as the result of aviation activities is not as generally or as completely excluded from life insurance contracts as that of death as the result of war. In the early days of aviation, of course, when there were no statistics by which to measure the added risk, it was common to exclude aviation in most policy forms. As the insurers gained experience, however, and particularly as the safety of flying increased, it became possible to demonstrate statistically that the added risk was minimal in many areas and to measure it with reasonable accuracy in others. Consequently, the use of such devices as a flat extra premium and exclusions from the accidental means death benefit made it possible to cover the risk of death as the result of flying in all but its most hazardous forms.

Insurers still use exclusions concerning military flying and such hazardous activities as crop dusting. By and large, however, the risk of death as a fare-paying passenger on a regularly scheduled flight of a common carrier is rarely excluded from the risk assumed, and many individuals who fly their own planes can now be insured at standard rates for reasonable amounts. Aviation limitation riders, therefore, are rarely used today except in individual cases involving such hazardous pursuits that an extra premium is not a practical solution to the problem. The legal problems resulting from the use of aviation riders are, of course, reducing as the use of the rider itself is reduced.

D. GUARANTEED INSURABILITY

Reducing term coverages, level term coverages, and term coverages on one or several other members of the insured's family can be and often are added to the basic life insurance contract by rider. Usually they do not present legal problems differing in any major respect from those applicable to the basic policy. When the guaranteed insurability rider is added, however, a new and different set of facts is presented, along with the possibility of new problems. Briefly, the guaranteed insurability option provides insurance against the risk of becoming uninsurable and offers the option of purchasing, at various dates in the future, additional policies of not more than a stated amount, without evidence of insurability.

The risk of becoming uninsurable has long been recognized as an important reason for purchasing insurance on the lives of children, but until recently the only hedge against it was to purchase as much insurance as possible in the early years. In 1957, however, this risk was first recognized as insurable, with the offering of the guaranteed insurability coverage under which one did not have to purchase the entire amount of insurance at the time of his first application.

The basic idea is simple. If this coverage is applied for, a section is included in the policy which grants the insured, at the time he applies for the first policy, the right to purchase additional policies, without evidence of insurability, at specific intervals over a considerable length of time, usually terminating with his attainment of age 40. Illustrative of the basic promise under such a rider is the following:

> *Benefit.* On each of the Option Dates specified above the company agrees that, subject to all the terms and conditions of this section, the owner may purchase a new policy on the life of the insured without evidence of insurability, as follows:
>
> (1) The policy and this Optional Additional Insurance Section must be in force on the Option Date.
>
> (2) The amount of insurance which may be purchased on any Option Date under this Optional Additional Insurance Section shall not be less than $5,000 nor shall it be greater than the Option Amount.
>
> (3) Proper written application and the first premium for the new policy must be received by the company at its home office or a regional office on or within sixty days prior to the Option Date.
>
> (4) The Policy Date of the new policy shall be the Option Date on which such policy is purchased.
>
> (5) The new policy may be any whole life or endowment plan regularly issued by the company on the Option Date for the amount of insurance being purchased; provided, however, that such new

policy will not include any provisions granting benefits in the event of total and permanent disability or granting additional insurance specifically against death by accidental means unless agreed to by the company on receipt of such evidence of insurability as may be requested at the time the option is exercised.

The new policy shall be issued upon a form in use on the Option Date, at the then premium rate for the attained age of the insured in the then premium class of the insured, and subject to any limitations of risk then outstanding against this policy or then being applied to all such newly issued policies for the insured's age and sex.

(6)   The new policy will be endorsed to provide that the time periods of the Incontestability and Suicide provisions thereof will commence on the date of this Optional Additional Insurance Section.

(7)   The right to purchase a new policy under the terms of this Supplementary Agreement as of any particular Option Date shall, if not exercised, expire on that Option Date, but such expiry shall not affect the company's obligation to issue a new policy as of any subsequent Option Date.

In this provision, the option date is the date on which the insured is permitted to purchase a new policy. Generally, there are several option dates, which depend upon the insured's age when he applies for the benefit. The option amount is the face amount of the base policy up to a stipulated maximum.

This provision gives the insured-owner the right to purchase a new policy, for an amount not less than $5,000 nor more than the option amount, on the anniversary of the policy date following his attained age of 25, 28, 31, 34, 37, and 40, subject to the conditions specifically set forth.

Such conditions limit the company's possible liability and impose some restraint on possible antiselection. However, the possible liability is considerable, since a person at age 21 could purchase $10,000 of life insurance with this provision, become uninsurable prior to age 25, and still acquire as much as $60,000 more insurance by age 40 at standard premium rates. The potential value of the option under these circumstances is obvious.

Many companies also offer a guaranteed insurability rider under which the option to purchase an additional policy may be advanced in the event of marriage or the birth of a child. These are rather aptly called the "marriage and stork" options, and they often provide some automatic term life insurance for a specified period after the event mentioned has occurred. For instance, if the rider provides this privilege and the next available option date is 1976, the owner would ordinarily be required to wait until that date to take advantage of it. If he were married in 1975, however, the 1976 option date would be advanced to 1975 and he could make his 1976 purchase in 1975. As previously noted, term life insurance equal to that available under the option might be provided for a specified period—90 days, for instance—or until the exercise of the option, if sooner, following his marriage. The same privilege would be available to him on the birth of a child. In either case, the option, once used, would not be available on the date originally specified but succeeding options would be unaffected.

Many companies also provide a special privilege for the insured who is disabled on the option date. If premiums are being waived on the option date because of the insured's total disability, the coverage may include the privilege of purchasing a specially designated policy, such as life paid up at 85, for example, and having premiums on the new policy waived, as well as those under the base policy. (A special policy is customarily designated in order to preclude antiselection—for example, if the policy-owner could otherwise purchase an endowment policy.)

This is a relatively new coverage, and legal problems have not had much time to develop. It is notable, however, that the New York Insurance Department has anticipated the possibility of one type of problem. This is the operation of the contestability and suicide provisions under each new policy issued under such options. The department has, therefore, issued a specific directive requiring that each new policy issued under this type of option contain an amendment specifically providing that the incontestability and suicide periods of the new policy run from the policy date of the original policy—that is, the policy containing the guaranteed insurability rider. Thus the insured not only purchases a new contract without evidence of insurability but he also purchases an incontestable policy on each option date, after the expiration of two years from the date the original policy is issued.

SUMMARY

Accidental Death

Benefits payable in the event of death by accident are often provided by rider and fall into two main classes: the accidental means death benefit and the accidental death benefit. The accidental means death benefit is payable in cases where death results from a cause that is itself accidental. That is, both the cause and the result must have been accidental. By contrast, an accidental death is the accidental result of an act that may not itself have been accidental. The accidental death benefit is more frequently offered today than the accidental means death benefit, although many companies continue to use the accidental means language.

Court cases concerning the accidental means benefit fall into three large groups. One group is made up of cases in which the policy wording is interpreted to carry out the intent of the insurer and provide a true accidental means death benefit. A second group views the distinction as being so highly technical that it is not enforced in their jurisdictions. A third group maintains some distinction but takes a very liberal view of what constitutes accidental means.

Where an intentional act has been performed in the manner intended, with only the result being accidental, it is not considered to be death by accidental means in jurisdictions where the accidental means distinction is strictly upheld. The trend, however, is to hold that any "slip or mishap" in the action taken is sufficient to meet the accidental means requirement. Thus the presence of an unknown factor or a mistake may transform an intended action into accidental means.

Decisions differ as to whether death as the result of an unusual sensitivity to a medication is death from accidental means, but as a general rule, this situation is not interpreted as accidental means in the strict sense of the term.

If the insured dies as the result of an injury intentionally inflicted by another without the insured's consent, it is considered to be death by accidental means. If the insured is the aggressor, however, or if he takes deliberate risks, it is not death by accidental means.

If injury or death is the natural and probable result of the insured's voluntary act, it is not the result of accidental means and there is no accident. One of the tests used in this situation concerns whether the result was foreseeable. If it was foreseeable, there was no accident; if it was not foreseeable, the death or injury will be held to have been accidental.

Other requirements are specified to define the kind of risk that is intended to be covered. One of these requires that death shall have occurred within 90 days of the injury. Other common requirements in the accidental means definition are that the means must have been violent and evidenced by external and visible marks. Insurers also commonly list a number of situations in which neither the accidental death nor accidental means death benefit will be paid. Commonly called "risks not assumed," these include death resulting from suicide or self-destruction, gunshot wounds inflicted by the insured, taking poison, committing or attempting to commit a felony, and many others, although an individual insurer probably will have only a few exclusions in its policies.

Generally, if death results from a combination of accident and pre-existing disease, it is considered accidental if the accident was the proximate cause of the death. "Proximate cause" means a cause that is either directly responsible for the result or that begins an unbroken chain of events, each causing the next, which leads to and brings about the alleged result.

Waiver of Premium for Disability

Disability benefits have been offered by life insurers in connection with life contracts since shortly before 1900. Offering a disability income benefit, however, proved a hazardous move, since rates were not adequate for the benefits provided. Life company experience with the coverage during the 1930s was extremely hazardous. More recently, life insurers have resumed offering the coverage, but at much more scientific rates. The more commonly offered benefit, however, is the waiver of premium for disability benefit.

Definitions. The usual definition of disability requires disability such that the insured is "wholly prevented from performing any work, following any occupation, or engaging in any business for remuneration or profit." The disability must also have continued uninterruptedly for at least six months before the benefit is available.

Deciding when a disability is total has been difficult under this definition, and court decisions bear this out. Most life insurers and the majority of courts interpret this general definition to mean disability that prevents the insured from working at his customary occupation or any other for which his education and training might reasonably fit him. Some courts have held that it is only necessary that he be unable to work at his usual occupation, and still others take the literal view that he is not totally disabled if he can work at anything. Definitions reflecting each of these views are used by some insurers, but by far the majority define total disability as the inability either to work at any occupation or to work at an occupation for which the insured is fitted by education, training, and experience.

Benefits are also usually payable if the insured loses the sight of both eyes, the use of both hands or both feet, or the use of one hand and one foot, regardless of whether the insured is able to follow an occupation for profit.

According to the majority of court decisions on the subject, a permanent total disability is merely a total disability that lasts for an indefinitely continuous period of time. The requirement that total disability must have continued for a specified period such as four or six months is interpreted as a waiting period, to establish how long such a disability must continue in order to qualify the insured for the benefit; it does not create a presumption of permanence in the literal sense of the term and many companies no longer use the term "permanent" in their definitions.

Risks not assumed under this coverage include injuries resulting from suicide attempts or any hazards of war.

Riders That Limit Coverage

The war limitation rider is used to limit coverage under a policy so that war deaths are not covered. If this limitation is worded to exclude deaths that result from war, it is commonly referred to as a result clause. If it is worded to exclude death "while in military service," it is a status clause. Most insurers today use the result type of clause, and insurers whose policies must meet the provisions of the New York Insurance Law are required to use this type of wording.

Court decisions differ as to whether the word "war" should be given its strict constitutional meaning, thus requiring a declaration of war by Congress, or its ordinary and accepted meaning—as armed hostilities. One court has distinguished between these concepts as "legal war" and war "in the material sense." War in the legal sense requires a contest by armed forces that is authorized by the constitutional authority of the warring nations.

Guaranteed Insurability

A popular coverage offered in connection with the life insurance contract today is often referred to as "guaranteed insurability." This benefit is provided as an option in connection with regularly issued life insurance contracts and simply provides the privilege of purchasing additional life insurance at later, specified dates, in amounts within specified limits, without evidence of insurability. Riders of this kind sometimes permit options to be exercised at an earlier date than specified (advanced) in the event of marriage or the birth of a child. Although this coverage is simple in wording, there is a possible legal problem relating to the interpretation and operation of the contestable and suicide periods under the policies purchased as a result of the exercise of the options. A regulation of the New York Department of Insurance requires that such policies be amended at issue to provide that the contestable and suicide periods shall be interpreted as running from the date of issue of the original policy.

ILLUSTRATIVE CASE

The following case illustrates some of the problems which have been discussed earlier in this chapter. Extensive citations have been omitted from the opinion in the interest of brevity, but otherwise the actual reasoning of the court is presented in full in order that the student may see for himself the approach taken by a court in considering questions of this kind.

RALEY, *Appellant*, v.
LIFE & CASUALTY INS. CO. OF TENNESSEE, *Appellee*[27]
District of Columbia, Municipal Court of Appeals

CAYTON, Ch. J.: The question on this appeal is whether an industrial accident insurance policy covered death caused by sunstroke. The action was brought by appellant as widow and beneficiary under the policy, which was written on the life of Thomas F. Hoy. It was stipulated[28] that Mr. Hoy collapsed at an intersection in Arlington, Virginia, on a June afternoon in 1952, and was taken to a hospital where he died several hours later. It was also stipulated that the "sole and exclusive cause of the death of Thomas F. Hoy was exposure to the sun's rays, that is to say, sunstroke." An official weather report, submitted under the same stipulation, revealed that an extreme heat wave was in progress in this locality at the time of the mishap. The trial court ordered judgment for the insurance company and plaintiff brings this appeal.

The policy insured "against loss of life through accidental means" and recited, "if the insured sustains drowning or bodily injury effected solely through violent, external and accidental means, and if such drowning or bodily injury is the direct, independent and proximate cause of the death of the insured within 90 days from the date of such injury, and if such death is not caused or contributed to by disease or infirmity, the Company will on surrender of the policy pay the principal sum specified herein. . . ."

It seems clear, as the insurance company concedes, that because the policy was executed and delivered in this jurisdiction, the rights of the parties are to be decided according to District of Columbia law. . . .

Urging us to declare that under the law of this jurisdiction a policy of this kind does not cover death caused by sunstroke, appellee insurance company relies on *Landress* v. *Phoenix Mutual Life Insurance Company*, 291 U.S. 491 (1934). There the Supreme Court, in a sunstroke case, said: ". . . the carefully chosen words defining liability distinguish between the result and the external means which produces it. The insurance is not against an accidental result. The stipulated payments are to be made only if the bodily injury, though unforeseen, is effected by means which are external and accidental. . . ." The court ruled that the insurance company was not liable.

If the language just quoted must be regarded as governing all situations of this kind, the answer in this case would be plain and the beneficiary would be out of court. (We later discuss the dissenting opinion of CARDOZO, J., which has been widely quoted and generally approved.)

*   *   *   *   *

Thus whatever the effect of the *Landress* decision in the State of Tennessee where the case arose, it cannot be said to have declared general common law or to be binding on State or Federal courts generally. A large number of Federal as well as State courts have departed from the view expressed in *Landress* and expressly ruled that death by sunstroke is a death caused by

---

[27] 117 A. (2d) 110 (D.C. C.A., 1955).
[28] Stipulated points are facts that are agreed to and thus do not have to be proved.

accidental means and is not merely an accidental result. The decided trend of recent decisions establishes that the majority view today is that sunstroke is covered by this type of policy, and that disability or death induced by sunstroke is caused by "accidental means." . . .

Another group of cases, not dealing specifically with sunstroke, advances the general proposition that the term "accidental means" is synonymous with "accidental result" and "accidental death." . . .

We refer also to several well considered workmen's compensation cases in which the same general views have been expressed. . . .

In their brief, counsel for appellee urge that workmen's compensation cases should be disregarded. They say: "The spirit and intent of the workman's compensation law vary considerably from the principles of contract and insurance law, and to apply the reasoning of workman's compensation cases to the issue here would be error."

While we recognize that these are two different fields of insurance law, we cannot agree that for the purpose of the single question before us there is any reason in logic or common sense for applying a stricter rule in one than in the other. In both situations the same basic test applies in determining whether an "accidental means" produced the fatality.

Cases taking the contrary view are listed in the majority opinion in the *Landress* case, and in Appleman, Insurance Law and Practice, Vol. 1, Sec. 447.

We have already mentioned that in *Landress, supra,* there was a dissenting opinion by CARDOZO, J. That opinion has several times been quoted, adopted and followed by other courts, and it seems wise to quote parts of it here:

> Sunstroke, though it may be a disease according to the classification of physicians, is none the less an accident in the common speech of men. . . . The suddenness of its approach and its catastrophic nature . . . have made that quality stand out when thought is uninstructed in the mysteries of science. . . . Violent it is for the same reason, and external because the train of consequences is set in motion by the rays of the sun beating down upon the body, a cause operating from without.
>
> In my view this man died from an accident. What killed him was a heat-stroke coming suddenly and unexpectedly upon him while at work. Such a stroke is an unusual effect of a known cause, often, no doubt, threatened, but generally averted by precautions which experience, in this instance, had not taught. It was an unlooked for mishap in the course of his employment. In common language, it was a case of accidental death.

Textwriters have pointed to the dissent, not only as stating the "better" rule, but as expressing the view now adopted by a majority of courts. Vance on Insurance, 3d Ed., p. 949; Richards on Insurance, Vol. 1, Section 17, p. 59. Appleman, Insurance Law and Practice, Vol. 1, Section 447. At page 555 the author says: "The dissenting opinion of Justice Cardozo presents one of the most brilliantly reasoned opinions in the field of insurance law, and certainly the best at expressing the reasons in back of the rule adopted by the majority of jurisdictions."

In this jurisdiction there has been only one appellate decision on the subject and that made the flat declaration that death from sunstroke is an accidental injury. *Fidelity & Casualty Co. of New York v. Burris,* 61 App. D.C. 228, 59 F. 2d 1042 (1932). There the deceased was engaged in manual labor on an intensely hot day. He collapsed on his way to a water barrel and was taken to a hospital where he died later that same day "from heat prostration or sunstroke." The broad language of the opinion, per GRONER, J., gives the answer to our question:

> The decision of the case turns, we think, upon the answer to two questions: *First, is death from sunstroke an accidental injury?* Second, did the sunstroke arise "out of and in the course of employment"? *Both questions should be answered in the affirmative.* [Italics supplied.]
>
> The term "accidental injury," as used in the act, means any unexpected misfortune or mischance resulting in some form of bodily injury—an injury due to accident or caused by some sudden or unexpected occurrence. Deceased admittedly was killed by sunstroke. That was the injury. It was sudden and unexpected, and hence accidental. . . .

It is true that it was a workmen's compensation case, but there was nothing in the decision limiting its application to that class of case, or indicating or even suggesting that a different result would have been reached if an industrial insurance policy were involved. Nor, as we have already said, is there any logical reason for not applying the same rule to industrial policies.

Other and much more recent decisions in this jurisdiction also point to a holding of liability in this case. It has always been the law that ambiguities are to be resolved in favor of the insured (or beneficiary) and against the insurance company which prepared the policy. That rule has recently been extended and strengthened. In *Hayes v. Home Life Ins. Co.,* 83 U.S. App. D.C. 110, 112, 168 F. 2d 152, 158 (1948), it was said that customers of insurance companies: ". . . are, in vast majority, not informed in the obscurities of insurance expertise and not equipped to understand other than plain language. If the companies were permitted to write clear clauses of liability at one point and obscure negations of liability at another, and to maintain successfully the prevalence of the latter over the former, the temptation to sell on one clause and defend on the other would be dangerous."

That decision was cited and followed as recently as this year in *Buchanan v. Massachusetts Protective Asso.,* D.C. Cir., U.S. App. D.C., 223 F. 2d 609. There the court stressed the duty of an insurance company to spell out in plainest terms—terms understandable to the man in the street—any exclusionary or delimiting policy provisions, and said that the court would: "insist upon language which unambiguously conveys such an intent to the mind of an ordinary layman. Failing such unambiguous language, doubt should be resolved in favor of the insured."

With these rules to guide us, we think our course in this case is clear. We think we must rule that the collapse and death of Mr. Hoy was not only accidental in final result, but that an "accidental means" produced the fatal injury. Laying aside "insurance expertise," and laying aside also a purely technical, scientific or medical approach to the situation, it must be said that Mr. Hoy's death was caused by "violent, external and accidental means" as surely as if he had been struck down by a bolt of lightning, or by a tree or other physical object hurled against him by a strong wind.

Reversed, with instructions to enter judgment for plaintiff.

QUESTIONS FOR REVIEW

1. Define the terms "accidental death" and "death by accidental means."
2. Briefly discuss the three general approaches taken by the courts with respect to death by accidental means.
3. Generally speaking, if death results from an intentional act on the part of the insured, it is not considered death by accidental means. Discuss the difference, if any, in the holdings if:
    a. An unknown and unexpected factor is involved.
    b. The intentional act is that of another person.
4. What is the purpose of the 90-day requirement in the accidental death (means) rider?
5. State the general rule in connection with death from accidental means if disease is a contributing cause.
6. Define proximate cause.
7. Briefly summarize a typical definition of total disability and outline three interpretations of this definition that have been followed by the courts. Which interpretation represents the majority view?
8. Discuss the term "permanent disability" with respect to:
    a. A literal interpretation.
    b. The view of the majority of the courts.
    c. The significance of the "waiting period."
9. Distinguish between a war limitation rider of the status type and one of the result type. Which is more generally used at the present time?
10. What legal problem might be presented in connection with the incontestable and suicide clauses as the result of the exercise of an option under a guaranteed insurability rider? Briefly summarize one solution that has been used.

Chapter Outline

Chapter 8

The Contract
Is Contested

THE INCONTESTABLE clause was voluntarily included in the life insurance contract by forward-looking life insurers during the latter half of the 19th century. An incontestable policy provision was required by the Uniform Policy Provisions legislation that grew out of the Armstrong Investigation, and such provisions have since become so widely required by statute that it is safe to say that an incontestable provision is a required part of every individual life insurance contract issued in any state today. The purpose of this chapter is to outline the major legal principles that have been developed in connection with this policy provision.

A. VALIDITY AND CONTRACT LAW

8.1 The Meaning of Validity

As previously discussed, certain basic requirements relating to offer, acceptance, consideration, legal capacity, and legality of purpose must be met before an agreement will have effect as a binding informal contract. Even when these requirements have been satisfied, however, there are other factors that under special circumstances may affect the validity of a contract.

Some of these factors are of such fundamental importance that their presence or absence, as a matter of law, will make an attempted contract void, that is, no contract at all. This is true, for instance, of a contract of life insurance issued to someone who has no insurable interest in the life to be insured. Other factors have less serious consequences and merely

255

give the injured party the privilege of avoiding the contract, without liability on either side, or permitting it to stand in accordance with its terms. Used in this sense, the validity of a contract means its legal sufficiency, as contrasted with mere regularity of form.

8.2 Factors Affecting Validity

Among the more common factors that may affect the validity of a contract are a mistake or mistakes of one or both of the parties to it, misrepresentation or concealment of a material fact by one of them, and fraud. Each of these general subjects has many subdivisions, and none can be discussed here in detail. The more basic legal principles, however, will be outlined.

A Mistake of Law. As might be supposed, the legal effect of a mistake in making a contract depends upon the kind of mistake that is involved. Thus, it is customary to distinguish between a mistake of law and a mistake of fact. If contracting parties are mistaken concerning the legal effect of certain facts with reference to which the contract is made, they are said to have made a mistake of law. The general rule is that if there has been no error in connection with the facts, a mistake of law will not affect the validity of a contract. (However, in some states, a mutual mistake of law has the same general effect as a mutual mistake of fact.)

A Mistake of Fact. Under some circumstances, a mistake of fact may be serious enough to affect the validity of a contract. The mistake must concern a material fact—that is, a fact that has had a definite influence on the decision of the parties—and ordinarily it must have been a mutual mistake—that is, both parties must have been mistaken as to the same fact. However, the legal effect of a mutual mistake is different under different circumstances.

A mutual mistake concerning the existence of the thing bargained for—an automobile, for example—will destroy the validity of a contract. Also, if the mistake makes the contract extremely burdensome on one of the parties and avoidance would work no special hardship on the other, the contract may be rescinded by the injured party.

Other mistakes have less serious results. For instance, if a mutual mistake has been made in drafting a contract, the usual remedy is to permit the contract to be reformed to reflect the actual intent of the parties. This means that the contract will be interpreted as if the mistake had not been made. A mutual mistake of this kind, therefore, does not affect the validity of the contract; it only means that it will be enforced according to the intention of the parties, not the way they wrote it.

Misrepresentations. In general contract law, if one party misstates a material fact and, as a result, induces the other to make a contract he would not have made if he had known the truth, the party who has been misled has the legal right to avoid the contract. This is true in most jurisdictions even if the misrepresentation was innocently made; and it especially applies if the contracting parties occupy a relationship of unusual trust and confidence, such as guardian and ward, parent and child, trustee and the beneficiary of the trust.

Concealment. When the misleading results from silence (concealment), the legal effect is somewhat different. Generally speaking, the fact that one party did not volunteer information that the other might have liked to have does not necessarily give the second party the right to avoid a contract. However, if the parties occupy a confidential relationship, they have a duty to reveal information of material significance; and if it is not so volunteered, the injured party will have the right to rescind the contract.

Fraud. If either party to a contract is guilty of fraud, the contract is voidable at the election of the other. However, fraud has never been completely defined. This is partly because circumstances vary from case to case and partly also because the dividing line between being defrauded and being careless is a very thin one. In general, however, fraud is any misrepresentation of a material fact that is made with the knowledge that it is not true or with a reckless disregard of whether it is true or not, and made with the intention that another will act in reliance upon the statement, where the latter is entitled to rely upon the misrepresented fact, does rely upon it, and suffers injury as the result.

Basic in fraud is the matter of intent. The guilty person must either have known that the information was false and thus have intended to mislead the other, or he must have acted with a reckless disregard of the truth or falsity of his statement. Obviously it is impossible to say with certainty what anyone intends or has intended. However, if the circumstances are such as to make it clear that he knew that the information was false or that he spoke with a reckless disregard of whether what he said was true or false, his intent to defraud will be presumed.

Second, the misstatement must be one of fact. By its very nature, a misstatement of fact relates either to the present or the past. With respect to the future, the only misrepresentation possible is a misstatement of intention, and that can constitute fraud only if a promise is made with the intention of not keeping it. Misstatements of opinion or of value will not ordinarily be considered fraudulent unless they are made by an expert who has information not available to the other party and who makes the misstatement with the intention that the other will act in reliance upon it. A misstatement of law falls in the same category. Fraud, therefore, usually concerns a misstatement of a present or past fact.

Third, the injured person must have relied upon the misstatement and must have suffered damages as the result. If he knew the truth, or if he could have ascertained it merely by looking at something readily available, he cannot maintain that he was the victim of fraud. Under such circumstances, he would not have been justified in relying upon the misstatement. If the truth is hidden, if the subject matter is so technical that he cannot be expected to understand it, or if means of ascertainment are not available, he may rely on the statement and, if injured, claim fraud. He must, however, also have suffered some damage—that is, some financial loss. If there is no financial loss, there is ordinarily no actionable wrong, that is, no right to seek legal redress.

8.3 Avoidance and Rescission

A person who has the right to avoid or rescind a contract must take some action to enforce his right, having the contract set aside by court action if necessary. If he does not take some action of this kind, the contract will be considered valid and must be performed.

The injured party may also lose the right to rescind a contract if, with knowledge of the facts, he affirms the transaction, does not object within a reasonable length of time, or retains property and uses it after knowledge of the truth. These rules are all important in connection with life insurance contracts.

B. VALIDITY AND THE LIFE INSURANCE CONTRACT

8.4 Material Misrepresentation

The right to rescind where there has been material misrepresentation is especially applicable in connection with the life insurance contract. In order for the insurance principle to function, it is necessary that the lives to be insured be so selected that the mortality actually experienced will approximate that assumed under the mortality tables used. For purposes of making this selection, the insurer requests detailed information concerning the health of the proposed insured, his family history, occupation, etc. Often there is a medical examination and a routine inspection.

Nevertheless, many applications are handled on a nonmedical basis, the company making its risk appraisal decision almost entirely on the basis of the representations in the application. If those representations are not true, the insurer will have been induced by misrepresentation to make a contract that it would not have made if the truth had been known to it.

The Test of Materiality. Generally speaking, the test of materiality is whether the company would have taken different risk appraisal action on the application if it had known the truth about the fact or facts misrepresented. Assume, for example, that the applicant states his date of birth as September 17, 1934, when it was actually September 19, 1934. This would be misrepresentation, but it would not be material. The decision to accept the application or reject it would not have been different if the company had known the truth.

Often the answers to questions in the application concerning ill health and treatment by a physician are equally immaterial. For instance, suppose the applicant records a visit to his personal physician in August, 1973, and states as the reason for the visit, "ankle sprain." If, as a matter of fact, the condition was not technically a sprain, the distinction would not ordinarily be material to the risk. But if the proposed insured had been receiving treatment for a condition such as leukemia or a heart condition, the truth becomes highly important. Here, a misstatement of the nature of the condition might easily cause the insurer to issue a policy that it would not have issued if it had known the truth. Any misstatement concerning a condition of this kind, therefore, would probably be a misstatement of a material fact.

Material misrepresentation in the application for a life insurance contract is most commonly discovered in connection with the investigation of early death claims. (It is not significant with respect to claims under older policies because of the incontestable clause, as will be discussed later.) When material misrepresentation is discovered in connection with an early claim, the claim may be denied on that basis. Since the company would not have issued a policy if it had known the truth, it is entitled to deny the claim and refund the premiums the policyowner has paid.

Often, however, material misrepresentation is discovered under policies while the insureds are still living. Perhaps a disability claim is being investigated, or a second application for insurance on the same life is being reviewed. When an application is received, it is routine practice for an insurer to search its records for previous applications submitted or policies already in force on the life of the proposed insured. (Otherwise, the insurer would have no control over the aggregate amount of insurance it issues on any one life.) In any such situation, information may be discovered that will lead to an investigation revealing health history that has not been disclosed or has been misrepresented.

Whenever information of this kind is revealed, prompt action is usually taken to have the policy rescinded. Usually this means that the insurer, after verifying its information (completely enough to support its action in court, if necessary), notifies the policyowner that it is electing to rescind the policy and is returning the premiums paid. If the policyowner refuses the refund of premiums, the company initiates the appropriate court action to have the policy rescinded legally.

Most life insurance companies take very prompt action in any situation where material misrepresentation, concealment, or fraud is discovered in connection with an in-force life insurance policy, for two reasons. One is that the right to rescission may be lost if the injured party, knowing all the facts, nevertheless treats the contract as continuing in force or fails to object within a reasonable length of time. The other reason is the fact that the incontestable clause, a provision peculiar in life insurance law, establishes a deadline—in most states, two years from the issue date of the policy—beyond which the company cannot initiate legal action to have a life insurance contract rescinded.

C. THE INCONTESTABLE CLAUSE

8.5 The Policy Provision

It will be recalled that the typical incontestable clause is relatively simple. Briefly, it provides that after the policy has been in force during the lifetime of the insured for a period of two years from the issue date, it will be incontestable except for nonpayment of premium and except for provisions granting disability benefits or the accidental death or accidental means death benefit. Incontestability means that the insurer cannot challenge the validity of the policy—that is, initiate an action to rescind it on the basis of material misrepresentation, concealment, or fraud in the application.

From the legal point of view, this clause is unique. In fact, it is directly opposed to one of the most cherished maxims of general contract law—that fraud vitiates a contract. In life insurance, except for a very few decisions to the contrary, this maxim must be revised to read something like this: "Fraud vitiates a contract unless it is a life insurance contract and the contestable period has expired."

What, then, is so unusual about the life insurance contract that insurers should be required by law to include in it a provision directly contrary to a basic maxim of general contract law? To answer this question it is necessary to know something about the history of insurance generally and particularly the doctrine of warranties.

8.6 Warranties and Representations

Statements made by the parties to a contract have been discussed thus far primarily as representations, and the significance of materiality has been pointed out. In the early days of insurance, however, the statements of the insured were warranties, and warranties were and still are quite different from representations. A representation is a statement made in connection with the formation of a contract, which tends to influence the other party's decision to complete the contract. In contrast with this situation, a warranty is part of the contract itself and is a statement or condition relating to a fact or action to be taken. The warranted fact must be exactly true or the action must be performed in exactly the manner stated, or the contract can be declared void. In fact, warranties are sometimes said to be material by agreement.

In the early days, before life insurance as we know it today had been developed, warranties played a very important role in insurance agreements. During the latter half of the 18th and the early part of the 19th centuries, warranties in insurance contracts were enforced with complete technical exactness by the courts of England and the United States. If warranted facts were not true exactly as stated, the insurer could avoid the contract.

This did not usually result in hardship in marine insurance, where the doctrine was first applied. Ordinarily, no extensive period of time had elapsed between the making of the contract and any dispute that might arise concerning its validity. When the same technical rules were applied to the life insurance contract, however, the results were very different. Often, a life insurance contract had been in force for a number of years when its validity was challenged. By that time, the person who had made the warranties—the insured—was usually dead, and the beneficiary, who rarely had had anything to do with the negotiations for the policy, was seriously handicapped in a dispute about the technical exactness of statements about which he knew nothing. Technically right, perhaps, the insurers nevertheless found that by the latter half of the 19th century their readiness to litigate with respect to every deviation from the absolute truth in the application was creating an atmosphere of serious distrust.

To counteract some of this feeling, the companies began including in their policies a provision waiving their right to contest the policy after it had been in effect for a stated period of time. The first such step was taken by the London Indisputable Life, an English company, which included a provision in its charter in 1848 relinquishing the right to contest a policy for any reason whatsoever. In the United States, as previously mentioned, the Manhattan Life Insurance Company introduced the incontestable clause in 1864, in the form in which we usually think of it—as a provision in the policy.

By the time of the Armstrong Investigation, in 1905, a majority of life insurers in the United States were using an incontestable clause. The Standard Policy Law enacted in New York following the Armstrong Investigation included an incontestable clause and made its use mandatory. Later, the Committee of Fifteen, which was appointed in the wake of the Armstrong Investigation, recommended model state legislation which also included an incontestable clause. This was subsequently enacted into law by considerably more than half the states.

Requiring an incontestable clause as a matter of law, however, did not succeed in solving the problems presented in connection with the validity of the life insurance contract. Unfortunately, a new question arose almost immediately: What is a contest of the policy?

8.7 What Is a Contest?

It is generally agreed by lawyers and students of the life insurance contract that life insurance companies included the incontestable clause in the first place as a waiver of their right to contest the policy for misrepresentation, concealment, or fraud in the application. These are all factors which go to the essential validity of the policy. Nevertheless the wording of the clause has cast considerable doubt on this point. For instance, a typical incontestable clause, as previously noted, reads as follows:

> This policy shall be incontestable after it has been in force during the lifetime of the insured, for a period of two years from the earlier of the policy date or the issue date, except for nonpayment of premiums.

One of the most logical questions concerning this clause is this: Why is the nonpayment of premiums excepted if the only purpose of the clause is to prevent a contest in the event of material misrepresentation, concealment, or fraud in the application? Sometimes provisions relating to military and naval service are also listed as exceptions, and similar questions can be asked about them.

If these exceptions had never been included in the clause, there would probably have been little question as to the legal effect of the clause. The word "contest" would have been accepted as meaning a challenge of the validity of the contract, based on rules applicable to contracts generally. The incontestable clause would have been accepted for what it was undoubtedly intended to be, a pledge of good faith in the form of a waiver, after two years, of any legal right the insurer might otherwise have had to challenge the validity of the contract with respect to technical defects in its inception.

When a life insurance company denies a claim on the basis that premiums were not paid when due or within the grace period, or because the insured was killed as the result of military or naval service, it is denying the claim on a completely different basis than when it asserts that it has no liability because the contract was invalid by reason of material misrepresentation or concealment of a material fact in the application. In fact, when the insurer contends that it has no liability because premiums were not paid as required or the insured met his death as the result of military service, it is assuming the validity of the contract and alleging a violation of its terms or failure to fulfill its conditions. To include such defenses as these as exceptions in a provision concerning a contest of the validity of the contract is to create a serious doubt concerning the meaning of the word "contest."

This doubt is increased by the application of a standard rule of construction to the effect that when one thing is specifically expressed in a policy provision or legal document, other similar items not so expressed are presumed to be excluded. Lawyers often state this rule in the Latin: *Expressio unius est exclusio alterius.* When this is applied to the incontestable clause, the conclusion is that having expressed one or two "exceptions" which are in reality defenses, the company should be required to except all possible defenses or be held to have waived them. In any case, this point of view has been taken by a number of courts. In those jurisdictions, therefore, it would seem that the only way an insurer could be certain it would be permitted to rely on any limiting provision of the policy in denying a claim would be to incorporate that provision into the incontestable clause. The suicide clause, for instance, the misstatement of age clause, aviation exclusions, and any of the ordinarily accepted conditions specified in the policy have been thought to conflict with the incontestable clause and have been challenged on that basis at one time or another.

8.8 Conflict with Other Policy Provisions

The Suicide Clause. The suicide clause is probably the clause that has been challenged most frequently on the ground of conflict with the incontestable clause. The suicide clause, it will be remembered, provides that in case of self-destruction of the insured within one or two years from the policy date, the company's obligation under the policy is limited to a return of the premiums paid. Thus, if the insured's death is by suicide during the specified period, the insurance will not be paid. Is this a "contest" of the policy?

A number of the early court decisions held that a denial of the claim for the full amount of the insurance in this situation was a contest of the contract. Assume a policy specifying a suicide period of two years and a contestable period of one year. If the insured's suicide occurred in the second policy year, the courts held that the company could not deny the claim on the basis of suicide because that amounted to a contest of the policy, and the contestable period had expired. Most later cases, however, have held that the fact that the policy had become incontestable does not bar a defense of suicide if the suicide occurs within the specified period. In fact, one court stated that, under these circumstances, a defense based on suicide was just as valid as a defense based on the grounds that the insured was still alive.

Holdings of this latter kind represent the majority view and are based on the general theory that under a policy including a suicide clause, death by suicide is a risk which was not intended to be covered until the lapse of the stated period of time. Thus when a suicide claim is denied because the suicide occurred during the specified period, the insurer is carrying out the terms of the contract, not contesting it.

Misstatement of Age. Because the age of the insured has such a vital relationship to the risk of death, a misstatement of age clause was commonly used by life insurance companies even before the introduction of the incontestable clause. With the growing use of the latter, however, the question arose as to whether an adjustment for misstatement of age could be made after the expiration of the contestable period. In other words, was this also a contest of the policy, which would be barred by the incontestable clause after the expiration of the contestable period?

In some of the earlier policies, misstatement of age was listed in the incontestable clause as one of the exceptions. Thus, the incontestable clause was held not to prevent an adjustment for misstatement of age in those cases, since it was specified as an exception in the clause.

Where a separate misstatement of age clause is used, the majority of courts have reached the same conclusion—that there was no conflict between the two clauses—but for a different reason. For instance, in one 1939 case[1] the court held:

> No person can testify to his own age except from hearsay. No doubt many persons do not have accurate information as to their correct ages. Yet the correct age of insurants is the chief corner-stone of the life insurance structure. If a person obtains insurance by stating a given age, nothing further being said on the subject in the policy, then, under the statute, it may be that the company can not question the correctness of the age stated. But is there anything in the statute which prevents a person from obtaining insurance at a stated age, qualified by a provision in the contract for adjustment according to correct age? We do not so read the statute. Nor do we know of any dictate of public policy to prevent such an age adjustment clause.

D. SOME MILESTONE CASES

8.9 The Monahan Case

The case of *Monahan* v. *Metropolitan Life Insurance Company*,[2] decided in 1918 by the Illinois Supreme Court, marked one of the first important milestones in the development of the language of the incontestable clause. The case involved an incontestable clause that read as follows:

> After two years this policy shall be non-contestable except for non-payment of premiums. . . .

---

[1] *Langan* v. *United States Life Insurance Co.*, 344 Mo. 989, 130 S.W. (2d) 479 (1939).

[2] 283 Ill. 136, 119 N.E. 68 (1918).

Note that the clause made no mention of the "lifetime of the insured," as is usually the case today. At that time, it had not occurred to anyone that such wording was needed. If the insured died during the contestable period, and if there had been material misrepresentation or fraud in the application, it was not questioned that the company could deny the claim on that basis no matter when the claim was presented. Thus, if the insured died toward the end of the contestable period and claim was presented after the expiration of the period, it was assumed that the insurer could deny the claim on the basis of material misrepresentation if that was involved. In other words, it was assumed that the obligations of all parties to the contract were fixed as of the date of death and any defense that was available to the insurer on that date would continue to be available no matter when claim was filed.

This assumption was tested in the Monahan case. The facts of that case were these: the insured died during the contestable period, there was material misrepresentation in the application, and the beneficiary waited until the expiration of the contestable period and then presented claim. The claim was denied, and the beneficiary brought suit.

The Illinois Supreme Court interpreted the clause literally. Since the contestable period had expired at the time of the suit, the court said, the company was precluded from defending on the basis of material misrepresentation in the application. In short, the fact that the insured died during the contestable period did not mean that a defense available at that time would continue to be available to the company after the expiration of the period specified.

Following this decision, the insurer's only remedy in another situation presenting the same set of facts was to take action immediately, without waiting for the death claim to be submitted, and bring suit for rescission prior to the expiration of the contestable period. In many cases this would have been inconvenient; in others, impossible.

For these reasons, steps were taken almost immediately to amend the various state statutes to permit the use of an incontestable clause including the words "during the lifetime of the insured." New York amended its standard provisions law to this effect in 1921, and Illinois adopted the same kind of law in the same year. The Illinois law also included wording permitting the insurer to exclude from the incontestable clause policy provisions concerning disability benefits and benefits in the event of death as the result of accidental means.

Shortly afterwards the National Convention of Insurance Commissioners recommended legislation permitting the inclusion of the phrase "during the lifetime of the insured" in the incontestable clause, and the statutes of most of the states have now been amended in this manner. As a result, when a life insurance policy includes an incontestable clause with this phrase, it is generally agreed that if the insured dies before the policy has been in force long enough to become incontestable, the policy never becomes incontestable. In other words, when death occurs before the end of the contestable period, the policy has not been in force for "two years during the lifetime of the insured." Thus, the policy will never become incontestable no matter how long the beneficiary waits before making claim, and another Monahan case would be impossible.

8.10 Metropolitan Life Insurance Company v. Conway

Probably the clearest statement of the majority opinion concerning the nature and effect of the incontestable clause is found in *Metropolitan Life Insurance Company* v. *Conway*.[3] This case arose not between beneficiary and life insurance company but between life insurance company and the Superintendent of Insurance of New York. The latter had refused to approve an aviation rider which limited recovery to the payment of the reserve if the insured's death occurred under circumstances defined in the rider. He took the position that the provisions of the rider were inconsistent with the incontestable clause as required by the New York law. It was as if the Superintendent were saying to this company: "After two years from date of issue the incontestable clause prohibits you from contesting the policy. Yet you are now requesting permission to include in your policies a provision expressly declaring that if the insured should, at any time, meet his death by reason of aviation activities, you will not be liable for more than the reserve."

The company's position was that even though a policy became incontestable after two years, the insurer was nevertheless free to specify risks it was unwilling to assume at the outset and throughout the life of the contract. Thus under a policy so drafted as to provide that if the insured died as the result of aviation activities the insurer would pay only the policy reserve, the company, in paying only the reserve, would, in effect, be carrying out the terms of the policy, not contesting it.

The case presented the basic question squarely. Does the word "contest" as used in the incontestable clause mean a dispute of the policy based on circumstances or conditions giving the company the right to avoid it as a matter of law? Or does it mean any defense on any grounds whatsoever by which the company may be legally justified in paying less than the face amount of the policy?

The appellate court held with the insurance company that an aviation rider was not a provision permitting the company to "contest" the policy if the insured were killed while engaged in aviation activities, and therefore the rider was not in conflict with the incontestable clause. The New York Court of Appeals upheld that decision in one of the most famous

---

[3] 252 N.Y. 449, 169 N.E. 642 (1930).

and classic expressions of life insurance law. The decision was written by Justice Cardozo, later Justice of the United States Supreme Court, who said:

> We agree with the Appellate Division in its holding that rider and statute in this instance are consistent and harmonious. The provision that a policy shall be incontestable after it has been in force during the lifetime of the insured for a period of two years is not a mandate as to coverage, a definition of the hazards to be borne by the insurer. It means only this, that within the limits of the coverage the policy shall stand, unaffected by any defense that it was invalid in its inception, or thereafter became invalid by reason of a condition broken. Like questions have arisen in other jurisdictions and in other courts of this state. There has been general concurrence with reference to the answer. . . .
>
> The meaning of the statute in that regard is not changed by its exceptions. A contest is prohibited in respect of the validity of a policy, "except for nonpayment of premiums and except for violation of the conditions of the policy relating to military or naval service in time of war." Section 101, Subd. 2. Here again we must distinguish between a denial of coverage and a defense of invalidity. Provisions are not unusual that an insured entering the military or naval service shall forfeit his insurance. A condition of that order is more than a limitation of the risk. In the event of violation, the policy, at the election of the insurer, is avoided altogether, and this though the death is unrelated to the breach. No such result follows where there is a mere restriction as to coverage. The policy is still valid in respect of risks assumed.

The basic point of this case is the distinction between a contest of the validity of the policy and the denial or reduction of coverage because of a special provision in the policy. Thus the denial of a claim because the insured was killed while flying his own plane, if the policy included such a restriction, was, in reality, carrying out the terms of the policy, a very different thing from contesting its validity.

8.11 The Minority Decisions

Although the Conway decision represents the majority line of decisions concerning the nature of the incontestable clause, it has not been followed by all the states. In fact, the same question of the legality of aviation riders was presented to the Louisiana Supreme Court just two years after the Conway case was decided, and the Louisiana court took the opposite (minority) view. In this case[4] the court said:

> The provision . . . making the contract incontestable after a stated period, means something more than that the insurer cannot then contest the validity of the policy on the ground of breach of a condition; it means

---

[4] *Bernier* v. *Pacific Mutual Life Insurance Co.*, 173 La. 1078, 139 So. 629 (1932).

that the company cannot contest its obligation to pay, on due proof of death of the insured, the amount stated on the face of the policy, except for a cause of defense that is plainly excepted from the provision making the policy incontestable.

Thus, the court in the Bernier case in effect held that the incontestable clause was "a mandate as to coverage" and that a company could not "contest its obligation to pay" except for a reason plainly reserved in the wording of the clause itself. A few other courts have taken a similar view, although not always for the same reasons.

E. THE LEGISLATIVE PATH

Justice Cardozo's clear language has been a very strong influence toward the view that the incontestable clause relates to the validity of the contract and not the coverage, and it has been followed in the majority of jurisdictions. However, it has not been followed unanimously, as the Bernier case proves. Because of these divergent opinions, therefore, attention has been turned toward a **possible resolution** of the problem by means of legislation.

The Life Insurance Association of America and the American Life Convention appointed a committee in 1947 known as the Holland Committee to draft recommended statutory provisions. Among the recommendations of this committee was a statutory provision adopting the Conway doctrine, as follows:

A clause in any policy of life insurance providing that such policy shall be incontestable after a specified period shall preclude only a contest of the validity of the policy, and shall not preclude the assertion at any time of defenses based upon provisions in the policy which exclude or restrict coverage, whether or not such restrictions or exclusions are excepted in such clause.

The gist of this statute is that the incontestable clause shall not be considered a mandate as to coverage. At the same time, legislation was recommended concerning risks that the life insurer may except from the coverage of the policy. This was in the form of "prohibited provisions" legislation and read as follows:

On or after _____, no policy of life insurance shall be delivered (or issued for delivery) in this state if it contains any of the following provisions:

      °   °   °   °   °

(b) A provision which excludes or restricts liability for death caused in a certain specified manner or occurring while the insured has a specified status, except that the policy may contain provisions excluding or restricting coverage as specified therein in event of death under any one or more of the following circumstances:

(1) Death as a result directly or indirectly of war, declared or undeclared, or of any act or hazard of such war;

(2) Death as the result of aviation;

(3) Death as a result of a specified hazardous occupation or occupations;

(4) Death while the insured is a resident outside continental United States and Canada; or

(5) Death within two years from the date of issue of the policy as a result of suicide, while sane or insane.

Neither of these statutes has been widely enacted, although the latter, which has been called a legislative "mandate as to coverage," has been adopted in approximately one third of the states in this or similar form.

F. OTHER STATUTORY MODIFICATIONS

8.12 Warranties and Representations

Although the concept of warranties is primarily of only historical interest in life insurance today, its former significance is clearly reflected in many statutory provisions in state insurance laws. One of the most widespread, for instance, is the requirement that the life insurance contract contain a provision declaring that in the absence of fraud, all statements in the application shall be deemed representations and not warranties.

8.13 The Effect of Misrepresentation

Most, though not all, of the states have enacted special statutes concerning the use of material misrepresentation in the application for a life insurance policy to defeat or avoid the policy. Of these, about half state the requirements in the alternative—that the misstatement must either have been made "with intent to deceive" or materially affected or increased the risk. Illustrative of this type of statute is Section 766 of the Illinois Insurance Law, which reads as follows:

. . . No such misrepresentation or false warranty shall defeat or avoid the policy unless it shall have been made with actual intent to deceive or materially affects either the acceptance of the risk or the hazard assumed by the company.[5]

This statute summarizes the traditional view of the legal effect of material misrepresentation. Several other states have similar statutes.

---

[5] Illinois Revised Statutes, Chap. 73, Sec. 766 (1973).

Slightly different wording is used to impose essentially the same requirements in another group of states, as illustrated by the following Massachusetts statute:[6]

> No oral or written misrepresentation or warranty made in the negotiation of a policy of insurance by the insured or in his behalf shall be deemed material or defeat or avoid the policy or prevent its attaching unless such misrepresentation or warranty is made with actual intent to deceive, or unless the matter misrepresented or made a warranty increased the risk of loss.

The fact that several states have essentially similar statutes on the question, however, does not necessarily mean that the courts will interpret them similarly. In fact, that assumption cannot even be made with respect to the same statute in the same state, from year to year. In at least two cases,[7] for instance, the Illinois statute quoted above has been interpreted as if the word "or" in the clause, "unless it shall have been made with actual intent to deceive *or* materially affects . . .," should read "and." This would require the insurer to prove that any misstatement relied upon was not only false and material to the risk but also made with intent to deceive. Two landmark cases,[8] however, have held that the statute should be interpreted as it is written—to permit an insurer to avoid a policy of life insurance if a statement or statements are made in the application that are untrue and material to the risk or if they are made with intent to deceive.

Some statutes specifically forbid an insurer from using misstatements in the application to deny a claim unless the statements were fraudulently made. Ohio, for example, requires it to be "clearly proved that such answer is wilfully false, that it was fraudulently made, that it is material, and that it induced the company to issue the policy, that but for such answer the policy would not have been issued. . . ."[9] Similar requirements are sometimes imposed by the courts, particularly in states where there is no specific statute concerning the legal effect of material misrepresentation.

The Cause of Loss. A few states take the position that material misrepresentation may not be relied upon as a defense to a claim under the life insurance contract unless the representation in question related to the actual cause of loss. This is true, for instance, in Kansas and Rhode

---

[6] Laws of Massachusetts, Volume 5A, Chapter 175, Sec. 186.

[7] *Hamberg* v. *Mutual Life of New York* (1944) 54 N.E. (2d) 227, and *LaPenta* v. *Mutual Trust Life Insurance Co.* (1954) 4 Ill. App. (2d) 60, 123 N.E. (2d) 165.

[8] *Weinstein* v. *Metropolitan Life Insurance Company* (1945) 60 N.E. (2d) 207, and *Campbell,* Appellant v. *Prudential Insurance Company,* Appellee (1958) 147 N.E. (2d) 404.

[9] Ohio General Code, Section 9391.

Island, as well as Missouri, where the statute in question[10] reads as follows:

> Sec. 376.580. No misrepresentation made in obtaining or securing a policy of insurance on the life or lives of any person or persons, citizens of this state, shall be deemed material, or render the policy void, unless the matter misrepresented shall have actually contributed to the contingency or event on which the policy is to become due and payable, and whether it so contributed in any case shall be a question for the jury.

Under a statute of this kind, the insurer would not be permitted to defend a claim denial on the basis of material misrepresentation in the application if the misrepresented facts related to a malignancy and the insured died of a heart attack. If there is a question as to whether the malignancy contributed to the heart attack, it is a question of fact for the jury.

The Role of the Medical Examiner. Other states—specifically, Iowa and Wisconsin—have statutes that prohibit an insurer from defending a claim denial on the basis of material misrepresentation of the health of the insured in any case where a medical examiner has certified to the soundness of the proposed insured's health. The Iowa statute reads as follows:

> In any case where the medical examiner, or physician acting as such, of any life insurance company or association doing business in the state shall issue a certificate of health or declare the applicant a fit subject for insurance, or so report to the company or association or its agent under the rules and regulations of such company or association, it shall be thereby estopped from setting up in defense of the action on such policy or certificate that the assured was not in the condition of health required by the policy at the time of the issuance or delivery thereof, unless the same was procured by or through the fraud or deceit of the assured.[11]

In the case of *McNabb* v. *State Farm Life Insurance Company*,[12] decided in 1953, the Iowa Supreme Court quoted the requirements that must be met by the company in the light of the statute, as follows:

> We have frequently held that to establish the affirmative defense of fraud required by this section, the proof must be clear, satisfactory, and convincing and must show (1) a material representation of an existing fact (2) its falsity (3) scienter[13] (4) intent that it be relied upon (5) that the examining physician relied and acted thereon and (6) that the company was thereby defrauded.

In the McNabb case, the applicant in his application denied having received medical treatment of any kind during the past five years. As a

---

[10] Vernon's Annotated Missouri Statutes, Sec. 376.580.
[11] Sec. 511.31 Iowa Code Annotated.
[12] 116 F. Supp. 641 (D.C. Iowa, 1953).
[13] Knowledge on the part of the person making the statement.

matter of fact he had been a patient in an institution for the treatment of mental disorders for several months, less than two years prior to the date of the application, and during that time had received several shock treatments. The court concluded:

> Upon the entire record the court finds that the false statements quoted in this memorandum were fraudulently made, concerned material matters, that they were believed and relied upon by defendant's examining physician and the defendant and induced the issuance of the policy in suit.

Thus, the insurer's defense of fraud was upheld.

G. CONCEALMENT AND FRAUD

8.14 Concealment

The law with respect to concealment and fraud is closely related to the law of material misrepresentation. Each concerns the essential validity of the contract and, if established, gives the insurer the legal right to avoid it. Specifically, however, the law is more technical as to concealment and fraud than with respect to material misrepresentation, and both concealment and fraud are more difficult to prove.

As previously mentioned, the mere fact that one party does not disclose information which the other would have considered of value does not permit the latter to avoid the resulting contract, as a general rule. However, in relationships of special trust and confidence there is a duty to disclose any information that would be of value to the other party in considering whether or not he wishes to enter into the contract. Since the relationship between the life insurance company and the applicant is one of trust and confidence, there is a duty on the part of the applicant to disclose information which he knows or ought to know is material to the risk, even though no question relating to that particular subject may have been included in the application.

In a sense, the failure to volunteer material information is misrepresentation by concealment. The word itself implies intent—the intentional hiding or withholding of information. The information the life insurance company considers material will ordinarily be requested by means of the detailed questions in the application. If information not so referred to is material to the risk, it is ordinarily so unusual in nature that it can hardly be assumed to have been innocently withheld. In any case, the rule is that concealment of a material fact in connection with the application for a life insurance contract will justify the life insurance company in avoiding the contract only if such information was withheld with fraudulent intent.

One interesting case[14] on the subject dealt with a situation in which

---

[14] *DeBellis* v. *United Benefit Life Insurance Company*, 372 Pa. 207, 93 A. (2d) 429 (1953).

the concealment was accomplished by means of telling the absolute truth. In this case, Rinaldo Joseph DeBellis applied for a life insurance contract in the amount of $5,000, with an accidental death benefit of $5,000. Five months after the policy was issued (in 1947), his body was found under a railroad bridge; he had been stabbed to death. The death certificate listed the deceased as Joseph DeLuca. This was the first notice the insurer had had that the insured was known by that name; and the company denied the claim, alleging that the insured had made false and fraudulent representations in his application for the insurance.

At the trial, the insurer presented evidence to show that the insured had been involved in a shooting in 1938 and had been treated in a hospital under the name of Joseph DeLuca. He had been convicted of a conspiracy to commit a felony and given a sentence of from three to six years in the penitentiary, from which he was paroled in 1941. He was returned to prison for violating his parole later that year and then transferred to another prison. Throughout all these years, the insured had been known as Joseph DeLuca, and he was serving a sentence on parole under that name when he applied for the life insurance contract in question, using the name Rinaldo Joseph DeBellis.

The court discussed the basic question of misrepresentation by concealment as follows:

> The principal question in the case is whether in the circumstances the insured was guilty of intentional misrepresentation sufficient to avoid the policy in concealing his true identity, and in answering "yes" to the question as to his habits being "correct and temperate." There is no case in point because, perhaps, never before has anyone ever had the temerity to procure insurance under such circumstances. On behalf of the plaintiffs it was argued that when the insured was asked his name, and he gave the name given him at birth, as he was not asked whether he had an alias or any other name, he made no misrepresentation. The law is not so naïve. The contention overlooks entirely the doctrine that in an insurance contract the utmost good faith is required of the insured because the insurer takes the risk largely on the representations of the insured. The contention also overlooks the principle that there may be misrepresentation by concealment. As stated in the early case of *Smith* v. *Columbia Insurance Co.*, 17 Pa. 253, at page 261:
>
> "It is not sufficient for the insured to answer all the questions propounded to him. Like a witness on the stand, he is bound to tell the whole truth without waiting to be interrogated. The contract of insurance is eminently a contract of good faith."

The court then discussed the principle of concealment in fire insurance and concluded that the law was no different in life insurance. The decision continues in these words:

> It is true that ordinarily, where no question is asked of the insured and he makes no representations, he may presume that nothing more as to

the risk is desired from him; but where there is something unusual about the situation which apparently increases the risk, he is bound to disclose it: 45 C. J. Section 115. Of course, not every nondisclosure will forfeit the policy, but as stated by Circuit Judge William H. Taft in the well-known case of *Penn. Mutual Life Insurance Co. v. Mechanics' Savings Bank and Trust Co.*, 72 Fed. 413:

". . . It is clearly just to require that nothing but a fraudulent nondisclosure shall avoid the policy. Nor does this rule result in practical hardship to the insurer, for in every case where the undisclosed fact is palpably material to the risk the mere nondisclosure is itself strong evidence of fraudulent intention."

. . . What is the purpose of an insurer in asking for an applicant's name? It is not merely to learn the name in the abstract, but to identify the person dealt with so that inquiry may be made about him. We cannot conceive of any greater fraud on an insurance company than an applicant giving his name as "X" and failing to disclose that he is also known as "Y," when, in fact, under the name of "Y" he has a long criminal record and was actually at the time he applied for the insurance under the name of "X" serving a parole sentence under the name of "Y," which would not expire for nine years.

We think the trial judge on the evidence presented in the case, partly on the admissions in the pleadings and otherwise on uncontradicted evidence of the facts referred to without regard to other misrepresentations, should have directed a verdict for the defendant, since on this major point in the case there was no fact in dispute. The misrepresentations here, as to the applicant's name and as to his habits being "correct and temperate," were so gross the trial judge should have declared it as a matter of law.

8.15 Fraud

In any situation involving material misrepresentation by concealment, the basic problem is to prove that the applicant withheld the material information intentionally. This is also the problem in those states that require proof that material misstatements have been made with intent to deceive before the insurer may rely on them to deny a claim or rescind the policy. In fact, the difficulty in connection with any action involving an allegation of fraud is the problem of establishing intent. However, if the facts are sufficiently clear, the courts will presume an intent to defraud.

For example, in one Pennsylvania case[15] the applicant had had at least 13 consultations with four different physicians in a city 100 miles from her home within two years of the date of application. Yet she stated in her application that there had been no consultations with any physician within the past seven years. The court said:

---

[15] *Bailey v. The Pacific Mutual Life Ins. Co. of Calif.*, 336 Pa. 62, 6 Atl. (2d) 770 (1939).

The consultations were clearly of such important character and of such recent occurrence as could not be forgotten, and the insured must have been fully cognizant that she hid them from the insurer by her false answer. In this connection, we said in *Evans* v. *Penn. Mutual Life Ins. Co.*, 322 Pa. 547, 553:

"The circumstances preceding and attending the making of the statements may be such that the insured must be said to have been aware of their falsity at the time, or that an inference of fraud is otherwise irresistible, as for instance where an unreported illness or disability of insured was so serious and so recent that he could not have forgotten it."

H. DEFENSES NOT BARRED BY THE INCONTESTABLE CLAUSE

8.16 Fraudulent Impersonation

The general rule with respect to the incontestable clause, like most rules, has its exceptions. Generally, after the expiration of the contestable period, all defenses relating to the validity of the contract are barred. One of the most common exceptions, however, concerns the situation in which an application is completed for insurance on the life of a specified person but a different person takes the medical examination. In such instances, the general rule is that the incontestable clause does not operate to bar a defense after the expiration of the contestable period because no contract was ever formed.

It will be recalled that there is a difference between requirements for the formation of a valid contract and factors going beyond such formation and relating to the essential validity of the contract. This particular line of cases points up that distinction with force and clarifies the operation of the incontestable clause in the language of basic contract law.

One of the best illustrations of this line of reasoning is found in the case of *Obartuch* v. *Security Mutual Life Insurance Company*,[16] which began as a suit for the death benefits under two $10,000 policies on the life of Frank Obartuch. The company admitted that the contestable period had elapsed but denied liability on the grounds that the application was either not signed or not knowingly signed by Frank Obartuch and that someone unknown to the company was fraudulently substituted for the alleged insured at the medical examination.

The court's conclusions of law were as follows:

1. That it is contrary to public policy for any person to obtain life insurance by substituting an individual other than the named insured for medical examination, and a policy secured by such substitution is void;

2. That the incontestable clause in the policies in suit does not preclude the defense that the person examined by the defendant's medical examiner

---

[16] 114 F. (2d) 873 (C.C.A. Ill., 1940).

was not Frank Obartuch, but someone else who impersonated said Frank Obartuch;

3. That said policies did not constitute a valid contract with Frank Obartuch and, if valid at all, were contracts upon the life of the person examined by the defendant's medical examiner;

4. That there was never any valid contract of life insurance upon the life of Frank Obartuch because he never knowingly signed any application therefor or authorized any other person to sign an application for him. . . .

The court then noted other cases in which the incontestable clause had been held not to bar a defense of fraudulent impersonation and concluded that "there is no effective incontestable clause when the policy is clearly shown never to have been accepted by the insured in his lifetime as a contract." It continued:

In the *Maslin* case, the court held that the defense of impersonation was not barred by the incontestable clause on the theory that no contract was made with the named insured. True, as plaintiff points out, the named insured neither signed the application nor submitted to medical examination, but the matter of substitution was stressed by the court. On page 370, it said:

". . . There cannot be the slightest doubt that the person whom an insurance company intends to make a contract with and intends to insure is the person who presents himself for physical examination. . . .

"The defendant's only contract was with the man who made the application and took the examination."[17]

In the *Ludwinska* case, a similar situation is considered. The person named as the insured was an imbecile and the application for insurance was made by her sister who also impersonated the named insured at the medical examination. The court held that if anyone was insured it was the sister and not the one named in the policy. On pages 30 and 31 (Atl.), it is said:

". . . The contract must be made by someone capable of contracting under the insurance law. Without this neither the incontestable clause contained in the policy nor the policy itself have any life. The clause can rise no higher than the policy; the incontestable clause cannot of itself create the contract. . . .

"Insurance companies do not insure names. They insure lives. . . ."

In the *Logan* case, which referred to a statute requiring the incontestable provision, the court, on page 292, said:

". . . This statute certainly has reference to cases where there is a contract between the insured and the insurer. If the insured never made any application to the association for insurance, either by making the application herself, or authorizing another to do so for her, then there never was a contract between the insured and the insurer and the statute above quoted could not have application at all."

---

[17] But this was not the person insured under the policy.

In the *Harris* case, this court considered a situation where the policy was placed for inspection in the hands of the one who applied for the policy. In the meantime, the person died and the named beneficiary sought to recover. It was held that no contract existed and that the incontestable clause did not bar a defense. On page 130, of 80 F. 2d, it is said:

". . . The expressions of these courts, while not the whole basis of the decisions, tend to uphold our view that there is no effective incontestable clause when the policy is clearly shown never to have been accepted by the insured in his lifetime as a contract. . . ."

Lack of Insurable Interest. Following this same reasoning—that the incontestable clause is not operative if a contract was never formed—it is held that the incontestable clause does not bar a defense based on lack of insurable interest. It is well established that one cannot take out a valid and enforceable policy of insurance for his own benefit insuring a person in whose life he has no insurable interest. Such a contract of insurance is void as a matter of public policy. The contract is "void in its inception," and since the incontestable clause is a part of that contract, it necessarily fails with the contract of which it is a part. In short, no contract came into existence in the first place and the incontestable clause, therefore, is of no avail. As quoted above from the Ludwinska case, ". . . the incontestable clause cannot of itself create the contract."

I. SOME MISCELLANEOUS QUESTIONS

8.17 Date from Which the Contestable Period Runs

Many policy provisions reflect the usual statutory language and make the policy incontestable after it has been in effect for two years from "date of issue." Since the policy date and the date when the policy was issued are often different, there may be a very real question as to which of these dates is the one from which the contestable period shall be computed.

The majority of courts hold that if the insurance does not become effective until after the date of issue, the contestable period begins to run from the issue date. However, where the policy bears an issue date later than that on which the insurance becomes effective, the period will be held to begin on the earlier date. In this as in other instances, the terms of the policy will be construed most favorably toward the insured and the beneficiary; hence an interpretation giving the beneficiary the benefit of incontestability at the earliest possible moment.

8.18 How a Policy Is Contested

The meaning of the word "contest" as used in the incontestable clause and as it relates to the contract itself has been discussed at some length.

However, exactly what the company must actually do in order to "contest" a contract, in the procedural sense of the term, has not been explained. Although it is not the purpose of this book to discuss procedural law in any real detail, the idea of the "contest" of a policy as a matter of procedure is sufficiently important to receive a note of explanation.

Ordinarily, a contest is held to mean some affirmative or defensive action in court in which the insurer and the insured, or his representatives or beneficiaries, are parties. The word "contest" implies litigation. Thus, the insurer must begin an action in equity to have the contract rescinded or be sued for the policy proceeds and defend on the basis of misrepresentation or concealment of a material fact or fraud in the application. Either of these actions will constitute a contest of the validity of the contract in the sense the word is used in the incontestable clause.

A mere denial of a claim or a notice that the company intends to rescind or repudiate the contract does not constitute a contest. Furthermore, a suit by the insurer to have a policy reformed so that it will conform to the actual agreement of the parties has been held not to be a contest within the meaning of the incontestable clause.

The difference between an action in equity to have the contract rescinded and a defense to a claim in a court of law is considered sufficiently significant by some insurers that they omit the words "during the lifetime of the insured" from the incontestable clause. When these words are included in the incontestable provision, the death of the insured during the contestable period fixes the rights of the parties as of the date of death. The company may then deny the claim and defend the denial on grounds of material misrepresentation, concealment, or fraud, whenever suit is brought for the proceeds of the policy.

If these words are not included in the provision, the insurer will lose the right to defend the suit on those grounds if the suit is brought after the expiration of the contestable period. It thus does not have an "adequate remedy at law" and is entitled to bring an action in equity during the contestable period to have the policy canceled. The fact that an equity case is heard by the court without a jury is thought by some insurers to be a sufficient advantage to justify the extra responsibility of bringing an action to have the policy rescinded during the contestable period, rather than to wait and interpose the appropriate defense when sued.

J. DISABILITY BENEFITS

When the incontestable clause was originally introduced, it applied to life coverages only, because they were the only coverages offered in the life insurance policy. The early legislation requiring the clause related only to life coverages also for the same reason. No provision was made for excepting disability benefits because such benefits were not offered in connection with the life contract.

In the years that followed the Armstrong Investigation, life insurers began offering disability benefits in connection with life insurance; and when the question was presented to the courts, the incontestable clause was generally held to apply to the disability benefits as well as to the life insurance. Nevertheless even in this period, some courts recognized the essential difference between the coverages and held that the statutory incontestable requirements for life insurance did not apply to disability benefits, even though both were provided in the same policy.

Neither of the basic arguments supporting the incontestable clause for life insurance applies to any significant degree to disability insurance. In a disability situation, claim is often made before the contract has run for any considerable period of time, and proof and witnesses, including the insured, are ordinarily readily available. Equally significant is the fact that the person to be penalized in most contests concerning disability benefits is the contracting party himself. Granting him immunity from the consequences of his own misrepresentation, even fraud in some instances, is difficult to justify.

In 1922, therefore, the National Convention of Insurance Commissioners recommended that statutes requiring the incontestable clause be amended to permit life companies to except disability and accidental death benefits from the operation of the incontestable clause. This option was first offered in 1923, when the New York legislature amended the New York Insurance Law to allow an exception in the incontestable clause of "provisions relating to benefits in the event of total and permanent disability and provisions which grant additional insurance specifically against death by accident." A provision of this kind has since been incorporated into the statutory law of about half the states.

Incidentally, New York has since amended its law to require that disability benefits be made incontestable, but the requirements are separately stated from those relating to life coverage, and the period of time, three years, is different. Thus the essential difference in the nature of the two coverages has continued to be recognized.

8.19 The Court Decisions

Where No Exception Is Made. By the weight of authority, if no specific exception is made in the incontestable clause, disability benefits and accidental death benefits are held subject to its provisions in the same sense as is the life coverage. After the expiration of the contestable period, the policy cannot be rescinded for fraud or misrepresentation with respect to any of the benefits, and claim denials cannot be defended on those grounds.

An insurer can, of course, always show that a risk was not assumed in the first place. Also, the company may introduce evidence to show that disability is not total or permanent (since this is not contesting the policy). It should be recalled, however, that this distinction between "contesting" the policy, on the basis of factors going to the essential validity of the contract, and showing that the risk was not assumed, or that conditions have not been met, is not unanimously agreed upon.

Where Disability and Accidental Death Provisions Are Excepted. Where disability and accidental death provisions are excepted from the operation of the incontestable clause, there is some disagreement among the courts. By the weight of authority, such exceptions should free these benefits entirely from the operation of the clause, and prior to 1934 the cases so held. In that year, however, a United States Circuit Court of Appeals, in *Ness v. Mutual Life Insurance Company*,[18] held that the incontestable clause applied to the accidental death and disability clauses of the policy even though the clause specifically excepted "restrictions and provisions applying to double indemnity and disability benefits as provided in sections 1 and 3."

In this case and in two others in which it was followed, the exceptions as to "sections 1 and 3" did not include all of the sections relating to the benefits to be excepted. Thus there was some basis for the holding that the exception created an ambiguity which must be decided in favor of the insured. However, this same reasoning was later applied to a different set of facts in which there was no such ambiguity, and this established a difficult precedent so far as any logical application of legal principles was concerned.

The insurer's right to exclude such benefits was upheld in the case of *Equitable Life Assurance Society of the United States v. Deem*,[19] where the court said:

> The policy as a whole includes three separate kinds of insurance, which constitute in reality three major promises of insurance protection, life, accident and disability. It seems entirely clear that the insurer intended to avail itself of the statutory authority to make the incontestable clause inapplicable to the latter two of these risks, and thus excepted from the clause those two provisions of the policy relating to them.

And later:

> While ambiguities which fairly exist in insurance policies must be resolved in favor of the insured, it is not permissible for courts by a strained and over-refined construction of ordinary words to create an ambiguity which would not otherwise exist. . . . And while the incontestable clause

---

[18] 70 F. (2d) 59 (C.C.A.N.C., 1934).
[19] 91 F. (2d) 569 (C.C.A. W.Va., 1937).

is a valuable feature of life insurance and is to be liberally construed to effectuate its beneficent purpose, there is no reason to deny to the insurer the option given by statute to except from its operation the additional features of disability and double indemnity benefits, where its purpose to do so has been definitely expressed. "To make a contract incontestable after the lapse of a brief time is to confer upon its holder extraordinary privileges." We must be on our guard against turning them into weapons of oppression.

Thus, where the incontestable clause contains an express exception, it is believed that the majority of the courts have upheld the company's right to contest the validity of the disability provisions even after the expiration of the contestable period. However, many courts have denied the companies this right. Numerous cases have arisen on this question since 1930, and the decisions are highly conflicting.

SUMMARY

Validity and Contract Law

The Meaning of Validity. In addition to the basic requirements that must be met before an agreement becomes a binding informal contract, there are several factors that may under some circumstances affect the validity of the life insurance contract. One of these is failure to meet the insurable interest requirement. Other factors are mistakes of the parties, misrepresentation or concealment of a material fact, and fraud.

Mistakes. Some of the more common rules concerning the legal effect of a mistake of fact are as follows: A mistake concerning the existence of the subject of the contract destroys the validity of the contract. If by reason of a unilateral mistake of a material fact, the contract is excessively burdensome on one of the parties and if rescission will not mean a substantial hardship on the other, rescission may be granted. A mutual mistake will also permit reformation of a contract in most instances.

Material Misrepresentation. If by misstating a material fact, one party to a contract induces the other to make a contract he would not have made if he had known the truth, the injured party may avoid the contract at his option. Misrepresentation by concealment of a material fact also gives the right to rescind the contract if the parties occupy a confidential relationship.

Fraud. Fraud is any misrepresentation of a material fact that is made with the knowledge that the statement is not true, and made also with the intention that another will act upon the information, where the other person does so act and suffers injury as the result.

Avoidance and Rescission. Where a person has the right to rescind or avoid a contract, he must take some action to perfect his right and have the contract set aside by court action if necessary. If he does not do this, the contract will be considered valid.

Validity and the Life Insurance Contract

In most respects, the general rules concerning material misrepresentation, concealment, and fraud apply, with not too much variation, to the life insurance contract. The test of materiality is whether the insurer would have taken different risk appraisal action on the application if it had known the truth.

When facts giving the insurer the right to rescind are discovered during the lifetime of the insured, the remedy is an action in equity to have the contract rescinded. If such information is discovered after the death of the insured, the insurer's remedy is in a court of law as a defense to the claim. Either action, however, is subject to the contestable period as defined in the incontestable clause.

The Incontestable Clause

The incontestable clause is unique to life insurance and, in fact, is directly opposed to one of the basic principles of general contract law—that fraud vitiates a contract. It was included in the life insurance contract because a strict application of the doctrine of warranties, developed in connection with marine insurance, worked a definite hardship when invoked in connection with the life insurance contract. Introduced at first by the insurers on a voluntary basis, the incontestable clause was later required by the standard provisions laws that followed the Armstrong Investigation. Nevertheless, making an incontestable clause compulsory did not resolve all the questions concerning a contest of the life insurance contract. The next question concerned the meaning of a contest.

The word "contest" is generally considered to mean simply a contest of the validity of the contract. However, the exceptions listed in the clause itself have raised some questions. For instance, the nonpayment of premiums has nothing to do with the validity of the contract, yet it is frequently listed as an exception in the incontestable provision. This fact, and the application of a generally accepted maxim, "the expression of one thing is the exclusion of others," has created some confusion. As a result, the incontestable clause has frequently been challenged as conflicting with other provisions of the contract.

Most of these conflicts have been resolved on the basis that the incontestable clause relates solely to the validity of the contract. Thus, it is generally held that death by suicide is a risk not assumed under the contract, and denial of a claim on that basis does not constitute a contest of the policy. It is also generally agreed that the incontestable clause does not prevent the insurer from making adjustments for misstatement of age.

Milestone Cases

The case of *Monahan* v. *Metropolitan Life Insurance Company*[20] dealt with a situation where the insured died prior to the end of the contestable period but the beneficiary presented claim only after the period had expired. The insurer denied the claim on the basis of material misrepresentation, but the court held that the right to deny was lost at the expiration of the contestable period. As the result of this case, the standard policy provisions legislation was revised to permit insurers to provide that the policy will be incontestable after it has been in force for two years from the policy date, "during the lifetime of the insured." When this wording is used, it is generally held that the insurer's defense will be preserved if the insured dies during the contestable period, even though the period expires before claim is presented.

In *Metropolitan Life Insurance Company* v. *Conway*,[21] Justice Cardozo analyzed the effect of the incontestable clause when an aviation limitation rider is used with the policy. The use of this rider had been disapproved by the Superintendent of Insurance of New York on the grounds that it conflicted with the clause. Justice Cardozo said that the clause was not a mandate as to coverage and that it related only to contests of the validity of the contract. Thus the insurer was free to decide for itself what risks it was willing to assume. Within those limits, at the end of two years, the contract would be free of any defense that it was invalid in the beginning. Since that time, the majority of courts have followed this reasoning. Nevertheless, there have been some decisions to the contrary, and because of these decisions, an attempt has been made to define the meaning of the clause by statute. However, this has not been widely successful. Related legislation has defined the risks a life insurer may except from coverage and thus provides a legislative guide as to coverage.

Other Statutory Modifications

One of the standard policy provisions declares that all statements in the application in the absence of fraud shall be deemed representations and not warranties. Other statutes have been enacted in the majority of the states defining what the insurer must prove if it relies upon a material misrepresentation to deny a claim. Many of these statutes provide that a

---

[20] 283 Ill. 136, 119 N.E. 68 (1918).
[21] 252 N.Y. 449, 169 N.E. 642 (1930).

misrepresentation or false warranty shall defeat a claim or avoid a policy only if it has been made with actual intent to deceive or materially affects either the acceptance of the risk or the hazard to be borne by the insurer. Some of the states require that the misrepresentation shall have been made fraudulently. One or two states require that the misrepresentation must relate specifically to the cause of death. Other states specify that if a medical examiner certifies to the health of the proposed insured, the company cannot later deny a claim except for fraud.

Concealment and Fraud

Concealment of a material fact in connection with the application for a life insurance contract is ordinarily considered to justify avoidance of the contract only if concealment was fraudulent.

Fraud differs from material misrepresentation primarily by requiring proof of intent. If the facts are sufficiently clear, however, fraudulent intent may be presumed.

Defenses Not Barred by the Incontestable Clause

Where an application for life insurance is completed by one person as the proposed insured but another person takes the medical examination, it is generally held that the incontestable clause does not bar the company from showing that no contract was ever made insuring the purported insured. This same line of thought is followed in cases where the insurable interest requirement is not met. Both these instances concern contracts that are void in the inception. Since no contract was ever formed, the incontestable clause, like the contract itself, never became effective.

Miscellaneous Questions

In deciding when the contestable period begins to run, any ambiguity will be resolved against the insurer to give. the beneficiary the benefit of incontestability at the earliest possible moment.

In the procedural sense, a contest of the policy means an affirmative or defensive action in a court of law.

Disability Benefits

The original incontestable clauses related only to the death benefit under the life insurance contract, because no disability benefits were ordinarily provided at that time. Thus, when legislation was enacted requiring an incontestable clause, it was held to relate only to the life insurance coverage. However, the reasons for limiting an insurer's right to contest a life insurance policy after the death of the insured are not so persuasive with respect to disputes that arise during the lifetime of the insured. Consequently, present statutes permit disability benefits to be excepted from the operation of the incontestable clause in most states. In New York disability benefits must be made incontestable after three years. Disability benefits are usually held to be subject to the incontestable clause, however, if there is no specific exception in the clause.

ILLUSTRATIVE CASES

The following cases have been selected to show two different approaches to the question of material misrepresentation. Their significance lies in the fact that each decision governs in its own particular jurisdiction.

JOHN HANCOCK MUTUAL LIFE INS. CO. v. *BERG*[22]

The plaintiff, which issued a policy of insurance on the life of the above named incompetent, moves for summary judgment on its first cause of action to rescind the accidental death benefit provision and on its second cause of action to rescind the waiver of premium after total disability provision.

The complaint alleges and the answer admits that the incompetent represented in his application for the policy that he had never received any disability benefits from any source, had not consulted or been treated by a physician for nervous or mental symptoms, and had not been treated by a physician or confined to any hospital for the past five years; that such representations were false, were material, and were relied on by the plaintiff in issuing the policy.

The defendant claims that the provisions sought to be rescinded are now incontestible [*sic*] and in any event that an incompetent is not chargeable with misrepresentations, since he was incapable of knowing the meaning of his acts.

While the life insurance provision of the policy is now incontestible I do not believe the provisions sued on are incontestible. By the terms of the policy the accidental death benefit provision is contestible during the life of the policy and the waiver of premium after total disability provision is contestible if total disability occurs within three years from the date of issue of the policy. The proof submitted by the plaintiff establishes and in fact the answer alleges that the incompetent was totally disabled within three years from the date of issue of the policy.

The court is aware of the rule of law that a contract with an incompetent person who has not been adjudicated[23] is not valid and while the other party may not rescind it because of the incompetency, the incompetent party may if

---

[22] 268 N.Y.S. (2d) 638 (1966).

[23] An incompetent person who has not been adjudicated is one who has not been declared incompetent by a court.

the other party can be placed in status quo.[24] This rule was developed to protect not only the incompetent but also an innocent party who had conferred a benefit on an incompetent party.

In the instant case, the plaintiff is not seeking to rescind because of the incompetency, but because of the material misrepresentations. If it were because of the former, the incompetency would act as a shield to protect the incompetent. However, there is no reason to allow the incompetency to be used as a sword and that is what the effect would be if an incompetent were not responsible for misrepresentations. Consequently, the court holds that an incompetent is responsible for misrepresentations, and that a contract based on such may be rescinded by the innocent party. That the misrepresentations were innocently made is of no consequence. [Citations.]

CIESIELSKI v. *PRUDENTIAL INSURANCE COMPANY OF AMERICA*[25]

On August 31, 1957, Anthony Luta applied for life insurance and was required, as is the practice in such matters, to answer in writing certain questions with regard to the state of his health, current and past. One of the questions read:

> Have you ever been treated for or had any known indication of
> (e) ulcer of stomach or intestines, or rectal disorder?

He answered this question "No."

On July 9, 1958, he died of carcinoma of the aesophagus [*sic*]. The insurance company refused to pay the face amount of the policy to the beneficiary, claiming fraud and misrepresentation on the part of the insured.

In the ensuing litigation, the Trial Court submitted to the jury the question as to whether the insured had made false statements or had acted in bad faith. By its verdict the jury answered that there had been no fraud. The insurance company has appealed, urging upon us that the documentary records in the case entitle it to judgment n.o.v.,[26] since it should have had binding instructions at the trial.

To begin with, the insurance policy expressed that all statements made by the insured in the application were representations and not warranties. Therefore, for the appellant to prevail it must show that the insured knowingly[27] practiced a deception on the insurance company. *Burton* v. *Pacific Mutual Life Insurance Co.*, 368 Pa. 613, 84 A. 2d 310; *Travelers Insurance Co.* v. *Heppenstall Co.*, 360 Pa. 433, 61 A. 2d 809.

Did Luta know he had cancer? There is nothing in the record to establish such awareness. The medical records introduced by the defendant show that this dread disease had indeed fastened its mortal coils about the insured's digestive tract, but mercifully he was ignorant of the knowledge. He had complained

---

[24] In other words, although the competent contracting party cannot rescind a contract made with an incompetent, the latter is permitted to rescind if the competent party can be restored to the position he was in before the contract was made.

[25] 416 Pa. 146, 205 A. (2d) 42 (1964).

[26] A judgment in spite of a jury finding to the contrary.

[27] In other words, in Pennsylvania, knowledge was necessary.

to his physician, Dr. Klueber, of difficulty in swallowing certain foods; the doctor sent him to a hospital for x-ray studies; Dr. Sheedy, the radiologist who read the x-rays, informed Dr. Klueber that he found evidence of carcinoma and Dr. Klueber sent Luta to a general surgeon, Dr. Tetlow who confirmed the radiologist's conclusions. But no one of these doctors told Luta that he had cancer. Nor did he suffer any symptoms which might warn him that a time bomb was ticking away in his body.

Ignorance of the law may be no excuse, although this strait jacket, often cruel in its application, has undergone some relaxation during recent decades, but there can be no question that ignorance of facts when one is not negligent in ascertaining the facts, can never bind one to the unknown. What does not enter one's conscious world is as if it did not exist insofar as legal or moral responsibility for it is concerned, assuming, all the time, of course, that the person involved in no way sought to avoid the facts. There is not the slightest suggestion in the record that Luta endeavored to draw a veil over the knowable.

There were no facts adduced at the trial to suggest that Luta had any reason to believe that a cable was pulling him toward the cemetery. Indeed, in this respect, nature played an inscrutable trick by assuring him that he was in good health. After taking some medication prescribed by Dr. Klueber he experienced such an exuberance of salubrity that he told a Joseph Ciesielski, who so testified, that he "felt like a new man." This sense of renewed vigor was such that he worked up to the date of his death. Thus, neither doctor, nor druggist, nor ever-babbling circumstance suggested to Anthony Luta that his days were numbered. Nor was there anything written in the notebook of memory to remind him that he should answer the questions in the insurance application in any manner other than the way in which he did answer them.

Reduced to basic essentials, the question in this case was one strictly of fact and that question was resolved by the fact-finding tribunal with no stumbling over application of the law, as correctly submitted by the Trial Judge.

Judgment affirmed.

QUESTIONS FOR REVIEW

1. In general terms, what is the legal effect so far as a contract is concerned if the parties have made—
   a. A mistake of law?
   b. A mutual mistake of fact?

2. Define fraud.

3. In the absence of a statute, what is the general rule concerning the rights of an insurer which has issued a policy in reliance on a misstatement of a material fact in the application?

4. State briefly the test of materiality where a misstatement of fact has been made on the application for a life insurance contract.

5. Briefly summarize the reasons why it seemed necessary to modify the legal rules relating to warranties when these concepts were applied to life insurance contracts.

6. In which of the following situations is the company's defense against a death claim a contest of the policy:
   a. A denial on the basis that the policy has lapsed for nonpayment of premium.
   b. A denial because the death was the result of aviation activity where there was an aviation exclusion.
   c. A denial based on the misrepresentation of a material fact in the application.

7. Explain the effect the incontestable clause would have if:
   a. Death was the result of suicide within two years.
   b. There had been a misstatement of age.

8. Briefly discuss the significance of the words "during the lifetime of the insured" as they may appear in the incontestable clause.

9. In general terms, what did Judge Cardozo mean when he said that the incontestable clause is not a "mandate as to coverage"?

10. List two situations in which the validity of the policy may be challenged after the expiration of the contestable period. Explain why the incontestable clause is inapplicable in each situation.

Chapter Outline

Chapter **9**

The Ideas of Waiver
and Estoppel

THIS CHAPTER discusses two legal devices that are not reflected in the life insurance policy itself but that have been developed and used by courts for many years in the interest of policyowners and beneficiaries, the doctrines of waiver and estoppel. These doctrines have long been used in various areas of the law, but they have been used with particular frequency in connection with questions involving the life insurance contract.

A. WAIVER AND ESTOPPEL DEFINED

9.1 Distinct Concepts

It is sometimes said, and many court decisions would seem to bear it out, that there is little, if any, difference between waiver and estoppel. There is, however, a clear technical distinction between the two concepts; and this large and very important area of life insurance law often becomes seriously confused if it is not approached with a clear understanding of the basic meanings of the terms.

9.2 What a Waiver Is

A waiver is the intentional and voluntary giving up of a known privilege or right. The person who gives up the right or privilege may expressly say that he is doing so, or his words or actions may be of such a nature as to admit of no other reasonable interpretation. In more legal language, these ideas are summarized by saying that a waiver may be express—as is true when a person specifically states that he is waiving a right or privilege—or implied—as in the situation where words or actions clearly indicate that intent.

It must also be remembered that whatever one may do for himself, he may do through an agent. Thus, an authorized agent may waive a privilege or power for his principal. In the case of the life insurer, waiver is always by an agent since, in technical terms, even an officer of the company is acting as an agent for the company.

Contractual Waivers.   A waiver for which there is consideration is said to be a contractual waiver. This is most clearly illustrated by the waiver of premium for disability benefit. Under it, the insurer intentionally and voluntarily promises to give up its right to enforce the condition of premium payment during any period of the insured's total disability, as described and defined. Since there is consideration for this promise, the waiver is contractual.

Noncontractual Waivers.   Most waivers are less formal and without consideration. In this sense, a waiver is merely the voluntary relinquishment of a known right or privilege. In the true sense of the word, a waiver always requires the intent to relinquish the right in question and full knowledge of the circumstances involved.

The basic idea of waiver as a legal principle is not difficult to understand. It is in the practical application of this principle that one encounters problems. Actually, many conditions in the life insurance contract may be waived by the insurer. For instance, premiums are to be paid on the due date or within the grace period. If the right to enforce this requirement is voluntarily given up, no matter how or why, the right to require the payment of premiums when due or within the grace period has been waived. It is not necessary that one intends to set in motion the legal consequences of a waiver; he need only intend to take the action he actually took. The legal consequences flow from the actions taken, not the intentions.

The importance of this distinction—between what one intends and the legal consequences of one's actions—as well as the basic principles involved in the concept of waiver are illustrated in the case of *Hoffman* v. *Aetna Life Insurance Company*.[1] The case concerned two group life insurance contracts, and the question was whether they had lapsed at the time of the insured's death. Premiums were paid on a monthly basis to a resident agent of the insurer, who reported premium collections on a daily basis to the insurer.

The specific facts in the Hoffman case were these: Premiums were never paid on the day they were due. In fact, some of the premiums were not paid for as long as 60 days after the due date. Eventually, however,

---

[1] 22 N.E. (2d) 88 (Ohio, 1938).

all premiums were paid to and including the premium due on June 1, which the agent reported as paid on June 13.

Increased insurance was made effective as of June 10 and an adjusted premium became payable. A payment was made on June 15 but it was not enough to cover the increased premium; and no further premiums were paid, although the insurer set up on its records the premiums due for July, August, and September.

On August 23, one of the employees was killed in an accident, and the insurer was promptly furnished proof of his death. The evidence indicated that sometime between September 1 and September 15, the insurer noted on its records that the policies had lapsed for nonpayment of the premium due on July 1 and notified the beneficiary on December 12 to that effect.

The jury was requested to answer the question "as to whether the insurance company voluntarily relinquished known rights, benefits, privileges or advantages," and the jury decided that the insurer had waived its right to insist upon a forfeiture of the insurance by accepting premium payments as much as 60 days overdue.

The court of appeals denied an application for a rehearing, saying:

> We have always understood that, in an ordinary contract, where the parties, by negotiation, fix the terms of the contract and both of them have a part in choosing the language in which such terms are expressed, a provision as to times of payments may be waived by a course of conduct; and that where failure to make installment payments as stipulated gives to one of the parties the right to claim an advantage and he repeatedly accepts past due payments, he waives the right to claim such advantage and cannot claim it as to subsequent payments unless he gives the other party notice of his intention to insist upon payments as specified.
>
> We know of no good reason for saying that such principle does not apply to insurance contracts, where the insured has no part in determining the wording of the contract.

In other words, the court held that the insurance company had waived the requirement that premiums be paid on the due date or within the grace period by accepting, without objection, premiums paid as much as 60 days late. The company could insist upon timely payment even after such a course of conduct, but only after giving notice of its intention to do so.

9.3 What an Estoppel Is

The concept of estoppel is similar to waiver in a sense, and the concepts are frequently used interchangeably. However, estoppel involves some additional considerations. Actually, there are two kinds of estoppel: legal estoppel and equitable estoppel. Legal estoppel is primarily concerned with estoppel by record or deed and dates back to the earliest days of the common law. In this sense, whenever a person has executed a deed or other formal document in which he has made certain statements of fact, he will not thereafter be permitted to deny the truth of those statements. In other words, he is estopped to deny (prohibited from denying) the statements he made in the deed.

The concept with which life insurance law is concerned is *equitable* estoppel. This concept was first used in courts of equity and later applied in courts of law. Like many legal principles, equitable estoppel is more easily illustrated than defined; and the case of *Clauson* v. *Prudential Insurance Company of America*[2] furnishes a good illustration.

The Clauson case involved a suit under a group life insurance contract issued to Chrysler Motors Corporation, effective as of July 1, 1957. The contract provided for life insurance on a term basis for persons owning qualified Chrysler dealerships. The amount of insurance for each dealer was to be determined annually as of July 1, based on the number and type of motor vehicles shipped to the dealer, in accordance with a system of insurance credit points.

Mr. Clauson, the insured, was a Chrysler dealer and entitled to coverage under the contract, but he stated at the outset that he was not interested unless he could be insured for $50,000. The Boston City manager for the Dodge division of Chrysler told Clauson that he was eligible only for $30,000; but after some negotiations they agreed upon $50,000, and a certificate was issued in that amount. Notice was never given to Clauson that the amount of insurance was other than $50,000, and his contribution toward the premium for the coverage was based on that amount.

When Clauson was accidentally killed, his widow (and beneficiary) presented claim in the amount of $50,000. The Chrysler Company then checked its records and determined that Clauson had been eligible only for $30,000. The insurer paid the $30,000 to the beneficiary and offered to refund to the estate the amount of Clauson's contributions in excess of those that would have been required for that amount of insurance. The beneficiary sued.

The court found that the contract required Chrysler to make a determination of the number of insurance credit points on an agreed basis, that the company did not make that determination prior to issuance of the certificate, and that this failure to make the determination was the result of a joint decision by Chrysler and Prudential, with no notice being given to Clauson.

"There remains for determination the question," the court said, "of

---

[2] 195 Fed. Supp. 72 (U.S.D.C. Mass., 1961).

whether the plaintiff may invoke the doctrine of equitable estoppel as entitling her to recover in this action" (in other words, win her suit for the additional proceeds). The law of equitable estoppel in Maryland, the jurisdiction of this case, had been stated in a case decided in 1866, and the court quoted from that case as follows:

> The rule is this; _____ where one by his acts, declaration or silence, where it is his duty to speak, has involved another person, in reasonable reliance on such acts or declarations, to enter into a transaction, he shall not, to the prejudice of the person so misled, impeach the transaction. He need not have acted fraudulently, or willfully have misled the other party. The object of the rule is not to punish for fraud or falsehood, but to adjust equitably a loss between two parties one of whom must bear it, and it is considered that he should bear it who has caused it. This is a most benefi-cent principle, for it enforces good faith and gives security to that trustfulness which must enter much into business transactions and it applies itself not to any special class or sort of cases, but to all dealings between man and man. But it must be observed that equity applies this principle of estoppel cautiously and only in a case clear upon the circum-stances. . . .[3] Hence it is required that the matter of estoppel, i.e., the facts out of which it arises, be clearly established in evidence; and then the facts so established must present these two requisites, viz:
>
> 1. That the party claiming the estoppel was misled and induced to enter into the transaction upon the faith of the declaration, act or silence of the other, or upon the fact or relation which he seeks to restrain the other party from denying.
> 2. That his being so misled was not through his own negligence, or want of attention to proper means of information. . . .

Applying this rule to the facts of the Clauson case, the court concluded that it presented a clear case for the operation of an estoppel. First, Mr. Clauson would not have entered into the transaction if he had known that the amount of insurance he was entitled to was only $30,000. Second, he could not be considered negligent in assuming that Chrysler would do what the policy provided it would do—that is, check its own records before issuing the certificate. Furthermore, Chrysler's collection of the premium calculated on that basis could only further substantiate his belief that the company's records had been checked and that his records had been correct. This argument is concluded as follows:

> Even if prior to his death Mr. Clauson might have been made whole[4] by a refund of a portion or all of his contributions, no such action can make his widow whole after his death because the risk has been determined and

---

[3] Here the court is saying that the doctrine of equitable estoppel will not be lightly invoked, since it would always interfere with the usual legal procedures and remedies.
[4] That is, the wrong might have been corrected.

a relatively slight change of position has been rendered very much greater by circumstances beyond the control of any party. As is the case with any aleatory contract, a party who has failed to make a timely assertion of his rights may be foreclosed from taking advantage of them after a lapse of time in which the risk has been determined.[5]

The court decided, therefore, that the insurer was "estopped to deny that the amount of insurance to which Harvey G. Clauson, Sr., was entitled under the policy was different from that stated in the certificate." Judgment was entered for the plaintiff in the amount of $20,000, with interest and court costs, since the company had already paid $30,000.

The difference between this case and the previous case involving a waiver should be readily apparent. In the waiver case the company had the right to insist upon payment of premiums on the due date. It chose not to insist upon this right and, in fact, accepted some premiums as much as 60 days late. In legal effect, therefore, the insurer relinquished a right it might otherwise have insisted upon, and could not reassert that right without notice to the insured of its intention to do so.

In the estoppel case, the facts were quite different. Here the insurer permitted the insured to believe that he was insured for $50,000; it issued a certificate in that amount and collected premiums for that amount. As a matter of fact, the insured would have sought insurance elsewhere if he had not thought he was insured in that amount. After his death, the company checked its records and determined that he was entitled to $30,000 only. Thereupon it paid that amount to the beneficiary and offered to refund to the estate the excess premium. Here one of the parties would have to suffer a loss, and, in accordance with a well-established equitable principle, the court held that that loss should fall on the party whose actions had contributed most toward causing it—the insurer. This decision was reached by applying the principle of estoppel.

To summarize, the principle of estoppel is invoked in a situation where one person, A, has, by his words or actions, caused another person, B, to enter into a transaction in reliance upon those words or actions (in good faith and without negligence on B's part) that he would not have entered if he had known the truth. Under such circumstances, if B has suffered a loss as a consequence of relying upon A's actions or declarations, A will be estopped—that is, forbidden—to deny that the circumstances were as he permitted them to appear to be.

9.4 Waiver and Estoppel Compared

Similarities of the Concepts. Basically, waiver and estoppel are separate and distinct concepts. Nevertheless, just as the two sides of a coin

---

[5] *Clauson* v. *Prudential Insurance Company of America, op. cit.*

are different and yet together constitute a whole, so waiver and estoppel often occur together and constitute two views of the same essential situation. Thus if an insurer takes such action as to indicate that it is waiving its right to declare a policy void, and if the policyowner relies upon that action to such an extent that it would be inequitable to permit the insurer afterward to insist upon the forfeiture of the policy, it may be equally correct to say that the forfeiture was waived or that the insurer was later estopped to deny the waiver. In either case, the decision is for the policyowner; and often the courts are not too technical in their analyses. As a result, the two concepts are often discussed together and frequently viewed as essentially the same.

Basic Differences. In specific situations, the differences are often important. For instance, where an agent without authority is alleged to have waived a condition, most courts hold that if the lack of authority was known to the applicant or insured, such an alleged waiver will be ineffective. With an equitable estoppel, the situation is different. The actions, even of an unauthorized agent, may create a situation resulting in an equitable estoppel[6] against the life insurance company. It is important, therefore, to keep the basic distinctions in mind.

Waiver is an agreement, though not necessarily a contract, and it is closely related to contract law. Estoppel is more closely related to the law of torts and concerns actions so inequitable as to preclude the person who was responsible from availing himself of a defense that would otherwise be his. Waiver results from intentional actions even though the actions may at times have implications of which the person was not completely aware. An estoppel is enforced contrary to the intentions of the person against whom it is invoked, and he is said to be estopped to claim rights he would otherwise have had.

Courts of equity often use the phrase "equity and good conscience," and it is a good phrase to bear in mind. Although equitable estoppel is frequently applied in courts of law, it is essentially an equitable doctrine, and it carries with it many of the attributes of the court of equity. An equitable estoppel ordinarily requires words or actions of such a nature that they lead the other party to rely on them in good faith and to suffer a loss as a result. The court then says—in effect, and sometimes in actual words—that the person who permitted the situation to arise or was responsible for it cannot "in equity and good conscience" be heard to say that the facts were not as he represented or permitted them to seem to be.

Thus, the law will not permit an insurer to interpose an otherwise valid defense against a claim if, with full knowledge that the contract is voidable, it has delivered a policy, accepted premiums, or otherwise

---

[6] See discussion of agency by estoppel in Chapter 3, section 3.14.

conducted itself as if the contract were valid. This, of course, assumes that the insured is innocent of wrong.

B. SOME COMMON RULES CONCERNING WAIVERS

9.5 The Importance of Intent

It is essential to all forms of waiver that the person alleged to have waived something must have had the intention, express or implied, to do what he actually did. For that reason, there are several well-settled rules on the subject. One of these, previously mentioned, is that the unauthorized act of an agent cannot create a waiver, although it may raise an estoppel. Another rule concerns acts of the insurance company which might under some circumstances create a waiver—acts such as furnishing forms for proof of loss, etc. The rule is that such actions will not have that effect if, by notice either in the policy or elsewhere, the company expressly denies that a waiver is intended. However, once a privilege or power has been waived, the waiver cannot thereafter be revoked.

Many actions taken by an insurance company when it has knowledge of a breach of a condition will be interpreted as showing an unequivocal intent to continue the contract in force. Thus, if an insurer learns of a violation of one of the conditions set forth in the policy, the collection of subsequent premiums will be held to waive its right to avoid or terminate the contract on the basis of such a violation.

9.6 Some Waivers Are Forbidden

As a general rule, a party to a contract may waive any privilege or power available to him under that agreement. Thus, any provision that is for the benefit of the insurer may be waived by it, even though it is a standard provision required by statute. However, there are several exceptions to the rule as it applies to the life insurance contract.

Perhaps the most basic exception to this general rule is based upon the public interest. One cannot relinquish any right conferred by any rule of law or statute that has been enacted in the public interest. This rule is stated in one case[7] concerning nonforfeiture provisions as follows:

> . . . Under the nonforfeiture statutes . . . and the judicial decisions construing them, the law jealously guards and protects the rights of policyholders in the excess reserves built up in the early years of level premium life insurance policies. The benefits conferred by these statutes cannot be abrogated, waived, or contracted away, either by agreement in the policy

---

[7] *Fayman* v. *Franklin Life Insurance Co.*, 386 S.W. (2d) 52 (1965).

or by agreement made between the parties prior to default. If any advance agreement is made for the disposition of the reserves upon default, for which statutory authority cannot be found, it is unenforceable and void. The public policy involved overrides the freedom of contract of the parties before default with reference to these benefits and prior to the time the nonforfeiture statutes become effective. . . .

A second exception is so obvious that it seems almost unnecessary to state it—that one cannot waive a fact. Thus, the insured cannot agree that the person who is really the agent of the insurer shall be considered the agent of the insured, even though an agreement to this effect is set forth in the policy itself, as was once the practice. Such a provision cannot operate as a waiver of the truth. If the agent is the representative of the insurance company, he is its agent and this fact cannot be waived.

This rule is clearly stated in the case of *Sternaman* v. *Metropolitan Life Insurance Co.*,[8] as follows:

> The power to contract is not unlimited. While, as a general rule, there is the utmost freedom of action in this regard, some restrictions are placed upon the right by legislation, by public policy, and by the nature of things. Parties cannot make a binding contract in violation of law or of public policy. They cannot in the same instrument agree that a thing exists and that it does not exist, or provide that one is the agent of the other and at the same time, and with reference to the same subject, that there is no relation of agency between them.

There are also certain rules of the common law in which public policy is so deeply concerned that parties to a contract will not be permitted to waive them. One example is the rule prohibiting the making of insurance contracts that are not supported by an insurable interest. Such an unlawful agreement cannot be made enforceable either by waiver or estoppel.

9.7 Cannot Create Coverage by Waiver

Generally speaking, the law does not impose upon any person a contractual duty unless his promise is supported by consideration or is under seal. Thus if an insurer is not liable with respect to a given type of loss, the general rule is that liability will not be created by waiver or estoppel. This is illustrated most clearly, perhaps, in cases where the policy does not cover losses if the insured is beyond a specified age. Under the majority view, the insurance company cannot by waiver create liability for losses beyond that age. If the company inadvertently bills the policyowner for premiums beyond the limiting age, the company must refund the premium, but it is not liable if a loss occurs beyond the specified age.

---

[8] 57 L.R.A. 318 (N.Y., 1902).

There are, however, holdings to the contrary; and in at least one case[9] it has been held that an equitable estoppel may be imposed if premiums are accepted beyond the limiting age.

9.8 Releases

If one has a legal right to receive a sum of money from another, he may release the right by agreement with consideration or under seal, but it cannot be waived. Nor does the payment of one sum constitute consideration for the release of a right to payment of another. This latter principle is illustrated most frequently in situations where the beneficiary makes claim for the death benefit and the accidental death benefit under a life insurance policy. If the insurer determines that the accidental death benefit is not payable, payment of the death benefit does not constitute consideration for the release of the beneficiary's possible right to the accidental death benefit.

Assume that Helen Jones is the beneficiary of a life insurance policy insuring the life of her husband, Charles. Charles has a minor automobile accident and a heart attack and dies under such circumstances as to make it highly doubtful that he died as the result of accidental means. Helen makes claim for the accidental means death benefit as well as the amount of insurance under the basic policy. The insurer pays the benefit under the basic policy but denies the claim for the accidental means death benefit. The law is clear that payment of the death claim is not consideration for the beneficiary's release of her claim for the accidental means death benefit as well. In fact, life insurance claims people sometimes say that payment of the claim for the basic benefit may "finance" the beneficiary's suit for the accidental means death benefit.

On the other hand, if there is a true dispute as to the amount properly payable, and if the parties come to an agreement and payment is made, the agreement will be held to be effective as against later proof that a larger sum was in reality due and payable. For example, it might be impossible to determine the exact date of the insured's death in some instances, such as death in a wilderness or a drowning incident where the body is not found until weeks or months later. In such instances, it may not be possible to determine the exact amount payable because the date of death is uncertain. However, if the insurer and the beneficiary, recognizing the impossibility of exactly determining the date of death, agree to a compromise settlement and payment is made, this agreement will be upheld even though it becomes possible later to prove the exact date of death and that a larger amount should have been paid. In situations of this

---

[9] See *Pitts* v. *New York Life Insurance Company*, the Illustrative Case at the end of this chapter.

kind, the parties are said to have resolved their problems by an "accord and satisfaction." They reach an agreement or "accord," and it is satisfied by the payment. An accord and satisfaction has always been held to be an effective discharge of an obligation to pay a disputed sum of money.

9.9 Policy Provisions concerning Waivers

Many policies contain provisions specifically declaring that only certain named officers may waive any terms of the contract. Even those who have this authority are often required to execute such a waiver in a specified manner, usually by written endorsement of the policy. One company accomplishes this in a provision that reads as follows:

> Only the president or vice-president, or the secretary of the company has authority to alter this contract or to waive any of its provisions.

The general rule is that a provision of this kind is solely for the benefit of the company and that it as well as any other similar provision of the policy may be waived. In short, the very policy provision that attempts to limit the exercise of the power to waive may itself be waived!

A provision of this kind, therefore, operates merely as notice to the owner of limitations on the authority of the agent under the policy. After receipt of the policy, the insured is considered to have knowledge of the limitations. If the company does not waive the policy provision or permit an estoppel to arise, thereafter a subsequent attempted waiver on the part of the agent will be ineffective. It should be noted, in connection with estoppels, that the question is not whether the action of the agent is authorized but whether it was within the course of his employment.

C. ESTOPPEL AND MATERIAL MISREPRESENTATION

9.10 Avoidance of the Contract

The doctrine of equitable estoppel is frequently invoked in situations where the agent, in completing the application for insurance, has inserted incorrect answers to the questions even though the applicant has given him correct answers. It is relatively standard practice for a life insurance agent to fill in the blanks in a life insurance application for the applicant, asking each question and filling in the blanks with answers the applicant gives him. After completing the application in this way, the agent asks the applicant to sign it. The applicant does so and, in legal effect, thus makes the answers his own.

Assume, however, that in writing the answers to the application questions, the agent is given correct answers by the applicant but, knowing that the application may not be accepted if the truth is stated, he inserts false answers which he knows will not be questioned. May the insurer in this situation—and during the contestable period of the policy—deny the claim after the death of the insured, or rescind the policy during his lifetime, on the basis of material misrepresentation in the application? Or is it estopped to do so?

The general rule, as stated in the early cases, was that an insurer in this situation could not rely upon the falsity of such answers to deny the claim or rescind the policy. The reasoning was that the agent was representing the insurer, his knowledge was imputed to the insurer, and the insurer was therefore estopped to use the falsity of the answers in the application to support its denial of a claim or rescission of the contract. However, this rule assumes that correct answers were given by the applicant, that there was neither fraud nor collusion on his part, and that he did not know of the false answers inserted by the agent. The knowledge of the applicant, therefore, is an important factor in the application of this rule; and, since it is customary today to make the application a part of the policy, the question often turns on whether the applicant is or is not under a duty to read the application and thus become aware of the false answers.

9.11 Applicant's Duty to Read the Application

The decisions are mixed with respect to whether the applicant has a duty to read the application for a life insurance policy. What is sometimes referred to as the majority rule, however, is that he is under a duty to read the application—as he must read anything he signs—and he will be held responsible for its contents. This rule is summarized in the case of *Theros* v. *Metropolitan Life Insurance Company*,[10] as follows:

> It is also the majority rule that an insured is under a duty to read his application before signing it, and will be considered bound by a knowledge of the contents of his signed application. This is merely an application of fundamental contract law. While courts generally are inclined to treat insurance contracts as special and do not always vigorously apply all the principles of contract law, that tendency should not be allowed to overrun the bounds of legitimate exception.

The court noted also that there was no evidence to show that the insured was

> . . . by fraud, accident, misrepresentation, imposition, illiteracy, artifice or device reasonably prevented from reading the application before signing it. Therefore, he is, by law, conclusively presumed to have read the application and his beneficiary is bound by the contents thereof.

---

[10] 407 P. (2d) 685 (1965).

In other words, the insured is presumed to have knowledge of the misstatements in an application he has signed and that is made a part of the policy that was delivered to him.[11] Thus the insurer is not estopped to deny the truth of the answers recorded by its own agent, since the applicant knew of the false answers and did nothing about it.

Some understanding of the legal basis for the minority view is given in the dissenting opinion in the Theros case. There the judge summarized the legal position of the parties and continued as follows:

> The critical question is this: Did Mr. Theros know that Mr. George put down the false statements, rather than the correct information he gave Mr. George, and knowingly participate in the falsification?
>
> How is this question to be answered? Mr. Theros is dead and his testimony is unavailable. There are two sources to look to in order to determine what actually happened: (a) whatever deduction may be drawn from the fact that Mr. Theros signed the application; and (b) the testimony of the agent, Mr. George.
>
> As to (a), the court's decision states that from his signing of the application, in the absence of a showing of fraud, duress or something of that nature, the deceased is conclusively presumed to have read it. With deference to the view of my colleagues to the contrary, it is my opinion that an analysis of the situation here presented will reveal that the "presumption" referred to cannot properly be regarded as conclusive, and that it does not establish the fact so absolutely as to be incontestable.
>
> ❖   ❖   ❖   ❖   ❖
>
> As to (b), beyond any question of presumption there is evidence relating directly to the question whether the deceased knew of the false answers: the testimony of the defendant's agent, Mr. George. While in one part of his testimony he made statements indicating that Mr. Theros knew the contents of the application, he also made statements to the contrary. That being so, it would be the prerogative of the fact-trier to determine which to believe.

Thus, the majority view is that the applicant has a duty to read the application before he signs it and will be charged with knowledge of any false statement inserted by the agent. However, as suggested by this dissenting opinion, there are strong equities on the other side. Often, too, the special facts of the case are sufficient to overcome the presumption that the owner has read the policy.

Two examples will illustrate such special situations. In one case,[12] the evidence showed that the applicant gave correct information concerning the diabetic condition of her daughter (the proposed insured), but the agent recorded incorrect answers which made it appear that the

---

[11] See *Couch Cyclopedia of Insurance Law* (2d ed.; Rochester, N.Y.: Lawyers Cooperative Publishing Co., 1959), 35.211.

[12] *Hart v. The Prudential Insurance Company of America,* 47 Cal. App. (2d) 298, 117 P. (2d) 930 (1941).

daughter's health was good. After her death, the company denied the claim on grounds of misrepresentation of material facts in the application. The company contended that even if the agent inserted false answers, the applicant was presumed to have knowledge of the false statements since the application was attached to the policy. The mother testified that there was no copy of the application in the policy, however, and that was the finding of the court. The holding, therefore, was against the company.

In another case,[13] the applicant had suffered a severe head injury while in service. The evidence showed that at the time the application was filled out he discussed this with the agent, who said: "Well, as long as you do not have a medical discharge they don't care about all this. As long as you have an honorable discharge and not a medical discharge you can sign this application." The head injury, therefore, was not mentioned in the application, and the company denied the claim for that reason.

Of the insured's duty to read the application under these circumstances, the court said:

> Defendant correctly states that when the insured has a copy of the application in his possession he is presumed to have read it, and to be aware of any misstatements therein even though they were not due to his own fault. . . . The rule would not apply here to charge Boggio with knowledge he did not have when he signed the application unless he could have ascertained that his statements were false in the sense that they withheld information sought to be elicited by the questions contained in the application. This was not the case. He relied on Angelino's [the agent's] statement that the questions did not call for information as to the injury received in the service unless it had led to medical discharge. Having had the question interpreted for him in this manner, repeated reading of the questions and answers would not have led him to believe that his service injury was material. He knew at all times that his answers were literally untrue but not that they would be deemed untrue by the company in determining whether he was an insurable risk.

9.12 Collusion

There is almost general agreement concerning the legal position of the insurer where the agent writes false answers that were agreed upon with the proposed insured—in other words, where the applicant and the agent conspire to submit a fraudulent application. In situations of this kind, the agent is definitely acting outside the scope of his authority, the applicant or beneficiary cannot be allowed to benefit from this misconduct, and the company is fully justified in relying upon the material misrepresentation as grounds for avoiding the contract.

---

[13] *Boggio* v. *California Western States Life Ins. Co.*, 239 P. (2d) 144, Cal. App. (1952).

D. THE PAROL EVIDENCE RULE

9.13 Equitable Estoppel

Because equitable estoppel, in effect, assumes something contrary to the intention of the party against whom it is invoked, it also frequently involves proving a set of facts contrary to the terms of the contract itself. It will be remembered, however, that the parol evidence rule precludes the admission of evidence tending to deny or contradict the terms of a written contract.

At the same time, it may also be recalled that the doctrine of equitable estoppel was adopted by common-law courts from courts of equity. The parol evidence rule, as a rule of evidence, applies to actions involving juries. Since equitable actions do not involve juries, there were no parol evidence problems in equitable estoppels so long as they were confined to courts of equity. A conflict with the parol evidence rule was almost inevitable, however, when the concept of equitable estoppel was adopted by common-law courts.

As a general rule, if the alleged estoppel is based upon actions or statements that occurred or were made after the contract became effective, it will be upheld. With respect to estoppels based on events occurring before or at the inception of the contract, however, there is a difference of opinion. Several courts have held that the parol evidence rule prevents the admission of evidence establishing such estoppels.

A Landmark Case. One very early, but significant case[14] in the development of the doctrine of equitable estoppel in connection with the life insurance contract involved a warranty in the application that was not true. The application was signed by the insured, all of the statements in it were warranted to be true, and it was made a part of the contract. The warranty in question concerned the age of the mother of the insured at the time of her death. Alleging the untruth of this warranted age, the life insurance company denied the claim.

Evidence was offered to show what actually took place at the time of the application. Witnesses testified that the agent asked the insured the age of her mother at her death, and the insured said she did not know. Someone else who was present volunteered an answer which was inserted in the application by the agent. It was later found to be incorrect. If admitted in the trial, this evidence would support an equitable estoppel. The question was whether oral evidence could be admitted under such circumstances and for such a purpose.

The court held that the evidence was admissible, and the finding was against the insurer. On appeal to the United States Supreme Court, the decision was unanimously upheld, as follows:

---

[14] *Union Mutual Life Insurance Co.* v. *Wilkinson,* 13 Wall. 222, 20 L. Ed. 617 (1872).

It is in precisely such cases as this that courts of law in modern times have introduced the doctrine of equitable estoppels, or, as it is sometimes called, *estoppels in pais.* The principle is that where one party has by his representations or his conduct induced the other party to a transaction to give him an advantage which it would be against equity and good conscience for him to assert, he would not in a court of justice be permitted to avail himself of that advantage. And although the cases to which this principle is to be applied are not as well defined as could be wished, the general doctrine is well understood and is applied by courts of law as well as equity where the technical advantage thus obtained is set up and relied on to defeat the ends of justice or establish a dishonest claim. . . . The modern decisions fully sustain this proposition, and they seem to us founded in reason and justice, and meet our entire approval. This principle does not admit oral testimony to vary or contradict that which is in writing, but it goes upon the idea that the writing offered in evidence was not the instrument of the party whose name is signed to it; that it was procured under such circumstances by the other side as estops that side from using or relying on its contents,[15] not that it may be contradicted by oral testimony, but that it may be shown by such testimony that it cannot be lawfully used against the party whose name is signed to it.

This holding has been followed by the courts of most of the states, although there have been a few exceptions.

9.14 Waivers

One very characteristic situation involving alleged waivers concerns the stipulation often found in the life insurance policy that it shall not take effect until the policy has been delivered and the first premium has been paid. If the applicant does not have the cash at the time of delivery but with the agent's acquiescence pays the premium with a promissory note, can parol evidence be introduced after the insured's death (and before payment of the note) to show this agreement?

At first it would seem that parol evidence in this case would contradict one of the terms of the contract. However, an analysis of the situation leads to a different conclusion. The effectiveness of the contract is conditioned upon payment of the premium, but there is nothing to prevent the agent from removing or altering this condition if he has adequate authority. In that situation, he waives the condition of prepayment of the first premium. The question, therefore, concerns the making of the contract and not the terms of a contract already made. The parol evidence rule does not apply to circumstances involved in the making of the contract.

---

[15] In other words, this was not a violation of the parol evidence rule since oral evidence was not used to vary the terms of the contract. On the contrary, it was used only to show that the contract was completed under such circumstances that the insurer was estopped to rely upon it.

The cases, therefore, hold that an insurer may, through an authorized agent, waive this condition and that this waiver may be shown by oral evidence. The contract itself is not varied.

Now assume that the life insurance policy is avoidable by the company because of the breach of a policy condition by the policyowner. At a later date the insurance company learns of the breach, expressly states that it is of no importance, and premiums are thereafter accepted. This type of case illustrates a subsequent waiver of a breach of condition, and it is generally agreed that a waiver of this kind can be shown by oral evidence.

E. THE DUTY TO ACT

Under general contract law, silence does not ordinarily change one's legal responsibilities unless there are special circumstances that place one under a duty to speak. This is true also with respect to the contract of life insurance. The insurer, therefore, is under a duty to speak only when it would be inequitable to remain silent.

For example, the breach of a policy condition by the policyowner places the insurer in essentially the same position as the discovery of material misrepresentation. It does not avoid the contract, but it gives the insurer the right to avoid it if it wishes. If the company exercises this right, the legal relationships created by that particular contract are extinguished. Contractual duties cannot thereafter be re-created without a new contract. However, if the company fails to exercise this right and with full knowledge of the breach remains silent, what is the legal effect of its inaction?

As a general rule, the courts hold that the breach of a condition subsequent gives the insurer only the right to disaffirm the contract, and that this right must be exercised within a reasonable time after knowledge is acquired or it will be regarded as having been waived. The policy may be worded in such a way as to require the power to be exercised in a particular way, as by instituting legal proceedings. If this is true, legal proceedings must be instituted. Otherwise, the privilege will be held to have been waived after a reasonable period of time. The right may also be extinguished by the expiration of any period fixed by statute or by the incontestable clause.

F. THE DOCTRINE OF ELECTION

The doctrine of election is often mentioned in connection with the overall subject of estoppel, although it is a very special application of it. Fundamentally, it involves a choice among two or more inconsistent or irreconcilable legal remedies of such a nature that having elected one course of action, the plaintiff will be estopped from pursuing any of the others thereafter.

Assume, for example, that a life insurance company takes action to cancel a life insurance contract which includes provisions for the payment of disability benefits. The insured brings an action against the company for the fraudulent breach of the contract and is awarded damages. Subsequently the insured brings another action for disability benefits which would have accrued to him prior to the date of the previous suit had it not been for the cancellation of the contract by the company. Note that in the first suit, the insured alleged that the contract was breached and that he was entitled to damages as a consequence. In the second suit he demanded benefits that would have been payable if the contract had not been breached. This is clearly a case of the attempted pursuit of a second course of action inconsistent with the first.

In one case presenting this set of facts, the court quoted from a prior decision as follows:

> . . . If a party should invoke a remedy appropriate to a certain state of facts, and there should exist another remedy appropriate to a different state of facts, inconsistent with and repugnant to the first state of facts, his invocation of the first remedy is an election which by the bare commencement of the action will bar his right to invoke the other remedy.[16]

Applying the law to the facts of this case, the court held that the insured was bound by his first choice of remedy—the award of damages—and could not proceed with the second action—for the payment of disability benefits. The first action was brought on the basis that the policy was canceled and damages were due. Under those circumstances, the insured could not bring a second action to require payment of benefits that would only be payable if the contract were enforced. The insured had elected to treat the contract as canceled, and that election barred his right to pursue the second, inconsistent remedy.

SUMMARY

Waiver and Estoppel Defined

A waiver is the intentional and voluntary giving up of a known privilege or right. It may be express or implied. Some waivers are contractual, as in the case of the waiver of premium for disability under the life insurance contract; others are without consideration and thus not enforceable as contracts. As a general rule, the acceptance of past-due

---

[16] *McMahon* v. *McMahon*, 122 S.C. 336; 115 S.E. 293, quoted in *The Pacific Mutual Life Insurance Co. of Calif.* v. *Rhame*, 32 F. Supp. 59 (D.C. S.C., 1940).

premiums will be considered a waiver of the insurer's right to insist upon payment on the due date.

The principle of equitable estoppel is defined as a situation where one person by his acts, words, or silence causes another to take action he would not otherwise have taken. Under such circumstances, the person responsible will be estopped to deny that the circumstances were as he made or permitted them to appear to be, if to do otherwise would cause loss to the second person.

Waiver and estoppel are distinct concepts, although they are often used almost interchangeably. Actually, the concept of waiver gives legal effect to an intentional act on the part of one of the parties to a contract, while equitable estoppel is used to prevent a party from pleading the truth in a situation which he has misrepresented or permitted to appear otherwise than as it was.

Some Rules concerning Waivers

Waiver always requires an intentional action on the part of the person alleged to have waived a privilege or right, although the intent need not be a specific intent to waive in the legal sense of the word. One needs only to have intended to take the action he took. It is not necessary that he intended to waive any rights.

Some waivers are forbidden by law. Thus, one cannot waive a right conferred by law if the public interest is concerned, and one cannot waive a fact. Nor can insurance coverage be established by waiver. A right to receive payment of an agreed sum of money cannot be waived; but if there is a dispute concerning the amount, an agreement and payment of the amount agreed upon will be binding.

Policy Provisions

Although many policies contain a provision that only certain named officers of the insurer may waive any provisions of the contract, this provision itself may be waived.

Avoidance of the Contract

In cases involving material misrepresentation in the application, it is sometimes alleged that correct answers were given the agent but that they were incorrectly recorded. The general rule is that if the applicant gave truthful answers to the questions and they were falsely recorded by the agent, the insurer is estopped from using the false answers to avoid the contract unless there was fraud or collusion on the part of the applicant and the agent, or actual knowledge on the part of the applicant.

If a copy of the signed application is made a part of the contract, the majority rule is that knowledge of the false answers on the part of the applicant will be presumed. This is based on the general rule that a person who signs a written instrument is presumed to know its contents. However, there is a strong minority line of cases on this subject, and as a general rule relatively slight evidence will be sufficient to support the contention that the applicant did not or could not know of the false answers.

In cases of collusion between the agent and the applicant, however, the agent is acting outside the scope of his authority and the insurer is not estopped from relying on the false answers in the application to avoid the contract.

The Parol Evidence Rule

Equitable Estoppel. In applying the principle of equitable estoppel, it is frequently necessary to prove a set of circumstances that conflict with the terms of the life insurance contract. This, of course, conflicts with the parol evidence rule and has sometimes been challenged on that basis. If the alleged estoppel has occurred after the contract became effective, however, it will generally be upheld.

If the estoppel concerns circumstances preceding or occurring at the inception of the contract, the parol evidence rule has sometimes been held to preclude the admission of oral evidence to show the estoppel. One of the leading cases on this subject—*Union Mutual Life Insurance Co.* v. *Wilkinson*[17]—upholds the admission of oral evidence, in the words of the court, "not to vary or contradict that which is in writing" but to show that "the writing offered in evidence was not the instrument of the party whose name is signed to it." Most, though not all, of the states have followed this line of reasoning.

Waiver. An agreement with an authorized agent to waive payment of the first premium may be shown by oral evidence even though the policy is conditioned on such payment. This is not considered to be in conflict with the parol evidence rule because it involves circumstances surrounding the making of the contract, not the meaning of any of its provisions.

The Duty to Speak or Take Action. Silence or inaction do not ordinarily affect one's legal responsibilities unless he has a duty to speak or to take some action, and this principle is held to apply to the insurer in connection with the life insurance contract. Thus if a company learns of a breach of a condition subsequent, it must exercise its right to disaffirm the contract within a reasonable time—i.e., take some action—or it will be held to have waived the right.

---

[17] 13 Wall. 222, 20 L. Ed. 617 (1872).

The Doctrine of Election. If a wronged person has a choice of two inconsistent or irreconcilable remedies and elects to pursue one of them, his election of that remedy will prevent or estop him from later instituting an inconsistent action.

ILLUSTRATIVE CASE

It has been noted that liability cannot as a general rule be extended by waiver. The concept of equitable estoppel is highly flexible, however, and the following case is included here as an illustration of the kind of circumstances which may be held to create an estoppel, as well as an excellent discussion of the subject.

PITTS v. NEW YORK LIFE INSURANCE COMPANY[18]
Supreme Court of South Carolina

Action by the beneficiary of a policy of insurance on the life of her husband to recover double indemnity by reason of his accidental death. The case was tried before the Honorable Clarence E. Singletary, Presiding Judge, without a jury; appeal is from his judgment in favor of the plaintiff.

On July 1, 1920, appellant insured the life of Reuben B. Pitts under a ten-year term policy for $10,000, or $20,000 in the event that his death should result from accident. On July 30, 1925, this policy was converted into an ordinary life policy, with like provision for double indemnity in case of death by accident, and with provision for payment of disability benefit of $100.00 per month if the insured should become disabled before age sixty. As so converted, its annual premium was $405.20, of which $10.00 was stated to be for the double indemnity coverage and $28.20 for the disability coverage, with the provision that after the insured should reach the age of sixty years the premiums to become due would be reduced by the amount of the premium charged for the disability coverage. It excluded the double indemnity coverage in case of death resulting from certain causes, among them "engaging as a passenger or otherwise, in submarine or aeronautic operations."

On January 27, 1933, pursuant to application by the insured and the beneficiary, the double indemnity provision was amended by endorsement reading as follows:

> In accordance with the request of the insured, the double indemnity benefit is hereby modified to permit the double indemnity provision to apply if the insured's death occurs as the result of riding as a fare-paying passenger in a licensed passenger aircraft provided by an incorporated passenger carrier and operated by a licensed pilot on a regular passenger route between definitely established airports.
>
> It is also understood and agreed that the entire provisions for double indemnity as included in the policy will apply only if death occurs prior to

---

[18] 148 S.E. (2d) 369 (1966).

the anniversary of the policy on which the insured's age at nearest birthday is 65.

Any premium due on and after the anniversary on which the age of the insured at nearest birthday is 65 will be reduced by the amount of premium charged for the double indemnity benefit.

In 1942, when the insured reached age sixty, appellant reduced the annual premium by $28.20, the amount charged for the disability coverage. The insured became sixty-five years of age in 1947, but in that year and each year thereafter appellant continued to bill him without reduction of the premium by the amount ($10.00) charged for the double indemnity benefit; and the insured continued to pay the premiums as thus billed until his death, at the age of eighty-one, on March 25, 1963.

That the insured's death resulted from accident is not disputed. Appellant paid the face amount of the policy, $10,000, but refused to pay under the double indemnity provision. Its offer to refund the double indemnity premiums paid subsequent to August 1, 1947, together with interest on each such payment, was rejected.

In her complaint respondent [the beneficiary] alleged that appellant, having failed and neglected, after the insured had reached the age of sixty-five, to reduce the premium by the amount charged for the double indemnity benefit as it was obligated to do by the terms of the 1933 endorsement before mentioned, "has waived its right to rely upon the provisions of the said endorsement and is now estopped" to deny liability for such benefit. In its answer appellant alleged that its failure to note that the premium should be reduced in 1947 was the result of a clerical error, and that the continued payment by the insured and acceptance by it of the unreduced premium after the insured had reached the age of sixty-five were the result of inadvertence and mutual mistake and were contrary to the express terms and conditions of the policy.[19]

It appears undisputed that appellant did not discover the error in its records, and the resulting erroneous billing of premiums, until after the insured's death.

The trial judge held that by having billed the insured for the full premium and accepted payment of the same each year for sixteen years after the insured had reached the age of sixty-five years appellant had waived a right to deny coverage under the double indemnity provision of the 1933 endorsement; and he accordingly ordered judgment for the plaintiff for $10,000.00, with interest from the date on which the face amount of the policy was paid to the beneficiary. That ruling is here challenged by several exceptions.

Policy provisions under which an insurer may assert non-coverage fall into two classes: (1) those providing for forfeiture; and (2) those limiting or excluding coverage. The former may be waived; with regard to the latter, the weight of authority is said to support the view expressed in 29A Am. Jur., Insurance, Section 1135, page 289, as follows:

---

[19] The basic question of the case is summarized in this paragraph. Did the insurer, by continuing to bill for and collect the premium for the accidental death benefit beyond the limiting age, waive its right to rely upon that termination date, as contended by the plaintiff; or is this a situation where the doctrines of waiver and estoppel do not apply?

The rule is well established that the doctrines of implied waiver and of estoppel, based upon the conduct or action of the insurer, are not available to bring within the coverage of a policy risks not covered by its terms, or risks expressly excluded therefrom, and the application of the doctrines in this respect is therefore to be distinguished from the waiver of, or estoppel to assert, grounds of forfeiture. Thus, while an insurer may be estopped by its conduct or its knowledge from insisting upon a forfeiture of a policy, the coverage, or restrictions on the coverage, cannot be extended by the doctrine of waiver or estoppel.

To the same effect is the following, from 16 Appleman, *Insurance Law and Practice*, Section 9090, page 629:

> It has been broadly stated that the doctrines of waiver and estoppel cannot be used to extend the coverage of an insurance policy or create a primary liability, but may only affect rights reserved therein. While an insurer may be estopped, by its conduct or its knowledge or by statute, from insisting on a forfeiture of a policy, under no conditions can the coverage or restrictions on coverage be extended by waiver or estoppel.

❖   ❖   ❖   ❖   ❖

The essential elements of equitable estoppel are: (1) ignorance of the party invoking it of the truth as to the facts in question; (2) representations or conduct of the party estopped which mislead; (3) reliance upon such representations or conduct; and (4) prejudicial change of position as the result of such reliance. *Johnson v. Wabash Life Ins. Co., supra.* The presence of these elements is not essential to the establishment of implied waiver, which results merely from conduct of the party against whom the doctrine is invoked from which voluntary relinquishment of his known right is reasonably inferable. But the two doctrines are related, and have this in common: that the applicability of each in a particular situation results from conduct of the party against whom it is invoked which has rendered it inequitable that he assert a right to which, in the absence of such conduct, he would be entitled.

Whether an insurer, by accepting and retaining the premium for a coverage that by the terms of the policy is excluded or terminated, may be estopped to deny such coverage, must of course depend upon the circumstances of the particular case. For estoppel is an equitable doctrine, essentially flexible, and therefore to be applied or denied as the equities between the parties may preponderate. *Peoples National Bank of Greenville v. Manos Bros., Inc.*, 226 S.D. 257, 84 S.E. 2d 857, 45 A.L.R. 2d 1070. Where the insurer over a long period of time after the date prescribed by it for the termination of a particular coverage has continued to demand, accept and retain the premium fixed by it for that coverage, it may reasonably be inferred that the insured, who in the normal course of things relies upon the insurer's billing, has been misled by such conduct to believe that the insurer has continued to accept the coverage. Upon the same premise, excusable ignorance on the part of the insured as to the true fact, i.e., that the insurer has made a mistake in its billing, may likewise be inferred.

In the present case, as has been noted, the premium for the double indemnity coverage, $10.00, was separate and distinct from, and in addition to, that charged for the normal coverage, $367.00. Although by the terms of the policy the double indemnity coverage was to expire in 1947, when the insured became sixty-five, the undisputed fact that appellant continued for sixteen years thereafter to bill him for such coverage, and to collect and retain it, in our opinion furnished sound and adequate basis for the three elements of estoppel —ignorance, misleading, and reliance—before mentioned. The fourth element, prejudicial change of position, is also present. For not only did the insured expend the amount of such premium, in response to the erroneous billing, during each of the sixteen years between 1947 and 1963, but the insurer's claim for relief from the consequences of its error comes not until after the death of the insured and therefore, we think, too late. Cf. *Privette* v. *Garrison*, 235 S.C. 119, 110 S.E. 2d 17, where the equitable doctrine of laches[20] was held applicable as a bar to the assertion of a right by one party to a transaction against those claiming under the other party, then deceased.

We need not, and do not, decide whether the rule of non-waiver is applicable in the present case, for we think that under the facts apparent in the record here the insurer is estopped to deny the coverage in question. The issue of estoppel was before the Court; it was one of law, the essential facts being undisputed; and the result reached was the just and correct one. Affirmance in that result[21] is proper in such case under Section 8 of Rule 4 of this Court.

QUESTIONS FOR REVIEW

1. Briefly explain what a waiver is. Give an example of
   a. A contractual waiver.
   b. A noncontractual waiver.

2. Define and illustrate the concept of equitable estoppel. Contrast this with legal estoppel.

3. In what way may waiver and estoppel be considered similar?

4. List and briefly discuss two basic differences between the concepts of waiver and estoppel.

5. Briefly explain why each of the following statements is true or false:
   a. The unauthorized act of an agent cannot effect a waiver, although it may provide a basis for an estoppel.
   b. The unauthorized act of an agent cannot effect a waiver or create an estoppel situation.
   c. The unauthorized act of an agent may effect a waiver under some circumstances, although it is most likely to provide a basis for an estoppel.

---

[20] *Laches* may be defined as unreasonable negligence to assert a right, by reason of which the right is lost.

[21] The appeals court affirmed the original decision in favor of the beneficiary. This decision is particularly significant because it first pointed out that additional coverage—beyond that stipulated in the contract—could not be provided under estoppel, and then went on to decide that, under the circumstances of this case, a decision contrary to the general rule was the equitable one.

6. List three kinds of attempted waivers that will not, as a matter of law, be held effective.

7. A has a legal right to receive a stated sum of money from B, but he signs a written waiver of this right. What is the general rule concerning the legal effect of this waiver?

8. Many life insurance policies contain a provision listing the officers who are authorized to waive terms of the contract. Are such provisions always effective? Explain.

9. Summarize the rule concerning the right of the insurer to avoid a policy during the contestable period where its own agent and the applicant are guilty of collusion in completing the application containing false answers to the questions asked.

10. Briefly outline the basis of conflict between the parol evidence rule and the principle of equitable estoppel. How was this conflict resolved in the Wilkinson case (where the admission of oral evidence was upheld; see section 9.13)?

PART III

The Contract
in Operation

This section discusses the various transactions and questions that may arise during the period in which the life insurance contract remains in force.

Chapter Outline

Chapter **10**

The Policyowner Pays
the Premium

IN A BROAD general sense, the operation of any insurance company turns upon the regular collection of premiums, their investment, and the prompt payment of claims. The long-range nature of the life insurance contract and the level premium, legal reserve system make the subject of premium payment, and particularly the consequences of nonpayment, considerably more complicated with respect to the life insurance contract than in connection with other kinds of insurance. The purpose of this chapter is to outline the major problems that can arise in connection with the payment of the life insurance premium and to discuss the legal principles most frequently applied in reaching their solutions.

A. THE NATURE OF THE LIFE INSURANCE PREMIUM

10.1 From the Policyowner's Point of View

The many billions of dollars in life insurance premiums that are paid in this country every year are paid in amounts ranging from a very small amount in some instances to several thousands of dollars in others. Often they are paid over long periods of time. Literally, therefore, nearly all premiums are paid in instalments. Nevertheless, there are some very basic differences between life insurance premium payments and the instalment payments the policyowner may make on his car, refrigerator, or other household appliances.

No Promise to Pay. First and most fundamental is the fact that there is no promise to pay the life insurance premium. When a person buys a

321

car, he receives something tangible at the outset; and he promises to pay the purchase price in a stated number of future instalments of a specified amount. The something tangible which he receives is consideration for his promise to pay, making that promise a valid and enforceable contract on which he can be sued if necessary.

When a person applies for and is issued a life insurance policy, he receives conditional promises from the life insurance company and, in addition, the privilege of keeping the policy in force by paying the premiums. Courts have almost unanimously held that an unpaid insurance premium is not an indebtedness and that the payment of premiums is not an obligation in the legal sense of the word. Insurance premiums, therefore, may be considered as amounts to be paid, but they are payments the policyowner can discontinue any time he wishes, and the insurance company is powerless to compel him to continue. On the other hand, if he keeps the policy in force by payment of premiums, the promises on the part of the insurer are legally enforceable. The fact that so many policyowners continue to pay premiums on their policies year after year, without compulsion other than the nature of the contract, is a most convincing, silent tribute to the value of this privilege.

10.2 From the Company's Point of View

Life insurance, as we know it today, did not truly come into existence until the adoption of the level premium, legal reserve plan. This plan transformed a relatively limited kind of agreement into a plan of insurance, with premium payments tailored to the average person's earning pattern and his life insurance needs. Directly in some respects, indirectly in others, the level premium, legal reserve plan permitted the development of the highly flexible contract that we know today. Under it, relatively modest premium payments at regular intervals may assure a sizable estate for the policyowner's dependents at his death or for himself at retirement.

Funding a plan of such flexibility and unique value is not a simple matter, and it could not be accomplished at all on a basis of individual contracts unrelated to each other. In considering the payment of premiums, therefore, as in the area of risk selection, it is necessary to bear in mind that the life insurance contract is not merely an enforceable agreement between an individual and the life insurance company; it is also an insurance device.

The Legal Problem. Prior to the level premium, legal reserve plan, the life insurance premium presented no special legal problem. An annual premium under a life insurance policy had very much the same legal effect as the premium for fire insurance coverage or the premium under any other policy of insurance. Payment of the premium by the insured for a given term was consideration for the protection provided by the insurance company for the same period.

Because of the special characteristics of the life insurance risk, however, it was not economically feasible to keep these early life insurance contracts in force for the whole of life. Life insurance for more than a limited period of time, therefore, did not become practical until the development of the level premium, legal reserve system. Under this plan, life insurance entered the long-range era, with commitments often running for many years; and the premium for any given year was no longer related only to the insurance protection for that year.

The level premium is possible because funds accumulated in the early years are invested and held for use in later years, when the level premium would otherwise be inadequate. It is fundamental, however, that these funds are held for the benefit of all policyowners, and there is no such thing as an individual account for an individual policy. Nevertheless, in the field of legal problems, it is most frequently an individual policy that is in question. For that reason, we turn to the individual policy to see how it is affected by the level premium, legal reserve system.

Under the Individual Policy. Except for the first year or so, the level premium paid in the early years for a whole life or endowment policy (or any life insurance policy running more than a year, except, perhaps, a decreasing term policy) is more than sufficient to provide for both the current year's mortality needs and the insurer's expenses. If a level expense portion is deducted from the gross premium, there remains a level net premium which provides for more than the policy's share of the current year's death claims. Any balance becomes a part of the company's invested assets, and equivalent reserve liabilities are established to provide for the time in later years when the level net premium would not by itself be sufficient to provide for the policy's share of the current year's claims.

As the insured grows older, a larger amount of the net premium is needed to provide that policy's share of the current year's mortality costs, and a smaller amount can be invested. However, the invested assets attributable to the legal reserve continue to grow, since, for a while at least, additional funds are being received and interest is being earned on those funds which have previously been set aside. When an individual insured dies, the amount of that policy's proportionate segment of the company's policy reserves offsets a corresponding amount of the claim.

In other words, under the level premium, legal reserve system, the net amount at risk[1] is reduced annually for each policy. This avoids any need for premium increase and permits a guaranteed level premium.

---

[1] The net amount at risk is the difference between the benefit payable and the amount of the reserve. This difference is the amount which must be made up by the mortality portion of the net premiums received during the year.

Since the level premium, legal reserve system has such technical[2] and far-reaching implications, it is not surprising that there was at first some question concerning the legal nature of this life insurance premium, which the policyowner may pay if he wishes, but which he doesn't really have to pay.

10.3 The Legal Nature of the Premium

The Early View. In one of the early life insurance cases in which this problem was considered,[3] the court took the position that each premium subsequent to the first purchased two things. First, it paid the cost of the insurance for the year in question, and second, it paid for the right to renew the insurance for another period of the same length. Although this approach was followed by a few other courts, it seems clear that it overlooks the basic level premium idea—that the contract is designed to function on a long-term basis and the premium is related to that same basis even though it is payable annually.

The Better View. It seems highly appropriate that one of the clearest opinions, as far as an interpretation of the life insurance premium is concerned, was written by an actuary-lawyer turned judge. Mr. Justice Bradley, a student of actuarial science and a practicing lawyer, had served as consulting mathematician for one of the leading life insurance companies for several years before becoming a member of the United States Supreme Court. With this background, he was almost uniquely equipped to write the opinion in the case of *New York Life Insurance Co. v. Statham,*[4] which concerned the legal effect of the suspension of premium payments under a life insurance policy by reason of the Civil War. For present purposes, the important part of that decision is as follows:

> We agree with the court below [the court from which the appeal was taken], that the contract is not an assurance for a single year, with a privilege of renewal from year to year by paying the annual premium, but that it is an entire contract of assurance for life, subject to discontinuance and forfeiture for non-payment of any of the stipulated premiums. Such is the form of the contract, and such is its character. It has been contended that the payment of each premium is the consideration for insurance during the next following year—as in fire policies. But the position is untenable. It often happens that the assured pays the entire

---

[2] The exact relationship of mortality, interest, and expense, in any specific case is dependent upon a varying set of technical factors, which are controlled to a large extent by state insurance law and regulation.

[3] *Worthington v. Charter Oak Life Insurance Co.,* 41 Conn. 372, 19 Am. Rep. 495 (1874).

[4] 93 U.S. 24 (1876).

premium in advance, or in five, ten, or twenty annual instalments. Such instalments are clearly not intended as the consideration for the respective years in which they are paid; for, after they are all paid, the policy stands good for the balance of the life insured, without any further payment. Each instalment is, in fact, part consideration of the entire insurance for life. It is the same thing, whether the annual premiums are spread over the whole life. The value of assurance for one year of a man's life when he is young, strong, and healthy, is manifestly not the same when he is old and decrepit. There is no proper relation between the annual premium and the risk of assurance for the year in which it is paid. This idea of assurance from year to year is the suggestion of ingenious counsel. The annual premiums are an annuity, the present value of which is calculated to correspond with the present value of the amount assured, a reasonable percentage being added to the premiums to cover expenses and contingencies. The whole premiums are balanced against the whole insurance.

Thus, the basic question was whether the life insurance contract could be separated into yearly promises and yearly premiums. It seems obvious that with the level premium, legal reserve system, this is impossible. To make this system work, it is necessary to consider premium payments on a long-term basis. The court's interpretation in the Statham case takes this long-range approach and gives it legal significance. It places both the company's promises and the insured's premium payments on a continuing basis, with the effectiveness of the promises being conditioned on the payment of premiums.

10.4 Initial and Subsequent Premiums

It is generally considered that the premiums under the life insurance contract must be divided into two groups. The first or initial premium constitutes the consideration for the insurance company's promises and puts the contract into force. Most insurance policies are expressly declared not to be effective unless and until they are delivered and the first premium is paid during the lifetime and continued insurability of the insured. At that time, by the clear implication of this wording, the insurance becomes effective, and the insurer is bound on its promises. Thus, the first or initial premium is the consideration "requested and given in exchange" for the company's promises, the "legally adequate" consideration which makes the life insurance contract a valid and binding agreement.

The promises of the life insurance company become effective at the time of delivery of the policy and payment of the first premium, or at an earlier date if there is a conditional receipt. They will continue to be effective if the insured continues to pay the premiums as they fall due. It is this "if" which puts the promises of the company on a conditional basis and makes the payment of succeeding premiums a *condition precedent*.[5]

It is not always easy to distinguish between a condition and a promise, but the consequences of nonperformance in the two cases differ widely. A person who fails to perform a contractual promise may be liable in damages for breach of contract. A person who does not perform a condition loses only the right to require the promisor to perform his promise. He has no liability for his own failure to perform. It is generally agreed that payment of renewal life insurance premiums as they become due is a condition and not a promise. Therefore, the policyowner has no liability if he does not pay a renewal premium when it becomes due.

B. THE PAYMENT OF PREMIUMS

10.5 The Initial Premium

Payment May Be Presumed. A great deal of life insurance law centers around the payment or nonpayment of the initial premium because of the essential role it plays in the formation of the life insurance contract. Ordinarily, the policy provides that insurance will not become effective unless and until the first premium is paid. However, many policies, particularly those issued in the past, have contained a provision referring to the "initial premium, receipt of which is hereby acknowledged." This statement has played an important part in many cases, where it has been held to establish a presumption that the initial premium was paid.

This is statutory law in California, where Section 484 of the Insurance Code provides as follows:

> Section 484. Acknowledgment of receipt of premium in policy is conclusive evidence of payment. An acknowledgment in a policy of the receipt of premium is conclusive evidence of its payment, so far as to make the policy binding, notwithstanding any stipulation therein that it shall not be binding until the premium is actually paid.[6]

The application of this principle is illustrated in a specific instance in the case of *Lincoln National Life Insurance Co.* v. *Mathison,*[7] as follows:

> . . . The policy issued to Mathison contained a clause reading as follows: "This insurance is granted in consideration of the payment of $486.25, the receipt of which is hereby acknowledged. . . ." In the Kamischer[8]

---

[5] The student may wish to review the discussion concerning conditions in Chapter 4, section 4.7.

[6] Insurance Code Annotated of the State of California, Deering's California Codes, 1963.

[7] 150 F. (2nd) 292 (U.S.D.A., S. Calif., 1945).

[8] *Kamischer* v. *John Hancock Mutual Life Ins. Co.,* 1 Cal. App. (2d) 629, 37 P. (2d) 126, (C.C.A. Cal. 1945).

case, the court held that this language is in effect an acknowledgment of a receipt of the premium, and by reason of the code provisions the insurance company was precluded from the defense that the premium was not paid.

A slightly different view was taken in one North Carolina case,[9] where the court said:

> If the premium in fact is not paid, the acknowledgment of payment, so far as it is a receipt for money, is only prima facie, and the amount can be recovered; but so far as the acknowledgment is contractual, it cannot be contradicted so as to invalidate the [policy].

In other words, the acknowledgment did not amount to payment in fact, and the insurer was entitled to receive the money. It did, however, have contractual effect, and therefore the validity of the policy could not be questioned. Thus, in this case, as in the Lincoln National case, the validity of the contract was upheld by reason of the acknowledgment of payment.

Even if the policy does not state that receipt of the first premium "is hereby acknowledged," the fact that the beneficiary has possession of the policy at the time of the insured's death has strong legal significance, as brought out in the case of *Woloshin* v. *The Guardian Life Insurance Company of America.*[10]

In that case, the policy was in the possession of the insured at the time of his death, just one month after the policy was issued. The insurer refused to pay the death benefit, contending that the initial premium was never paid. The question was whether possession of the policy by the beneficiary at the date of death creates a presumption of delivery and payment of the first premium of such a nature as to require that it be submitted to the jury. The court said:

> The evidence does not support the contention of defendant [the insurer] that the policy was delivered to Woloshin for inspection merely and that the delivery, therefore, was not absolute. The agent mailed the policy to him with a bill for the premium. No interim receipt was taken pending payment. Delivery of the policy was made on the credit of the assured and resulted in a contract between the parties conditioned only by its terms. But assuming that the question of conditional delivery were in issue, that question, clearly, was for the jury.
> The beneficiary's lawful possession of a life insurance policy after the death of the insured, and especially when, as here, there is no allegation of fraud, accident, artifice, or mistake, to impeach this possession, *prima facie* sustains the burden of proof resting on the plaintiff, by raising a

---

[9] *Smith* v. *Atlantic Joint Stock Land Bank*, 212 N.C. 79, 192 S.E. 866 as quoted in *Creech* v. *Sun Life Assur. Co. of Canada et al.*, 224 N.C. 144, 29 S.E. (2d) 348 (1944).

[10] 146 Pa. Super. 152, 22 A. (2d) 54 (1941).

strong presumption that the policy was not only manually delivered but was also *legally*[11] delivered to the insured, and puts the defendant in a position where, to avoid an adverse verdict, it must offer evidence of the conditional delivery alleged, sufficiently convincing to countervail the strong presumption of legal delivery arising from the lawful possession of the policy by the beneficiary. . . .

The court also referred to another case as authority for the rule that where a policy contains an acknowledgment that the first premium is paid and is unconditionally delivered, there is a legally conclusive presumption that payment has been made. If the policy does not acknowledge receipt of the first premium, the beneficiary's possession of the policy creates a prima facie case, but the presumption that the premium was paid is rebuttable. Thus, the rule is that in the absence of fraud, possession of a life insurance policy by the beneficiary at the death of the insured creates a presumption that the initial premium was paid. The life insurance company is free to introduce evidence to show that the premium was not paid, if such evidence is available. However, if there is no admissible evidence, or if it is legally insufficient to overcome the presumption, the latter stands as a matter of law. In this case, the receipt of the initial premium was not acknowledged in the policy, but the beneficiary had possession of it. The court held, therefore, that the question of whether the initial premium had been paid was a question of fact to be decided by the jury; and this is the prevailing view.

Payment Can Be Waived. An insurance company or its agent may be held to have waived payment of the first premium. Under these circumstances (as in cases where payment is presumed), the insurance becomes effective without the actual payment of the premium. Illustrative of such a situation is the case of *Henderson* v. *Capital Life and Health Insurance Company,*[12] decided in 1942. There, a mother applied for a policy on the life of a minor child, and the policy was delivered while she was away from home. The father of the insured testified that the agent left the policy and receipt book and said that he would collect the first premium on his next visit. Before that next visit, the insured had died.

Upon learning of the death, the agent went out to the house and picked up the policy and receipt book, saying that he would do everything he could to obtain the proceeds of the policy for them. However, the proceeds were not paid, and the agent refused to return the policy to the owner. On suit, the lower court held that the actions of the agent in delivering the policy without collecting the initial premium constituted a waiver of the payment of the first premium, and the reviewing court upheld that decision, saying:

---

[11] The reader may wish to refer to the general definition of delivery, in the legal sense of the term, in Chapter 4, sections 4.24 and 4.25.

[12] 199 S.C. 100, 18 S.E. (2d) 605 (1942).

. . . Under the well settled rule, the company may waive the time and method of the payment of premium. It will be observed that the policy by implication acknowledges receipt of the initial premium. It has been repeatedly held in this State that the manner and method of the payment of the initial premium may be waived and that credit may be extended for the initial premium. . . .

I think the effect of the plaintiff's testimony in this case was that credit was extended for the initial premium until the agent made his next visit, but if it be construed as a promise on the part of the agent to advance the premium for the plaintiff, and to be reimbursed on his next visit, such would be evidence of waiver by the company, particularly in view of the fact that the policy contained no stipulation that it was not to be effective until the premium was paid and, as above stated, impliedly recognized the payment of the initial premium.

10.6 Renewal Premiums

An insurance company has the right to specify how, where, and to whom renewal premiums shall be paid, and ordinarily the policy provisions on these matters will be held to govern. In any specific question, however, the facts of the individual case must be considered. Thus, it is not enough merely to know what the policy provides. One must know also what the parties actually did and the general principles of law most frequently applied in resolving such questions. The following discussion concerns some of the more typical questions that arise in connection with the payment of renewal premiums.

10.7 Time of Payment

Renewal premiums must be paid on or before the date specified in the policy, unless an extension of time is given by the company. In this respect, it is sometimes said that "time is of the essence," which simply means that if the premium falls due on June 20th, payment on June 21st is too late. However, payment may be made at any time prior to midnight of the due date, and if a premium is due on Sunday or a legal holiday, payment on the following day will usually be sufficient.

Premium Due Date. In a conditional receipt situation, it is a relatively simple matter to date the policy as of the date the insurance becomes effective. Where the initial premium is not paid with the application, however, the situation is different. There, if insurance does not become effective until the policy has been delivered and the initial premium paid "during the continued good health of the insured," a period of several days may elapse between the date of the policy and the date the insurance becomes effective. In such cases, the first annual premium may pay for less than 12 months of insurance if the premium due date is an anniversary of the policy date. For instance, the policy may be dated November 15, 1974, with the insurance becoming effective on December 20, 1974, and the next annual premium falling due on November 15, 1975. Some of the problems resulting from this type of situation have been presented to the courts a sufficient number of times that several relatively standard rules have been developed.

First, where delivery of the policy is not required to put it into effect, if the insurance takes effect on payment of the first premium and the policy expressly states the date from which the premium period is to run, that date will control.

The Minority View.   Where the contract takes effect only upon delivery, however, court decisions are divided. There is a strong minority line of decisions that premium periods are to be computed from the date the policy was delivered and the first premium paid, regardless of the date specified in the policy for the payment of premiums. This was the conclusion of the court in the case of *Lentin* v. *Continental Assurance Co.*,[13] where the court reviewed and discussed the entire question, summarizing the minority view as follows:

> The other view adopted has been that where the contract expressly provides that it shall take effect only on the condition of payment of the first premium, or of delivery, that such provision controls both as to the date upon which premiums must be paid and as to the expiration date of the policy, nothing more appearing except that the insurance company has dated the policy on a date prior to the payment of the first premium, or delivery, and has provided for the payment of subsequent premiums on the policy date.

A number of cases are cited supporting this view, and the court concluded as follows:

> . . . The rationale of these cases is that since the premiums are payable in advance, a mere dating of the policy at a time prior to its effective date and the subsequent payment of premiums on the date of the policy's date are not sufficient to change an explicit provision in the contract that it takes effect as of a later date. To hold to the contrary would result in the insured's paying for insurance over a period during which the insurance company was under no liability to him and in which he had no insurance. This, we believe, is the better view, for to hold that the payment of the first premium, which contemplates that it be for a year's insurance, guarantees insurance for a period less than a year, is to give the insured something substantially less than what his express agreement with the company called for.

The court, therefore, followed the minority rule and held that the initial premium paid for a full year of protection from the date of delivery and payment of the premium.

---

[13] 105 N.E. (2d) 735 (Ill., 1952).

The Majority View. The majority holding, however, is that if the policy expressly states a date for future premium payments, even though the policy is not effective until a later date, the date specified in the policy must control. These cases take the position that under circumstances of this kind there is no ambiguity and the contract must be enforced as written. This reasoning is followed, for example, in the case of *D. & P. Terminal, Inc.* v. *Western Life Insurance Company*,[14] decided in 1966 by the United States Court of Appeals, Eighth Circuit. That decision reads in part as follows:

> There is no question in the present case of the "effective date" of the policy. See *Beister* v. *John Hancock Mutual Life Insurance Company*, 356 F. 2d 634 (8 Cir. 1966). The only question is the date premiums were to be paid to avoid a lapse in coverage. These dates were specifically decided and clearly set out in the insurance contract. We cannot write another contract for the parties, expressing dates contrary to those established by the parties. [Citations.] When the intention of the parties is clear and unambiguous, as it is here, the Court may not assume an ambiguity. It is the duty of the Court to give effect to this intention. [Citation.] According to the contract, the premiums were due November 5, February 5, May 5, and August 5. Failure to pay on these dates, plus any grace period, would cause a lapse in coverage.

Backdated Policies. If the policy is backdated at the insured's request to give him the benefit of a lower premium, he will be held bound by his agreement. In such cases, the premium period begins to run from the actual date of the policy, regardless of when the policy was delivered. Nevertheless backdating, at best, means some period of time when there was no coverage and for this reason a number of states, as previously noted,[15] have laws limiting the length of time a policy can be backdated. The most typical limit is six months.

Grace Period. As noted earlier, the insurance laws of most states require that policies issued in, or issued to be delivered in, their states must include a grace period of a month or 31 days, within which any premium other than the first premium may be paid without default. Payment in such cases may be made at any time prior to midnight of the last day of grace. Generally speaking, also, the premium may be paid after the death of the insured so long as it is paid during the grace period. There are a few holdings to the contrary, but this is by far the prevailing rule.

Two basic points concerning the grace period are worthy of note. One is that there is no grace period for the initial premium, which is consistent with the view that the contract (and any provision in it) is ineffective, for lack of consideration, until the initial premium has been paid. The second

---

[14] 368 F. (2d) 743 (U.S.C.A., 8th Cir., 1966).
[15] See discussion in Chapter 6, section 6.12.

point is that while the grace period runs from the due date of the premium in default, there is no assurance that the due date specified in the contract will necessarily be upheld in a court action, as illustrated by the Lentin case previously discussed.

Extension of Time. Since the prompt payment of premiums is for the insurer's benefit, the company may waive this requirement at its discretion and grant extensions of time for the payment of any premium it wishes. As a matter of fact, such extensions are granted under special circumstances in the usual course of business. Consequently, another legal question is sometimes raised: If an extension is granted, does a grace period follow the expiration of the extended time period? The general holding is that it does not. For instance, if the grace period ends on June 15, and the insurer gives the policyowner an additional two-week period in which to pay the then-due premium, is the policyowner entitled to a grace period after the end of the two weeks? The general view is that he is not.

10.8 Payment by Promissory Note

The insurer may make whatever terms it wishes with respect to the medium in which the premium must be paid, and it has the right to demand payment in cash. Alternatively, it may accept promissory notes, post office money orders, personal checks, bank drafts, or it may make whatever other arrangements it may wish with the policyowner. Payment by personal check is the customary method of payment today, of course, but payment by promissory note presents so many technical questions that the subject deserves some further discussion.

There is no question but that an insurer may waive the requirement that a premium be paid in cash or check and accept a promissory note if it wishes. However, waiver is highly technical at times, especially if an agent is involved; and a promissory note is a separate legal instrument adding its own set of technical rules to those already effective in connection with the life insurance contract. As a result, most cases involving promissory notes present numerous questions both of fact and law.

In legal effect, the unconditional acceptance of a promissory note, instead of cash or a check, in payment of a life insurance premium is the equivalent of payment of the premium. If the insured defaults in payment then, the default relates to payment of the note, not the premium. In the event of such default, therefore, the insurer cannot take action to declare the policy lapsed for nonpayment of the premium. For this reason, when an insurer accepts a promissory note, it usually attempts to make it quite clear that the note will not operate as payment of the premium if the note itself is not paid when due. This is done by including in both the policy and the note or notes provisions for the forfeiture of the policy if the note or notes are not paid when due. Provisions of this kind are uniformly held to be valid and enforceable.

10.9 Payment by Check

If there is no agreement to the contrary, payment of a premium by check is conditional upon the check's being honored, even though a premium receipt has been given. If the check is dishonored and a premium receipt has been given, the company has a choice of action. It may lapse the policy for nonpayment of the premium or it may take action with respect to the dishonored check. If it elects to lapse the policy, it should act promptly, return the check, request the premium receipt, and declare the policy forfeited. If the company elects to take action with respect to the dishonored check, the right to lapse the policy may be held to have been waived. If the company takes no action, but retains the check, its waiver of the right to lapse will be presumed.

The legal effect of electing to rely on a dishonored check in a situation of this kind is illustrated in the case of *Sjoberg* v. *State Automobile Insurance Association, Des Moines, Iowa.*[16] This was a suit on a $5,000 health insurance policy after the insured was killed in an automobile accident. The insurer contended that the policy had lapsed prior to the date of death because of nonpayment of the last premium. The facts showed that the death occurred on August 5 and that the last quarterly renewal premium, due July 1, was paid by personal check on July 8, well within the grace period. The check was returned, however, with the notation "insufficient funds." The company did not return the check, rescind the receipt, and declare the policy canceled, as would have been its right. Instead, the local agency was requested to contact the insured and secure a bankable check or other remittance. This had not been accomplished at the date of death.

The court noted the general rule that if there is no agreement to the contrary, payment by check is conditional upon the check's being honored, and it said:

> . . . There is authority, however, that if a check is unconditionally accepted as payment of the premium even though it turns out to be worthless the acceptance will prevent a forfeiture.
> . . . In the case at bar the defendant [the insurer] on the occasion of a prior default followed strictly the terms of the policy. On the occasion in question instead of doing so it gave the insured a full receipt of the premium upon receiving his check. There was some delay in the presentation of the check for payment but when it was returned dishonored de-

---

[16] 48 N.W. (2d) 452 (N.D., 1951).

fendant did not repudiate the transaction but wrote his agents to contact insured to get "bankable check or other remittance." The agent notified the insured thereof. Neither the letter nor the conversation between defendant's agent and the insured referred to a forfeiture of the policy. Instead the whole tenor of both was to effect the collection of the check. Such negotiations indicate an intention to keep the policy in force. . . . They indicate defendant's election to rely upon the check rather than upon forfeiture and reinstatement.

In a case[17] where the insurer redeposited a premium check that had been dishonored once for insufficient funds and, when it was again dishonored, took no further action, the holding was different. In that case, the policy was issued on May 14, 1967, and premiums were payable on a monthly basis. The premium that became due on February 14, 1969, was not paid by the due date; but on March 10, a check was mailed to cover both the February and March premiums. It was presented for payment on March 19 and returned dishonored for insufficient funds. It was presented again on April 2 and again dishonored.

On April 9 the insured died by accidental means. On that same day the beneficiary mailed a money order to the insurer in the amount of the two past due premiums. The insurer refused to accept the money order and declared the policy lapsed.

The beneficiary brought suit in the United States District Court for the Western District of Washington, based on the theory that by redepositing the check the insurer had waived its rights to declare the policy lapsed. The decision was for the insurer and, on appeal, the United States Court of Appeals agreed, saying:

> It is clear beyond question that when payment of that check was refused and dishonored by the bank for the second time on the 3rd of April, six days prior to the death of Mr. Biggoe, that again indisputably effected a second lapse, and there being no action by defendant subsequent to that time that in any way whatever could give rise to a claim of either waiver or estoppel, the lapse was fully effective not later than the 3rd of April 1969, six days prior to the insured's death.

In other words, merely redepositing the check was not sufficient to constitute a waiver or estoppel situation. Additional action on the part of the insurer would have been necessary, and no further action was taken except the prompt refusal of the money order when it was received.

Postdated Checks. As a general rule, if a postdated check is paid according to its terms on the date it bears, it is considered effective payment of a life insurance premium as of that date.

---

[17] *Bigjoe, Appellant* v. *Pioneer American Ins. Co.,* 71 Life Cases 513 (Wash., 1971).

C. OTHER WAYS OF PAYING PREMIUMS

10.10 Premiums Paid in Advance

Although most insureds wish to pay their premiums as they fall due, there are some who are concerned that they may not be able to meet the payments in the future on the dates specified. This is especially true of persons whose incomes are somewhat irregular. In other cases, an older person may wish to make a gift to a grandchild of a policy on the latter's life and pay the premiums in advance until the child is grown, or to some other specified date in the future. To accommodate such specialized needs, most companies have some provision for accepting premiums paid for a specified number of years in the future.

As a general rule, premiums paid in advance are accepted on a discounted basis for not longer than 20 years, and a receipt is given the payor that specifies the circumstances under which the money so paid may be withdrawn, as well as the disposition of any premiums that may remain unearned at the death of the insured.

Legal Problems. Generally speaking, it is considered within the authority of a life insurance company to accept premiums paid in advance, on the theory that it is an activity reasonably related to the company's basic corporate business. In other words, it is in the nature of an implied power, which is necessary or appropriate in connection with the express power of a life insurance company. However, when these sums are subject to withdrawal at the request of the payor, it is apparent that the insurance company is providing a service which resembles that provided by banks, a fact which some of the state legislatures and officials have noted with varying results.

The two principal legal problems presented by this method of premium payment are: (1) may the payor withdraw premiums paid in advance prior to the date the respective premiums fall due; and (2) what disposition should be made of the unapplied balance of the fund remaining at the death of the insured?

Withdrawal Rights. Life companies ordinarily grant the right to withdraw the unapplied portion of the fund at the payor's discretion, subject to some limitations. Sometimes there is a limitation as to the date on which withdrawal may be made, and in other instances only the entire amount unapplied may be withdrawn. In other cases the request is specifically made subject to deferral at the company's option.

Settlement at Death. Often, of course, some advance premiums may still be unearned at the death of the insured. To whom should they be paid? The receipt given at the time the money is accepted may provide that such funds will be paid to the beneficiary or to the payor's estate. In most cases, the prepaid premiums are deposited by the insured. To return the remaining sum to "the payor" at the insured's death, therefore, means paying it to his executor or administrator. As a matter of convenience it is ordinarily preferable to make it payable to the beneficiary if the sum is not large.

10.11 Preauthorized Check Plans

A preauthorized check plan is a plan for paying premiums by means of instruments termed "checks," which are, in more legal terms, sight drafts drawn by the insurer to its own order, as authorized by the policyowner, on the bank in which the latter maintains a checking account. The plan requires an authorization from the policyowner, for the company to draw the draft, and the policyowner must also authorize the bank to accept and process the drafts in the regular course of business. A separate agreement between the bank and the insurer provides that the latter will indemnify the bank for any liability it might incur by reason of participating in the plan. The exact provisions of this indemnity agreement vary, although recommended forms have been worked out by several interested associations.

Those persons who favor preauthorized check plans take the position that we are living in a monthly payment economy and that these plans only cooperate with policyowners who are already paying most of their bills on a monthly basis. They also point out that the plan frees the policyowner from having to remember to pay his life insurance premium, and thus he avoids the risk of inadvertently letting a policy lapse and being temporarily, or permanently, without coverage.

Preauthorized check plans were opposed by some bankers in the past, primarily on the grounds that since the policyowner is not notified each time the insurance company forwards a draft on his account, overdrafts may occur and present problems with respect to the effectiveness of the insurance. It is the purpose of the indemnity agreements between the banks and the life insurance companies to prevent, insofar as possible, these potential difficulties on which the objections are based.

Generally speaking, if a preauthorized check or draft clears through regular banking channels, the premium is paid just as effectively as if the policyowner himself had drawn the check. If for some reason the check does not clear, the insurer, ordinarily, will take the same action it would take when any other check is returned for insufficient funds.

10.12 The Automatic Premium Loan

The automatic premium loan provision included in the policy itself permits the company to effect a policy loan against the cash value of the policy if the premium is not paid at the expiration of the grace period. At the present time, inclusion of this type of provision is compulsory only in Rhode Island. However, even there the applicant may elect an automatic paid-up nonforfeiture benefit in lieu of the automatic premium loan. The automatic premium loan provision is thus essentially on an elective basis, and on that basis it is found in the policies of most companies. In such cases, the policyowner must elect to have it operative before it will be invoked by the company. If the policyowner makes such an election, however, the provision will be invoked only when necessary to prevent lapse and only if the policy has a loan value at the time sufficient to pay the past-due premium. The company simply establishes a policy loan in an amount sufficient to pay the premium and interest on the loan to the next premium payment date. It is customary to notify the policyowner that the loan has been made.

Advantages. If properly used, the automatic premium loan can be a decided advantage both to the policyowner and to the insurer. Certainly it keeps the policy in force, preventing an inadvertent lapse; and it has the further advantage of maintaining the disability and accidental death provisions in force (which would not be true if the policy continued under one of the nonforfeiture options, as will be discussed later). Even if the insured is able to meet the insurability requirements, reinstatement of the policy is an inconvenience; and if he is uninsurable, reinstatement is, of course, unavailable. The fact that there is an additional loan against the policy is of minor significance, since the policyowner is always free to repay the loan, with interest, at his convenience.

Disadvantages. Perhaps the most general criticism of the automatic premium loan is that it makes it too easy for the insured to defer payment. Used indiscriminately, it can give a false sense of security, and often the establishment of the first loan is the beginning of a process which ultimately ends in lapse. The continued use of the loan inexorably drains the cash value, so that at the time of lapse there is always a smaller value, if any value at all, to be applied under the nonforfeiture options.

10.13 Allotment Plans

Under the federal government allotment plan, members of the military service have the privilege of authorizing the regular deduction of sums from their pay for the purpose of paying premiums on their life insurance. These deductions are made on a monthly basis and, once initiated, they will continue to be made until the policyowner or someone on his behalf authorizes their discontinuance.

Salary allotment plans accomplish the same purpose in connection with private employment. There the employee authorizes the employer to withhold the amount of the insurance premium from his salary and to forward it directly to the insurer.

Like preauthorized check plans, the payment of premiums in advance, and the automatic premium loan, allotment plans are merely mechanical means to assure that premiums will be paid when they fall due. Special problems sometimes arise in connection with their operation, particularly concerning the responsibilities of the various parties involved, but the basic principles with respect to payment of premiums are not changed. Premiums must still be paid when they fall due, and the responsibility is upon the policyowner to pay them, not upon the life insurance company to see that they are paid.

D. PERSONS TO WHOM PREMIUMS MAY BE PAID

Most life insurance policies issued today contain a provision that all premiums subsequent to the first shall be payable to the company at its home office, or to an authorized agent in exchange for an official receipt signed by the secretary and countersigned by the agent. As a result, there are few problems if the premium payment is sent to the home office or a regularly designated office to receive such payments.

Nor does payment to an agent present any problem if the agent actually remits the premium to the company's home office. If he does not do so, however, a question of his authority may be raised. Payment to an agent, it will be remembered, is payment to the principal, even though the agent may only have apparent authority to accept such payment. However, if the agent does not have actual authority to receive the premium, it must be shown that he had such apparent authority as to justify a reasonable person in relying on it.

E. WHO MAY PAY THE PREMIUM?

10.14 The General Rule

Ordinarily, the owner of the policy pays the premiums or they are paid by someone else at his direction and with his approval, as by his agent. Nevertheless, other persons sometimes pay such premiums without the express consent of the owner, sometimes over extensive periods of time. In such cases, questions often arise as to possible legal rights of these persons as the result of their payments.

The general rule is that anyone who wants to do so may pay a life insurance premium for someone else. Life insurers have no duty to look behind the payments and ascertain whether or not the payors have any rights under the policies in question, and as a matter of practice they do not do so. Unless the payor already has a specific interest in the policy, however, he will acquire no rights by reason of having paid the premiums. In the absence of fraud or mistake, a person who has no interest in a policy but who pays a premium is a mere volunteer. He acquires no rights under the policy by so doing and has no claim for the premiums which he paid.

10.15 When the Beneficiary Pays

This general rule is probably most frequently tested with respect to the beneficiary. Assume, for example, that John Smith owns a policy on his life and has named his wife as beneficiary, revocably. John takes no interest in his policy or his family, and the wife keeps the premiums paid as they fall due. Several years later, there is a divorce and John remarries. Then he wants to change the beneficiary of his policy. The general rule in this situation is that payment of the premium by the beneficiary will not prevent the policyowner from changing the beneficiary designation in accordance with the policy provisions. (Under these same circumstances, the beneficiary who has been named irrevocably is safe, of course, since an irrevocable beneficiary designation cannot be changed except with the beneficiary's consent.)

In other words, the beneficiary may pay the premiums on a life insurance policy after the insured has discontinued such payments, but the "mere expectancy" of a revocable beneficiary cannot generally be enlarged by such payment. Payment of the premium will preserve whatever rights a beneficiary already has, but payment is always made subject to the provisions of the policy concerning later beneficiary changes.

Nevertheless, in situations of this kind, other problems are frequently involved. For instance, a wife may have possession of the policy and refuse to surrender it for endorsement (if endorsement is required) of a beneficiary change the policyowner wishes to make. Sometimes community property rights are involved. Sometimes, also, a divorce decree may have determined the ownership of insurance on the lives of both spouses. Until all such possibilities have been ruled out, therefore, it is not very safe to rely upon the general rule.

10.16 When the Assignee Pays

Unless there is a different agreement, the policyowner who has assigned his policy collaterally has the duty, as between himself and the assignee, to pay the premiums. (Between policyowner and the insurer, payment of premiums is not a duty, of course, but a privilege.) If the collateral assignee agrees to pay and does pay, he is entitled to recover the amount of premiums paid. The absolute assignee, of course, is in the same position with respect to paying the premium as the original owner was.

The Company's Position. The company's position with respect to the identity of the premium payor is excellently illustrated in the case of *Atlas Life Insurance Company* v. *Davis*,[18] decided in 1950. There the insured had paid the premiums by military allotment for a time and then requested that the allotment be discontinued. A department of the government paid the premiums after that, although it was without authority to do so. After the death of the insured, the company contended that the policy was not in full force and effect because payment of premiums was made without authority. The court said:

> It is undisputed that the policy was issued, and that the company received and retained all the premiums due upon said policy. The facts under the pleadings stand admitted. It is apparent, therefore, that the issue involved is whether the payment of premiums by a third party, or one other than the insured, is sufficient to maintain a policy of life insurance in force and effect. We think it was, since, from the insurer's point of view, it is immaterial who pays the premiums and payment by a third party is sufficient.

F. PREMIUM NOTICES

10.17 In the Absence of a Statute

The general rule is that a life insurance company has no legal responsibility to send premium notices unless there is a statute or a policy provision requiring it. As a matter of fact, a number of states have such statutes, but even without them companies would send notices, simply because it is good business to do so. Sending premium notices has proved to be an effective means of keeping life insurance contracts in force, particularly during their early years; and the practice, for that reason, has become routine.

Even in the absence of a controlling statute, however, there are two situations in which the company will be required to send premium notices, as a matter of law.

First, if the insurer specifically agrees to give notice of premiums due, it will, of course, be required to do so. Thus, if the policy includes a provision to that effect, the company must send the notice as specified.

A second situation in which premium notices are required arises when the company has consistently sent premium notices over an extended period of time, even though not required to do so either by statute or a policy provision. In such situations, the insurer may be precluded from discontinuing the practice without specific notice to that effect. The courts are not in complete agreement on this point, but the majority holding is that where it has been customary to give notice, a company

---

[18] 232 P. (2d) 146 (Okla., 1950).

cannot discontinue the custom without warning, and then declare a forfeiture of the policy if the policyowner does not pay the next premium when due. The theory is that by following such a course of conduct for a sufficient length of time that the policyowner has been led to rely upon it, the company is thereafter estopped from relying upon what would otherwise have been its right to declare a forfeiture.

10.18 Statutes Requiring Notice

New York, Illinois, Kansas, and a few other states have statutes which limit the right of a life insurance company to declare a policy forfeited for nonpayment of premium unless premium notices have been sent. The Illinois statute is illustrative.[19] It states that a policy cannot be declared forfeited for nonpayment of premiums or interest within six months after default in the payment of a premium unless a premium notice has been mailed to the insured or assignee at least 15 and not more than 45 days prior to the due date of the premium. The affidavit of a company employee having the responsibility of mailing the notices, that notices were prepared, duly addressed, and mailed, is presumptive evidence that the notice was given as required. Specifically excepted from the requirements set forth in the statute are life policies on which premiums are payable monthly.

The New York statute is very similar to this, as is the Kansas statute, although the latter is considerably more detailed. An Ohio statute applies only to foreign (out-of-state) companies and requires them to send premium notices to all insureds and to third-party owners or assignees who reside in Ohio.

Statutory premium notice requirements are held to be for the benefit of the policyowner and any application or policy provision that attempts to waive the notice requirement will be held void.

G. DIVIDENDS

10.19 Participation in Surplus

In general business usage, a dividend represents an apportionment of the earnings of the enterprise that is paid to the stockholders as their share of the profits. In insurance, the word often has a very different meaning. Stock life insurers are concerned with dividends in the usual sense of the word—that is, stockholders' dividends. The most common use of the word in life insurance, however, concerns policyowners' dividends, and that is a very different concept.

---

[19] Illinois Revised Statutes, Chap. 73, Sec. 846 (1973).

Policyowners' dividends are paid in connection with participating life insurance policies. Under such policies, the premiums are established at such a level that the company expects to be able to operate on a smaller amount. The difference is a margin of safety. If the financial results of the company operations are as expected, a part of the premium is returned to the policyowner at the end of specified intervals, and that refund is called a "dividend." Since policyowners' dividends clearly have nothing to do with corporate profits, they are, in legal effect, premium abatements. For this reason, life insurance dividends are not subject to personal income tax, and they are always taken into account in calculating the "cost" or "investment" in a life insurance contract or annuity for income tax purposes.

The right to elect how policy dividends are to be applied is one of the valuable rights a policyowner has under a participating life insurance policy; carrying out the policyowner's wishes in this respect is one of the important responsibilities of the insurer to its policyowners.

10.20 The Dividend Options

Participation in the surplus of a company has been legislatively recognized as a possible source of abuse since the days of the Armstrong Investigation, and for that reason it has been made the subject of statutory regulation by most of the states. Typically, such statutes specify the rights of policyowners (of participating policies) to participate in the surplus of the insurer and the method or methods of distribution of the surplus. The Illinois statute, for example, requires that the participating policy include "a provision that the policy shall participate annually in the surplus of the company beginning not later than the end of the third policy year. . . ." This statute continues:

> . . . and the insured under any annual dividend policy shall have the right each year to have the dividend arising from such participation either paid in cash, or applied in reduction of premiums, or applied to the purchase of paid-up additional insurance, or be left to accumulate to the credit of the policy, with interest at such rate as may be determined from time to time by the company. . . .[20]

The statutes in effect in many of the states require, as this one does, that participation shall be on an annual basis. A few of the statutes, notably those of Illinois and New York, specify the optional methods that must be provided in the policy for the application of dividends. Other states provide for optional methods of dividend application although they do not spell them out in detail in the statute.

---

[20] Illinois Revised Statutes, Chap. 73, Sec. 836(1)(e) (1973).

Most participating life insurance contracts provide four basic dividend options, permitting the dividends to be:

1. Paid to the policyowner in cash.
2. Applied to reduce the premium.
3. Applied to purchase paid-up additions to the policy.
4. Accumulated at interest.

The "Fifth" Dividend Option. Many companies provide a special option under some plans that permits the dividend to be used to purchase term insurance for one year. Called the one-year term dividend option (or, less formally, the "fifth dividend option"), this provides an additional amount of insurance if the insured should die during the year following the application of the dividend.

The additional insurance under this option is sometimes limited to the amount of the cash surrender value of the policy, in which case the amount of the dividend in excess of that needed may be paid in cash or applied under one of the other options. The result is that with this option the policyowner may borrow up to the full cash surrender value of his policy and still leave the face amount of the policy to the beneficiary at his death. The one-year term insurance purchased under the option will be enough to repay the maximum loan until a rather advanced age.

The Automatic Dividend Option. Typically, state laws concerning policyowners' participation in surplus provide that if options are offered, the insurer shall specify which option will take effect automatically; that is, if there is no election by the insured. A few states specify which option this must be, and unfortunately they do not all specify the same one. Thus, Nebraska and North Dakota provide that if no option is elected, dividends shall be payable in cash; Indiana requires the interest option; Ohio requires the paid-up additions option; and Massachusetts either the paid-up additions option or the interest option. This difference in requirements from state to state is taken into consideration by some insurers who provide in their policies that if no option is elected by the insured, "the dividend shall be applied to purchase a (paid-up) dividend addition or as may be required by the laws of the State in which the policy is delivered."

A recent review of a representative sampling of participating contracts shows that paid-up additions is by far the most frequently used automatic dividend option.

Notice Required. If dividends are to be applied to reduce premiums, it is obvious that the policyowner will not know the exact amount of premium he must pay unless and until he receives a premium notice. In such cases, the company is legally obliged to send a premium notice. Otherwise nonpayment of the premium when due cannot be held to work a forfeiture of the policy.

10.21 Other Dividend Privileges

It is relatively standard practice also to include the privilege of applying the accumulated dividends to pay up the policy or to mature it as an endowment if the policyowner wishes.

10.22 Insurer's Duty to Apply Dividends

The general rule is that an insurer cannot declare a life insurance policy forfeited for the nonpayment of a premium if it has in its possession unapplied dividends sufficient to pay the premium then due and the policyowner has not elected to have the dividend applied otherwise. Under these circumstances, the insurer is obligated to use the dividends to pay the premium then due and thus prevent the policy from lapsing. If the dividend is not sufficient to pay the entire premium that is due, however, the insurer is not obliged to make a partial payment.

A relatively frequent question in this area concerns the situation where the dividends held are sufficient to pay a quarterly or semiannual premium but the premium due is on the annual basis. Is the insurer obligated in this instance to change the mode and apply the dividend to pay the smaller premium?

This question has been answered differently in different jurisdictions, as might be expected. The problem is analyzed in one case[21] and the basic principles summarized as follows:

> In *Lamar* v. *Aetna Life Ins. Co.*, 85 F. 2d 141, 142 (10th Cir.), two principles were stated, "(1) It is the general rule of law that where an insurer has in its possession sufficient unapplied dividends presently due the insured to pay the stipulated premium, it should apply them in extinguishment of the premium and thus avoid lapse of the policy unless the insured directs otherwise. And the law will make the application if the insurer fails to act, the consent of the insured thereto being presumed. . . . (2) But it is equally well settled that such dividends must be sufficient in amount to discharge the premium in full, otherwise the doctrine has no application and lapse is not prevented." In all the cases cited for the latter principle the dividends were insufficient to pay even the smallest premium instalment provided for in the policy, but the reference appears to be to the full stipulated premium. As to the first principle, the stipulated premium in the case at bar is an annual one.
>
> The issue is to be decided with reference to all policyholders whose policies may be treated as lapsed by the insurer, the living as well as those who die. The rights of the insurer are to be fairly considered. The proposition which we consider, but not as advocated by the plaintiff, may be stated in this form: Whenever at the expiration of a grace period there is a declared dividend to the credit of the insured who has elected to have

---

[21] *Simmons* v. *Cambridge Savings Bank*, 191 N.E. (2d) 681 (Mass., 1963).

dividends applied to reduce premiums, and that dividend is sufficient to pay a premium on a quarterly basis, but not on the stipulated annual basis, the insured, who had the right to change the basis of payment but had not done so, unless he notifies the insurer that he intends to let the policy lapse, is to be taken by his silence to authorize payment on a quarterly basis.

As to the insured and the plaintiff, the beneficiary, it is obvious that they would have preferred that the quarterly premium be paid than that the policy lapse. In this case assent could retroactively be presumed. But in order to reach this result, it would be necessary to hold that every policyholder living at the expiration of the grace period should prospectively be taken to assent to a change in the method of payment where no notice of an intention to let the policy lapse is given to the insurer. This would involve a revision of the policy which we feel unable to make under sound principles of construction of contracts.

In this case, therefore, it was decided that the insurer was under no obligation to change the annual mode of premium payment to a more frequent mode even though the dividends held would have been sufficient to pay the smaller premium. To hold that the insurer must do so, the court reasoned, would be to remake the contract, and this it would not do.

Funds held by the insurer under a special agreement are a different matter. Thus in *Sugarman* v. *Equitable Life Assurance Society of the United States*,[22] the court held that the proceeds of a matured policy held by the insurer at interest were subject to the deposit agreement and must be handled in accordance with its terms. Thus, the insurance company had no authority to depart from the terms of that agreement and apply any part of those funds toward the payment of premiums due on another policy.

H. EXCUSES FOR NONPAYMENT OF PREMIUMS

10.23 Relating to the Policyowner Only

There is almost no excuse for the nonpayment of premiums which will prevent the forfeiture of a life insurance policy on that account, unless the policyowner can show that he was ready and willing to pay and that an act or acts on the part of the insurer prevented payment. Thus, physical or mental disability of the policyowner, poverty, accident, illiteracy, even disappearance, have been and are generally held not to excuse the failure to pay premiums.

A moment's reflection will show the soundness of this as a general proposition of law. Payment of premiums is a condition precedent.

---

[22] 71 A. (2d) 148 (N.J. Sup. Ch., 1950).

Performance of the company's promises is subject to this condition, and there is no right to have the promises performed unless the condition has been fulfilled. For this reason, nonpayment of premiums is a good defense in a suit against the life insurance company, and excuses for nonperformance of the condition have little bearing on the case unless they relate to conduct on the part of the promisor, in this case the life insurance company.

10.24 Relating to the Insurer

Waiver and Estoppel. Policy provisions with respect to the payment of premiums and the lapsing of the policy if premiums are not paid when due or within the grace period are considered to be included in the policy for the benefit of the insurer and, consequently, they may be waived by the insurer. An extension of time for the payment of a premium is a practical example of such waiver.

One of the most frequently recurring legal problems in this area has resulted from the habitual acceptance of late premiums without objection. This is generally held to preclude the insurer from later insisting on a forfeiture for nonpayment of a premium when due or within the grace period, a principle sometimes referred to as "estoppel by course of conduct." Thus, in one case[23] the court said:

> On the issue of waiver and estoppel the evidence is that for a period of six years all premiums had been paid by Mrs. Boggs to Hansen [the agent of the insurer], either in cash or by her personal check, and that no one of these payments was exchanged for the company's receipt signed by the president or secretary as required in the policy. It is also in evidence that each and all of these payments were made in this manner while the insured was in default, and in many cases after the period of grace had expired. During this period of six years, eighteen separate premiums became due. Fourteen of these were accepted by appellant [the insurer] after the period of grace had expired. In only one instance—September, 1940—the appellant demanded and received an application for reinstatement.
>
> . . . we conclude that the course of conduct in relation to the payments of premiums running over a period of six years was such that the respondents [the beneficiaries] were entitled to assume that the terms of the policy need not be adhered to strictly, and that the appellant was estopped from insisting upon a strict compliance with those terms until it had given the respondents reasonable notice of its change in policy.

The insurer may avoid this kind of situation by expressly providing in any notice of default that a late premium will be effective only if paid

---

[23] *Gleed* v. *The Lincoln National Life Insurance Co.,* 65 Cal. App. (2d) 213, 150 P. (2d) 484 (1944).

during the lifetime of the insured and whatever other conditions it wishes to impose. This is illustrated in the case of *Hutchinson* v. *The Equitable Life Assurance Society of the United States*,[24] as follows:

> . . . The plaintiff [the beneficiary] contends that Florida applies a blend of waiver and estoppel to an insurer who follows a course of dealing with the payment of premiums so as to induce the insured to believe that a delay in his premium payment will not give rise to a forfeiture. Plaintiff then concludes that this principle applies to the instant case.
>
> The fallacy of plaintiff's argument is that the default notices expressly stated that there would be no reinstatement if the insured died prior to receipt of the defaulted premium; thus there was no course of conduct by the insurer which in any way could have led the insured to believe that a default payment would be accepted after his death or that the policy had not lapsed. Accordingly there can be no waiver or estoppel.

Refusal of Tender. The actions of insurance company representatives may also be held to excuse nonperformance of the premium payment condition if they have refused what in general contract law is called a "tender of performance." As it relates to a condition, a tender of performance is similar to, though not exactly the same as, the tender of payment of a debt.

Offering to pay a life insurance premium is a tender of performance of this condition precedent if the offer is accompanied by ability and willingness to pay and is itself not subject to a condition. Such an offer is sometimes said to be the equivalent of performance, but this is not strictly true. It is the equivalent of performance in this sense: it establishes the liability of the promisor whose promise was subject to the condition in question. Thus a refusal of a tendered premium on the part of a life insurance company will excuse the nonpayment of the premium, and this is the equivalent of payment in the sense that the insurer will be precluded from declaring the policy forfeited for nonpayment of premium. However, the company remains entitled to the premium; and, in the event of the death of the insured, the premium may be deducted from the death benefit.

The legal effect of a tender of the life insurance premium that is refused is illustrated in the case of *Harms* v. *The John Hancock Mutual Life Insurance Company*.[25] This case involved a policy that was issued on November 22, 1944. The premiums were payable on a quarterly basis in the amount of $25.40. The first two quarterly premiums were paid when due or within the grace period, but the third premium was never paid. The grace period expired on June 22 and the insured died on July 3. The basic question to be decided by the court was the legal effect of an offer to pay the premium, made by the mother of the insured (and

---

[24] 335 F. (2d) 592 (U.S.C.A., 5th Cir., 1964).
[25] 34 N.W. (2d) 687 (Wis., 1948).

beneficiary of his insurance), which was made within the grace period and refused by an agent of the insurer. The court discussed and decided the question as follows:

> . . . The insurance in this case was solicited by an agent of the defendant insurer named Balistreiri who collected the first two premiums and called at plaintiff's house on June 20, 1945 to collect the last quarterly premium. This was two days before the expiration of the grace period. Defendant's agent informed Mrs. Hatch that he had come to collect her son's insurance. She told him that the son was sick and would not have a paycheck until July 5th and that she would have to pay the premium herself although she wished that the youngster would pay for his own insurance. She extracted three ten dollar bills from her pocketbook and told the agent that he might as well take it. The agent declined and said that he would hold the matter open until the 10th of July so that the boy would have a chance to pay it. As he left plaintiff said, "Well, Mr. Balistreiri, it's right here," and the agent said, "It's all right, Mrs. Hatch. I will hold it open until the 10th of July."
>
> The jury found that plaintiff Josephine Hatch offered to pay and that the agent put off the matter as above indicated.
>
> It is contended by appellant [the insurer] that the agent having no authority to issue policies could not grant an extension of time for the payment of a premium. This contention misses the point and the case is governed adversely to appellant by *Baumann* v. *Metropolitan Life Ins. Co.,* 144 Wis. 206, 128 N.W. 864. The point is that the amount of the premium was offered to a collecting agent of the company who declined to take the money and under those circumstances it must be held that plaintiff was deterred from making such payment by conduct or statements on the part of such agent which induced in her an honest belief that a failure to then make the payment or tender would not then be relied upon by the company to work a failure or forfeiture of the policy.

Therefore the insurer was estopped from declaring the policy lapsed for failure to pay the premium.

10.25 Relating to War

The legal effect of nonpayment of premiums because of war presents a unique situation. When communications of any kind are impossible between policyowner and insurer because their respective countries are at war, the reasons for nonpayment of premiums are clearly beyond the control of either. The legal effect of nonpayment in this situation, therefore, tests legal principles perhaps more harshly than any other set of circumstances that might affect the payment of premiums. It is not surprising that the conclusions reached in the several jurisdictions in which the question has been considered have not always been in accord.

State Court Decisions. The question, as most frequently litigated, is simple: What is the status of a life insurance contract at the end of a war between the respective countries of the insured and the insurer when because of that war and for that reason alone it has been impossible for the insured to pay the premiums?

This question was litigated extensively at the close of the Civil War in cases which set forth the basic alternatives which are still being propounded today. Summarized, state court decisions fall generally into two groups: One group is composed of holdings that the contract is not terminated by nonpayment of premiums because of war, and the payment of premiums is only suspended; the other group holds that the contract is completely terminated by reason of nonpayment of premiums, in accordance with the provisions of the policy.

The earliest holding in point of time, a Kentucky case, was decided on the principle that cancellation of the contract for nonpayment of premiums would effect a forfeiture, which the law traditionally "abhors." Thus the decision was in the beneficiaries' favor, the court saying: "None of the parties can be presumed to have contemplated such a disabling war or to have intended by the condition of avoidance more than voluntary failure to pay, when there was a legal ability to receive the premiums."[26] In other words, the court held that the parties did not contemplate forfeiture for nonpayment of premiums under circumstances when it was not legally possible either to pay or to receive them.

The Supreme Court of Virginia further developed this view—that war only suspends a contract of insurance; and the courts of New York and New Jersey took much the same position, that the effect of war was to suspend rather than cancel the contract and that at war's end, the contract could be resumed by payment of the back premiums.

Meanwhile, the Georgia Supreme Court, in the case of *Dillard* v. *Manhattan Life Insurance Company*,[27] reached an analysis more in accord with present-day thinking, as follows:

> Indeed, a contract of life insurance is, at best, nothing but an undertaking that the company will take the annual premiums paid, invest them safely, and pay to the insured the product, after deducting the expense of the business. Indeed, if every person insured lived to an average age, this would be exactly the contract, but as any individual may die at any time, the company agrees to pay what his premiums would amount to, making up its losses on him by the payments of those who live beyond the average age. The regular annual payment agreed upon under the contract is thus a condition precedent of the contract and not a condition subsequent.

---

[26] *New York Life Insurance Company* v. *Clopton*, 7 Bush. (Ky.) 179 (Summer Term, 1870).

[27] 44 Ga. 119 (July Term, 1871).

The court then pointed out the basic principle that failure to perform a condition precedent does not work a forfeiture because the right which is subject to it never vested in the first place. "A failure to perform a condition precedent is a failure to do the thing necessary to acquire the right," the court said. "Hence the conclusion is reached that the plaintiff should recover nothing."

These two lines of decisions have sometimes been referred to as the New York and Connecticut rules.[28] The New York rule is that war merely suspends the contract; after the war, back premiums may be paid and the contract revived. The Connecticut rule holds that the contract terminates according to its terms if premiums are not paid, regardless of the cause.

The Federal Cases. The most significant federal decision included an additional point—the idea that equities were involved even though nonpayment of the premium was a failure to perform a condition precedent. In this case, the case of *New York Life Insurance Company* v. *Statham*, previously mentioned,[29] the court said:

> We are of opinion, therefore, first, that as the companies elected to insist upon the condition in these cases, the policies in question must be regarded as extinguished by the non-payment of the premiums, though caused by the existence of the war, and that an action will not lie for the amount insured thereon.
>
> Secondly, that such failure being caused by a public war, without the fault of the assured, they are entitled *ex aequo et bono*[30] to recover the equitable value of the policies with interest from the close of the war.

It should be remembered at this point that by the decision of *Erie* v. *Tompkins*, the federal courts are today obliged to apply the common law of the state where the question under consideration arose. For example, in cases arising under the law of Virginia, the federal courts would now follow the common law as defined by that state. The decision in the Statham case, therefore, does not have the weight at the present time that it would have had prior to the decision in the Erie case.

The Versailles Treaty. The effect of World War I on life insurance contracts previously in force between nationals of enemy countries was specifically defined in the Treaty of Versailles.[31] Such contracts were not to be considered as having been terminated by the outbreak of the war, and any amount which during the war might have become payable under a contract was specifically declared to be recoverable after the war, with

---

[28] See William R. Vance, *Handbook on the Law of Insurance*. 3d ed. by Buist M. Anderson (St. Paul: West Publishing Co., 1951), p. 148.

[29] See section 10.3 above.

[30] "In equity and good conscience."

[31] Treaty of Versailles, Part X, Sec. V, Annex, Clause III of Annex to Sec. V, pars. 11 and 15.

interest at 5 percent from the date on which it became payable. Contracts which had lapsed because of nonpayment of premiums during the war could be surrendered for cash as of the date of lapse, or be restored within three months following the date of the treaty, upon payment of arrearages of premiums with interest at 5 percent.

World War II. Of the numerous treaties signed at the close of World War II, none repeated the provisions of the Versailles Treaty, which, in effect, merely suspended those contracts of insurance on which premiums had not been paid by reason of the war. In the early years of World War II, legislation had been proposed which would have kept in force all contracts of insurance written by American companies on the lives of nonenemy persons unable to escape enemy-occupied countries, but it was not enacted. Generally speaking, therefore, American insurance companies took the position that since many of their contracts contained automatic nonforfeiture provisions, the most equitable course of action was just to carry out all contracts in accordance with their terms.

I. RECOVERY OF PREMIUMS PAID

Fundamentally, the life insurance policy transfers a risk of loss from an individual to a group of insureds as of the moment the insurance takes effect. The company thus assumes the risk, and the policyowner pays the premium. Generally speaking, therefore, in any question concerning recovery of the premium paid, the basic question is: "Has the risk been assumed by the company?"

10.26 Where the Risk Has Been Assumed

As a general rule, if an effective contract has been entered into, the premium payor is not entitled to a return of premiums paid. Thus the mere fact that the company has reorganized without the consent of the insured, though with proper legal authority to do so, does not give the insured the right to a return of the premium paid to the reorganized company. Also, if overpayments or assessments are paid voluntarily and with full knowledge of the facts, they cannot ordinarily be recovered by the payor. However, if the money is paid under a mistake of fact, or through fraud on the part of the agent, it is ordinarily recoverable.

Illustrative of payment under a mistake of fact are those cases where premiums are paid after the death of the insured. For instance, in one Utah case[32] the wife of the insured continued to pay the premiums on his life insurance after he had disappeared while herding sheep. He apparently became lost, and although his horse returned to camp, he did

---

[32] *Cook v. Cook,* 174 P. (2d) 434 (Utah, 1946).

not. There was an alleged agreement between the wife and the mother of the insured (the mother was the beneficiary) concerning the insured's property, and the wife paid the premiums until her husband's body was found some two years later. The case itself concerned the rights of the wife as the result of having paid the premiums voluntarily, and the court held that the mere payment of the premiums gave her no rights whatsoever as against the named beneficiary under the policy. However, the company had already refunded the amount of premium she had paid, since it was paid under a mutual mistake of fact—that is to say, their ignorance of the death of the insured.

10.27 Where the Risk Has Not Been Assumed

As a general rule, the premium payor can recover any premiums paid by him if the insurance has not taken effect as a binding contract. Obviously if the application is rejected, the applicant is entitled to return of the premium. Also, if the policy issued is not in accordance with the application, the applicant may refuse to accept it and is then entitled to recover back the premium paid.

10.28 Illegal Contracts

The decisions of the courts are not in complete accord with respect to recovery of premiums paid under illegal contracts of insurance. As a general rule, if the contract is illegal or invalid for lack of insurable interest, for example, the premium payor can recover the premium if the parties are not *in pari delicto*. This is a frequently used Latin phrase, which, roughly translated, means "in equal fault." Thus if the applicant acted in good faith and if he had no part in the wrong, he is not ordinarily penalized by reason of the illegality of the contract and can recover the premium paid. If the parties are *in pari delicto*, however, the premium cannot be recovered. Some courts simply take the position that if the contract is illegal they will leave the parties where they found them. Under this approach, the premium cannot be recovered regardless of the good faith of the payor.

SUMMARY

The Nature of the Life Insurance Premium

Although life insurance premiums are usually paid in instalments, they differ from most other instalment payments made by the policyowner in one fundamental respect. There is no promise, and thus no obligation on his part, to pay the life insurance premiums.

In the language of contract law, the initial premium constitutes the consideration for the promise or promises of the insurer and puts the contract in force. Payment of renewal premiums as they fall due is a condition precedent, performance of which is necessary to keep the promises of the insurer in force, although nonperformance of the condition imposes no liability on the policyowner.

Presumption of Premium Payment

In the absence of fraud, possession of the policy by the insured or beneficiary at the insured's death creates a presumption that the initial premium was paid. This presumption is especially strong if the policy specifically acknowledges receipt of the premium. The prevailing view, however, is that evidence can be introduced to show that the initial premium was not paid. Under some circumstances, also, the insurer or its agent may waive payment of the first premium and extend credit for that amount so that payment can be made at a later date.

Renewal Premiums

Renewal premiums must be paid on or before the date specified in the policy unless an extension of time is granted. As a general rule, the premium due date specified in the policy will govern. There is, however, a strong minority line of cases that hold that 12 months of insurance coverage must be provided in exchange for the initial premium. In accordance with this line of reasoning, if the insurance under a policy does not go into effect until delivery of the policy during the lifetime and continued good health of the insured, the premium period must be computed from the date the insurance actually took effect. The majority view, however, is that if a date is expressly stated in the policy for premium payment, that date will control. This includes policies that are backdated to save age.

Who May Pay the Premium

The general rule is that anyone who wishes to do so may pay a premium on a policy on the life of someone else. However, he will acquire no rights under the policy by doing so. Thus a revocable beneficiary cannot enlarge his "mere expectancy" under the contract simply by paying premiums.

As between the policyowner and a collateral assignee, the policyowner has the duty to pay the premiums. An absolute assignee stands in the same position with respect to premium payment as the original owner.

Persons to Whom Payment May Be Made

Most policies require renewal premiums to be paid to the home office or to an authorized agent. Payment to an unauthorized agent will be effective if it reaches the home office on time. Otherwise, there must be sufficient apparent authority on the part of the agent to justify a reasonable person in believing that the agent had the authority to accept premium payments. In that case, the insurer may be estopped to deny that the agent had the authority the premium payor thought he had.

Payment by Promissory Note

Legally, the acceptance of a promissory note instead of cash in payment of a life insurance premium is the equivalent of payment. It is important, therefore, if promissory notes are accepted, that both they and the policy contain provisions for the forfeiture of the policy if there is a default in payment of the note.

Payment by Check

Payment of a premium by check is generally held to be conditional upon the check's being honored. If a premium receipt has been given and the check is dishonored, the company may, if it wishes, lapse the policy for nonpayment of premium. In that case, it should return the check, request the receipt, and declare the policy forfeited. Alternatively, the insurer may take action to secure payment of the check. In the latter case, however, the company is presumed to have waived its right to forfeit the policy.

A postdated check is considered payment effective as of the date of the receipt if the check is honored on the date it bears.

Other Ways of Paying Premiums

Insurers sometimes accept the discounted value of premiums paid in advance, holding the amount so paid on deposit, out of which each premium is paid as it falls due. Because this resembles the practices of banks in accepting deposits, this practice has been criticized. For this reason, the right to withdraw may be limited except for total withdrawal. Ordinarily, the receipt for the funds specifies the withdrawal rights available as well as the disposition that will be made of the remaining balance, if any, at the death of the insured.

A preauthorized check plan is a plan under which the insurer is authorized to draw drafts in its own favor on the bank where the policyowner has an account, and to process such drafts in the regular course of business. The bank is authorized to honor such drafts as they are presented and is protected under an indemnity agreement with the insurer.

The automatic premium loan is a provision in the policy that, if elected, authorizes the insurer to establish a policy loan for the purpose of paying a premium otherwise unpaid at the end of the grace period, if the loan value is sufficient for this purpose.

Allotment plans permit members of the armed services to authorize the regular deduction from their salaries of sums sufficient to pay the premium on their life insurance with private insurers. Salary allotment plans serve the same purpose in private employment.

Premium Notices

In the absence of a statute to the contrary or a policy provision, the life insurer has no duty to send notices of premiums as they fall due. Most private insurers would do this, however, simply because it is good business. If the insurer has specifically agreed to send notices, it is required to do so; and if it has sent notices for an extended period of time, it may be subject to an estoppel if it discontinues the practice without specific advance notice to that effect.

A few states have statutes specifically forbidding an insurer from declaring a policy lapsed for nonpayment of premiums unless premium notices have been sent. Statutes of this kind are for the benefit of the policyowner, and the general rule is that he cannot waive the requirement by agreement in the application or the policy.

Dividends

A life insurance policy dividend is a premium abatement. Most participating policies provide four basic dividend options, under which dividends will be:

1. Paid in cash.
2. Applied to reduce the premium.
3. Used to purchase paid-up additional insurance.
4. Left to accumulate at interest.

In addition, some companies provide a special option under which the dividend may be applied to purchase term insurance for the next succeeding year in an amount equal either to the cash value of the policy or for whatever amount the dividend will purchase.

Usually one dividend option is automatic if no election is made, and some states specify which option will be automatic.

It is also common practice to permit application of the accumulated dividends to pay up the policy or mature it as an endowment.

The company is legally obliged to send premium notices if dividends are applied to reduce premiums.

Generally speaking, a policy cannot be declared forfeited if the insurer has in its possession unapplied dividends sufficient to pay the then-due premium and the policyowner has elected to have the dividends used to reduce the premium. However, this fund must be sufficient to pay the entire premium, since the insurer is not obligated to use it for partial payment.

Excuses for Nonpayment of Premiums

There is no excuse for nonpayment of premiums unless the policy-owner can show that he was ready and willing to pay the premium and an act or acts of the insurer prevented him from doing so.

Both waiver and estoppel may operate to prevent a forfeiture of a policy for nonpayment of a premium under some circumstances, and a refusal of tender has much the same effect.

Relating to War

Court decisions vary concerning the legal effect of nonpayment of premiums because of war between the state or country where the insured resides and the domicile of the insurer. In considering Civil War cases, the state courts took two positions, now sometimes referred to as the New York and the Connecticut rules. The New York rule is that if premiums are not paid because of war, the contract is merely suspended and may be revived at war's end by payment of back premiums. The Connecticut rule is that nonpayment of premiums as the result of war has the same legal effect as nonpayment for any other reason; it terminates the contract according to its terms.

Federal cases held that the insured or his beneficiaries were entitled to recover the equitable value of the policy with interest at the end of the war.

After World War I, the Versailles Treaty specifically provided that any amounts that might have become payable under a life insurance contract during the war were recoverable after the war, with interest at 5 percent from the date on which they became payable.

No similar treaty was made with respect to the effect of World War II on life insurance contracts, and insurers generally considered that their contracts would be continued or terminated according to their terms.

Recovery of Premiums Paid

The general rule is that once the risk has been assumed by an insurer, the policyowner is not entitled to recover any premium paid. If the risk has not been assumed, the premium is recoverable. However, if a premium has been paid under a mutual mistake of fact (for instance, after the death of the insured), it is ordinarily recoverable.

ILLUSTRATIVE CASE

The following case illustrates the interweaving of several principles that have been discussed thus far—the power of an agent, as distinguished from his authority, for example; the concepts of waiver and estoppel; and the fact that there are several ways in which a life insurance premium may be paid.

McGOWAN v. PRUDENTIAL INSURANCE COMPANY OF AMERICA[33]
United States District Court, W. D. Pennsylvania

GOURLEY, Chief Judge:
This civil jury proceeding arises from a suit on an insurance policy to recover accidental death benefits and family income benefits. Verdict was in favor of plaintiff.

The immediate matters before the court are Motions for Judgment N.O.V. and New Trial on behalf of defendant.[34]

JUDGMENT N.O.V.

(1) In support of said motion it is contended there was not sufficient evidence to support the jury's findings that the agent's representations created an estoppel and if they did, there was not sufficient evidence to support his authority to do so.

An exhaustive and meticulous review of the record indicates substantial evidence from which the fact finder could infer that the agent's representations to the plaintiff gave her a basis to believe that the policy was still in force and that the plaintiff relied thereon.

As to the agent's authority, counsel for the defendant relies on the disclaimer in the policy under "Miscellaneous Provisions"—

> No agent has power on behalf of the company to make or modify this contract, to extend the time for paying a premium, to waive any forfeiture, or to bind the company by making any promise or representation or by giving or receiving any information.

---

[33] 253 F. Supp. 415 (U.S.D.C., Pa., 1966).

[34] Judgment *non obstante veredicto* means a judgment in favor of one party to a suit in spite of the fact that a verdict has been reached for the other party. Here the defendant (the insurer) has moved for judgment on its behalf in spite of the finding for the plaintiff and, if that is not granted, a new trial.

(2) However, there was substantial evidence to indicate that the defendant company had clothed the representative with the authority to do what he stated to the assured he did in fact do, that the policy was kept in force through the automatic loan provisions thereof.

Furthermore, the master contract between the agent and defendant, which defines the agent's duties and obligations with regard to policyholders, expressly states—

> . . . to render to policyholders of a company all service incidental to the maintenance and care of the company's business which may be required by the policyholders or by the company.

(3) Where there is an express provision in the policy against waiver of agents, notwithstanding this, the receipt of the premium and delivery of a receipt therefor by the agent did constitute a waiver in view of the scope of the agent's authority. The basis of the decision was waiver and not estoppel, but the important point, in this thesis, is the ruling as to the extent and scope of the authority of an agent in the expediting of an express provision in the policy against waiver. *Globe Mut. L. Ins. Co.* v. *Wolff*, 95 U.S. 326, 24 L. Ed. 387.

It is further contended that the principles enunciated in *Continental Assur. Co.* v. *Jensen*, 46 F. 2d 902 (3 Cir.), are inapposite to the instant case. In that case an insurance agent told the assured that he [the agent] was paying the premium and did not do so, and it was determined that this created an estoppel so that the assured was able to collect on the policy. The Court stated, "The misrepresentation which the plaintiff relies upon as a basis of estoppel in this case was made by an agent. It was not expressly authorized by the company nor was it brought to the company's attention subsequently and ratified by it. Is the company bound by it? This depends, as I take it, upon whether it was a statement made in connection with a matter which was within the general scope of the agent's authority."

Although the facts in this case are somewhat different, I believe the rule enunciated therein is applicable in this proceeding.

In *Davis* v. *Home Insurance Company*, 74 Pa. Super. 92, the court said, "let it be noted that this agent's statement that he had affixed a permit for other insurance to the policy was a plain bald statement of fact. It was no expression of an opinion by the agent. It was a simple declaration that the agent had in fact done that which he had a perfect right to do and there was no reason why the insured should not have relied on that statement of fact."

(4) The authority of an agent is governed by the following legal doctrine:

> An authorization is interpreted in light of all accompanying circumstances, including among other matters: (a) the situation of the parties, their relations to one another, and the business in which they are engaged; (b) the business methods of the principal; (c) facts of which the agent has notice respecting the objects which the principal desires to accomplish; (d) the nature of the subject matter, the circumstances under which the act is to be performed. (The American Law Institute, Restatement of the Law, Agency, 2d Section 32.)

In this proceeding there is no question that the agent had broad authority to conduct his business, and, in fact, there was testimony to show that it was his custom to have his clients provide him with signed copies of blank forms so that he could expedite matters such as instituting automatic premium loans and other matters.

I conclude that whether or not the assured relied on the statements made by the agent and whether or not the agent had authority to state that the automatic loan provision had been effected was a factual question properly submitted for determination by the jury.

The Court has stated many times before that it is not the Court's prerogative to substitute its judgment for that of a jury.

Motion for Judgment N.O.V. is denied.

QUESTIONS FOR REVIEW

1. What is the essential difference between the payment of a premium for a whole life policy and the payment of an instalment under a conditional sales agreement?

2. Distinguish between initial and subsequent premiums under a life insurance policy with respect to their legal significance.

3. Describe briefly the legal problem that may result if a promissory note is accepted as payment of a life insurance premium and the note is not paid when due.

4. If a personal check is returned for insufficient funds and a premium receipt has been given, what actions are open to the insurer?

5. What is the general rule concerning the payment of life insurance premiums by someone other than the policyowner?

6. Briefly summarize the preauthorized check plan for paying life insurance premiums. What are the principal arguments for and against the plan?

7. What are the principal advantages of the automatic premium loan? The disadvantages?

8. Under what circumstances is a life insurance company required to send premium notices?

9. Discuss briefly the insurer's duty with respect to the application of dividend accumulations when a premium remains unpaid at the end of the grace period.

10. Under what circumstances may the insurer be precluded from declaring a policy lapsed for nonpayment of premiums even though the premium has not in fact been paid when due or within the grace period?

11. Briefly discuss two basic situations under which the applicant or policyowner may be entitled to the return of a premium which has been paid.

Chapter Outline

A. The "Values" of the Contract

B. The Meaning of Property
 11.1 Personal Property
 11.2 The Life Insurance Contract Is a *Chose* in Action

C. The Transfer of a *Chose* in Action
 11.3 What an Assignment Is
 11.4 Assignments Classified

D. Assignment of the Life Insurance Contract
 11.5 After Death of the Insured
 11.6 Prior to the Death of the Insured
 11.7 Formal Requisites for an Assignment
 11.8 Responsibility of the Insurer
 11.9 Assignments Intended to Be Absolute
 11.10 Assignments Intended to Secure Indebtedness

E. Assignments in Practice
 11.11 Property Settlements and Divorce Decrees
 11.12 Business Insurance

F. Some Practical Solutions
 11.13 The Policy Provision
 11.14 The A.B.A. Assignment Form

G. How Assignments Are Released

H. Transfer of Ownership by Endorsement

Chapter 11

The Policy as Property

BECAUSE of its steadily increasing cash value, any whole life insurance contract is considerably more than just a way to provide for the payment of a specified sum of money at the insured's death. A whole life insurance contract today provides present (lifetime) rights of undeniable value; and the policyowner cannot be deprived of them except as the result of his own actions. In many respects, therefore, a life insurance contract (other than term insurance) is very similar to such other evidences of present property rights as corporate bonds, mortgages, and stock certificates.

The purpose of this chapter is to discuss the more frequent ways in which the life insurance contract may be considered and used as personal property and to outline some of the legal principles that need to be observed if the property uses of life insurance are not to nullify or seriously impair its primary value as insurance.

A. THE "VALUES" OF THE CONTRACT

In one of the famous cases on insurable interest, *Grigsby* v. *Russell*,[1] Mr. Justice Holmes spoke of the property characteristics of life insurance as follows: ". . . life insurance has become in our day one of the best recognized forms of investment and self-compelled saving. So far as reasonable safety permits, it is desirable to give to life policies the ordinary characteristics of property." And later in the same case: "To deny

---

[1] 222 U.S. 149, 32 S. Ct. 58, 56 L. Ed. 133, 36 L.R.A., N.S. 642, Ann. Cas. 1913B, 863 (1911).

361

the right to sell . . . is to diminish appreciably the value of the contract in the owner's hands."

This "value of the contract in the owner's hands" and the possibilities of dealing with it in many respects as he would deal with any other kind of personal property have given the cash value policy a usefulness it would not otherwise have had. Such a policy may be surrendered for cash, used as collateral for a loan, sold, or given away. All of these are property uses.

In considering the property aspects of the life insurance contract, however, it is imperative to remember that the value of a life insurance contract to the beneficiary at the death of the insured (its value as insurance) is ordinarily much greater in dollars and cents than its value to the policyowner during the insured's lifetime. The property aspects of the contract were developed incidentally to its fundamental and basic purpose, which is to provide a specified benefit, payable upon the death of the insured, to a named beneficiary.

Because of this basic purpose, life insurance has been the object of many protective laws which have not been enacted with respect to any other kind of property. When Justice Holmes prefaced his statement with the words, "So far as reasonable safety permits," he was recognizing the fact that the life contract involves rights and characteristics that do not lend themselves to an indiscriminate application of the rules and principles applicable to such instruments as certificates of stock, negotiable instruments, and bonds. If the growing uses of life insurance as property are not to jeopardize its fundamental and still major purpose of protection, the property rights which the contract evidences must be exercised with an ever-present awareness and consideration of the value of the contract to the beneficiary.

Nevertheless, there is no good reason why the life insurance contract cannot have a wide usefulness as property without seriously impairing its basic value as insurance. Many of the possible conflicts between the rights of the beneficiary and those of the assignee can be avoided by a better understanding of the legal effects of the provisions of the policy and the policyowner's actions. Most useful are the provisions in many modern policies that define the ownership rights under the policy and the legal effects of an assignment. Thus, there seems no reason to believe that these conflicts cannot eventually be resolved on a middle ground which will retain the best of the uses of life insurance as property while maintaining the policy in its fullest possible effect as insurance.

B. THE MEANING OF PROPERTY

The word property is popularly associated with objects of a tangible nature such as land, buildings, furniture, automobiles, and the like.

Legally, however, property does not mean the objects themselves but rather the rights that inhere in them. Rights of possession, of control, of disposition (rights of *user,* the lawyer might say) are all ownership rights, and ownership rights constitute property in the legal sense of the word. The person in whom ownership rights are vested is known as the owner.

Kinds of Property. If the rights of ownership inhere in land or objects permanently attached to it, such as buildings, the property is referred to as real property. If one's ownership rights concern movables (such as furniture, automobiles, jewels, paintings) or intangibles (such as certificates of stock or bonds), the property is classified as personal property. (The terms "real" and "personal" are derived from the forms of legal action which were used in the early days of the common law to enforce one's rights of ownership, and they are descriptive of the property only in that sense.)

11.1 Personal Property

There are two kinds of personal property: (1) *choses* (things) in possession and (2) *choses* in action. (It may be helpful to recall that for some time after the Norman Conquest, French was spoken in the courts and by the aristocracy of England. Hence the French word *chose* for what the Saxon would have called "thing.")

The phrase *choses* in possession refers to tangible objects which are capable of being possessed; for instance, the movables mentioned above. *Choses* in action, on the other hand, refers to ownership rights which are evidenced by something tangible but which evidence does not have value in or of itself. With a *chose* in action, one may have to take legal action to recover the value it represents. In other words, a *chose* in action does not have value in itself but is an evidence of a right to values. A certificate of stock is an example. The paper on which it is printed has only minimal value, but the rights which it evidences may and sometimes do have very great value.

It is in this connection that the legal sense of the word property has its clearest application, meaning not the thing itself but rather the rights which inhere in it. Thus rights of property and ownership are virtually synonymous and mean not one right but rather a collection or "bundle" of rights which one person, known as the owner, may exercise, knowing that his right to do so will be protected by law.

11.2 The Life Insurance Contract Is a *Chose* in Action

The Policy, an Evidence of Value. The many valuable rights which are exercisable by the policyowner prior to the maturity of a life insurance contract give it a number of what Justice Holmes termed the "ordinary characteristics of property." Such rights as the right to effect a policy loan, to withdraw or direct the application of dividends, to surrender the policy for its cash value, are all ownership rights. Considered in this light, then, the life insurance contract has many of the same characteristics as bank accounts, evidenced by passbooks; creditor interests, evidenced by mortgages, bonds, and notes; or corporate ownership, evidenced by certificates of stock. In this respect, the life insurance contract can be considered a *chose* in action, and, as such, it is governed by the same laws which govern any other *chose* in action and may be dealt with in the same way.

Property Uses. Since the life insurance contract represents lifetime rights of value, it is sometimes advantageous to transfer those rights either for value (a sale), gratuitously (a gift), or as security for a loan (a pledge). In cases of divorce, any life insurance owned by either spouse will be a part of the property to be considered and a proper subject for a property settlement. In case of death, third-party ownership policies may pass with the decedent's other personal property to his executor or representative for distribution to his heirs or legatees (those to whom he leaves personal property by will).

In all these situations, the life insurance contract is subject to the same laws which govern any other *chose* in action, but it is complicated by a value which is not usually associated with any other *chose,* the right to receive a benefit payable on the death of the insured. This latter right is ordinarily conferred upon a beneficiary, and by methods different from the transfer of a *chose* in action—procedures outlined in the policy itself.

How the law of property fits in with, and must be modified by, this most basic of all rights under the life insurance contract has been the subject of a great many conflicting court decisions. The majority of such questions, however, have arisen in connection with assignments, and for that reason, the major part of the following discussion will concern that subject.

C. THE TRANSFER OF A *CHOSE* IN ACTION

11.3 What an Assignment Is

Perhaps the most important characteristic of ownership is the right of an owner to transfer his ownership rights or any portion of them to another, on almost any basis he may choose. With respect to a nonnegotiable *chose* in action, transfer of title is accomplished by means of an assignment.

An assignment may be defined as a transfer of some or all of the rights of ownership with respect to a *chose* in action, made by one person, known as the assignor, in favor of another, known as the assignee. Originally a *chose* in action was not transferable. Even now, unless there is a statute which declares otherwise, the assignee of a *chose* in action may take legal action only in the name of the assignor. This limitation has been removed in most states by statute, however, and in the United States it is generally accepted that a *chose* in action can be freely assigned, whether as a gift or for a consideration; and the assignee is free to bring suit, if necessary, in his or her own name.

11.4 Assignments Classified

Absolute and Collateral Assignments.   An assignment made for the purpose of transferring all of one's ownership rights to another, irrevocably, is called an absolute assignment. If an assignment is made for the purpose of transferring some or all of one's ownership rights to another, but on condition that they are to return ("revert" is the legal word) to the assignor on the repayment of money currently being borrowed or otherwise owed, it is called a collateral assignment. In other words, under a collateral assignment, the owner is transferring all or a specified part of his ownership rights as security for a loan, with the understanding, express or implied, that the assignment will be canceled and the ownership rights returned to him when he repays the loan.

Gifts and Sales.   If no payment is made by the assignee, an absolute assignment is said to be made without consideration. In that case, it is a gift. A gift has been defined as a "voluntary transfer of his property by one to another without any consideration or compensation therefor."[2] It must be a present transfer of an interest in property. If the gift is to take effect only in the future, it is a mere promise to make a gift and is unenforceable because of lack of consideration. If the transfer is made for a consideration, it is the equivalent of a sale.

D. ASSIGNMENT OF THE LIFE INSURANCE CONTRACT

11.5 After Death of the Insured

The beneficiary's rights under a life insurance contract become definitely established at the death of the insured. After that time, therefore, the rights under a life insurance policy are no different from any other rights to a fixed amount of money. Rights of this kind are freely assignable, and even a policy provision prohibiting assignment is generally held ineffective to prevent an assignment after the insured's death. This rule is expressed in an illustrative case[3] as follows:

---

[2] *Gray* v. *Barton*, 55 N.Y. 68, 14 Am. Rep. 181 (1873).

[3] *Lain* v. *Metropolitan Life Insurance Company*, 388 Ill. 576, 58 N.E. (2d) 587 (1944).

The general rule, supported by a great wealth of authority, is that general stipulations in policies, prohibiting assignment thereof except with the insurers' consent, or upon giving some notice, or like conditions, have universally been held to apply only to assignments before loss, and, accordingly, not to prevent an assignment after loss, of the claim or interest of the insured in the insurance money then due in respect to the loss.

After maturity, therefore, the life insurance contract can be assigned as freely as any other claim for a stated sum of money. It is assignments made prior to maturity of the policy that present problems.

11.6 Prior to the Death of the Insured

The freedom to assign a life insurance contract however and to whomever the owner wishes is especially valuable in business and estate planning. It is often highly advisable for persons in business to own insurance on the lives of their associates—partners, employees, fellow stockholders. When the reason for such ownership ceases, it is a simple matter for the owner to assign the policy by absolute assignment to the insured for its then value (i.e., to sell it to him), and both persons are benefited. Similarly, in estate planning it is sometimes advisable for some of a person's life insurance to be owned by his or her spouse. This can be accomplished by having the intended owner complete the application for the insurance in the case of new insurance or by having the owner of a policy already issued execute an absolute assignment in favor of the spouse.

So long as the third-party owner, or the assignee, as the case may be, is also the beneficiary, no difficulties are usually encountered. Whenever the ownership of a life insurance policy is transferred, however, the beneficiary designation should be reviewed and changed, if necessary, to reflect the intentions of the new policyowner. For, in almost every instance, the most valuable right under a life insurance contract is the right of the beneficiary to receive the proceeds at the insured's death. Ordinarily, also, the avowed purpose of the applicant is to make this benefit available to the designated beneficiary. It is easy to lose sight of this basic purpose, however, when assignments are made. As a result, the conflict between the property rights of the assignee and the insurance rights of the beneficiary has provided a large legal heritage of decisions.

In an effort to avoid such problems, policies providing only a limited amount of insurance, such as industrial policies, sometimes include a provision prohibiting or strictly limiting any assignment of the policyowner's rights. By and large, however, the freedom to use a life insurance contract as property is a valuable privilege; and the majority of ordinary life insurance contracts do not restrict the owner's right to assign them.

11.7 Formal Requisites for an Assignment

Assignments are (and should be) usually in writing, and it is customary to deliver the evidence of the rights being transferred (the stock certificate, bank book, insurance policy, etc.) by manual delivery to the assignee at the time the assignment is executed.

A Writing. In the absence of a statute or a policy provision, it is not legally necessary that an assignment be in writing. In fact delivery of the *chose* without any writing may be sufficient under some circumstances to effect what is called an equitable assignment—that is, a situation which in fairness must be interpreted as an assignment even though the technical requirements for an assignment have not been met. The case of *Sundstrom* v. *Sundstrom*[4] illustrates some of the possibilities growing out of this principle. In that case there were two claimants under the policy, the mother of the insured and his wife. The policy was first issued with the mother as the named beneficiary. Some time after the insured's marriage he changed the beneficiary designation to his wife. Later still, the wife sued for divorce, and the insured again changed the beneficiary back to his mother.

The case presented an especially difficult set of facts. The wife had worked and supported the insured, who had arthritis and was able to work only sporadically. Together they had paid his parents the money the latter had charged him for furnishing care prior to his marriage. When that indebtedness had been reduced to a relatively small sum, the insured changed the beneficiary to his wife and gave her the policy, telling her that it was to be hers. Seven years later the wife was very seriously injured in an automobile accident. After a few weeks her husband closed out their joint bank account and went back to his parents, taking with him the life insurance policy. The wife sued for divorce; but before the decree became final the insured had died, after having changed the beneficiary back to his mother. On this set of facts the court held that there was an equitable assignment in favor of the wife, reasoning as follows:

> We are convinced that this evidence, if believed by the trial court, fully warranted it in finding that the insured had made an equitable assignment of the policy to respondent [the wife] in 1932. It is apparent that he was at that time a hopeless cripple. For four years, his wife had faithfully worked to help support him, and had given him every attention possible. More than that, her earnings had been the principal means by which his personal, premarital debt to his parents had been reduced from five hundred eighty dollars to seventy dollars. Presumably he not only felt a deep affection for her, but also was sincerely grateful for all that she

---

[4] 15 Wash. (2d) 103, 129 P. (2d) 783 (1942).

had done. In addition, he had agreed to transfer the policy to her as soon as *they* got "the folks" paid up. The language employed by him when he delivered the policy to her indicated that it was his intention then and there to invest her with full ownership of the proceeds thereof.

It is true that no formal written assignment of the policy was executed, as required by the provision of the policy hereinabove quoted. But that provision, as we have seen, is designed solely for the protection of the insurance company, and its rights are in no way involved here. Although the transaction between the insured and the respondent with reference to the transfer of the policy was simple and informal, it was only natural for a husband and wife to deal with each other in that way at a time when the relationship between them was one of affection and when there was no occasion for either of them to suspect the other of possible future double-dealing. Nor would it be expected that a wife, even if she were aware of the express requirements of the policy and were familiar with legal phraseology, would insist, under the circumstances then existing, that the terms of the transaction be reduced to writing. The evidence amply justifies the conclusion that it was the insured's intention on October 28, 1932, to transfer to respondent a present interest in the ultimate proceeds of the policy, that he delivered the policy to respondent for that purpose, and that by the form of expression which he then used he made an absolute appropriation of such proceeds to her, relinquishing further control or power of revocation with reference thereto. That being the case, the trial court had sufficient grounds for holding that the insured effected an equitable assignment of the insurance policy to the respondent.

Delivery of the Policy. As a general rule, in order to constitute a valid assignment of a life insurance contract, either the policy or a written assignment must be delivered to the asignee. However, the majority of the decisions have been to the effect that where there has been a duly executed assignment, delivery of the policy is not essential to the assignment's validity.

Notice to the Company. Generally speaking, it is not essential to the validity of an assignment that notice of it be given to the insurer. Certainly an assignment of which notice was not given would be valid as between the parties to the assignment. It is also generally held that a policy provision requiring the filing of a copy of the assignment with the insurer is for the benefit of the company and may be waived by it.

Nevertheless, as a practical matter, the performance of the contract is very much affected by the question of notice. The company cannot be guided by the terms of an assignment of which it knows nothing, and it has no duties beyond discharging its promises to the persons who, by its records, are entitled to payment.

The person whom the insurer is obligated to pay is the beneficiary. If, on the death of the insured, claim is made by the beneficiary and the claim is settled by payment to him or her, without notice of an assignment, the assignee will have no action against the company. The assignment provisions in most life insurance policies make it clear that an assignment will not be recognized until notice of it has been given to the company.

Rights of Successive Assignees.   A question sometimes arises as to the respective rights of successive assignees who have given notice to the insurer of their assignments but in a different order from that in which the assignments were made. For instance, John Davis assigns his life insurance policy (face amount, $5,000) to the firm for which he works as collateral security for amounts advanced to him. He does not deliver the policy to his employer, however, and, later, he assigns it to the First National Bank as security for a loan. The bank notifies the insurer of its assignment immediately; the employer gives notice later, but before the proceeds of the policy have been paid. If the proceeds are not enough to pay both assignees in full, which one must suffer the loss?

There are two leading rules by which this type of problem is resolved. One is known as the English rule, the other as the American rule. According to the English rule, the assignee who first gives notice is the one who is entitled to the proceeds, if he—the assignee—has had no notice of a prior assignment. Several states have followed this rule, which ignores the order in which the assignments were made. The majority rule, however—that is, the American rule—is that the assignee under the first assignment made has the preferable claim, regardless of the order in which notices of the assignments were given. Courts in some 14 or 15 states have followed this rule. In any situation presenting a question of this kind, however, the insurer always has the right to pay the policy proceeds into a court and ask the court to decide which is the proper payee. This legal remedy, called "interpleader," is discussed in Chapter 17.

11.8 Responsibility of the Insurer

The Policy Provision.   The assignment provision included in most life insurance policies today expressly states that the company assumes no responsibility for the "validity or effect" of any assignment of the contract. The provision most commonly used also requires that written notice of the assignment be given the insurer at its home office.

The reasons for these requirements are found in the circumstances surrounding typical life insurance assignment situations. In most instances, the assignment of a life insurance contract is something over which the insurer has almost no control. The validity of an assignment is governed almost entirely by factors with which the insurance company is powerless to deal: the law of the state where the assignment is made; the competency of the parties making the assignment; the nature and extent of the rights assigned; the provisions of the instrument setting forth the conditions of the assignment; even the purpose of the assignment. All may have an effect on the validity and effect of the assignment. The insurer has no control over any of these factors and is not a party to the transaction. Therefore, it is not required to assume any responsibility for the validity or effect of the assignment.

The responsibilities of the company in an assignment situation, so far as the law is concerned, are set forth in the case of *New York Life Insurance Company* v. *The Federal National Bank of Shawnee, Oklahoma.*[5] There the insured (policyowner) and the beneficiary joined in an assignment of his life insurance policy. The assignee borrowed the full loan value of the policy; and, after the death of the insured, the balance of the proceeds was paid to the assignee. Later the beneficiary was declared incompetent, and the bank, as guardian of the beneficiary's estate, sued the life insurance company to recover the face amount of the policy, alleging that the assignment was invalid because of mental incapacity of the insured at the time. On appeal, the court held that the insurance company had no duty to inquire into the competency of the insured-assignor at the time of the assignment. When payment has been made in good faith to a beneficiary or assignee of record, the company cannot be required to pay a second time. Pertinent excerpts from this decision are as follows:

> No case has been cited, and our search has failed to reveal one, which has compelled an insurance company to pay a policy a second time when in good faith it has paid the amount of the policy to a new beneficiary or to an assignee, on the ground that the assignment or the change in beneficiary was void because of lack of mental capacity of the insured at the time the change was made, and that is so even though the original beneficiary did not join in the application for change of beneficiary or in the application for the assignment of the policy. The cases upon which the appellee [the bank] relies to sustain its contention in this respect are not in point. . . .
>
> . . . There is yet another reason why the Bank may not prevail. That part of the policy which gave the insured the right to assign contains this provision: "The company assumes no responsibility for the validity of any assignment." This provision was a part of the contract made at a time when the parties were competent to contract, and must be given effect. There is no ambiguity or uncertainty as to the meaning of this provision. It can only mean that the Company shall not become liable by virtue of the assignment which for any reason was invalid. There was a good reason for the inclusion of such a provision. The Company had a large number of policy-holders. Many requests for the assignment of policies would be received. The Company no doubt realized that fraud, duress or undue influence might be practiced in many instances which would go to [affect] the validity of the assignment, or that assignments might be invalid for

---

[5] 151 F. (2d) 537, 162 A.L.R. 536 (C.C.A. Okla., 1945).

many other reasons, including impaired mental capacity or even lack of mental capacity to make the assignment. If the Company was to be charged with liability if an assignment was invalid for any of these reasons, it would of necessity be compelled to deny the right to assign, or in each instance would be compelled to carefully investigate the application before it was granted. This would place an impossible burden upon the Company. It was for these reasons that the Company in substance said to the insured: "We will give you the right to assign, but we shall not be liable if for any reason the assignment is invalid."

Clearly, in this case, the court upheld the right of the insurer generally to rely upon the policy provision concerning assignments as protection in situations where the validity of the assignment was challenged after payment had been made to the assignee. The court added a notable comment, however, as follows:

. . . This provision would not, of course, protect the Company in case of an irregular assignment because that would put it upon notice, or in cases in which it had knowledge of the mental condition of the insured, or in cases in which it had knowledge of facts which should put it upon inquiry. But this is not such a case.

In other words, the insurer's payment must have been made in good faith. An assignment that is irregular on its face cannot be ignored, and if the insurer knows that the assignor is not mentally competent, it cannot disregard that knowledge either. Thus any facts that might arouse suspicion in the mind of a reasonable person must be investigated. In the absence of such circumstances, however, the insurer does not have to investigate the circumstances surrounding an assignment before making payment to an assignee.

11.9 Assignments Intended to Be Absolute

As a general principle, a policyowner may assign a life insurance policy on his own life to anyone he chooses and on any terms he may wish. The law generally takes the position that property should be freely transferable; and in many instances, it is important to have the right to transfer a life insurance contract. In most states, this presents no problem, but there are some very strong decisions in a few states that hold that an assignee must have an insurable interest. This minority view is illustrated by the case of *Werenzinski v. Prudential Insurance Company of America,*[6] decided by the Pennsylvania Supreme Court in January, 1940. This case concerned four insurance policies issued on the life of Cybuck, a man who tended the furnace in an apartment house owned by Werenzinski, did various odd jobs around the apartment house, and sometimes slept in

---

[6] 339 Pa. 83, 14 Atl. (2d) 279 (1940).

the basement. The policies were issued to Cybuck and were payable to his estate, but were later assigned to Werenzinski. The insured was found one evening lying in front of one of the boilers in the basement, so badly burned that he died.

The insurance company contended that the assignee was not entitled to the proceeds of the policies because he did not have an insurable interest in the life of the insured. The judge instructed the jury

> . . . that the controlling question was as to who paid the premiums after the making of the assignments; if they were paid by plaintiff [the assignee] the policies would then represent wagering contracts and plaintiff would be barred from recovery, but if the insured continued to pay the premiums the verdict should be for plaintiff even though admittedly he had no insurable interest in Cybuck's life.

The jury decided in favor of the insurance company, but the court granted a new trial because the question of whether the assignments were made in good faith was not submitted to the jury.

The supreme court held that it was error to grant the new trial, saying:

> There was ample evidence to warrant the conclusion, which the jury must have reached, that plaintiff, at least after becoming the assignee of the policies, paid the premiums, and if this was so the law would not permit plaintiff to recover, irrespective of any question of good faith.
>
> There are two propositions so well established both by decision and statute that there can be no doubt in regard to them. The first is that a person may take out a policy of insurance on his own life and name as beneficiary whomsoever he pleases, regardless of whether or not such beneficiary has an insurable interest, or, having taken out a policy, he may assign it to one without an insurable interest, provided, in either event, the insured continues at all times to pay the premiums; under such circumstances no question arises of a wagering contract obnoxious to public policy. . . . The other proposition is that a person cannot take out a valid and enforceable policy of insurance for his own benefit, and pay the premiums thereon, on a life in which he has no insurable interest. . . .
>
> A more doubtful situation, from the legal standpoint, exists when a policy of insurance taken out by one on his own life, and thus valid in its inception, is subsequently assigned by the insured to a person having no insurable interest and the assignee thereafter pays the premiums. If such assignment is merely a subterfuge, planned or contemplated when the policy was issued, to enable the assignee thereby to accomplish what he could not have done directly, namely, to obtain insurance on a life wherein he had no insurable interest, it would not be sustainable. But where the assignment is not in execution of such a pre-existing purpose to circumvent the law, but arises from subsequent happenings, may the assignee recover on the policy? There has been a wealth of discussion pro and con

on this subject in judicial opinions and in textbooks, and there is a sharp division of authority. In the great majority of jurisdictions it is held that such an assignment is valid, even though the assignee pays the premiums. . . . The best arguments in support of this view are to be found in *Grigsby* v. *Russell*, 222 U.S. 149 (followed in *Midland National Bank* v. *Dakota Life Insurance Co.*, 277 U.S. 346, 350). But there are a number of states, among which Pennsylvania has consistently maintained its place, where it is held that the assignment of a policy, whether in "good faith" or not, to one who has no insurable interest and who thereafter pays the premiums is as contrary to public policy, and therefore as legally objectionable, as the original issuance of the policy to such a person would have been. This viewpoint has been maintained in Pennsylvania through a course of so many years and by such a number of repeated affirmations that, if it were now sought to change it in order to bring it into harmony with the prevailing doctrine, the appeal for that purpose would have to be directed to the legislature and not the courts.

The court thus decided that Werenzinski was not entitled to the proceeds, leaning heavily on the fact that this view (admittedly a minority view) had been followed in Pennsylvania for a very long time. Any change, therefore, the court said, "should be directed to the legislature and not the courts." This statement is especially interesting in view of the fact that in 1951, the Pennsylvania legislature amended the insurance law of Pennsylvania by adding the following sentence:

> If a policy of life insurance has been issued in conformity with this section, no transfer of such policy or any interest thereunder shall be invalid by reason of a lack of insurable interest of the transferee in the life of the insured or the payment of premiums thereafter by the transferee.[7]

Thus Pennsylvania was removed from the states which follow the minority rule with respect to the requirement of an insurable interest on the part of an assignee. The student may find this case and the later action of the Pennsylvania legislature interesting for a different reason, also, as pointing up the respective roles of courts and legislatures in defining and shaping the law of the life insurance contract.

The Majority View. The prevailing view, as noted in the case just quoted, is that if the policy is taken out by the insured himself or by someone else who has an insurable interest in the life insured, and if the transaction is in good faith and not solely for the purpose of later assigning the policy to one who could not have taken it out originally, the owner can assign it to whomever he wishes. It does not matter that the assignee has no insurable interest in the life insured or that he pays the premiums. This rule is well stated by the Missouri Supreme Court in the

---

[7] 40 Purdon's Pennsylvania Statutes, Sec. 512.

case of *Butterworth et al.* v. *Mississippi Valley Trust Co.,*[8] decided in June, 1951. There the court said:

> There is some difference of opinion. But the prevailing view, and the greater weight of authority and the better and more soundly reasoned conclusions of the courts, was tersely expressed by Mr. Justice Holmes in *Grigsby* v. *Russell,* 222 U.S. 149, 32 S. Ct. 58, 56 L. Ed. 133, wherein, ruling this precise question, he said, in part: "And cases in which a person having an interest lends himself to one without any, as a cloak to what is, in its inception a wager, have no similarity to those where an honest contract is sold in good faith." The principle of the good faith of the assignment transaction runs like a scarlet thread through the better reasoned cases. The decided trend of adjudications unquestionably is to establish the rule that an insurable interest in the insured by the assignee of a policy of life insurance is not essential to the validity of the assignment if the party to whom it was issued in good faith had an insurable interest, and if the assignment was in good faith and not made to cover up a gambling transaction. We unequivocally approve that rule.
>
> . . . Without the power of assignment life insurance contracts would lose much of their value. In a commercial age and with a commercial people, and in recognition of commercial practices, the courts are not unaware of the frequent necessity for the transfer by assignment of such contracts in the usual course of every day business. To limit the assignment of such contracts otherwise valid to those having an insurable interest, and to thus ignore the bona fides of assignments of convenience or necessity, would not only impair the value of such contracts as a plan of estate building and economic protection but would work unconscionable injury to policyholders who are no longer financially able to or who no longer desire to continue such contracts.

Assignment with Fraudulent Intent. A number of assignment cases have reached the courts because the circumstances of their making indicated that they were not made in good faith. That is, a person would apply for insurance on his own life and then assign the policy to someone who had no insurable interest. Thus the assignee was permitted to obtain a policy he could not otherwise have gotten. The law is very strict with respect to anything that suggests trafficking in human lives, and whenever the facts of an assignment case suggest that it was in reality only a wagering contract, the assignment will not be upheld. Under such circumstances, the majority of courts have held the policy valid but the assignment void for lack of insurable interest on the part of the assignee.

11.10 Assignments Intended to Secure Indebtedness

Collateral Assignments. Life insurance contracts are most commonly assigned as security for indebtedness. Usually termed a collateral assign-

---

[8] 240 S.W. (2d) 676 (Mo., 1951).

ment, a transfer of this kind closely resembles a pledge as security for the payment of a debt. The typical collateral assignment transfers only a part of the ownership rights under the policy, rarely the right to designate or change the beneficiary, and the transfer is always on condition that the assignment shall be canceled and the rights so transferred shall revert to the assignor on payment of the debt.

As a general rule, there is not too much question with respect to the rights transferred under such an assignment during the lifetime of the insured. However, questions sometimes arise, and when they do they are typically answered in accordance with the general principles of property law. Thus, the assignment will usually be given effect in accordance with its terms. This principle is illustrated in the case of *Greenberg* v. *Equitable Life Assurance Society of the United States.*[9]

In the Greenberg case, the insurer received from the collateral assignees a request for the cash surrender values of two life insurance policies. Before payment had been made, the insureds' attorney notified the company that the insureds had not consented to the request and that if the funds were paid as requested, the insureds would initiate an action against the company. The insurer then filed a bill of interpleader.

The United States District Court for the District of Minnesota held that the company must pay the cash surrender value to the assignees since the assignment provided that this right was granted them. The company contended that it was on notice as to a dispute, but the court said:

> . . . The unqualified right of an assignee cannot be limited by the mere assertion of a claim by the assignor which is not ultimately substantiated. . . .
>
> The primary purpose of the assignment privileges granted to the insured is to enable the latter to utilize that asset in business transactions as collateral or otherwise. If the unqualified right of a banking institution, for instance, to an assigned insurance policy for a loan could be thwarted by unsupported claims and contentions by an assignor as to the validity of the assignment, it must be apparent that no banking institution could assume to accept such an asset as collateral in a business transaction with the insured.

Right to Repayment of Debt Out of Death Benefit. The most typical, and most difficult, problem in connection with collateral assignments arises at the death of the insured. Under most standard collateral assignment forms, the assignee is given the right to have the indebtedness repaid out of the proceeds of the policy. If the policy is payable to the estate of the insured—that is, if no beneficiary is designated—the rights of the assignee are unquestioned. However, when a beneficiary has been

---

[9] 167 F. Supp. 112 (D.C. Minn., 1958).

designated and the designation has not been revoked at the time the assignment was made, a definite question can be raised unless the beneficiary has joined in executing the assignment or otherwise consented to it.

If the beneficiary has been designated irrevocably, the beneficiary's rights are superior to those of the assignee unless the beneficiary has consented to the assignment. If the beneficiary designation is revocable, however, the court decisions are divided.

In a few states, the courts have taken a very strict view. In effect, they hold that the revocable beneficiary has a right that is vested, subject to being divested. That is, the beneficiary has a right to the proceeds at the death of the insured which can be terminated only by following the procedures outlined in the policy for changing the beneficiary. If that has not been done, the assignee has no right to the proceeds.

Illustrative of this minority point of view is the case of *Continental Assurance Co.v. Conroy*,[10] where the court said:

> It has long been the law in New Jersey that there are two sets of interests in an insurance policy; that of the beneficiary to the proceeds of the policy if he survives the insured, and that of the insured's representatives to the proceeds of the policy if the insured outlives the beneficiary. . . . Moreover, a beneficiary is said to take a vested interest which can be defeated only by a change of beneficiary made in accordance with the procedure specified in the policy. . . . When the insured in the present case assigned his policy to the trustees he made no attempt to comply with the provisions of the policy concerning the substitution of beneficiaries. Therefore, all that was transferred to the trustees, by virtue of this assignment, was the contingent interest of the insured's representatives to the proceeds of the policy in the event that the insured outlived the beneficiary.

The majority rule in this type of situation is that the assignee under a collateral assignment has a right to the proceeds of the policy that is superior to that of a revocable beneficiary even though the latter did not consent to the assignment. The underlying reasons for this rule are suggested in one case as follows:

> From an every day, practical standpoint it is desirable to hold that an assignee of a policy containing a clause permitting a change of beneficiary and an assignment of the policy secures a right in the proceeds of the policy superior to the rights of the named beneficiary. If an assignee, in the absence of the consent of the beneficiary, does not obtain such right it will be practically impossible for an insured to borrow on a policy in time of need of financial aid in those cases where compliance with the form prescribed in the policy cannot be followed. No bank or individual would be likely to lend on the security of a policy where the right to

---

[10] 209 F. (2d) 539 (C.A. N.J., 1954).

enforce the reduction of the security to cash would only mature in case the insured outlived the beneficiary, and where the continued life of the policy depends upon the payment of the annual premium. As stated in the case of *Matter of Whiting* (3 Fed. Rep. 2d 440, 441): "To hold that the beneficiary of such policy has a vested interest would be tantamount to destroying the 'changed beneficiary' provisions of the policy itself." (Cf. Vance on Insurance (2d ed.), 646; 48 Yale L. J. 315.)

That the question is a practical one is illustrated by the large number of decisions involving the issue.[11]

As a matter of practice, the insurer will generally request evidence of the amount of the assignee's claim at the death of the insured. Settlement of the death claim is then made by paying that amount to the assignee in one sum and the remainder to the designated beneficiary—in one sum, or under a settlement option, if elected.

Absolute Assignments. Although absolute assignments are used primarily for the sale or gift of a policy, they are sometimes used for the purpose of securing an indebtedness. In such instances, if the purpose of the assignment can be shown—that is, that it was intended to serve as security for a debt and was not intended to be a permanent transfer of all rights to the assignee—the general rule is that it will be treated as if it were a collateral assignment, and the assignee's rights will be determined on that basis.

Illustrative of this type of holding is the case of *Albrent* v. *Spencer,* a Wisconsin case decided in March, 1957.[12] There the insured made an absolute assignment of policies on his life, together with stock he owned in a freight and storage corporation, as collateral security for the payment of a note on which approximately $140,000 was due. After the insured's death, the assignee collected the entire proceeds of the policies, satisfied the indebtedness, and retained the difference, allegedly amounting to approximately $90,000. The court summarized the basic question in the case as follows:

> We consider that the case presents the issue of whether it is against public policy for a creditor of the insured to avail himself of an absolute assignment of a previously pledged life insurance policy issued upon the life of the debtor, which assignment is intended to end the creditor-debtor relationship. . . .

This question was considered in the following way:

> . . . It offends one's sense of justice that a creditor should realize more out of the proceeds of the policy than the principal and interest due on the loan for which the policy was pledged plus any expenditure of the

---

[11] *Davis et al.* v. *Modern Industrial Bank et al.,* 275 N.Y. 405, 18 N.E. (2d) 639, 135 A.L.R. 1035 (1939).

[12] 81 N.W. (2d) 555 (Wis. 1957).

creditor for premiums necessary to protect his security. To uphold the result reached below in the instant case would be to encourage creditors to bring pressure upon necessitous debtors to convert the rights of the creditor from that of pledgee to that of owner in order that he might gamble upon the life of the insured in the hope of realizing the difference between the amount due on the loan and the face of the policy. In the instant case it is alleged that such difference amounted to the huge sum of approximately $90,000.

The reference to "the result reached below" is to the decision of the lower court, which upheld the rights of the absolute assignee to the total proceeds of the policy. The appellate court says that this decision would encourage creditors to insist that they be made owners rather than pledgees and thus be able to gamble on the life of the insured for the difference between the amount of the indebtedness and the total proceeds payable on the death of the insured. The court decided, therefore, not to uphold the decision of the lower court and instead to hold that cases of this kind present an exception to the general or majority rule.

> While it must be conceded that the majority rule is that, where an owner of a life insurance policy has an insurable interest therein he may make a valid assignment of the policy to a third party having no such insurable interest, (29 Am. Jur., Insurance, p. 313, Sec. 357) it clearly is in the interest of public policy to engraft an exception on to such rule to cover situations such as that which confronts us here. A desirable exception and one that we are compelled to adopt is that any purported absolute assignment by a debtor to a creditor of a policy, which had previously been pledged as security to the creditor, is only valid between the immediate parties to the extent of enabling the creditor to realize the cash surrender value of the policy. If the creditor after receiving such absolute assignment and the creditor-debtor relationship is terminated, continues to hold the policy for the purpose of gambling upon the life of the insured, he becomes a constructive trustee[13] for the benefit of the estate of the deceased of any proceeds received upon the death of the insured, to the extent that such proceeds exceed the amount that would have been due such assignee if the creditor-debtor relationship had not been extinguished.

E. ASSIGNMENTS IN PRACTICE

Any transfer of the ownership rights under a life insurance contract, except by endorsement, is, in legal effect, an assignment. This includes a wide range of different transactions having the effect of transferring, or establishing a lien on, the owner's rights under the policy.

---

[13] If the creditor holds the policy until the death of the insured and at that time collects more than the debt would have been, he is construed to hold the excess as a trustee for the benefit of the estate of the insured.

Usually, such situations are readily identifiable. For instance, there is usually a written assignment, defining the terms of the transfer, often titled "Assignment of Life Insurance Policy as Collateral," and the beneficiary usually has joined with the owner in executing it. In such cases, the legal effects are clear. There are, however, many other documents that may effect a transfer of ownership rights under a life insurance policy, and the legal effects are not always so clearly indicated.

11.11 Property Settlements and Divorce Decrees

One situation in which the rights of the policyowner may be modified or transferred as the result of agreements outside the contract is found in connection with property settlements and divorce decrees. A property settlement between the insured and the beneficiary, for instance, often operates to modify the insured's rights under the policy. Thus, the insured may be required to keep a policy in force for the benefit of his former wife or forbidden to revoke her designation as beneficiary until she remarries or the youngest child reaches age 21, or any of a number of other possibilities. Note, however, how very different the benefits are to the wife whose designation cannot be changed until her youngest child is 21 from those she would have if the policy were required to be kept in force for her benefit until that date. (Clearly, not changing the designation would not benefit her if the policy were allowed to lapse.) It is important also to note the differences between the responsibilities of the insurer if it has received notice of a property settlement from those it would have in the absence of notice.

The responsibilities of the insurer in the absence of notice, as well as the situation of the former wife, are clearly illustrated in the case of *Elledge* v. *Aetna Life Insurance Company*.[14] There, two policies of insurance on the life of the husband were referred to in a property settlement dated May 30, 1959, as follows:

> It is mutually agreed and understood that as to the insurance policies described in item No. 6 above, each of same is on the life of Husband and have as beneficiary Wife. It is further agreed and understood that Husband will not change the beneficiary on any of said policies and will not borrow on same nor surrender same for cash value, they being hereby considered and designated as the property of Wife.

The policies had been issued in 1929 and 1934, and premiums had been waived because of disability of the insured since 1956. A relatively small loan had been granted on each policy prior to the divorce, and the insured applied for and was granted maximum loans on both policies after the divorce. He later attempted to change the beneficiary on both

---

[14] 406 S.W. (2d) 374 (Ark., 1966).

policies and was furnished forms for this, but was unable to submit the policies for endorsement as required, since his former wife had them.

Late in 1963, Mrs. Elledge notified the insurer of the divorce settlement, and early in 1964 she forwarded a certified copy of the property settlement.

On July 12, 1964, the insured died. In the suit that followed, the insurer offered to pay the proceeds into court (the face amount less the policy loans) and asked the court to decide between the claims of the former wife, Mrs. Elledge, and Mrs. Patton, whom the insured had wished to name as beneficiary when he attempted to make the change. The court awarded the proceeds of one policy to Mrs. Elledge and the other to Mrs. Patton and both appealed the decision.

On appeal, the supreme court of Arkansas held that Mrs. Elledge should have the proceeds of both policies, but held also that the insurer was not in error in deducting the amount of the loans since the loans were granted prior to the date when it was notified of the property settlement. The pertinent part of the decision is as follows:

> · The principal reason why appellant's [Mrs. Elledge's] argument must fail is that she did not comply with Section 15 of the policies until long after the loans were made. That section provides as follows:
>
>   "No assignment of this policy shall be binding upon the Company unless and until the original or a duplicate thereof is filed at its Home Office. The Company does not assume any responsibility for the validity of an assignment."
>
> Of course, there was no way for Aetna to know of the assignment unless it was notified, and the burden of notification was very clearly placed on appellant. Apparently, she eventually discovered this requirement, for she notified the company of the assignment on December 18, 1963, and sent a certified copy of the property settlement on February 10, 1964, but this was nearly two and one-half years after the loans had been made.

The court then cited a previously decided case[15] in which the same question had been presented, quoting from it as follows:

> . . . Independent of the provisions of the policy, the law of this State, as elsewhere, seems to be clear that the debtor has the right to deal with the creditor until he has actual notice of an assignment. . . .
>
>   . . . "And although such an assignment is good as between assignor and assignee, it has been held that it is necessary to give notice to the company in order to constitute an assignment valid as against a subsequent assignee, and free from acts of an assignor as to surrender of the policy to the office. *And the policy itself may provide that notice must be*

---

[15] *Patten* v. *Mutual Benefit Life Insurance Company*, 192 S.C. 189, 6 S.E. (2d) 26, 126 A.L.R. 91 (1939).

*given to the company, and in such a case the provision should be complied
with to render the assignment a valid one."*

Thus under general principles of law the company had the unquestionable right to make loans on the policy and to treat with the insured as the
sole owner thereof until it received notice of the assignment.

11.12 Business Insurance

Assignments are frequently used in business insurance and, as a
general rule, present no special problems. Here, as elsewhere, however,
it is important to bear in mind that a transaction may be the equivalent
of an assignment even though it is not so called. This is clearly illustrated in the case of *Brand* v. *Ersman et al.*[16]

In that case, three partners of a partnership known as Robert A.
Brand & Company had a partnership agreement that provided that at
the death of any partner during the existence of the partnership, the
value of his share of the business would be paid to his representatives or
next of kin. Pursuant to this agreement, the partnership applied for and
paid the premiums on a policy of insurance on the life of each partner.
Under each policy, the spouse of the insured partner and the other
partners were named beneficiaries, equally, but the firm itself was the
owner and all ownership rights were reserved to it.

Three years later, the partners sold "all of the assets" of the partnership, including all "contracts . . . rights or *choses* in action . . . subject, however, to all of the debts and obligations against the said
partnership. . . ." Thereafter, the purchasing firm, known as Blair Manufacturing Company, had possession of the policy insuring Brand and
paid the premiums on it. Brand died in 1946, and the Blair Manufacturing Company collected the proceeds of the insurance on his life. His
widow, one of the named beneficiaries, claimed the proceeds should
have been paid to her. The court, however, held as follows:

> The Brand firm purchased the policy to discharge an existing obligation
> of the firm and to enable the firm to discharge a future obligation. The
> terms of the policy gave the firm complete control over it. As an asset of
> the firm it was assigned when the firm assigned all its assets and delivered
> its policy to the assignees [Blair Manufacturing]. There can be no doubt
> that the assignment ended the rights of the beneficiaries named in the
> policy, for the policy expressly provided that "the interest of any beneficiary or beneficiaries shall be subject to any assignment of this policy
> made as provided herein."

Apparently, there was a question concerning the form of the assignment,
but the court pointed out that only the insurer could raise this question

---

[16] 84 App. D.C. 194, 172 F. (2d) 28 (1948).

since the policy provision was for its benefit. The widow's claim was, therefore, denied.

F. SOME PRACTICAL SOLUTIONS

11.13 The Policy Provision

The Brand case not only illustrates the problems arising when life insurance is assigned with "all other assets" of a business firm but also points up the significance of the policy provision concerning assignments and the fact that assignments may take different forms. One way to reduce legal problems in this area, therefore, is to draft the contract provision in such a way that the results of an assignment are clearly defined.

As previously noted, in any serious dispute concerning an assignment, the insurer would pay the proceeds into court and ask the court to decide who is rightfully entitled to the money. Nevertheless, this procedure only protects the company from the possibility of having to pay twice. It does not protect anyone from the expense and delay of the court proceedings; and it does not protect the beneficiary from having the proceeds reduced by court costs and fees, to say nothing of having the entire amount payable tied up until the question is resolved.

It seems probable that most of the conflicts resulting from assignments could be avoided if, at the time the assignment is executed, the beneficiary arrangements under the policy were kept clearly in mind and changed, if necessary, to avoid a conflict. It would seem equally true that many conflicts could be avoided simply by specifying in the assignment provision itself what the effect will be if the policy is assigned. One company does this with the following policy provision:

> The company assumes no responsibility for the validity or effect of any assignment of this policy and no assignment will be recognized until it has been duly filed with the company. An assignment of this policy shall operate to the extent thereof to transfer to the assignee the interest of any beneficiary whom the assignor has the right to change, and to render any part of the sum payable to which the assignee is entitled payable in one sum, notwithstanding any settlement agreement endorsed hereon at the time the assignment is executed.

A policy provision of this kind clarifies the respective rights of the beneficiary and any assignees. Under this provision, execution of an assignment automatically revokes the beneficiary designation to the extent necessary to protect the assignee. At the death of the insured, therefore, the rights of the various parties should be readily ascertainable.

11.14 The A.B.A. Assignment Form

Many of the problems that once arose in connection with assignments have been avoided by the development and use of a standard form of assignment for collateral purposes—the American Bankers Association Form of Assignment, or the A.B.A. Assignment Form No. 10, as it is called. (A copy of this form is reproduced in Appendix D.)

The A.B.A. Assignment Form No. 10 was developed by the Bank Management Commission of the American Bankers Association with the collaboration of the Association of Life Insurance Counsel. It is officially termed an "Assignment of Life Insurance Policy as Collateral," but it is considerably more exacting than the usual collateral assignment form. Thus it was hoped that the A.B.A. form would satisfy those lenders who once demanded an absolute assignment, while nevertheless making clear that the purpose of the assignment is collateral security for a loan.

Under Part B of this form, the following rights are specifically declared to pass, by the assignment, to the assignee and to be exercisable by him: the right to collect the net proceeds of the policy at the insured's death or on maturity of the policy; the right to surrender the policy for cash; the right to effect a policy loan; the right to receive dividends; and the right to exercise all nonforfeiture rights.

Other rights are specifically reserved to the owner, and so do not pass by the terms of the assignment. They are the rights to collect disability benefits payable in cash, to designate and change the beneficiary, and to elect an optional mode of settlement.

The assignee agrees, under Form 10, that the balance of any sums collected, after satisfying the indebtedness, will be paid to the persons who would have been entitled to the money if there had been no assignment. The assignee also agrees that the rights to surrender the policy or make a policy loan will not be exercised unless there has been a default on the part of the policyowner and notice of default has been mailed to him. Finally, the assignee agrees to forward the policy to the insurance company for endorsement of any change of beneficiary or settlement agreement which the policyowner wishes to make.

As this form is more widely used, it is believed that conflicts will occur less frequently and the dual nature of the whole life policy—as property as well as insurance—will give it added value without increasing the possibility of problems.

G. HOW ASSIGNMENTS ARE RELEASED

Life insurance companies assume no responsibility for the validity or legal effect of an assignment of a life insurance policy, and ordinarily take the same approach to any documents purporting to release an assignment already made. The company is interested only in having evidence of such a release before the policyowner will be permitted to resume the exercise of rights under the policy without the consent of the assignee.

As a general rule, an absolute assignment is the equivalent of a sale or gift. If it has been used for collateral purposes, however, the assignee should release his rights to the policy at such time as the indebtedness in question has been satisfied. The appropriate evidence of such a release is an absolute assignment back to the original assignor.

Effective releases under a collateral assignment may range in form all the way from a formal recital of the rights so released, signed and witnessed, to a simple statement on the letterhead of the assignee in question, to the effect that the indebtedness has been satisfied and that all rights and title to the captioned policy are thereby released. The important consideration is not the precise form of the release but its legal significance, and in any case of doubt as to the latter, the advice of competent counsel should be obtained.

H. TRANSFER OF OWNERSHIP BY ENDORSEMENT

Probably the most convenient way to transfer ownership of a life insurance policy, if the owner wishes to transfer all his rights irrevocably, is to request a transfer of ownership by endorsement. Most present-day life insurance policies grant this privilege in a policy provision similar to the following:

> The owner may transfer ownership to a new owner and designate or change a contingent owner to succeed to the rights of the owner on his death, otherwise ownership will pass to the estate of the owner. A transfer of ownership is not an "assignment" and the owner is not an "assignee" within the meaning of those terms as used in this policy.
>
> A transfer of ownership, including a designation or change of a contingent owner, may be made only by written request accompanied by the policy for endorsement. The transfer will not take effect until endorsed on the policy by the Company, but when so endorsed, will be effective as of the date of the request for transfer, subject to any action taken by the Company before endorsement.

A provision of this kind permits the policyowner to change the ownership of his policy in much the same way he would change the beneficiary. He executes a request for transfer and sends it to the insurer along with his policy for endorsement; and the ownership is changed as of the date specified in the policy provision. Since this procedure is completed through the insurer itself, the latter makes no attempt to disclaim any responsibility for the validity or legal effect of the endorsement (as it does under the assignment provision of the policy).

SUMMARY

The Values of the Contract

The value of the life insurance contract to the owner (its cash value) makes it a kind of personal property that can be borrowed on, sold, given away, or inherited. The value to the beneficiary after the death of the owner, however, is the contract's principal value. It is important, therefore, when using the contract as property, that its basic value as insurance should be kept in mind, so that the rights of beneficiaries and assignees may be, at all times, clearly defined.

The Nature of Property

Property in the legal sense means rights of ownership. Rights that inhere in tangible things such as land, or objects permanently attached to it, are said to constitute real property. Rights that relate to movables such as furniture, automobiles, jewels, etc., are said to constitute tangible personal property. Rights that are evidenced by such instruments as stocks or bonds are referred to as intangible personal property.

Personal property consists of *choses* in possession and *choses* in action. The latter term refers to ownership rights that are evidenced by a contract, certificate, or similar document which has no value in or of itself. The life insurance contract is a *chose* in action.

The Transfer of a *Chose* in Action

Ownership rights represented by a *chose* in action are transferred from one person to another by means of an assignment. The person executing an assignment is the assignor; the person in whose favor it is executed is the assignee.

If an assignment transfers all the ownership rights evidenced by the *chose,* it is an absolute assignment. If it transfers only some of the rights, as collateral security for the repayment of an indebtedness, with the understanding that if the indebtedness is repaid as promised the rights so transferred will revert to the assignor, the assignment is said to be a collateral assignment.

An absolute assignment made for a consideration is a sale; if made without consideration, it is a gift.

Assignment of the Life Insurance Contract

After the death of the insured, the life insurance contract is simply a promise to pay a stated sum of money and is freely assignable. Even a policy provision prohibiting assignments is generally held inoperative to prevent this type of assignment.

An assignment made during the lifetime of the insured presents a possibility of conflict between the rights of the assignee and the beneficiary. This is sufficiently strong that policies providing only limited amounts of insurance, such as industrial policies, often prohibit or severely restrict any assignment.

Ordinarily, an assignment is in writing and, together with the stock certificate, bankbook, policy, or other evidence of the rights being transferred, is manually delivered to the assignee.

Notice to the insurer that a life insurance contract has been assigned is not necessary to the validity of the assignment, but in the absence of such notice the life insurer will have no liability if it pays to the named beneficiary, the owner, or to a later assignee.

As a general rule, a policyowner may assign a policy of insurance on his own life as freely as he wishes, either as a gift or as a sale. There is, however, a minority line of decisions holding that an assignment of this kind is invalid unless the assignee has an insurable interest. The prevailing view is that if the transaction is one in good faith, it is immaterial that the assignee has no insurable interest.

Life insurance contracts are most commonly assigned as security for indebtedness. In such cases, there may be a question concerning the assignee's right to repayment of the debt out of the proceeds payable at the death of the insured.

Although there are strong minority decisions to the contrary, the general rule is that a collateral assignee's right to the proceeds of the policy, to the extent of the indebtedness, is superior to the rights of a revocable beneficiary even though the latter did not consent to the assignment. The policy provision on assignments frequently spells out specifically that the assignee's rights supersede those of the named beneficiary.

Even if the assignment is absolute in form, the courts will treat it as a collateral assignment if it can be shown that it was executed as security for the repayment of a debt or debts.

The rights of successive assignees may present a conflict if the assignee whose assignment was executed earlier in point of time does not give notice until a later assignment or assignments are made and the later assignee gave notice first. The majority rule in the United States is that the assignee who has the earlier assignment has a prior right to repayment out of the policy proceeds even though he did not give notice before notice was given by a later assignee.

Assignments in Practice

It is important to remember that any transfer of ownership rights under a life insurance contract by an instrument outside the policy is, in legal effect, an assignment. Property settlements in connection with divorce decrees present one very common instance in which such rights may be transferred from the policyowner to another even though the transaction may not be labeled an assignment. Similarly, the transfer of all the assets of a business may include a life insurance policy or policies, in which case the general law of assignments may be held to apply.

Legal problems resulting from assignments usually take the form of a conflict between the rights of the assignee and those of the beneficiary of the contract. One practical way to resolve this problem is to provide in the policy itself what the legal effect of an assignment will be and how settlement will be made if an assignment is in effect at the time of the insured's death.

A second major factor in resolving assignment problems is the use of the American Bankers Association Form of Assignment, commonly referred to as the A.B.A. Form No. 10. This form clearly states which rights pass by the assignment and which do not.

Collateral assignments may be released by any clear statement to that effect.

ILLUSTRATIVE CASE

The following case has been selected as illustrative because it points up in a very practical way the legal nature of an assignment and the rights and obligations of the several parties concerned.

MASSACHUSETTS MUTUAL LIFE INSURANCE COMPANY v. PINELLAS CENTRAL BANK & TRUST COMPANY[17]

SEBRING, H. L., Associate Judge.

This appeal is from summary final judgment in favor of the plaintiff [the bank] upon the following undisputed facts.

Massachusetts Mutual Life Insurance Company issued a policy of life insurance to one Carl F. Falzoni, effective as of February 22, 1960, premiums thereon to be payable monthly in advance. After the policy was issued, Falzoni assigned and delivered it to Pinellas Central Bank and Trust Company as collateral security for a loan.

Two days after the loan was made, Massachusetts Mutual received from the bank a copy of the assignment of the policy and a letter of transmittal informing the insurer that the policy had been assigned as collateral security for a loan, and inquiring as to the cash surrender value of the policy, the amount of accumulated dividends, the amount of any outstanding loans against the policy, and the method of payment of the policy in the event of the death of the insured. On the same day the insurer received from Falzoni a written request for a change of premium payments from monthly to quarterly pay-

---

[17] 175 So. (2d) 245 (D.C.A. Fla., 1965).

ments and also a written request for a change of premium payments from quarterly to annual periods. Accompanying the requests was a quarterly premium payment which extended the policy coverage up to February 22, 1961 and an annual premium payment which extended the policy coverage from February 22, 1961 to February 22, 1962. These requests for changes in premium payment frequencies were made by Falzoni at the express direction of the bank, and the bank furnished the money with which to pay the premiums up to February 22, 1962.

The next annual premium on the policy became due and payable on February 22, 1962. When payment was not made on or before the due date, the insurer advised Falzoni that the premium was past due, and when this brought no payment from Falzoni during the 31-day grace period allowed by the policy, the insurer availed itself of the policy provisions providing for the automatic application of accumulated dividends and cash surrender value to past due premiums, and applied first the accumulated dividends, and then a portion of the cash surrender value, to the payment of the past due premium.

On November 2, 1962, the bank surrendered the policy of insurance to the insurer with the request that the cash surrender value be paid to it. In pursuance of this request, the insurer mailed the bank a check in the amount of $398.78, which represented the difference between the gross cash surrender value of the policy and the amount that had been applied from the cash surrender value to the payment of the past due premium. The bank refused to accept the check as full payment of the cash surrender value, contending that the insurer had no right to avail itself of the automatic premium loan provision of the policy after it had been notified by the bank of the assignment of the cash surrender value of the policy and when it knew that the gross cash surrender value was not sufficient to pay Falzoni's indebtedness to the bank. The insurer refused to pay the additional sum, and the bank thereupon instituted this action for the recovery of this amount. Upon hearing upon pleadings and affidavits the trial court granted a motion for summary final judgment in favor of the plaintiff for the amount claimed, with interest and attorneys' fees, and this present appeal was taken from the judgment.

(1) We know of no theory upon which the plaintiff could have lawfully recovered the gross cash surrender value of the policy, under the undisputed facts of the case.

(2) When Falzoni made the assignment of the policy to the bank, it acquired the policy "subject to all the terms and conditions of the policy and to all superior liens, if any, which the insurer may have against the policy."[18] As the result of this assignment the assignee was placed in the same status with respect to rights and liabilities under the policy that the insured occupied before the transfer. *Moon v. Williams*, 102 Fla. 214, 135 So. 555. After the assignment the bank held the policy as collateral for a loan—the exact amount of which is not shown by the record and which, so far as we can find, was never disclosed to the insurer—subject to all the conditions of the policy so

---

[18] It is basic in the general law of assignments that the assignee cannot, as the result of an assignment, obtain more extensive rights than the assignor had. Thus all the defenses that would have been valid against a claim on the part of the policyowner for the total cash value of the policy were good as against the bank.

far as they imposed duties and obligations upon Falzoni. Among these duties and obligations were that premiums were to be payable in advance before their due date; that a default in premium payment would occur upon non-payment of any premium on its due date; and that if any premium in default was not paid before the end of a grace period, fixed in the policy at 31 days after the due date of the defaulted premium, the policy would lapse and terminate as of the due date of the premium in default.

The bank also acquired the policy subject to a condition inserted therein at the requestion [*sic*] of Falzoni, that in the event any premium remained unpaid on the last day of the grace period, dividend accumulations on the policy would be automatically applied by the insurer to pay the premium in full, if the dividend accumulations were sufficient for this purpose, and, if they were not, and the insured had elected to come under an "Automatic Premium Loans" provision available only in policies on which premiums were payable annually, semi-annually or quarterly, that the insurer would automatically lend to the insured, at 5% per annum, an amount sufficient to pay the balance of the unpaid premium, provided the security under the policy for the repayment of the loan was then sufficient.

It is averred in the answer of the defendant, and stands undenied, that the bank knew that it was customary to include automatic premium loan provisions in life insurance policies. But, however that may be, it is clear that the bank had the policy in its hands on or before December 14, 1960, the day the policy was assigned, and hence had full opportunity to examine its provisions, including the provisions as to the due date and as to premium payments and the consequences that would ensue in the event the premiums were not paid in accordance with the terms of the policy. That the bank knew of the automatic premium loan provision in the policy seems evident, we think, by the fact that the moment the bank accepted the policy as security for a loan, it directed Falzoni to request a change in the premium payment plan so as to bring the policy within the Automatic Premium Loans provision, and advanced money to him with which to pay a quarterly plus an annual premium on the policy.

(3) After Falzoni thus made himself eligible to participate in the Automatic Premium Loans provision, we think it became the duty of the insurer to apply accumulated dividends and cash surrender values to the payment of past due premiums if the insured failed to pay them, and might well have rendered itself liable to the insured or his beneficiary if it had allowed the policy to lapse. [Citations]

(4) While it may be that the insurer never gave the bank notice that a premium payment was due on the policy, we think that this makes no difference, because there was nothing in the policy or in any arrangement between the parties requiring notice to be given. Under these circumstances, the insurer was under no duty to inform the assignee of the time when payment of premiums was required; if the bank desired this information it had the duty to make periodic inquiries of the insurer as to the dates premiums were due and the amounts thereof. [Citations]

It follows from our view of the case that the trial court committed reversible error when it entered the summary final judgment in favor of the

plaintiff. Accordingly, the judgment should be reversed and remanded with directions that an appropriate judgment be entered in accordance with law.[19]
It is so ordered.

QUESTIONS FOR REVIEW

1. List and briefly discuss two kinds of personal property. In which class does the life insurance contract fall?
2. Briefly define an assignment.
3. Differentiate between an absolute and a collateral assignment.
4. Under what circumstances does an absolute assignment constitute the making of a gift? When is it a sale?
5. List the formal requirements for a valid assignment. Is notice to the insurance company essential for the validity of the assignment? Is it essential for any other purpose?
6. Why do most policies state that the company assumes no responsibility for the validity or effect of an assignment?
7. State the majority rule concerning the relative rights of the beneficiary and a collateral assignee—
    a. When the beneficiary has joined in the assignment.
    b. When the beneficiary has not joined in making the assignment.
8. According to the prevailing assignment rules, what portion of the proceeds of a $10,000 life insurance policy would be recoverable by the assignee in each of the following cases:
    a. The assignment is absolute and made as a gift.
    b. The assignment is absolute and made for the purpose of securing the payment of a $6,000 debt to the assignee.
9. State the majority rule concerning the requirement of an insurable interest on the part of an assignee.
10. What is meant by the release of an assignment?

---

[19] The reviewing court is saying here that the trial court was wrong in holding that the bank was entitled to the total cash surrender value of the policy. The judgment was, therefore, reversed and judgment given for the insurer.

Chapter Outline

A. The Policyowner's Right to Change the Beneficiary
    12.1 The Policy Provision
    12.2 The Nature of the Right
    12.3 How the Right May Be Limited

B. The Beneficiary's Rights
    12.4 Beneficiaries Classified
    12.5 Revocable and Irrevocable Beneficiaries

C. Limitations of the Policyowner's Rights
    12.6 Incompetency
    12.7 The Right May Be Waived
    12.8 The Owner May Be Estopped
    12.9 The Effect of Divorce

D. How the Right Is Exercised
    12.10 The Endorsement Method
    12.11 The Filing Method
    12.12 Endorsement at Insurer's Option
    12.13 "Substantial Compliance"
    12.14 Change of Beneficiary by Will

Chapter 12

The Policyowner Changes the Beneficiary

NEXT TO his right to designate a beneficiary or beneficiaries, the policy-owner's right to change the designation if he wishes, and as often as he wishes, is one of the most significant rights he may acquire under the contract. The purpose of this chapter is to discuss the nature of this right, the procedures by which it is exercised, and some of the more common legal problems that may result from carelessness, mistakes, or complicated fact situations in connection with such changes.

A. THE POLICY OWNER'S RIGHT TO CHANGE THE BENEFICIARY

12.1 The Policy Provision

Most modern life insurance contracts provide that the owner of the policy may designate and change the beneficiary as often as he wishes. An illustrative policy provision reads as follows:

> BENEFICIARY. During the lifetime of the insured, the owner may designate and change the beneficiary as often as he may wish by filing with the company a written request in a form satisfactory to the company. No such change will be effective unless recorded by the company, but upon being so recorded, shall take effect as of the date the request was signed, provided that any interest created thereby shall be subject to any payment made or other action taken by the company before such recording.
>
> The interest of any beneficiary who dies before the insured shall vest in the owner unless otherwise provided.

This right to change the beneficiary depends upon the wording of the contract, and it is very generally held that the right does not exist unless it is specifically reserved at the time the contract is made. As a general rule, however, the right to change is specifically reserved, as indicated in this policy provision.

12.2 The Nature of the Right

From the legal point of view, the right to designate a beneficiary differs in a basic sense from the other ownership rights under the life insurance contract. For it is closely related to what has long been known as a "power of appointment" in the law of property.

A Power of Appointment. A power of appointment has been defined as:

> A power or authority conferred by one person by deed or will upon another (called the "donee") to appoint, that is, to select and nominate, the person or persons who are to receive and enjoy an estate or an income therefrom or from a fund, after the testator's death, or the donee's death, or after the termination of an existing right or interest.[1]

In general terms, a power of appointment relates to the future disposition of property. More specifically, it is a right conferred on a person who is not an owner, allowing him to say who will be the future owner of certain specified property. Mr. Smith, for example, may leave his farm to his wife for her lifetime, but not wish to say which of his children are to inherit it at her death. He may, therefore, give her the right to say who will receive the farm at her death. In this situation, she is said to have a power of appointment with respect to that particular property. That is, she has the right to say, by will or by deed, who will take title to the farm at her death, although she does not own the property or have the right to sell it. A power of appointment, therefore, may be defined as a power given to a person who is not the owner of certain designated property to name (or appoint) the person or persons who will be owner or owners on and after a date in the future that is specified by the person who grants the power.

This may seem a little technical, but its application to the life insurance contract is clear. The owner of a life insurance policy has many ownership rights under the contract; but he does not, in any sense, "own" the death benefit. So far as that benefit is concerned, he has only a power of appointment, just as did Mrs. Smith with respect to the farm. It is this fine distinction that makes the conflict between the rights of an assignee and a beneficiary under the life insurance contract so technical.

---

[1] *Black's Law Dictionary* (4th ed.; St. Paul: West Publishing Co., 1951), p. 1334.

12.3 How the Right May Be Limited

Even though the owner has reserved the right to change the beneficiary, his right to change the beneficiary at any given time is not automatically guaranteed. For instance, he may become incompetent as a matter of law to make a beneficiary change. He may, by his own acts, have waived the right, or he may have acted in such a manner that he will be estopped to make another change; and the right to change the beneficiary may also be limited in other ways, as by a divorce decree.

B. THE BENEFICIARY'S RIGHTS

12.4 Beneficiaries Classified

Contracts made between two or more persons for the purpose of benefiting a third are not confined to life insurance, although the life insurance contract is an outstanding example. In any situation of this kind, the person to be benefited is called a beneficiary. In contract law generally, these persons are further classified as creditor beneficiaries, donee beneficiaries, and incidental beneficiaries.

The *creditor* beneficiary is one to whom some debt or other legal obligation is due from one of the parties to the contract, where the debt or obligation is to be extinguished by the performance of the contract. If the contract is made for the benefit of a third person but without consideration—i.e., as a gift—the beneficiary is called a *donee* beneficiary. An *incidental* beneficiary is one who will benefit indirectly from the performance of the contract, but whose benefit was not the primary reason for making the contract.

12.5 Revocable and Irrevocable Beneficiaries

As a general rule, the beneficiary of a life insurance contract today is a donee beneficiary. The right to change the designation is also usually reserved; and the designation is, therefore, revocable. In most jurisdictions, a revocable beneficiary is considered to have a mere expectancy (because the policyowner can terminate the beneficiary's right at will, simply by changing the designation). Thus, the revocable beneficiary has no legally enforceable right to the proceeds of the policy until after the death of the insured. This is not true of an irrevocable beneficiary; but under present-day policy wording, the rights even of an irrevocable beneficiary are contingent upon his surviving the insured. Therefore, even if the policyowner has designated a beneficiary irrevocably, he may outlive the person so designated. In that event, he will again have the right to designate and change the beneficiaries under his policy.

C. LIMITATIONS OF THE POLICYOWNER'S RIGHTS

12.6 Incompetency

One basic possible limitation of the power of a policyowner to make a valid change of beneficiary concerns his legal capacity. The owner may be a minor, for instance, in which case his competency to make a valid beneficiary change will often be dependent upon the special statutory provisions previously referred to concerning the rights of minors. He may be incompetent because of advanced age or mental illness, in which case the legal question concerning his capacity to make a valid beneficiary change may be considerably more difficult to resolve.

The Minor Policyowner. At common law, the capacity of a minor to exercise contractual rights and be bound by his decisions is, as previously noted, decidedly limited. This obviously affects his right to change a beneficiary designation under a life insurance contract, but exactly how and to what extent has never been very clearly expressed by the courts.

Statutory Modifications. Considerably more than half the states have statutes modifying to some degree the minor's incapacity with respect to life insurance contracts. Sometimes these statutes grant a considerable amount of freedom from the usual contractual restrictions, but almost without exception, these statutes limit the persons whom the minor may designate as beneficiaries.

The New York statute is illustrative. It permits a minor aged 15 or over to enter into an insurance contract on his own life or the life of anyone in whom he has an insurable interest—

> . . . for the benefit of such minor or for the benefit of the father, mother, husband, wife, brother or sister, child or children, or any grandparent of such minor, and to exercise and enjoy every right, privilege and benefit which the minor has or to which he may become entitled under any life insurance contract on the life of such minor or person in whom the minor has an insurable interest whether or not such contract was applied for by such minor, *subject to the foregoing limitation as to designation of beneficiary.*[2] [Emphasis added.]

Under this statute, the minor has the right to change the beneficiary under the described contracts, but only to another of the persons named in the statute.

Mental Incompetency. A mentally ill or otherwise mentally incompetent policyowner does not have the power to make an effective change of beneficiary. The test of competency in this respect is very much the same as the test of capacity to make a will or execute a deed. It has been summarized by one court as follows:

---

[2] New York Insurance Law, Sec. 145.

The test to be applied in determining the mental competency of deceased at the time the change in beneficiary was attempted is: Did he have sufficient mental capacity to understand the extent of his property and how he wanted to dispose of it, and who were dependent upon him.[3]

The mental capacity of the policyowner to make such a change would, of course, ordinarily be questioned, if at all, by the person standing to lose because of the purported change—that is, the beneficiary previously designated. The burden then would be on that person to prove that the policyowner did not have the capacity to make a valid change at the time he attempted to do so.

Guardians. The general rule is that the guardian of an incompetent or minor policyowner cannot make a valid change of beneficiary on behalf of his ward. Occasional cases have held that this can be accomplished if it is supported by an appropriate court order. Generally, however, the exercise of the power to change a beneficiary falls in the same legal category as executing a will; neither can be done by the guardian for his ward. Both his will and a change of beneficiary must be executed by the ward himself or not at all.

The Position of the Insurer. As a general rule, the insurance company that pays the proceeds of a policy to a beneficiary designated by an incompetent policyowner will be protected from having to pay again if the incapacity of the policyowner was unknown to the company. The same rule applies where payment is made to an assignee of record, if the insurer did not know that the assignment was made at a time when the policyowner was incompetent. In either instance, it is generally held that, in the absence of any facts that would suggest incompetency, the insurer is not required to inquire into the competence of the policyowner to make a change of beneficiary or an assignment. So long as the insurer acts in good faith, it is under no duty to investigate. The rule is quoted in one leading case[4] as follows:

> The law of the case is not difficult. As I ruled at the trial, if the insured was insane when a change of beneficiary was made by him, and the insurer without notice of such insanity, acted in good faith upon the paper as genuine, indorsed the policy accordingly, and on his death, still in ignorance of his insanity, paid the money in good faith to the beneficiary as changed, the company would have been protected.

12.7 The Right May Be Waived

Even though the right to change the beneficiary is reserved so far as the policy is concerned, it may nevertheless be waived. For instance, in

---

[3] *Harris* v. *Copeland*, 59 N.W. (2d) 70 (Mich., 1953).
[4] *The New York Life Insurance Co.* v. *Federal National Bank*, 162 A.L.R. 536, 151 F. (2d) 537 (U.S.C.C.A. 10th Cir., 1945).

one case in 1955,[5] the insured had made a property settlement with his first wife prior to their divorce in which he had agreed to maintain insurance in the amount of $10,000 in force on his life, naming her as beneficiary. A trust was established for her support, and the insurance policies were delivered to the trustee. Later these policies became worthless and others were substituted. Later still, the insured notified the trustee that he was designating his present wife as beneficiary under the policies instead of the former wife. The court held that by reason of the property settlement the insured had waived his right to change the beneficiary, saying:

> . . . As against his wife and trustee he waived his right to change the beneficiary in these two policies outstanding at the time of his death which together amount to less than $10,000. Indeed it appears that Moore had designated his first wife as the beneficiary in these two policies in 1947. He informed her in December, 1950, that she was the beneficiary in the two policies now in question. We think the inference is plain that Moore recognized his obligation to maintain insurance for her benefit and that all parties understood that the policies in question were substituted for the certificate of the group insurance which had become worthless. We think the plaintiff acting as trustee for her mother acquired an equitable interest in the policies by virtue of the contract with her father and her right to enforce the contract and to collect the proceeds of these policies was superior to that of the defendant second wife.

12.8 The Owner May Be Estopped

The policyowner may sometimes be estopped to make a later change of beneficiary. For instance, if he has designated a person as beneficiary for the purpose of securing an existing debt, he will not be permitted to change the beneficiary until the debt has been paid. Similarly, if he has delivered the policy to the named beneficiary with the intention of making a gift, a later beneficiary change may not be permitted. In one case, such a delivery, with words of gift intent, was held to be an equitable assignment, and a subsequent attempted endorsement of a change of beneficiary was held ineffective.

12.9 The Effect of Divorce

In the absence of a special statute, the divorce of the policyowner and the beneficiary does not, in and of itself, affect the policyowner's right to change the beneficiary designation. However, applicable statutes are in effect in a few states. Under a Michigan statute, for example, a wife's interest as beneficiary is automatically terminated by a divorce

---

[5] *Handrahan, Trustee etc.* v. *Moore, etc.*, 124 N.E. (2d) 808 (Mass., 1955).

decree unless the decree itself provides differently. Under a Kentucky statute, the wife's rights are automatically terminated by divorce, even though she was designated irrevocably; and both Missouri and Minnesota have statutes permitting the insured husband to change the beneficiary designation after divorce even if the designation was, by its terms, irrevocable. In other words, the statutes differ from state to state; but whenever the rights of a beneficiary are terminated, the policyowner's right to change the beneficiary is, in effect, restored. Thus, in Missouri and Minnesota, the rights he relinquished when he designated his wife as irrevocable beneficiary are restored when he is divorced from her. Even where no special statute is in effect, however, if there has been a property settlement, the policy rights of either or both of the parties to a divorce proceeding may be very much affected.

Clearly, the exact legal effect of any property settlement depends upon the terms of the settlement in question. However, some of the possible effects of a property settlement made in connection with the divorce of the policyowner and the named beneficiary are vividly illustrated in the case of *Mutual Life Insurance Company of New York* v. *Franck.*[6] This case concerned the disposition of two 15-year endowment life insurance policies of $5,000 each. The policies were issued in 1919 with the wife of the insured, Coral, named as beneficiary of each.

In 1921, the insured and the beneficiary executed a property settlement in which the insured promised to name his wife the sole irrevocable beneficiary of the policies, and the policies were delivered to her. The insured and the beneficiary were subsequently divorced. The divorce decree repeated the requirement that the wife be named sole irrevocable beneficiary and required that the insured continue to pay the premiums on the policies.

In 1923, the insured purportedly made his executors, administrators, and assigns the beneficiaries of both policies. Later that same year he borrowed from Beulah Franck (then Beulah Wheeler) the money to pay the premiums then due; and in 1924, he and Beulah were married. No more premiums were paid, but the insured again, as the court said, "purported to change" the beneficiary, this time to his present wife. He also obtained the policies and gave them to her.

In 1931, when the insured died, both the first and second wives claimed the proceeds of the policies. The insurer paid the proceeds into court, asking the court to decide who was rightfully entitled to the money. The second wife was awarded the amount of the premium which she had loaned the insured, but the court held that the first wife had an equitable interest as beneficiary that could not be terminated without her consent. The pertinent part of the decision reads as follows:

---

[6] 50 Pac. Rep. (2d) 480 (D.C.A. 3d Dist., Cal., 1935).

. . . It has been determined that while a named beneficiary of a policy which provides for a change thereof by the insured, secures only a contingent interest therein, a subsequent agreement of the insured in consideration of a settlement of property rights in contemplation of a divorce by the terms of which he covenants to make her sole, irrevocable beneficiary of the policy, vests her with an equitable interest therein which may not be defeated without her consent.

The court then cited a previous case[7] that had presented a similar set of facts, and it quoted from that case the following discussion of the effect of the property settlement agreement:

. . . When Dexter Shoudy, in anticipation of the divorce between himself and his wife, offered as one of the terms of settlement of their property rights "to keep in effect for her as long as she remained single" said policies, and when this offer was accepted by her, the quality of her interest as a beneficiary in said policies became changed from that of a mere expectancy to a more fixed and permanent relation. She had thenceforth an equitable interest in said policies of which she could not be divested by the mere act of the insured in changing the name of the beneficiary.

D. HOW THE RIGHT IS EXERCISED

The general rule with respect to changing the beneficiary under a life insurance contract is simple. The owner changes the beneficiary only by following the procedure set out in the policy. It is well settled that the insurer may prescribe or regulate the procedure by which the policyowner may change the beneficiary. In fact, this procedure for changing the beneficiary is one of the conditions in the contract of insurance. Ordinarily, then, the policyowner must satisfy the condition before the designation is effectively changed.

12.10 The Endorsement Method

Most present-day policies require that a written request for a beneficiary change be submitted to the home or other administrative office of the company. Additional requirements differ, but for a long time, one relatively standard requirement was that the policy be submitted for endorsement. Illustrative of this type of requirement is the following provision:

The owner may change the beneficiary at any time while the insured is living, by submission to the Home Office of a written request satisfactory to the company, but such change shall become effective only when the

---

[7] *Shoudy* v. *Shoudy*, 55 Cal. App. 344, 352, 203 P. 433.

policy has been received at the Home Office and the change of beneficiary endorsed hereon by the company. After such endorsement has been made, the change shall take effect and any interest of any previous beneficiary shall cease as of the date of such written request whether or not the Insured is living at the time of such endorsement but without prejudice to the Company on account of any payment made by it prior to such endorsement.

This procedure is commonly referred to as the endorsement method. Note that the policy had to be sent to the insurer and that the new beneficiary designation had to be endorsed (typed) on the policy before the change became effective.

12.11 The Filing Method

Of recent years, a growing number of insurers have been requiring only that the written request for change of beneficiary be filed with the company. Illustrative of this type of wording is the policy provision which appears in Sec. 12.1.

This is commonly referred to as the filing or recording method of changing the beneficiary. Under it, the insurer does not endorse the new beneficiary designation on the policy and, therefore, the policy does not have to be submitted to the insurer. The company retains a copy of the new designation in its files and returns one copy to the policyowner to be kept with the policy.

12.12 Endorsement at Insurer's Option

A third method, used by some companies, effects a kind of compromise between the other two methods by providing that a beneficiary change may be made by filing a written request, but reserving the right to require the policy for endorsement of the change if the company deems it necessary or advisable. Usually this would not be done unless the requested designation suggested a possible problem that could only be resolved by a review of the policy.

A recent tabulation of beneficiary change provisions in the policies of 110 leading life insurance companies disclosed that 24 followed the endorsement method, 65 permitted a change by filing or recording the request for change with the company, and the others followed the filing method but reserved the right to require that the policy be submitted if requested by the company.

12.13 "Substantial Compliance"

It is generally held that the method and procedure set forth in the policy for making beneficiary changes is an exclusive method. Therefore, it is usually held that the policyowner cannot change the beneficiary by the use of any other method. However, there is an equally well-established exception known as the "substantial compliance" rule.

Under the substantial compliance rule, if the policyowner has done everything in his power to comply with the procedure set out in the policy but has failed because of circumstances beyond his control, the change of beneficiary will ordinarily be held to be effective. In other words, substantial compliance with the procedural requirements set forth in the policy will be effective to change the beneficiary in situations where it would be inequitable to hold otherwise.

As might be suspected, the number of cases in this area is tremendous, and a conflict of authority exists. In fact, it has been said that the individual facts of these cases weigh perhaps more heavily than in any other area of the law of the life insurance contract. Nevertheless, the majority of jurisdictions follow this principle of substantial compliance.

Substantial compliance holdings rest on a common equitable principle that equity regards as done that which ought to be done. The rule is often applied in cases where the beneficiary and the insured have been divorced and the beneficiary deliberately withholds the policy in order to prevent the insured from having it endorsed. In such cases, if the insured has executed a request for the change, has sent it to the company, and has otherwise done everything in his power to comply with the policy requirements, the fact that he cannot send the policy to the insurer for endorsement will not ordinarily prevent the change from being effective. This rule was applied in one case[8] as follows:

> The insured's intent that the proceeds of the policy in suit should be payable to his sister, and should not be payable to his wife, was clear. In attempting to effect a change of beneficiary in substantial compliance with the terms of the policy, the insured did all that it was practicable for him to do, in view of the fact that he did not have the policy, that his wife had it, and was holding it in order to prevent a change of beneficiary. It is a reasonable inference that a demand upon her for the policy would have been futile, and we do not believe that the insured was required to sue her for its possession. We think that the right of the appellee (the sister) to the proceeds of the policy, under the facts as found by the District Court, was, in equity, superior to the claim of the appellant [the wife]. The appellant was in no position to take advantage of the failure of the insured and the insurer to bring about an indorsement upon the policy of the change of beneficiary. The requirement that the policy be delivered to the Company for indorsement was not for the protection of the appellant, but was for the protection of the Company. *Royal Union Mutual Life Insurance Co. v. Lloyd*, 8 Cir., 254 F. 407, 410. The Company, by bringing the action in interpleader, has waived any

---

[8] *Doering v. Buechler*, 146 F. (2d) 784 (C.C.A. Minn., 1945).

defense it may have had to the claim of either party. *Carter* v. *Thornton,* 8 Cir., 93 F. 2d 529, 532.

In addition to illustrating the application of the doctrine of substantial compliance, this case also illustrates another rather generally accepted principle—that by bringing the action in interpleader, the company waived any defenses it might have had to the claim of either party. The requirement of endorsement was included in the policy for the protection of the insurer. By bringing the action of interpleader, the insurer waived this requirement; and the fact that the policy was not endorsed as required had no bearing on the court's consideration of the case. This approach—that endorsement is not strictly required—is sometimes supported on the basis that endorsement is merely a ministerial act—that is, an act that does not require the exercise of discretion—and the insurer cannot refuse to perform it.

Degree of Compliance. In applying the substantial compliance rule, it is, of course, always necessary that some appreciable degree of compliance be shown. It is generally agreed that a mere statement of intention on the part of the policyowner is not enough. Nor is it enough that he requested forms or even completed a written request if the request was not then delivered or mailed to the insurer.

If the policyowner has performed all the acts necessary to effect a change of beneficiary except to deliver the policy for endorsement, the reason or reasons for not delivering the policy may govern. Thus if the beneficiary has wrongfully withheld it, compliance with all other requirements will usually be held to satisfy the substantial compliance rule. However, if the policyowner has simply neglected to submit the policy for endorsement, the change of beneficiary will not ordinarily be effective. In other words, he must comply with the policy requirements unless he is prevented from doing so by circumstances beyond his control.

12.14 Change of Beneficiary by Will

Cases concerning attempts to change the beneficiary of a life insurance policy by will must be divided into two large groups. One group includes policies which do not provide any specific method for making beneficiary changes. When this is true—and it was true of some of the earlier policies—the general rule is that a new beneficiary may be designated by will.

If a definite procedure for making beneficiary changes is specified in the policy—and this, of course, is usually the case today—the general rule, as previously noted, is that that procedure must be followed in making the change or it will not be effective. The majority rule, therefore, is that if the policyowner attempts to change the beneficiary by will, the change will not be effective if the policy spells out a specific procedure for changing the beneficiary. This holding is often explained on the basis that, since the will is effective only at the death of the insured and since the rights of the beneficiary vest at that time, the designation is no longer subject to change after the death of the insured. This view is taken in the case of *Cook* v. *Cook*[9] decided by the California Supreme Court in 1941. There the court said:

> . . . Of course, there are instances in which an insured may transfer his policy by will. Where the policy has no named beneficiary but is payable to the estate of the insured, the policy may be disposed of by will or pass by intestate succession if the insured dies intestate (14 Cal. Jur. 585; *In re Mattley's Estate*, 110 Cal. App. 439).[10] . . . There may be other instances, but the rule cannot have any application to the facts in the instant case. A will does not become operative until death; prior to death it is revocable at the whim of the testator, and the objects of the testator's bounty have no vested rights. In that respect it is very similar to the rights of a beneficiary under a life insurance policy in which the insured reserves the right to change the beneficiary such as we have in the instant case. However, upon death the beneficiary's right becomes vested, and that being the case, no expression in the insured's will purporting to assign his life insurance policy or change the beneficiary can be effective. At death he no longer has a policy to assign. It has passed to his heirs, if no beneficiary was designated; if a beneficiary is named it passes to such beneficiary. He cannot then change the beneficiary because the right of the named beneficiary has vested.

Nevertheless, there are some cases upholding the effectiveness of a beneficiary change by will even where a specific procedure is set forth in the policy. One group of cases, for instance, holds that even when a procedure is specified, if it is not stated to be exclusive, an effective change may be made by will. This approach is sometimes supported on the theory that the insured did everything in his power to effect the change. In other words, the substantial compliance approach has been taken. In other cases, this result is reached on the basis that the procedural requirement is for the benefit of the insurer and can be (and in the instant case has been) waived. The majority view, however, is that an attempted change of beneficiary by will is not effective.

SUMMARY

The Right to Change

Most life insurance contracts today provide that the policyowner may designate and change the beneficiary as often as he wishes. This right,

---

[9] 17 Cal. (2d) 639, 111 P. (2d) 322 (Cal., 1941).

[10] This, of course, is always true and has nothing to do with the question of beneficiary changes.

however, differs from other ownership rights under the policy since it is, in effect, the power to say who may receive a fund which the policyowner himself does not own. It thus resembles a power of appointment more closely than a true ownership right. A power of appointment is the power to designate a person or persons who will own property to which the person exercising the power is not himself entitled.

In general contract law, beneficiaries of contracts made by two other parties are classified as creditor beneficiaries, donee beneficiaries, or incidental beneficiaries. A creditor beneficiary is one to whom a debt or some other obligation is due from one of the parties to the contract, a donee beneficiary is a beneficiary who has given no consideration for his or her designation, and an incidental beneficiary is one who will benefit only indirectly from the performance of the contract.

Limitations of the Policyowner's Right

The Incompetent Owner.   In the absence of a special statute, if the policyowner is a minor, his capacity to change a beneficiary designation is decidedly limited. Statutes are effective in a number of states, however, giving minors of a specified age and upward the right to own and exercise the rights under contracts of life insurance under specified conditions. Ordinarily such contracts must be payable to the minor or his estate or to certain designated members of his family. His right to change the beneficiary would ordinarily be limited to changes to others of the named group of persons.

An insane or mentally incompetent policyowner does not ordinarily have the capacity to make an effective change of beneficiary, and a guardian of an incompetent or minor policyowner cannot usually make an effective change for his ward.

As a general rule, an insurer will be protected if it pays money to a beneficiary who has been designated by an incompetent owner if the incompetency was not known by the insurer. That is, the company is not required to inquire into the competency of a policyowner who requests a change, unless it has knowledge of facts that would put it on notice.

Other Limitations.   A policyowner may waive the right to make a later change of beneficiary, as, for instance, by agreeing in a property settlement to keep a life insurance contract in force for the named beneficiary or by naming the beneficiary irrevocably. He may also be estopped from making a later change if he takes such actions that he creates an equitable estoppel. Property settlements in connection with divorce decrees constitute one frequently occurring source of waiver or estoppel in this area.

Exercise of the Right

Endorsement or Filing Methods. Policy provisions setting forth the procedures for changing the beneficiary may require the policyowner to send in a written request and submit the policy for endorsement. This is termed the endorsement method. If a written request is required only to be filed with or recorded by the insurer, the company is said to follow the filing or recording method. Most present-day insurers follow the filing method, but some also reserve the right to require the policy for endorsement at their discretion.

Substantial Compliance. As a general rule, if the policy specifies a procedure for changing the beneficiary, that procedure must be followed or the change will not be effective. However, if the policyowner has done everything in his power to comply with this procedure and has been prevented from fully complying by factors beyond his control, his attempted change may be held to be effective on the grounds that he has substantially complied with the requirements set forth in the policy.

Beneficiary Changes by Will. If the contract specifically recognizes a change of beneficiary by will or if it does not set forth any procedure for changing the beneficiary, a beneficiary change by will is generally held to be effective. If a special procedure is required by policy provision, as is generally the case today, that procedure must be followed in order to make an effective beneficiary change.

ILLUSTRATIVE CASE

The following case is included here only to illustrate the many ways a relatively simple question can be presented in the area of beneficiary designations.

CORDER v. PRUDENTIAL INSURANCE COMPANY[11]

MATTHEW J. JASEN, Justice.

This is a motion by plaintiff for summary judgment.[12]

An insurance policy was issued to deceased Anna M. Corder in the amount of $5,000.00 on April 27th, 1960. The beneficiaries listed in said policy were Wesley D. Corder, husband of the insured, if living, otherwise Willa Eakman, mother of the insured. On April 15th, 1963 the named insured died. Subsequently, the plaintiff brought action to collect said proceeds from the insurance company who in turn interpleaded Willa Eakman as Administratrix of the Estate of Anna M. Corder. The administratrix answered the complaint herein and interposed a counterclaim that the proceeds of the insurance policy

---

[11] 248 N.Y.S. (2d) 265 (1964).

[12] An immediate judgment granted by the court without further proceedings, generally on the basis of the documents filed with the court and without the oral testimony of witnesses.

in question be paid to her. . . . This court on December 30th, 1963 permitted the insurance company to deposit the proceeds of said policy with the Treasurer of the County of Erie, to be disposed of in accordance with the direction of this court.[13]

It is the contention of the plaintiff that he is the named beneficiary and therefore entitled to the proceeds.

The mother-administratrix in opposing this motion proceeds upon two theories. First, by reason of fraud of the plaintiff the proceeds of the policy belong to the estate of the insured, and secondly, that plaintiff was not the husband of the insured and that therefore the insurance contract is void by virtue of the deceased's breach of warranty in representing him as her husband.

As to the contention of fraud, the administratrix fails to set forth any evidentiary facts sufficient to raise a question of fact.

The remaining argument of the administratrix is that inasmuch as the plaintiff was not the husband of the insured he has no insurable interest and therefore no valid right to the benefits under the policy.

It is conceded that the Wesley D. Corder, who brings this action is the Wesley D. Corder named as beneficiary by the deceased in the insurance policy, and that he is the particular person intended by the insured to be the beneficiary of said proceeds.

(1) Where the deceased effects the insurance upon her own life, it is well-established law that she can designate any beneficiary she desires without regard to relationship or consanguinity.

Section 146 of the Insurance Law provides in part that:

1. Any person of lawful age may on his own initiative procure or effect a contract of insurance upon his own person for the benefit of *any person*. . . . [Emphasis supplied.]

* * * * *

(2) Since the undisputed proof shows that the application for the policy was made by the insured deceased, there is no issue of insurable interest on the part of the plaintiff.

The use of the term "husband" in this connection, was merely descriptive of the relationship which the assured claimed existed between her and the beneficiary. Even though the named beneficiary was not actually the insured's husband, it does not alter the basic fact that the plaintiff is the person to whom the deceased had intended that the proceeds of the policy be paid. . . .

For the reasons stated, motion for summary judgment granted.

QUESTIONS FOR REVIEW

1. What is meant by "power of appointment"? How does this describe the right to designate a beneficiary under a life insurance contract?

---

[13] This means that the named beneficiary sued to collect the proceeds and the insurer filed an interpleader action, asking the court to decide between the named beneficiary and the administratrix of the insured's estate. The administratrix interposed a counteraction and the court permitted the insurer to pay the proceeds into court and have the court decide who was entitled to payment.

2. List three situations in which the rights of an owner to change a beneficiary may be limited.

3. What is the general rule concerning an insurer's liability if it pays the proceeds of a life insurance contract to a beneficiary who was designated by a mentally incompetent owner?

4. Briefly outline circumstances under which the right to change the beneficiary under one's life insurance contract may be waived. Briefly describe how an equitable estoppel may operate against a policyowner with respect to a change of beneficiary.

5. Distinguish between the endorsement and the filing methods of beneficiary changes.

6. Briefly summarize the rule of substantial compliance with respect to beneficiary changes.

7. Why are most attempts to change a beneficiary by will held to be inffective?

Chapter Outline

Chapter 13

The Policyowner "Borrows" on His Policy

THE OWNER of a life insurance contract with loan values has two strings to his bow, so to speak, if he needs money on a temporary basis. On the one hand, he may use his policy as collateral security and borrow money from a bank or other lending institution. Alternatively, under the policy loan provision, he may receive directly from the insurer an advance not to exceed the cash surrender value (less interest to the next premium payment date).

In effecting a policy loan, however, the owner is taking advantage of a privilege which differs in a very basic, legal way from his right to use the contract as security for a bank loan. The purpose of this chapter is to discuss the legal nature of a policy loan, show how it differs from a bank loan, and note some of the more important legal problems that may be encountered in connection with such loans.

A. THE "LOAN" PROVISIONS

13.1 Historical Development

Like the nonforfeiture benefits, policy loans were first made available by insurers on a voluntary basis. The automatic premium loan, or a practice similar to it, was in use as early as 1845[1] and was well established by the 1890s. Thus, the earliest policy loans were established for

---

[1] See Krueger and Waggoner, *The Life Insurance Policy Contract* (Boston: Little, Brown & Co., 1953), p. 189.

the purpose of keeping the policy in force, a practice that is understandable both from the policyowners' and the insurers' points of view. Later, the loan privilege was expanded to permit borrowing for any purpose the policyowner might have in mind. This latter type of loan is often referred to as a request loan, or cash loan, to distinguish it from the premium loan.

The Request Loan. Today a policy provision permitting a policy loan under cash value policies is required in every state in which the Uniform Standard Provisions Law has been enacted. Since this includes the states in which most of the major life insurers are domiciled, a policy loan provision of this type is probably included in most policies, other than term insurance policies, that are issued today.

The Automatic Premium Loan. The automatic premium loan provision, on the other hand, is a required provision only in Rhode Island, and even there it is not imperative if specified nonforfeiture provisions are included. The automatic premium loan provision is a valuable right, however, and for that reason, most life insurers include it in their policies on a purely voluntary basis.

13.2 An Illustrative Policy Provision

An illustrative policy loan provision was quoted in part in Chapter 6, but the complete provision is considerably more extensive than that excerpt would indicate. Typically, this policy provision reads as follows:

Loan Provisions.

(1) *Policy Loan.* At any time while this policy is in force, other than as extended term insurance, the company, upon satisfactory assignment of this policy will advance to the owner on the sole security of this policy any amount which shall be within the limit of the then maximum loan value, if any, less any existing indebtedness to the company secured by this policy. The policy need not be presented for endorsement unless required by the company.

The company reserves the right to defer the granting of any loan, other than to pay premiums on policies in this company, for a period not exceeding six months from the date the request for such loan was received.

(2) *Automatic Premium Loan.* If this provision is elected in the application or otherwise in writing before the end of the grace period, a loan shall be automatically granted on this policy to pay a premium in default. The owner may revoke such election as to its subsequent application by giving written notice to the company.

No such loan will be granted if the loan value, less any existing indebtedness, is not sufficient to pay the premium then due under this policy.

(3) *Loan Value.* The maximum loan value shall be that amount which, with interest at the rate of five per cent per annum to the date on which

the next premium is due or, if no further premiums are payable, to the next anniversary of the Policy Date, equals the cash value as of such date.

(4) *Loan Interest.* Interest on loans shall accrue from day to day at the rate of five per cent per annum and shall constitute an indebtedness to the company against this policy as and when it accrues. Interest shall be payable on each anniversary of the Policy Date subsequent to the date of loan until the loan is repaid. Any interest unpaid when due shall be added to and form a part of the loan and bear interest at the same rate. If at any time the total indebtedness to the company on this policy, including accrued interest, exceeds the then maximum loan value, the accrued interest shall become due and this policy shall be void thirty-one days after the company has mailed notice to the last known address of the owner and the assignee of record, if any.

(5) *Loan Repayment.* All or any part of a loan may be repaid, with accrued interest on the amount so repaid, at any time while this policy is in force other than as extended term insurance. Any existing indebtedness to the company secured by this policy shall be deducted from the sum payable at the time of any settlement.

13.3 An Advance, Not a Loan

The promise expressed in this policy loan provision has special significance in indicating the legal nature of the transaction. Note that it states that ". . . the company . . . will advance . . . any amount which shall be within the limit of the then maximum loan value. . . ." It does not say that the company will "loan" this amount.

This is clearly in accord with court decisions on the subject, one of the most important of which was a decision of Justice Oliver Wendell Holmes, as follows:

> The so-called liability of the policyholder never exists as a personal liability, it never is a debt, but is merely a deduction in account from the sum that the plaintiffs (insurance company) ultimately must pay.[2]

Regardless of the policy language used, therefore, the policy "loan" is in reality an advance rather than a loan.

No Promise to Repay. Perhaps the most significant indication that a policy loan is not a loan in the legal sense of the word is the fact that the policyowner does not promise to repay it. Note again the language of the policy provision: "All or any part of the loan may be repaid. . . ." The provision does not say that it must be repaid.

Furthermore, there are situations under which, as a general rule, such a loan may not be repaid. For instance, the policy must be in force, other

---

[2] *Board of Assessors* v. *New York Life Insurance Co.,* 216 U.S. 517, 30 S. Ct. 385, 54 L. Ed. 597 (1910).

than as extended term insurance. As a general rule also, a policy loan cannot be repaid after the death of the insured, but must be deducted from the death benefit. (A number of companies, however, permit such repayment after the death of the insured in order that the total proceeds may be placed under an option or otherwise distributed in accordance with the settlement arrangement planned by the policyowner.)

These requirements and practices are all consistent with the view that a policy loan is not an indebtedness in the legal sense of the word, and therefore not a charge against the estate of the owner-insured at his death.

Understandably, the loan can be made "on the sole security" of the policy because the company has in its possession at all times an amount equal to or in excess of the amount of the loan. Thus the loan is 100 percent secured by the cash value of the contract.

No Promise to Pay Interest. Interest is provided for, but here again the provision does not contemplate a personal liability on the part of the policyowner. Interest is payable, but it does not have to be paid. If at any time the total loan and accrued interest exceeds the then maximum loan value, the accrued interest becomes due, but it still does not have to be paid by the policyowner. The policy simply terminates 31 days after notice has been mailed to the owner and the assignee of record, if any; and the insurer uses the cash value to pay off the "loan."

13.4 Not Borrowing "Own Money"

The statement is sometimes erroneously made that the policyowner is really only borrowing his own money when he establishes a policy loan. Whether viewed from a strictly insurance or the legal point of view, this is not true. The policyowner does not have an accumulating fund in his own name. The funds of the company are held and invested for the benefit of all policyowners, and individual policyowners have specified shares only if they wish to surrender their policies. If a policy is kept in force until the death of the insured, the amount of insurance will be paid to the beneficiary, regardless of how much or how little the cash surrender value may have been immediately before the date of death. Deductions provided by the policy—such as a premium due but unpaid, or a policy loan—will be taken into account in making settlement, but the insurer does not operate like a savings bank in any sense of the term.

13.5 The Interest Charge

The fact that interest is charged on these advances does not make them loans in the legal sense, although courts have held that insurers are subject to the same laws with respect to interest rates that lenders are.

Thus, if there is no statute permitting otherwise, it has been held that simple interest only may be charged. The Standard Policy Provisions Law permits compound interest, and most policies accordingly provide that if the interest is unpaid, it will be added to and become a part of the principal of the loan.

Although interest is charged for several reasons, the most important is the fact that policy values are based on the assumption that portions of the premium unused in the early years will be invested at the assumed rate of interest. If any part of these values is advanced to the policyowner interest free, the intricate structure of the level premium would be seriously affected.

This does not mean, however, that the interest rate for policy loans should bear any direct relationship to the rate assumed in calculating the policy values. For one thing, insurers do not wish to encourage policy-owners to borrow on their policies except as an emergency measure; and second, the handling of policy loans, many of which are in small amounts, is a surprisingly expensive procedure.

Several of the states have statutes establishing the maximum rate of interest that may be charged on policy loans—generally 5 or 6 percent. When interest rates generally became much higher, in the early 1970s, a considerable amount of interest was shown in the possibility of legislation permitting a flexible policy loan interest rate that might vary with the trend of interest rates generally. Such legislation would have to be enacted in a significant number of the states, however, to be of any practical value to insurers; and to date there has been no noticeable trend in that direction.

13.6 Procedural Requirements

Endorsement of the Policy. At one time there was some discussion concerning whether the policy actually had to be delivered to the insurer in connection with the granting of a policy loan. It will be remembered that the quoted policy loan provision speaks of "assignment of the policy," and policy loan provisions have frequently required delivery of the policy for endorsement by the company. It is generally acknowledged today, however, that as a *chose* in action, the life insurance contract may be assigned without actual delivery, just as is true of other *choses* in action, so long as the assignment can be proved. Delivery of the policy, therefore, is primarily for the benefit of the insurer and therefore may be waived by it. Handling the policy each time a loan is granted also means a considerably more expensive and inconvenient procedure. For these reasons, most insurers no longer require that the policy be submitted for endorsement of a loan agreement, although they may reserve this right.

Deferment. The second paragraph of the policy loan provision quoted above provides that the company may defer the granting of any loan, except a premium loan, for a period not to exceed six months from the date the request is received. This is required by statute, and it is intended only as a safety measure. It is possible that extremely unusual economic conditions might cause policyowners to seek loans in such large numbers that the financial condition of life insurers might be affected. This provision would permit some control over the utilization of the privilege under such conditions. As a practical matter, however, policy loan requests are ordinarily processed immediately, and this privilege thus furnishes one of the most easily accessible sources of ready funds a policyowner can have other than money in the bank.

B. THE LEGAL EFFECTS

When the policyowner borrows from a bank, pledging the policy as security, he is personally obligated to pay the loan. The lender is entitled to payment out of the proceeds of the policy—that is, the cash value during the life of the insured, the death benefit after his death—but his first line of recovery is payment from the policyowner himself.

The legal results flowing from this fact are not usually very significant. Most collateral assignment forms give the assignee the right to surrender the policy for cash, without the owner's consent, in case of default in payment of the loan. All give the assignee the right to recover the amount of the unpaid debt out of the proceeds of the policy at the death of the insured. Where the total estate of the insured consists of insurance, therefore, the ultimate effects of the policy loan and the bank loan are approximately the same. In both cases, the amount of the unpaid loan is deducted from the insurance proceeds payable, and the named beneficiary receives the remainder. However, if the insured leaves at his death property other than the insurance, the results may be quite different.

The executor or administrator is charged with the duty of paying the debts of the decedent out of his probate estate; and life insurance payable to a named beneficiary never becomes a part of that estate. If the policy has been assigned to a bank as security for the repayment of a loan from the bank, the debt is eligible for payment out of the probate estate. In this case, therefore, unless the will provides differently, the beneficiary receives the full proceeds of the insurance. By contrast, if the insured had made a policy loan that was not repaid before his death, the loan would be deducted from the amount payable by the insurer, and the beneficiary would receive only the remainder. If the insured leaves a sizable estate other than insurance, therefore, and if others will share in that estate, the beneficiary is in a considerably less favored position if the policyowner-insured has effected a policy loan than if he has pledged the policy as collateral for a bank loan. This is illustrated in the case of *In Re Estate of Schwartz,* the Illustrative Case at the end of this chapter.

SUMMARY

The Policy Loan Provision

The earliest policy loan practices took the form of loans to pay premiums, and such loans were permitted as early as 1845. Later, the request or cash loan was made available. Today a policy loan provision is required in all but short term policies issued in any state in which the Uniform Standard Provisions law is in effect. The automatic premium loan provision is not required in any state except Rhode Island, but it is a valuable privilege which many insurers make available on a purely optional basis.

As a legal concept, a policy loan is not a loan at all, but rather an advance of some of the cash values to which the policyowner is entitled by contract. Thus, it is secured by these values, and in that sense 100 percent secured at all times.

The policyowner does not promise to repay a policy loan (although he may repay it), and it will be deducted from the proceeds of the policy if it is not repaid prior to the insured's death. Interest is charged; and if not paid when due, it will be added to and become a part of the principal.

A policyowner is not borrowing his "own money" in any real sense, for he has a right to the cash value only if he surrenders the contract. He has no accumulated fund in his own name.

Interest is charged primarily because the premium is computed on the assumption that all funds not used for current costs will be invested by the insurer at not less than a specified rate of interest. In considering the interest rate for policy loans, however, it is important to bear in mind that insurers do not wish to encourage their policyowners to borrow on their policies, as well as the fact that handling policy loans is an expensive procedure. Some states specify by statute the maximum interest rate that insurers may charge for policy loans.

Requiring the policy to be submitted to the insurer for endorsement in connection with a policy loan is a procedural requirement for the convenience of the insurer. Since handling the policy is an added expense, many insurers no longer make it a requirement for effecting a loan.

The company is required to reserve the right to defer the granting of a policy loan (except for payment of premiums) for a period not to exceed six months. This is merely a precautionary provision, however, in the event that extremely unfavorable economic conditions might warrant invoking such a decision. As a matter of company practice, policy loan requests are acted upon immediately.

The Legal Effect

Since a policy loan is not a loan in the legal sense of the word, it is generally held that the beneficiary is not entitled to reimbursement out of the general estate of the insured for the amount of policy loans deducted from insurance settlements.

In the case of loans from other institutions than the insurer, where the policy is pledged as collateral, the insured's personal representative, unless otherwise provided in the will, must repay the loan out of the assets of the probate estate to the extent such assets are available.

ILLUSTRATIVE CASE

In the following case, decided by the Pennsylvania Supreme Court in 1952, the insured had two policies on his life, with loans on both. Suit was brought on the theory that the beneficiaries were entitled to reimbursement out of the general estate to the amount of the loans, which were deducted from the proceeds of the policies, and the trial court agreed. The opinion of the Supreme Court of Pennsylvania is given almost in full because of the excellent analysis of the legal nature of the policy loan and the rights of the beneficiaries under policies in which loans were in effect.

IN RE ESTATE OF SCHWARTZ[3]
Pennsylvania Supreme Court, Eastern District

STEARNE, J.:   The question involved is whether a "policy loan" upon a life insurance policy is a debt of such a nature as enables the designated beneficiary, upon the insured's death, to require the loan to be repaid from the insured's general estate, thus enabling the beneficiary to receive the full insurance proceeds. The court below ruled that it was such a debt and directed its repayment. This appeal follows.

George J. Schwartz, the decedent, was insured by two policies of life insurance, each in the amount of $5,000. In one policy decedent named two of his daughters beneficiaries, and in the other he designated his first wife. Neither policy reserved the right to change beneficiaries. But each policy *obligated* the company to make "loans" to the insured to the limit of its cash surrender value. "Loans" were granted in the aggregate amount of $3,466.80.

By his will the testator-insured directed his executors "to pay my funeral expenses and all my just debts as soon after my decease as may conveniently be done." It was upon the theory that the "policy loans" created a debtor-creditor relationship between the insured and insurer, that the learned court below decreed that the beneficiaries were entitled to reimbursement from the general estate in order that they should receive the full face amounts of the policies.

In support of its ruling the court below relied upon our decision in *Wilson*

---

[3] 369 Pa. 574, 87 A. (2d) 270 (1952).

Estate, 363 Pa. 546, 70 A. 2d 354, wherein we decided that in an assessment of transfer inheritance tax, credit must be allowed for an indebtedness of the decedent-insured where a loan was made to him by a bank, and his life insurance policy, payable to designated beneficiaries, was pledged as collateral security. We said, p. 551:

> Decedent (settlor) merely assigned the insurance policies as collateral for his loan. As with any other collateral, when a loan is repaid the collateral is returned to the owner. Had the creditor bank used decedent-settlor's insurance collateral to liquidate its loan, the designated insurance beneficiaries could have enforced their claim against the estate of the decedent under their right of *subrogation,*[4] to the same extent as if they had been the original creditor.

In the case now before us, contradistinguished from the facts in *Wilson Estate, supra,* the "debt" was owed to the insurance company and not to a third person with the insurance policy assigned as collateral. This raises the narrow but important question whether any sound difference exists between the fundamental natures of these transactions. More accurately: does such an insurance "loan" from the insuring company upon the policy itself create a debtor-creditor relationship?

The learned court below, and counsel at argument stated that they have been unable to find any reported case in this jurisdiction which has decided this question. Our own research has disclosed none. But courts in at least six other jurisdictions have considered the problem. They unanimously agree that a "loan" granted pursuant to a policy right does not create a debtor-creditor relationship. The nature of such a "policy loan" has recently been discussed in *Fidelity Union Trust Co.* v. *Phillips,* 5 N.J. Super. 529, 68 A. 2d 574. It is said, p. 575:

> A clear distinction is drawn between a loan made by an insurance company to an insured against a life policy, and a collateral loan made by a third party secured by an assignment or pledge of the policy on the life of the borrower. The former "is not a loan in the strict technical sense, for there is no obligation of repayment on the insured, but rather an advancement on the cash value of the policy, the repayment of which will reinstate the depleted insurance without the issuance of a new policy and the submission of evidence of insurability. A 'loan' by the insurer in such circumstances does not give rise to the relationship of debtor and creditor." *David* v. *Metropolitan Life Insurance Co.,* 135 N.J.L. 106, 50 A. 2d 651, 653 (Sup. Ct. 1947), affirmed 136 N.J.L. 195, 54 A. 2d 731 (E. & A., 1947). Mr. Justice Holmes declared in *Board of Assessors* v. *New York Life Insurance Co.,* 216 U.S. 517, 30 S. Ct. 385, 386, 54 L. Ed. 597, 1910, "This is called a loan. It is represented by what is called a note, which contains a promise to pay the money. But as the plaintiff

---

[4] The right given to a creditor to be substituted for another and to succeed to the other's rights. In this situation, the court says, the beneficiaries had the right to be substituted for the original creditor—that is, the creditor bank—and thus be repaid out of the estate of the decedent.

(insurance company) never advances more than it already is absolutely bound for under the policy, it has no interest in creating a personal liability, and therefore the contract on the face of the note goes on to provide that if the note is not paid when due, it shall be extinguished automatically by the counter-credit for what we have called the reserve value of the policy. In short, the claim of the policyholder on the one side and of the company on the other are brought into an account current by the very act that creates the latter. The so-called liability of the policyholder never exists as a personal liability, it never is a debt, but is merely a deduction in account from the sum that the plaintiffs ultimately must pay." Therefore, when an insurance company advances to an insured a sum of money against his policy, and upon the death of the insured retains the amount required to satisfy the "loan" or advance, the beneficiary named in the policy is not entitled to recover from the estate of the insured the amount by which the insurance had been depleted by borrowings by the insured upon the policy.

❋   ❋   ❋   ❋   ❋

Substantially the same rule was adopted by this Court in *Black's Estate,* 341 Pa. 264, 19 A. 2d 130. The insurance policy there included a provision almost identical with that now under consideration, except that payment by insurer was more accurately termed an "advance" rather than a "loan." Decedent had bequeathed his business to his son subject to payment of all his personal and business debts. A dispute arose between the son and the widow, as residuary legatee, as to whether certain items were debts or obligations payable out of the business. Concerning a cash advance to decedent from his insurance company, we said (p. 270):

> The auditor and court below held that the advance was not such a debt as was required to be paid out of the business of decedent. With that conclusion we are in accord, for the association could not make any claim against the estate of the decedent. It could not have proceeded against the decedent at the date of his death. Consequently there was no indebtedness, as clearly appears from a perusal of the agreement. The policyholder had the right to repay the advance made but he could not be compelled to do so.

While counsel for appellees point to factual distinctions between that case and the present one, such distinctions have no bearing on the legal principle here involved.

Legal digests and text writers appear to be equally unanimous.

> Although a policy loan is termed a "loan," it differs from an ordinary commercial loan, and, in fact, is not a "loan" in the ordinary sense of the word. It is merely a deduction from the sum insurer ultimately must pay, and is more accurately described as an advance. 44 C.J.S. Insurance, sec. 337, p. 1291.

Accord: 29 Am. Jur. Insurance, sec. 463; Goldin on Insurance in Pennsylvania (2d ed.) page 631; 2 Couch on Insurance, sec. 335; Cooley's Briefs on Insurance (2d ed.) page 157.

Appellees argue that the insured's will and his testamentary scheme, considered in the light of his family circumstances, reveal that he intended his insurance beneficiaries to receive the full face amount of the policies. But the insured's *testamentary intent* is not the controlling consideration. We are obliged first to determine his *contractual* intent at the time he entered into the contracts of insurance wherein the rights of the insurance beneficiaries were created. We cannot interpret the meaning of contracts entered into on June 11, 1913, by speculating on testamentary intent adopted by insured in his testamentary scheme of April 2, 1949, nearly thirty-six years thereafter. The terms of the insurance contracts are clear and unambiguous; they give the insured an absolute right to demand at any time an advancement of any sum of money up to the reserve value of the policies. Under no discernible doctrine could it be held that the insured was incurring a *personal liability* by exercising this contractual right. The insured could, of course, have directed by his will that the "policy loans" be paid[5] out of his general assets so that the beneficiaries would receive the face amounts of the policies. As he chose not to do this we have no power to do it for him. We cannot construe a direction to pay "debts" as applicable to an advancement of money which did not create a personal liability. As an insurance policy loan does not create a debtor-creditor relationship, the beneficiaries of these policies so encumbered are entitled only to the *net* proceeds.

Decree reversed at appellees' cost.

QUESTIONS FOR REVIEW

1. Summarize a typical policy loan provision.
2. Why is a policy loan not considered a loan in the generally accepted legal sense of the word?
3. Why is interest charged on policy loans?
4. What is the purpose of the provision reserving the right to defer the granting of a request policy loan?
5. A has a $10,000 life insurance policy subject to a policy loan of $3,000, and B has a policy in the amount of $10,000 which he has assigned collaterally to X Bank as security for a $3,000 loan. Assuming that neither leaves other property at his death and that the policies are in force, what amount would be payable to the beneficiary under each policy at the death of the insured? Would either be entitled to reimbursement out of the general estate if other property were available? Explain.

---

[5] It should be remembered, however, that the insurer is under no contractual obligation to accept repayment of the loan after the insured's death.

Chapter Outline

A. "Testamentary" Disposition

    14.1 The Law of Wills and Testaments

    14.2 Exceptions

    14.3 The Question of Contracts

B. Testamentary Disposition and the Optional Modes of Settlement

    14.4 Election by the Policyowner

    14.5 Election by the Beneficiary

    14.6 The Cases

    14.7 Legislation

    14.8 Matured Endowments and Cash Surrenders

Chapter **14**

Life Insurance and the
Law of Wills

A TESTAMENTARY DISPOSITION of property is a disposition not intended to take effect until the death of the owner. Generally speaking, documents intended to have this effect must be executed in accordance with the statute of wills of the jurisdiction concerned or they will be held to be ineffective as a matter of law. No one would think of contending today that the life insurance contract violates the law of wills, but other types of life insurance arrangements, particularly those involving the optional modes of settlement, have occasionally been challenged as "attempted testamentary dispositions," not executed in accordance with the statute of wills, and therefore invalid.

In the majority of cases involving this challenge, the validity of the instrument has been upheld. Nevertheless, it presents a significant question of law, which it is the purpose of this chapter to discuss.

A. "TESTAMENTARY" DISPOSITION

14.1 The Law of Wills and Testaments

Technically and historically, an instrument that directed the disposition of land and attached buildings (real property) following the death of the owner was called a will; and a document serving the same purpose with respect to personal property was called a testament. The terms were used together, therefore, to designate an instrument—one's "last will and testament"—that directed the disposition of all of a person's property, both real and personal, at his death. This terminology has been retained in the technical language of the law.

Regardless of when it is executed, a will does not take effect until the death of the person who made it (the testator). Often it is secret, or at least highly confidential, until that time; it is usually subject to change as long as the testator lives; and often, too, the last will a person makes is made at a time when his faculties are dimming and persons who seek to benefit at his death may be in a position to exert a great deal of influence over him. Important also is the fact that controversies as to the testator's intent and the legal effect of the document arise only after the death of the best witness, the testator.

From an early date, therefore, the law has specified certain requirements that must be met before an instrument purporting to direct the disposition of property after the death of the owner can be given effect. In spite of the apparent clarity of these laws, a large body of case law has been developed in connection with questions concerning instruments, intended to have the effect of wills, that have not been executed in accordance with the statute of wills.

The basic principle on which these statutes and court decisions rest is this: that any attempt to say how one's property shall be distributed after his death must be executed in accordance with the statute of wills of the jurisdiction concerned or it will be held invalid and ineffective. Generally, the jurisdiction where the decedent made his home at the time of his death will govern the disposition of his personal property; the jurisdiction where the real property is located will govern the disposition of that property. If the instrument in question was not executed in accordance with the statute of wills of the proper jurisdiction, the owner is said to have died "intestate" (without a will) and the property in question will be distributed according to the statute of intestate succession (which is simply a statute saying how the property of a resident of the state in question shall be distributed if the owner dies without leaving a valid will).

14.2 Exceptions

In spite of this relative strictness, the law has recognized, from an early date, some ways to arrange the ownership of property so that it will shift to others at the owner's death without the necessity of a will. Property owned in joint tenancy is one example. At the death of one joint owner, ownership automatically vests in the survivor or survivors. Another method of transferring ownership at one's death without the formalities of a will is through a special kind of gift called a "gift *causa mortis.*" A gift *causa mortis* is a gift made in contemplation of one's death, when death seems imminent, but on condition that if death does not occur as anticipated, of the illness or injury then suffered, ownership of the property in question will return to the person making the gift.

14.3 The Question of Contracts

Traditionally, there is a strong question as to whether contracts are ever to be considered as governed by a statute of wills in the sense that they must meet the requirements there set forth or be held invalid. Basically, a statute of wills relates to the transfer of property for which no consideration has been given. Certainly, it does not relate to a sale of the property. Moreover, the dangers of fraud, undue influence, and other similar possibilities, which are felt to make strict requirements necessary for wills, are not as compelling in the case of contracts, where other requirements are thought sufficient to accomplish the same general purposes. It has sometimes been flatly stated, therefore, that the rules concerning testamentary disposition of property have no application to contracts, although there is judicial authority to the contrary.

The life insurance contract, because it becomes payable on the death of the insured, would seem more likely to present a question of attempted testamentary disposition of property than most other third-party beneficiary contracts. Nevertheless, the validity of the life insurance contract so far as a testamentary disposition question is concerned seems to have been firmly settled at a relatively early date, and there seems never to have been any very strong threat that the beneficiary designation might be held to be an attempted testamentary disposition of property.

It has been suggested that the nature of the early contracts of life insurance may have been largely responsible for this favorable holding. Since these early contracts usually had no lifetime values, there was no property until the insured's death. Furthermore, since the early policies were often purchased by the beneficiary, even if there had been lifetime values, they would have belonged to the beneficiary from the first, and again there would have been no question of testamentary disposition. The development of lifetime values and ownership usually by the insured himself was sufficiently gradual that the possible problem had been resolved before the circumstances developed that might have given firmer grounds for challenge. Even where the insured is the policyowner, however, the property to be distributed at his death does not, in fact, ever belong to him. It is only when payments are being made under an optional settlement that a serious question of testamentary disposition may be presented.

B. TESTAMENTARY DISPOSITION AND THE OPTIONAL MODES OF SETTLEMENT

14.4 Election by the Policyowner

When the policyowner is someone other than the insured and elects an optional mode of settlement for the beneficiary or beneficiaries of a life insurance policy, the settlement arrangements are somewhat more elaborate than is true of a one-sum beneficiary designation; but the fact remains that the property to be retained by the insurer and paid out in accordance with the optional settlement elected is not the property of the policyowner, and it does not become payable at his death but at that of the insured. Even when the policyowner is the insured, the property is not his. The situation is different, however, where the beneficiary elects an optional mode of settlement, following the death of the insured, and designates the person or persons to receive any proceeds unpaid at his (the beneficiary's) death. There have been very few cases on the point, and most of them have been decided against the person or persons raising the testamentary disposition question. However, the nature of life insurance and the practices of life insurance companies with respect to the settlement of claims make it important to consider any possible problem that might interfere with the prompt settlement of claims and the absolute reliability of life insurance obligations. The cases on this subject, therefore, are considerably more important than their number would indicate.

14.5 Election by the Beneficiary

The special circumstances presented when the beneficiary elects an optional settlement can be illustrated most clearly by an example. Assume a policyowner, for example, John Smith, whose life insurance policy in the amount of $50,000 is payable to his wife, Mary, in one sum. Following John's death, Mary elects to leave the proceeds with the company under the interest option, with full right of withdrawal, and requests that the supplementary contract be so drawn that any sum remaining at her death shall be payable equally to those of her children who are then living, and to the children of any deceased child by right of representation.

Here, obviously, there is no question about the existence of property—the policy proceeds—and no question as to the person who owns it. Mary has as complete a right to the policy proceeds as if the money were on deposit in a bank. She agrees with the insurance company to leave this money under the interest option. She also agrees and directs that if she dies while any amount remains, it is to be paid in equal sums to her children, or to their children if any child is then deceased. Undoubtedly, this can be viewed as a disposition of her property not to take effect until her death.

Noninsurance cases can be cited showing that similar arrangements involving bank deposits have been held ineffective to pass an interest to the persons named to take at the death of the depositor. In other words, they were held invalid as attempted testamentary dispositions not executed in accordance with the statute of wills. How, then, does the life insurance situation differ? The following cases are reviewed briefly in an attempt to answer this question.

14.6 The Cases

Three principal cases since 1942 have upheld the validity of supplementary contracts in which an optional method of settlement was elected by the beneficiary, with directions that any funds remaining with the insurance company at her death be paid not to her personal representatives but directly to named persons. In technical terms, this is a "gift over." The effect, of course, is to transfer rights to another person at one's death without using a will. Where the distribution under the laws of intestacy would be to persons different from those designated under the contract, however, it is always possible that someone may challenge the arrangement on the grounds that it is void as an attempted testamentary disposition of property which does not comply with the statute of wills. This is exactly what happened in each of the following cases.

1. The Mutual Benefit Life Insurance Company v. Ellis et al. This case arose in New York and was decided in 1942 in the United States Circuit Court of Appeals, Second Circuit.[1] The wife was beneficiary of four life insurance policies on the life of her husband, and she elected to take the proceeds not under one of the standard options but under a somewhat different agreement between herself and the company, under which the income was to be paid to her during her life with the principal payable at her death to her husband's three sisters. At her death, the sisters made claim for the payment (basing their claim on the provisions of the settlement agreement), and the administrator of the beneficiary's estate also made claim (on the grounds that the agreement constituted an invalid attempted testamentary disposition of the property). The company paid the money into court and asked the court to decide among the claimants.

The district court held that the sisters were entitled to the money "upon the theory that the certificate was either a supplementary insurance contract or created a valid trust in their favor." The appellate court said: "We are in accord with the result of the decision but on the ground that the sisters were entitled to recover as third-party donee-beneficiaries." In other words, the appellate court reached the same decision, but on different grounds.

The most pertinent part of the court's decision went as follows:

> The crucial question is whether the sisters acquired the right to recover the proceeds of the policies as third-party donee-beneficiaries, or

---

[1] C.C.A. N.Y., 125 F. (2d) 127, 138 A.L.R. 1478 (1942).

whether they were precluded from this because the agreement to pay them was invalid as an ineffective attempt to dispose of property upon Mrs. Addie's death without the formality of a will . . .

. . . A sufficient answer to the argument that it would violate the Statute of Wills to enforce the agreement for the sisters lies in the fact that their right to enforce is based upon a contractual obligation and not on any interest in the property of the decedent. The appellant cites no Colorado decision having any bearing on the present situation except *Smith v. Simmons,* 99 Colo. 227. There a bank to which certain bonds were delivered by the owner, with a letter instructing it as to the disposition of the bonds after the owner's death, was held an agent and not a trustee, and the bonds were therefore held a part of the transferor's estate, of which she had made no proper testamentary disposition. In the case at bar, however, the title to the proceeds of the policies passed to the company, leaving only contractual rights in Mrs. Addie and the sisters. The Colorado decisions are to the effect that such a right, though subject to be divested in the manner provided in the contract, is a vested right arising when the contract is made and enforceable unless and until terminated pursuant to the provisions of the instrument of settlement. . . .

For the foregoing reasons, we hold that the appellees were entitled to recover as third-party donee-beneficiaries.

The court thus held in favor of the sisters whom the beneficiary had designated to receive the proceeds at her death, basing its decision on the theory that the insurer held title to the proceeds under a contract to pay them out as directed. According to Colorado law, rights of this kind were vested subject to being divested and did not "pass" at the beneficiary's death. Instead, the rights vested in the sisters when the supplementary agreement was completed with the insurer and, as a technical matter, this was not a disposition "to take effect at death."

2. Toulouse v. New York Life Insurance Company. This case[2] involved a 20-year endowment policy which matured during the lifetime of the insured. At its maturity he requested that $6,000 be left with the company under Option 1 and that any amount remaining with the company at his death be paid in equal shares to his four nieces and a nephew. The company issued a supplementary contract providing for settlement in accordance with his request.

There were no withdrawals, and at the death of the insured the accumulated values in the possession of the company amounted to $7,164.31. The executor of the insured's estate brought an action to recover that amount, contending that the part of the supplementary contract relating to distribution to the nieces and nephew was void "as an attempted testamentary disposition in violation of the statute of wills." The company, on the other hand, contended that the supplementary contract constituted a "valid third-party donee-beneficiary contract."

---

[2] 245 P. (2d) 205 (Wash., 1952).

In considering the question, the court pointed out that the right to take advantage of optional methods of settlement in a life insurance contract is a valuable one. The beneficiary acquires a vested interest in the company's performance of that portion of its contract of insurance, a right which is in the nature of a property right and would be protected.

The court referred to the case of *Mutual Benefit Life Insurance Co.* v. *Ellis* and pointed out that, contrary to the facts in that situation, the rights of the nieces and nephew in the supplementary contract under consideration were "derived from the original insurance contract through the exercise of Option 1."

"Appellant has cited no cases," the court continued, "and we have found none holding that supplementary insurance contracts such as the one in the present case are void, as testamentary dispositions in violation of the statute of wills."

Appellant had cited a case which involved the question of a gift, and the court discussed that case, but continued:

> We are not here concerned with the law of gifts, *inter vivos* or *causa mortis;* but with the question of whether or not the supplementary insurance contract between the insurance company and Mr. Sherlock confers any rights on Mr. Sherlock's nieces and nephew named therein, to whom the company promised to pay any of the proceeds of the original insurance policy (plus accumulated interest) which might be in its possession when Mr. Sherlock died. Their rights under that contract are based upon the contractual obligation of the company to do what it agreed with Mr. Sherlock it would do. Mr. Sherlock might have defeated their rights by withdrawing all the money, but he had no right under the agreement to substitute someone else in their stead as the third-party donee-beneficiary; he could make no change in exhibit No. 5 (the supplementary agreement), in which the insurance company's obligations were set forth. By analogy to insurance policy cases the supplementary insurance contract gave the named nieces and nephew a vested interest (*Massachusetts Mutual Life Insurance Co.* v. *Bank of California,* 187 Wash. 565, 60 P. 2d 675)—not in any specific property or to any amount of money, but in the performance of the contract by the insurance company.

The court concluded, with the gist of the decision as follows:

> The mere fact that the death of one of the parties to a contract is designated as a contingency upon which a promise to deliver property to a third-party donee-beneficiary turns, is not alone sufficient to make such a contract a testamentary disposition and subject it to the statute of wills. *Warren* v. *United States,* 68 Ct. Cl. 634, certiorari denied, 281 U.S. 739, 74 L. Ed. 1154, 50 S. Ct. 346. . . . As was said in the last cited case and quoted with approval in *In re Howe's Estate,* 31 Cal. 2d 395, 399, 189 P. 2d 5, 1 A. L. R. 2d 1171, "their right to enforce is based upon a contractual obligation and not on any interest in the property of the decedent."

The majority opinion in this case would be comforting support to the life insurance company title department if it were not for the very strong dissenting opinion. In the dissenting view, Justice Donworth takes issue with the theory that the supplementary contract grew out of the insurance contract by reason of the election of Option 1.

> It is very plain to me that this so-called supplementary contract is an entirely new contract between the parties which is not supplementary to, nor in anywise connected with option 1 of the endowment policy in so far as it purports to designate substitute payees upon Mr. Sherlock's death. There is nothing in the endowment policy relating to the payment of the proceeds to any person other than Mr. Sherlock *after the close of the endowment period.*
>
> . . . This supplementary contract is a new contract having nothing whatever to do with life insurance. The fact that the depository of the proceeds was a life insurance company is immaterial. It might have been a bank or an individual.

The dissenting judge notes the fact that the majority opinion assumes that the interest of the nieces and nephew is a vested one, by analogy to the beneficiary under a life insurance policy where the insured has not reserved the right to change the beneficiary designation. The dissenting opinion, however, points out that the insured in this case reserved the right to destroy the rights of the nieces and nephew by withdrawing all of the funds at his discretion. "The rule is," the judge continued, "that if an insured retains the power to extinguish the rights or interest of a beneficiary, even though he cannot change his designation of the beneficiary, then the beneficiary has a mere expectancy or contingent interest."

> It cannot, therefore, be maintained that even by analogy to the law of life insurance the named nieces and nephew acquired at any time prior to Mr. Sherlock's death vested rights to the balance of the fund.

✿   ✿   ✿   ✿   ✿

> . . . It is fundamental that a valid gift *inter vivos* can be completed by delivery to another person for the benefit of the donee. But it is equally fundamental that in such a case the donor must irrevocably divest himself of dominion and control over the subject matter of the gift. In the present case, Mr. Sherlock expressly retained control and dominion over the funds during his lifetime, and the transaction must, then, fail both as an abortive attempt to make a gift *inter vivos* as well as an abortive attempt to make a testamentary disposition of the funds.
>
> By the decision in this case, it is held for the first time that the owner of personal property may avoid probate proceedings and the expense of administering his estate by the simple expedient of reducing his assets to cash and entering into a contract with a bank, insurance company or individual (similar in form to the supplementary contract here involved), while still retaining control over the money during his lifetime.
>
> If such a revolutionary change is to be made in this state in the method

of transmitting property at death, which has heretofore been recognized as exclusive, only the legislature should make it effective. It surely did not amend or repeal the statute of wills by enacting the section of the insurance code (RCW 48.23.300) which is quoted in the majority opinion.

3. Hall v. Mutual Life Insurance Co. of N.Y. In January, 1952, the New York Supreme Court, sitting in special term, decided this case[3] and held invalid, as an attempted testamentary disposition, a supplementary contract issued in settlement of a life insurance policy on the life of the beneficiary's father. The beneficiary elected settlement under the interest option and named her then husband as the person to whom any sums remaining at her death were to be paid. The power to change this supplementary beneficiary was not reserved, although, as in the Toulouse case, the beneficiary could withdraw all or any part of the amounts so held any time she wished. Nine years after the supplementary contract was issued, the husband and wife were separated and later divorced. The wife remarried and died shortly afterward.

The arguments of the Toulouse majority and minority opinions were utilized in this case. The husband urged that the supplementary contract was an extension of the policy and that the use of the optional modes of settlement had been authorized by the legislature. The executors of the wife's estate took the view, put forth by the minority opinion in the Toulouse case, that the supplementary contract was a new and independent contract which "insures nothing; it is simply a contract for the deposit of a fund, fully in existence, upon which interest is to be paid. Being neither a contract nor part of a contract of insurance, the gift over is claimed invalid as an attempt to effect a testamentary disposition without conforming to the Statute of Wills."

This view was adopted by the special term court, which held that, as a new and independent contract, "its provision for payment over of any unpaid balance of principal on the death of the policy beneficiary, was an invalid testamentary disposition for failure to comply with the requirements of the Statute of Wills (Dec. Est. Law, Section 21)."

The Second Court Decision. The New York Supreme Court, Appellate Division, summarized the situation in a second decision in the case,[4] and stated its own point of view thus:

> The mere statement of the respective contentions of the parties reveals a battle of words and nominal distinctions stirred up by the issue. It may seem blunt and over simple, but the fact is that a supplementary contract partakes both of an insurance contract and an independent contract for the deposit of a fund. It is fruitless and a vain concern to try to fit what is so obviously a transaction that bridges two categories of legal thinking,

---

[3] 109 N.Y. Supp. (2d) 646 (1952).
[4] 122 N.Y.S. (2d) 239 (1953).

into one or the other, simply because the law and lawyers as a convenience to thinking, and to make possible communication between finite minds, have invented separate categories of thought and words to mark the separation.

It is obvious that the policy beneficiary has the right to a settlement option only because that right was given by the policy. Nor could an insurance company grant such a contract independent of a policy. Moreover, we may take judicial notice that with changes in interest rates it is sometimes to the disadvantage of the insurance company to enter into the supplementary contract; but it loses its freedom by virtue of the insurance policy it had issued. On the other hand, it is equally true that once the insured had died, all the insurance aspects of the contract of insurance were fully terminated, at least in the actuarial and legal sense. The supplementary contract clearly provides for the continued holding, or deposit, of the fund now arisen, very much in the manner of a bank if the fund were given to the bank. But this provision obviously could not have arisen unless it were inchoate[5] in the original insurance contract. From another aspect too, the deposit is related to the policy of insurance: There is no doubt that the insured in purchasing this policy and in paying his premiums was definitely buying optional modes of settlement. It is common knowledge that the methods of settlement are very frequently a very valuable part of the policy. That is particularly true these days, if the options arise from an older policy where the terms are likely to be more beneficial. In this case the policy was issued in 1925.

Accordingly, it would seem the more sensible view to determine the question on the basis of whether we are dealing with a social evil or hazard or a social good, and to be controlled in that view by legislative intention, if it has been expressed or may be implied.

. . . In the instant case, the supplementary contract was fully executed and accepted by both parties, the insurance company and the policy beneficiary. The trivial variance, whether the interest payments were to be made annually or quarterly and with respect to the right to withdraw principal, did not change the contract from being supplemental to the original policy of insurance. Again we are faced with the need not to confuse the word with the meaning of the word. For the purpose of binding the insurance company *without other action by the insurance company*, insured or policy beneficiary must accept the option in the unvarying terms offered in the policy. The slightest variance may avoid the company's liability—so the court held in the *Gram* case. That is fundamental law of contract. A qualified acceptance is simply a counter offer. That does not mean, and cannot possibly mean, that as to third parties, any variation in the executed supplementary contract from the terms of the policy constitutes a new contract, and not one derived from the policy. To so hold would mean that the principles and realities applied to modifications of contracts are not to be applied to contracts of life insurance.

---

[5] Begun but not completed.

. . . It does not merit extended discussion to prove the very high public interest in the extension of the life insurance system, as a major provision for thrift and security for individuals and families. . . . Part and parcel of this system for many decades, is the optional mode of settlement, with power to make gift over [of] the unused principal. This is no evil to be hobbled; no course of conduct with incidence of recurring injustice to be limited by safeguards, slowing but necessary.

The court, therefore, did not try to decide the question solely on technical, legal principles. Instead, it considered the public interest aspects of life insurance and pointed out that it was not necessary to limit the use of optional settlements. Probably the most significant factor behind the decision, however, was the fact that, by reason of the adverse holding in the special term court, the New York legislature had enacted an amendment to the Personal Property Law providing that even where it involves a gift over in the event of death, a supplementary contract is not repugnant to, or in violation of, the statute of wills. Interpreting the enactment of this amendment as the most recent expression of legislative approval of exactly the kind of arrangement under attack in this case, the court concluded:

The supplementary contract is a valid extension of the policy of insurance providing for the continued deposit of the fund for the purpose of paying interest thereon, and the gift over on the death of the policy beneficiary is not subject to the statutes governing the making of testamentary dispositions.

14.7 Legislation

Legislation along the lines enacted in New York as the result of the first adverse holding of the court in the Hall case has been proposed in a number of other states and enacted into law in some of them. Generally speaking, opposition has come principally from those persons who believe that, by proposing legislation on the subject, the life insurance industry is, in effect, conceding that there is a problem. It is their position that since so few cases are ever litigated it is really wiser to assume that the practice is valid. Those who favor legislation take the position that it is always possible that a case may be presented where the persons who would benefit by a decision upholding the validity of the supplementary contract would not be the ones who, in fairness, would seem most entitled to the money. In such situations, it is quite possible that a court could, on perfectly valid grounds, reach a conclusion which would be adverse to the interests of the many thousands of persons having rights at the present time to insurance funds left with life insurance companies under supplementary contracts.

14.8 Matured Endowments and Cash Surrenders

It should be noted that this type of problem is not confined to the proceeds of life insurance payable on the death of the insured. The Toulouse case involved the proceeds of an endowment policy, and the same question could be raised if the policyowner elected to take the cash surrender value of the policy under an optional settlement and provided for any balance to be paid to someone else in the event of his death before the entire proceeds had been paid out.

SUMMARY

A testamentary disposition of property is a disposition made by one's last will and testament. A will does not take effect until one's death, and any instrument intended to have that effect must be executed in accordance with the applicable statute of wills.

Although a life insurance policy provides for the payment of money at the death of the insured, the death benefit is never the property of the policyowner, whether he is the insured or some other person. It was settled at an early date, therefore, that the life insurance contract does not constitute an attempted testamentary disposition of property.

When the beneficiary-payee elects an optional settlement of any benefit payable under the contract, the situation is different. If the settlement agreement provides for a gift over to named persons at the primary payee's death, the agreement has, in a few instances, been challenged as an attempted testamentary disposition of property not executed in accordance with the statute of wills. As a general rule, such dispositions are upheld for two principal reasons: (1) they are contractual, and (2) it is in the public interest to thus encourage the use of life insurance.

QUESTIONS FOR REVIEW

1. Briefly define the following terms:
    a. Last will and testament.
    b. Intestacy.
2. State two possible reasons why the life insurance contract has not generally been considered subject to the statutory requirements concerning wills.
3. In what general area of life insurance has the testamentary disposition question posed a definite legal threat?
4. How has this question been resolved in New York? What are the advantages of such a solution? Some disadvantages?

Chapter Outline

A. If the Premium Is Not Paid
   - 15.1 The Policy Lapses

B. The Nonforfeiture Benefits
   - 15.2 The Standard Nonforfeiture Laws
   - 15.3 The Cash Surrender Value
   - 15.4 Extended Insurance
   - 15.5 Paid-up Insurance

C. Requirements for Reinstatement
   - 15.6 Evidence of Insurability
   - 15.7 The Meaning of Insurability
   - 15.8 Satisfactory to the Company

D. The Application for Reinstatement
   - 15.9 Effect of Application
   - 15.10 Two Main Groups of Court Decisions
   - 15.11 The Legal Nature of the Right
   - 15.12 Addition of Conditions
   - 15.13 Contestability of the Reinstated Policy
   - 15.14 Reinstatement and the Suicide Clause

Chapter 15

The Policy Lapses
and Is Reinstated

IF A LIFE insurance premium is not paid when due (or within the grace period), either in cash or by automatic premium loan, the policy is said to lapse. Thereafter, the contract is effective only as provided by any nonforfeiture section included in the policy. However, most life insurance contracts contain a reinstatement provision which enables the policyowner to return his policy to a premium-paying status and restore all benefits and privileges previously enjoyed.

The purpose of this chapter is to outline some of the problems relating to lapsation and the reinstatement process and to consider the major legal problems involved in the operation of the contract after reinstatement has been effected.

A. IF THE PREMIUM IS NOT PAID

15.1 The Policy Lapses

It is easy to say that if a life insurance premium is not paid by the end of the grace period (and if no automatic premium loan is available or effective), the policy lapses, but there is a considerable difference of opinion as to the meaning of the word "lapse." It is sometimes used to mean termination of the contract except as to any nonforfeiture benefits that may be involved; and it is sometimes used to mean termination of the policy without benefits. In the former case, the contract doesn't actually lapse until any applicable nonforfeiture benefit has expired.

Because the word has no precise general definition, it is not very useful except in a context that makes clear the meaning one wishes to convey.

It is probably better insurance usage to say that a policy lapses when it changes from a premium-paying basis to a nonpremium-paying but non-paid-up status, regardless of whether it contains any nonforfeiture benefits or, if provided, any such benefit becomes effective. If a nonforfeiture benefit becomes effective, the policy "expires" when the benefit terminates. Using these definitions, a policy may be said to lapse for nonpayment of a premium due on October 2, 1975, for instance, if the premium is not paid before the end of the grace period; and it expires at the termination of any extended term insurance that may be available. This usage has the added advantage of avoiding any controversy as to whether the policy lapses on the due date of the unpaid premium or at the end of the grace period.

Most life insurance contracts are consistent with this view, as indicated in this illustrative grace period provision:

> *Grace Period.* A grace period of thirty-one days shall be allowed for the payment, without interest, of any premium after the first. During this period the insurance under this policy shall remain in force. However, if the premium due on the due date remains unpaid at the end of the grace period, this policy shall lapse. If the death of the insured occurs within the grace period, the past due premium will be paid from the sum payable under this policy.

B. THE NONFORFEITURE BENEFITS

The owner of a legal reserve life insurance policy has three choices if his policy lapses for nonpayment of premiums after it has acquired a cash value. He may surrender it for its cash value, in which case the contract will be terminated. Alternatively, he may leave the cash value with the company and elect one of the nonforfeiture insurance benefits, typically either reduced paid-up or extended term insurance. One of these non-forfeiture insurance benefits is required by law to be specified as the automatic nonforfeiture option.

15.2 The Standard Nonforfeiture Laws

Nonforfeiture benefits are required by the Standard Nonforfeiture Laws, prepared and recommended by the National Association of Insurance Commissioners. The laws, as previously noted, have been enacted by the legislature or otherwise made effective in every state. Briefly, they require that with the exception of some short-term policies, all life insurance contracts must provide cash and other nonforfeiture values in accordance with formulas specified in the law. These formulas must be set forth in the policy, together with the values of the contract at the end of each of the first 20 policy years.

This approach differs from the method of computing cash values and nonforfeiture benefits required by legislation in effect prior to the 1948 C.S.O. laws. (The prior legislation had required the policy to show the reserve basis and provide a cash value equal to the reserve minus a "surrender charge" of not more than $25 per $1,000 of insurance.) Nevertheless, the basic legal principle remained the same. Only the methods of computing the values were changed. The policy must contain a provision specifying the cash value on surrender and providing at least one other optional benefit—either extended term or a reduced paid-up policy.

15.3 The Cash Surrender Value

The cash surrender value of a life insurance contract has been defined as the cash value (as determined by rules set forth in the governing statute and the nonforfeiture section of the policy) of a policy that has been surrendered to the insurer by a person having the contractual right to surrender it.[1] As a general rule, the person having this right is the owner, but this does not mean that he cannot by assignment transfer that right to another.

Legal Nature of the Right. One of the most frequently recurring questions in connection with the nonforfeiture section of the life insurance contract concerns the legal nature of the right to surrender the policy for its cash value. This question has arisen occasionally with respect to the election of one of the nonforfeiture insurance options, but it arises most typically when the owner attempts to surrender the policy for its cash value and the insured dies before the surrender transaction has been fully completed. In such instances, a technical question may very well be raised, since the death benefit may be payable if the necessary steps for surrender were not completed before the death of the insured. The difference between the cash surrender value and the amount of the death benefit is usually enough to make a court action worthwhile if there is any appreciable degree of doubt concerning completion of the surrender process.

The problem has been analyzed in different ways in a few cases, but the general rule is that the right to elect to take the cash surrender value of the contract is exactly what it is called in most life insurance policies— an option—and that the insurance company is in the same position as any other party to a contract who provides an option to the other party. As a general legal principle, then, the right to take the cash value is a continuing, irrevocable offer from the insurer to the policyowner, which

---

[1] 29 Am. Jur. 906.

becomes effective as a binding agreement when it is accepted according to its terms. Even when the insured dies before the cash value has in fact been paid, the majority of courts have held that the policyowner's acceptance of the offer is effective and final. This view is expressed in one case[2] as follows:

> . . . While we have found no Texas decisions directly in point, the general rule is that when the insured elects to exercise the option to surrender the policy and collect the cash value by an unequivocal notification to the company to that effect, the obligation of the company thereupon became a matured indebtedness to the insured for the amount of the cash surrender value, and any contingent liability (to pay the death benefit) thereby came to an end.

In another case,[3] the court points out that the option is one of the rights the policyowner (the insured in this case) bought and paid for, as follows:

> The privilege to exercise the option of surrendering the policies for their cash value was one bought and paid for by the insured; such option is an offer contained in the policy contract and is from the company to the insured and it is his right to accept the offer, within a specified time, and his acceptance completes the contract; the company has no right to accept or reject; its obligation to pay is absolute.

As is true of any other offer, however, an option must be accepted according to its terms. Thus the requirements set forth in the contract must be complied with. In the contracts of one insurer, these requirements, as they apply to the nonforfeiture options, are stated as follows:

> At any time after this policy has acquired a cash value, and while the insured is living but not more than 90 days after the due date of the first unpaid premium, the owner may elect one of the following provisions. Such election shall be in writing and filed with the home office of the company.

The last sentence in this provision states the requirements of the insurer with respect to the nonforfeiture options. Since these requirements are included for the benefit of the insurer, they may be waived; but in the absence of a waiver, they must be complied with if a binding agreement is to result. Thus, if different terms are requested by the policyowner as a part of his request for cash surrender or if the policy is not submitted, if requested, the purported acceptance is in reality a counteroffer, which itself must be accepted by the insurer.

---

[2] *Green* v. *American National Insurance Company*, 452 S.W. (2d) 1 (C.C.A. Texas, 1970).

[3] *Pack* v. *Progressive Life Insurance Co.*, 239 Mo. App. 1, 187 S.W. (2d) 501, 505, as quoted in *Magers* v. *Nat'l. Life and Accident Insurance Co.*, 329 S.W. (2d) 752. See also *Franklin Life Ins. Co.* v. *Smithers*, 285 F. (2d) 875 (1961).

In other words, most of the cash surrender problems can be resolved by applying rules of general contract law. This point is illustrated in an especially interesting way in the case of *Board of Trustees of the Unitarian Church* v. *Nationwide Life Ins. Co.*[4] In this case, the request for the cash surrender value was completed by the policyowner prior to the death of the insured but was not mailed until after the insured's death. The insured died on November 17, and the request was not mailed until November 26. The court held, therefore, that the election to take the cash surrender value was based on a mutual mistake of fact—that is, the insured was dead and the face amount of the policy was payable when the request to receive the cash value was mailed. Since neither party knew this, the court held that the policyowner's election of the surrender value was not binding.

Surrender by an Incompetent. It is generally settled that if a life insurance contract is surrendered by an insane policyowner who is also the insured, and a cash value is paid that is less than the face amount of the insurance, the insurance company may nevertheless, upon the subsequent death of the insured, be required to pay the beneficiary the difference between the cash value, plus any other credits such as premiums, and the face amount which would have been due. In other words, the surrender may be avoided after the insured's death by his personal representative or heirs, just as would be true of any other contractual transaction of an incompetent.

15.4 Extended Insurance

Extended insurance is insurance in the face amount of the policy less any loan unpaid on the due date of the unpaid premium, extended for such period as the cash surrender value will provide. In most policies, this period is specified for each of the first 20 years, and, on request, it will be computed for other years.

Extended term insurance was the nonforfeiture option required by the earliest nonforfeiture laws, and it is still the most common automatic nonforfeiture benefit. Through the years a number of legal problems relating to this benefit have been decided by the courts, although present nonforfeiture statutes and policy wordings have done much to reduce the number of such problems that are encountered today.

One question that occasionally arises in this area concerns the right of the insurer to provide the extended insurance only with respect to the face amount of the policy, exclusive of additional benefits such as the accidental death benefit. This was the question in the Louisiana case of *Smith* v. *Great Southern Life Insurance Company.*[5] In this case, the

---

[4] 88 N.J. Sup. 136, 211 A. (2d) 204, 15 A.L.R. (3d) 1313 (1965).
[5] 176 So. (2d) 623 (C.A. La., 1965).

insured had obtained a policy on November 22, 1954, in the amount of $25,000 and in December, 1954, had added a double indemnity benefit under a supplemental contract. The latter provided in part as follows: "Failure to pay any premium when due under said policy or this Supplemental Contract shall automatically terminate this contract and all rights hereunder."

Premiums were paid until October 22, 1961, from which date the face amount of the policy was automatically continued as extended term insurance. The insured was accidentally killed on July 5, 1962, when he was struck by an airplane propeller. The company paid the face amount—$25,000—but refused to pay the accidental death benefit, basing its refusal on the wording of the supplemental contract quoted above.

The beneficiary sued for the accidental death benefit, contending that "Louisiana's public policy of extending insurance whenever possible, as well as the prohibition against an insurer taking premiums and failing to afford coverage" required that payment be made, and that insurance contracts should always be construed, if ambiguous, so as to afford coverage rather than deny it.

The court, however, said that this position was not supported by the contract, which expressly stated that the failure to pay any premium when due would automatically terminate the supplemental contract and that this wording was not in contradiction of the nonforfeiture statute. The company's position, therefore, that the accidental death benefit was not payable, was sustained.

A second type of question that occasionally arises with respect to the extended term insurance option concerns the effect to be given an outstanding policy loan in computing the amount of insurance to be extended. Present practice is to deduct the amount of the loan from the cash value and then to extend the amount of insurance that would have been payable on the due date of the last unpaid premium (face amount less the loan balance) for as long a period as the net cash surrender value will provide. This, of course, means that the amount of the loan is deducted from both the cash value used and the amount of insurance payable. The understandable, though not too logical, reaction of many people is that the loan is thus being deducted twice. A moment's thought reveals that this is not true, for any loss produced by the deduction of the loan from the amount of insurance is effectively balanced by the longer term for which the lower amount of insurance is provided. This approach is justified on the basis of fairness, since any other treatment of outstanding loans would provide a larger amount of insurance for the policyowner who lapsed his policy with an outstanding loan against it than if that same policy had been maintained on a premium-paying basis. For example, if the amount of insurance is $10,000 and a loan is in effect for $3,000, only $7,000 would be payable at the death of the insured as long as the loan remained unpaid and the policy remained on a premium-paying basis. If the policy went on extended term insurance on October 11, therefore, the loan must be deducted from the face amount and only the remainder carried as extended insurance or a larger amount would be payable at the death of the insured after October 11 than before. For this reason (and because for a given cash value, the reduced amount of insurance can be continued for a longer period), insurers reduce the face amount by the amount of the outstanding loan and continue the reduced amount as extended term insurance. The cases generally support this treatment.

15.5 Paid-Up Insurance

Generally speaking, the policyowner may, if he prefers, elect to have the net cash surrender value of his policy used to purchase fully paid insurance of the same duration and kind as the policy provides, in whatever amount the cash surrender value will purchase. This has been defined legally as "insurance for a limited amount for the life of the insured as distinguished from temporary extended insurance for the full amount of the policy."[6] It should be noted, however, that this definition applies only to whole life insurance. As actually used today, the benefit is available under endowment contracts and longer term contracts. In any case, it means paid-up insurance of the kind and for the duration provided by the policy immediately prior to the date of lapse. Thus, if the original policy was an endowment at 65, the reduced paid-up insurance will be endowment at 65.

At best, the nonforfeiture benefits of a life insurance policy are decidedly less advantageous than those provided while the policy is on a premium-paying basis. Sections of the policy that provide for disability and accidental death benefits are usually terminated on the date the policy lapses; and the nonforfeiture coverages themselves are limited. Extended term insurance is by its very nature impermanent; and reduced, paid-up policies typically provide benefits of only a fraction of the face amount of the policy. As a consequence, when the policyowner's life insurance needs are greatest, the extended term coverage may have expired or the reduced paid-up amount may be so small as to be of little benefit.

Thus, except in those rare instances where the need for life insurance protection has passed, the owner of a lapsed life insurance contract needs, sooner or later, to decide whether he wants to apply for new insurance or restore the lapsed policy to a premium-paying status. If he decides on the latter course, he will apply for reinstatement of his policy.

---

[6] 29 Am. Jur. 906.

C. REQUIREMENTS FOR REINSTATEMENT

The reinstatement provision of a life insurance contract generally provides that if the policy lapses for nonpayment of premium, it may be reinstated at any time within three (or sometimes five) years from date of lapse. The insured must furnish evidence of insurability, including good health, "satisfactory to the company," and all unpaid back premiums must be paid, plus interest. If a policy loan was in effect at the date of lapse, it must be repaid or restored as a lien against the policy.

It will be noted that the policyowner is not only required to furnish evidence of insurability, he must also pay all unpaid back premiums, with interest. Thus, if more than a slight period of time has passed since the policy lapsed, the policyowner may find it financially advisable to apply for a new policy.

If the older policy has been in effect for several years, however, it may include privileges of special value, particularly optional settlements, which either are no longer offered or, if available, provide for less favorable interest or mortality assumptions. Prematurity rights attain significant value sooner in a reinstated policy than in one newly issued, and this is usually an advantage. Ordinarily, also, the procedure for reinstatement is simpler than that involved in applying for a new policy. Other things being equal, therefore, there are often persuasive reasons why the policyowner may prefer to reinstate a policy already issued rather than to apply for a new one.

15.6 Evidence of Insurability

Why Necessary. Even though the right of reinstatement is a contractual right, it is nevertheless necessary for the insurer to require evidence of insurability in order to avoid antiselection. It has previously been noted that life insurance involves the application of the law of large numbers to a group of insureds whose risks of death are reasonably comparable. For this reason, the insurance company must have the opportunity at the outset to select the persons with whom it is willing to contract. To put it differently, all persons included in an insured group must be selected on an impartial basis in accordance with established principles of insurability.

Complete freedom to reinstate or not to reinstate, as the policyowner might choose, would destroy this impartial balance. It is understood that the insurability of the individual insureds will change as the contracts continue in operation. It might be argued, therefore, that to reinstate a lapsed policy after the insured has become uninsurable would place the company in no worse a position than if he had become uninsurable while the policy continued on a premium-paying basis. This would be true if all lapsed policies were eventually reinstated. As a matter of fact, however, they are not; and it is the insureds who have become uninsurable who ordinarily are most interested in reinstatement. Those who are still insurable may not be so interested. For this reason, the mortality experience of the company would be very adversely affected if reinstatement were permitted without restrictions of any kind. Evidence of insurability is required in order to prevent this kind of adverse selection. (It should be noted that because insurability is required for reinstatement, one who is eligible to reinstate a lapsed policy would always have available the alternative procedure of having a new policy issued.)

15.7 The Meaning of Insurability

The word "insurability" has such a definite and technical meaning in life insurance that it is somewhat surprising to find that there is an extensive history of litigation over its meaning with respect to the reinstatement process. At the present time, it seems hardly open to question that the word, as used in connection with reinstatement, should have exactly the same meaning, except as to age, that it had when the original application was received. Thus the company is free to consider such factors as habits, occupation, finances, and so on, as well as the good health of the applicant in an application for reinstatement just as if it were considering an application for a new policy of life insurance. However, this has not always been true.

Prior to 1906, the usual requirement for reinstatement was expressed as "good health." After the Armstrong Investigation, however, the standard policy provision statute used the phrase "evidence of insurability satisfactory to the company." Today the phrase "evidence of insurability" is most commonly used, often with the words "including good health" to make the requirement as clear as possible.

With only a few exceptions, the courts have held that "insurability" is a broader term than "good health" and thus includes other factors as well. One of the clearest expressions of this point of view is found in the case of *Kallman* v. *Equitable Life Assurance Society*.[7] In this case the policyowner met the requirements of insurability as far as health was concerned, but reinstatement was refused because of his financial situation and the large amount of life insurance (in excess of $159,000) he was already carrying. The company's refusal was challenged in a court action a few months after the applicant had committed suicide. The court upheld the company's decision, saying:

> The distinction between "good health" and "insurability" might be illustrated in the case of a criminal condemned to death. On the eve of his execution he might be found to be in perfect physical condition, but

---

[7] 248 A.D. 146, 288 N.Y.S. 1032 (1936).

it could not be reasonably contended that his situation did not affect his insurability. There are numerous circumstances which affect insurability. In *Ginsberg* v. *Eastern Life Insurance Co. of New York,* 118 N.J. Eq. 223, 178 A. 378, affirmed 120 N.J. Eq. 110, 184 A. 348, the Court said that it is common knowledge that an insurance company will not reinstate a policy where it is known that the insured is financially insolvent and the circumstances (show) probability of suicide. . . .

We are of the opinion that the language of the statute and of the policy "evidence of insurability satisfactory to the company" does not limit the inquiry upon an application for reinstatement to the good health or good physical condition of the insured. . . . Here, the insured's pecuniary circumstances coupled with his heavy over insurance, entirely out of line with his incoming financial condition, had a definite bearing upon his longevity and created a moral hazard which directly affected his insurability.

Minority Decisions. Two cases are frequently cited as authority for holding that evidence of insurability must be confined to evidence of good health. One is the case of *Sussex* v. *Aetna Life Assurance Company,*[8] a Canadian case decided in 1917, and the other is *Missouri State Life Insurance Co.* v. *Hearne,*[9] a Texas case decided in 1920. In the Hearne case, the decision in the Sussex case was cited with approval. It seemed probable, however, that special facts of the earlier case led to a more limited interpretation than would usually be applicable and that this point may not have been clearly apparent to the court in the later case.

In the Sussex case, the insured had been a commercial traveler when he obtained the insurance, but he was a member of the armed services when he applied for reinstatement of the policy. The policy itself contained a provision reading as follows: "This policy contains no restrictions regarding change of occupation, residence, travel, or service in the militia or army or navy in time of war or in time of peace. . . ."

The insurance company refused to reinstate the policy except with restrictions concerning service in the armed forces, but the trial court held that "proof of insurability" meant only the condition of the insured's health. Since the policy specifically said it contained no restrictions regarding "service in the militia or army or navy," this seemed a reasonable conclusion. However, so narrow an interpretation of the phrase "proof of insurability" would not necessarily be applicable in every situation, as was suggested in the Hearne case, where the court broadened it to include an insurable interest.

In summary, therefore, there is some limited authority to support the contention that insurability means nothing more than good health and an insurable interest. The weight of authority, however, is to the effect that insurability is definitely a broader term and includes all matters which

---

[8] 33 Dominion Law Reports 549, 38 Ontario Law Reports 365 (1917).
[9] 226 S.W. 789 (Tex. Civ. App., 1920).

would have been considered by the company on an original application except age.

15.8 Satisfactory to the Company

There have been a number of different interpretations of the meaning of the phrase "satisfactory to the company" as applied to evidence of insurability. For instance, it has been held that the judgment and conscience of the officers of the company are absolutely controlling,[10] and yet, by contrast, it has also been held that if there is reasonable compliance with the insurer's requirements relating to insurability, reinstatement should be compelled.[11]

The majority rule is that the courts will consider the practices of other insurance companies and judge whether the decision of the company is reasonable on that basis. This position is summarized by the court in the case of *Kennedy* v. *Occidental Life Insurance Company*,[12] as follows:

> The overwhelming weight of authority is to the effect that an agreement to reinstate an insurance policy upon "satisfactory evidence" of insurability does not give the insurer the power to act arbitrarily or capriciously, but that evidence which would be satisfactory to a reasonable insurer is all that is required.

D. THE APPLICATION FOR REINSTATEMENT

15.9 Effect of Application

The conditions set forth in the reinstatement provision of a life insurance policy are conditions precedent. Therefore, if they are not met when the policyowner applies for reinstatement, the reinstatement will not become effective. Thus, if the conditions are not met when application for reinstatement is made and if the insured dies before a decision is made by the insurer, the beneficiary can receive only whatever nonforfeiture benefits may still be in effect under the lapsed policy. In other words, simply completing an application for reinstatement is not enough to effect reinstatement if all of the conditions are not met.

Assume, however, that the requirements set forth in the policy provision have been met. The policyowner has furnished evidence of insurability, including evidence of good health, and submitted his check for all back premiums with interest. This information reaches the company just before notice of the insured's accidental death. Here, it seems obvious

---

[10] *Conway* v. *Minnesota Mutual Life Insurance Company*, 62 Wash. 49, 112 P. 1106 (1911).

[11] *Lane* v. *New York Life Insurance Co.*, 147 S.C. 333, 145 S.E. 196 (1928).

[12] 18 Cal. (2d) 627, 117 P. (2d) 3 (1951).

that the situation is different. The company has not accepted the application, it is true; but it has not declined it either. Thus, since the expressed conditions have been met, there is a clear-cut legal question as to whether the company must specifically approve the application for reinstatement in order for it to become effective.

15.10 Two Main Groups of Court Decisions

There are two main groups of court decisions as to whether the insurer must approve an application for reinstatement before it becomes effective. One group takes the position that if the specified conditions have been met and application has been made for reinstatement, it is of no consequence that the insured may have died before the company has had the opportunity to act upon the application. In other words, if the specified conditions have been met, reinstatement is automatic as of the date of the request, when it has been received.

Illustrative of this line of decisions is a Colorado case[13] in which the insured had applied for reinstatement, furnishing evidence of insurability satisfactory to the company and otherwise meeting all requirements specified in the policy provision. Before the company had approved the application, the insured was killed in an automobile accident. There had been some delay in checking his answers to the application questions concerning visits to a physician, but the visits proved not to have involved a condition of any significance as far as insurability was concerned. The court held that, under these conditions, reinstatement was effective, saying:

> . . . Where a policy contains a provision of this kind, where proof of insurability which is not open to valid objection as to form or substance is submitted within the authorized time, where payment of all premiums then in arrears plus interest thereon is tendered, where the insured thus fully complies with the conditions of his contract, and where his death is wholly accidental and in no way involved in his proof of insurability, the policy is reinstated and the restoration relates back to the time of the submission of the application and the tender of the premiums.

Under this line of decisions, if all conditions have been met, the reinstatement automatically becomes effective as of the date of the request, and changes in insurability between that date and the date of approval by the company do not affect the situation.

A second group of cases treat the application for reinstatement as an offer which must be accepted like any other contractual offer, although they may reach this conclusion by different routes. Thus, some courts take the position that reinstatement itself is a contract, separate and

---

[13] *Bowie* v. *Bankers Life Co.*, 105 F. (2d) 806 (C.C.A. Colo., 1939).

distinct from the life insurance contract. Others view reinstatement as a transaction that creates a new contract of life insurance. Under either of these approaches, the reinstated policy is held not to become effective until the application for reinstatement has been accepted in accordance with basic principles of contract law, or until a reasonable length of time has elapsed following the request for reinstatement. This means that the standard requirements of offer and acceptance are held to apply, and thus it is necessary that the offer be accepted during the lifetime of the offeror, in this case the policyowner.

A number of courts take the position that the insurance company must be permitted a reasonable length of time in which to approve or disapprove the application for reinstatement. If the insured should die during that period of time, the policy is not in effect on the reinstated basis. What constitutes a reasonable length of time is a question of fact to be decided by the jury; and, as so determined, it has varied from as little as one week to as much as 15 months.

As a general rule, the courts hold that an unreasonable delay in approving or declining an application for reinstatement has the effect of waiving the insurance company's right to decline reinstatement of the policy. Illustrative of this point of view is the language of the court in the case of *Froehler* v. *The North American Life Insurance Co. of Chicago*,[14] an Illinois case decided in 1940. Strictly speaking, this case involved the question of material misrepresentation in the application for reinstatement. However, the evidence showed no reason to believe that the insured knew of his impaired physical condition (a brain tumor) at the time he completed the application for reinstatement. With respect to the question of delay, the court said:

> In his original policy of insurance the deceased bought and paid for a right to be reinstated after default in payment of premium upon furnishing evidence of insurability satisfactory to the company, and the payment of all past-due premiums with interest. The record shows that he was solicited to reinstate his policy and that he furnished the company all the evidence that it required of his insurability. It is unnecessary for us to decide, and, therefore, we do not decide, whether the company might thereafter have required further evidence. . . .
>
> The record shows without dispute that the insured had furnished all the evidence he had been asked to furnish and that that evidence was entirely satisfactory. The jury found it was honestly given and the situation was no different than if the insured had been struck by lightning or hit by a truck on May 15, 17, or 19, 1933. The company had no contractual right to hold the deceased's money while it delayed for an unreasonable length of time a fulfillment of the contractual right to reinstatement. Two juries have found that it did so, and at the same time

---

[14] 374 Ill. 17, 27 N.E. (2d) 833 (1940).

have found that the insured, honestly and in good faith, complied with the terms of his contract by furnishing all the evidence of insurability required by the company.

A similar result was reached in the case of *Waldner* v. *Metropolitan Life Insurance Company,*[15] where the court said:

> . . . The defendant could not indefinitely hold the application for reinstatement without disapproving it, retain the money of the insured until long after her death, and thereafter escape liability on the ground the insured had not provided satisfactory proof of insurability. In *Andrus* v. *Insurance Assn.,* 168 Mo. 151, 67 S.W. 582, it was said:
>
> "The company must take one horn of the dilemma or the other. It cannot retain the benefits and deny the existence of the contract. If it does not wish the receipt of the premium to have the effect in law of reinstating the policy or of preventing a forfeiture, it must refuse to receive the money until the health certificate is filed and until the president and medical director act."

15.11 The Legal Nature of the Right

As a general rule, the parties to the contract are held to have the right to specify in the policy the requirements that must be met to make a reinstatement effective. Thus if the policy itself requires that the application for reinstatement be approved by the company, that requirement will be enforced. However, in one leading case—*Kennedy* v. *Occidental Life Insurance Co.*[16]—the nature of the reinstatement process was held to be such that a requirement of this kind, included in the application for reinstatement, was invalid. This case contains such an excellent summary of the different approaches to this question that it is quoted here at some length:

> Courts are not in agreement as to the legal effect of reinstatement clauses in insurance policies. Some courts have held that an application for reinstatement of a lapsed policy constitutes an offer to enter into a new contract which must be accepted by the insurer before any contract exists between the parties. . . . Under this theory the insurer's agreement to waive the lapsing of the policy will be treated as consideration for the agreement of the insured to be bound by any new terms imposed in the application for reinstatement (*Foley* v. *New World Life Ins. Co., supra*) and no recovery may be had for any loss occurring before the insurer has accepted the application for reinstatement, either expressly or, perhaps, by allowing an unreasonable time to lapse without acting thereon. . . .
>
> We are of the opinion, however, that reinstatement under a policy such as is present in this case does not involve the formation of a new contract.

---

[15] 149 Kan. 287, 87 P. (2d) 515 (1939).
[16] 18 Cal. (2d) 627, 117 P. (2d) 3 (1951).

By the terms of the policy the insured is given a right to reinstatement after lapse upon compliance with certain conditions. During the period in which reinstatement is possible the policy is not void but merely suspended. The right to revive the policy by reinstatement is a valuable contractual right, the consideration for which is found in the premiums paid and to be paid under the original policy, and the insurer has no arbitrary or discretionary right to refuse reinstatement if all the conditions therefor have been complied with. These views are supported by the weight of authority. . . .

Applying this theory of the nature of reinstatement, we hold that the provision in the application for reinstatement that it should not be effective until approved at the home office of the company during the lifetime of the insured cannot vary the terms of the original policy. The insured had a contractual right to be reinstated under the terms of his policy and any agreement to impose different terms is unsupported by consideration. . . .

Summary. Most commentators on this question simply say that some courts hold reinstatement to be automatic if the requirements have been met and application made prior to the date of the insured's death. Other courts hold that the application for reinstatement must be accepted by the company and that such acceptance must be accomplished during the lifetime of the insured or it will not be effective. In the Kennedy case, quoted above, the court says that the weight of authority supports the view that reinstatement is a valuable contractual right and the insurer has no arbitrary or discretionary right to refuse reinstatement if all the conditions have been complied with.

It is almost impossible to state that one view or another is the "majority" holding. This is because so many of the cases which, numerically, might support one view or the other are early cases involving different policy wording and different economic circumstances. The law of the life insurance contract is constantly changing, and the impact of financial and economic factors is nowhere more important than in this area of the effect of lapse and reinstatement. In considering trends, however, the language of *Kennedy* v. *Occidental Life Insurance Company* is undoubtedly significant as indicating a trend toward emphasizing the "contractual right" approach to reinstatement—that is to say, that reinstatement is a contractual right which the policyowner has bought and paid for and the insurer cannot arbitrarily refuse reinstatement if the conditions have been met.

By what seems to be the majority line of decisions, the application for reinstatement is acknowledged to be different from an application for a new policy. Reinstatement is itself a contractual right, and ordinarily it cannot be exercised after the contract has been terminated by surrender for cash. This is clearly spelled out in the standard statutory language requiring the policy provision, as follows:

> A provision that if in event of default in premium payments the value of the policy shall have been applied to the purchase of other insurance as provided for in this section, and if such insurance shall be in force and the original policy shall not have been surrendered to the company and cancelled, the policy may be reinstated within three years from such default, upon evidence of insurability satisfactory to the company. . . .[17]

As a general rule, companies are more liberal than the statute requires, with respect to the status of the policy, when granting reinstatement. If the statute were interpreted literally, reinstatement would be allowed only under cash value policies and then only as long as the policy remained in force under one of the nonforfeiture provisions. Under the typical policy provision concerning reinstatement, however, it is not necessary that the policy shall have remained in force under one of the nonforfeiture options; and term insurance policies customarily include the reinstatement provisions even though no nonforfeiture benefits are available under them. However, it is relatively standard practice to specify in the reinstatement provision that reinstatement will be available "if the policy has not been surrendered for its cash value." Thus reinstatement is permitted, subject to the conditions set forth in the policy provision, if the policy has not been surrendered and terminated.

At the time of reinstatement, therefore, the contract is already in operation in a limited sense. The motor is still idling though the car is not in motion. The application for reinstatement is, in a sense, only the shifting of gears that moves the policy out of the extended term or reduced paid-up insurance status, or even a lapsed status, and puts it back into operation on a premium-paying basis. Accordingly, the majority of courts hold that reinstatement is not a separate contract and that the process of reinstatement is not the effecting of a new contract but rather the exercise of a contractual right.

Because the policyowner has this contractual right to restore the original policy to full force and effect, the status of the reinstated contract has presented a number of questions through the years. For one thing, does the insurer have the right to impose new conditions in connection with the restored policy? For another, is the reinstated policy contestable, assuming that the original period of contestability has expired? A third question relates to the effect of suicide of the insured following reinstatement but after the original suicide period under the policy has expired.

15.12 Addition of Conditions

Because reinstatement is a contractual right, it is generally held that the insurance company cannot impose additional conditions in connection with reinstatement. This problem arises in a number of areas. Perhaps the

[17] Illinois Revised Statutes, Chapter 73, Sec. 836 (i) (1971).

most important is that of the war hazard clauses. Assume, for example, that at a time when the company was issuing policies without war hazard limitations of any kind, it issued to one Joseph Conley a policy for $12,500 at age 24. Two years later the policy lapsed for nonpayment of premiums. Now, two years later, Joe applies for reinstatement. He offers evidence of insurability and pays the unpaid back premiums with interest. At this time the company is issuing all its policies with a war hazard rider if the applicant is between the ages of 18 and 45. Can the company include a war clause in Joe's reinstated policy, as it is currently doing in every new policy issued to anyone in Joe's age group?

The cases seem clear that the company cannot do this. The policy owner has a contractual right to restore his original policy to premium payment status if he furnishes evidence of insurability, including good health, and pays the back premiums with interest. Once he has done this, the company cannot impose additional conditions that were not included in the original policy.

Illustrative of this holding is the case of *Schiel et al.* v. *New York Life Ins. Co.,*[18] which arose in Arizona and was decided in 1950 by the United States District Court, District of Arizona. In this case the insurer had permitted reinstatement of a policy on the life of a young prospective pilot, but only on condition that the double indemnity provision in the lapsed policy be omitted from the policy after reinstatement and an aviation exclusion clause be included. The original policy was free of all conditions pertaining to legitimate occupations, whether involving the armed services or not. The court said:

> . . . The Company made no claim that Schiel had become uninsurable for ordinary life purposes in the amount originally written; in fact it conceded by its conduct that he was insurable for those purposes and in that amount. It declined, however, to reinstate the ordinary life policy except upon a condition importing a concept of insurability at variance with the policy as written. This we think it might not do.
>
> An understanding of the view taken may require some further analysis of the terms of the original policy. The clause relating to occupation has been quoted earlier. It provides that the policy is free of conditions as to residence, travel, occupation, and military and naval service, *except as to provisions and conditions relating to double indemnity, etc.* . . . In respect of the ordinary life coverage, however, the insurer had contracted that the policy was free of conditions pertaining to any legitimate occupation, whether in connection with the armed services or otherwise. The condition imposed on reinstatement of the ordinary life coverage for all practical purposes nullified the occupation clause (in the original policy). Under guise of reinstatement the insurer undertook to rewrite the contract in such fashion as to repudiate a risk assumed at the outset. If it could do

---

[18] 178 F. (2d) 729 (C.A. Ariz., 1949).

that it could with equal facility have excluded altogether the risks of military service or travel, whereas the insured's liberty of action in all those matters was a measure of his insurability fixed and determined by the original contract. Without further laboring the point, we add only that the word "reinstate," as used in the policy, is entitled to be given its ordinary meaning, which is to restore to a former state or position.

This case states what is undoubtedly the general rule, that the provisions of a reinstated policy cannot be modified by new conditions imposed in connection with the reinstatement process. It is summarized in a more recent case as follows:

> An application for reinstatement, however, if accepted by the insurer, does not alter the terms and conditions of the basic contract of insurance; they customarily are already embodied in the policy itself, including any endorsements or documents attached. Upon reinstatement, the terms and conditions of the original policy do not change; premium rates, cash surrender value, loan value, beneficiary designation, an insured's indebtedness under the policy—in short, all basic obligations and rights—remain the same. The reinstatement provision is merely another contingent contractual feature of the policy pursuant to which the insured, having permitted his policy to lapse, is entitled, upon compliance with the conditions therein, including production of satisfactory evidence of insurability, to reinstatement of the original contract.[19]

15.13 Contestability of the Reinstated Policy

There are three main groups of court decisions concerning the operation of the incontestable clause following reinstatement of a life insurance policy. One group takes the position that once the original contestable period has expired, the insurer is powerless to contest the policy on any grounds going to the essential validity of the contract. Thus, even if reinstatement has been procured by fraud or material misrepresentation, if the original contestable period has expired, the policy remains incontestable for any reason after reinstatement.

Illustrative of decisions falling in this group is the case of *Munn* v. *Robison et al.*, a case that arose in Arkansas and was decided in 1950.[20] In that case the company sought to deny liability under policies in the amounts of $1,000 and $6,000 on the grounds of fraud in the applications for reinstatement. The plaintiffs challenged this defense on the grounds that the incontestable clause had expired prior to the reinstatement.

With respect to reinstatement and the incontestable clause, the court said:

---

[19] *Occidental Life Insurance Company of California* v. *Fried,* 245 F. Supp. 211 (U.S.D.C.D. Conn., 1965).

[20] *Munn* v. *Robison, et al.,* 92 F. Supp. 60 (D.C. Ark., 1950).

Among the provisions of the policy is one giving the insured the absolute right, under the facts of this case, to reinstate. John Hancock accepted and approved each application for reinstatement, which, under the Arkansas law, is conclusive that the condition "production of evidence of insurability satisfactory to the Company" was satisfied. Thus, while the policy may have lapsed for non-payment of premiums, it was, by virtue of this provision, not a "dead" contract, because the reinstatement was made under a then existing right of the insured conferred thereby[21] rather than a gratuitous privilege conferred by John Hancock. And, it is settled beyond dispute in Arkansas that "the reinstated policy is not a new contract, but is the same old policy." *N.Y. Life Ins. Co.* v. *Dandridge*, 202 Ark. 112, 149 S.W. 2d 45. As expressed in *N.Y. Life Ins. Co.* v. *Campbell*, 191 Ark. 54, 57, 83 S.W. 2d 542:

"It necessarily follows from what we have said, and the cases cited in support thereof that the reinstatement of the insured by appellant created no new contract between them, but simply revives and reinstates the original contract and all provisions thereof, and subsequently the rights and obligations of the respective parties thereto must be measured thereby."

In *N.Y. Life Ins. Co.* v. *Dandridge, supra,* the court said:

"Most of the courts, holding a contrary view to ours, seem to base their reasons on the idea that reinstatement creates a new contract and that the incontestable clause, although barred by lapse of time, is revived and becomes available to contest a reinstated policy for fraud. Our idea is that to so hold, something must be read into the policy that is not there, but might have well been there, had the company so desired. Such a holding changes the incontestable clause to read that "this policy shall be incontestable after two years from its date of issue or after the date of any reinstatement thereof." It is well settled that courts do not or should not, make contracts for the parties, and the contract as written will be most strongly construed against the party writing it."

The majority line of decisions holds that the contestable period runs again for the same period after reinstatement, but that the new contestable period applies only to statements made in the reinstatement application. A third and very minor group of cases hold that only the original contestable period is effective with respect to the policy as a whole, but reinstatement itself is a separate agreement, which, since it has no incontestable provision, can be contested for fraud at any time. An excellent summary of the three different views of this question is found in *Johnson* v. *The Great Northern Life Insurance Company*,[22] a North Dakota Supreme Court case decided in January, 1945. In it the court said:

. . . Neither the statutes nor the policy under consideration contain any provision to the effect that the incontestable clause in any way limits the

---

[21] In other words, the right of reinstatement was conferred by the policy, not gratuitously granted by the insurer.

[22] 73 N.D. 572, 17 N.W. (2d) 337 (1945).

right to contest a reinstatement. In such circumstances there seem to be three rules which find support in the authorities. One of these is that an incontestable clause in a policy has no application whatever to a reinstatement and the reinstatement may be contested at any time. Another is that an incontestable clause will prevent a contest of a reinstatement if the time in which the original policy was contestable has expired. The third rule is that the incontestability provision applies to the reinstatement in the same manner as it did to the original issuance of the policy; that is to say, the time within which the reinstatement may be contested is the same period thereafter as that within which the original policy might have been contested, and the grounds for such contest are limited to those which arise out of the negotiations leading to the reinstatement.

The rule last stated appears to be the majority rule. . . . It is also the rule which seems to us to be best founded upon reason. We would reject the rule first above stated, because, while not contrary to the contract or to express statute, it is contrary to legislative policy fairly to be inferred. This rule rests also upon the conception that the reinstatement is a new contract which is contrary to our holding in *Rott* v. *Provident Life Insurance Co., supra.* The second rule completely eliminates any requirements of good faith in the negotiations for reinstatement and is contrary to our holding in *New York Life Insurance Company* v. *Hansen, supra.*

We therefore adopt the rule last stated and hold that defendant may contest its reinstatement of the instant policy only during the same period of time thereafter as was fixed for contesting the original policy, or upon grounds expressly excluded from the operation of the incontestability provision.

The majority rule was further explained in the case of *Sellwood* v. *Equitable Life Insurance Co.,*[23] as follows:

. . . The authorities reason that, since it is fundamental that fraud vitiates everything into which it enters . . . it cannot be supposed that the parties intended that an insured should have what Judge Learned Hand . . . characterized as "a license forever to cheat the insurer"; and that the reasons for the public policy that, absent fraud, statements by an insured in an application for insurance should be deemed to be representations and not warranties and that a limit should be set on the time within which the insurer should have the right to contest the policy for false statements of the insured in an application, apply to an application for reinstatement the same as to one for the original issuance of the policy itself. This view has been adopted by many authorities, regardless of whether the reinstatement be regarded as the continuation of the original contract of insurance or the making of a new one. . . . We adopt the rule that, upon reinstatement of a lapsed life insurance policy, the incontestable clause runs anew as to misrepresentations in the application for reinstatement. This rule is not only supported by the weight of authority, but also is a just and fair one.

---

[23] 42 N.W. (2d) 346 (Minn., 1950).

As more and more states resolve the question by statutory enactment, they adopt this majority rule. For instance, the Florida Insurance Code, adopted in 1959, contains the following:

> A reinstated policy of life insurance . . . may be contested on account of fraud or misrepresentation of facts material to the reinstatement only for the same period following reinstatement and with the same conditions and exceptions as the policy provides with respect to contestability after original issuance.[24]

Attachment of Copy of Application. As a general rule, when a request for reinstatement reaches the company, the policy is in the hands of the policyowner. For that reason, the courts have generally held that it is not necessary that a copy of the reinstatement application be attached to the policy in order for the insurer to avail itself of a defense based upon fraud or misrepresentation in the application. However, some of the states have enacted statutes requiring the insurer to furnish a copy of the application to the policyowner or beneficiary on request, and where there is an applicable statute it will, of course, be given effect.

15.14 Reinstatement and the Suicide Clause

Where the operation of the suicide clause of a reinstated policy is concerned, the majority of courts have held that reinstatement merely continues the original contract in force so that the original suicide period, having once expired, is not thereafter revived by the reinstatement process.

Most of the courts reach this conclusion on the theory that reinstatement does not create a new contract but merely revives the original policy and continues it in force as from its original date. In one of the outstanding cases presenting the question,[25] Judge Learned Hand favored this theory but felt it necessary to yield to the weight of authority in his jurisdiction. Cases in his jurisdiction had favored the theory that a reinstated policy must be considered as having been reissued on the date of reinstatement. Even adopting that view, however, Judge Hand held that the suicide clause must be read as effective from the original issue date, the majority conclusion. This much-cited case presents an excellent example of Judge Hand's approach to a legal problem, as follows:

> Were we free to decide the point as *res nova*,[26] we should say that the reinstatement of a lapsed policy is not a new contract at all, when the insured can revive it merely by satisfying the company of his insurability

---

[24] Florida Insurance Statutes, Sec. 627.0221.

[25] *Tatum* v. *Guardian Life Insurance Company,* 75 F. (2d) 476, 98 A.L.R., 341 (C.C.A. N.Y., 1935).

[26] A "new subject in question," one not previously considered by the courts of the jurisdiction.

and by paying the arrears. Those are the conditions upon what by the lapse has become a conditional obligation; but which is still an obligation from which the insurer cannot withdraw at will, being bound to approve if he is in fact satisfied. We should not be disposed therefore to go along with *International Ins. Co.* v. *Mowbray*, 22 F. 2d 952 (C.C.A. 7). As in other similar situations satisfaction is a question of fact, which, once proved, makes the obligation absolute. . . . The insurer's approval is only an admission of satisfaction with which the insured might dispense if the insurer refused it, when in fact satisfied; he might even compel the reissuance of the policy by specific performance. *Mutual Life Co.* v. *Lovejoy*, 203 Ala. 452, 456, 83 So. 591. . . . In that view of course the policy, when reinstated, remains what it was before; its terms cannot be read as though it had its inception at the time of reinstatement; and those cases which allow the insurer to contest the reinstatement for a fraud occurring after the policy has become incontestable, are only instances where the insured has never in fact fulfilled the prescribed conditions. Though he has procured an admission from the insurer, the fraud in its procurement destroys its evidential force. Cases like *Teeter* v. *United States Life Ins. Ass'n*, 159 N.Y. 411, 54 N.E. 72, holding that the reinstated policy again becomes incontestable when the original period has elapsed after reinstatement, may possibly accord with this view; but if so, it must be confessed it is only by a considerable wrench of the language.

However, the great weight of authority is flatly against our analysis of the situation. . . . we feel bound to yield to the preponderant opinion. But although we are therefore to consider the policy as though it had been issued anew on February 14, 1933, it by no means follows that in construing it we must read it as though it spoke throughout from that date. By its very terms the policy is "reinstated:" the parties have thus chosen a word which presupposes, not a new contract, but the revival of an old one. The insured must pay not a single premium, but all arrears; and thereafter only at the old rate, however many years have passed. All benefits—e.g., the surrender and loan value, term and paid-up insurance —go again into force as of the original date; they do not begin anew. Moreover, in the case at bar the defense of suicide was limited to one year from "the date hereof;" that is, the date upon the policy. In several cases the insurer has been held strictly to this when it varied from the date of actual inception. . . . Perhaps too the contrast between that phrase in the policy at bar and "the date of issue" in the incontestability clause may be taken as some indication of a change of intent. Judged textually, therefore, there is very good reason for holding that the clause speaks from the original date. It is of course true that our interpretation exposes the insurer to a risk which it would otherwise escape. An insured who had let a policy lapse might at any time within three years conceive the notion of getting it reinstated and then killing himself. Nevertheless we are disposed to hold that even on the theory of a new contract, which we should not ourselves have adopted, the reinstated policy is to be referred *pro tanto* to the date of the original; at least that the insurer who prepared the instrument must bear the doubts, so far as there are any. In the only decisions in which the point has arisen this has been the result. . . .

Those cases which allow the insurer to prove fraud in procuring the reinstatement though the period of incontestability has passed, do not indeed fall in so easily with the accepted view as with our own. They may nevertheless be made to fit with it. Though the new contract be a reissue of the policy as of the date of the renewal, it would force beyond all reason the meaning of the incontestability clause to say that it barred a fraud which did not even exist when the policy became incontestable. The cause is one of limitation, not a license forever to cheat the insurer; unless construed in that preposterous way it must be an exception to the general principle that the policy as reinstated speaks from its old date. It may be the only exception; at least the suicide clause is not one.

Judgment affirmed.

SUMMARY

If the Premium Is Not Paid

If a life insurance premium is not paid when due, or within the grace period, the policy is said to lapse. The word "lapse" may mean termination of the contract without further benefits, or it may mean termination except as to any nonforfeiture benefits that may be provided. If it is used in this latter sense, the policy is said to expire when the nonforfeiture benefits are exhausted.

The Nonforfeiture Benefits

If a life insurance contract lapses for nonpayment of premium after it has acquired a cash value, the policyowner may surrender it for its cash value or elect to have the policy continued, either as reduced paid-up or as extended term insurance. One of these latter benefits must be specified in the policy as the automatic nonforfeiture option.

Cash Surrender. The legal effect of a request for the surrender value of a life insurance contract becomes important in cases where the insured dies after having made application for the surrender value, but before payment has been made. Different views have been taken of this problem at different times. One analysis is that in electing to take the cash surrender value, the policyowner is making an offer. Acceptance on the part of the insurer is necessary before the surrender has been completed. The majority view is that the right to surrender a policy for its cash value is no different than any other policy option. Thus, it is a continuing, irrevocable offer on the part of the insurer which, if accepted in accordance with its terms, becomes a binding contract. Once the policyowner has exercised his right, therefore, the insurer has no alternative but to comply.

Extended Insurance. Extended insurance is insurance for the face amount of the policy less any unpaid loan, extended for such period of time as the net cash surrender value will purchase. The insurer is permitted to exclude the accidental death coverage from this nonforfeiture benefit. It is also customary to deduct the amount of any unpaid loan from the cash value as well as from the amount of insurance extended.

Paid-up Insurance. Paid-up insurance is insurance of the same duration and kind as provided by the policy, but in a reduced amount determined by the amount the net cash value will purchase.

Reinstatement

To restore a life insurance policy to its full value after lapse, it is necessary to reinstate it. The reinstatement provision permits this at any time within three (sometimes five) years after lapse, if all unpaid back premiums are paid, with interest; evidence of insurability is furnished; and any policy loan unpaid at date of lapse is repaid or restored as a lien against the policy.

Evidence of insurability is required in order to avoid adverse selection, and insurability for this purpose is generally held to have the same meaning, except as to age, that it had when the original application was considered.

The reinstatement requirements are conditions precedent and must be met at the time the policyowner applies for reinstatement or the reinstatement will not become effective. Whether the reinstatement is effective even though not yet approved at the death of the insured is a question that has been answered differently by different courts. One group of decisions takes the position that if the conditions have been met at the date of the insured's death, it is not necessary that the company shall have specifically approved the application for reinstatement. Where the view is taken that reinstatement is itself a separate contract, or where the process is viewed as creating a new contract, the customary view of offer and acceptance is followed; and it is necessary that the offer be accepted by the insurer during the lifetime of the offeror before the reinstatement will be effective.

It is generally held that the insurer must approve or disapprove the reinstatement application within a reasonable length of time or it is presumed to have approved it.

The parties to a life insurance contract are generally held to have the right to specify in the policy the requirements that must be met to reinstate a policy. Court decisions on the subject vary, but it would seem that the better approach is to consider that the policyowner has a contractual right to reinstatement and the insurer has no right to refuse if all the conditions have been complied with.

The Policy after Reinstatement

The majority of court decisions hold that a reinstated contract is not a new contract, although the exact nature of the legal status of the reinstated contract is sometimes in doubt. Because reinstatement is a contractual right, it is generally held that an insurer cannot impose new conditions—such as the addition of a war hazard limitation rider—in connection with the reinstatement.

The operation of the incontestable clause has also presented a problem. Some courts have taken the position that once the original contestable period has expired, the company may not thereafter contest the validity of the contract. A second group holds that a new contestable period begins with each reinstatement, so far as the reinstatement application is concerned; and a third group holds that reinstatement itself is a separate agreement, to which the incontestable provision does not apply. Thus it may be contested for fraud at any time.

Probably the majority rule is that the incontestable clause applies to reinstatement in exactly the same way it does to the original application process, and that reinstatement may be contested on a basis of material misrepresentation in the reinstatement application for a period of two years from the effective date of the reinstatement. This rule has been enacted into the insurance laws of some of the states.

Most courts hold that reinstatement has no effect on the suicide clause and once the suicide period has expired, the suicide of the insured is one of the risks assumed.

QUESTIONS FOR REVIEW

1. What two meanings are frequently given to the word "lapse"?
2. Summarize present statutory requirements concerning policy provisions for nonforfeiture benefits.
3. Outline the majority view as to the legal nature and operation of the cash surrender option.
4. What is the legal position of an insurer if a cash surrender value has been paid to an incompetent insured who later dies and whose personal representative then attempts to avoid the cash surrender transaction?
5. Outline briefly the limitations of the nonforfeiture benefits as compared to the benefits provided by a policy in force on a premium-paying basis.
6. List the requirements for reinstatement found in the usual reinstatement provision of a life insurance policy.
7. Why is evidence of insurability one of the requirements for reinstatement?
8. What is the majority decision concerning the meaning of the phrase "satisfactory to the company" in connection with the evidence of insurability required for reinstatement?

9. In legal terms, in what way does the application for reinstatement differ from the application for a new policy?

10. List and briefly discuss three different legal theories concerning the application of the incontestable clause with respect to reinstatement. Which is the majority rule?

11. State the majority rule with respect to the operation of the suicide clause after reinstatement of a policy.

Chapter Outline

Chapter 16

Other Rights by Operation of the Law

THE LIFE INSURANCE policy has previously been considered as property, with an emphasis upon the rights the policyowner may exercise solely because he owns the policy. Other people, too, may have or obtain rights under a life insurance contract by operation of the law, rather than by the terms of the contract. Wives or husbands in community property states, creditors of the insured under some circumstances, trustees in bankruptcy—these and others, under appropriate circumstances, may assert rights under the contract that are not expressly provided by the contract itself. Indeed, some of these rights may even be contrary to some of the policy provisions. The purpose of this chapter is to discuss the more important of these rights and the circumstances under which they may arise.

A. THE LIFE INSURANCE CONTRACT AND COMMUNITY PROPERTY

The settlers of this country who had a major voice in the formation of the Constitution of the United States and the constitutions of the earlier states of the union brought their ideas of law primarily from England. Thus, the life insurance contract had its origin and most of its development in a legal climate based upon the common law.

The explorers of the South and West, however, brought their ideas of law from the countries of their origin also—in this case France and Spain. For that reason, the legal systems of Arizona, California, Idaho, Louisiana, Nevada, New Mexico, Texas, and Washington are strongly influenced by, if not actually based upon, the legal systems of France and

Spain. As a result, all include a concept which is foreign to anything in the common law, the concept of community property.

16.1 What Community Property Is

The term "community property" refers to the property a married couple acquires during their marriage, in a community property state. Under community property law, husband and wife are considered to constitute a "community," and all property acquired during the marriage, through the skill or labor of either husband or wife, is considered as owned by both spouses in equal shares.

The effect of community property law upon the ownership rights under a life insurance contract differs under different circumstances and often from state to state. The fact that the life insurance contract developed primarily under common-law principles means that ownership rights are, in most states, interpreted in accordance with common-law principles. In community property states, however, the general principles of common law relating to ownership rights came into conflict with a completely different concept of ownership—that marriage itself establishes rights of ownership in the policyowner's spouse. Court decisions have resolved some of the questions that have resulted; special statutes have resolved others. As is true of common-law jurisdictions, however, the same question may be decided one way in one community property jurisdiction and differently in another. The following discussion attempts to outline some of the major areas of concern in community property jurisdictions and some of the ways in which the more significant questions have been answered.

16.2 General Rules of Community Property Law

There are a few general rules of community property law which are helpful as starting points in considering life insurance problems. First, property is either community property or it is not, at the time it is acquired; and its status does not change throughout the marriage. Property acquired before marriage is separate property and remains separate property. Property acquired after marriage, except by gift or inheritance, is community property and remains community property.

Second, property acquired with community funds is community property. Thus, a contract of life insurance purchased with community funds constitutes community property, and the spouse of the owner has community property rights in it. For example, if premiums are paid or assets are purchased out of the husband's earnings, the policy or other assets constitute community property, but this is equally true if premiums are paid or assets purchased out of the wife's earnings. Ordinarily, if both community property and separate funds are used in acquiring property, the property so acquired is owned by the husband and wife in the same proportions as the funds that were used.

Finally, although ownership of community property is in the husband and wife equally, the right of management is usually[1] in the husband, subject to some very definite limitations. For instance, the husband has the right to control or sell community property, but he cannot ordinarily make a gift of it except for the benefit of the community, and he can never exercise his right of management to defraud his wife.

16.3 When a Life Insurance Policy Is Community Property

In considering the question of community property rights in connection with the life insurance contract, there are two broad classes of policies: (1) those purchased prior to marriage, and (2) those applied for and issued to the policyowner after marriage.

Policies Purchased before Marriage. When a person applies for and is issued a life insurance policy prior to marriage, the policy is separate property at the time it is issued; and in most community property states, it remains separate property even though premiums are paid on it after marriage out of community funds. Decisions in Louisiana, New Mexico, and Texas follow this rule. At the death of the insured, if the spouse is not the beneficiary, the community is entitled to reimbursement out of the proceeds for any premiums paid out of community funds.

In California and Washington, if a policy is issued prior to the marriage of the insured but premiums are paid out of community property after the marriage, the contract is owned by the husband and wife in proportions equal to the ratio of community funds to separate funds which were used in payment of premiums. The proceeds at the death of the insured are treated as part community property and part separate property in the same proportions.

Policies Purchased after Marriage. When a person applies for and is issued a policy of life insurance during marriage, the premiums are customarily paid out of community funds, and the principal questions arise in connection with the beneficiary designation. If the policy is payable to the insured's estate and premiums have been paid out of community funds, the policy is ordinarily considered community property and the wife has a one-half interest in the proceeds. There are decisions to this effect in California, Louisiana, New Mexico, Texas, and Washington.

Where the wife is the named beneficiary and the premiums are paid out of community funds, the policy is also ordinarily considered to be

---

[1] Arizona and California have enacted legislation providing that management of community property shall be in husband and wife, jointly.

community property during the lifetime of the insured; but the proceeds, when paid, are the separate property of the wife. Thus, in California, if the wife is the beneficiary, premiums paid out of community property are considered gifts to her, and the proceeds are her separate property, although the policy is community property while the insured is living.

In New Mexico, the proceeds of a life insurance policy are the separate property of the wife if she is the named beneficiary when it is issued. However, the policy itself is community property, and it is subject to the management of the husband during the marriage and prior to his death.

16.4 Community Property Problems

Generally speaking, there are three distinct areas in which a community property problem is likely to arise under a life insurance contract. The question of management and control arises in connection with the exercise of prematurity rights, such as the rights to change the beneficiary and to surrender the policy for cash. Questions relating to the husband's power to make a gift arise in connection with beneficiary designations. Lastly, community property questions are particularly likely to arise in connection with the disposition of the proceeds at the death of the insured. In this discussion, therefore, the right to change the beneficiary will be considered first; second, the right to surrender the policy for cash; and third, the rights involved at the time the death benefit becomes payable.

The Right to Change the Beneficiary.   Naming someone other than the wife as beneficiary is essentially the same as making a gift to that person. Therefore, in states that recognize the husband's right to make gifts of community property, the courts also hold that he has the right to change the beneficiary designation under a policy insuring his life from his wife to someone else. If the husband's right to make gifts is not recognized, then he is held not to have the right to make a beneficiary change of this kind.

For example, Texas holds that the husband may make moderate gifts without the wife's consent as long as they are not in fraud of the wife's interests. Arizona courts also follow this theory, and Nevada has the same basic philosophy, although the point seems not to have been decided in connection with life insurance. In California, the husband cannot make a gift of more than one half the community property without his wife's consent. In that state, a change of beneficiary from the wife to someone else is valid unless the wife objects, but she has a right to one half of the proceeds if she gives notice of her claim prior to payment of the proceeds to the named beneficiary.

In Washington, the insured cannot name anyone other than his estate or his wife as beneficiary of a policy of life insurance on his life, if it is community property, without her consent. Such a designation is not merely voidable; it is void, and the wife is entitled to the entire proceeds.

The position taken by Louisiana courts is not quite so strict. There a change of beneficiary from the wife to the mother of the insured has been upheld as within the rights of the insured.

Surrender for Cash. The courts of three states—Texas, Washington, and California[2]—have specifically ruled that the cash surrender value of a life insurance contract is community property if premiums were paid out of community funds. Since surrender of the life insurance contract for cash is a management transaction, however, and since the husband is usually the manager of the community property, this would not seem ordinarily to present a problem. The fact that there are very few cases on this point would tend to bear this out.

The Death Benefit. The most significant community property problems in connection with the life insurance contract arise at the death of the insured; and, as might be expected, they manifest themselves most frequently under policies payable to someone other than the insured's wife. In such cases, under most community property laws, if the wife has not consented to the beneficiary designation or change, she retains her community property interest in the policy proceeds. The nature of this interest under the law of California is illustrated and described in the case of *Bazzell* v. *Endriss,* decided by the California District Court of Appeal, November 12, 1940.[3]

This case involved a claim by the widow of the insured for half of the proceeds of the policy (payable to the mother of the insured) on the grounds that premiums had been paid out of community property and she (the widow) had not consented to a gift to the mother. In the trial court, the decision was for the widow; and the sister of the insured, as executrix of the mother's estate, appealed. The basis of her claim was that the insured was indebted to his mother in an amount in excess of the amount of insurance and, therefore, the designation of the mother as beneficiary was not a gift.

The court quoted from an earlier case,[4] where the court had said:

> It is no doubt the settled law of this state that, where the premiums on an insurance policy issued on the life of a husband . . . are paid entirely from community funds, the policy is a community asset, and, in view of the provisions of section 172 of the Civil Code, the husband cannot make a valid gift thereof without the written consent of the wife; and that where the husband attempts to do so, by naming a third party as beneficiary, the

---

[2] See 172 S.W. (2d) 307 (Texas); 324 P. (2d) 1103 (Washington); and 6 Cal. Rptr. 45 (California).

[3] 41 Cal. App. (2d) 463, 107 P. (2d) 49 (1940).

[4] *Union Mutual Life Ins. Co.* v. *Broderick,* 196 Cal. 497, 507.

transaction as to the wife's share is voidable and subject to her right of revocation.

A similar view was also taken in a later case[5] as follows:

From the leading case of *New York Life Ins. Co.* v. *Bank of Italy*, 60 Cal. App. 602 [214 Pac. 61], through the many intervening cases, down to *Travelers Ins. Co.* v. *Fancher*, 219 Cal. 351 [26 Pac. (2d) 482], the only test applied to this problem has been whether the premiums (on a policy issued on the life of a husband . . . are paid entirely from community funds. If so, the policy becomes a community asset and the nonconsenting wife may recover an undivided one-half thereof "without regard" [as said in *Dargie* v. *Patterson*, 176 Cal. 714, 721, 169 Pac. 360] "to the amount or condition of the estate remaining in his [the husband's] hands at the time of his death," and we might add, without regard to the disproportionate size of the premium when compared with the face of the policy.

The court then analyzed these holdings and the decision in the lower court involving the present case as follows:

In the first cited case it was held that the change of beneficiary was made by reason of the fact that the insured was indebted to his sister, and that under such circumstances the change was made for a consideration and was not a gift. In the second case the trial court found against an indebtedness of the insured to his mother and the judgment for the widow was sustained.

In the present case the insured's mother was named at all times as the beneficiary. There is considerable evidence that the insured at various times, before and after marriage, had given certain sums of money to his mother. Bank accounts indicated also that the mother had withdrawn various amounts and delivered them to the insured for use in his business, for his hospital bills and different unexplained purposes. Appellant, the sister of the insured, testified that in April of 1937 her brother had said "I owe Mother $3,000." There was no showing that the mother had, since her husband's death, any source of income except that given her by her son, plus some indefinite amount earned by keeping a rooming house.

The court found that the naming of the mother as beneficiary constituted a voluntary gift without valuable consideration, and that at no time did the wife consent to a gift of her community interest in the policy. Reading the record in its entirety, and taking into consideration statements that prior to marriage the insured had contributed to his mother's support, and that she in turn had loaned money to establish him in business and to pay his hospital and other bills; also the fact that the widow paid the last premium during the insured's illness, and considering conflicting evidence and inferences that could be drawn from the testimony, we find ample evidence to sustain the trial court's conclusion. . . .

The trial court judgment for the widow was therefore affirmed.

The wife's interest in the proceeds of life insurance under the law of

---

[5] *Mundt* v. *Connecticut Life Ins. Co.*, 35 Cal. App. (2d) 416, 421 (1939).

the state of Washington is illustrated in the case of *California-Western States Life Insurance Company* v. *Jarman, Admx., Respondent, Tollette, Appellant,*[6] decided by the Washington Supreme Court in 1947. In that case, after an interlocutory (temporary) decree of divorce, the husband applied for and was issued a policy of life insurance on his own life, naming his mother as the beneficiary. On his death prior to the date the divorce decree would have become final, the company filed a bill of interpleader and asked the court to decide between the rights of the wife under the Washington community property laws and the mother as the named beneficiary under the policy. The court held in favor of the wife, as follows:

> Is the mother of an insured, named as his beneficiary in a life insurance policy, entitled to the proceeds of such policy, where her son paid one monthly installment of the annual premium while living separate and apart from his wife, who had obtained an interlocutory decree of divorce which did not become final because the insured died prior to the expiration of the statutory period of six months? That is the sole question, which is not an open one in this state, presented in the case at bar.
>
> In *Occidental Life Ins. Co.* v. *Powers*, 192 Wash. 475, 74 P. (2d) 27, 114 A.L.R. 531, we held that, when the premiums on life insurance are paid with community funds, the proceeds of the policy on the life of the husband constitute community property, and that the wife's interest in the community property is a vested interest, of which she cannot be deprived without consideration.
>
> . . . In *Hanley* v. *Most*, 9 Wn. (2d) 429, 115 P. (2d) 933, we cited with approval *Occidental Life Ins. Co.* v. *Powers, supra,* and held that a life insurance policy, on which the premiums were paid out of community funds, constitutes community property, and that the husband may not, without the consent of his wife, substitute his mother and his secretary as beneficiaries of such policy. . . .
>
> All property, with certain exceptions not pertinent in the case at bar, acquired after marriage by either husband or wife, or both, is community property. Everything that is produced by either spouse, whether it be by toil or talent, is earned by the community and belongs to the community. . . .
>
> . . . In the case at bar, there is no evidence to overcome the presumption that the proceeds of the insurance policy is community property; hence, that presumption is conclusive.
>
> . . . The right of respondent to the proceeds of the policy of insurance was not in any wise changed by the entry of the interlocutory order in the divorce action, for the reason that the marital status of the parties was not changed, and for the further reason that their respective property rights were never adjudicated. . . .
>
> . . . We are committed to the rule that an interlocutory decree of divorce abates and becomes a nullity for all purposes on the death of one

---

[6] 185 P. (2d) 494 (Wash., 1947).

of the parties prior to the entry of the final decree (21 Wash. L. Rev. 178), and that an interlocutory divorce decree, which had not become final at the time of the death of the insured, does not prevent a divorced wife from taking the proceeds of an insurance policy as a wife for the reason that, during the term of an interlocutory decree of divorce, the marital relation exists in law as well as in practical effect. 2 Couch, Cyclopedia of Insurance Law 1278.

. . . In the case at bar, the community property, the nature and extent of which are not disclosed by the record, remained in the hands and under the management of the husband. That property included the property then in existence; the interest, accumulations, and earnings—it included all property acquired after the marriage (Rem. Rev. Stat., Section 6892 [P.P.C. Sections 434–27]) which was not, and of course cannot now ever be, dissolved by a court.

The judgment for the wife was, therefore, affirmed.

16.5 Deferred Settlements

The significance of the wife's community property rights, as contrasted with the provisions of the contract itself, is interestingly emphasized in the case of *Tyre* v. *Aetna Life Insurance Co.*[7] In that California case, the insured named his wife as beneficiary under a $20,000 life insurance policy and elected a settlement agreement providing a life income to her with a 10-year certain period. In the event of her death prior to the end of the 10-year period, the guaranteed payments were to be continued to her children.

The wife did not consent to or know about the requested settlement agreement. After the insured's death, therefore, she requested the insurer to pay her the face amount in cash. The insurer refused, and she brought an action for $10,000 in cash as her community property interest, the remaining $10,000 to be paid under the life income option. The insurer contended that it was obligated under the contract to carry out the terms of the settlement agreement, and the trial court agreed, as did the District Court of Appeal. The Supreme Court did not agree, and reversed the decision, stating:

> Plaintiff could not avoid a contract entered into for a valuable consideration by her husband in the course of his lifetime management of the community personalty even though it was made without her consent and temporarily affected her control immediately following his death.

✸ ✸ ✸ ✸ ✸

> In the present case, however, the husband's election to have the policy proceeds paid as an annuity instead of in a lump sum was not an exercise of his nontestamentary power of management during his lifetime, but an

---

[7] 353 P. (2d) 725 (Cal., 1960).

attempt to dispose of proceeds after his death. Until he died he could elect to have the proceeds paid as a lump sum or as an annuity actuarially worth that sum. Of course, as between the husband and defendant there was consideration for the change in method of payment. The right to an annuity was consideration for the surrender of the right to a lump sum payment. Similarly there is consideration between the insurance company and the insured when the insured changes the beneficiary from one person to another. Nevertheless, it is settled that even though the insurance contract provides that the insured husband has the right to change the beneficiary without the wife's consent when she is named as such, any such change of beneficiary without her consent and without a valuable consideration other than substitution of beneficiaries is voidable, and after the death of the husband the wife may maintain an action for her community share in the proceeds of the policy. [citations.] These cases recognize that although the payment of insurance proceeds is a matter of contract between the insured and the insurer, the insured's exercise of his unilateral right under the contract to select the beneficiary is testamentary in character. Similarly, the insured's exercise of his unilateral right under the terms of the policy to determine whether the proceeds shall be paid as a lump sum or in the form of an annuity is testamentary in character. Section 201 of the Probate Code gives the husband testamentary control over only one-half of the community property, and the word "testamentary" as used in that section is not limited to formal testaments. Thus, although a wife can set aside a husband's unauthorized gift of community property in its entirety during his lifetime [citations], she is limited to the recovery of her one-half share after his death on the theory that his testamentary powers validate the gift of his half interest. [citations.] Similarly, a wife's gift causa mortis of community property [citations] and a husband's gift of a community life insurance policy [citations] have been upheld as to the spouse's community interest by reference to the testamentary power.

Just as the husband cannot deprive his wife of her community interest by exceeding his testamentary powers to make gifts of more than half the community property to third persons, so he cannot defeat her interest by making a testamentary gift to her under conditions that restrict her management and control of the property. Her remedy in both situations is to disavow the gift and stand on her community rights.

Termination of the Community by Divorce. The husband-wife community is terminated by death, divorce, or annulment of the marriage. In some of the community property states, a husband and wife cannot make an agreement which would alter the nature of their community property interests. This is the gist of statutes in effect in Arizona, Louisiana, and Texas. However, in Arizona, California, Nevada, New Mexico, and Washington, the parties may make a property settlement agreement in contemplation of divorce or separation.

For a long time, Texas required a beneficiary to have an insurable interest at the time life insurance proceeds were payable in order to be entitled to the proceeds. In connection with a divorce question, therefore, it was held that, since divorce terminated the wife's insurable interest in the life of her husband, it also terminated all her rights in a policy of life insurance on his life. In later decisions, however, the courts recognized a difference between the interest a wife might have in the proceeds of the policy payable at death and the cash surrender value of the contract.

Illustrative of this later point of view is the case of *Womack* v. *Womack*,[8] decided by the Texas Supreme Court in 1943. This case involved four life insurance policies. Three were on the life of the husband and had a total cash surrender value of $1,542.84. The other policy insured the life of the wife and had a cash surrender value of $252.00. All the policies had been purchased during the marriage and all premiums had been paid out of community property funds.

The insureds were divorced in 1941 and divided the other property between them. However, the legal question as to whether the cash surrender value of the policies constituted community property was left open for later determination by the court. The trial court held that the cash surrender value of the policies did constitute community property, and the decision was affirmed by the Court of Civil Appeals; but an appeal was taken to the supreme court because of a conflict with the decision in another case. The only question before the court was whether the cash surrender value of life insurance policies was community property.

The supreme court affirmed the decisions of the trial court and the Court of Civil Appeals as follows:

> Article 4619, Vernon's Annotated Civil Statutes, as amended in 1927, defines community property as follows:
>
> "All property acquired by either the husband or wife during marriage, except that which is the separate property of either, shall be deemed the common property of the husband and wife; and all the effects which the husband and wife possess at the time the marriage may be dissolved shall be regarded as common effects or gains, unless the contrary be satisfactorily proved."
>
> The word "property" has been frequently defined and its meaning determined by many decisions of the courts. In the case of *Titus* v. *Terkelsen*, 18 N.E. (2d) 444, 445, 302 Mass. 84, the court, in discussing the word "property," said:
>
> "It is a word of comprehensive meaning. *Holbrook* v. *Brown*, 2 Mass. 280, 282; *Raymer* v. *Tax Commissioner*, 239 Mass. 410, 413, 132 N.E. 190. In its ordinary legal signification it 'extends to every species of valuable right and interest, and includes real and personal property. . . .' "
>
> . . . It is true that in the early decisions of the courts of this country,

---

[8] 142 Tex. 299, 172 S.W. (2d) 307 (1943).

including the decisions of the courts of this State, it was held in some of them that policies of life insurance were not property. The history of Article 4619, as amended, clearly shows that the Legislature intended to give the term "community property" a broader meaning than it was originally given. Many of the modern decisions hold that a life insurance policy is property. In the case of *Grigsby* v. *Russell,* 222 U.S. 149, 56 L. Ed. 133, Mr. Justice Holmes, speaking for the Supreme Court of the United States, said:

"Life insurance has become in our days one of the best recognized forms of investment and self-compelled saving. So far as reasonable safety permits, it is desirable to give life policies the ordinary characteristics of property."

The word "property" in our bankruptcy laws is construed to include the "cash surrender value" of life insurance policies, and such property rights pass to the creditors of the insured. The courts recognize the right of the insured to pay his creditors the "cash surrender value" of his policy and retain the policy. . . . The courts of this State have held that the "cash surrender value" of a policy is property, and may be considered and treated as community property. . . .

. . . The trial court and Court of Civil Appeals correctly held that the cash surrender value of the policies was community property, and that respondent was entitled to judgment for one-half thereof.

The rule announced in the case of *Whitesell* v. *Northwestern Mutual Life Insurance Company, supra,* as well as in any other cases holding contrary to the rule announced herein, is expressly overruled.

In California, the rights of the wife, as beneficiary, do not cease upon divorce. Unless the husband is precluded by some legally enforceable claim on the part of the wife (an assignment, for example), he may change the beneficiary designation to whomever he wishes after the divorce. However, if community funds have been used to pay the premiums and he changes the beneficiary, the wife is entitled to reimbursement for her share of the premiums so paid. Also, in California, if the divorce decree does not dispose of a life insurance contract, the rights of the parties may be litigated in a later court action.[9]

Exoneration Statutes. In spite of the apparent technicalities of these laws, most community property states have statutes which make payment of the death benefit in good faith to the beneficiary or assignee of record, and without knowledge of an adverse claim, sufficient to discharge the insurer of liability. Illustrative of this type of statute—generally referred to as an "exoneration statute"—is the following from the California Code:[10]

Payment in accord with terms of policy or assignment: Discharge of insurer: Notice of claim to payment or interest in policy. Notwithstanding

[9] *In re Williams' Estate,* 36 Cal. (2d) 289, 223 P. (2d) 248 (1950).
[10] California Insurance Code, Sec. 10172.

the provisions of Sections 5105 and 5125 of the Civil Code, when the proceeds of, or payments under, a life insurance policy become payable and the insurer makes payment thereof in accordance with the terms of the policy, or in accordance with the terms of any written assignment thereof if the policy has been assigned, such payment shall fully discharge the insurer from all claims under such policy unless, before such payment is made, the insurer has received, at its home office, written notice by or on behalf of some other person that such other person claims to be entitled to such payment or some interest in the policy.

B. RIGHTS OF CREDITORS

Creditors, as they are concerned with the life insurance contract, may be divided into two large general groups. First, there are many creditors who are parties to or assignees or beneficiaries of life insurance contracts. Their rights are derived directly from the contract and have been discussed in Chapter 11. Second, there is a group of creditors who have no connection with any particular life insurance contract, but who may attempt to assert rights to the contract as property, in accordance with the statutory procedures open to creditors generally with respect to the property of their debtors.

16.6 Rights under the Contract

Generally speaking, a creditor who has had the foresight to protect himself against possible loss by insuring the debtor's life in his own favor is entitled to the proceeds in their entirety. This is true even though the amount of the insurance may be more than the amount of the indebtedness, so long as the difference is not so great as to suggest that the insurance was secured for wagering purposes.

A collateral assignee, as previously noted, usually has a right to share in the proceeds of life insurance to the extent of the indebtedness remaining unpaid at the death of the insured. Finally, if an absolute assignment has been executed for collateral purposes, it will be treated as if it were a collateral assignment, thus giving the assignee the right to share in the insurance proceeds but only to the extent of his indebtedness.

These rules, discussed and illustrated in Chapter 11, are repeated here as a reminder that the creditor is always free to apply for and own life insurance on the life of his debtor or to request a collateral assignment in his favor of a policy already in effect. If he does not pursue one of these courses, however, the possibility of his perfecting a claim under a life insurance contract as property is strictly limited. In this area, the contract's primary purpose as insurance has been and remains paramount so far as court decisions and statutory law are concerned.

16.7 Rights by Operation of the Law

Every state has its own procedures which a creditor may employ to sue a debtor, obtain a judgment, and then take further action to have property of the debtor sold to satisfy the judgment. These procedures differ from one state to another, and they differ also with respect to the nature of the property concerned. Most important to the present discussion is the fact that some kinds of property are specified by statute to be "exempt" from the claims of creditors, and life insurance occupies a high position on this list. As a matter of fact, a discussion of the rights of creditors in and to contracts of life insurance effected by debtors might more aptly be titled "privileges of debtors." This is especially true if a third person is named as beneficiary.

16.8 The Exemption Statutes

Why We Have Them. There is a traditional line of thinking, particularly in this country, to the effect that granting to the hopelessly insolvent debtor the right to retain a homestead and the "tools of his trade," in the interest of his possible rehabilitation, will prove to be a benefit to society in the long run. Exempting life insurance proceeds from the claims of creditors of the insured only extends this thinking to the members of the insured's family. Proponents of generous exemption statutes thus take the position that while a man should, perhaps, be "just before he is generous," he should also be encouraged to make whatever reasonable provisions may be possible for the welfare and support of his widow and orphan children. Society itself has an interest in this type of protection.

What They Are. Every state has its own type of exemption statute, and individual questions are, of course, governed entirely by the statutory and other applicable law of the jurisdiction concerned. In a general consideration of the question, however, the statutory exemption provisions with respect to life insurance contracts may be divided into three groups. The first group consists of a number of statutes that are derived from the original married women's statutes. These statutes enabled a married woman to apply for and own insurance on her husband's life and, incidentally, included a provision exempting such insurance from the claims of the husband's creditors. Second, several states, particularly the western states, have statutes that establish a liberal exemption in favor of life insurance but limit the amount to the insurance that can be purchased by a stated maximum amount of premiums annually. A third type of statute follows the lead of an early New York exemption statute and establishes a sweeping exemption in favor of most life insurance policies insuring the life of the insured-debtor or owned by him and insuring the life of another.

The Married Women's Statutes. It has previously been mentioned that at common law married women were unable to make contracts, but that this disability has been removed or modified by statute in every jurisdiction today. The first Married Women's Act was passed in New York in 1840. It made it possible for a married woman to contract for life insurance on the life of her husband, naming herself as beneficiary. It also provided that the life insurance so contracted for would be free from the claims of the husband's creditors. Today this type of law, in effect in several states,[11] has significance not only because it enables a married woman to apply for and own life insurance but also because it is effective as an exemption statute.

Illustrative of this type of statute is the following from the law of Ohio:[12]

> § 3911.11 Wife may insure life of husband. A married woman may by herself and in her own name, or in the name of a third person with his assent as her trustee, cause the life of her husband to be insured for her sole use, for any definite period or for the term of his natural life, and, if she survives such period or term, the amount of insurance becoming due and payable by the terms of the insurance shall be payable to her, free from the claims of the representatives of the husband or any of his creditors.

Exemptions Limiting the Amount by Premiums Paid. Several of the western states[13] have statutes which are very broad in scope, often extending the exemption to the claims of the beneficiary's creditors as well as those of the insured. However, these statutes often limit the amount of the insurance to which they apply. For instance, the California statute limits the exemption to that amount of life insurance which can be purchased with an annual premium of $500. Thus, Section 690.9 of the Civil Procedure Code expressly declares as "exempt from execution or attachment" (by creditors):

> All moneys, benefits, privileges, or immunities, accruing or in any manner growing out of any life insurance [owned by the debtor] if the annual premiums paid do not exceed five hundred dollars ($500), or if they exceed that sum a like exemption shall exist which shall bear the same proportion to the moneys, benefits, privileges, and immunities so accruing or growing out of such insurance that said five hundred dollars ($500) bears to the whole annual premium paid:[14]

---

[11] Alabama, Delaware, District of Columbia, Massachusetts, and Ohio.
[12] Page's Ohio Revised Code Annotated, Title 39: Insurance, Sec. 3911.11.
[13] In addition to California, they are Idaho, Montana, Nevada, and Utah.
[14] California Civil Procedure Code, Sec. 690.9.

The New York Type of Exemption Law. The third type of exemption statute mentioned above is modeled after the statute which was originally Section 55-a of the New York Insurance Law. Statutes taking this general approach have been enacted in a number of other states. The original New York law read as follows:

> If a policy of insurance, whether heretofore or hereafter issued, is effected by any person on his own life or on another life, in favor of a person other than himself, or, except in cases of transfer with intent to defraud creditors, if a policy of life insurance is assigned or in any way made payable to any such person, the lawful beneficiary or assignee thereof, other than the insured or the person so effecting such insurance, or his executors or administrators, shall be entitled to its proceeds and avails against the creditors and representatives of the insured and of the person effecting the same, whether or not the right to change the beneficiary is reserved or permitted, and whether or not the policy is made payable to the person whose life is insured if the beneficiary or assignee shall predecease such person; provided, that, subject to the statute of limitations, the amount of any premiums for said insurance paid with intent to defraud creditors, with interest thereon, shall enure to their benefit from the proceeds of the policy; but the company issuing the policy shall be discharged of all liability thereon by payment of its proceeds in accordance with its terms, unless before such payment the company shall have written notice, by or in behalf of a creditor, of a claim to recover for transfer made or premiums paid with intent to defraud creditors, with specification of the amount claimed.[15]

It will be noted that this statute exempts the proceeds and cash values of policies on the life of the debtor and those on the life of someone else if they are owned by him. The exemption is available regardless of beneficiary designation, as long as someone other than the debtor or his estate is named. Enacted in 1927, this law was in force in New York all during the Depression, but it was repealed in 1939. The present exemption from claims of creditors statute will be found in Section 166. It provides the same kind of protection but is considerably more detailed.

Miscellaneous Statutes. These three general groups account for the majority of exemption statutes in effect at the present time. Nevertheless, there are numerous miscellaneous laws in effect in different states which establish exemptions in greater or lesser degrees and in different ways. Louisiana, for instance, has a law which entitles the beneficiary, assignee or payee to the "proceeds or avails" of a life insurance policy or endowment policy as against the creditors of the insured or policyowner and exempts them also from liability for the debts of such beneficiary, payee, or assignee.[16]

---

[15] New York Insurance Law, 1927, Sec. 55-a.
[16] Sec. 4105 G.S. Louisiana, 1939.

16.9 The Prematurity Values

Although the cash surrender value of a life insurance policy is generally considered to be, and in many ways treated as, a type of personal property, creditors have not been very successful in reaching this cash value. This is true even of policies payable to the insured or his estate, since the provisions of the policy ordinarily govern the situation. If the policyowner must take affirmative action to surrender his policy for cash—and usually this is true—the courts generally take the position that he cannot be compelled to do so. Until the policyowner takes the necessary action, therefore, the insurance company is under no duty to pay the value to him, there is no immediate right to the cash surrender value, and thus there is no property (in the conventional sense of the word) for the creditor to proceed against.

Threading through the cases is a clear recognition that it is in the public interest to maintain life insurance for its basic insurance purpose. Thus, in one case, the Minnesota exemption statutes were held to apply to endowment policies as well as life insurance, even though the statutes in that state did not expressly include endowments. There the court said:

> It is also to be noted that Sections 61.14 and 61.15 are remedial statutes enacted for the public good to effectuate the beneficent purpose of protecting a debtor's dependents by giving them a preferred status over his creditors as to the proceeds of a life insurance policy upon his life; as such, these statutes are to be given a liberal construction to accomplish their intended purpose. See *Grimestad* v. *Lofgren*, 105 Minn. 286, 291, 117 N.W. 515, 517; Annotation, 164 A.L.R. 914. Insofar as such dependents are the beneficiaries, the insurance proceeds by statutory command inure to their separate use and benefit and are exempt from seizure by such creditors. It is elementary that statutes are to be interpreted and construed in keeping with the object to be attained. Section 654.16. If we were to hold that the cash-surrender option of the insured, or any other interest of the insured under the policy prior to its maturity, is a property right which is not exempt, but is available to the insured's creditors, the protective benefits would be wiped out, and we would thereby defeat the statutory purpose.[17]

16.10 Benefits on Maturity

Life insurance benefits payable to the estate of the insured are paid to the executor (if there is a will) or the administrator (if there is no will). The executor or administrator has certain duties as a matter of law, and one of these duties is to pay the debts of the decedent. In the absence of

---

[17] *Fox et al.* v. *Swartz et al.*, 51 N.W. (2d) 80 (Minn., 1952).

a statute to the contrary, life insurance proceeds paid to the insured's estate are used for this purpose exactly as are any other moneys or property.

If the proceeds are payable to a named beneficiary, the situation is different. There the rights of the beneficiary vest (belong to him absolutely) at the moment of the insured's death. The personal representatives (executors or administrators) of the insured, and hence his creditors, have no right to any part of the proceeds. It is important to note here that the theory of insurance, as the pooling of contributions out of which death benefits are paid, plays an important part in this analysis. The insured has made a contract with the company to pay a benefit to the named beneficiary on his death. As consideration for the performance of that contract, he has paid premiums for a specified length of time or until his death. It is not the insured's money, however, that the insurer pays to the beneficiary. The insurer pays only the death benefit it has agreed to pay. As a general rule, therefore, the death of the insured does not result in a transfer of any of the insured-decedent's funds in the ordinarily accepted sense of the word.

16.11 The United States as Creditor

An important exception to the general rule is found in a pair of cases decided by the United States Supreme Court in 1958. These cases clarified the rights of the United States government to collect income tax owed by the deceased insured out of the proceeds of life insurance on his life, payable to a named beneficiary. For some time prior to that date, this question had been variously decided, sometimes favorably to the government, sometimes unfavorably. In the cases of *Commissioner* v. *Stern*[18] and *United States* v. *Bess*,[19] the United States Supreme Court clarified this question and brought some degree of order out of what had been disorder.

In both cases, the court held that the state procedures for perfecting claims against property would be given effect in favor of the United States government just as they would be for any other creditor. In one case, the policy proceeds were effectively protected by the operation of the statute of the state concerned, which was Kentucky. In this case, *Commissioner* v. *Stern*, the court held that since there was no evidence that Stern had paid premiums in fraud of creditors, the state exemption

---

[18] 58–2 USTC ¶9594, 357 U.S. 39, 2 L. Ed. (2d) 1126, 78 S. Ct. 1047 (1958), aff'g *Stern* v. *Commissioner*, 57–1 USTC ¶9429, 242 F. (2d) 322 (CA–6, 1957), rev'g 15 TCM 114.

[19] 58–2 USTC ¶9595, 357 U.S. 51, 2 L. Ed. (2d) 1135, 78 S. Ct. 1054 (1958), aff'g *U.S.* v. *Bess*, 57–1 USTC ¶9528, 243 F. (2d) 675 (Ca–3, 1957), aff'g 55–2 USTC ¶9673, 134 F. Supp. 467 (D.C. N.J., 1956) in part.

statute was effective against the claims of the United States government just as it would have been with respect to any other creditor.

The other case, *United States* v. *Bess,* arose under the law of New Jersey. There the court held that a lien had attached to the cash surrender value prior to the death of the insured, and that the lien was enforceable after his death to the amount of the cash surrender value. A dissenting opinion expressed the point of view that none of the proceeds could be reached in the hands of the beneficiary because the cash value was extinguished at the insured's death and the lien with it. Although this is the minority opinion, it is especially significant as expressing the ordinarily accepted insurance view with respect to the cash value of a life insurance policy—that the cash value is available only during the lifetime of the insured and is merged into the proceeds at his death.

These two cases were highly significant because they clarified a question until then unanswered, and also because they held that the law of the state concerned applies and will be given effect in connection with federal income taxes just as would be true in connection with the claims of any other creditors.

16.12 The Federal Tax Lien Law

In 1966 a new Federal Tax Lien Law was enacted, clarifying the effect of federal tax liens for tax delinquencies. Briefly, it provides, with respect to life insurance owned by the taxpayer, that if the policyowner has not made other arrangements to satisfy the lien within 90 days after it has been established, the amount of the loan value is to be paid to the government by the insurer, but the policy remains in force.

The law also confirms the insurer's right to make policy loans without regard to possible federal tax liens if it has had no actual notice of a lien at the time the loan was made. In the case of automatic premium loans, it is necessary only that the insurer shall have had no notice of a lien at the time the automatic premium loan agreement was made.

16.13 Creditors of the Beneficiary

The creditors of the beneficiary ordinarily stand in a somewhat better position with respect to effecting a lien or otherwise satisfying their judgments out of the proceeds of life insurance. The proceeds definitely are the property of the beneficiary as of the date of the death of the insured, and the insurance concept no longer cloaks the money with the idea of pooled contributions which do not "belong" to any one person. Nevertheless, the idea of preserving the insurance moneys for the purposes intended, that is, protection for a person's dependents, remains uppermost. As a consequence, a number of statutes exempt the proceeds of life insurance from the claims of the creditors of the beneficiary[20] as well as the insured, and the spendthrift trust provision is frequently used.

The Spendthrift[21] Trust. Under a true trust, one person, called the trustee, holds a property interest under an agreement with the grantor which requires the trustee to keep or use that interest for the benefit of another person, called the beneficiary. Under a spendthrift trust, property is conveyed to a trustee under the same kind of agreement, except that the agreement also provides that the beneficiary's interest "shall not be transferable by the beneficiary and shall not be subject to the claims of the beneficiary's creditors as long as it is in the hands of the trustee." This provision makes it a true spendthrift trust, that is, a trust designed to protect a beneficiary from his own weaknesses as far as money is concerned.

In the latter half of the 1800s, there was considerable conflict as to whether the grantor of a trust could include in the trust agreement any provision of this kind that would protect the money or property of the trust from the claims of the beneficiary's creditors. At the present time, however, such provisions are valid in all but a few states, in some by special statute, in others without. The theory is that the creditors of the beneficiary are not harmed by it. Prior to the creation of the trust they had no rights in the property; after the creation of the trust, they had no rights. Thus, they are not harmed by such a provision.

This is not true, however, with respect to the creditors of the grantor himself. Before the creation of a trust, his creditors have rights which they can attach against his property. Therefore, any attempt to deprive them of those rights by creating a trust in the grantor's own favor that is exempt from claims of his creditors will be considered void as to his creditors.

In view of the strong emphasis upon protection of life insurance from the claims of creditors, it was only natural that those persons responsible for drafting settlement agreements under the optional modes would think of the spendthrift trust as a possible means of protecting the proceeds from the claims of the creditors of the beneficiary. However, since the life insurance company's relationship with the beneficiary is not one of trustee-beneficiary, special statutes were required before this could be done. Such statutes have now been enacted in well over half the states. There are a few differences, but in general there is a very definite similarity among the various statutes and often identical wording is used.

---

[20] This is true, of course, only so long as the proceeds, or any part of them, have not been paid to the beneficiary. As soon as the money has been paid to the beneficiary, it may be attached by his creditors.

[21] The modern use of this term does not in any sense imply that the beneficiary *is* a spendthrift.

Illustrative of this type of statute is a provision of the Illinois Code,[22] as follows:

> Any domestic life company shall have the power to hold the proceeds of any policy issued by it under a trust or other agreement upon such terms and restrictions as to revocation by the policyholder and control by beneficiaries, and with such exemptions from the claims of creditors of beneficiaries other than the policyholder as shall have been agreed to in writing by such company and the policyholder. Upon maturity of a policy in the event the policyholder has made no such agreement, the company shall have power to hold the proceeds of the policy under an agreement with the beneficiaries. Such company shall not be required to segregate funds so held but may hold them as part of its general company assets. A foreign or alien company, when authorized by its charter or the laws of its domicile, may exercise any such powers in this State.

The student will note first that this statute confers certain powers upon the domestic life insurance company and thus cannot apply to foreign or alien companies, whose powers are granted or modified only by the state under whose laws they are organized. Nevertheless, if such foreign or alien companies are authorized by their domiciliary state laws to exercise such powers, they are given the right by this statute to exercise them in Illinois.

Secondly, the company is given the power to hold policy proceeds under an agreement which provides for exemptions from the claims of the creditors of the beneficiaries, but not those of the policyowner. This means that if the policyowner is the payee under a settlement agreement relating to funds payable on surrender for cash, for instance, or the maturity of an endowment, he cannot make an agreement with the company which will preclude his own creditors from any rights in the funds. This simply recognizes the previously mentioned point that the policyowner is in a very different position with respect to his own creditors from the position he occupies with respect to the creditors of a third person for whom he might like to establish a trust. Cash surrender proceeds are payable to him, as are endowment proceeds in many instances. Therefore, when he attempts to leave such funds with the insurer for his own benefit but exempt from the claims of his own creditors, he is attempting to deprive them of rights they otherwise would have had. The Illinois statute does not permit him to do this.

Spendthrift provisions included in settlement agreements are drafted in many different forms. One illustrative example reads as follows:

> No payee other than the insured . . . under settlement agreement elected by the insured shall have any right in advance of actual receipt of payment from the company, to transfer, assign, alienate, encumber,

----

[22] Illinois Revised Statutes, Chap. 73, Sec. 853 (1965).

anticipate, or commute any instalment or payments, or to make any change in the provisions elected; and, except as otherwise prescribed by law, no payment of the interest or principal shall, in advance of actual payment of the company to payee, be subject to the debts, contracts, or engagements of any payee, nor to any judicial process to levy upon or attach the same for the payment thereof.

16.14 When Premiums Are Paid out of Embezzled Funds

Even the most cursory examination of the law makes it clear that life insurance is a highly preferred kind of property as far as the claims of creditors are concerned. For instance, insolvency alone is not enough to bar the operation of the exemption statutes, and the only general exception, so far as the exemption statutes are concerned, deals with transfers in fraud of creditors.

Generally speaking, it is just as difficult to decide what constitutes fraud in this area as in any other, and the exemption statutes are very liberally interpreted. In one specific set of circumstances, however, neither the policyowner nor the beneficiary is protected. That is the situation where embezzled funds have been used to pay the premiums. The courts are in very general agreement in such cases that the person from whom the funds are embezzled has the right to follow those funds and enforce a right against the proceeds. However, they differ with respect to the amount which may be recovered.

As a general rule, the courts hold that the proceeds of life insurance on which premiums have been paid out of embezzled funds are "impressed with a constructive or resulting trust" in favor of the person whose money was thus wrongfully used. This only means that the situation will be construed (or interpreted) as if the proceeds were held in trust for the person whose money was embezzled. The same general result has been reached by saying that the wronged person is entitled to a lien against the proceeds.

The principal question arises in connection with the amount of money the wronged person may recover out of the proceeds. As a general rule, if all the premiums were paid out of wrongfully acquired funds, then all the proceeds are held to be payable to the person to whom the funds rightfully belonged. If only part of the premiums were wrongfully acquired, then the person from whom the funds were taken is generally held to have a right to a share of the proceeds of the insurance equal to the proportion of premiums so wrongfully acquired. A few decisions have held that the wronged person is entitled only to recover the premiums wrongfully appropriated.

One of the more interesting decisions in this general area is a Louisana Supreme Court decision, *Succession of Joseph L. Onorato,*[23] decided in

---

[23] 219 La. 1, 51 So. (2d) 804, 24 A.L.R. (2d) 656 (1951).

March, 1951. The reader will remember that Louisana is one of several states whose law is based on French or Spanish (in this case, French) law rather than the English common law, which formed the background of legal thinking of the majority of the states.

In the Onorato case, the insured had been an agent for the collection of rents. In the course of his duties, he misappropriated more than $26,000 belonging to others, and out of this he paid more than $5,000 in premiums for insurance on his own life. In this case, the court held that the persons from whom the funds were taken had the right to recover the amount of those premiums out of the proceeds of the insurance. The way this conclusion is reached under the civil law of Louisiana and the similarity of basic principles with those of the common law are illustrated by the following excerpts from the opinion of the court:

> ". . . it is a natural and immutable law, that he who is the owner of a thing should always continue to have the property of it, until he has divested himself of it voluntarily, or until he be divested of it by some just and legal way . . ." I Domat's Civil Law (Strahan's tr), pp. 49, 59, 60, 62.
>
> There flows from this natural law the doctrine recognized in the civil law that, as between the owner and the thief, one whose property has been stolen may recover it even though the thief has changed the form of the property. As stated in 10 Scott, The Digest of Justinian, 35:2:53 (14), p. 268, "Where anyone steals a silver ingot belonging to me, and makes cups out of it, I can either bring suit for the theft of the ingot, or a personal one for the recovery of the property.
>
> "The same rule applies to grapes, and their unfermented juice, and seeds; for the action for the theft of grapes, their unfermented juice, and their seeds, can be brought, as well as a personal action."

❖   ❖   ❖   ❖   ❖

Under these principles of law, in the event a thief steals money and with the funds of his theft purchases or buys insurance, the owner can recover from the proceeds of the insurance the amount of the money so taken. The title of the owner cannot be considered as inferior to that of the thief or his representative, for, as pointed out above, the thief himself has no title whatever to the property stolen.

The courts of other states almost without exception hold that, when embezzled or stolen funds are used to purchase exempt insurance, the exemption does not deprive the owner of recourse to the proceeds from such insurance. This holding is based on what is termed the common law constructive trust theory, which, as the writer appreciates it, is that the embezzler gets legal title when he uses the funds so entrusted to him to purchase other property, but he holds the equitable title in trust for the one from whom he has embezzled or stolen the funds.

Under the doctrine of our civil law, the embezzler never gets any kind of title against the one from whom he steals, for, when he purchases with stolen funds, the title is in the one from whom he stole the funds. Whatever may be the distinction between the two doctrines, the underlying principle of each is justice, equity, and fair dealing.

. . . In our opinion, in this case the civil law doctrine should not be applied to the extent that the proceeds of exempt life insurance, when the premiums are paid or the insurance purchased with stolen funds, should be given to the owner of the property thus stolen, but he is entitled to recover the amount of the stolen funds which was used by the thief in payment of premiums or purchase of the insurance itself. By permitting this recovery, the fraud is made ineffective, equity and justice are served, and the public good and the policy of the statute creating the exemption are in no way impaired since the family and loved ones of the insured are assured of the proceeds that the misappropriated money bought.

C. INSURANCE AND THE BANKRUPTCY ACT

Under the federal Constitution (Article I, Section 8), Congress is authorized to "make uniform laws on the subject of bankruptcies throughout the United States." From the earliest times, however, Congress has followed the practice of giving effect in bankruptcy laws to the exemption statutes of the various states with respect to life insurance proceeds. This practice holds even though the result has been to that extent a departure from uniformity.

16.15 The Exemption Statutes

Of the two sections of the Federal Bankruptcy Act which are specifically concerned with this problem, Section 6 is the more important and reads in part as follows:

> This title shall not affect the allowance to bankrupts of the exemptions which are prescribed by the laws of the United States or by the State laws in force at the time of the filing of the petition . . .

In determining whether insurance policies will or will not be included in the assets which pass to the bankruptcy trustee for the benefit of creditors, one rules out first those policies which have no cash surrender value. In those cases there is no property to which the trustee may take title. Then those policies which have a cash surrender value must be reviewed in the light of the special exemption statutes of the state of the policyowner's legal residence (in legal terms, his *domicile*).

Because of the wide variations in the wording and application of the state statutes, it is impossible to discuss the question of when an insurance policy will be exempt from bankruptcy proceedings in general terms that will have any real meaning. The question always comes down to an analysis and interpretation of the particular exemption statute of the specific state in question, as well as the pertinent court decisions. This is true whether the states are community property states or common-law states, whether the right to change the beneficiary was reserved or not reserved, whether the amount of insurance is large or small.

16.16 The Cash Surrender Value

Another provision of the bankruptcy law gives some protection against the claims of creditors even though the policy may be payable to the estate of the insured and have a cash surrender value to which the trustee in bankruptcy takes title. This provision is found in Section 70-a of the Act and permits a bankrupt to keep a policy, even though payable to his estate or to other beneficiaries which may not fall within the class specifically designated under the exemption statute, if he pays an amount equal to the cash surrender value to the trustee within 30 days after the ascertainment of the amount.

Of particular importance is the fact that the title of the trustee in bankruptcy does not extend to any values under the policy except the cash surrender value. Thus, in one case—*Burlingham* v. *Crouse*[24]— where a trustee took title to a policy on a given date in accordance with the bankruptcy law and the insured subsequently died, it was held that the trustee was entitled only to the sum which would have been available to the bankrupt as a cash asset at the time of the bankruptcy.

16.17 Later Developments

A case such as the Burlingham case, decided in 1913, may tend to suggest that the subject of bankruptcy and life insurance is of academic interest only. This possibility was definitely terminated by the decision of the United States Court of Appeals for the Fourth Circuit, handed down January 5, 1955, in the case of *Lake* v. *New York Life et al.*[25] This was a consolidation of five suits brought by a trustee in bankruptcy to recover the cash surrender values of life insurance policies under which the companies had granted policy loans amounting to some $45,000 following, but without knowledge of, the bankruptcy of the insured. The companies were held liable to the trustee for the full amount of the cash surrender values of the policies, and in April, 1955, the United States Supreme Court refused to review this decision of the Circuit Court of Appeals.

As a result of this decision, every loan made by a life insurance company and every cash surrender value it pays subjects it to possible double liability if the policyowner is bankrupt at the time of the payment.

---

[24] 228 U.S. 459 (1913).
[25] 218 F. (2d) 394 (C.A. Md., 1955).

Actual notice of the bankruptcy to the company is not required. For this reason, whenever a request for a loan or a cash surrender is received which involves a substantial amount of money, precautions are ordinarily taken by the insurer to ascertain whether the payee is in bankruptcy or not. For example, one company has a bankruptcy search made in the district court in which the policyowner resides in every instance where the payment requested amounts to $10,000 or more. Other companies have different monetary limits. However, this possibility of double liability is very real, and unless corrective legislation is enacted, precautions will have to be taken by the insurers themselves if they are to protect themselves against it.

SUMMARY

In addition to rights specifically granted by the terms of the contract, a number of people may have or obtain rights under a life insurance policy solely by operation of the law. These include wives or husbands in community property states, creditors of the insured in some instances, and trustees in bankruptcy. Because such rights may prevail even though contrary to the terms of the contract itself, it is highly important that this possibility be kept in mind in any consideration of the life insurance contract.

Community Property Rights

The explorers of the Southwest brought with them the concept of community property from the countries of their origin—France and Spain. Briefly, the concept relates to the property a man and his wife acquire during their marriage. Husband and wife are considered to constitute a community, and all property acquired during the marriage, other than by gift or inheritance, is community property and owned by them in equal shares.

The life insurance contract is a form of property, and the community property concept applies. If the contract is formed prior to marriage, it constitutes separate property of the insured at that time. If premiums are paid out of community funds after marriage, the contract may remain separate property or it may be considered part community property and part separate property. In some states the contract is considered to remain separate property, but if the wife is not the beneficiary, she is entitled to reimbursement out of the proceeds for any premiums paid out of community funds. In California and Washington, the proceeds of such contracts are considered community and separate property in the same ratio as community and separate funds were used to pay premiums.

When the contract is applied for after marriage, the premiums are ordinarily paid out of community funds. In such cases, if the policy is payable to the insured's estate, the wife is usually considered to have a one-half interest in the proceeds. If the wife is the named beneficiary, the entire proceeds are usually considered to be her separate property.

As a general rule, the husband has the right of management and control of the community property during the marriage. However, he cannot ordinarily make a gift of his wife's interest without her consent, and designating someone other than the wife as the beneficiary is essentially the same as making a gift to that person.

Some states take the position that the husband can make moderate gifts without the wife's consent so long as they are not in fraud of the wife's interest. In California, however, the husband cannot make a gift of more than one half of the community property without the wife's consent. A change of beneficiary from the wife to someone else is valid unless the wife objects, but she has a right to half of the proceeds in such a case if she notifies the insurer before payment has been made. In Washington, if the policy is community property, the husband cannot name anyone as beneficiary other than the wife or his estate without the wife's consent. Such a designation is void, and the wife is entitled to the entire proceeds.

Generally, the surrender of a policy for cash is within the managerial authority of the husband, but payment of the death benefit to anyone other than the wife or the estate of the insured may present a problem if the wife has not consented to the beneficiary designation. Cases in both California and Washington uphold the right of the wife to the proceeds of insurance on the life of the husband under such circumstances where premiums have been paid out of community funds.

The community is terminated by death, divorce, or annulment of the marriage. Consequently, a property settlement may properly take the cash surrender value of a life insurance contract into consideration. In California, if the contract is not disposed of in the property settlement, the rights of the spouse of the insured may be litigated in a later action.

In most of the community property states, exoneration statutes protect the insurer if it makes payment to the beneficiary or assignee of record without notice of an adverse claimant to the proceeds.

Rights of Creditors

Creditors frequently request an assignment in their favor of life insurance on the life of a debtor. Alternatively, they may apply for and obtain insurance on the debtor's life, payable to themselves as beneficiaries. If they do not follow one of these courses, however, their possibilities of perfecting a claim, as creditor, to the life insurance contract, as property, are decidedly limited.

Life insurance occupies a high position on the list of kinds of property that are exempt in most respects from the claims of creditors. Although the statutes granting such exemptions differ from state to state, they can be divided into three large groups. A number of states have so-called married women's statutes, which permit a married woman to insure the life of her husband in her favor and also exempt the proceeds from the claims of the representatives of her husband or his creditors.

Some of the western states have statutes that exempt a portion of the proceeds of any life insurance contract, up to a specified limit. Typically they establish the limit as the amount of insurance a specified amount of annual premium will buy.

A third type of statute is modeled generally on a New York statute that exempts the proceeds of any life insurance owned by a person on his own life or the life of another, and payable to someone other than his estate.

Although the prematurity values of life insurance are generally acknowledged to be property, they are not very readily available in connection with the claims of creditors. If the owner must take affirmative action to obtain these values, the courts usually take the position that he cannot be compelled to do so.

The benefits payable on maturity will be payable either to the estate of the insured or to a named beneficiary. In the former case, the proceeds will usually be available to help pay the creditors of the insured. In cases where the insurance is payable to a named beneficiary, it is not usually available to meet the claims of creditors of the insured. One important exception to this is found in claims of the United States for income taxes owed by the deceased insured.

The Federal Tax Lien Act, enacted in 1966, specifically provides that if a policy is subject to a federal tax lien, the policyowner may pay the loan value to the government and continue the policy in force. It also protects an insurer in policy loan transactions as long as the company does not have actual notice of the lien.

Creditors of the Beneficiary

Although the proceeds of life insurance definitely become the property of the beneficiary at the date of the insured's death, a number of state statutes exempt these funds from the claims of creditors of the beneficiary as well as of the insured. A spendthrift trust clause is also sometimes used to afford protection to payees under settlement agreements.

Premiums from Embezzled Funds

As a general rule, if premiums were paid on life insurance out of wrongfully acquired funds, the person whose money was wrongfully used has a right of recovery from the proceeds of the insurance. If all the premiums were wrongfully acquired, then the wronged person has a right to all the proceeds. Otherwise, he is usually considered to be entitled to that proportion of the proceeds equal to the proportion of misappropriated premiums to total premiums.

The Bankruptcy Act

Life insurance owned by a person who is declared bankrupt is included in the property of the bankrupt that must be taken over by the trustee in bankruptcy, but state exemption statutes will be given effect. Section 70-a of the Federal Bankruptcy Act permits an insured to retain a life insurance contract if he pays the cash surrender value to the trustee within 30 days after ascertainment of that value.

In 1955, in the case of *Lake* v. *New York Life et al.*, the United States Court of Appeals held that a trustee in bankruptcy could recover from the insurer the full cash surrender value of policies on which the owner had effected policy loans while bankrupt, although that fact was not known to the insurers at the time the loans were made.

QUESTIONS FOR REVIEW

1. Give a brief definition of the term "community property." From what legal system is this concept derived?
2. State the basic rules of community property relating to:
   a. The time at which the status of property as community property is determined.
   b. What determines whether property is or is not community property.
   c. Rights of management of community property.
3. As a general rule, where a life insurance policy is applied for by a married man, what are the rights of his wife in community property states:
   a. If the proceeds are payable to his estate?
   b. If she is named as beneficiary and the designation is not changed?
   c. If she is named as beneficiary and the designation is later changed?
4. Briefly discuss the right of the husband to change the beneficiary on his policy of life insurance if it is community property.
5. What is the general rule concerning the husband's right to surrender a life insurance policy for cash when it is community property?
6. What is the effect of an "exoneration statute" with respect to the payment of proceeds under a life insurance policy by a life insurance company?
7. What is meant by the term "exemption statute" with respect to the rights of creditors to life insurance values?
8. List and briefly describe three different types of exemption statutes in effect in various states.

9. As a general rule, if all premiums paid on a life insurance policy are paid out of embezzled funds, what are the rights of the person from whom the money was embezzled?

10. Under what circumstances may a trustee in bankruptcy release a life insurance contract after he has taken title to it?

Chapter Outline

Chapter 17

Remedies

GENERALLY SPEAKING, the parties to the life insurance contract have available to them the same remedies as are available to any other contracting parties. Nevertheless, some kinds of problems arise more consistently than others in connection with the life insurance contract; and as a consequence, the remedies applicable to those problems are more frequently used. The remedy of interpleader, for instance, is particularly useful in resolving disputes concerning beneficiaries; and disputes of this kind arise frequently. Rescission and reformation are also valuable in connection with problems that are relatively typical. It is the purpose of this chapter to discuss these and other remedies which are especially useful in resolving problems and disputes in connection with the life insurance contract.

A. INTERPLEADER

The remedy of interpleader permits any person, corporation, or association holding money or property belonging to someone else to submit to a court the question of who is rightfully entitled to it. Whenever two or more persons claim the same property and the holder cannot decide between or among them, he may file a bill of interpleader in a court, deposit the money with it, and the court will decide among the claimants. The funds or property can then be paid to the person or persons rightfully entitled to it, and the entire question can be settled in one court proceeding instead of the several that might be required if each claimant brought a separate suit.

495

17.1 Interpleader and the Life Insurance Company

The remedy of interpleader is especially appropriate for the life insurance company. After years of policy transactions, beneficiary changes, assignments made and released, policy lapses and reinstatements, there are frequently conflicting claims among successive beneficiaries, beneficiaries and assignees, and persons claiming by reason of property rights in community property states or oral transactions of various kinds. When an insurer is faced with claims from more than one person in circumstances of this kind, its position may be quite difficult. Payment to one claimant, if he or she is not the one legally entitled to the proceeds, usually means that the company will have to pay the same claim twice. Only a court of law can make the necessary decision among the claimants; and the insurer gets the question before a court by filing a bill of interpleader.

The bill of interpleader permits the life insurance company to pay the money due into a court and require these various claimants to "interplead" their claims. A final court decision settles the question, and the company is discharged of all further liability. If one of several claimants sues the company before a bill of interpleader has been filed, the company ordinarily has the right to defend by filing a cross bill of interpleader.

Unfortunately, there is always some expense involved in connection with interpleader, and this expense, as a general rule, is payable in part or in its entirety out of the proceeds of the policy. Thus, the funds which actually reach the payee or payees are ordinarily somewhat diminished by reason of the interpleader action. For this reason, and also because any court action means delay in performing a service that is ordinarily performed promptly, life insurance companies do not generally initiate interpleader actions if there is any other reasonable way to reach a satisfactory settlement.

17.2 Illustrative Cases

Several of the cases discussed earlier in this text have reached the court when the insurer filed a bill of interpleader. For instance, the Illustrative Case at the end of Chapter 5 was an interpleader action to determine the proper beneficiary in a case involving a person who was described as a "trustee under trust agreement dated September 3, 1935." The case cited in Chapter 11, section 11.10, illustrated the use of an interpleader action to determine the rights of assignees.

Only two additional cases will be discussed here. One of them is the case of *Nixon* v. *Life Insurance Company of Virginia*,[1] where the court

---

[1] 124 A. (2d) 305 (D.C. Mun. App., 1956).

gives an especially good summary of the nature and purpose of the remedy of interpleader; and the other is the case of *Tomalewski* v. *State Farm Life Insurance Company*,[2] which illustrates the use of the remedy in an unusual set of facts.

In the Nixon case, the insured had two life insurance policies with the same insurer, neither of which had designated a beneficiary by name. Both policies, however, contained a "facility of payment" clause, which read as follows:

> The Company may make any payment provided for in this Policy, to husband or wife, or any relative by blood, or lawful beneficiary, or connection by marriage of the Insured, or to any other person who may appear to be equitably entitled to the same by reason of having incurred expense on behalf of the Insured for his or her burial, or for any other purpose; and the production by the Company of a receipt signed by any or either of said persons, or of other sufficient proof of such payment to any or either of them shall be conclusive evidence that such benefits have been paid to the person or persons entitled thereto, and that all claims under this Policy have been fully satisfied.

After the insured's death, the plaintiff, Hazel Nixon, delivered the policies to the insurance company and made claim to the proceeds. She based her claim on the fact that for the last four years of his life the insured had lived at her house, during which time she had furnished him clothing, housing, and food, assisted him in his business, and paid premiums on the policies, all without compensation. The widow of the insured also claimed the proceeds, both in her own right and as administratrix of the insured's estate. The insurance company did not attempt to decide between the claimants but, instead, filed a bill of interpleader.

The claimants answered, admitting that the policies contained a facility of payment clause, and set forth the bases of their claims. The court heard the opening statements of the claimants' lawyers but did not take any evidence to support or disprove either claim. Instead, it ruled that the proceeds should go to the administratrix as a matter of law. The plaintiff appealed, contending that the court should have examined the evidence and made a decision on the merits. The appellate court agreed with this contention, saying:

> Appellant's contention, which we think dispositive of this case, is that the court below should not have ruled that the administratix of the deceased-insured was entitled to the proceeds of the policies as a matter of law. Her position is that the court should have heard proof of the merits of her claim and exercised its equitable power to decide who was entitled to the disputed funds. A consideration of the nature and purpose of interpleader together with an examination of the cases, convinces us that appellant is correct in this contention.

---

[2] 354 F. Supp. 1359 (D.C. Pa., 1973).

Interpleader is a long established equitable remedy designed to avoid multiplicity of claims and circuity of action. Its foundations are in equity and where allowed the court is called upon to determine to which of the various claimants the money deposited with the court should be awarded. Where, as here, the remedy is invoked by the insurer, we think the better rule is that it is the duty of the court to pass upon the merits of the claimant's rights to the proceeds.

At this point appellee contends, as she did in the trial court, that no beneficiary having been specifically named in the policies, the proceeds must be distributed to the representative of the insured's estate. She cites authority in support of this contention but our examination discloses that much of it is distinguishable from our present case. Most of the cases cited concern policies which themselves are distinguishable in that they expressly make the proceeds payable to the administrator or executor of the insured *unless* at its option the insurance company elects to pay under the facility of payment clause. . . .

. . . Similarly, in *Ellis* v. *Metropolitan Life Ins. Co.*, Mo. App., 3 S.W. 2d 397, where the insurance company interpleaded both the insured's administratrix and a woman with whom he had boarded before his death, the latter contending the deceased was indebted to her for board, lodging and washing, and the payment of premiums, the court in the exercise of its equitable powers, reversed the trial court and directed a judgment against the administratrix and in favor of the adverse claimant. It is to be noted that the court so acted even though the policy expressly named the administrator as beneficiary.

. . . This procedure is in keeping with the fundamental nature and purpose of proceedings by way of interpleader by preventing circuity of action, a course sure to result from the trial court's action relegating the appellant to an independent suit either against the administratrix or the distributees of the estate. We fail to see any valid reason why the insurance money should pass through decedent's estate, or how the orderly processes of justice would be served by such circuitous procedure. Indeed, it is manifest that such a requirement would have the effect of merely postponing for decision that which is now subject to the court's disposition in one proceeding, not to mention the additional hardship and expense to appellant who would be obliged to file suit in the same court. . . .

The Tomalewski case illustrates the use of the remedy of interpleader to get a question before the court in an unusual set of facts. The insurer used a three-part application form and relied upon the beneficiary designation in the application. In this case, the beneficiary section, which was on page 1 of the application, was not completed (although the application was signed) until after the pages were reversed to complete a military service questionnaire on the back. The applicant then made his decision concerning beneficiaries and instructed the agent to fill in the appropriate blanks. The agent did so, but the carbon paper had been reversed in the process. The result was that the original copy of the application (which was retained in the insurer's office) showed Viola O. Tomalewski, mother of the insured, as the primary beneficiary and Thaddeus J. Tomalewski, father of the insured, as successor beneficiary. The agent's copy read the same, but the beneficiary section of the third copy, which was included in the policy, was blank. The wording that should have been included on the third copy appeared on the reverse side of the agent's copy because of the error in reversing the carbon paper.

Two months after the policy was issued, the insured married; and on December 8, 1971, he died. The mother claimed the proceeds as the named beneficiary, and the widow made claim on the basis that no beneficiary was named and the proceeds were, therefore, payable to the estate of the insured. The insurer, therefore, filed an interpleader action.

The widow relied on a statute that provided that if a correct copy of the application was not attached to the policy, the company could not introduce the application as evidence "in any controversy between the parties to, or interested in, the policy, nor shall such application . . . be considered a part of the policy." But the court said:

> The widow relies on 40 P.S. 441 which provides that "correct" copies of the application are to be attached to the policies; and that if this is not done the application shall not be received in evidence "in any controversy between the parties to, or interested in, the policy, nor shall such application. . . . be considered a part of the policy." This section is designed to compel the company to place clearly before the policy holder any matter which it may seek to use as a defense. "The Insurance Company Law expressly provides that the copy of the application, attached to a policy, must be a correct copy. If it is not an exact duplicate of what was submitted by the insured, the entire application must be disregarded and may not be used thereafter as the basis of a defense by the insurer." [Citation.] This does not preclude use of Company files as business records, however. [Citation.]
>
> What confronts us here is not use of the inexact data as a defense by the insurer but as proof substantiating the rights of the beneficiary by use of the business records of the Company and of its agent. The Company has here made no defense but admitted by interpleader its liability on the policy.
>
> Moreover, our decision here with respect to disposition of the policy proceeds would not preclude an independent . . . action for negligence against the Company based upon its agent's negligence.

The court said, in effect, that it would be unduly technical to hold that the application for the policy consisted only of the first page of the application form, with the beneficiary section left blank, and continued:

> We therefore hold that the legally significant text is to be found in the complete original copy in the Company's file. Accordingly, the policy

proceeds must be paid to the designated beneficiary, Viola O. Tomalewski, the insured's mother.

The court thus held that the records of the company could be used in determining the correct beneficiary but did not rule out an action against the company on the basis of the agent's negligence.

17.3 Requirements for Interpleader

Three essential requirements must be met before a bill of interpleader may be filed. First, there must be no adequate remedy at law; second, the holder must not himself have an interest in the fund or funds; and finally, the claims must all relate to the same fund.

In filing a bill of interpleader it is basic that there must be no adequate remedy at law by which the plaintiff may protect himself from the threat of multiple suits. As a matter of fact, the purpose of the remedy is not so much to protect from double liability (which, of course, it does) as to protect from the threat of multiple litigation (if each claimant to the death benefit brought suit individually against the insurer). This point is brought out in one case, as follows:

> The jurisdiction of a federal court to entertain a bill of interpleader is not dependent upon the merits of the claims of the defendants. . . . It is our opinion that a stakeholder, acting in good faith, may maintain a suit in interpleader for the purpose of ridding himself of the vexation and expense of resisting adverse claims, even though he believes that only one of them is meritorious. As the Supreme Court said in *Myers* v. *Bethlehem Corporation*, 303 U.S. 41, 51: "Lawsuits also often prove to have been groundless; but no way has been discovered of relieving a defendant from the necessity of a trial to establish the fact."[3]

Another court has said:

> The fundamental basis for interpleader is to permit the holder of a fund who admits he is not the owner of it to put the fund in the hands of the court, so that claimants with substantial contentions may fight out their claims to it and so that the holder will be shielded from the danger of deciding at its peril who is rightfully entitled to the fund, as well as from the burden of defending and danger of losing separate lawsuits brought by each claimant.[4]

The person who seeks the remedy of interpleader must, as these quotations indicate, be a disinterested "stakeholder." In other words, he must not have a claim of his own to the money or property in question. This is

---

[3] *Hunter* v. *Federal Life Insurance Company*, 111 F. (2d) 551 (C.C.A. Ark., 1940).

[4] *United Benefit Life Insurance Company* v. *Katz*, 155 F. Supp. 391 (D.C. Pa., 1957).

especially true in the insurance cases where the insurer admits it is holding insurance proceeds that are payable to someone else.

Also, the claims must have a common origin and the claimants must claim the same thing. The mere fact that one may be faced with a number of lawsuits is not enough; they must all relate to claims to the same money or property.

17.4 The Federal Interpleader Act

The first Federal Interpleader Act was passed in 1917 and repealed in 1926, when a new law was enacted. In 1936, another act was passed to replace the 1926 law, and in 1948 a revision of the Judicial Code resulted in the present code section under which the remedy is available. Under this Section 1335, Title 28, U.S.C., federal courts have jurisdiction in cases involving a "certificate, policy of insurance, or other instrument of value or amount of $500 or more."

Under the Code, the claimants must be legal residents of different jurisdictions. In other words, there must be "diversity of citizenship." Incidentally, the remedy of interpleader is also available under the laws of most of the individual states.

A Bill in the Nature of a Bill of Interpleader. A bill in the nature of a bill of interpleader is very much the same as a bill of interpleader except that the person or corporation holding the money need not truly be a disinterested stakeholder. In other words, he may have some interest in the outcome, although perhaps not actually a claim to the money itself.

B. RESCISSION

Chapter 8 contains a discussion at some length of the insurer's right to cancel (avoid) a contract of life insurance if there was fraud, material misrepresentation, or concealment in the application. As pointed out in that discussion, this right is enforced by means of the equitable remedy of rescission, under which a court of equity may declare the contract canceled and of no legal effect.

17.5 When Not Available

If evidence of fraud, material misrepresentation, or concealment is discovered after the death of the insured (but prior to the expiration of the contestable period), the facts so revealed may ordinarily be used in defense of a suit by the beneficiary, and the company has an adequate remedy at law. An equitable remedy, therefore, is not available under these circumstances.

Assume, for instance, that John Doe, insured, dies of leukemia three months after issuance of a policy. The death certificate states that the illness was of two years' duration, and investigation supports this statement. The illness was actually diagnosed some two years prior to death, and the insured was informed of the diagnosis. Nevertheless, the answers to the application questions relating to his health gave no hint of ill health of any kind. This, of course, is misrepresentation of a material fact, and the company will deny the claim for the death benefit in accordance with its usual procedures. If the beneficiary sues, the company will show that information material to the appraisal of the risk was misrepresented at the time of the application, and this will ordinarily constitute an effective defense to the suit.

17.6 No Remedy at Law

If evidence to justify avoidance of the contract is discovered during the lifetime of the insured, however, and prior to the expiration of the contestable period, the only remedy open to the company is to ask a court of equity to rescind the contract. The insurer cannot wait until the insured dies, for that may be beyond the contestable period, and there is no other means by which the company can have its obligations under the contract canceled.

In this connection it will be recalled that in the Monahan case,[5] although the insured died during the contestable period, the beneficiary waited until the expiration of that period to bring her suit. The court then held that the company was precluded by the incontestable clause from contesting the validity of the policy. Subsequently, legislation was enacted to permit the companies to include in the incontestable clause the phrase "during the lifetime of the insured." The effect of this was to preserve to the company the right to defend a claim denial at any time, on grounds of material misrepresentation or fraud, in any case where the insured died during the contestable period of the policy. Thus a life insurance company continues to have a remedy at law in cases involving fraud or misrepresentation if the insured dies during the contestable period and the policy's incontestable clause includes the phrase "during the lifetime of the insured."

Some companies consider this a somewhat dubious advantage, however. Because the company has an adequate remedy at law, it cannot go into a court of equity when the insured dies during the contestable period, even though it might be advantageous to have the question decided by the judge rather than a jury. For this reason, some insurance companies continue to use incontestable clauses that do not include the words "during the lifetime of the insured." As a result, they do not have

---

[5] See Chapter 8, section 8.9.

an adequate remedy at law and are permitted to bring an action in equity to have the policy rescinded during the contestable period. It is necessary, however, that the action actually be brought during the contestable period in such situations.

17.7 Illustrative Case

The case of *Massachusetts Mutual Life Insurance Company* v. *Goodelman*,[6] decided by the United States District Court for the Eastern District of New York, in April, 1958, illustrates how the equitable remedy of rescission is available if the phrase "during the lifetime of the insured" is not included in the incontestable clause.

This case concerned a policy that was issued on February 27, 1956, insuring the life of Leon Goodelman in the amount of $100,000. The insured died on December 22, 1957, only slightly more than two months before the expiration of the contestable period. Before the end of the period, the insurer elected to rescind the policy and tendered payment of the premium paid on it, basing this action on the contention that the policy was procured by false representation and concealment of facts, since the insured was suffering from diabetes and arteriosclerosis when the application was completed. On February 20, 1958, the company instituted a court action for rescission of the contract, taking this action because the incontestable clause did not contain the words "during the lifetime of the insured." After the expiration of the contestable period, the beneficiary sued the insurer for the proceeds of the policy (a procedure referred to in the following discussion as "the second action") and filed a motion requesting that the action in equity (for rescission) be dismissed on the ground that the insurer had an adequate remedy at law. The court considered the motion to dismiss and denied it, as follows:

> The ground urged by defendant for dismissal of the instant action for rescission is that the sole issue between the parties is basically legal in nature; that the plaintiff has a complete and adequate remedy at law in that it can assert its claims of fraud and misrepresentation in the aforesaid second action and thus assure the present defendant of her right to a trial by jury of that action.
>
> The principal issue on this motion is whether the Mutual Company had the right to resort to a court of equity with its claims for rescission or should have delayed action until the beneficiary sued on the policy and then interposed its defenses in such action. Mutual contends that if it had delayed bringing its action beyond the two year period from date of issue of the policy, it would have lost its right to defend by the operation of the incontestability clause in the contract. It reads as follows:

---

[6] 160 F. Supp. 510 (D.C. N.Y., 1958).

"Incontestability. This policy . . . shall be incontestable after it has been in force for a period of two years from its date of issue."

It is crystal clear from a mere reading of the provision that if Mutual had any remedy pertaining to the policy, such remedy must be asserted within the two year period, in this case prior to February 27, 1958. It could not be availed of beyond that time. Similar clauses have been so construed in *Mutual Life Insurance Co.* v. *Hurni Packing Co.*, 263 U.S. 167, and *Killian* v. *Metropolitan Life Insurance Co.*, 251 N.Y. 44. The beneficiary's contention that the clause is not in compliance with Section 155 of the New York Insurance Law has no merit.

Mutual was not precipitate in instituting its action for rescission. It delayed doing so until its claim was about to be outlawed by the incontestability clause. In fact, barely one week remained for it to take action or forfeit its right to do so. In a similar recission case, *American Life Insurance Co.* v. *Stewart*, 300 U.S. 203, the plaintiff's right to resort to equity by way of claim for rescission was upheld, Mr. Justice Cardozo writing for the Court, said:

"If the policy is to become incontestable soon after the death of the insured, the insurer becomes helpless if he must wait for a move by some one else, who may prefer to remain motionless till the time for contest has gone by. . . . Accordingly an insurer, who might otherwise be condemned to loss through the mere inaction of an adversary, may assume the offensive by going into equity and there praying for cancellation."

The motion is denied.

The court thus held that the insurer did not have a remedy at law and must bring its action in equity. If the incontestable clause had included the words "during the lifetime of the insured," the insurer would have had a remedy at law and could not have instituted an action in the equity court.

In spite of the decision in this case, insurance companies are not always successful in their attempts to have life insurance contracts rescinded, as is illustrated by the case of *Franklin Life Ins. Co., Plaintiff Appellant* v. *William J. Champion & Co., Defendant Appellee.*[7] There the life of the president of a realty company—William J. Champion, Jr.—was insured for $100,000 under a policy issued to the company on June 18, 1959. Three quarterly premiums were paid, but the premium due on June 18, 1960 was not paid when due or within the grace period. The policyowner tendered payment of the June 18 premium by check, which was received by the insurer on July 30, 1960. The insurer notified the policyowner that the policy was in default and requested completion of a reinstatement application. The application included a question concerning the name or names of physicians the insured had consulted

---

[7] *Franklin Life Insurance Company* v. *William J. Champion and Company*, 353 F. (2d) 919 (C.A., 1965).

during the past and the question: "Are you now in good health?" The answer to the first of these questions was "Dr. Nelson Taylor" and the answer to the second was "yes."

The insurance company requested and obtained a statement from Dr. Taylor; and on the basis of that statement and the answers contained in the reinstatement application, the policy was reinstated as of August 30, 1960.

On August 31, the insured suffered a very severe headache. On September 1, he consulted Dr. Taylor; on September 2, he was admitted to a hospital, where tests were made that disclosed that he was suffering from a lesion of the brain. On March 30, 1961, he died.

The insurer denied the claim for the proceeds of the policy on the basis that the insured had stated in the reinstatement application that he was then in good health, which clearly was untrue. Suit was brought in the United States district court, and the court entered a judgment for the full amount of the policy.

The insurer appealed the decision on the grounds that even though the statement may have been made in good faith—that is, without knowledge of its falsity—it was nevertheless untrue; and, if material to the risk (as it was), it would be grounds for rescission. The court considered the question in this way:

> The principal issue in the case is whether Mr. Champion's answer in his application for reinstatement, that he was in good health, rendered the reinstatement of the policy void. We assume that the answer was made in good faith, as the district court so found, and there was evidence to sustain the finding. There seems to be no question that at the time he was suffering from carcinoma of the brain; and the evidence supports the finding of the district court that he was completely ignorant of having the disease, and had no reasonable ground to suspect that he was not in good health.

✿ ✿ ✿ ✿ ✿

> Appellant [the insurer] contends that such an untrue statement is ground for rescission of the insurance contract, if it materially affected assumption of the risk by the insurer.
>
> The general rule and weight of authority hold that the statement of an applicant for insurance that he was in good health is a representation only that he believed he was in good health. In *Bronx Savings Bank* v. *Weigandt*, 1 N.Y. 2d 545, the Court of Appeals of New York said:
>
> > "A representation as to good health in an application for insurance . . . is not an affirmation of fact and does not provide a basis for rescission in the absence of proof of actual fraud."
>
> Speaking of such representations in *Sommer* v. *Guardian Life Ins. Co. of America*, 281 N.Y. 508, the Court of Appeals said:
>
> > "The applicant does not guarantee the literal truth of the statement, nor do the parties condition their contract upon the existence of good

health. The representation is not part of the contract; it is a 'statement inducing the formation of the contract as distinguished from an affirmation of fact or a promise incorporated in and material to the contract.' 3 *Williston on Contracts* (Rev. Ed.), Sec. 673; *Vance on Insurance,* pp. 89, 390; 4 Couch, *Cyclopedia of Insurance Law,* Sections 824, 885. Such statements must be construed in the light of their purpose to furnish to the company information which will enable it to decide whether it shall make a contract of insurance in which the information furnished will not be incorporated as an affirmation of fact.

"The courts, both state and federal, have generally construed statements that an applicant was in good health or free from disease as a representation only that the applicant in good faith believed and was justified in believing that his health was not impaired by any condition which would ordinarily be regarded as a 'disease.' "

It is interesting to note that in the extended discussion of this case, the court refused to consider the insured's statement as a warranty:

. . . The insurance company undoubtedly knew that Mr. Champion could state only his own opinion that he had no disease and that he was conscious of no malady or condition which impaired his health. To hold otherwise would be to construe Mr. Champion's statement as a warranty of the truth, when it was no more than a bona fide representation that he believed the statement to be true. *Sommer* v. *Guardian Life Ins. Co. of America,* 281 N.Y. 508. Again, it is to be pointed out that the insurance was reinstated only when the insurance company received the medical report of Dr. Taylor, upon which it, obviously, relied in reinstating the policy.

The court then held that there was no basis for rescission on the ground that the insured had concealed any medical treatment in the application for reinstatement and that the decision of the district court—against the insurance company—should be affirmed.

C. REFORMATION

Life insurance policies are prepared with the utmost care, and machine procedures are utilized as much as possible to assure as high a degree of accuracy as is attainable. Whenever work is done, however, mistakes will sometimes be made; and a mistake in a life insurance policy is almost always serious.

Perhaps 20-year endowment values were inadvertently included in a 20-pay life policy. Possibly a typist moved a decimal point one place to the right; perhaps figures have been reversed. In any case, there is only one thing to do, administratively speaking. The policyowner must be informed of the error; the nature of the error must be explained; permission to correct the error must be requested.

Assume, however, that permission to correct the error is not granted.

The policy states the value as $7,893.27 (instead of $789.33), and the policyowner states that he intends to enforce it according to its terms. It is at this point that the insurer's lawyer considers the equitable remedy of reformation.

17.8 What Reformation Is

Reformation is the remedy by which a written instrument is re-formed or construed in such a way as to express the true intentions of the parties when the contract, as actually written, fails to do so. Reformation has been possible in courts of equity for many years; but, like all equitable remedies, it is "extraordinary" in nature and will be granted only for compelling reasons. Before a contract can be reformed, therefore, it must clearly be shown that it does not, as it is written, express the agreement of the parties, either because of mistake or fraud. If the error is the result of a mistake, it must be a mutual mistake or a mistake on the part of one party with fraud or inequitable conduct on the part of the other.

17.9 The Purpose of the Remedy

The purpose of reformation is not to make a new contract but to re-form the one presently existing so that it will be in the form in which it was intended to be expressed in the first place. The purpose is not to substitute a new contract but to make the original contract effective as intended.

17.10 Illustrative Case

In *Flax* v. *Prudential Life Insurance Co.*,[8] decided by the United States District Court in February, 1956, the plaintiff sued for $5,495.26, plus 7 percent interest from February 19, 1955, under a policy which originally provided for a death benefit of $1,864.00, with $463 as a pure endowment at the end of 20 years. The company contended that the correct amount due was $1,994.65 and that the $5,495.26 sued for was based on what the law has continued to term a "scrivener's error," meaning, of course, the error of one who wrote the contract. The court said:

> . . . The defendant [the insurer] had no knowledge of the existence of the mistake until during the month of June 1954, at which time, in the course of processing an application by the plaintiff for a loan on the policy, it discovered it. The defendant immediately notified the plaintiff of the mistake and requested him to join in the reformation of the policy to rectify it, which he has refused to do.

The policyowner sued to obtain the amount erroneously stated in the policy and the insurer filed an answer and counterclaim, asking reforma-

---

[8] 148 F. Supp. 720 (D.C. Cal., 1956).

tion of the contract so that it would read as it would have read if the error had not been made.

The court pointed out that the policy was issued while the applicant was a resident of New York and said that since the case involved parties whose residences were in different states, the law of New York governed in deciding the contractual rights of the parties to the contract. It then continued:

> New York courts have held uniformly that incontestability clauses of the type inserted in this policy do *not* prevent a contest of the policy on the ground of fraud or mistake. To the contrary, these courts make these defenses available to the insurer whenever an action is instituted to enforce any of the terms of the policy. They take the view that when, either through mutual mistake or unilateral mistake by one party which is known to the other, the policy does not express the intention of the parties, reformation may be had either when an action is instituted by the insured to enforce its provisions or in a direct action brought by the insurer to make the policy speak verity.
>
> In one of the cases, an action was brought by the insurer to reform a disability policy so that it would stipulate that the disability insurance to be paid to the insured would be $100 per month instead of $1,000, which had been inserted through a scrivener's mistake. The policy was issued in 1926 and the action was not begun by the insurer until 1937. Notwithstanding this, the trial court granted reformation. The judgment was affirmed by the Appellate Division whose decision, in turn, was affirmed by New York's highest court, The Court of Appeals.

✻   ✻   ✻   ✻   ✻

> . . . So we come to these important considerations: (a) Was there a mistake in the execution of the rider which was attached to the policy when the insured on March 20, 1936, exercised one of the options under the policy converting it into paid-up insurance? (b) Was the mistake of a type for which relief can be granted in action of this character?
>
> Answers to these questions require a brief consideration of the circumstances under which, generally, equity will grant relief for mistakes. From time immemorial, it has been the function of equity as administered in the federal courts to remedy what is known as "scrivener's mistakes"— mistakes performed by the person who drafted the instrument in such a manner that it did not express what was actually agreed. In an early case, the Supreme Court of the United States has stated the principle and the reasons for it in this manner:
>
> "There are certain principles of equity, applicable to this question, which, as general principles, we hold to be incontrovertible. The first is, that where an instrument is drawn and executed, which professes or is intended to carry into execution an agreement, whether in writing or by parol, previously entered into, but which, by mistake of the draftsman, either as to fact or law, does not fulfill, or which violates, the manifest intention of the parties to the agreement, equity will correct the mistake,

so as to produce conformity of the instrument to the agreement. The reason is obvious: the execution of agreements, fairly and legally entered into, is one of the peculiar branches of equity jurisdiction; and if the instrument which is intended to execute the agreement be, from any cause, insufficient for that purpose, the agreement remains as much unexecuted, as if one of the parties had refused, altogether, to comply with his engagement; and a court of equity will, in the exercise of its acknowledged jurisdiction, afford relief in the one case, as well as in the other, by compelling the delinquent party fully to perform his agreement, according to the terms of it, and to the manifest intention of the parties. So, if the mistake exists, not in the instrument, which is intended to give effect to the agreement, but in the agreement itself, and is clearly proved to have been the result of ignorance of some material fact, a court of equity will, in general, grant relief, according to the nature of the particular case in which it is sought."

The principle has been followed in later cases and it is now an accepted norm of equity jurisprudence as administered in the federal courts that reformation will be granted for mistake. Even a unilateral mistake may be the basis for relief when it is known to the other party to the contract.

❖   ❖   ❖   ❖   ❖

The case before us is an almost perfect illustration of the classical instance referred to in the books, that of a person looking at cheap jewelry and seeing what he, at once, recognizes as being a valuable jewel, which, by mistake, had been placed with the "paste," purchases it at a price wholly unrelated to its real value. In the circumstances, as the Restatement puts it:

"The shopkeeper is entitled to restitution because the shopkeeper did not, as A knew, intend to bargain except with reference to cheap jewelry."

The plaintiff is an experienced businessman and should have known that in modern business and insurance practice, a clause which would make the surrender value of a policy more than double its maturity value, without additional obligations on his part, was not within its contemplation. His coverage at the inception of the policy (omitting the endowment) was $1,864, which was increased on conversion to $2,755.

❖   ❖   ❖   ❖   ❖

. . . To summarize: The plaintiff either did or did not know of the mistake. If he did, it appearing that the mistake was not known to the insurer, we have the type of unilateral mistake for which relief by way of reformation is granted. If he did not know the mistake, we have a case of mutual mistake for which reformation also lies. Indeed, relief may be granted by disregarding the printed words which the scrivener erroneously failed to delete.

❖   ❖   ❖   ❖   ❖

. . . Entering into business undertakings, parties do not intend to overreach each other, but rather mean to make equitable and conscionable agreements.

One of California's Court of Appeals has summed up the principle in these words:

"In every contract there is an implied covenant of good faith and fair dealing."

         ❁   ❁   ❁   ❁   ❁

. . . So, if plaintiff's present demands were allowed, he would receive something which he did not bargain or pay for—something for nothing. The language of the Persian poet applies:

> Sue for a Debt he never did contract,
> And cannot answer—
> Oh, the sorry trade.

It would be neither good morals nor good law to sanction the application of such a policy to business relations.

On the other hand, a ruling for the defendant avoids a palpable injustice and still allows the plaintiff the full benefit of the contract he intended to make.

Judgment will, therefore, be for the defendant.

The court thus held that the insurer could pay the amount that should have been stated in the policy.

A similar set of facts is found in the case of *Johnson et al. v. Consolidated American Life Ins. Co.*[9] This case concerned a $5,000 policy on the life of an eight-year-old girl which, at the end of eight years, could have been surrendered for a paid-up policy for the full face amount and a cash payment. The typist erroneously typed $5,000 as the cash payment instead of $19.20. This was one of two policies purchased by the father of the insured, one policy on her life and the other (which contained no error) on the life of her two-year-old sister.

At the end of eight years, the father of the insured requested the paid-up policy and the $5,000. The insurer tendered the paid-up policy and $19.20, which was refused. The insurer then filed suit for reformation of the policy on the basis that the error was mutual. The court discussed the question of mutual error in this way:

> Insured contends that there was no mutual mistake because the proof shows that the clerical error was made by some employee of Insurance Company and that neither Insured nor her father had anything to do with the mistake.
>
> The general rule in this state and elsewhere is that reformation of a contract is justified only (1) if the mistake is a mutual one, or (2) where there is a mistake on the part of one party and fraud or inequitable conduct on the part of the other. *Allison v. Allison,* 203 Miss. 15, 33 So. 2d 289 (1948). No fraud is alleged or proved in this case.

---

[9] *Johnson et al. v. Consolidated American Life Insurance Co.,* 244 So. (2d) 400 (Miss., 1971).

The mistake that will justify a reformation must be in the drafting of the instrument, not in the making of the contract. 45 Am. Jur., Reformation of Instruments § 46 (1943). When the Insurance Company accepted the application and premium, the contract came into being. What were the terms of the policy thus intended by both parties to be issued? The application showed the face amount of the policy, age of the insured, the amount of the premium, and the kind of policy. When these data were applied to Insurance Company's schedules and tables and the policy forms, the precise terms of the policy were thus determined. This is what the parties intended. In Option 3 of Theresa Ann's policy the second type-written figure was intended to be $19.20, but in drafting the policy the figure $5,000 was mistakenly written instead of $19.20. The mistake was made by Insurance Company, but in legal contemplation both parties intended the figure to be $19.20. Therefore, the mistake was mutual. *Smith v. Federal Land Bank of New Orleans,* 178 Miss. 600, 173 So. 2d 673 (1937); *Berry v. Continental Life Ins. Co.,* 224 Mo. App. 1207, 33 S. W. 2d 1016 (1931).

D. THE DECLARATORY JUDGMENT

A declaratory judgment, as the name implies, is a judgment that declares the rights of the parties to an action or sets forth the opinion of the court on a given question. It does not require either of the parties to take any action or to pay money to the other. Thus, it differs markedly from the usual court decision; and, particularly in the United States, its use is a relatively recent development in the law. Prior to 1919, only a few states had declaratory judgment statutes, and even the development of the Uniform Declaratory Judgments Act did not stimulate interest in this form of relief to any marked extent. This uniform act was adopted in not more than about half the states. Since the enactment of the Federal Declaratory Judgment Act in 1934, however, there has been an increased interest in this type of legal remedy.

17.11 Nature of the Declaratory Judgment

The most important thing about the declaratory judgment is that it does not involve any procedure for carrying out the decision of the court. A declaratory judgment stands by itself, as a clarification of rights or facts in a given case.

Originally, it was thought that the remedy would be concerned primarily with questions of status or property rights and the construction of various legal instruments, such as wills. Applied to the life insurance contract, this function has many possibilities, one of which is illustrated in the case of *Liner et al., Plaintiffs* v. *Penn Mutual Life Insurance Company.*[10] The Liner case involved the interpretation of two life insur-

---

[10] 145 N.Y.S. (2d) 560 (A.D. 4th, 1955).

ance policies that had been intended to provide funds for educational expenses. Both policies provided that on the death of the insured, the proceeds were to be held under the interest option, with interest payable to the widow of the insured, as trustee during the minority of the beneficiaries—a son and a daughter. The widow was given the right to withdraw $500 each year in one sum under each policy until the company received an affidavit from a college specifying that the beneficiary was enrolled there. After receipt of the affidavit, $1,250 a year could be withdrawn in one sum or in two installments of $625.

Both policies contained accidental death coverage and the insured died under such circumstances that this additional benefit was payable. The question was whether the specific amounts that could be withdrawn would be doubled, since the amount payable was doubled. The beneficiaries asked for declaratory judgments to that effect, while the insurer contended that the accidental death benefit merely doubled the sum payable and had no effect on the withdrawal privileges, which remained unchanged. The first court held in favor of the contention of the insurer, and the beneficiaries appealed.

The appellate court discussed the question in this way:

> The first policy was issued in 1940, when the insured's son Richard was less than one year old. The policy was in the principal amount of $5,000 with double indemnity. Upon the death of the insured, the net proceeds were to be retained under Option D and interest paid to Richard for life. After reaching age 17, Richard could withdraw twice in each year "an amount equal to but not to be more nor less than the sum of $625.00." It will be noted that the principal was to be conserved until Richard was ready for college; thereafter, $1,250 could be withdrawn annually, so that proceeds would be exhausted during a four year college course. During Richard's minority all sums due to him were to be paid to the insured's widow as trustee, and she was to exercise the right of withdrawal for him. On Richard's death the net proceeds remaining were to be paid to her in one sum. By a "supplemental agreement attached to and made a part of the policy," the company agreed to pay the double indemnity benefit "in addition to and together with the sum insured by this policy." It should be noted that the application for this policy provided that after Richard attained age 17, one-eighth of the proceeds could be withdrawn twice yearly for educational purposes. In place of the proportion (one-eighth) the policy contains a figure ($625) which is one-eighth of $5,000, and it would seem that the policy was not intended to vary the application. The numerical equivalent of the fraction employed by the insured in his application adequately expressed his primary intention and could only fail to do so in case of his extremely unlikely death by violent, external and accidental means.
>
> Further evidence that the insured regarded $625 as the practical equivalent of one-eighth may be found in the fact that in his subsequent application for a policy to benefit his second child Victoria, he again pro-

vided that one-eighth of the proceeds could be withdrawn twice yearly. For the proportion, the policy as issued again substituted the numerical equivalent. The policy for Victoria was issued in 1942, when she was only a few months old. Payment of the double indemnity benefit was to "be made in the same manner as and shall be in addition to the sum insured or death benefit." The policy was substantially like that taken out for Richard, except that before Victoria attained age 17 her mother as trustee was entitled to withdraw $500 per year. It undoubtedly occurred to the insured, as it would to any sensible man, that if he were to die leaving two young children, his wife might have a difficult time. Accordingly, he permitted a limited withdrawal before Victoria reached age 17. Thereafter, "an amount not to exceed $1,250.00 in any one year" could be withdrawn. The withdrawal privileges were to be non-cumulative.

On July 9, 1943, the insured executed a change of beneficiary of both policies. The beneficiary clauses of both policies are now identical. The insured continued to elect Option D. The interest is payable to his widow as trustee during the minority of the beneficiary. The widow may also exercise the withdrawal privileges during the beneficiaries' minority. Before the receipt by the company of an affidavit from a college to the effect that the beneficiary is enrolled there, $500 may be withdrawn each year in one sum. After receipt of such an affidavit, $1,250 may be withdrawn each year in one sum or in multiples of $625. The withdrawal privileges are non-cumulative. Upon the death of the primary beneficiary, the remainder shall be paid to the widow in one sum.

The purpose of the insured throughout these transactions was to protect his children during approximately the first twenty years of their lives and to insure that they would receive a college education. The period during which he desired to assist them was substantially certain and known to him; it would not vary according as he might or might not die an accidental death. Regardless of the manner in which he might die, he wished to assist his children through college so that they could take care of themselves. That would require twenty years, not forty. Yet the insurance company interprets the withdrawal privileges so that the duration of the protection period varies according to the way in which the insured met his death. We think the desired protection period would be the same in either case.

The insured obviously contracted for double indemnity for the reason that a sudden death from violent, external and accidental means would deprive him of all opportunity to make further provision for his children. He accordingly provided that in that event the principal amount of each policy should be doubled. But the extra $5,000 must be distributed at the same time and in the same way as the basic death benefit. The supplemental agreements use the language "in addition to and together with" and "in the same manner as and . . . in addition to" the basic $5,000. An article on double indemnity has stated:

"Double indemnity is a desirable supplement to the primary life insurance. It is intended to provide double payment to the beneficiary at the time of greatest need when the insured meets an untimely and premature death as the result of accidental injury." (Kelly, Recent Developments in Double Indemnity Law, 33 Corn. L. Q., 360).

The "time of greatest need" in the present case is the time immediately after the insured's death, when his children are still dependent. It is then that he intended them to have the benefit of the double indemnity provisions. "Double indemnity" means twice as much, not twice as long.

We conclude that the withdrawal privileges under Option D should be doubled. Nothing else would satisfy the purpose of the insured to provide for his children during a fixed period of their lives which would not vary according to the manner of his death, and nothing else would satisfy his direction set forth in the supplemental contract that the extra $5,000 be distributed "in addition to and together with" the basic death benefit.

The judgments are reversed and judgments granted to the plaintiffs declaring that $1,000 may be withdrawn each year until receipt of the affidavit mentioned in the change of beneficiary and $2,500 per year thereafter.

The declaratory judgment has been found helpful in many claim situations. For instance, if claim is presented for disability benefits and the company denies liability on the grounds that the insured is not disabled within the terms of the policy, the company may be faced with a claim based on repudiation of the policy. An action for a declaratory judgment in such cases is one of the most effective ways of clarifying the rights of the parties and the status of the contract.

Another difficult problem is presented in connection with claims under which the company pays the face amount of the policy but denies the accidental death benefit. In such cases, the company pays the face amount of the policy without prejudice to the rights of the beneficiary under the accidental death section of the policy. This discharges the company with respect to the face amount of the policy but leaves its liability open as far as the accidental death portion is concerned. It is sometimes said that payment of the face amount, in practical effect, often "finances" a lawsuit. If there is any real possibility that suit may be filed against the company, an immediate action for a declaratory judgment offers one way to have the facts ascertained while evidence is fresh and before witnesses have scattered.

This same advantage is occasionally offered in connection with a denial of a claim for the face amount of the policy. Even though the company is convinced of the soundness of its decision, it nevertheless remains vulnerable to a possible suit by the beneficiary until the expiration of the statute of limitations or the period of time specified in the policy. During that time, witnesses may die or become widely scattered, and ascertainment of the truth may become progressively more difficult.

An additional difficulty is encountered in some states in the form of statutory penalties imposed for wrongful and vexatious delay in settling life insurance claims. An unfavorable decision after the expiration of the period specified in these statutes means not only liability but also a statutory penalty. In such cases, an action for a declaratory judgment furnishes one method of clarifying the rights of the parties and may enable the company to support its position by a court decision and thus avoid the statutory penalty.

Most life insurance companies do not particularly want to support a denial of a claim, per se. They do not deny a claim unless they believe such action is completely justified. Numerous factors may be involved, however, including evidence in the hands of the beneficiary or his attorney which has never been made available to the life insurance company. In any event, the declaratory judgment presents one way for the insurer to bring the question into court and thus affirm its good faith in the action it has taken.

E. ANTICIPATORY BREACH

Another rather technical remedy sometimes discussed in connection with the life insurance contract is that of anticipatory breach. A breach is the legal term given to the situation where a promisor fails to perform his contract when the time arrives for such performance. The promisee then has a right to sue at law for damages for breach of contract, although he does not usually have this right prior to the time specified for performance.

The repudiation of some contracts prior to the time specified for performance gives the wronged party a present right to sue, if he wishes, for what is termed an "anticipatory breach." Under such circumstances, he may, of course, wait until the time for performance and sue then, or, alternatively, he may treat the contract as at an end and ask to have it rescinded.

Ordinarily, if a life insurance company denies a claim for the benefit payable on death, no matter how completely justified the denial may seem, the beneficiary may treat this action as a breach and sue for damages. Let us say, however, that the company becomes insolvent. It seems obvious here that the company will not pay at such time as payment may fall due, because it will not be able to do so. Yet the beneficiary or the insured has no action for breach since there has not been a breach in the true, legal sense of the word until the actual time for the performance. The same general situation obtains where an insurance association refuses to accept premiums and requests that its members accept a different plan of insurance. In one case[11] of this kind, the refusal

---

[11] *Wartsky et al.* v. *Progressive Order of the West,* 4 Commerce Clearing House Life Cases 893 (N.J., 1940).

of the association to continue to accept premiums was held to be an anticipatory breach, giving the members of the association the right to sue. The New Jersey Supreme Court said:

> By the great weight of authority, when there has been a renunciation of an executory contract by one party, the other has the option of treating the contract as terminated for all purposes of performance and to maintain an action at once for damages occasioned by such repudiation without waiting the time fixed by the contract for performance, or the latter may elect to treat the contract as still binding and, when the day of performance arrives, proceed to enforce his contract as of that time. Such renunciation is not a breach of the contract unless it is treated as such by the adverse party. Upon such a repudiation of an executory agreement by one party, the other may make his choice between two courses open to him, but can neither confuse them or take both.

When the life insurance contract includes provisions for disability benefits payable in instalments and the company denies the insured's claim for those benefits, the breach is a present one, but the insured's right of action against the insurer concerns only the benefit due at that time. Benefits to fall due in the future are not includable in the damages sought. This point has led to attempts to use "anticipatory breach" actions in suits for damages measurable not only by the amount of the benefit presently due but by all the instalments which might become due in the future as well. It is this element of futurity which suggests the anticipatory breach approach.

Nevertheless, in the law of contracts generally, the doctrine of anticipatory breach is not ordinarily held to apply if the promise involves only the payment of money. Nor does it usually apply to any contracts except those which involve mutual and interdependent obligations, and it will be recalled that the life insurance contract is unilateral in nature. The obligations under the life contract are not interdependent; they are the obligations of the company alone.

It is not surprising, therefore, that court decisions upholding the application of the doctrine of anticipatory breach in the case of the life insurance contract are in the minority.

The majority holdings are summarized in the case of *John Hancock Mutual Life Insurance Company* v. *Cohen*,[12] as follows:

> We conclude the general rule to be that the doctrine of anticipatory breach has no application to suits to enforce contracts for future payment of money only, in installments or otherwise. *Cobb* v. *Pacific Mutual, supra; Flinn* v. *Mowry, supra; Brix* v. *People's Mutual Life Ins. Co., supra; Sulyok* v. *Penzintezeti*, 111 N.Y.S. 2, 75, 82; 105 A.L.R. 460; Restatement, Contracts, §§ 316–318; 5 Williston on Contracts, 3740–3743; 12 Cal. Juris. 2d, Contracts, §§ 246–250; see also Calif. L. Rev. 216.

---

[12] 254 F. (2d) 417 (U.S.C.A. Cal., 1958).

SUMMARY

Interpleader

Interpleader is an equitable remedy that enables a person or corporation holding money or property belonging to others and claimed by different persons to deposit it with a court and request that the claimants prove their respective rights. The funds or property will then be paid to the persons the court decides are entitled to it.

Before this remedy will be granted, the person seeking it must show that he has no adequate remedy at law, there must be adverse claimants, and the holder of the property must not himself have an interest in the fund.

A bill in the nature of an interpleader may be filed if the holder of the funds has some interest in the outcome and is not a truly disinterested stakeholder.

Rescission

The remedy of rescission is available to an insurer if material misrepresentation or fraud in the application for the policy is discovered during the lifetime of the insured and prior to expiration of the contestable period. In such cases, the company has no adequate remedy at law and may, therefore, petition the court to rescind or cancel the contract.

Reformation

Reformation is the remedy by which a written instrument is reformed or construed in such a way as to express the actual intentions of the parties. It is available when, as a result of mistake or fraud, a contract as written does not express the intent of the parties. As a general rule, if the error is the result of a mistake, the mistake must either have been mutual or, if unilateral, there must have been fraud or inequitable conduct on the part of the other party.

The Declaratory Judgment

A declaratory judgment is available under the Federal Declaratory Judgments Act and similar statutes in some of the states. It permits one to petition a court to review the facts or interpret a contract and declare the rights and liabilities of the parties. It differs from the usual court decision in not having any machinery to require the parties to carry out the judgment.

Anticipatory Breach

If a contract is repudiated prior to the time performance is required, the person who would at that later time be entitled to performance may bring an action for anticipatory breach. Although the doctrine is not generally held to apply to actions for future instalments of money, it is sometimes used as an attempt to enforce claims to future payments under disability provisions of life insurance contracts.

ILLUSTRATIVE CASE

The usefulness of the remedy of interpleader is demonstrated again and again in cases involving the life insurance contract. The following case is included as an illustration of its use as well as the significance of factors outside the contract on the rights of a policyowner.

METROPOLITAN LIFE INS. CO., Plaintiff v. *MARCOULIER ET AL., Defendants*[13]

HARPER, District Judge: This is an interpleader action filed by the Metropolitan Life Insurance Company against Karen Sue Marcoulier, her minor children (Michael, Katherine and Russell), and Janet A. Marcoulier, to determine the right to the proceeds of a life insurance policy issued by the above mentioned insurance company on the life of Leo R. Marcoulier. Defendants, Karen Sue Marcoulier and her minor children, are domiciled in the State of Missouri. Defendant, Janet A. Marcoulier, is a citizen of the State of Washington, employed by the Defense Department, and at the time of the trial residing in the Netherlands. This court has jurisdiction pursuant to 28 USCA 1332 and 28 USCA 1335.

This court tried the issues raised by the adverse claimants. The material facts are not in dispute and are as follows:

(1) On May 16, 1959, defendant, Karen Sue Marcoulier, married Leo Marcoulier, who was at that time and until his death a career soldier in the United States Army. Three children were born of that marriage. The three children, the defendants Michael, Katherine and Russell, are all minors, and their aunt, Zora Kathleen Blackmon, was appointed by this court as their guardian ad litem.[14] These three defendants will hereafter be referred to as "minor children."

(2) In 1962, the life insurance policy in issue was secured from the Metropolitan Life Insurance Company. The policy provides that the insured is Leo Marcoulier. The policy further provides that "the owner may change the beneficiary designated to receive any amount payable by reason of the death of a person insured under this policy. . . ." With regard to benefit payments,

---

[13] *Metropolitan Life Insurance Company* v. *Marcoulier et al.*, 322 F. Supp. 246 (U.S.D.C., Mo., 1971).

[14] A guardian appointed to represent them in the suit.

the policy provides that "the amount payable if the insured dies will be paid to the insured wife, if living, when the insured dies."

On January 14, 1964, the insured designated his minor children as beneficiaries of the policy, and in March of that year he and the children's mother, Karen Sue were divorced. In May, the insured and his former wife entered into an agreement under which the insured was to support the children and continue in force the insurance policies on which the children were named beneficiaries.

In September, 1964, the insured notified the insurance company that Silvia Marcoulier was his wife and he named the children as contingent beneficiaries. In September, 1968, after being divorced from Silvia, he married Janet. He died on June 6, 1969.

The proceeds of the policy were claimed on behalf of the children because of the divorce settlement and Janet claimed the proceeds because the policy provided that the proceeds would be paid to the insured's wife. The insurer then filed a bill of interpleader.

o   o   o   o   o

All claimants present arguments as to the validity of the French divorce decree in 1964. However, it is unnecessary for this court to pass upon this issue as the minor children are entitled to the proceeds of the policy regardless of the validity or invalidity of the French decree. The decree of support was rendered in Massachusetts, and this court will apply the laws of that state.

o   o   o   o   o

. . . the decree as rendered by the Massachusetts probate court is binding as there was no subsequent modification of the decree.

In determining under the laws of Massachusetts that the decree as rendered is binding, it is necessary to examine the provisions of the stipulation in order to determine what, if any, obligations Leo Marcoulier owed to the minor children. Defendant, Janet Marcoulier, maintains that the terms of the stipulation did not require that the children remain as beneficiaries, but only that the policy would be kept up and not allowed to lapse. The provision in issue provides:

> That the insured, Leo R. Marcoulier, shall continue in force such insurance policies presently outstanding in which the said minor children are named as beneficiaries therein.

Under *Farrington* v. *Boston Safe Deposit & Trust Company,* 181 N.E. 779, 781 (Mass. 1932), it is only the language of the decree that is to be interpreted by the court. There are a total of six provisions within the stipulation. All six provisions concern themselves with providing for the welfare of the minor children. Five of the provisions relate to the rights and duties of the consenting parties during the lifetimes of the parents. The provision in question relates to the payment of life insurance premiums and the policy beneficiaries. The language of the decree makes the minor children beneficiaries of the life insurance policy. Such is the natural and obvious meaning of the decree and the stipulation. If this court were to maintain that the above mentioned provision did not require Leo Marcoulier to retain the minor children as beneficiaries, the court decree would have no real meaning.

Therefore, it is the opinion of this court that the Massachusetts probate court decree of May 18, 1964, prevented Leo Marcoulier from thereafter changing beneficiaries without first obtaining a modification of the above mentioned decree. The decree is final under Massachusetts law and is entitled to full faith and credit in this court. United States Constitution, Article IV, §1. Accordingly, the proceeds of the policy are payable to the minor children.

Even if this court were to hold that the decree entered by the Massachusetts court was not valid, the stipulation between defendant, Karen Sue Marcoulier, and Leo Marcoulier for the benefit of the minor children would vest the proceeds of the policy in the same manner as accomplished by the court decree.

QUESTIONS FOR REVIEW

1. Briefly outline the nature of the equitable remedy of interpleader. List two requirements that must be met before it is available.
2. How does a bill "in the nature of" a bill of interpleader differ from a bill of interpleader?
3. What is the legal effect of the rescission of a life insurance contract?
4. Why is the remedy of rescission not generally available after the death of the insured?
5. What is the purpose of the legal remedy of reformation? Under what circumstances will reformation be granted?
6. Briefly discuss the nature and purpose of a declaratory judgment. Under what circumstances may the remedy prove especially advantageous to a life insurance company?
7. Describe two sets of circumstances under which suit might be brought against a life insurance company for anticipatory breach.

PART IV

The File Is Closed

Chapter Outline

Chapter 18

The Contract
Is Performed

A LIFE INSURANCE contract is "performed," as that word is used in contract law, when the last of the promises it contains is carried out. Under the typical life insurance policy, this is accomplished when the insured has died and the amount of insurance is paid by the company.

The purpose of this chapter is to explore the ways in which this promise and those most closely related to it are carried out and some of the most significant legal problems that may be involved.

A. REVIEWING DEATH CLAIMS

Death claims are reviewed in a life insurance company for the basic purpose of verifying that the conditions specified in the contracts have been met. Specifically, the premiums must have been paid as required, the term of the policy must not have expired, and the insured must have died.

The review of early death claims (those arising within the contestable period) for the purpose of verifying that requested underwriting information was furnished at the time of application and that the policy was not obtained through material misrepresentation, concealment, or fraud has already been discussed. The fact that the policyowner or beneficiary could receive a great deal more in benefits than he or she had paid in premiums under a life insurance policy constitutes a great temptation to the unscrupulous to attempt to obtain such policies by fraud. For this reason alone, early death claims would be carefully reviewed.

At the same time, however, the importance of life insurance to the survivors of the insured is clearly kept in mind in the claim department of a life insurance company, and most life insurers consider it an essential part of their responsibilities to pay death claims as promptly as possible. Certain basic questions must be answered when a claim is received; but as soon as those questions are settled, the claim will be paid. These questions will be discussed in the following pages, beginning with the basic one: "Is the benefit payable?"

18.1 Is the Benefit Payable?

Several factors are involved in any determination of whether the benefit is payable. Most important is the question of whether the policy was in force, either on a premium-paying or a paid-up basis or under one of the nonforfeiture options. Did death occur during the suicide period and, if so, is there a possibility that the insured took his own life? Is accidental death coverage involved, and did the death occur under circumstances that might present a problem on this point?

The validity of the contract is significant also, if death occurred during the contestable period. In reviewing such early claims, therefore, the reviewer will be alert for evidence of material misrepresentation or fraud.

Evidence of Death.   Generally speaking, a certified copy of the death certificate is accepted as satisfactory evidence that the insured is dead. Nevertheless, this does not mean that it cannot be challenged and other evidence presented to show that the certificate is incorrect. In some instances, also, the reported cause of death is open to question. The evaluation of the death certificate as competent evidence of the facts it sets forth, therefore, constitutes a separate legal question in and of itself.

18.2 To Whom Is the Benefit Payable?

Obviously, claim should be made by the beneficiary. However, in cases where the policyowner has indicated his wishes to change the beneficiary but has not completed the procedures necessary to make the change effective, determining the correct beneficiary may present a very definite legal problem. In this connection, it should be borne in mind that legal problems of this kind are not the rule; they are the exception. Hundreds of claims are processed and paid without question. When a legal problem is revealed, however, the claim is given individual consideration and the problem must be resolved before payment is made.

No Named Beneficiary.   Under most ordinary life insurance contracts, if there is no surviving beneficiary at the death of the insured, the policy provides that the insurance will be paid to the executor or administrator of the insured. Sometimes this is the wish of the policyowner, and sometimes it merely results from the death of all named beneficiaries. In any event, when the personal representative is the claimant, the insurer will require evidence of his appointment. Ordinarily, in such cases, a certified copy of the Letters of Administration or comparable documents are requested.

The Trustee-Beneficiary. Policies are sometimes made payable to trustees. Here the proceeds will be claimed by the trustee, but the insurer will need evidence of the trustee's appointment and power to act. Certified copies of the trust agreement itself are necessary in some cases. In this, as in all cases, the important thing is to be quite certain that the person to whom payment is made is the person entitled to payment, both by the terms of the contract and the law.

Minor Beneficiaries. Some of the most difficult claim questions are presented in connection with minor beneficiaries. The minor's capacity to receive and give a valid receipt for the proceeds of the life insurance contract is affected by many laws and circumstances. As previously noted, in specific circumstances, many of the states have statutes which make the minor capable of effecting a binding contract of life insurance as if he were an adult. However, these statutes must be carefully checked. For instance, the Illinois statute, quoted in Chapter 2, removes the disability of certain minors with respect to the purchase of contracts of insurance on their own lives or the lives of family members. Nevertheless, it does not remove the minor's disability with respect to his right to receive and to be bound by his receipt for the proceeds of insurance on the life of someone not listed in the statute. Thus if insurance on the life of a parent is payable to a minor child, a different kind of enabling statute is necessary before the minor beneficiary can give a release that he cannot afterwards disaffirm.

Illustrative of this type of statute is the statute in effect in New York which permits a minor of the age of 18 years to receive and give a binding receipt for insurance proceeds in a single sum of not more than $3,000 or for periodic payments of not more than that amount in any one year, under a settlement agreement with the life insurance company. The statute reads as follows:

> Any minor domiciled in this state, who shall have attained the age of eighteen years, shall be deemed competent to receive and to give a full acquittance and discharge for a single sum or for periodical payments, not exceeding three thousand dollars in one year, payable by a life insurance company under the maturity, death or settlement agreement provisions in effect or elected by such minor under a life insurance policy or annuity contract, provided such policy, contract or agreement shall provide for the payment or payments to such minor and provided that prior to such payment the company has not received written notice of the

appointment of a duly qualified guardian of the property of such minor; but no such minor shall be deemed competent to alienate the right to such payment or payments or to anticipate the same.[1]

In the majority of instances where insurance proceeds are payable to a minor beneficiary, they are paid to the legally appointed guardian of the minor's estate. In such cases, claim is filed by the guardian and supported by a certified copy of the court order appointing him. It should, perhaps, be noted that this appointment is just as necessary in the case of a surviving parent who is named guardian as it is if a nonrelative has been appointed. The parent is the guardian of the person of the child, but except under the civil law and laws derived from it, a parent, as such, has no right to receive or control any part of the estate of the child. Thus payment of the proceeds of a life insurance policy naming a minor beneficiary can safely be made only to the guardian of the estate of the minor. No one else has the power to give an effective receipt for such payment.

A number of states have laws making it possible to pay to and receive an effective receipt from persons other than the legally appointed guardian of the estate of a minor where the amount in question is less than a stated sum. For instance, the Illinois law makes such a provision for situations where the estate is not in excess of $2,500, and provides as follows:

> Upon receiving an affidavit that the personal estate of a minor does not exceed $2,500 in value, that no guardian has been appointed for his estate, and that the affiant is a parent or a person standing *in loco parentis* to the minor, any person or corporation indebted to or holding personal estate of the minor may pay the amount of the indebtedness or deliver personal estate to the affiant. In the same manner, and upon like proof any person or corporation having the responsibility for the issuance or transfer of stocks, bonds or other personal estate may issue or transfer the stocks, bonds or other personal estate to or in the name of the affiant. Upon the payment, delivery, transfer or issuance pursuant to the affidavit, the person or corporation is released to the same extent as if the payment, delivery, transfer or issuance had been made to the legally qualified guardian of the minor and is not required to see to the application or disposition of the property.[2]

Pennsylvania has an unusual kind of law which makes it possible to name a guardian for the beneficiary designated in a life insurance policy. This statute reads as follows:

> Any person, who hereafter makes a deed or gift *inter vivos* or exercises a right under an insurance or annuity policy to designate the beneficiary

---

[1] New York Insurance Law, Sec. 145. (Alienate means to assign.)
[2] Illinois Revised Statutes, Chap. 3, Sec. 326 (1965).

to receive the proceeds of such policy, may in such deed or in the instrument creating such gift or designating such beneficiary, appoint a guardian of the estate or interest of each beneficiary named therein who shall be a minor or otherwise incompetent. Payment by an insurance company to the guardian of such beneficiary so appointed shall discharge the insurance company to the extent of such payment to the same effect as payment to an otherwise duly appointed and qualified guardian.[3]

B. THE INSURED TAKES HIS LIFE

18.3 Suicide, a Legal Concept

Suicide has been defined as "the deliberate termination of one's existence, while in the possession and enjoyment of his mental faculties."[4] Mere self-destruction is not suicide in the legal sense of the word. For this reason, the words "sane or insane," which are often included in life insurance policies, extend the meaning of suicide considerably beyond its usual legal significance.

In the Absence of a Policy Provision. Where there is no express suicide provision and the policy is payable to the estate of the insured, the majority of courts have held that intentional self-destruction while sane is not a risk that is covered by the policy. If the policy is payable to a third person, however, payment has been allowed. It seems the universal court holding that if there is no express policy provision to the contrary, self-destruction while insane is covered by the policy exactly as any other death would be.

The Policy Provision. By far the majority of present-day life insurance policies contain a provision expressly excepting suicide from coverage for a limited period of time. Usually this period is two years, sometimes one, and it is included for the purpose of effecting an equitable compromise between two acknowledgedly incompatible considerations.

On the one hand, the best interests of the policyowners as a group must be considered. To make no effort to prevent persons from applying for life insurance for the purpose of securing the benefits to their dependents by taking their own lives would clearly be unfair to the other policyowners, who would have to share the resulting higher costs of the insurance. It might also have a tendency to encourage the taking of one's own life and thus be against public policy.

On the other hand, however, the fact that the insured met his death by suicide—perhaps many years after having applied for the policy—should not be used as an excuse for not paying the claim. The generally recognized purpose of life insurance is to provide protection against the

---

[3] Purdon's Penna. Statutes, Title 20, Probate, Estates and Fiduciaries Code, Sec. 5115.

[4] *Black's Law Dictionary* (4th ed.; St. Paul: West Publishing Co., 1951), p. 1602.

economic loss resulting from the insured's early death; and the economic loss to the insured's dependents is just as great if his death is the result of suicide as if he lost his life in an automobile accident.

A policy provision under which premiums are refunded, but no other benefit is payable if the insured dies by suicide within the first two years after the policy is issued, is generally believed to furnish sufficient protection against those persons who might be tempted to make a profitable occasion of their already decided upon departure from this life. Few people, it is thought, will apply for life insurance, with the intention of waiting two years and then committing suicide. At the same time, the beneficiary of the insured who commits suicide after the expiration of two or more years will have the same protection that he would have in the event of death in any other manner.

Statutes. Some, though not nearly all, of the states have special statutes defining the period during which the risk of suicide may be excluded from a life insurance contract. These statutes differ widely. Colorado and North Dakota, for example, provide that after one year from the date the policy is issued, suicide shall not be a defense against a life insurance claim. The Missouri statute is one of the most unusual, since it provides that suicide shall not be a valid defense unless it was contemplated by the insured when he applied for the insurance. This statute reads as follows:

> In all suits upon policies of insurance on life hereafter issued by any company doing business in this state to a citizen of this state, it shall be no defense that the insured committed suicide, unless it shall be shown to the satisfaction of the court or jury trying the cause, that the insured contemplated suicide at the time he made his application for the policy, and any stipulation in the policy to the contrary shall be void.[5]

As a practical matter, it would be almost impossible to prove an intent of this kind in most suicide situations, even if it existed. The effect of this statute, therefore, is to nullify the suicide provision in any life insurance policy issued to a citizen of Missouri. The statute has been litigated extensively, but it has been held constitutional and has even been held to apply to a policy that was issued at a time when the insured was a resident of another state but was reinstated after he became a resident of Missouri.

Interpretation of the Suicide Provision. Policy provisions excepting death by "suicide" are generally interpreted to refer only to self-destruction of the insured while sane. When the words "sane or insane" are used, there is a conflict in the court decisions. Where the policy provides that suicide, sane or insane, is a risk not assumed, the majority of courts have held that self-destruction while insane is a valid exclusion. However, a

---

[5] Mo. Stat. Ann., 1949, Tit. 24, Sec. 376.620.

strong minority group of courts take the position that self-destruction, if the insured is so insane as not to realize the natural consequences of his act, is not suicide "sane or insane." In other words, it is not suicide in the legal sense of the term. In these latter cases especially, the question of what constitutes a state of insanity is important.

It is notable that the New York Insurance Department by administrative ruling forbids the use of the phrase "sane or insane" in policies submitted to that department for approval.

Presumption against Suicide.　At the present time, the majority of suicide cases relate to questions of fact and whether the self-destruction in question was actually suicide. As an aid in deciding such questions, the courts have developed a very strong presumption against suicide. In other words, the courts take the point of view that self-destruction is against the natural inclinations of the average person. Therefore, if the facts of a case can be interpreted in more than one way, the legal presumption is that the insured did not take his life. When an insurer denies a claim on the grounds of suicide, therefore, the burden is on it to prove the suicide by evidence sufficient to convince the jury.

The importance of the burden of proof concept in this area is illustrated in the case of *Angelus* v. *Government Personnel Life Ins. Co.*,[6] decided by the Washington supreme court. This case deals solely with the question of suicide as an affirmative defense, which means a defense that must be specifically interposed by one of the parties in a lawsuit. In this case, it was the insurer who interposed the defense and then had the burden of proving it. The more applicable portions of the decision read as follows:

> The sole question is: Did decedent commit suicide?
> Plaintiff establishes a *prima facie* case with evidence that the insured died while the policy of life insurance was in effect. Liability follows a showing of death, unless there is an affirmative showing that death was within an exception contained in the policy.
> In this case, suicide is an affirmative defense. The insurance company must establish, by a preponderance of the evidence (*Selover* v. *Aetna Life Ins. Co.*, 180 Wash. 236, 38 P. 2d 1059 [1934]), that the wound that caused the death of the insured was intentionally self-inflicted. (*New York Life Ins. Co.* v. *Newport*, 1 Wn. (2d) 511, 517, 519, 96 P. 2d 449 [1939].) Although not necessarily controlling, the presence or absence of motive for suicide is an element to be taken into consideration.
> There is very little, if any, dispute as to the facts surrounding the death of the insured. The disagreement is over the conclusion to be drawn from these facts.
> The following appears from the written statements gathered by the investigating officer:

---

[6] 321 P. (2d) 545 (Wash., 1958).

Decedent, twenty years old at the time of his death on October 31, 1955, was attached to a Marine fighter squadron as an aircraft radar technician. He was assigned to a guard company for temporary duty, which was to terminate the day of his death.

His guard duties required that he be familiar with a .45 calibre automatic pistol. On numerous occasions, while acting as corporal of the guard, he had given instruction on the use of the automatic pistol and on safety precautions to be observed while handling it.

Throughout decedent's tour of duty with the guard, all pistols assigned to personnel on post or on duty were kept with a loaded clip inserted, but no round of ammunition was in the chamber. It was common knowledge among members of the guard that all pistols in actual physical custody of guard personnel were loaded.

Decedent is described as a happy-go-lucky individual with no known disturbing problems. He was a good worker, cheerful, and competent in his temporary additional duty assignment. One of his associates states:

"He was an exceptionally good natured marine and I never knew him to worry or sweat anything. I had known him a good while and was a very close friend of his. It always appeared to me life was just a big joke to him and I told him several times he ought to take things more seriously."

About eleven a.m. the day of his death, decedent talked with Corporal Last, who reported that he "seemed to be in a very good mood. He was especially happy because he was off guard and had liberty that night."

About five p.m. of the same day, Sergeant Nelson asked decedent "when he was coming back to work with me in fire control. He told me that he would be down in the morning and ready to go to work."

About five-thirty p.m. decedent and Corporal Tishler, with whom he was going on liberty, entered hut No. 5. Decedent talked with Corporal Ball, who stated:

"He was laughing and seemed to be in very good spirits as he was going on liberty and he was kidding me because I had the duty. He walked into the head [lavatory] to comb his hair and I heard him laugh and then the report of the .45."

While Corporal Tishler was combing his hair, decedent grabbed a pistol belt hanging on a peg, pulled the pistol out of the holster, "jacked a round into the chamber," put the pistol to his head, and said "here's to it," and fired the pistol. He died several hours later.

On previous occasions, decedent had been observed playing a modified version of "Russian Roulette" with a .45 calibre automatic pistol, the same type which caused his death. He would squeeze the release on the clip, allow it to slide down, then pull the slide to the rear, and release it. If the clip dropped about half an inch, the slide would not pick up a round from the clip and place it in the chamber. The clip was then locked in place, the pistol placed at his temple, and the trigger pulled. In truth, this is not "Russian Roulette," which is played with a revolver and not an automatic pistol. His safety depended upon sleight-of-hand and not chance.

He would never do it unless he was just trying to "shake someone up." He always laughed afterwards.

One witness stated that *the clip was not in the weapon* when it was recovered from the floor after the shooting. Another witness stated, when describing the weapon after the shooting,

"The pistol was fully cocked with one (1) round in the chamber and three (3) rounds in the magazine *when recovered.*"

This suggests the hypothesis that the decedent believed he had released the clip and caused it to drop, so that the slide had not "jacked a round into the chamber" of the pistol. If this be true, he was mistaken.

In *United Benefit Life Ins. Co.* v. *Schott,* 296 Ky. 789, 796, 177 S.W. 2d 581, 150 A.L.R. 1359 (1943), a case factually akin to the instant one, the court said:

"The brandishing and flourishing of the weapons, in the manner described by Fields and McDowell, do not impress us as having been more than the mere blustering and swaggering of a swashbuckler. Persons intent upon committing suicide are not apt to behave in that manner."

We agree with the trial court; appellant did not establish suicide by a preponderance of the evidence.

The judgment is affirmed.

18.4 Suicide versus Accidental Death

A special problem is presented in this area in connection with deaths that occur under such circumstances that they might be interpreted either as death from accidental means or suicide. In such cases, the concepts of presumptions and burden of proof are especially important. In one case,[7] for instance, the insured died as the result of injuries suffered in connection with a dynamite explosion. The court said:

There is no need to detail the evidence at length. It may be said in resumé that there was no eye witness to the explosion, that some circumstances and certain statements made by the insured immediately after it occurred point strongly to suicide but that other circumstances indicate persuasively that it was an accident, and that no motive for suicide was shown. In Colorado, death by unexplained violence is presumed to have been accident, evidence establishing death by violence without explanation as to the manner in which the violence was inflicted constitutes prima facie proof that the death was accidental, *Occidental Life Ins. Co.* v. *United States Nat. Bank of Denver, Colo.,* 98 Colo. 126, 53 Pac. 2d 1180; and, if under the evidence death by violence can be explained on any reasonable hypothesis other than suicide, it is the duty of the court or the jury to do so, *Prudential Ins. Co. of America* v. *Cline,* 98 Colo. 275, 57 Pac. 2d 1205. Taken as a whole and fairly construed, the evidence did not conclusively establish suicide. Instead, it presented an issue for the jury.

---

[7] *Parfet* v. *Kansas City Life Insurance Co.,* 128 F. (2d) 361 (C.C.A. Colo., 1942).

C. DEATH AS THE RESULT OF WAR

Two basic questions arise in connection with the payment of the death benefit under a life insurance policy that has been issued with a war hazard limitation. One is the question of whether the hostilities involved actually constituted war. The second question is whether the insured met his death under circumstances that would bring it within the terms of the exclusion.

The question of the meaning of "war," as that word is used in war hazard limitation riders, has been previously discussed. The circumstances under which such limitations or exceptions apply are illustrated in the case of *Eggena* v. *New York Life Insurance Company*.[8] This case involved a war exclusion under an accidental death benefit, but the basic principle remains the same. In the Eggena case, the insured was a member of a tank crew who was killed while riding as an observer in a tank that was proceeding in a routine training convoy to a bivouac area. The accident occurred in Arkansas, and the argument was made that the death did not result directly or indirectly from "war or any act incident thereto," and thus the accidental death benefit was payable. The court discussed several prior cases and said:

> The case at bar is what is known as a result case, as distinguished from one involving the status. Various courts have held that the war clause is not applicable where death is due to some cause common to both military and civilian life. . . .
>
> . . . In many cases where recovery was permitted death was attributed to causes which affected both civilians and those engaged in military service alike, such as pneumonia and various accidents common to all. . . .

In this case, the court concluded that this was not an accident "common to all" and that the military exclusion applied, as follows:

> Here deceased came to his death riding in an army tank as a member of a crew in training for war, which is not a cause of death common to civilian life. A clause excluding liability in the event death results directly or indirectly from war, we are satisfied, must apply to a member of the military forces, a member of an army tank crew, on active duty, while in the line of duty, acting under orders from superior officers and carrying out a military assignment as a part of his training during the prosecution of war. The death of insured was the direct result of an act incident to war.

D. DEATH AS THE RESULT OF AVIATION

The aviation exclusion found in some, though not many, life insurance policies today limits the benefit payable if death occurs as the result of

---

[8] 18 N.W. (2d) 530 (Iowa, 1945).

certain specified aviation activities. Ordinarily, the exclusion is used in cases where there is an added risk by reason of aviation activities on the part of the proposed insured and the applicant does not wish to pay the increased premium necessary to cover the additional risk.

The increasing safety of aviation in general has been reflected in a gradual but steady liberalization of aviation restrictions, and today the exclusions used ordinarily do not apply if the insured is being transported as a passenger only. Often liberalizations of company policy apply to previously issued policies also, so that the actual handling of a claim may reflect practices more liberal than the wording of the contract itself would indicate.

Cases reaching the courts have involved many questions of policy wording, and a great many cases interpret specific phrases such as "fare-paying passenger" and "regularly scheduled flight." Another type of question which has sometimes been presented relates to what are essentially war deaths occurring while the insureds are in flight. In such cases as these, if the life insurance policy does not contain a war hazard exclusion, the aviation exclusion has been held to apply only to civilian aviation.

Another class of case presenting a relatively close question involves the death of an insured who brings his plane down safely but alights on a desert or a lake, for example, and loses his life by reason of perils incident to the terrain. In one such case,[9] the insured's plane landed safely on a lake, but he was drowned trying to swim to the shore. There the court said:

> Defendant [the insurer] contends that drowning, after a forced landing of a land-based plane in cold water, is an undisputable risk associated with aerial flight in a private plane and further that it was a risk intended to be excluded from the operation of this policy. If this argument is logical it would mean also that if a person were forced to land his private plane in a pasture, where, after safely alighting, he was gored to death by a vicious bull, an insurer would not be liable on a policy containing the clause [excluding aviation] now under consideration. Likewise, such a landing made in a public highway, followed by the accidental death of the insured after alighting from his plane and resulting from being struck by a passing automobile, would be similarly excluded from such a policy.
>
> There is no evidence in this record that the death of the insured resulted directly or indirectly from injuries sustained by him while in the airplane or in falling or descending therefrom or therewith. Furthermore, there is no evidence from which such an inference can be reasonably drawn. After leaving the plane he swam a considerable distance in cold water and drowned. The exclusion clause of the policy does not apply to this case.

---

[9] *McDaniel* v. *Standard Accident Insurance Co.*, 221 F. (2d) 171 (C.A. Ill., 1955).

E. MYSTERIOUS DISAPPEARANCE

Claims based upon the mysterious disappearance of the insured present a somewhat different problem. Here the basic question does not relate to how death occurred but rather to whether it did. People often disappear without explanation, leaving questions relating to property rights and responsibilities, including insurance problems, to be worked out as satisfactorily as possible. Because this is not unusual, the law has developed some basic principles and presumptions in connection with the distribution of property under such circumstances, some of which are used in connection with the life insurance contract. One of the most important is the presumption of death after an absence of seven years.

The Presumption of Death. The presumption of death after an unexplained absence of seven years has been developed since 1800. Prior to that date, in the absence of evidence to the contrary, an absent person was presumed to be living even though he might have been 90 or 100 years old at the time a question arose. As generally stated today, however, a person will be presumed to have died (*a*) if he has been missing from his home or usual residence for a period of seven years; (*b*) if such absence has been continuous and without explanation; (*c*) if persons most likely to hear from him have heard nothing; and (*d*) if he cannot be located by diligent search and inquiry. At the present time, this presumption is recognized in almost all the states, either by statute or judicial recognition of the common-law rule.

It is generally agreed that the presumption may be rebutted. This means that the person who wishes to show that death has not occurred may present evidence to that effect. If such evidence is not offered, the presumption will stand and the person will be declared dead. If evidence is presented to show that he is still living, the question of his survival is one of fact, to be decided by the jury.

18.5 Unexplained Absence

Sometimes it is shown that a missing person was a fugitive from justice. The majority of courts do not hold that this showing destroys the presumption, but only that it then becomes a question for the jury to decide. Similar rules are ordinarily followed in connection with missing persons who were in serious financial or domestic troubles at the time of their disappearance. Such information does not necessarily mean that the person is still living; but it does furnish a reason, other than death, for his absence.

18.6 Date of Death

Often it is not enough merely to establish the fact of death. In life insurance questions, the actual date of death is often important. Many life insurance policies on the lives of persons missing for extended periods of time lapse for nonpayment of premiums prior to the expiration of seven years. Obviously it is to the advantage of the beneficiary to prove, if possible, that the insured actually met his death sometime prior to the date the policy lapsed.

There are two rules with respect to establishing the date of death. Under the majority (or English) rule, the missing person is presumed to be dead at the end of the seven years, but the exact time of death is left open to be established as a question of fact. Under the minority rule, the missing person is presumed to have died at the end of the period. Under the latter rule, the person wishing to establish death prior to the end of the seven-year period has the burden of introducing evidence to that effect. Thus, in either case, it is necessary to present evidence relating to the exact date of death. The principal difference relates to the amount and kind of evidence that will suffice. Under the minority rule, it is usually necessary to show that the insured was exposed to some specific peril before an earlier date of death can be established. Under the majority rule, on the other hand, evidence of character, habits, domestic relations, and other circumstances may ordinarily be presented for the consideration of the jury in reaching its conclusion.

Regardless of the rule that may be applied, the only safe procedure for a beneficiary of a life insurance policy, when the insured has disappeared, is to continue the payment of premiums until the end of seven years, when the question of the death of the insured can be judicially decided. If it can then be proved that the insured met his death on some date prior to the end of the period, any overpayment of premiums will be recovered.

Uniform Act. The Uniform Absence as Evidence of Death and Absentees' Property Act, in effect in Maryland, Tennessee, and Wisconsin, was prepared several years ago by the National Conference of Commissioners on Uniform State Laws. It abolishes the presumption of death after seven years' absence and provides that the issues of death and the date of death be submitted to the jury in every case.

18.7 Reappearance

One of the truly complicating aspects of this problem of mysterious disappearance, as it relates to the life insurance contract, is presented when the insured reappears after having been declared dead and after settlement of the death benefit or benefits has been made. Suppose that the Ajax Life Insurance Company paid the insurance proceeds to the beneficiary of a life insurance policy on John Doe's life after John's unexplained absence for seven years, and then two years later John reappears. What, if any, are the rights of the company?

General Rules. The general rule is that if the full benefit provided by the policy has been paid to the beneficiary in good faith and the insured later reappears, the amount paid may be recovered by the insurance company on the basis that it was paid under a mistake of fact. If less than the full amount provided by the policy has been paid, as in a compromise settlement, for example, it cannot be recovered. The ruling principle here is that the compromise settlement of a doubtful claim will not be disturbed.

These rules (concerning the recovery of money paid) are illustrated in the South Carolina case of *Pilot Life Insurance Co.* v. *Cudd.*[10] There the insurer paid $1,013.36 to the beneficiary of a life insurance contract in June, 1943, on the strength of a Certificate of Presumptive Death issued by the Maritime War Emergency Board. In 1945 it was learned that the insured was a prisoner of war in a Japanese Prisoner of War Camp and on October 8, 1945, the Maritime War Emergency Board issued a certificate correcting the Certificate of Presumptive Death. The insurer requested the return of the insurance money and the beneficiary refused. The insurer then initiated a court action to recover the money, alleging that it had been paid under a mistake of fact. The decision in the trial court was for the insurer and the defendant appealed.

The supreme court pointed out that the case raised the following issues:

1. Was such payment a mutual mistake of fact or error of judgment on the part of the company?
2. Was such payment a voluntary one?
3. Was such payment a compromise settlement by plaintiff?

The court reviewed the facts that led to the payment in the first place and then continued:

> That the insured is alive and back in the United States at this time is undisputed.
>
> This case was tried as an equity case and from this there is no appeal; therefore, it will be so considered by this Court.
>
> It is a firmly established general rule that money paid to another under the influence of a mistake of fact, that is, on the mistaken supposition of the existence of a specific fact which would entitle the other to the money, which would not have been paid if it had been known to the payor that the fact was otherwise, may be recovered, provided the payment has not caused such a change in the position of the payee that it would be unjust to require a refund. The ground on which the rule rests is that money paid through misapprehension of facts belongs, in equity and good conscience to the person who paid it.

---

10 208 S.C. 6, 36 S.E. (2d) 860 (1945).

Both parties to this action had been advised that the insured had sailed from Ceylon and that his ship and all aboard had been unheard from and were presumed lost as a result of enemy action. Both parties exhausted their sources of information and all accepted the death of the insured as a fact. The U.S. Government also thought and so certified as a result of which appellant filed her claim and accepted the payment of the policy by respondent. It is obvious that both parties accepted as a fact that the insured had died shortly after sailing from Ceylon. There is no evidence of fraud, therefore, the question resolves itself into whether or not there was a mutual mistake. Appellant contends that there was no mutual mistake but rather a mistake or error of judgment on the part of the insurer. That settlement was made under the realization of an uncertainty and that the settlement was a compromise of a doubtful liability.

All the facts available to one of the parties was [sic] available to, and known by, both and their reactions thereto were the same. The acceptance of the death of the insured as a fact was a mutual mistake of fact equally concurred in by both parties. The whole situation having arisen because of the acceptance by the parties as a fact that the insured came to his death shortly after he sailed from Ceylon, when such fact did not exist. To follow appellant's line of argument would be to allow the beneficiary to be enriched to the amount of $1,013.36 for which the essential prerequisite was the death of the insured when in fact he is still alive. A mistake of fact having existed the proposition is elementary that repayment to the insurers could be compelled: *Masonic Life Ass'n* v. *Crandall*, 41 N.Y.S. 497, 11 L.R.A. (N.S.) 234.

In *Riegel* v. *American Life Ins. Co.*, 19 L.R.A., 166, 11 L.R.A. 857, we find the reverse of the position of the parties in this case. The plaintiff-beneficiary held a policy for $6,000.00 on the life of a debtor, Leisenring, who had not been heard from for about thirteen years. The beneficiary was paying premiums on this policy in an annual amount of $153.90, which premiums were burdensome to her and an arrangement was worked out whereby she surrendered the $6,000.00 policy and accepted a new policy, paid up, for $2,500.00 and was thereupon relieved from the payment of premiums. This, of course, was based upon the assumption of fact by both parties that the insured was alive. A short time later it was discovered that Leisenring, the insured, had died some time prior to the arrangements between the beneficiary and the insurer, and thereupon the beneficiary brought action against the company for recovery on the original policy of $6,000.00. The insurer there defended very much upon the grounds that appellant here contends for and filed a demurrer. contending that there was a compromise settlement based upon a doubtful fact. The Circuit Judge sustained the demurrer and dismissed the action, holding that "Where both parties treat upon the basis of the fact being doubtful, and the transaction shows that both parties took the risk of the doubt, equity will not interfere, but will leave the parties where they were." This order was reversed on appeal by the Supreme Court of Pennsylvania which said:

"The case presented on these facts was that of a contract entered into under the influence of a mutual mistake, and a claim for relief from such contract. The mistake was in relation to the fact of Leisenring's death. Both parties evidently supposed, and acted on the supposition, that he was alive, and that the annual premiums upon his life, which had become burdensome to Mrs. Riegel must be continued indefinitely, until his death should take place.

"At the time she made it (the contract of settlement) she was already relieved from the burdensome premiums, and the entire amount of the policy was honestly due her from the Company. What was the effect of the mistake upon her? Simply to take from her the difference between the two policies and give her absolutely nothing for it. . . . The Company parted with nothing. She secured nothing. The whole transaction was a mistake, and if the decree of the court below stands, the result will be to take $3,500.00 from Mrs. Riegel, and give it to the Insurance Company."

After the case was tried on its merits and the lower Court had held that the beneficiary was not entitled to relief, the Supreme Court reversed that Order and held that the original policy of $6,000.00 should be reinstated and that amount paid to the beneficiary. In discussing the right of the beneficiary to relief because the parties had proceeded upon the mistaken assumption that the insured was alive, when in fact he was dead, the Court quoted portions of its opinion on the first appeal. The Court points out that the Circuit Judge, on the hearing on the demurrer, had treated the arrangement as a compromise, but that it did not partake of a compromise because "both parties to the transaction were acting, in respect thereto, on the basis that Leisenring was alive," and the Court says, with respect to such a situation:

"The general rule is that an act done or a contract made under a mistake of a material fact is voidable and relievable in equity. . . . It makes no difference in application of the principle that the subject-matter of the contract be known to both parties to be liable to a contingency which may destroy it immediately; for, if the contingency has, unknown to the parties, already happened, the contract will be avoided as founded on a mutual mistake of a matter constituting the basis of the contract. . . .

"It cannot be doubted that in exchanging the old for the new policy both parties acted on the basis that Leisenring was then alive. Their every act in the transaction was predicated on that as an assumed fact. . . . If the exchange was not made on the asumption by both parties that Leisenring was then alive, the Company stultified itself by issuing a paid-up policy on the life of one who was then in his grave; and the plaintiff was guilty of extreme folly of paying $3,500.00 for exemption from a liability which, by the previous death of Leisenring, had ipso facto ceased. . . . she and the company were both at that time ignorant of the fact that the life on which the original risk was taken had previously dropped. . . . The central fact underlying the transaction, and to which every circumstance connected therewith clearly points, was the assumption by both parties that Leisenring was then in full life."

The logic of this case is inescapable and simply by reversing the position of the parties very appropriate to the case now before us.

* * * * *

Appellant argues strenuously and at length that what occurred in the payment of the face of the policy was voluntary and made in compromise, and, therefore, is not the subject of rescission.

"That cannot be said with propriety to be voluntarily done, where a formal assent thereto is induced by mistake . . . as to facts material to control the operation of the will therein any more than where such formal assent is extorted by the application of a force which fetters and obstructs its free working." *Kenneth* v. *S. C. Railway Co.*, 15 Rich. L. 284; 98 Am. Dec. 382.

A compromise as shown by the principal authority cited by appellant (*Taylor* v. *Insurance Company*, 196 S.C. 195, 12 S.E. 2d 708) involves the essential element of a dispute or a controversy. The Taylor settlement was upheld because there was a bona fide basis for dispute between the parties as to whether the insured had committed suicide. But here there was no dispute, nor claim for double indemnity nor controversy between the parties. Both parties had substantially the same information and proceeded upon the same mistake of fact.

The court concluded that the payment was based upon a mutual mistake of fact, that it was not a compromise payment, and that it was made voluntarily. Therefore, the insurer was entitled to recover the amount so paid.

F. ESTABLISHING THE PROPER PAYEE

After it has been determined that the benefit is payable, there may nevertheless be questions as to the person or persons to whom it is to be paid. Here we have the basic problems of attempted but not completed changes of beneficiary; the beneficiary who murders the insured; the beneficiary designation which is, in effect, changed by reason of divorce; and the interposition of numerous persons whose rights are based on the law in general, as opposed to those whose rights are based entirely on the terms of the contract itself. Of these, perhaps the most basic question arises in the situation where the insured meets his death at the hands of the beneficiary.

18.8 The Beneficiary-Murderer

There is probably no principle better established in the law of the life insurance contract than the rule that a beneficiary of a life insurance policy who feloniously kills the insured will not be permitted to receive the proceeds. The rule is grounded in public policy. To permit a murderer to receive the insurance benefit payable upon the death of the very person he has murdered would violate one of the basic tenets of the law, which is to protect human life and discourage anything tending to encourage murder.

As this principle is applied in the settlement of life insurance claims, there are two major divisions. One group of cases involves those situations where the policy in question was issued to an applicant who, at the time of application, was contemplating the murder of the person whose life was being insured. The other group is comprised of cases where the policy was applied for and issued in good faith but the beneficiary later murdered the insured.

Where the Policy Was Procured with Intent to Murder. In cases where the beneficiary procured the policy with intent to murder the insured, the company may be held to have no liability on the grounds that the policy as issued did not constitute a valid contract in the first place. Illustrative of this kind of case and this particular type of holding is *Colyer's Admr., Appellant* v. *New York Life Insurance Company*,[11] decided by the Kentucky Court of Appeals in June, 1945. The facts of this case are stated in the court's own words, as follows:

> On April 10, 1942, Finley Duncan brutally murdered his 20-year old brother-in-law, Edward Colyer, who had been making his home with Duncan for several years. Duncan sought to establish his innocence by saying that Colyer met his death in an automobile accident. He was sentenced to the penitentiary for his natural life. *Duncan* v. *Commonwealth*, 294 Ky. 783, 172 S.W. 2d 665. On March 12, 1942, through Duncan's instigation, a $10,000 accident policy was issued on Colyer's life with Duncan and his wife as beneficiaries. On March 16, Duncan made application for a guarantee reserve life policy on Colyer, paying approximately $1,000 travel and $700 auto death benefits, with Duncan as beneficiary. The policy was issued the following April 1. . . .

On April 6, another policy was issued on Colyer's life in the amount of $2,000, with Duncan as beneficiary. Duncan took the policies home and put them under a mattress on April 8. On April 9, he contrived the death of Colyer, attempting to make it appear to be an automobile accident. He was tried and sentenced to life imprisonment.

The court differentiates other cases and states the law which controls in this instance as follows:

> . . . but those decisions are based upon a valid insurance contract and involve situations where the intent or purpose of the beneficiary to do away with the insured arose after the issuance of the policy. In the case at bar it is clearly established that there was a predetermination on the part of Duncan, before the policy was issued, to kill Colyer. Under such a circumstance there can be no recovery, either on the part of the bene-

---

[11] 300 Ky. 189, 188 S.W. (2d) 313 (1945).

ficiary or the estate of the insured, because the contract of insurance was void from its inception. In fact there was no contract of insurance between Colyer and the Company. While this precise question seems not to have been before this Court heretofore, there is ample authority to support the statements just made. 29 Am. Jur., Insurance, Section 1313 and the Annotation to the case of *Smith* v. *Todd*, 155 S.C. 323, 152 S.E. 506, 70 A.L.R. 1529. One of the leading cases on the subject is *New York Mutual Life Ins. Co.* v. *Armstrong*, 117 U.S. 591, 29 L. Ed. 997, 6 S. Ct. 877. That case is referred to in the American Jurisprudence citation and also in the Annotation in 70 A.L.R. The *Armstrong* decision also holds that evidence as to the procurement of other policies by the beneficiary at or about the same time is admissible.

The conclusions just stated seem to us to be inescapable when it is considered that, at or about the time Duncan was negotiating with the Company relative to a policy on Colyer's life, he secured two other accidental policies on Colyer with himself as beneficiary; that he wanted a double indemnity policy; and that only two days after the policy in question was issued he brought about Colyer's death through an alleged automobile accident. As a matter of fact, reference to the case of *Duncan* v. *Commonwealth, supra,* will show that Duncan knocked Colyer in the head; tied his legs together; placed him on the floor back of the front seat of the car; set the car on fire; and caused it to run over a 200 foot embankment.

Under the circumstances, we think the judgment should be and it is affirmed.

That is, no death benefit was payable. It should be added that although this presents an interesting kind of decision, this rule has not been applied in any large number of cases.

Policies Applied for and Issued in Good Faith. By far, the majority of the cases involving the murder of the insured by the beneficiary concern policies applied for and issued in good faith. The beneficiary guilty of murder will not be permitted to receive the proceeds in this situation, but there is no question about the insurer's liability under the policy. Thus, the insurer is obligated to pay the proceeds to someone, but there are two basic questions to be answered before that person can be ascertained. First, the exact nature of the beneficiary's crime must be established in order to be sure the basic rule applies. Second, if the designated beneficiary is ineligible to receive the benefit, the correct payee must then be established.

18.9 Was It Murder?

A very basic question in the settlement of a life insurance claim where the beneficiary has killed the insured concerns the nature of the crime the beneficiary has actually committed. There are a number of gradations of felonious killing, and not all are classified as murder. Thus, the fact that the beneficiary has killed the insured is not necessarily sufficient to deny him the right to receive the proceeds of any life insurance on the victim's life.

There are also a number of technical rules of evidence relating to whether one can introduce evidence of a conviction of a criminal case into a civil case. A suit concerning the payment of life insurance proceeds is a civil action and the rules of evidence that are involved in that type of case are different from the rules that apply in a criminal case. Thus, if John Brown, insured, is killed by Anne Brown, his wife and primary beneficiary under his life insurance policy, she may be acquitted of the charge of murder; but because of different rules of evidence, she may not necessarily be entitled to receive the insurance proceeds.

18.10 The Alternative Payee

Once it has been determined that the beneficiary who would otherwise be entitled to receive the policy proceeds was guilty of murder, the question immediately arises as to the proper disposition of the proceeds under those circumstances.

The basic rule with respect to distribution of the proceeds where the beneficiary murders the insured is stated in the case of *Austin* v. *United States of America*,[12] where the court said:

> The fact that public policy prevents the payment of the insurance benefits to the murderer does not void the insurance policy; the liability of the insurer is just the same when death is the result of murder as when it is produced by any other cause, and if there is any person who has a right to the benefits of the policy, his rights will be enforced.

The problem then becomes one of determining whether there is a person or persons who have a right to the benefits of the policy. In answering this question, one turns first to the applicable statutory law, if any, of the state in question. Several of the states have statutes specifically relating to this question in connection with insurance proceeds, and other states have general statutes disqualifying murderers from inheriting property from the persons they have murdered. The statutes which specifically relate to the disposition of insurance proceeds sometimes provide that if the primary beneficiary murders the insured, the proceeds of the policy shall be payable to any contingent beneficiary or beneficiaries who may be named. Others make no such provision, and the general statutes, of course, do not touch upon the question.

In the absence of an applicable statute, the provisions of the policy must be carried out. If only one beneficiary was named, settlement is not

---

[12] 125 F. (2d) 816 (C.C.A. Ill., 1942).

usually difficult. In that situation, if the beneficiary is disqualified from receiving the proceeds, most policies provide that payment is to be made to the estate of the insured.

Where there is a contingent beneficiary or beneficiaries, the question is more complex. In most policies, if a contingent beneficiary is named, payment is to be made to the primary beneficiary, "if living," otherwise to the contingent beneficiary. Even though the primary beneficiary is disqualified from receiving the proceeds, however, the fact that he or she survived the insured (which is usually true) would seem to prevent the contingent beneficiary from becoming entitled to the proceeds.

A few statutes specifically provide that in such situations, payment shall be made to the contingent beneficiary. This, of course, solves the problem, since policy provisions are always governed by applicable statutory law. Where there is no such statute, however, court decisions on the subject differ. Some courts have held for the insured's personal representative; others for the contingent beneficiary.

Thus, in one case[13] the California supreme court held that the general rule disqualifying the primary beneficiary from receiving the proceeds of insurance on the life of the person he had murdered should not be used to impair the rights of the contingent beneficiary. Accordingly, the court held that the contingent beneficiary should receive the proceeds.

Illustrative of some of the questions that can arise, and also important as showing the application of the general principle in cases related to murder of others than the insured, is the case of *United States* v. *Kwasniewski*[14] decided by the United States District Court for the Eastern District of Michigan, June, 1950.

In the Kwasniewski case, the insured, Raymond C. Grzenkowicz, died while in the military service, leaving his insurance benefits payable in monthly installments to his mother, Stella Yucha Kwasniewski, as principal beneficiary and Joseph Kwasniewski, his stepfather, as contingent beneficiary. After benefits had been paid from March until September, Joseph shot and killed Stella. A bill in the nature of a bill of interpleader was filed to determine those persons among the brothers and sisters of the insured, his natural father, and the stepfather, to whom the remaining benefits should be paid.

Because the killing took place under circumstances of severe emotional stress, a defense of temporary insanity was interposed, and the defendant was acquitted in the criminal case. Nevertheless, the circumstances of the death, sufficient for an acquittal in the criminal case, were held not sufficient to avoid the disqualification of the accused under the rule of public policy we have been discussing. The court said:

---

[13] *Beck* v. *West Coast Life Insurance Company,* 241 P. (2d) 544 (Cal., 1952).
[14] 91 F. Supp. 847 (D.C. Mich., 1950).

It is a fundamental rule of common law that no man shall be permitted to profit by his own wrongful act. Courts have consistently held that a beneficiary who intentionally and feloniously kills the insured is barred from claiming insurance proceeds on the life of the insured. The same principle applies to a case involving killing of a principal beneficiary by a contingent beneficiary. . . .

It is claimed on behalf of Joseph Kwasniewski that he killed the principal beneficiary during a period of temporary insanity; that such killing was not intentional and felonious; that he was acquitted of the murder charge in the criminal proceeding, and hence is not barred from claiming the insurance funds. The fact that the person who would acquire property as a result of the death of the person killed has been acquitted of the killing does not prevent the application of the rule. Restatement of the Law, Restitution, Property Acquired on Death, Sec. 187, subd. e, f.

The record of the criminal proceeding in which Joseph Kwasniewski was acquitted of the murder charge is not binding upon this court. *Metropolitan Life Insurance Co.* v. *McDavid, et al.*, 39 F. Supp. 228. Testimony was submitted in the present case relating to the circumstances which led to the death of Stella Yucha Kwasniewski. Although the jury found in the criminal proceeding that Joseph Kwasniewski killed his wife during a period of temporary insanity which warranted acquittal of the murder charge, it cannot be said, for the purposes of the instant suit, that the killing was not intentional and felonious.

Although he was acquitted of the murder charge, therefore, Kwasniewski was not permitted to claim the insurance proceeds.

18.11 Other Problems Relating to the Identity of the Beneficiary

Simultaneous Deaths. We have previously discussed the problems incident to the rights of persons, beneficiaries and insureds, who lose their lives so nearly at the same time that it is impossible to say with certainty which of them has survived the other. The remedy of interpleader is often used to clarify this problem.

Incomplete Changes of Beneficiary. Another important area where questions often arise concerns policies where the policyowner has initiated the procedures necessary for changing the beneficiary designation but has been unable, for one reason or another, to complete the change. The effect upon the rights of the various persons concerned are different depending upon the state in which the problem arises. In some states, as discussed in Chapter 12, the courts have taken a strict approach with respect to the policy provision concerning beneficiary changes; in others, they have viewed it more liberally. However, in any case in which there is a doubt, the company will ordinarily pay the proceeds into court and ask the court to make the determination.

G. THE AMOUNT TO BE PAID

18.12 Computation of the Amount

If death was the result of suicide during the suicide period, the liability of the company under most policies is limited to the amount of premiums paid, without interest. If death was the result of war or aviation activities and death from these causes was a risk not assumed under the contract, the liability is ordinarily stated as the amount of premiums paid or the amount of the reserve, whichever is the larger. In either case, settlement is made to the beneficiary in accordance with the provisions of the contract.

In the great majority of claims no exclusion is involved, and settlement is made up of some combination of the following items:

1. The death benefit, which is ordinarily the face amount of the policy but may be a reduced amount if the policy is under the reduced, paid-up nonforfeiture option. Also included under this item are paid-up additions, if any, and any adjustments required as the result of a misstatement of age.
2. Any accidental death benefit payable.
3. Any premiums paid in advance, including under some policies a refund of any premium paid beyond the month in which death occurred.
4. Any dividend accumulations.

Any unpaid policy loans with accrued interest and any premium payable but unpaid at the date of death will be deducted from the total of these items, and the remainder is the sum payable.

18.13 Settlement

Settlement of the sum payable may be made in one sum or under one or more of the optional modes of settlement. A settlement agreement may be in effect as a part of the policy, and if so, settlement will be made in accordance with its terms. If a settlement agreement is not in effect, most policies permit the beneficiary or beneficiaries entitled to a one-sum settlement to elect an optional mode. When settlement is made in accordance with an optional mode, it is customary to issue a new and separate contract (often called a supplementary contract) setting forth the provisions of the settlement.

SUMMARY

Reviewing Death Claims

The basic objective in reviewing death claims is to be sure the conditions of the contract have been met. Usually, this review is made as expeditiously as possible, because the prompt payment of death claims is essential if the insurer is to carry out its basic obligation to provide money when it is needed.

The first step in the review of any claim is to make sure a benefit is payable. The policy must have been on a premium-paying basis or paid up, and death of the insured must actually have occurred. Moreover, the possibility of suicide during the suicide period must be considered as well as the possibility that the accidental death or accidental means death benefit is payable.

Special considerations may be involved if the death benefit is payable to the estate of the insured, to a trustee-beneficiary, or to a minor beneficiary. In some states, however, special statutes make it possible to pay benefits in a limited amount directly to minor beneficiaries under some circumstances. A special review of the facts and the statutes that govern the settlement is necessary in these cases.

The Insured Takes His Life

Suicide may be legally defined as "the deliberate termination of one's existence, while in the possession and enjoyment of his mental faculties." Thus the fact that death is the result of the decedent's own actions does not necessarily mean that it was suicide.

If there is no policy provision expressly excluding death by suicide, the suicide of the insured does not excuse the insurer from paying the benefit to a named beneficiary. There are decisions holding that intentional self-destruction while sane is a risk not covered by the policy even in the absence of a policy provision, but self-destruction while insane is generally held to be covered.

Most present-day policies exclude the risk of death by suicide during a specified period, usually two years. A few states have governing statutes, one of which, the statute in Missouri, makes it necessary for the insurer to prove that the insured contemplated suicide when he applied for the policy before suicide will be a valid defense against a claim.

The courts take the approach that self-destruction is contrary to the natural inclinations of man, and if the circumstances of the death are susceptible to more than one interpretation, the presumption is that the insured did not take his own life. The person claiming that a death was suicide, therefore, has the burden of producing evidence to that effect.

Death as the Result of War

Where war exclusion clauses are involved, there are two basic questions. The first concerns when a state of war exists, and the second is whether the insured actually met his death under circumstances that bring it within the terms of the exclusion.

Death as the Result of Aviation

Most cases reaching the courts concerning aviation deal with the interpretation of such phrases as "fare-paying passenger" and "regularly scheduled flight." Another class of cases presents a question of the insurer's liability when the flier lands his plane safely but then dies as the result of hazards on the ground. Usually such deaths are not considered within the aviation exclusion and thus are covered by the policy.

Mysterious Disappearance

In most states there is a presumption of death after an unexplained absence of seven years. The person must have been missing from his home or usual residence for a period of seven years, his absence must have been continuous and without explanation, persons likely to have heard from him must have heard nothing, and it must have been impossible to locate him by diligent search and inquiry.

The Uniform Absence as Evidence of Death and Absentees' Property Act, in effect in Maryland, Tennessee, and Wisconsin, abolishes the presumption of death after seven years' absence and provides that the fact of death and the date of death shall be jury questions in every case.

If the insured reappears after having been declared dead and after the insurance benefit has been paid, the insurer is entitled to a return of the benefit, since it was paid under a mistake of fact. This is not true of compromise settlements, which the insurer cannot recover.

Establishing the Proper Payee

A beneficiary who feloniously kills the insured is not permitted to receive the proceeds—i.e., he cannot benefit from his own wrong. From the insurer's point of view, however, there are two different sets of circumstances under which this question may arise. One concerns policies which were applied for with the intent of murdering the insured. In this set of circumstances, the usual court decision is that the insurance company has no liability, on the grounds that the policy, as issued, did not constitute a valid contract.

The other type of situation concerns policies that were applied for and issued in good faith. Here the murderer-beneficiary is not permitted to receive the proceeds, but this does not relieve the insurer from liability under the policy. In other words, the contract is valid and the insurer is required to make settlement to someone, though it is not always easy to know whom. If only one beneficiary (the one who murdered the insured) was named, settlement will be made to the estate of the insured. Where a contingent beneficiary or beneficiaries were named, however, decisions differ. By the terms of the contract, a contingent beneficiary is not entitled to the proceeds if the primary beneficiary is living—and in the case of murder, the primary beneficiary would ordinarily survive the insured. Some courts have held, however, that payment should be made to the contingent beneficiary; others have held that payment should be made to the insured's estate. In some states a statute governs the situation.

A second question is important in such cases—whether the beneficiary actually murdered the insured. Not every killing is felonious, and the degree of proof required in a criminal proceeding differs markedly from that in a civil procedure. Such cases often present highly technical questions in this area, and the answers depend upon the facts of the individual case.

The Amount to Be Paid

If the death of the insured has not occurred under such circumstances as to be excluded from coverage under the contract, settlement will be in an amount arrived at as follows: from the sum of the death benefit provided by the policy, plus any accidental death benefit payable, plus any premiums to be refunded, and any accumulated dividends, will be subtracted any outstanding policy loans, with accrued interest, and any premium payable but unpaid on the date of death.

The sum payable may be paid in one sum or under an optional mode of settlement, if elected, in accordance with the terms of the contract. If an optional mode of settlement is effective, a separate contract is ordinarily issued, setting forth the terms of settlement and the payees.

ILLUSTRATIVE CASE

The following case is included here as an illustration of a legal problem in connection with claim settlement that may have to be resolved in court. This case concerns a certificate issued under a group life insurance policy, but the problem presented and the legal principles used in considering it are equally applicable to an individual contract.

THE PRUDENTIAL INSURANCE CO. OF AMERICA v. NEWSOM[15]

Defendant, Malinda Newsom, wife of Lawson J. Newsom, deceased, and Lonel Newsom, son of decedent, Lawson J. Newsom, were rival claimants of

---

[15] 408 S.W. (2d) 161 (Mo., 1966).

the proceeds ($1018.30) of a certificate of life insurance issued under a group policy by plaintiff, Prudential Insurance Company of America. Plaintiff filed a "Petition for Interpleader" joining both of the claimants as defendants and obtained an order from the trial court requiring the rival claimants to interplead their claims to the fund remaining on deposit in the registry of the court. Plaintiff deposited the sum of $1018.30 less $191.10 allowed it as expenses and attorneys' fees and was discharged from further liability. After a hearing on the interpleaded claims the court found in favor of Lonel Newsom and entered judgment accordingly. Malinda Newsom appealed.

Malinda Newsom claimed the fund on deposit by virtue of the provisions of an alleged last will and testament of her deceased husband, Lawson J. Newsom. Lonel Newsom claims the fund by reason of being named the designated beneficiary in said certificate of insurance. The respective claims were submitted to the trial court on the pleadings and an agreed statement of facts. We think the following properly summarizes all of the matters submitted to the trial court.

Lawson J. Newsom was employed by the Pullman Company as a porter prior to his death. On July 1, 1958, while so employed, the Prudential Insurance Company of America issued to him its certificate of insurance under a Group Policy issued to the Pullman Company. Among other benefits provided in the certificate of insurance issued to the aforesaid employee was a provision for death benefits which read:

> . . . If the Employee dies while insured for Employee Group Life Insurance under the Group Policy, the amount of Employee Group Life Insurance then in force on the life of the Employee will be paid to the Beneficiary.

When the aforesaid certificate of insurance was issued to the employee he named Georgia Newsom, his then wife as beneficiary. It appears that his wife, Georgia Newsom, died sometime prior to May 11, 1964.

Another provision contained in the certificate of insurance was the following:

> BENEFICIARY.—The Employee may, from time to time and without the consent of the Beneficiary, change the Beneficiary by filing written notice of the change through the Policyholder on a form furnished by or satisfactory to the Insurance Company, whereupon an acknowledgement of the change will be furnished the Employee for attachment to this Certificate. . . . When a new designation takes effect, any interest of any previous Beneficiary shall thereupon cease. . . .
>
> . . . Any amount of Employee Group Life Insurance for which there is no Beneficiary at the death of the Employee will be payable to the estate of the Employee.

On May 11, 1964, Lawson J. Newsom, the employee, executed a request for change of beneficiary from Georgia Newsom to "Lonel Newsom Son." Pursuant to said request for change of beneficiary a new certificate of insurance was issued to Lawson J. Newsom by the insurer designating Lonel Newsom, Son, as beneficiary for death benefits.

Lawson J. Newsom, after the death of his first wife Georgia, married defendant, Malinda Newsom, who was his wife on the date of his death, which occurred October 16, 1964.

On August 10, 1960 Lawson J. Newsom executed a "Last Will and Testament" which provided in part as follows:

SECOND. All the rest and residue of my estate, whether real, personal or mixed and wherever situated, including all cash in the Jefferson Bank and Trust Company and insurance from the Pullman Company, I give, devise and bequeath to my wife, Malinda Newsom.

On March 19, 1965 the Probate Court of the City of St. Louis, Missouri entered its order refusing Letters of Administration in the Estate of "Lawson Newsom a/k/a [also known as] Lawson J. Newsom" giving as its reasons for refusing the Letters of Administration that Malinda Newsom claimed to have discovered additional assets belonging to the decedent, to wit:

Whatever interest, if any, the deceased had in a Prudential Insurance Company of America, Policy No. G-40626, Certificate No. 709-10-2149, in the sum of $1,000.00 (issued in the name of Lawson J. Newsom).

It was agreed that part of decedent's funeral bill was paid by the wife, Malinda Newsom, and the balance was paid by the son, Lonel Newsom.

Malinda Newsom in her points relied on and in her argument in her brief says,

. . . The court will note that at the time of the change of beneficiary, from his deceased wife, Georgia to his wife's son Lonel Jr., the deceased had just come out of the Hospital from a prolonged illness on May 11, 1964, and at the time was not in a physical condition to be fully conscious of what he was doing and obviously he signed it under "Duress or undue Influence." . . .

There is not one bit of evidence in the record before us that bears upon or is in any way related to the decedent's physical or mental condition at the time he executed the change in beneficiary from his former wife Georgia to his son Lonel Newsom; nor is there one bit of evidence to support the apparent contention that he signed said change of beneficiary under duress or undue influence.

Another contention made by Malinda Newsom is that ". . . Since under the law, the husband cannot will away anything from the surviving wife, the designation of Lionel [sic] J. Newsom, Jr. as beneficiary is null and void and of no effect." She cites the case of *Smith* v. *Smith*, 327 Mo. 632, 37 S.W. 2d 902 in support of this contention. We confess we are unable to understand the meaning of the first sentence quoted above. We are aware that a surviving wife has certain statutory rights that cannot be defeated by the husband. However, such rights are not an issue in this case. The case of *Smith* v. *Smith, supra,* was a suit to contest a will. In that case the court held that in such a suit brought by a party in interest, the petition stating a cause of action, it cannot be dismissed without an adjudication upon the will. We do not have a will contest before us.

The sole issue before us for determination is whether the insured, after he has made an apparent attempt in his will to bequeath to his wife, Malinda, the death benefits of his insurance certificate, may thereafter change the beneficiary. We need not determine whether the provision in the will effected a change of beneficiary to Malinda Newsom. In this connection we point out that no attempt was made by the testator to comply with the terms of the policy regulating the change of beneficiary. We will assume, without so ruling, that testator by his will, effectively made his wife, Malinda, the beneficiary of the insurance benefits at the time he executed the will. Nevertheless, we think that the insured had the right after executing the will to again change the beneficiary.[16]

An insurance policy is a contract and should be construed according to the rules applicable to contracts, even as to the provisions in the policy designating the beneficiary and the right to change the beneficiary and this is also true of a certificate issued under a contract of group life insurance. The court will be governed by the language of the policy and the intention of insured as indicated therein. *Sims* v. *Missouri State Life Ins. Co.*, 223 Mo. App. 1150, 23 S.W. 2d 1075, 29A Am. Jur. Insurance, Section 1761, p. 836. It has been said that the language of the policy designating the beneficiary is to be treated as though it were of testamentary character, in that it is to receive, as nearly as possible, the same construction as if it were used in a will. *Sims* v. *Missouri State Life Ins. Co., supra.* For some reason, not understandable to us, Malinda Newsom takes this to mean that when the insured by his will made her the beneficiary of the insurance proceeds, he thereby revealed an intention that she have the proceeds, and having done so, testator thereafter, cannot change the beneficiary in the manner shown in this case. What is overlooked by Malinda Newsom is that the rule provides that the *language of the policy* designating the beneficiary is to be treated as though it were of testamentary character. The language of the certificate of insurance under review here is clear and unambiguous as to who is to receive the proceeds of the insurance at the death of the insured. It clearly provides that the proceeds will be paid to the beneficiary named in the certificate of insurance at the time of the death of the insured. This language needs no rule of construction to determine its meaning. Also under the language of the insurance certificate the insured enjoyed the privilege of changing the beneficiary at will without the consent of the previous beneficiary. He needed only to substantially comply with the provisions of the certificate. This he did.

The naming of a beneficiary in the certificate of insurance issued by the plaintiff herein was but an expression of the intention and will of the insured and was revocable and subject to change at any time. Malinda Newsom did not enjoy any vested right in the insurance certificate and the insured could change the beneficiary, as we have pointed out, at any time unless the laws of this state or the terms of the certificate of insurance itself prohibited or restrained the right of the insured to change the name of the beneficiary. We know of no such law or language in the certificate that would so prohibit the insured from making the change in the name of the beneficiary. He could change the name of the beneficiary with the same freedom as he could have changed the name of a

---

[16] The will naming Malinda was executed in 1960. The change of beneficiary was executed in 1964.

legatee or distributee in his will by the making of a new will before the first one took effect. [Citations.]

We rule that Lawson J. Newsom, the deceased, had the right to change the beneficiary of his insurance certificate under date of May 11, 1964, and to name Lonel Newsom, his son, as beneficiary thereof. The trial court correctly found that defendant, Lonel Newsom, was entitled to the sum of money on deposit in the registry of the court paid there by the plaintiff herein. The judgment of the trial court is affirmed.

QUESTIONS FOR REVIEW

1. List four sets of circumstances under which a death claim would ordinarily be disapproved.
2. As a general rule, who would be the correct payee of the death benefit if the beneficiary were—
    a. A minor child?
    b. A trust?
    c. The estate of the insured?
3. What is the principal argument for paying insurance proceeds even though the insured commits suicide? What is the principal argument against such payment?
4. What is unusual about the Missouri statute concerning suicide as a defense against paying life insurance proceeds? What is the practical effect of this statute?
5. Briefly summarize the difference between the status and the result types of war clauses.
6. Under what circumstances may a person be presumed to be dead after an absence of seven years?
7. What is the general rule concerning disposition of the proceeds of life insurance which have been paid on the assumption that the insured is dead, if he later reappears?
8. Briefly discuss the rules concerning payment of insurance proceeds when the beneficiary murders the insured—
    a. Where the beneficiary procured the policy with the intent to murder the insured.
    b. Where the insured applied for the policy in good faith and the murder was completely unrelated to the procuring of the policy.

PART V

Group Life Insurance

Chapter Outline

A. Historical Background
   19.1 The Early Plans
   19.2 The Early View

B. The Standard Group Life Insurance Definitions
   19.3 The 1956 Model Bill

C. Limitations on Amount of Insurance

D. Group Life Insurance Standard Provisions
   19.4 The Grace Period Provision
   19.5 The Incontestable Provision
   19.6 "Entire Contract" and Representations
   19.7 Evidence of Individual Insurability
   19.8 Misstatement of Age
   19.9 Settlement Provisions
   19.10 Individual Certificates
   19.11 Conversion at Termination of Individual's Coverage
   19.12 Conversion at Termination or Amendment of the Plan
   19.13 Extension of Death Benefit Provision
   19.14 Individual Certificates in Group Credit Life Insurance
   19.15 The Supplemental Bill Relating to Conversion Privileges

E. Insurance on the Lives of Dependents

F. Group Life Insurance Rates
   19.16 Regulatory Laws
   19.17 Creditor Group Life Insurance

G. Federal Employees Group Life Insurance
   19.18 Background
   19.19 Individual Certificates
   19.20 Amount of Insurance
   19.21 Beneficiaries
   19.22 Termination of Insurance
   19.23 The Costs of the Coverage
   19.24 Insurance Policies
   19.25 Legal Questions

H. Group Life Insurance and the Internal Revenue Code

Chapter 19

Group Life Insurance—
The Statutory Basis

THE EARLIEST group life insurance plans, in the form in which we know group life insurance today, were established in 1911 and 1912, insuring all the employees of two companies under master policies issued to the employers. The relationships of the people and companies concerned in each of these plans—insurer, employer, employees, and beneficiaries— were essentially the same as those under any of the more than 200,000 employer-employee plans in operation in this country today. In the years that followed, however, the group life concept was broadened and refined in a series of model group life insurance bills developed by the National Association of Insurance Commissioners and enacted into law at various times by many of the states.

The purpose of this chapter is to outline this series of legislative definitions and required policy provisions and to summarize the major legislative bases of other types of group life insurance plans that are in existence today.

A. HISTORICAL BACKGROUND

19.1 The Early Plans

The earliest group life coverages were written to cover loss of life among a group of persons during a voyage. On this basis, Manhattan Life Insurance Company, in 1854, insured the lives of 180 Chinese laborers who were transported from China to Panama to work on the canal. Between 1910 and 1912, however, the Equitable Life Assurance Society of the United States developed two group life insurance plans under which all the employees of an employer were insured under one policy issued to the employer, at a premium paid by the employer, but for the benefit of the employees' survivors. One of these policies was issued in 1911 to the Pantasote Leather Company of Passaic, New Jersey. The other was issued in 1912, to Montgomery Ward and Company, approximately two years after that company had first inquired about the possibility of obtaining such coverage.

In its general outline, the Montgomery Ward plan established a pattern for future employer-employee group life insurance plans. Briefly, it insured the lives of 2,912 employees of the company, for the benefit of beneficiaries selected by the insured employees, and at a premium to be paid entirely by the employer. The lives of all employees were insured, regardless of insurability; and the employer was not a beneficiary. Under the Ward plan, the employer paid the total cost of the insurance, a situation that is not always true today; but even today, some part of the premium cost of employer-employee plans must generally be paid by the employer.

19.2 The Early View

By 1915, several other major life insurers had begun to issue group life insurance, but there was widespread criticism of such plans. Many insurance people felt that it was essentially unsound to issue life insurance without individual underwriting; and the lower premium rates charged for group life insurance were felt to be unfairly discriminatory. Criticisms such as these were quieted somewhat in 1917, when the National Association of Insurance Commissioners developed a standard definition of permissible group life insurance and standard policy provisions for group life insurance policies.

B. THE STANDARD GROUP LIFE INSURANCE DEFINITIONS

The 1917 standard definition defined group life insurance as "that form of life insurance covering not less than 50 employees, with or without medical examination," under a policy issued to the employer and for a premium to be paid by the employer or jointly by employer and employees. All of the employees must be insured or "all of any class or classes thereof determined by conditions pertaining to the employment." The amounts of insurance were to be based upon a plan that would not permit individual selection; the employer could not be a beneficiary; and if the premium was to be paid by employer and employees jointly, the benefit must be offered to all eligible employees, and not less than 75 percent must be insured.

This standard definition has been revised a number of times since it was first developed. In 1946, for example, the definition was revised to reduce the number of required lives from 50 to 25, and in 1954 this number was still further reduced to 10. Today group plans covering as few as 10 lives are permissible under the laws of most states.

The 1946 revision included a number of additional types of groups in addition to employer-employee groups, recognized the right of an insurer to require evidence of individual insurability, and permitted coverage of retired employees. At this time, the National Association of Insurance Commissioners suggested that the amount of group life insurance permitted on any one life be limited to $20,000. This 1946 model bill was not widely enacted.

In 1948 a third model group life insurance bill was developed, which involved relatively minor changes; and in 1953 and 1956, additional revisions were recommended. Partly as a result of these frequent revisions, the exact provisions of the group life insurance law in effect in any particular state depend to a large extent upon when the law was first enacted or last revised.

In its general outlines, the 1917 model bill was enacted into law in 16 states and the District of Columbia, but remains in effect in only 6; and the 1946 model bill was enacted into law in only a limited number of states. Thus, there is no general pattern of legislation that is followed by a majority of the states. In fact, several states have no definition of group life insurance on their statute books, although all have some statutory requirements relating to group life insurance contracts.

19.3 The 1956 Model Bill

The 1956 model group life insurance bill recognizes as eligible groups the employees of an employer, the debtors of a creditor, the members of a labor union, the employees of two or more employers in the same industry, the members of one or more labor unions, or the employees of one or more employers and the members of one or more labor unions.

Employer-Employee Groups. A group policy may be issued to an employer insuring his employees or to the trustees of a fund established by an employer for that purpose. The eligible employees in either of these situations are defined essentially as they were under the 1917 definition: "all the employees of the employer, or all of any class or classes thereof determined by conditions pertaining to their employment." The policy may define the term "employees" to include employees of subsidiary corporations as well as employees, individual proprietors, and partners of affiliated businesses if the employer and the affiliated businesses are under common control through stock ownership or contract. Retired employees may be included, as may directors, if they perform the services of employees. Individual proprietors and partners, to be eligible, must be actively engaged in the business of the proprietorship or partnership and must devote a substantial part of their time to the business. At least 10 employees must be insured when the policy is issued, and the amounts of insurance provided must be based upon some plan precluding individual selection.

As was true under the 1917 definition, the premium for an employer-employee group must be paid by the employer or trustee. It may be paid entirely from the employer's funds or from funds contributed partly by the employer and partly by the employees, but it cannot be paid entirely from funds contributed by the employees. If the employees contribute toward payment of the premium, at least 75 percent of those eligible must be covered (excluding those whose evidence of insurability is not satisfactory to the insurer). If the premium is paid entirely from funds contributed by the employer, all eligible employees must be insured. However, those who cannot furnish satisfactory evidence of individual insurability may be excluded.

Group Creditor Life Insurance Plans.   The 1956 model bill defines group creditor life insurance as insurance under a policy issued to a creditor (the policyholder) to insure debtors of the creditor subject to requirements as follows:

1. The debtors eligible for insurance shall be (*a*) all of the debtors whose indebtedness is repayable (*i*) in instalments, or (*ii*) in one sum at the end of a specified period not longer than 18 months from the date the indebtedness was effective; or (*b*) all of any class or classes of such debtors "determined by conditions pertaining to the indebtedness or to the purchase giving rise to the indebtedness." Debtors of subsidiary or affiliated corporations and affiliated proprietorships and partnerships may be included if the business of the policyholder and the affiliated businesses are under common control. However, no debtor is eligible unless the indebtedness is a binding obligation upon him "at and from the date the insurance becomes effective upon his life."

2. The premium for group creditor life insurance shall be paid by the policyholder from his own funds or from funds collected from the insured debtors or from both. If the insured debtors pay part of the premium, evidence of individual insurability must be required unless at least 75 percent of the eligible debtors elect to pay the charges.

If no part of the premium is paid by the insured debtors, all eligible debtors must be insured under the policy except for those who cannot furnish evidence of individual insurability satisfactory to the insurance company.

3. At the time the policy is issued, the group of eligible debtors must be receiving new entrants at the rate of at least 100 persons per year or it

must reasonably be expected to receive 100 new entrants during the first policy year. The policy must reserve the right to require evidence of individual insurability if less than 75 percent of the new entrants become insured, and persons may be excluded from the eligible classes on a basis of age.

4. The amount of insurance on the life of any insured debtor cannot at any time exceed the amount of the instalment repayable debt he owes up to $10,000. The amount of insurance for a debtor whose indebtedness is repayable in one sum is limited also to the amount of his debt, or $10,000, whichever is the smaller.

If the indebtedness is repayable in one sum, the insurance may not remain in effect for longer than 18 months except in the event of default or extension of the loan. In either of these events, the insurance may be continued for six additional months.

5. The insurance must be payable to the policyholder (the creditor) and used to reduce or extinguish the indebtedness of the debtor to the extent of the amount paid.

Group Plans for Members of Labor Unions. The definition applicable to labor union groups includes a requirement similar to that included in the employer-employee group definition concerning the payment of premiums. The premium may be paid wholly from the union's funds, or partly from union funds and partly from funds contributed by the insured members for that purpose. If the premium is paid partly from funds contributed by the insured members, at least 75 percent of the members must be insured, excluding those who cannot furnish satisfactory evidence of individual insurability. However, a group policy insuring members of a labor union must cover at least 25 members when it is issued (by contrast with 10 employees under an employer-employee group).

Multiple Employer-Union Groups. The definition of a trusteed plan covering the employees of two or more employers or members of one or more unions, or both, requires that the premium be paid out of funds contributed by the employer or employers of the insured persons or by the union or unions, or by employers and unions. Group coverage is not permitted if any part of the premium is to be paid out of funds contributed for that purpose by the insured employees or members. Consistent with this premium payment requirement, no provision is made for coverage of less than all the employees or members, except for persons who cannot furnish satisfactory evidence of individual insurability.

A group policy insuring multiple employer or union groups must cover at least 100 persons when it is issued and an average of at least five persons per employer unit. If the plan is established by the members of an association of employers, the policy may be issued only under one of the following conditions:

1. The participating employers constitute at least 60 percent of those employer members whose employees are not already covered for group life insurance.
2. The total number of persons covered exceeds 600 when the policy is issued.

The policy cannot provide that if a participating employer discontinues its membership in the association, the group insurance covering its employees shall terminate for that reason.

C. LIMITATIONS ON AMOUNT OF INSURANCE

Although the 1956 definition of creditor group life insurance plans limits the amount of life insurance that may be provided on the life of any one debtor, no similar limitation is made a part of the definitions applicable to the other groups. Instead, a limitation is included as a separate provision following the separate definitions. This provision applies to group term life insurance and prohibits insurance in excess of $20,000 on any one life unless 150 percent of that person's salary exceeds $20,000. In the latter situation, term life insurance may be provided up to $40,000 or 150 percent of the insured person's annual compensation, whichever is less. (It is notable, however, that the trend among the states today seems to be toward higher limits or none at all.)

D. GROUP LIFE INSURANCE STANDARD PROVISIONS

The standard provisions section of the National Association of Insurance Commissioners model bill for group life insurance specifies certain provisions that must be included "in substance" in any policy of group life insurance that is delivered in the state. Other provisions may be used if they are more favorable to the persons insured or more favorable to the policyholder and equally favorable to the insured persons. There are 11 standard provisions and a supplementary bill relating to conversion privileges.

The standard provisions must be read in the light of the customary contractual arrangements used in group life insurance. Usually, the policy issued to the policyholder is called a master policy, and certificates—not policies—are issued to the persons whose lives are insured under the master policy. All 11 standard provisions must be included in the master policy, and 4 of these must also be included in the individual certificates.

The introduction to the standard provisions makes it clear that the standard policy provisions required for individual life insurance policies have no application to group life insurance. It also states that if the group insurance is on a plan other than term, the policy must contain nonforfeiture provisions that are equitable to the insured persons and the policyowner. However, these group nonforfeiture provisions need not be the same as those required for individual life insurance policies.

19.4 The Grace Period Provision

The first required provision for group life insurance policies concerns a grace period. In essence, a group life insurance policy must include a policy provision granting a grace period of 31 days for the payment of any premium due after the first. The policy must provide that the death benefit coverage will remain in force during this period unless the policyholder gives the insurer written notice to discontinue the coverage before the end of the period. The policy may provide that a pro rata premium will be payable for any time the policy remains in force during the grace period.

In general, the grace period provision has the same effect in group life insurance as its counterpart has in the individual life insurance policy—it continues the coverage in force for 31 days beyond the due date of a premium in default. Thus, if a covered employee should die during this 31-day period, the death benefit would be payable. However, this assumes that the person who died was still a member of the eligible group on the date of his death. If the policy provides that a person's insurance will terminate when his employment terminates, the grace period provision should have no application to extend his coverage beyond the date of termination of his employment; and the majority of court decisions have upheld this view. Thus an employee whose employment ceases during, but before the end of, the grace period and who subsequently dies (also during the grace period) would have no group coverage on the date of his death.

As pointed out by one court,[1] "The grace period provided by the policy is for the benefit of the employer, who, by the express terms of the policy, was required to pay the premiums. No obligation of that nature is imposed upon the insured."

19.5 The Incontestable Provision

The second required standard policy provision relates to contestability. The first sentence requires a provision to the effect "that the validity of the policy shall not be contested, except for nonpayment of premiums,

---

[1] *Adkins* v. *Aetna Life Ins. Co.*, Supreme Court of Appeals of W. Va., 43 S.E. (2d) 372 (1947).

after it has been in force for two years from the date of issue." In this respect, the provision closely resembles the incontestability provision of the individual life insurance policy. In a group policy, however, the incontestability provision must also provide that no statement made by any person insured under the policy concerning his insurability may be used in contesting the validity of that person's insurance after his coverage has been in force prior to the contest for a period of two years, during that person's lifetime, "nor unless it is contained in a written instrument signed by him." The 1956 standard provisions, therefore, require the inclusion of an incontestability provision that relates to two separate matters: the validity of the policy itself and the validity of the insurance of each individual whose life is insured under it.

As might be expected, most of the court decisions involving the question of contestability in group life insurance have concerned the validity of the insurance on the individuals covered by the policy. Many of these cases concern facts that may be summarized as follows: John Doe, who is not a full-time employee of the XYZ Corporation, nevertheless receives (by mistake) a certificate of insurance under the XYZ Corporation's group life policy. Two years and a few months later, John Doe dies. When his beneficiary submits the necessary claim documents, the claim is denied by the insurance company on the grounds that John did not meet the eligibility requirements of the policy—that is, he was never a full-time employee. Therefore, the insurer contends, he was never, in fact, insured. John's beneficiary maintains that this is not a permissible defense because of the incontestable clause.

The legal question is this: Is such a claim denial a contest of the validity of John's insurance coverage, in the sense that the word "contest" is used in the incontestability provision of the policy? If so, the beneficiary is right; the insurance company is barred from defending its denial on that basis, and the insurance is payable. If it is not a "contest" as that word is used in the incontestable provision, the insurer is right and is free to prove, if it can, that John was never in fact insured under the XYZ policy. If the company establishes this proof, the claim denial will be upheld.

As might be expected, there are court decisions holding both ways on this basic question. One case,[2] for instance, concerned the question of group insurance coverage for a lawyer who admittedly worked only a few days a month for the employer. A master policy was issued by the insurance company to the employer and enrollment cards were distributed to the employees for completion. The policy defined eligible employees as "full-time employees regularly working at least 30 hours per week at the employer's usual place of business."

---

[2] *Simpson* v. *Phoenix Mut. Life Ins. Co.*, 24 N.Y. (2d) 262, 299 N.Y. (2d) 835, 247 N.E. (2d) 655 (1969).

Leonard Simpson, the lawyer, completed an enrollment card which contained these words: "I request the insurance for which I may become eligible under said Group Policy."

The enrollment card was forwarded to the insurer, and a certificate was issued to Simpson, listing his name and the amount of insurance to which he was entitled. Premiums were paid by the employer as they became due. Simpson was killed after the expiration of the contestable period, and the claim presented by his beneficiary was denied on the basis that he had not been a "full-time employee working 30 hours per week." The facts were not in dispute. The question for the court was clear-cut: Did the incontestable clause, as a matter of law, prevent the insurance company from contending that Simpson had not been eligible for the insurance and therefore was not insured?

Both attorneys—for the beneficiary and for the insurance company—cited the case of *Metropolitan Life Ins. Co. v. Conway* as supporting their contention. There, as previously noted,[3] Chief Judge Cardozo said:

> The provision that a policy shall be incontestable after it has been in force for a period of two years is not a mandate as to coverage, a definition of the hazard to be borne by the insurer. It means only this, that within the limits of the coverage, the policy shall stand, unsupported by any defense that it was invalid in its inception, or thereafter became invalid by reason of a condition broken.

Each party believed that these words supported his case. The court, however, said the Conway case was "instructive" but not "dispositive." That is, it was helpful but didn't decide the question.

"The quoted passage," the court said, "establishes a frame of reference for decisions but does not unequivocally indicate which particular risks are conditions of insurance and thus borne by the insurer, if not discovered and contested within two years of issuance of the policy, and those hazards considered limitations on the risk an insurer is willing to assume and, therefore, not barred by the lapse of time."

In the Simpson case, the court decided that the question of whether Simpson was or was not a full-time employee could have been investigated and ascertained when the certificate was issued to him. After the contestable period had expired, therefore, the insurance company was precluded from raising the point as a reason for not paying the claim.

Several courts have held the opposing view—that the incontestability clause does not prevent an insurance company from denying a claim on the basis that the alleged insured was never an eligible employee within the terms of the master policy. In one case, the employee fraudulently obtained his job (and membership in an employee association which entitled him to insurance) by having his brother take the required

---

[3] Chapter 8, section 8.10.

physical examination. The court held that the incontestability clause did not prevent the insurance company from denying the employee's claim for disability benefits.

In another case, the person alleged to be insured was never in fact an employee of the employer, although premiums were paid on her behalf. The facts of this case[4] were not very clear, but the deceased had misrepresented her status as an employee, stating that she was an employee of the employer; and the requirement as to eligibility clearly appeared in the certificates which were issued to the insured persons. The court said that the incontestable clause prevents defenses that go to the validity of the policy, but that it was never intended to enlarge the coverage of the policy or to require the insurance company to insure persons it never intended to insure. The reasoning of the court is summarized as follows:

> However, the plaintiff urges that the defendant cannot contest the validity of the group policy because of the one-year incontestable clause within this policy, nor can it assert the invalidity of the individual insurance which the plaintiff claims the deceased possessed because of the two-year incontestable clause set forth in the certificate given to her. While aware of the authority which would seem to support this position (*John Hancock Mut. Life Ins. Co.* v. *Dorman*, 108 F. 2d 220 [9 Cir., 1939]), we do not believe that it represents the better view. 1 Appleman, Insurance Law and Practice, s. 331, p. 588.
>
> In *Fisher* v. *U. S. Life Ins. Co.*, in City of N. Y., 249 F. 2d 879 (4th Cir., 1957), the court held that the incontestability clauses were inapplicable because the party, never having been an employee, was never insured. In rendering the opinion, the court spoke as follows: "The incontestable clause, after the passage of the stipulated period, proscribes defenses which go to the validity of the policy whether because of noncompliance with conditions or the falsity of representations or warranties. It was never intended to enlarge the coverage of the policy, to compel an insurance company to insure lives it never intended to cover or to accept risks or hazards clearly excluded by the terms of the policy." *Id.*, 882. The opinion also quoted approvingly the statement of Chief Judge Cardozo in Matter of *Met. Life Ins. Co.* v. *Conway*, 252 N. Y. 449, 452: "The provision that a policy shall be incontestable after it has been in force during the lifetime of the insured for a period of two years is not a mandate as to coverage, a definition of the hazards to be borne by the insurer. It means only this, that within the limits of the coverage the policy will stand, unaffected by any defense that it was invalid in its inception, or thereafter became invalid by a condition broken." See also, *Washington National Ins. Co.* v. *Burch*, 270 F. 2d 300 (5th Cir. 1959); 1 Appleman, Insurance Law and Practice, s. 331, p. 588.
>
> In the Metropolitan case, the matter finally was succinctly summarized: "Where there has been no assumption of the risk, there can be no liability."

---

[4] *Fisher* v. *Prudential Ins. Co.*, 218 A. (2d) 62, 26 A.L.R. (3d) 625 (1966).

Id., 453. The opinion further criticized the Dorman case and suggested that its dicta which, as previously stated, appear to support the plaintiff, were unnecessary to the opinion.

In *Perkins* v. *Insurance Co.*, 100 N.H. 383, a requirement of the policy was that the insured be in good health when the instrument was issued. She was not, and after careful review of the authorities, we held that while, for reasons not material here, misstatements in the policy could not be relied upon by the company as a defense, nevertheless the agreement made good health a condition precedent to insurance coverage. We added that the parties had the right to so contract and that coverage never attached. Judgment was rendered for the defendant insurance company.

In *Duval* v. *Company*, 82 N.H. 543, a group insurance policy similar to the present one was issued, and the plaintiff was originally validly covered. However, he had ceased to be employed at the time of his death and the court held that "The insurance is effective only during the term of employment." P. 545. By a parity of reasoning, it would appear that if coverage ceases when employment ceases, it could never arise where there has never been any employment.

In recapitulation, we hold that since the deceased was never insured under the policy, the plaintiff cannot take advantage of the incontestability clauses.

In group life insurance, as with individual life insurance policies, the incontestable clause has been held not to prevent an adjustment for misstatement of age. In one case, for example, the person misstated his age when he was employed and would not have been eligible for the insurance at his true age. The court held that this defense was not barred by the incontestable clause. In another case the employer was named as beneficiary. The court held that the incontestable clause did not prevent the insurance company from refusing to pay the proceeds to the employer. In other words, the group life insurance statutes make the employer ineligible to be the named beneficiary. The incontestable clause cannot be used to circumvent that requirement.

19.6 "Entire Contract" and Representations

The third required group life provision included in the model bill of 1956 corresponds very closely with the "entire contract" provision required to be included in an individual life insurance policy. It thus requires that "a copy of the application, if any, shall be attached to the policy when issued. . . ." Since the application of the policyholder (the employer) does not contain a great deal of critical information, this requirement is not one of the most significant in the model bill. However, this provision must also include wording to the effect that "all statements made by the policyholder or by the persons insured shall be deemed representations and not warranties," and, finally, "that no statement made by any person insured shall be used in any contest unless a copy of the instrument containing the statement is or has been furnished to such person or to his beneficiary."

The legal effect of making all statements "representations and not warranties" is no different with respect to group life insurance than in the individual life insurance situation. This means, therefore, that misstatements must relate to matters material to the risk or they will not justify the insurance company in rescinding the policy.

The provision concerning a contest based on a statement or statements made by any person insured tacitly recognizes the fact that group policies often insure large numbers of individuals. Consequently, it would be virtually impossible, in many cases, to require that the instrument containing the statement be attached to and made a part of the policy, as would be true in individual life insurance. Thus, the law requires only that a copy of the instrument be furnished to the person insured or (after his death) to his beneficiary.

19.7· Evidence of Individual Insurability

The fourth required policy provision concerns the reservation of the right to require evidence of individual insurability under some circumstances. Generally, evidence of insurability will be required (in plans where the individual insureds make some contribution toward the premium) if an individual does not elect to participate in the plan during a specified period and then, later, decides in favor of such participation. Although many people might, in situations of this kind, elect to become insured for reasons having nothing to do with their insurability, an adverse change of health or occupation has no equal as a persuasive argument in favor of applying for coverage. Thus, situations of this kind would offer clear-cut opportunities for antiselection, and evidence of insurability is customarily required.

A comparable situation exists where an individual insured has converted his insurance at the termination of his group coverage and then, later, becomes eligible again for insurance in the same group. It is not unusual for the individual policy to which conversion is made to provide considerably less than the amount of insurance provided under the group plan. When the insured again becomes eligible for the group coverage, therefore, he has the opportunity to obtain the additional amount of coverage provided by the group plan. Therefore, there is an opportunity for antiselection, and evidence of insurability may be required for the additional amount of coverage under the group plan.

If the insurer plans to require evidence of insurability in either or both of the above-described situations, the conditions under which such evidence will be required must be set forth in the policy.

19.8 Misstatement of Age

Group life policies must contain a misstatement of age provision. The standard provisions law says this provision must specify "an equitable adjustment of premium or of benefits or of both" in situations where the age of a person insured has been misstated. Note that the adjustment may be made either in premiums or in benefits, in contrast with the required provision for individual life insurance, where the amount of insurance is adjusted to correspond to the amount of premium actually paid.

The New York version of this required group life insurance provision reads somewhat differently from the wording of the provision in the model bill. In New York, the group life policy must provide for the equitable adjustment of the premium unless the amount of insurance depends upon the age of the insured. In that event the policy shall provide for an equitable adjustment of the amount of insurance and the premium.[5]

In practice, this means that when the age of an insured has been misstated, the insurance will, in most instances, be paid in the amount provided by the certificate, and the adjustment will be made in the amount of premium payable by the policyholder. If the amount of insurance would have been different because of the age of the insured, the insurance will be payable in the adjusted amount and an appropriate adjustment will be made in the premium. As an example of the latter situation, the policy may provide that the insurance on all covered persons is to be reduced, at age 65, to not more than $5,000. If a vice president, apparently insured for $18,000 at his assumed age 64, is found to have been 65 on the date of death, his coverage under the policy will be adjusted to $5,000, and the premium for his coverage will be adjusted accordingly.

19.9 Settlement Provisions

The group policy must include a provision that any sum becoming payable because of the death of a person insured shall be payable to the beneficiary that person has designated. The policy may provide for the disposition of any sum or sums payable if there is no designated beneficiary living to receive part or all of the proceeds, and it may reserve the right to pay not more than $500 "to any person appearing to the insurer to be equitably entitled thereto" as the result of having incurred funeral or last illness expenses because of the death of the insured.

The first part of this standard provision guarantees to the insured person the right to designate the beneficiary for his insurance under the plan. Group life insurance definitions for employer-employee plans are

---

[5] Section 161, 1(c), New York Insurance Laws.

uniform in requiring that this must be someone other than the policy-holder. Subject to this limitation, however, the individual insureds are free to designate whomever they wish as beneficiary, and the general rules applicable to individual life insurance beneficiary designations also apply to beneficiary designations under group life insurance. Usually the designation is revocable, and the insured person is free to change the designation whenever and as often as he wishes, merely by complying with the procedures set out in the policy. Usually, these requirements are not elaborate. Generally a form "satisfactory to the insurer" is required, and the change must be submitted to the insurance company through the employer. Questions can and do arise as to the legal effect of certain fact situations, but the basic legal meaning of the provision has not generally been open to question.

Two other aspects of this standard provision law are also significant. One of these is the privilege on the part of the insurer to include in the policy a "succession beneficiary" designation in the event that no beneficiary has been designated by the insured at the time of his death or the beneficiary who was designated did not survive the insured. A group policy may provide that in situations such as these, the death benefit will be paid to the estate of the insured or, at the option of the company, to the first living person in a list of relatives of the insured. For example, the payment may be made to the spouse, father, mother, child or children, brother, or sister of the insured in such circumstances. The objective of a succession beneficiary provision such as this is to avoid the necessity of having a personal representative appointed merely to make claim for the group life insurance benefits of the insured. It may, therefore, effect a saving in money as well as time.

Finally, the standard provision also permits a clause customarily referred to as a "facility of payment clause," that permits settlement of an amount up to $500 to anyone who seems equitably entitled to it. Small amounts can then be paid to anyone who has assumed the expenses of last illness and burial of the insured.

One or two optional modes of settlement are usually provided under group life insurance contracts today, although it is not customary to permit elaborate settlement arrangements. Usually either the fixed period instalment option or the fixed amount instalment option is available, sometimes both. A life income option is sometimes provided, and may be available by special agreement with the insurer even when it is not expressly provided for in the policy itself.

19.10 Individual Certificates

The master group life insurance policy must also provide that the insurer will issue an individual certificate to the policyholder for delivery "to each person insured." This certificate must specify the insurance protection provided for the individual, the beneficiary to whom the benefits will be paid, and all the conversion rights and privileges that will be available under the plan if the individual's insurance under the plan, or the plan itself, should terminate.

The usual practice is to prepare a booklet for distribution to the covered employees, and today the individual certificate is often combined with this booklet to become, in effect, a booklet-certificate. The result is that in addition to the information required by the standard provision, the covered employee will also have the essential information concerning all the major elements of his coverage.

19.11 Conversion at Termination of Individual's Coverage

The eighth standard group life insurance provision is the first of two required provisions relating to the individual insured's right to convert his insurance to an individual policy in specified situations. This standard provision deals with the insured's conversion right when all or a part of his insurance (but not the group policy itself) ceases because his employment ceases or because he is no longer a member of an eligible class of employees. His employment may be terminated in any of several ways, of course. He may resign, he may be discharged, or he may be laid off. He may also be transferred from a class of employees eligible for the group life insurance to a class that is ineligible.

If a covered person's insurance terminates for any reason, he must have the right under the group policy to obtain an individual policy of life insurance from the group insurer, without evidence of insurability. However, the group insurer is not required to issue an individual policy unless the insured applies for it and pays the first premium within a 31-day period (the conversion period) following the date his coverage under the group policy terminates.

The individual policy does not have to contain disability benefits or any other supplementary coverages. It may be on any plan of insurance the insured may elect, except term insurance, that is being issued by the group insurer at the time of conversion, at the individual's attained age, and for the amount of insurance applied for. The amount of insurance may be the same or a lesser amount of insurance than that in force for the insured at the time his coverage under the group plan terminated. Thus, if any of his insurance matures on or before the date his group coverage terminates under the plan, it will not be counted in establishing the amount of insurance to be provided under the individual policy.

The premium for the individual policy must be at the customary rate for the kind of policy, the amount of coverage, and the class of risk in which the insured is placed at the time of conversion and for his attained age on the date the individual policy becomes effective.

Although this standard provision provides that the individual policy may be on any plan except term insurance, the New York Insurance Law modifies this to some extent. Under the New York law, the individual policy may be "preceded by one-year term insurance" if the individual requests it. Thus the person whose group life insurance terminates has the opportunity of continuing his life insurance coverage at one-year term insurance rates for a maximum of one year. This gives him the opportunity to continue his coverage at term insurance rates until he obtains employment elsewhere, perhaps then to be eligible for coverage under his new employer's group life insurance plan.

19.12 Conversion at Termination or Amendment of the Plan

The ninth standard provision required in group life insurance policies concerns the individual's right to convert his coverage in the event the group policy terminates or is amended to terminate the insurance for the class of employees of which he is a member. In this situation, the employee who has been insured for at least five years on the date of the termination of the policy has the same right of conversion that is granted the person whose insurance has terminated because his employment has terminated. That is, he may convert to an individual policy of his choice, other than term, within 31 days.

However, the amount of insurance to which the employee may convert may be limited to a smaller amount than is available when only the coverage—not the policy—is affected. If the group policy is terminated, or amended to terminate the coverage, the individual policy may provide not more than the lesser of $2,000 of insurance or the amount of insurance the individual insured had under the group policy, minus the amount of any insurance for which he will become eligible under a new group policy issued to the same policyholder, or reinstated within 31 days after termination of the group coverage in question.

To illustrate, suppose employee A is insured under his employer's group life insurance policy for $20,000. He has been insured under this policy for more than five years when it terminates. However, another group policy is issued to the same policyholder by another insurance company before 31 days have elapsed. Under the second policy, employee A has $15,000 of coverage. Under this standard required provision, in the first group policy, employee A (who has been employed for five years) must have the right to be issued an individual policy in the smaller of two amounts: either $2,000, or his former coverage minus the present coverage. In this illustration, the difference between his former and present coverages is $5,000; therefore, he is entitled to purchase an individual policy in the amount of $2,000.

19.13 Extension of Death Benefit Provision

The tenth required standard group life insurance provision also concerns the situation where an employee's group coverage terminates, but in this provision it is immaterial whether termination of the coverage results from the termination of his employment or termination or amendment of the policy. Briefly, this provision states that if an employee whose group life insurance terminates should die during the period in which he could have applied for and received an individual policy without evidence of insurability, the insurer will pay as a death benefit the amount of insurance for which an individual policy would have been issued, regardless of whether he has applied for such an individual policy. As a practical matter, this provision extends coverage under the group life insurance policy during the 31-day conversion period following the date the employee's coverage under the policy would otherwise terminate.

Each of these last three standard provisions (eighth, ninth, and tenth) must be included in the individual group certificates issued under an employer-employee group life insurance policy for delivery to the individual insureds.

19.14 Individual Certificates in Group Creditor Life Insurance

The eleventh required provision for group life insurance policies requires an insurance company to furnish to a group creditor life insurance policyholder individual certificates for delivery to the insured debtors. Each such form must contain a statement that the life of the individual debtor is insured under the policy and that if a benefit becomes payable, it will be applied to reduce the indebtedness or pay it in full.

19.15 The Supplemental Bill Relating to Conversion Privileges

A supplemental bill, prepared by the National Association of Insurance Commissioners, has been enacted by a significant number of the states. The effect of this law is to extend the period of time in which an individual who becomes eligible for conversion of his group life insurance may apply for and receive an individual policy without evidence of insurability. It does not extend the period during which a death benefit will be paid (that is, it doesn't extend the period of insurance). It only extends to a maximum of 60 days the period in which he may apply for an individual policy, unless he has received notice of his right to convert his coverage at least 15 days prior to the expiration of the conversion period. This additional period expires 15 days after the insurer has given notice and, in any event, the period is limited to not more than 60 days after the end of the conversion period provided in the policy.

E. INSURANCE ON THE LIVES OF DEPENDENTS

Under many group life insurance policies, it is customary to provide life insurance on the lives of spouses and children of insured employees. Many states do not have specific statutes relating to this coverage, but a few have provided especially for it. Illustrative is the statute[6] in New York, which reads as follows:

> 5. Any policy of group life insurance issued in accordance with paragraph (a), (b), (d), (e), (f), (g), (h) or (i) of subdivision one of this section may include provisions for the payment by the insurer of life insurance benefits upon the death of the spouse of the insured employee or member or his or her child dependent upon him or her for support and maintenance, provided that insurance upon the life of the spouse shall not exceed five thousand dollars or one-half of the amount of insurance on the life of the insured employee or member as provided in such policy, whichever is the lesser, nor shall the insurance upon the life of each dependent child so insured exceeded one thousand dollars.

F. GROUP LIFE INSURANCE RATES

19.16 Regulatory Laws

State insurance laws contain extensive sections relating to rates and rating organizations applicable to property and liability insurance, but life insurance companies have traditionally been exempt from rate regulation except in the area of group life insurance. Historically, this regulation of group rates began at an early date and was prompted by the fear that competition would result in the establishment of rates so low as to threaten the solvency of the group insurance companies.

New York's statute, the first of such rating laws to be enacted, gave the Superintendent of Insurance the power to establish minimum premium rates for group life insurance. A few other states followed this lead: Michigan and Pennsylvania in 1929, Ohio in 1935, and Maine in 1957. Today, however, only New York, Ohio, and Maine continue to set minimum premium rates for group life insurance. The New York statute[7] reads as follows:

---

[6] Section 204, subdivision 5, New York Insurance Laws.
[7] Section 204, subdivision 2, New York Insurance Laws.

2. The superintendent shall after consultation with the insurers licensed to write life insurance in this state from time to time issue regulations, . . . prescribing the minimum group life insurance premiums to be charged for the first year of insurance for a group not previously insured as such by any authorized insurer, based on an examination of the experience of such insurers and on reasonable assumptions as to interest, mortality and expense. No such regulation or amendment thereto shall be promulgated except upon notice and after hearing to all insurers affected thereby. The regulations of the superintendent made pursuant to this subdivision shall be subject to judicial review.

No domestic, foreign or alien life insurance company shall be permitted to do business in this state if it hereafter issues, within or without this state, any policy of group life insurance on which the premium shall be less than the premium prescribed in any applicable regulations promulgated by the superintendent. Anything in this chapter to the contrary notwithstanding, any group life insurance policy issued or delivered in this state may provide for readjustment of the rate of premium based on the experience thereunder, at the end of the first year or of any subsequent year of insurance thereunder, and such readjustment may be made retroactive only for such policy year. Any such rate readjustment shall be computed on a basis which is equitable to all group life insurance policies.

This New York law is highly significant for two reasons. First, the number of large companies domiciled in New York and subject to this law would, alone, give the law significance. However, as is true of other New York laws, it has what is called extraterritorial application. This means that the law applies not only to all New York companies wherever they operate but also to every group life insurance contract issued by any company licensed to operate in New York, regardless of where the contract is actually issued. As a result of this provision, any life insurance company that is licensed in New York must comply with this law with respect to all group life insurance contracts it issues. Thus, the New York rating law is extremely significant in the competitive position of any insurer licensed to operate in New York and doing a group life insurance business in other states as well.

It should be noted that these regulatory statutes apply only to first-year premium rates for group life insurance plans. In subsequent years, the group insurer is free to adjust the premium rate upward or downward, as indicated by the experience of the group.

In addition to this basic rate regulation of first-year premiums, New York and several other states also have rules concerning maximum employee contributions permissible under plans in which the employees share the premium costs (contributory plans). These rules are imposed to assure that the employer rather than the insured will assume the increasing costs as the individual insureds grow older. Otherwise, if the individuals were required to assume this increasing cost, the older members might tend to withdraw from the plan. The most typical maximum rate for employee contributions is $0.60 per month per $1,000 of benefit.

19.17 Creditor Group Life Insurance

The competitive situation that prevails in the group creditor life insurance field is exactly the opposite of the situation in group life insurance generally. In creditor group insurance, the policyholder is the beneficiary of the death benefit; in employee groups, this is forbidden. In some instances, the creditor group policyholder is also the agent and therefore receives a commission on the sale. Finally, the group creditor policyholder is not required to pay any part of the premium unless he wishes to do so, in contrast to employer-employee groups, where the employer must usually pay at least a part of the premium.

Under these circumstances, the life insurance company that offers its group creditor coverage at higher premium rates is not necessarily at a competitive disadvantage as far as the creditor (policyholder) is concerned. Although the debtors usually pay the premiums, they have nothing to say about the rates. Instead, all negotiations are in the hands of the creditor, who, although he may not pay any part of the premium, may nevertheless receive dividends or experience rating credits as well as a commission on the sale. Therefore, the higher the premium, the more attractive the coverage may be to the creditor-purchaser.

For these reasons, the statutes and rules and regulations with respect to group creditor plans are designed not to establish minimum premium rates for the first year of a group plan, but instead to establish maximum rates above which the insurer may not go without special permission. In the light of the factors mentioned, it is only reasonable that these maximums apply throughout the lifetime of the creditor group policy.

Different states have different methods of accomplishing this regulation. Some states require the insurance companies merely to file their rates. Some states require that benefits must be equal to a specified percentage of the premium. Other states (and New York is one of these) have established a scale of premium rates which the insurer may not exceed without permission of the insurance superintendent or commissioner.

G. FEDERAL EMPLOYEES GROUP LIFE INSURANCE

19.18 Background

It will be recalled that the federal government has full authority, as the result of the *Southeastern Underwriters* decision, to regulate insurance in all respects insofar as the business is transacted across state lines. This authority has not been extensively exercised, and where it has been, the regulatory activities have usually concerned subjects other than insurance contracts. In discussing group life insurance contracts, therefore, the principal statutes and regulations are on the state level. There is, however, one very significant federal law that has had a considerable influence in the group insurance area, and, therefore, some effect in the area of contractual arrangements and interpretations. This is the Federal Employees Group Life Insurance Act of 1954.[8]

In general terms, this act established a plan of life insurance for essentially all of the civilian employees of the federal government. Exactly who these people are is set forth in the definition of "employee"—a definition which includes members of Congress, congressional employees, the President, and several other specifically described employees. Excluded are noncitizen employees permanently stationed outside the United States and the Panama Canal Zone, and certain other types of employees who may be excluded by the Civil Service Commission on the basis of the seasonal or part-time nature of their employment.

The act provides that the Civil Service Commission shall purchase insurance that will cover each employee automatically on the date he becomes eligible as set forth in the law. If an employee does not want to be insured, he must notify his employing office. If the notice is received before he becomes insured, his insurance will not become effective. If it is received after his insurance takes effect, the insurance will continue to the end of the current pay period and then cease.

19.19 Individual Certificates

The Civil Service Commission (not the insurance company) is responsible for furnishing to each insured employee a certificate that states the benefits to which he is entitled, the beneficiary for those benefits, and the persons "to whom claims are to be submitted." The certificate must include a summary of all the provisions of the policy that affect the insured.

19.20 Amount of Insurance

The Federal Employees Group Life Insurance Act specifically provides that the amount of insurance available to each eligible employee will be an amount "approximating" the amount of his annual salary; and a schedule is included in the law, showing the amount of insurance for each salary range, in increments of $1,000. Thus, an employee whose

---

[8] U.S. C.A., Title 5, Sections 8701 *et. seq.*

annual salary is greater than $8,000 but not greater than $9,000 is entitled to $10,000 of insurance. If the salary is greater than $9,000 but not greater than $10,000, the amount of insurance is $12,000, and so on, with a maximum of $45,000. Optional additional insurance is available in the amount of $10,000, with the employee paying the total premium.

In the case of accidental death, an additional benefit is payable equal to the amount of insurance provided in the schedule. In the event of the loss of one hand, or one foot, or the loss of sight of one eye, a benefit is payable in the amount of one half of the accidental death benefit; and for loss of two or more of these members, an amount equal to the full accidental death benefit is payable.

19.21 Beneficiaries

Death claims are to be paid first to the beneficiary or beneficiaries designated by the insured employee in a "signed and witnessed writing" received in the employing office before the death of the insured. If there is no designated beneficiary at the death of the employee, the act provides, in effect, that the insurance proceeds shall be paid to the widow or widower of the employee, if living; otherwise to the child or children of the employee, and descendants of deceased children by representation, if any; otherwise, to the parent or parents of the employee, or the survivor, if any; otherwise to the "duly appointed executor or administrator of the estate of the employee." If there is no surviving member of any of these groups, payment shall be made to the "other next of kin of the employee entitled under the laws of the domicile of the employee at the date of his death."

If no claim has been made within one year after the death of the employee, by the person or persons otherwise entitled under the above sequence, or if payment to such a person is prohibited by federal statute or regulation, payment is to be made as if that person or those persons had predeceased the insured.

If neither notice nor claim has been made within two years after the death of the insured employee, payment may be made to the claimant who "in the judgment of the Commission is equitably entitled thereto."

19.22 Termination of Insurance

Any policy purchased by the Civil Service Commission to provide the coverage described in this act must contain a provision that the insurance of an employee ceases on his separation from the service "or twelve months after discontinuance of his pay, whichever is earlier." There must also be a provision for the temporary extension of life insurance coverage and a conversion privilege.

19.23 The Costs of the Coverage

The federal employees group life insurance plan is contributory, with the employee's share of the cost being withheld from his pay. The act specifies the amount of this contribution for each $1,000 of insurance, and provision is made for a government contribution in the amount of one half of the contribution made by the employee.

19.24 Policy Arrangements

The Federal Employees Group Life Insurance Act did not establish insurance for federal employees. Instead, it established a group life insurance plan and authorized the Civil Service Commission to purchase "from one or more life insurance companies" a policy or policies of insurance to provide the benefits outlined by the act. The company or companies from whom the insurance was to be purchased were required to (1) be licensed in each of the 48 states and the District of Columbia, and (2) have group life insurance in force in an amount equal to at least 1 percent of the total amount of employee group life insurance in the United States in all life insurance companies.

When the law became effective, in 1954, eight companies met these requirements. For ease of administration, however, the Civil Service Commission elected to purchase only one policy and to purchase it from the Metropolitan Life Insurance Company. This policy became effective on August 29, 1954. The other qualifying companies participated as re-insurers, although all transactions with the policyholder are handled by the Metropolitan Life Insurance Company. Provision is made in the law for reinsurance by smaller life insurers also; and at the present time, more than 360 life insurance companies are reinsuring a part of this business.

By reason of these reinsuring arrangements, the conversion privilege available to the individual insured employees differs somewhat from that provided under the usual employees' group life insurance policy. For example, in the typical instance, if the employees of the A.B.C. Manufacturing Company are insured under a group life insurance policy issued by the Argus Life Insurance Company, a terminating employee is entitled to have an individual life insurance policy issued to him by the Argus Life Insurance Company, without evidence of insurability. Under the federal employees group life insurance plan, however, the converting individual may purchase his individual policy from any participating insurer that has applied for authority to issue individual life insurance contracts and that has met the requirements set out by the Civil Service Commission. There is also a conversion pool for the purpose of spreading the excess mortality that is expected under converted policies.

19.25 Legal Questions

One of the unique legal problems involved in connection with the federal employees' group life insurance plan concerns the problem of whether a legal question is answered according to federal or state law. In fact, the answer differs according to the subject matter of the question.

In general, questions concerning the interpretation of the act itself are answered according to federal law. This is explained in one case[9] as follows:

> The construction of the federal statute is, in the first instance, a federal question. There is no well developed body of state law on the issue here presented, nor is there any overwhelming state interest that would suggest here that Congress intended that the courts look to the various states for the procedural rules to be applied in naming beneficiaries in federal insurance policies. In the interest of uniformity it is much better that the federal courts here develop a separate body of law rather than look to state law—and fifty different interpretations.

Questions involving the determination of family relationships, however, are answered in accordance with state law. This rule is summarized in the case of *Metropolitan Life Insurance Co.* v. *Thompson,*[10] as follows:

> . . . Plaintiff urges that this Act, the Federal Employees' Group Life Insurance Act, should be construed without reference to local law. Regretfully, I cannot agree. Family relationships are primarily matters of state concern; there is no federal law of domestic relations.

The question in this case was whether an illegitimate child would qualify as a child of the insured and thus be entitled to the proceeds of his natural father's insurance. The court held that under the applicable state law (of New York) he would not.

H. GROUP LIFE INSURANCE AND THE INTERNAL REVENUE CODE

No discussion of the statutory law of group life insurance would be complete without some mention of the effect of the federal tax laws on group life insurance. This book does not purport to discuss the taxation of life insurance, but the federal tax law has had a very definite effect on the development of group life insurance coverage and thus upon group life insurance contracts.

The original group life insurance definition and all modifications have specifically referred to group term life insurance. However, experiments have from time to time been made with group permanent life insurance,

---

[9] *Sears* v. *Austin,* 202 F. 2d 690 (1961).
[10] 250 F. Supp. 476 (1966).

and the present group standard provisions law specifically makes provision for such plans. It requires that if a group policy is issued on a permanent plan, the policy must include nonforfeiture provisions, although they need not necessarily be on the same basis as the nonforfeiture provisions required for individual life insurance policies.

The Internal Revenue Code regulations specifically provide that contributions made by an employer toward group term life insurance for his employees are deductible as a business expense for the employer and yet are not considered current income to the employees. This provision had the effect of encouraging employers to provide such insurance and has resulted in a very valuable fringe benefit to employees.

With the growth of group permanent life insurance, however, a different factor was injected. Under group permanent life insurance, values are accumulated, and the current protection is not the only factor to be considered. After some consideration, therefore, the Internal Revenue Service issued a regulation to the effect that the premium for group permanent coverages would be subject to taxation as additional compensation to the employee. The immediate effect was to discourage such plans; and the vast majority of group life insurance, therefore, has been issued on the term life insurance plan.

SUMMARY

Historical Background

Insurance on the lives of several people under one contract dates back as far as 1854. As we know it today, however, group life insurance had its beginnings in two group life insurance policies issued to the Pantasote and Montgomery Ward companies in 1910 and 1912, respectively. These policies insured all the employees of the employer under one policy issued to the employer as policyholder, insuring the employees for the benefit of beneficiaries designated by the insured employees.

At first there was criticism of group life insurance on the basis that life insurance without individual underwriting was unsound and that the lower premium rates for such plans were unfairly discriminatory. These criticisms were quieted when the National Association of Insurance Commissioners developed a standard definition of permissible group life insurance and a model group life insurance policy provisions law.

The Standard Group Life Insurance Definitions

The first standard group life insurance definition was developed in 1917. It defined group life insurance as insurance under a policy issued to an employer and insuring not less than 50 employees "with or without a medical examination" and for the benefit of someone other than the employer. The premium was to be paid by the employer or by the employer and employees. All the employees were to be insured or all of any class or classes determined by conditions of their employment. The amounts of insurance were to be established on a basis that would not permit individual selection; and if the employees paid any part of the premium, the benefit must be offered to all employees and at least 75 percent of them must be insured.

This definition has been revised to reduce the number of lives from 50 to 10, and expanded to include as acceptable groups the debtors of a creditor, the members of a labor union and trusteed plans covering the employees of two or more employers in the same industry, the members of one or more labor unions, or the employees and members of one or more employers and one or more labor unions.

Limitations on Amount of Insurance

The model law of 1956 includes a limitation of the amount of life insurance to be provided on the life of any one individual. This limit in the model bill is $20,000 unless 150 percent of the person's salary exceeds $20,000. In that event, the limit is $40,000 or 150 percent of the insured person's annual compensation, if less. The trend today, however, is toward much higher limits or none at all.

Group Life Standard Provisions

The NAIC model bill for group life insurance requires group life insurance contracts to include, in substance, 11 standard provisions. There is also a supplemental bill relating to required conversion privileges.

The standard provisions are as follows:

1. A grace period provision. This provision grants a period of 31 days for the payment of any premium after the first. The policyholder may terminate the policy prior to the expiration of this period; and, if this is done, the insurance will cease on the specified termination date. A pro rata premium may be payable for the portion of the grace period during which the insurance remained in effect prior to such termination.

2. An incontestable provision. This provision prohibits any contest of the validity of the policy after the expiration of two years after the issue date of the policy. It also concerns any statement as to insurability made by any person insured under the policy. It provides that no such statement may be used to contest the validity of the insurance of any such person unless the statement is in a written instrument signed by that person.

There are numerous court decisions concerning the effect of this provision and a definite split of authority on the subject. One line of cases holds that the insurer is barred by the incontestable provision from alleging (after the expiration of the contestable period) that a person was not eligible for the coverage when an individual certificate was issued to him. Another line of cases holds that such allegations do not constitute a contest of the validity of the insurance and therefore are not barred after the expiration of the contestable period.

3. *An "entire contract" provision.* The third required provision declares that a copy of the application, if any, of the policyholder shall be attached to the policy, when issued. It also provides that all statements made by the policyholder or by those insured under the policy shall be deemed to be representations and not warranties. Finally, it provides that no statement made by any insured person shall be used in any contest of the insurance unless a copy of the instrument containing the statement is furnished to that person or his beneficiary.

4. *A provision reserving the right to require evidence of insurability.* If the insurer intends to require evidence of insurability under any circumstances, the situations in which such evidence may be required must be set forth in this provision in the policy.

5. *A misstatement of age provision.* A group life insurance policy must include a provision specifying an equitable method of adjusting "premiums or benefits or both" in the event the age of any insured has been misstated.

6. *A settlement provision.* The group life insurance policy must include a provision guaranteeing the insured persons the right to designate the beneficiary; and, in employee groups, this must be someone other than the employer. The insured individual must also have the right to change the designation as often as he or she wishes.

The standard provisions law also gives the insurer the right to include in a group life insurance policy a "succession beneficiary" provision, if it wishes. This is a provision permitting the insurer, if no designated beneficiary is living at the insured's death, to pay the benefit to the first living person in a specified list of relatives of the insured in the order listed. The insurer is also permitted to include, at its option, a facility of payment clause. This is a provision permitting the insurer to pay up to $500 of the death benefit to anyone who seems equitably entitled to it.

7. *Individual certificates.* The group life insurance policy must also provide that the insurer will issue an individual certificate to the policyholder for delivery to each individual insured. Each such certificate must state the insurance protection furnished the insured person, the beneficiary to whom the insurance will be paid, and the conversion rights

provided in the event of termination of the individual's insurance under the plan or plans.

8. Conversion right at termination of the individual's insurance. This is the first of two required provisions relating to conversion rights. It concerns the rights available to the individual insured if his insurance ceases because his employment ceases, regardless of the reason, or because he is no longer a member of an eligible class of employees. In either case, he must have the right to obtain, without evidence of insurability, an individual life insurance policy from the group insurer. The individual policy must be applied for within 31 days from the date his group life insurance terminates, and may be on any plan of insurance, except term life insurance, that the insured elects and that is issued by the insurer at the time of conversion. New York requires that this individual policy must be preceded by one-year term insurance if the insured requests it.

9. Conversion at termination of the plan. The individual insured must also have conversion rights if his insurance terminates because the group policy terminates or if it is amended to terminate the insurance for the class of employees to which he belongs. In this event, the individual has essentially the same right of conversion as when his employment terminates except as to the amount of the insurance provided under the individual policy. If the individual's insurance ceases because the group policy is terminated or amended, the individual policy to which he is entitled need not provide insurance for more than $2,000 or, if less, the difference between his terminating coverage and the amount of group life insurance to which he may later become entitled (if this occurs not more than 31 days later).

10. Extension of death benefit provision. The group life insurance policy must also provide continuing coverage for the individual insured for 31 days after his group life insurance terminates, regardless of the reason for such termination.

11. Individual certificates in creditor group life insurance. This provision is required only in group creditor life policies. It provides that the insurer will issue individual certificates to the policyholder for delivery to the insured debtors.

The Supplemental Bill Relating to Conversion

A supplemental bill prepared by the NAIC relates to the conversion privilege and has been enacted by many states. It does not require a policy provision, but it does extend to a maximum of 60 days the period during which the employee may apply for individual insurance after his group life insurance has terminated, unless he has been notified of his conversion rights at least 15 days before the end of the conversion period.

This law does not require that insurance be provided beyond the end of the conversion period.

Insurance for Dependents

Insurance is sometimes provided on the lives of spouses and children of employees insured under group life insurance plans. Statutes specifically permitting this coverage are in effect in some of the states.

Group Life Insurance Rates

Several states—specifically New York, Michigan, Pennsylvania, Ohio, and Maine—either have or have had statutes providing for the regulation of group life insurance premium rates. Such statutes are intended to prevent the granting of inadequate rates as the result of competition. Only three states have such statutes today, but the laws of one of them— New York—are extraterritorial in effect.

Creditor Group Life Insurance

Premium rates for creditor group life insurance are regulated for exactly the opposite reason—to prevent the use of excessive premium rates.

Federal Employee's Group Life Insurance

The Federal Employees Group Life Insurance Act, enacted by Congress in 1954, establishes a plan of group insurance for almost all the civilian employees of the federal government, including the President and members of Congress. Insurance is provided for each eligible federal employee in accordance with a schedule related to his annual salary, up to a maximum of $45,000. Accidental death and dismemberment benefits are also provided.

Death benefits are payable to beneficiaries designated by the insureds, but if there is no designated beneficiary the act provides that the insurance can be paid to the first living person among the following, in the order listed: spouse of the insured, child or children, parents or a surviving parent. If there is no living payee in any of these classes, payment may be made to other next of kin of the employee entitled under the laws of the employee's state of residence at the time of his death. Each employee's group life insurance will terminate on the earlier of the date in which his employment terminates or 12 months after discontinuance of his pay. When the insurance terminates he is entitled to conversion privileges which permit him to purchase an individual policy with any life insurer that participates in the group plan.

Legal Questions

One of the most significant legal questions under the Federal Employees Group Life Insurance Act concerns the question of the applicable law—state or federal? Generally, questions involving the interpretation of the act are answered in accordance with federal law. Questions involving family relationships are answered in accordance with state law.

The Internal Revenue Code

Group life insurance is typically provided in the term life insurance plan and is so defined in the model group life definition. The use of this plan has been strongly influenced by the Internal Revenue Code, which provides that contributions made by an employer toward group term life insurance for his employees are deductible as a business expense but are not taxable as income to the employees. A similar privilege has not been available for group permanent life insurance, and the limited number of such plans reflects this fact.

ILLUSTRATIVE CASE

The following case has been selected as an illustrative case for this chapter because it demonstrates how the required incontestability provision is interpreted as it applies in group life insurance.

TAYLOR, Appellee v. AMERICAN HERITAGE LIFE INSURANCE CO., Appellant[11]

BOREMAN, Circuit Judge: Rose Antoinette Taylor, the widow of Jacob B. Taylor, instituted this action in the United States District Court for the Eastern District of Virginia against American Heritage Life Insurance Company (American Heritage) to recover, as beneficiary, the proceeds of insurance written on Mr. Taylor's life under a group insurance policy issued by American Heritage. American Heritage defended on the ground that Mr. Taylor had made material misrepresentations as to the condition of his health in his application for individual insurance coverage under the group policy. The district court did not consider the merits of this defense for the assigned reason that the policy, by its terms, was incontestable (except for nonpayment of premiums) since it was issued more than two years prior to the contest of Mrs. Taylor's claim by American Heritage. The lower court awarded Mrs. Taylor $10,045.24 (the face

---

[11] 448 F. (2d) 1375 (C.A. Va., 1971).

amount of the policy plus paid but unearned premiums), plus interest and costs. We reverse and remand for further proceedings.

Mr. Taylor was a member of the Fleet Reserve Association which held a master policy of group insurance issued by American Heritage under which eligible members of the Association could obtain life insurance. Each participating member was issued an individual certificate setting forth the benefits accruing from his subscription, together with a statement of his rights under the policy. The total amount of the premium on the group policy to be paid by the policyholder, the Fleet Reserve Association, was deemed to be the sum of the premiums due from the individual subscribers to the plan.

To be eligible to participate in the group plan an applicant member of the Association was required to provide American Heritage with satisfactory evidence of insurability. This requirement was normally met by responding to certain questions on an application form which each applicant was required to submit. No physical examination was required, unless the answers to those questions pertaining to health on the application form suggested the desirability of such an examination.

Mr. Taylor completed and signed his application for insurance on November 28, 1965. He responded as indicated to the following questions:

6. Are you now in good health? [x] Yes [ ] No.
   If not, give details below. . . .

9. Have you received medical or surgical treatment or advice during the last five years? [x] Yes [ ] No.
   If yes, give details below. . . .

11. Remarks: (If additional space is needed, use reverse side.)
    Gengivectomy [*sic*] performed Oct. 1965.

American Heritage issued a certificate of insurance to Mr. Taylor, effective January 1, 1966, without requiring a physical examination.

Although Mr. Taylor listed the gingivectomy, a surgical treatment for diseased gums, as the only medical or surgical treatment he had received in the five years prior to November 28, 1965, he had been, in fact, continuously and extensively treated, both surgically and medically, for cancer of the prostate since August of 1965. On December 19, 1966, less than a year after his insurance coverage began, Mr. Taylor died at Bethesda Naval Hospital, the immediate cause of death being shown as "carcinoma prostate with metastases, peritonitis." After his death, the necessary claim forms were submitted through the Fleet Reserve Association's insurance administrator. Since the *claim* forms indicated Mr. Taylor had cancer when he submitted his application for insurance which condition was not revealed in the *application*, American Heritage denied the claim. Mrs. Taylor instituted this action in the district court on February 27, 1968.

In the lower court, American Heritage took the position that it had been the victim of a material, knowing misrepresentation by Mr. Taylor and that such misrepresentation barred Mrs. Taylor's right to recover on the policy. However, the trial judge did not consider the merits of this defense since he concluded that this defense was unavailable to American Heritage by reason of the following provision of the master policy:

15. INCONTESTABILITY. This policy shall be incontestable after two years from its date of issue, except for non-payment of premium. No statement made by any person insured under the policy relating to his insurability shall be used in contesting the validity of the insurance with respect to which such statement was made after such insurance has been in force prior to the contest for a period of two years during such person's lifetime, nor unless it is contained in a written instrument signed by him.

Mr. Taylor's certificate of insurance was issued on January 1, 1966. American Heritage did not contest its liability in court until it filed its answer in the instant action brought by Mrs. Taylor in February 1968. The essence of the district court's holding was that American Heritage was estopped from raising the defense of misrepresentation because it failed to take legal action to contest its liability within two years of the effective date of Mr. Taylor's insurance.

American Heritage contended that the incontestability clause did not become operative since the insured died before the insurance had been in effect for two years. In rejecting this contention the district court considered only the first sentence of the incontestability clause as set out above, and relied on the authority of *Mutual Life Insurance Company of New York* v. *Hurni Packing Company*, 263 U.S. 167 (1923). In *Hurni*, the life insurance policy there in question, not a part of a group plan, contained the following language:

Incontestability. This policy shall be incontestable, except for non-payment of premiums, provided two years shall have elapsed from its date of issue.

Although the insurer's liability was not contested in that case within the two-year period, the insured had died within two years of the policy's issue date. The insurance company contended that the incontestability clause never became operative but the Supreme Court held to the contrary:

In order to give the clause the meaning which the [insurance company] ascribes to it, it would be necessary to supply words which it does not at present contain. The provision plainly is that the policy shall be incontestable upon the simple condition that two years shall have elapsed from its date of issue;—not that it shall be incontestable after two years if the insured shall live, but incontestable without qualification and in any event. 263 U.S. at 177.

Hurni is inapposite. That which was absent in the incontestability clause in that case is present in the second sentence of the incontestability clause at issue in the instant case. The second sentence, which was not fully considered by the court below, provides that "No statement made by any person insured under the policy relating to his insurability shall be used in contesting the validity of the insurance with respect to which such statement was made *after such insurance has been in force prior to the contest for a period of two years during such person's lifetime,* nor unless it is contained in a written instrument signed by him." (Emphasis by the Court.) It is clear that this provision would bar a contest of the insurance based on Mr. Taylor's asserted misrepresentation only if he had been insured under the policy for a period of at least two years before his death. *See Reliance Life Ins. Co.* v. *Everglades Discount Co.*, 204 F.2d 937 (5 Cir. 1953); *Greenbaum* v. *Columbian Nat. Life Ins. Co. of Boston*, 62 F.2d 56 (2 Cir. 1932); 18 Couch on Insurance 2d §72.48 (1968).

At first glance, the absolute nature of the language in the first sentence of the incontestability clause would appear to contradict the above interpretation of the second; indeed, the first sentence would seemingly render the second meaningless. However, closer inspection and analysis of the policy provide the resolution of this apparent conflict.

The first sentence of the clause states, "This *policy* shall be incontestable after two years from its date of issue, except for non-payment of premium." (Emphasis by the Court.) The reference is clearly and exclusively to the "policy." Here, American Heritage is not contesting the "policy," as issued to the Fleet Reserve Association, but the individual certificate of insurance issued to Jacob Taylor. Paragraph 23 of the policy (entitled "INDIVIDUAL CERTIFICATE") states that the certificates issued to individual subscribers "shall not constitute a part of this policy." By its terms, the first sentence of the incontestability clause does *not* refer to individual certificates of insurance.

Further, the master policy provides that, "This policy is delivered in the District of Columbia and is governed by the laws of that jurisdiction." To this end, *both* sentences of the incontestability clause substantially conform with §35-711(2) of the District of Columbia Code of 1961, which sets forth certain standard provisions of group life insurance policies issued within the District. §35-711(2) provides that:

§35-711. Standard provisions for policies of group life insurance.

No policy of group life insurance shall be delivered in the District unless it contains in substance the following provisions or provisions which in the opinion of the superintendent are more favorable to the persons insured, or at least as favorable to the persons insured and more favorable to the policyholder. . . .

(2) A provision that the validity of the policy shall not be contested, except for nonpayment of premiums, after it has been in force for two years from its date of issue; and that no statement made by any person insured under the policy relating to his insurability shall be used in contesting the validity of the insurance with respect to which such statement was made after such insurance has been in force prior to the contest for a period of two years during such person's lifetime nor unless it is contained in a written instrument signed by him.

Thus the District of Columbia Code specifically calls for the substantial inclusion of both the first and second sentences of the incontestability clause with respect to *group* life insurance policies.

By way of contrast, §35–703(3) of the District of Columbia Code, dealing with *regular* life insurance policies does *not* require the inclusion of absolute language of the type required for group plans and contained in the first sentence of the cause in question here. §35-703(3) provides in pertinent part:

§35-703. Standard provisions required in life insurance policies.

No policy of life insurance . . . shall be issued or delivered in the

District or be issued by a life company organized under the laws of the District . . . unless the same shall contain in substance the following. . . .

(3) A provision that, except as otherwise expressly provided by law, the policy . . . shall be incontestable after it has been in force during the lifetime of the insured for a period of not more than two years from its date . . . that all statements made by the insured shall, in the absence of fraud, be deemed representations and not warranties; and that no such statement or statements shall be used in defense of a claim under the policy unless contained in a written application. . . .

As we interpret the incontestability clause both sentences are to be given force and effect; they are not conflicting and neither is to be disregarded. Plaintiff's claim under the individual insurance certificate issued to Jacob Taylor is contested here and we hold that only the second sentence of the incontestability clause is pertinent to the certificate. It follows that the certificate was not incontestable since Mr. Taylor did not live for two years after its date of issuance.

The case is remanded to the district court to determine whether Mr. Taylor's application for individual insurance coverage contained such misrepresentations as would absolve American Heritage of liability.

Reversed and remanded.

QUESTIONS FOR REVIEW

1. On what principal grounds were the early group life insurance plans criticized?

2. Briefly summarize the 1917 standard group life insurance definition.

3. List four groups that are recognized as eligible groups for group life insurance under the 1956 model bill.

4. Which of the following is not a required provision for group life insurance policies under the N.A.I.C. model bill?
   a. A grace period provision.
   b. A misstatement of age provision.
   c. An incontestable provision.
   d. A provision requiring notice of right to convert to individual coverage.

5. Briefly summarize the conversion rights that must be granted under a group life insurance policy:
   a. If an employee's group coverage terminates because his employment terminates.
   b. If an employee's group coverage terminates because of termination of the group policy.

6. What is the purpose of statutes regulating noncreditor group life insurance premium rates? What is the purpose of rate regulation for creditor group policies?

7. How does the New York premium rating law affect group life insurers who are licensed to do a life insurance business in New York?

8. What is the purpose of the Federal Employees Group Life Insurance Act of 1954?

9. In what principal way does the conversion privilege of an employee of the federal government differ from the conversion privilege of a nongovernmental employee insured under his employer's group life policy?

10. Briefly summarize the rule for determining legal questions arising under the Federal Employees Group Life Insurance Act.

Chapter Outline

A. Rules of Interpretation

B. The Group Insurance Contract—An Overview

C. The Policyholder as an Agent of the Insurer

D. When Insurance Begins

  20.1 The Actively at Work Requirement

  20.2 Persons Insured Subsequent to Effective Date

E. Payment of Premiums

  20.3 Contributory and Noncontributory Plans

  20.4 Dividends

F. Change of Beneficiary

G. Assignments

H. When the Insurance Terminates

  20.5 What Employment Means

  20.6 When Is It Terminated?

  20.7 Date of Termination

  20.8 Extension of Death Benefit

I. Which Law Governs?

Chapter 20

Group Life Insurance—
The Case Law

ALTHOUGH the development of group life insurance has been strongly influenced by statutory law, court decisions have also played an important role. Many court decisions involving group life insurance interpret policy provisions that are required by statute, but many decisions also relate to the operation of the contracts generally and interpret policy provisions that are not required by statutory law.

This chapter will consider some of the major legal questions that have arisen under group life insurance contracts and the ways in which they have been resolved by court decisions.

A. RULES OF INTERPRETATION

Group life insurance contracts are interpreted according to the same rules that are followed in interpreting other life insurance contracts. Thus, ambiguities are interpreted in such a way as to favor the insured or beneficiary rather than the insurer.

Nevertheless, words are to be given their generally accepted meanings; and the courts will not construe policy language unless there is an ambiguity. This point is made clear in the Illustrative Case at the end of this chapter, as follows:

> Correlatively, the clauses in an insurance policy should be given their ordinary and usual meaning; if there is no ambiguity, a strained or distorted construction will not be indulged.[1]

---

[1] *Wells* v. *Driver,* 121 N.J. Super. 185, 296 A. (2d) 352 (1972).

It is generally agreed that the master policy is the contract of insurance, rather than the individual certificate that is issued to the insured person. The certificate is issued in order that the individual will have a statement of his coverage, but it is not a contract. However, if the terms of the certificate differ significantly from the provisions of the master policy, the terms of the certificate rather than those of the policy may be given effect.

B. THE GROUP INSURANCE CONTRACT—AN OVERVIEW

The insuring clause of a master policy of group insurance states that the insurer will provide benefits for persons specified in the policy, in consideration of premium payments by the policyholder. In addition to the required standard policy provisions discussed in Chapter 19, the master policy also contains provisions concerning the eligibility of the persons who are to be insured, details of the effective dates of the coverage of such persons, and provisions concerning the termination of the insurance.

The master policy contains extensive provisions concerning premium computation, and the formulas and rates are specified. Provisions are also included concerning the adjustment of premiums, and it is assumed that the premium rate will be adjusted as the makeup and experience of the group changes. Since first-year premium rates are regulated by a few of the states, even nonparticipating group life insurance policies usually provide for a refund of premium if the group experience proves more favorable than anticipated. Such refunds are called dividends in participating policies, but they are generally referred to as experience rating refunds in nonparticipating policies.

C. THE POLICYHOLDER AS AN AGENT OF THE INSURER

In employer group plans, the policyholder (usually the employer) often assumes many of the administrative duties under the group insurance contract, including enrolling the eligible employees and collecting employee contributions in contributory plans. It is not surprising, therefore, that it is sometimes contended that the employer is acting as an agent of the insurer in carrying out these administrative duties.

This question—whether the employer is or is not the agent of the insurer—is most likely to arise in one of three areas. It is probably most frequently raised in connection with situations in which a beneficiary contends that a deceased employee was insured and there is a question about the fact of coverage. For instance, it may be alleged by the insurer that an essential condition of the coverage was not met by the employee. Perhaps the employee had not worked the required number of hours per week. If the employer is considered the agent of the insurer, it is possible that the eligibility condition may have been waived by actions or statements of the employer. If the employer is not considered the agent of the insurer, the waiver may not be sustained. The question of agency in such a situation, therefore, may be vital to the beneficiary's case.

The question may also be significant in connection with the effectiveness of a beneficiary designation or change of beneficiary, and finally it may arise in connection with the presentation and payment of claims. In any of these situations, the employer will have had some administrative duties. Perhaps it is delivery of the individual certificate, acceptance and forwarding of beneficiary designations and changes, or receiving and forwarding claim forms. Whether the employer is performing these duties as an agent of the insurer or of the individual insured may be a crucial question.

The question of the employer's role as an agent is sometimes discussed in terms of majority and minority rules, in which case the majority rule is said to be that the employer is not the agent of the insurer. In accordance with this rule, notice to or knowledge of the employer is not considered notice to or knowledge of the insurer. Similarly, the actions taken by the employer with respect to the coverage provided by the group contract are not considered actions of the insurer.

The minority rule is just the reverse—that the employer is the agent of the insurer; and under this rule, the principles of agency law are applied in just the opposite way. Notice to or knowledge of the employer is considered notice to or knowledge of the insurer; and the actions of the employer are considered actions of the insurer.

The majority rule—that the employer is not the agent of the insurer—was followed in many of the earlier cases. It was a reasonable conclusion in a time when the employer assumed only a limited number of the administrative duties under a group life insurance policy covering his employees. As the employer undertook more and more of the details of administration (under so-called self-administered plans), however, there was an increasing tendency on the part of the courts to hold, in some instances at least, that certain responsibilities went with the duties.

Today, therefore, the safest answer to the question of whom the employer represents is that "it all depends. . . ." It depends upon the fact situation in the particular case; it depends upon the statutory law in some instances; and it depends upon how many of the administrative duties under the group plan are assumed by the employer. The best rule, today, therefore, seems to be that the employer-policyholder may be the agent of the individual insureds for some purposes and the agent of the insurer for others; and the multiplicity of present-day cases seems to make it impossible to support any more specific rule. Some examples may help to make this understandable.

Illustrative of cases holding that the employer may be considered to be the agent of the insurer for some purposes is the case of *Kaiser* v. *Prudential Insurance Co. of America*.[2] This case involved a change of beneficiary under a group policy which provided that any person insured under the policy could make a change of beneficiary at any time "by written notice through the Employer to the Company (the insurer) at its home office, on a form furnished by it."

The original beneficiary for the insurance in this particular situation was Berta Kaiser, the first wife of the insured. When she died, the insured changed the beneficiary to his daughter, Gertrude Kahl. Later, he remarried; and after his death, his second wife, Elizabeth, brought a suit against the insurer for the proceeds of the insurance. She alleged that the insured had submitted a change of beneficiary form to the employer designating her (Elizabeth) as the new beneficiary. The daughter also filed claim for the insurance money, and the insurer instituted an interpleader action, paying the money into court and asking the court to decide between the claimants.

Elizabeth Kaiser contended that the insured had done everything in his power to complete the change of beneficiary, and that since notice of the change was, under the terms of the policy, to be given to the insurer through the employer, the employer was the agent of the insurer for that purpose.

The insurance company, on the other hand, contended that the employer was not its agent and cited one of the leading older cases as well as a standard insurance reference as support for its position. Even though the employer was notified of the requested change, therefore, the insurance company maintained that the employer had no authority to tell the insured (as the claimant contended had been done) that the change of beneficiary had been completed. Moreover, if the employer was not the agent of the insurer, it had no authority to waive any of the policy requirements.

After considering these arguments, the court said that it might be reasonable to hold that the employer was not the agent of the insurer so far as payment of the premium was concerned, or reporting changes in the makeup of the insured group. In situations such as these, the employer's interests are on the side of the individual insureds, not the insurer. Then the court continued:

> . . . However, the employer has no such interest as against the insurer with respect to the distribution of the proceeds of the insurance. The employee is granted the right to designate the beneficiary and to change the beneficiary. The employer has reserved no control over the employee in regard to the naming or changing of the beneficiary. . . . The provision in the policy and certificate for acknowledgement of the notice

---

[2] 272 Wis. 527, 76 N.W. (2d) 311 (1956).

of change of the beneficiary is not for the benefit of the employer but obviously is designed principally for the benefit of the insurer. An employer is not precluded as a matter of law from acting as agent of the insurer with respect to receipt of notice from the employee as to change of beneficiary or in the matter of acknowledging that a change has been effected. . . . In view of these considerations, we are constrained to determine that the language of the policy and of the certificate in question relating to change of beneficiary must be construed to mean that the employer is the agent of the insurer in receiving notice of change of beneficiary and in acknowledging that such change has been effectuated.

Some of the conflicting decisions on this subject have been summarized by one authority[3] as follows:

> There is a distinct conflict of authority as to whether the employer acts as the agent of the insured or of the insurer in making the contract and keeping it in force. A number of cases have followed the more or less conventional rule that persons not regularly appointed agents or acting solely for the benefit of the company must be regarded as agents of the insured and have so held. In most respects, this rule would seem to be a sound one. The reason for it, however, could better be rested upon another ground. After all, the real insured is not the employee but the entity or group of employees; each employee is in the nature of a beneficiary entitled to receive certain privileges or benefits by reason of that insurance. Therefore, the employer, as representative of that entity, really is the agent of the insured.
>
> A number of cases, however, feeling that in this type of insurance liberal rules of construction ought to prevail and the individual employee not subjected to loss because of the acts of the employer, over whom he has no control, have held that the employer is the agent of the company rather than of the insured. While this view may not rest upon quite as sound a legal footing, it is, in some respects, a more equitable view. From the strict legal point of view, it is to some extent justified in that the employer collects the premiums from the employees and pays them over to the insurer, in that he often issues, cancels, and otherwise controls the individual policies which are issued to the employees, and, further, that the employees have no knowledge or control over the representations which the employer may make to the insurer.

It would seem that the question, therefore, of agency in group insurance, as in individual life insurance situations, is a question of the facts of the individual case. So-called majority and minority rules, therefore, are helpful, if at all, only as general guidelines.

One way to arrive at a clear-cut answer to this question is to have an appropriate statute, as illustrated in the case of *Weeks* v. *Pilot Life Insurance Company*.[4] In that case, the employee, Weeks, had been working

---

[3] Appleman, *Insurance Law and Practice,* Vol. I, at pp. 54–55.
[4] 180 S.E. (2d) 875 (S.C., 1971).

for more than two years and was covered by the group policy of his employer when he left work, in October, 1964, to visit a brother in Georgia. He did not tell his employer when or if he planned to return to work. The employer had been making weekly deductions from the employee's pay and had deducted enough money, at the time Weeks left, to pay part, but not all, of the premium for his coverage for October. The office manager, therefore, notified the insurer to cancel the insurance for Weeks as of October first.

Weeks returned to work on November 4 and asked about his insurance. The office manager did not know how to reinstate the coverage and was uncertain about the interpretation to be given a requirement that all employees whose employment commenced after a specified date must work 60 days before becoming eligible for the insurance. In other words, how did that requirement apply to an employee who had once been covered, whose insurance had terminated, and who had then returned to work? Accordingly, he waited until the insurer's service representative called and discussed the question with him. The representative told him that the requirement could be waived by the employer in such situations, if the waiver applied to all reinstated employees. He (the service representative) also instructed the office manager not to forward the insurance papers and premium for Weeks until the insurer had sent him a monthly statement. Accordingly, the employer's waiver, Weeks' application card, and premiums for the month of December were still in the possession of the employer when Weeks died. When claim was made, the insurer denied payment on the grounds that Weeks was not covered at the time of his death.

The lower court granted a motion for a directed verdict in favor of the insurance company. On appeal, however, the reviewing court said that the lower court had overlooked the fact that the employer and the office manager, Hancock, were both agents of the insurer, as a matter of law, because of a special statute to that effect.

The court also quoted from 14 Appleman, *Insurance Law and Practice,* 352 as follows:

> . . . Where the employer collects premiums under group policies by deductions from the wages of employees, he is regarded as the agent of the insurer, so that such deduction amounts to payment, as far as the insurer is concerned, even though not remitted to the insurer.

The court then said that there would probably have been no question about the coverage if the office manager had known how to handle the situation. Under the circumstances, any neglect on his part or on the part of the service representative must be the responsibility of the insurer rather than the employee. The court, therefore, concluded that the question should have been submitted to the jury to decide whether or not the insurer was estopped to deny coverage; the decision of the lower court (for the insurer) was reversed; and the case was sent back for a new trial.

D. WHEN INSURANCE BEGINS

The question of when insurance begins under a group life insurance plan arises in two separate situations. First, there is the question of when insurance becomes effective under the master policy. Second, there is the question of when insurance coverage begins for the individual insured.

As far as coverage under the group contract is concerned, the provisions of the policy govern. The policy usually specifies an effective date, and that date will control. The fact that a premium was paid a few days prior to that date will not establish earlier coverage; and neither conditional receipts nor binding receipts are customarily used in group life insurance.

20.1 The Actively at Work Requirement

It is relatively standard practice for a group life or health insurance policy to provide that insurance shall not become effective for any eligible person unless he is actively at work on the specified date. This requirement may not always be expressed in those exact words, but the idea is the same—to exclude from coverage anyone who is absent on the day specified, because of illness or injury. Sometimes the requirement is phrased in that way, so that coverage is not effective on the designated date for any employee who is absent because of illness or injury. Generally such absent employees become insured on the first day on which they return to work after becoming eligible.

Requirements of this kind are generally recognized and upheld as valid by the courts and are usually given effect in the generally accepted meaning of the words.

Illustrative of the interpretation usually followed is the case of *Jackson* v. *Metropolitan Life Insurance Company*.[5] In this case, the employee would have become eligible on August 1, 1968, provided he was actively at work on the date of his eligibility, for coverage under his employer's group insurance policy, which provided, in part as follows:

> . . . An employee employed subsequent to January 1, 1968, becomes eligible for insurance on the first day of the calendar month next following the month in which employment with the employer commences. The insurance on any employee becomes effective on the date of his eligibility, and insurance on any employee not actively at work on the date when

---

[5] 296 N.E. (2d) 679 (Ohio, 1973).

his insurance would otherwise become effective or on the next following date on which he is actively at work.

On August 1, however, the plant was shut down for inventory purposes. The employee would have gone back to work on August 5, but he died on August 4. Whether he qualified for insurance, therefore, depended upon the court's interpretation of the phrase "actively at work." In other words, was he actively at work on August 1?

In its decision, the court summarized the holdings of a number of cases, saying that the courts had uniformly interpreted the phrase, "which indicates that at least to them the meaning of the phrase is clear." For instance, in one case, the court had held that a striking employee was not actively at work within the meaning of the phrase. In another case, an employee did not qualify because he had been on leave of absence on the stipulated day because of disability. In still another case, the court had held that "actively at work" means "actually on the job and performing the employee's customary work."

The decision, therefore, was that the employee was not insured because he was not actively at work on the date he became eligible for coverage. The court said:

> In light of the well-understood meaning of the phrase "actively at work" and the harmony of the courts in their acceptance of that interpretation, we hold that where decedent was not performing his job or assigned duties on the date (August 1, 1968) he would have become eligible for coverage, because the plant was closed down for annual inventory, he was not "actively at work." Consèquently, decedent did not qualify for coverage under the provisions of the insurance policy.

20.2 Persons Insured Subsequent to Effective Date

As a general rule, group policies require that any person entering the group subsequent to the effective date of the policy must work for a specified period before becoming insured; and the courts generally uphold such provisions as valid. Exactly how this specified period is computed, however, may present a question—as is illustrated in the case of *Polan* v. *Travelers Insurance Company*.[6]

This case involved the interpretation of a requirement that employees complete three months of service before becoming eligible for insurance under a group policy. The employee was employed on April 20, 1965, and died on July 20, 1965, from the effects of an automobile collision on July 19, after he had worked the full day of July 19. The policy provided as follows:

---

[6] 192 S.E. (2d) 481 (W. Va., 1972).

(a) Employees whose employment commenced on or before April 7, 1952 are to be eligible on the effective date hereof; and
(b) other Employees are to be eligible on the date on which they complete three months of service.

It further provided that:

Each eligible Employee is to be insured hereunder from the date he becomes eligible; provided, however, that any Employee who is not actually at work on the date his insurance is to become effective shall not be insured until he actually returns to work.

The insurance company contended that under Pennsylvania law, the first day of employment must be excluded in counting the three-month period. Therefore, the three months would not have been completed until July 20 and the employee was not insured because he had not fulfilled the requirements for coverage.

The court pointed out that the basic question was the total period of time the employee was employed, saying:

It is undisputed, in fact it is stipulated, that Charles B. Polan commenced work on April 20, 1965 and worked that entire day. How, in computing the full period of his service in arriving at his eligibility can a day of that service be excluded? Certainly, he was entitled to credit for each and every day he worked to show that he completed three months service. To hold otherwise would create a fiction and constitute a denial of an admitted fact. Therefore, Charles B. Polan, having begun work on April 20, 1965, and having worked through July 19, 1965, completed three months of service and became eligible for coverage under the subject group insurance policy. To require him to have worked on July 20, 1965, to achieve eligibility, as contended by the appellant, would compel him to work three months and one day.

The court thus gave the words their usual and generally accepted meaning and held that the employee had fulfilled the necessary requirements to become insured.

The actively at work requirement, like many others, may be waived and the insurer may be estopped to enforce it. This is particularly likely to be the case in situations where the person was not actively at work but an individual certificate of insurance was nevertheless issued to him as a member of the group. Generally, the principle of estoppel does not apply if the certificate states clearly that insurance is not effective as of the effective date of the policy unless the employee is actively at work on that date and that the insurance will begin for that employee when he returns to active work, or at some other specified future date. However, court decisions are not all consistent on this point; and when premiums have been paid by the employer and accepted by the insurer, and a certificate has been issued, the insurer has been held estopped to deny the fact of coverage.

Holdings of this kind are not in accord with the general principle that coverage cannot be enlarged or imposed by waiver or estoppel. However, the actively at work requirement has been held to have been waived when an insurer knowingly accepted premiums on behalf of an ineligible employee (ineligible because he was not actively at work on the day in question).[7]

E. PAYMENT OF PREMIUMS

20.3 Contributory and Noncontributory Plans

Typically, a group life insurance policy provides that premiums will be paid by the policyholder. Employees may make contributions toward such payment; if they do so, the plan is a contributory plan. If they do not pay any part of the premium, it is a noncontributory plan. The details of premium payment in contributory plans complicate the question of coverage and thus may raise some legal questions that are different from those presented under individual policies.

Usually, under contributory group life insurance, the employee must sign an application and authorize the deduction of his premium contribution from his salary. The employer still pays the premium for the group coverage, but he uses the funds derived from employee contributions as well as his own funds for this purpose. Cases differ as to whether the individual's insurance continues after his employment terminates if the employer has deducted a premium from the employee's pay that would pay for a period beyond the termination date. For instance, if a premium has been deducted for a quarterly period ending March 31 but the employee's employment is terminated as of February 15, does his insurance under the policy continue to the end of the quarter because a premium has been paid for that period on his behalf?

In one case, the termination was held effective as of the date of termination of the employment, but there are several cases holding to the contrary. These cases hold that the employer is the agent of the insurer for the collection of premiums and the individual employee's coverage, therefore, cannot be terminated prior to the end of a period for which premiums are paid unless the employee is so notified.

20.4 Dividends

Individual insureds are not usually entitled to receive any dividends that may become payable under a group life insurance policy. The

---

[7] *Great American Reserve Ins. Co.* v. *Strain,* 377 P. (2d) 583 (Okla., 1962).

policyholder has paid the premium and is entitled to receive any dividends that become payable. Under some state laws, however, if the dividends exceed the premiums that the employer-policyholder has paid, the excess must be used for the benefit of the members of the group.

F. CHANGE OF BENEFICIARY

A typical change of beneficiary provision in a group life insurance policy provides that the beneficiary may be changed by the individual insured by submitting a signed written request "in form satisfactory to the insurer" and that the request shall be submitted to the insurer through the policyholder.

Legal questions sometimes arise as to whether the employer is the agent of the insured for the purpose of receiving changes of beneficiary, as discussed earlier; and questions also arise in situations where the beneficiary named in the individual certificate issued to the insured is different from the beneficiary shown in the employer's records or on a change of beneficiary form which was executed by the insured. In such situations, the court endeavors to decide what the intent of the insured may have been. Thus the individual facts of the case usually govern.

In general, the same legal principles that apply to beneficiary changes under an individual life insurance policy also apply to such changes under a group policy. Thus, any change of beneficiary must be made in accordance with the procedures set out in the policy itself, and if the insured has done everything in his power to complete the change, it will usually be held to be effective.

In one case,[8] however, when this argument was presented, the insured was held not to have done everything in his power to change the beneficiary, and the alleged change was not upheld. The insured had originally designated his mother as beneficiary under a group accident policy. The individual certificate included a change of beneficiary provision reading as follows:

> BENEFICIARY DESIGNATION AND CHANGE: The beneficiary or beneficiaries of an Insured Person shall be that person or those persons designated by the Insured Person and filed with the Company.
>
> Any Insured Person who has not made an irrevocable designation of beneficiary may designate a new beneficiary at any time, without the consent of the beneficiary by filing with the Company a written request for such change, but such change shall become effective only upon receipt of such request at the General Office of the Company. When such request is received by the Company, whether the Insured Person be then living or not, the change of beneficiary shall relate back to and take effect

---

[8] *Miller* v. *American Home Assurance Company,* 265 Fed. Supp. 112 (U.S. District Court, S.D. W. Va., 1967).

as of the date of execution of the written request, but without prejudice to the Company on account of any payment theretofore made by it.

The insurance was applied for on January 4, 1966, with the insured's mother as the designated beneficiary. On July 2, 1966, the insured was married to Phyllis Louise Miller, and on August 26, 1966, he was killed. Both the insured's mother and his widow sought to recover the proceeds of the policy, the mother on the basis that she was the named beneficiary and the widow on the basis that the insured had done everything in his power to change the beneficiary to her.

In support of the widow's position, it was shown that the insured had several times stated that if anything happened to him his wife would be well taken care of. He was also said to have pointed to the certificate and said to her that she would be well taken care of. Nevertheless, he did not give her the certificate or take any other action to change the beneficiary. After reviewing the facts, the court restated the general rule as follows:

> The majority of cases support the view that a change in beneficiary can be effected without a strict or complete compliance with the provisions of the policy regarding notice and endorsement. It is usually stated that substantial compliance by the insured with the conditions respecting a change of beneficiary is sufficient. The reason is that the right of the insured to change the beneficiary should be honored whenever possible and should not be defeated by delays, red tape, or mere technicalities.

The court concluded, however, that the statements and actions of the insured in this case were not all that a person could reasonably be expected to do under the circumstances, and that they were not sufficient to effect a change of beneficiary. The reasoning is summarized as follows:

> We are at a loss to see how the statements and action allegedly taken and relied upon can be considered all that a person in similar circumstances could be expected to do. We have no doubt that the ends of justice will be better served by refusing to change insurance beneficiaries under a course of events as dubious as those presently before the Court, even though it may occasionally result in an insured's final wishes being thwarted. To hold otherwise, even where proof justified it, which it does not here, would be to completely disregard the fact that a policy of insurance is a contract, admittedly one-sided, and that any and all benefits must be derived under and through it. To accept plaintiff Della Miller's[9] contention on the evidence presented would have the effect of making it an agreement solely between the beneficiary and the insured—a result for which we find no sanction in law.

G. ASSIGNMENTS

For many years, group life insurance policies were generally considered to be nonassignable. In fact, many master policies specifically

---

[9] The guardian of the widow, who brought suit on her behalf.

prohibited assignment by the individual insureds of their interests in the policy. For essentially the same reasons that industrial life insurance policies prohibited assignment, group life insurance policies (and the individual certificates) usually prohibited it also. The basic theory was that the purpose of group insurance was to provide a death benefit, and this might not be achieved if assignment were permitted.

Even where the policy did not prohibit the assignment of the employee's rights under the group policy, it was generally believed that it was not possible for the individual insured (the employee) to assign his interest under a group life insurance policy in such a way as to divest himself entirely of ownership. In other words, an absolute assignment was thought impossible. Two points were generally cited to support this view. One was the fact that premiums were frequently payable in part by withholding from the employee's salary and therefore he could always cancel his coverage by withdrawing his withholding authorization in a contributory plan. The other was that the employee could, even in a noncontributory plan, terminate his insurance by resigning. In other words, it was believed that the employee retained some control because he paid part of the premium or could terminate the insurance by resigning. These facts were considered sufficient to constitute incidents of ownership of which the employee could not, even by a purported absolute assignment, divest himself.

As long as the amount of insurance payable under a group life insurance plan was relatively modest, the question of assignment was not a significant factor. In recent years, however, benefits under group life insurance policies have sometimes reached significant amounts. A group death benefit of $100,000, for example, becomes a significant consideration when the federal estate tax is considered. Sooner or later, therefore, the estate planner would wonder whether there might not be a way of removing such a benefit from the estate of the insured for federal estate tax purposes.

Individual life insurance may be kept out of the insured's estate, as far as the federal estate tax is concerned, in either of two ways. Someone other than the insured (but having an insurable interest in his life, of course) may apply for and own the policy from the outset. Alternatively, the insured-owner may transfer ownership of the policy to a third person by absolute assignment. In either situation, no incidents of ownership would remain with the insured. Therefore, as long as the proceeds are not payable to the estate of the insured, they will not be includable in that estate for federal estate tax purposes.

A few attempts to apply this thinking to the group life insurance situation resulted in a revenue ruling from the Treasury Department of the United States declaring, in effect, that the proceeds of group life insurance will not be includable in the estate of the insured at his death provided three conditions are met. First, the law of the state where the insured lives must permit the insured to assign all incidents of ownership in the insurance, including the right to convert to permanent insurance on termination of employment and the right to change the beneficiary. Second, the policy must permit such assignment. Third, the insured must assign all such policy rights irrevocably.

This ruling has had two definite results. First many master policies of group life insurance were amended to delete the prohibition against assignment of the individual insured's interest; and, second, many of the states enacted laws specifically permitting such assignments.

The Supreme Court has held that it is not necessary to have an express statute permitting group life insurance to be assigned as long as there is no statute forbidding such action. This is a logical holding, based upon the generally accepted principle that people have the right to deal freely with any property interest unless there is a law expressly limiting this right. Because of the revenue ruling, however, many of the states, just to be on the safe side, have enacted laws expressly permitting the assignment of group life insurance.

H. WHEN THE INSURANCE TERMINATES

Group life insurance plans are formed for the purpose of providing insurance coverage to the members of certain employee groups, associations, or other qualifying groups. The individual becomes insured only after he has become a member of the group and, as a general rule, his insurance terminates when he ceases to be a member of the group.

Under employer-employee groups, the individual becomes insured only after he becomes an employee of the policyholder (and usually after he serves a probationary period); and although there are varying provisions for extending coverage under some circumstances, the typical policy provides that individual insurance coverage ceases when the employee's employment ceases. An illustrative policy provision might read as follows:

> The insurance of any participant shall automatically terminate on the earliest of the following dates:
> *a.* The date of termination of such participant's active status in any of the eligible classes of employment;
> *b.* The date of termination of this policy; and
> *c.* If this is a contributory plan, the date of expiration of the last period for which the participant has made a contribution if such participant fails to make, when due, any contribution toward the payment of premiums to which he has agreed in writing.

For purposes of this discussion, the important section of this provision is subparagraph (a). The effect of such a provision as this is clear. If the death of a particular person occurs prior to the date his employment terminates, he will have been insured and the benefit will be payable. If it occurs after that date, he will not have been insured on the date of death.

Questions arise most generally in two areas. First, there is the question of what is meant by termination of employment; and second, there may be a question of whether the facts of a given case amount to termination.

20.5 What Employment Means

There is rather general agreement that the word "employment" does not refer to a contract of employment but rather to the status of the employee with respect to his employer. It will be noted that the policy provision quoted above refers specifically to termination of the participant's "active status."

20.6 When Is It Terminated?

Employment is terminated when the status of employee and employer has been clearly and completely ended. It means a "termination of which the employee has knowledge," according to one court, and "something more than that the employee has stopped work or that the employer has stopped paying him." These latter conditions may exist in the case of sickness or layoff and do not necessarily mean that the employment has been terminated.

Exactly what actions constitute a termination of employment depends in every instance on the facts of the case. A few situations, however, have rather generally been held to constitute an effective termination of the employment status. Among these are the resignation of the employee, voluntary quitting, retirement, and discharge.

It is generally agreed that the employee who resigns or voluntarily quits work has terminated his employment, within the meaning of the contract language in a policy of group insurance. The employee's intention to sever his status may be inferred from other circumstances, however. Thus, where an employee did not formally resign but told his wife he would not return to work for the employer and applied for unemployment compensation, the court held that as a matter of law the employee had severed his employment prior to his death. The general rule is that retirement also constitutes termination of employment.

From the employer's point of view, the clearest manifestation of an intention to terminate the employment status is to discharge the employee. The legal effect of a layoff, however, presents a different question. Generally speaking, if the layoff is only a temporary measure and the apparent intention is to continue the employer-employee relationship, the employment will not be considered terminated.

20.7 Date of Termination

The exact date when an individual's employment terminates may be difficult to determine, because an apparently temporary leave of absence may become permanent either because of illness or otherwise. Leaves of absence for sickness or temporary layoffs, therefore, may present special and difficult problems. Because of this, many group policies include a special provision to the effect that when such temporary leaves or layoffs continue for a period of two (sometimes three) months, the employee's employment may be considered to have terminated as of a specified date unless the employer elects to consider it continued. Similar provisions specify that the insurance will not continue beyond a specified period unless the employer elects to have it do so. In either instance, the employer has the right to elect whether the insurance of the employee in question is to be continued in force.

20.8 Extension of Death Benefit

A special provision often included in group life insurance policies extends the coverage for a specified period, typically 12 months, in the event the employee is totally and permanently disabled. Under this type of provision, the insurer promises to pay the benefit the employee would have been entitled to immediately prior to termination of his employment, on receipt of due proof of his death during the extended period. Sometimes this period is defined as being equal to the period during which the employee's insurance has been in force at the date of termination of his employment, subject to a maximum of 12 months.

In order to qualify for payment of this benefit, the insured person must be proved to have been totally disabled at the termination of his employment and his death must have occurred within the period of time for which the insurance was extended.

I. WHICH LAW GOVERNS?

Group insurance policies are frequently issued by an insurer domiciled in one state, to an employer domiciled in a different state, insuring employees who may be residents of several different states. When a legal question arises, therefore, it is not always a simple matter to decide which law or laws are to be applied. As previously noted, questions of this kind fall into a special category and are resolved in accordance with conflict of laws rules. Group insurance problems frequently present conflict of laws questions.

The general conflict of laws rule is that questions relating to the validity of a contract are decided in accordance with the law of the place where the contract was completed—that is, the place where the last act took place that created a binding obligation. Usually, this rule applies to insurance contracts as well as other agreements.

In group insurance, the situation is somewhat more complex. Usually, the validity of a group insurance contract is determined by the law of the jurisdiction in which the policy was issued, although a few states have rules that forbid any insurer licensed in the state to issue a group policy anywhere that insures residents of that state unless the policy conforms to the insurance laws of the state of their residence.

A few courts, notably in New York, have followed what is referred to as a "center of gravity" or grouping of contacts rule, by which the law of the place that has the greatest interest in the question is applied.

These differing approaches to the question are summarized in the case of *Poffenbarger* v. *New York Life Insurance Company*.[10] There the beneficiary in a certificate of group life insurance sued the insurer for the death benefit provided under a group policy issued to trustees of the American Road Builders' Association Trust Fund. The trustee application for the policy was prepared in and mailed in the District of Columbia. The certificates (there were two) were delivered to the insured in West Virginia. The question was whether Poffenbarger was eligible for the insurance, and counsel for the beneficiary contended that the insurer could not challenge his eligibility because the contestable period had expired. The case thus turned on the court's interpretation of the incontestability clause; and, since the case was brought in a federal court, the next question was which state law should be applied in interpreting the clause—that of West Virginia, where Poffenbarger lived when the certificates were delivered to him, or that of the District of Columbia, where the application was completed. The court discussed this particular issue as follows:

> Since this is a diversity case the *Erie* doctrine requires that West Virginia law control the disposition of the issues, including any problem of conflict of laws. *Klaxon Co.* v. *Stentor Elec. Mfg. Co.*, 313 U.S. 487, 61 S.Ct. 1020, 85 L.Ed. 1477 (1941). If West Virginia law is applicable on the effect to be accorded the incontestability provisions of the group policy, it is unnecessary to review the welter of cases on this subject since the decision of our Supreme Court of Appeals in *Morris* v. *Missouri State*

---

[10] 277 F. Supp. 726 (D.C. W. Va., 1967).

Life Insurance Co., 114 W.Va. 278, 171 S.E. 740 (1933), is dispositive of the issue.

      ❉   ❉   ❉   ❉   ❉

Defendant contends, however, that in any event *Morris* should not apply since this case should be governed by District of Columbia law inasmuch as it was there that the group policy was delivered to the Trustees. It is well established in West Virginia that the *lex loci contractus* governs the nature, construction and validity of contracts. *Klinck* v. *Price*, 4 W.Va. 4 (1870). However, beyond that general principle, neither statute nor decisional law is available to indicate West Virginia's choice of the law to be applied in this troublesome area of group insurance contracts and the delivery of certificates thereunder. In the absence of state decisional law, it is the responsibility of the federal court to determine what the highest state court would find the law to be on this point if the same case were before it. See *Markham* v. *City of Newport News*, 292 F.2d 711 (4th Cir. 1961).

Counsel for both sides concede that on the facts presented here the West Virginia Court would be confronted with the choice of applying either the law of this state or the law of the District of Columbia. Some states have applied the law of the state in which the master policy was delivered, while others have applied the law of the state in which delivery of the certificate was effected.

      ❉   ❉   ❉   ❉   ❉

Assuming the West Virginia Court elected to apply the law of the District of Columbia, it would find no case law in that jurisdiction dispositive of the substantive issue. Under the circumstances it would be presumed that the law of the District would be the same as that of the forum.[11]

      ❉   ❉   ❉   ❉   ❉

Finally, it is not unreasonable to assume that our West Virginia Court in a case such as this might choose to apply the relatively new "grouping of contacts" theory of the conflict of laws. This theory would permit the forum to apply the law of the jurisdiction most intimately concerned with the outcome of the particular litigation. [Citation.] In the present case the State of West Virginia would appear to have a legitimate concern in the outcome of the litigation. This manifest interest of a state in the area of insurance on its residents was recognized in another context by the Supreme Court in *McGee* v. *International Life Ins. Co.*, 355 U.S. 220, 78 S.Ct. 199, 2 L.Ed.2d 223 (1957). It occurs to me that a West Virginia Court would and should recognize as significant the fact that the certificate was delivered in this state to the insured who was a resident of the state at the time, and that the plaintiff-beneficiary, as a West Virginia resident, is properly and logically entitled to litigate her claim in this forum. Additionally, it is noted that West Virginia legislation relative to group life insurance demonstrates a valid concern in regard to the issuance

---

[11] The law of the state where the case is heard—in this instance, West Virginia.

and delivery of such certificates in this state. See W.Va. Code ch. 33, art. 14.

The totality of these contacts and circumstances alone might well persuade the West Virginia Court to apply West Virginia law and recognize its holding in *Morris* as controlling on the facts of the present case. Certainly such a conclusion would not offend the basic principles of justice. The plaintiff's motion for summary judgment will be granted and counsel may submit an appropriate order incorporating this opinion by reference therein.

In this case, the court held that the law of West Virginia must be applied.

SUMMARY

Interpretation

Group life insurance contracts are interpreted according to the same rules as those that apply to individual life insurance contracts. The master policy is the contract; the certificate is issued only so that the individual insured will have a statement of his coverage.

The Group Contract—An Overview

The group life insurance master policy includes a general insuring clause, the provisions required by statute, provisions relating to eligibility for coverage, effective dates and termination dates of the coverage provided, and extensive provisions concerning premium payments and rates.

The Policyholder as an Agent of the Insurer

Many cases concerning group life insurance involve the question of whether the employer is or is not the agent of the insurer. It is sometimes said that there are two rules on this question—a majority rule and a minority rule. The majority rule is that the employer is not the agent of the insurer, and the minority rule is that the employer is the agent of the insurer. The more recent cases do not follow these rules rigidly but make the determination on the basis of the facts of the individual case. Therefore, it cannot reasonably be said that there is any general rule to apply to all situations. However, if there is an applicable statute, it will be given effect.

When Insurance Begins

Insurance under the master policy begins on the date specified in the policy and there is not generally any question of earlier coverage.

Usually, the policy provides that eligible individuals will not become insured on the specified date unless they are actively at work on that date. Generally, this means the employee must be actually on the job and performing his customary work. Employees entering the group after the date coverage becomes effective under the policy must usually work for a stipulated period before becoming eligible.

Payment of Premiums

Group life insurance premiums are typically paid by the policyholder. If they are paid in their entirety out of his own funds, the plan is said to be noncontributory. If he uses contributions from the insured members of the group as well as his own funds, the plan is a contributory one. Decisions differ as to whether the insurance of an individual continues after termination of his employment if the employer has deducted a premium from the employee's salary that would pay for a period beyond the termination date.

Dividends under group life insurance plans are paid to the policyholder, but if they exceed the amount of premium he has paid, they are sometimes required by statute to be used for the benefit of the insured members of the group.

Change of Beneficiary

Typically, the beneficiary under a group life insurance policy may be changed whenever the insured wishes, merely by completing the necessary form and submitting it to the insurer "through the employer." The same basic legal principles apply in connection with beneficiary changes under group life insurance contracts as under individual life insurance policies. Thus, if the insured has done everything in his power to complete the necessary procedures for a beneficiary change, the change will ordinarily be considered to have been completed.

Assignments

For a long time, it was generally considered that the individual insured under a group life insurance contract could not divest himself entirely of his ownership rights by making an absolute assignment. Today, however, it is generally believed that an absolute assignment of group life insurance will be effective if the master policy and individual certificates do not forbid absolute assignments, if the law of the state of domicile of the individual insured permits absolute assignments, and if the individual insured assigns all ownership rights irrevocably. In that case, an absolute assignment will have the effect of divesting the insured of all incidents of ownership and thus exclude the proceeds from the insured's estate for federal estate tax purposes.

Termination of Group Life Insurance

Typically, group life insurance coverage ceases for the insured individual when the employment terminates. Employment, in this sense, means a status; and it terminates when there is a definite intention on the part of the employee or the employer, or both, not to continue it. Thus, the employee may terminate the status by resigning and the employer may terminate it by discharging the employee. Leaves of absence or layoffs sometimes present borderline questions, but if the leave or layoff is only temporary, the status of employment will not be terminated. Many group life insurance contracts provide that when a leave of absence or layoff has continued for a specified period, such as three months, the insurance of the employee shall be terminated unless the employer elects to have it continue.

Extension of Death Benefit

Group life insurance policies frequently provide that if the insured is totally and permanently disabled, his insurance will be continued for a period of 12 months. If the insured is totally disabled at the time his employment terminates, therefore, and if he dies within the following 12 months, the insurance benefit will be paid.

Which Law Governs

Group life insurance master policies frequently insure individuals who live in several different states, so that the laws of the state where the policy was issued, the state where it was delivered, and the state where the certificate is delivered may all be different. In such situations, it is important to determine which state law will be applied in deciding a given question. Traditionally, questions relating to the validity of a contract are decided in accordance with the law of the place where the last act took place that was necessary to complete a binding agreement. With respect to the group life insurance contract, however, several states have applied the "center of gravity" or grouping of contacts rule. Under this rule, the law of the state that has the greatest interest in the particular question is applied.

ILLUSTRATIVE CASE

The following case has been selected because it illustrates and explains a number of important concepts in connection with the group life insurance conversion privilege. Because of its length, some portions have been deleted and others summarized.

WELLS, Plaintiff v. *WILBUR B. DRIVER COMPANY ET AL., Defendants*[12]

New Jersey Superior Court, Law Division

HANDLER, J.S.C.: This is an action by a beneficiary on a group life insurance policy issued by defendant, Prudential Insurance Company of America (hereinafter designated "Prudential") to defendant Wilbur B. Driver Company (hereinafter designated "Driver") for the benefit of Driver's employees. Plaintiff is the widow of George A. Wells, who had been an employee of Driver and an insured under the policy. The parties have moved for summary judgment.

Wells had been employed by Driver since 1947. He stopped working on April 30, 1969 due to neoplasm of the colon and received disability payments for six months thereafter. On November 10, 1969 Driver's personnel director and his assistant held a meeting with Wells and his wife during which there was a discussion of Wells' employment status. As a result Wells subsequently ceased working. He died on February 12, 1970 and Prudential paid plaintiff, as Wells' beneficiary, $5,043.15 on April 15, 1970 which amount the defendants contend represented the full amount of death benefits due under the group policy. Plaintiff asserts that she was entitled to insurance coverage in the amount of $18,300, and now claims the difference.

The Group Policy No. G-8489 herein was a non-contributory plan which provided life insurance coverage for each employee of Driver based upon the employee's compensation. Upon the death of an employee while insured the amount of insurance which would be payable was that set forth in a certificate issued to each insured employee periodically. Upon the attainment of age sixty-five or retirement the policy provided that the amount of an employee's life insurance was $5,000. Upon the termination of employment, there was also provided a right to convert all or a portion of the insurance to an individual policy without additional evidence of insurability. The employer under the contract was responsible for the administration of various phases of the insurance policy including maintenance of records concerning the particulars of each employee's insurance, the furnishing of periodic reports to Prudential indicating new employees, changes in amounts of insurance and terminations of insurance.

[The court here states that the insurance documents must be considered in the light of the applicable statute, which it quotes. The decision then continues:]

The statute does not further explicate what acts or circumstances constitute a "termination of employment" sufficient to trigger the conversion privilege . . . The policy itself however states specifically ". . . Termination of employment shall for all purposes of the Policy, be deemed to occur upon cessation of active full-time work . . . except that an Employee who is . . . retired will nevertheless be considered as still employed on a full-time basis until the Employer, acting in accordance with rules precluding individual selection, terminates the Employee's insurance by notifying the Insurance Company to that effect or by discontinuing premium payments for his in-

---

[12] 121 N.J. Super. 185, 296 A. (2d) 352 (1972).

surance. . . ." Issue is joined initially on whether there was such a termination of employment.

It is not unusual that a group insurance policy provide that termination of employment shall end an employee's insurance coverage [citations]. But it must be ". . . such a termination of the relationship of employer and employee as will make applicable and effective all parts of the insurance contract." [Citation.] A retired employee is one who has voluntarily withdrawn from employment and has ended his regular activity by arrangement with the employer. [Citations.] Consequently retirement is a termination of employment within the meaning of a "termination of employment" clause in a group insurance policy. [Citations.]

There was a meeting on November 10, 1969, between Driver's representatives and Wells, the subject of which was his retirement; a written request by Wells, for payment from the Driver's Employee's Security Plan was sent on the same date and there was a notation thereon to the effect that retirement was as of November 28, 1969; his retirement was also noted in the 1969 Christmas issue of Driver's publication. There was also correspondence from Driver's director of personnel to the administrator of group insurance and Driver's manager that Wells would retire December 1, 1969 and his last day on the payroll would be November 28, 1969. Thereafter Wells received wage security benefits, sabbatical payments and a pension payment the last of which was on or about January 9, 1970. These events can be assimilated only upon the rationale that Wells had retired from Driver.

A termination of insurance in the context of this case requires a coalescence of two events. There must in the language of the policy be a "cessation of active full-time work." Where such "cessation" is brought about through retirement there must also be either a notification by the employer to the insurer that the retired employee's insurance has been terminated or a discontinuance of premium payments for his insurance. Plaintiff contends that notwithstanding Wells' retirement, his insurance was not terminated because there was no subsequent notification of the termination of his insurance to the insurer or a discontinuance of premiums as required under the policy with respect to a retired employee.

* * * * *

Plaintiff also bases her claim upon the certificate apart from the insurance policy. It has been recognized that an insurance certificate does not of itself create any contractual relationship between the employee and the insurer. [Citation.] Ordinarily an insured holding a certificate of insurance is held to have constructive knowledge of the group insurance policy. [References.] In this vein defendants emphasize the clause in the certificate that "The provisions of the Group Policy principally affecting the Employee's insurance are described on this and the following pages of this certificate. All benefits described herein are governed by and are subject in every respect to the Group Policy which alone constitutes the agreement under which payments are made."

* * * * *

The certificate herein designated the amount of insurance at $18,300. It further provided that "If the Employee dies *while insured* under the Group Policy, the amount of insurance then in force on the life of the Employee will be paid to the beneficiary." This indicates with reasonable clarity the amount of insurance payable as a death benefit if insurance was in effect at the time of an insured's death. The certificate as required by *N.J.S.A.* 17:34–32(8) also fairly and accurately summarizes the rights and conditions with respect to the termination of insurance, the elements of the conversion right and the continuation of insurance during the 31-day conversion period. By necessary implication these clauses indicate that if there were such a termination of insurance and a failure to convert, there would be a loss or dimunition [sic] of insurance payable upon the subsequent death of the insured after the expiration of the conversion period. True the certificate does not state, as does the policy, the extent of this insurance drop, but the failure to specify the amount of reduction cannot in the context of this case be considered as so confusing or misleading to an insured as to induce the belief that there would be no loss of coverage whatsoever. To reach the result urged by plaintiff the certificate would have to be read as though the mandatory provisions pertaining to termination of insurance, the conversion privilege and the continuation of the insurance after the expiration of the 31-day period were non-existent.

Another and critical issue must be addressed in the context of this case— whether the failure to give a retired employee actual notice of the particular date when the termination of insurance is effective serves to continue full insurance coverage. It has been held that where insurance protection under a group insurance policy can be lost upon the termination of employment there will be implied an obligation on the part of the employer to give actual or definite notice thereof to the insured.

❂   ❂   ❂   ❂   ❂

Here Wells received no actual notice as to the particular date upon which his retirement would be or had become effective. Wells obviously knew, following the conference on November 10, 1969 and his subsequent receipt of various payments and benefits thereafter, that his retirement had been effectuated. But he was not advised as to any specific date that his retirement became effective so that he could estimate the accrual of the crucial period of time during which he would remain protected with continued insurance coverage and afforded an option to convert to an individual policy. Insofar as Driver did not notify Wells as to the actual date of the termination of his employment this constituted a breach of its implied obligation. Its dereliction in this respect is shared vicariously by Prudential. "Employment can be terminated only by notice given by the employer to the employee . . . [and] the insurer contracted to be bound by what transpired between the employer and employee." *Keane* v. *Aetna Life Insur. etc., supra.* 22 *N.J. Super.* at 305.

Assuming adequate notice of the termination date of employment, the court in *Keane* declined to consider the insurer liable on the policy for any failure to notify the insured of the actual termination of insurance. It stated that "The insurer nowhere conditioned its obligation upon such notice and we cannot revise the contract to embody that obligation." (*Id.* at 309.) Similarly in this case there is no explicit contractual undertaking set forth in the policy that a retired employee receive notice that premiums for his insurance were not paid or that his insurance was otherwise discontinued in order for there to be a termination of insurance. Nevertheless the policy and certificate herein provided that an employee who is retired will be considered "as still employed on *a full time basis* until the Employer . . . terminates the Employee's insurance by notifying the Insurance Company to that effect or by discontinuing premium payments for his insurance." [Emphasis added.] Thus in this case an insured employee by the very terms of the group policy and certificate was entitled to consider himself as fully employed for insurance purposes despite his actual retirement unless and until certain acts were performed. If, by necessary implication, an employer is obligated to notify an insured of the termination of his employment, this would import a comparable duty to apprise a retired employee of the actual date upon which there was a notification to the insurer or a discontinuance of premiums in order to conclude the employee's insurance coverage. It follows by a parity of reasoning that this implied obligation would fall within the pale of the insurer's contractual undertaking.

Wells received no notice at any time that as of a particular date his insurance would be terminated or decreased. There was a vague disclosure to the Wellses at the conference of November 10, 1969 that the insurance would be reduced to $5,000 following his retirement. This involved a discussion of *in futuro* events. Subsequent retirement benefits received by Wells occurred on varying dates. Moreover the last insurance certificate indicating the face amount of his insurance sent to Wells while he was alive was in the amount of $18,300. He was not privy to the interoffice reports of Driver or the report sent by Driver to Prudential in December 1969 which at best is merely an *indicium* of the discontinuance of premiums or a notification that Wells was then categorized as a retired employee. Without definite notice, knowledge could not be imputed to Wells that upon a particular date his group insurance terminated, that his right to convert to an individual policy had become activated and that the limited period of time during which he would remain fully protected was running.

In conclusion, the failure of Driver to furnish the insured with actual and definite notice of the exact date of the termination of his employment through retirement, compounded by the further failure to notify the insured that Prudential had been so notified of his actual retirement or that premiums had been discontinued as of a particular date served to continue Wells in the status of a fully employed employee for insurance purposes under the group insurance policy. As a consequence there was no effective termination of his insurance coverage or any portion thereof and insurance in the amount of $18,300 was payable to Wells' beneficiary as a claim upon his death on February 12, 1970. Accordingly, summary judgment in favor of plaintiff against defendants is granted.

QUESTIONS FOR REVIEW

1. List three areas in which the question of whether the employer is an agent of the insurer or the insured is likely to arise.
2. What has been considered the majority rule with respect to the employer as an agent? The minority rule?

3. How may this question of agency most reasonably be answered today?

4. List two reasons for the assumption, formerly held, that group life insurance was nonassignable.

5. What three requirements must be met before an absolute assignment of group life insurance is considered to be effective as far as the federal estate tax law is concerned?

6. Under which of the following situations may there be a question as to the termination of an employee's insurance under his employer's group life insurance plan?
   a. The employee resigns.
   b. The employee is discharged.
   c. The employee is laid off.

7. Briefly summarize the "center of gravity" or "grouping of contracts" rule in deciding conflict of laws questions under group life insurance.

PART VI

Health Insurance Contracts

Most of the principles of contract law that apply to life insurance contracts also apply to health insurance contracts, and in essentially the same way. However, many more varied benefits are offered under health insurance contracts than under life insurance contracts. For that reason alone, there are more opportunities for misunderstanding in health insurance than in connection with the life insurance coverages.

In numerous instances, therefore, legislatures have enacted specific laws designed to prevent misunderstandings and resolve problems that have arisen under health insurance contracts. This chapter will discuss some of the major areas in which such special legislative enactments and judicial decisions have seemed necessary.

Chapter Outline

A. Individual Health Insurance Contracts
 21.1 The Uniform Individual Policy Provisions Law
 21.2 "Entire Contract" Provision
 21.3 Grace Period Provision
 21.4 Reinstatement Provision
 21.5 Change of Beneficiary Provision
 21.6 Time Limit on Certain Defenses
 21.7 Notice of Claim
 21.8 Claim Forms
 21.9 Proof of Loss
 21.10 Payment of Claims
 21.11 Persons to Whom the Benefits Shall Be Paid
 21.12 Physical Examination and Autopsy
 21.13 Action at Law
 21.14 The Optional Provisions

B. The Benefit Provisions
 21.15 Disability Income Policies
 21.16 Hospital and Surgical Coverages

C. Definitions of Terms
 21.17 Injury and Sickness
 21.18 Hospital
 21.19 Physician

D. Exclusions and Limitations
 21.20 Benefits under Government Programs

E. Renewal Provisions
 21.21 Cancellable Policies
 21.22 Optionally Renewable Policies
 21.23 Noncancellable Policies and Guaranteed Renewable
 Policies

F. Preexisting Conditions

G. Group Health Insurance Policies
 21.24 Required Provisions
 21.25 Coordination of Benefits

Chapter 21

Health Insurance Contracts

HEALTH INSURANCE has been defined as insurance against loss of income or the expense of hospital or medical care resulting from sickness or accident. Health insurance is written under individual as well as group policies; and, together, such contracts have accounted for more than $10 billion in premium payments to U.S. life insurers and $8 billion in benefit payments by such insurers in each of the past several years.

This chapter will discuss the major statutory requirements that apply specifically to health insurance contracts and some illustrative court decisions.

A. INDIVIDUAL HEALTH INSURANCE CONTRACTS

By far the largest amount of health insurance today is written under group insurance contracts. In fact, such contracts account for considerably more than twice the premium income received from individual health insurance contracts. There are, however, more extensive statutory requirements relating to individual health insurance contracts than to group policies. The first part of this chapter, therefore, will concern individual health insurance policies and the major statutory requirements relating to provisions that must or may be included in them.

21.1 The Uniform Individual Policy Provisions Law

In General. From 1912 to 1950, individual health insurance policies were subject to a Uniform Standard Policy Provisions Law which required such contracts to contain certain standard policy provisions in the words and in the order set out in the law. The result of this requirement was a lack of flexibility and a tendency toward cumbersome policy language. In 1950, therefore, the National Association of Insurance Commissioners recommended a Uniform Individual Accident and Sickness Policy Provisions Law, which has since been adopted, with only a few variations, by all the states.

This legislation sets out two types of policy provisions: required and optional. Required provisions must be included in all individual health insurance contracts. Optional provisions may be used at the insurer's option, but they must be used if the subject matter to which they relate is included in the contract. In either case, it is not necessary to use the exact words in the exact order they are found in the law, and the insurer is free to use wording more favorable to the insured if it wishes.

Accident and sickness insurance is defined in this law as "insurance against loss resulting from sickness or from bodily injury or death by accident or both." One section of the law deals with the form of the individual health insurance policy and requires that the "entire money or other considerations therefor" be expressed in the policy, as well as the times at which the insurance takes effect and terminates.

The text of the policy must be presented in a type that meets minimum specifications set out in the law; and each policy form, rider, and endorsement must be identified by a form number in the lower left-hand corner of the first page. Requirements such as these are indicative of the minute detail with which all requirements are set out in the law.

Persons Covered.   The policy may insure only one person, or more than one if the policy is applied for by an adult member of a family and the additional persons are members of the family. The additional persons who may thus be insured include the husband, wife, dependent children, and any other person dependent upon the adult applicant; and the adult applicant is referred to as the policyholder.

Generally, children of the insured are eligible for coverage until they attain the age of 19, or the age of 23 if they remain in school. A number of states have enacted special laws that require insurers to retain as insureds under the parent's individual health insurance policy any child who reaches the limiting age but is dependent on the insured and incapable of self-support because of mental or physical impairment.

More recently, legislation has been enacted in some of the states requiring that health insurance policies insuring family members also provide coverage for newborn children from date of birth. Typically, such legislation permits the insurer to require that notice of the birth of the child be given, and that an application and an additional premium be submitted within a specified period.

Required Policy Provisions. Among the major policy provisions required by this legislation are the following:

1. An entire contract provision.
2. A grace period provision.
3. A provision permitting the policy to be reinstated.
4. A provision relating to change of beneficiary.
5. A provision entitled "time limit on certain defenses," which is essentially the same as an incontestable clause.

There are several required provisions relating to proofs of loss in the event of a claim, payment of claims, the company's right to require a physical examination or autopsy, and the time within which legal actions must be brought.

Optional Policy Provisions. Among the optional policy provisions are these:

1. Provisions relating to change of occupation.
2. Provisions relating to other insurance and earnings.
3. A provision excluding benefits in the event the insured is injured as the result of committing or attempting to commit a felony.
4. Overinsurance.

21.2 "Entire Contract" Provision

Each individual health insurance policy must provide that the policy "including the endorsements and the attached papers, if any, constitutes the entire contract of insurance." The statute also requires language to the effect that no change in the policy shall be valid until approved by an executive officer of the insurer and endorsed upon or attached to the policy. Finally, it specifies that no agent has authority to change the policy or to waive any of its provisions. The similarity of this provision to the provision required to be included in the life insurance contract is readily apparent.

21.3 Grace Period Provision

A grace period provision is also required to be included in individual health insurance contracts. Unlike the grace period provision required for life insurance policies, which is usually 31 days, the grace period for individual health insurance contracts may be as short as 7 days for weekly premium policies and 10 days for monthly premium policies; but it must be 31 days if the premiums are payable on any basis except weekly or monthly. As is true of life insurance, the coverage remains in force under a health insurance policy during the grace period.

If a claim arises during the grace period, the insurer may reserve the right to deduct any unpaid premium from any settlement, but this right is not made a part of the grace period provision. Instead, it is a separate, and optional, standard provision.

Some idea of the wide variety of health insurance policies that have been developed may be gained from the modifications required in the grace period provision for health insurance policies, as contrasted with the relatively simple grace period provision included in individual life insurance contracts. For instance, individual health insurance policies are sometimes cancellable by the insurer. Therefore, the law includes special wording for the grace period provision for those policies. In such instances, the policy may specify that the policy will remain in force during the grace period, "subject to the right of the insurer to cancel in accordance with the cancellation provision hereof."

Other health insurance policies may be renewable by the policyowner only at the option of the insurer (optionally renewable policies). For policies of which this is true, the grace period provision must be introduced with a statement that unless the insurer gives timely notice of its intention not to renew the policy beyond the period for which a premium has been paid, there will be a grace period of the specified length. This introductory language must be not less favorable to the insured than the following:

> Unless not less than five days prior to the premium due date the insurer has delivered to the insured or has mailed to his last address as shown by the records of the insurer written notice of its intention not to renew this policy beyond the period for which the premium has been accepted . . . (there will be a grace period, etc.)

Thus, the policy must contain a grace period provision, but if the insurer has notified the insured of its intention not to renew the policy beyond a specified date, there is no grace period for the premium that would otherwise become due on that date.

21.4 Reinstatement Provision

The reinstatement provision required to be included in individual health insurance contracts is also somewhat more complex than the reinstatement provision required in the life insurance contract. The individual health insurance contract must provide that if the policy lapses and an application for reinstatement is not required, acceptance of the overdue premium at a later date will automatically reinstate the policy.

If the insurer requires a reinstatement application, and if a conditional receipt is issued for the accompanying premium, reinstatement of an individual health insurance policy will be effective as of the date the application for reinstatement is approved. Even if the insurer fails to approve the application, the policy will be reinstated automatically unless the company notifies the policyowner of disapproval of the application within 45 days.

A reinstated policy of health insurance covers only losses resulting from accidents that occur after the effective date of the reinstatement, or sicknesses which begin more than 10 days after the reinstatement. (Thus, there is, in effect, a 10-day waiting period for sickness claims after reinstatement.)

This policy provision has been upheld in the courts many times, although some more recently decided cases take the position that if the condition resulting in the claim had its beginning while the policy was in force, the claim will be payable even though the policy later lapsed and was reinstated prior to the date the insured actually made claim.

Except for the 10-day waiting period applicable to sickness claims, the rights and responsibilities of the insured and the insurer are the same under a reinstated policy as they were prior to reinstatement, except as to "provisions endorsed hereon or attached hereto." Thus, a policy of health insurance may be reinstated subject to restrictive conditions that were not part of the policy prior to the lapse. In other words, the reinstatement of a lapsed policy does not necessarily mean that the old policy is fully restored to its former status. Benefits are reinstated, but they may be modified or limited as compared to the benefits originally provided.

21.5 Change of Beneficiary Provision

If an individual health insurance policy provides a death benefit, a change of beneficiary provision is also required. This provision must state that unless the owner has designated an irrevocable beneficiary, the right to change the beneficiary is reserved. It must also provide that the consent of the beneficiary or beneficiaries shall not be required in order for the policyowner to surrender or assign the policy or change the beneficiary, or change the policy in any other way.

21.6 Time Limit on Certain Defenses

In a general sense, the "time limit on certain defenses" provision required to be included in the individual health insurance policy is similar to the incontestable provision required in the individual life insurance contract. The basic purpose of this provision, as is true of the life insurance incontestable clause, is to limit the period of time in which an insurer will be permitted, legally, to defend a claim denial on the basis of material misrepresentation in the application. Thus the provision literally establishes a time limit for the use of certain defenses by the insurer in support of its denial of a claim. As a result, if the individual health insurance policy has been in force for the required period of time (which cannot exceed three years), the insurer will not generally be permitted to defend a claim denial on the basis of material misrepresentation in the application.

However, there are several significant differences between the time limit on certain defenses provision of the health insurance contract and the incontestable clause of the life insurance policy. These differences, for the most part, reflect the wider variety of problems that may be involved in health insurance claims than those arising under life insurance policies.

In outline, the time limit on certain defenses provision consists of two paragraphs. The first (paragraph *a*) must provide that after three years from the issue date of the policy "no misstatements, except fraudulent misstatements" made by the applicant shall be used to avoid the policy or to deny a claim for loss incurred or disability beginning after the expiration of the three-year period. (Several states have reduced the three-year period to two; and the insurer may always use a shorter period if it wishes, since that would be more favorable to the insured.)

This paragraph most nearly parallels the incontestable clause of the life insurance contract. Yet even here, the differences are readily apparent. First, the period is usually three years instead of two, as is customary for the incontestability clause of the life insurance contract. The second difference is that fraud is specifically excluded from the operation of the clause in health insurance policies. As previously noted, this is not true of the incontestability clause in life insurance.

The second paragraph of the time limit on certain defenses provision concerns the subject of preexisting diseases or conditions. It specifies that no claim for loss incurred or disability beginning after three years from the issue date of the policy shall be reduced or denied on the basis that the disease or physical disability existed prior to the effective date of the policy, unless that disease or physical condition was excluded from coverage under the policy by name or specific description.

Numerous rules and regulations have been promulgated to govern the treatment of claims in which a preexisting condition seems to have been involved. Because this is such an important consideration in health insurance, it will be discussed in some detail in a later portion of this chapter (section F., "Preexisting Conditions").

Optional wording is provided for the first paragraph of this time limit on certain defenses provision for policies that are referred to as either "guaranteed renewable" or "noncancellable." These terms will be discussed more extensively later, but at this point, it should be noted that they describe two different types of health insurance policies which give the insured the right to continue them by paying premiums as they become due and which the insurer cannot cancel or refuse to renew (except within stipulated limits) as long as the insured continues to pay the premiums. Individual health insurance policies of this kind may be continued on much the same basis as life insurance policies; and the optional wording for the time limit on certain defenses provision reflects that fact. This wording provides that after the policy has been in force for three years during the lifetime of the insured (excluding any period in which the insured is disabled), it will become incontestable with respect to the statements contained in the application. In other words, a noncancellable or guaranteed renewable health insurance policy may include an incontestable provision that is essentially the same as that found in the life insurance policy.

21.7 Notice of Claim

An individual health insurance policy must contain a provision specifically relating to notice of claim. The insurer must be given notice of claim within 20 days after the occurrence or commencement of any loss covered by the policy, or as soon thereafter as is reasonably possible. Note that this language recognizes the fact that an accidental death claim will be based on the "occurrence" of loss, while a disability income or hospital claim will be based on a loss that will "commence" on a specified day and may continue for some time. Notice, therefore, must be given within the specified number of days after the occurrence of loss in the one case and its commencement in the other.

Notice may be given by the insured or on his or her behalf, or by the beneficiary or on behalf of the beneficiary, to the insurer at a designated location, or to any authorized agent of the insurer. If enough information is given to identify the insured, the notice will be considered sufficient. If the policy provides loss of time benefits (disability income coverage) for a period of at least two years, it may also include a provision requiring notice of continuance of disability.

21.8 Claim Forms

An individual health insurance policy must provide that the insurer will furnish claim forms within 15 days of the date it receives notice of claim. Otherwise, the claimant will be considered to have fulfilled the requirements of notice of loss if he merely files written proof of the occurrence on which claim is based and describes the character and extent of the loss.

21.9 Proof of Loss

The policy must provide that proof of loss shall be given to the insurer in writing. If the policy provides for periodic benefit payments, proof of loss must be given within 90 days from the end of the period for which payment is due. This provision applies to disability income insurance policies. For benefits under other types of health insurance policies, proof of loss must be filed within 90 days after the date the loss is suffered. The policy must also provide that if it is impossible for the insured to comply with these policy requirements, it will be sufficient if he furnishes such proof within one year from the date proofs would otherwise have been required.

An illustrative policy provision concerning proof of loss would read as follows:

> Written proof of loss must be furnished to the Company at its said office, in case of claim for loss for which this policy provides any periodic payment contingent upon continuing loss, within ninety days after the termination of the period for which the Company is liable; and in case of claim for any other loss, within ninety days after the date of such loss. Failure to furnish such proof within the time required shall not invalidate nor reduce any claim if it was not reasonably possible to give proof within such time, provided such proof is furnished as soon as reasonably possible and in no event, except in the absence of legal capacity, later than one year from the time proof is otherwise required.

Note the basic difference between the requirement concerning notice of claim and proof of loss. Notice of claim must be given within 20 days, but proof of loss is a different matter. Proof of loss presumably may include a doctor's statement or, in the case of accidental death benefits, a death certificate. In any case, the insured or beneficiary is given 90 days in which to present proof.

21.10 Payment of Claims

The policy must specify that claims will be paid immediately upon receipt of proofs of loss unless periodic payments are involved. In that event, payments must be made as specified in the policy, but in no event less frequently than monthly.

21.11 Persons to Whom the Benefits Shall Be Paid

Any sum payable as a death benefit must be paid in accordance with the beneficiary designation, if there is a designated beneficiary. Otherwise payment will be made to the estate of the insured. If there are accrued unpaid benefits at the date of the insured's death, the insurer has the option of paying to the beneficiary or to the estate of the insured. All other benefits are payable to the insured.

21.12 Physical Examination and Autopsy

The policy must include a provision that the company, at its own expense, shall have the right and opportunity to have the insured examined and to make an autopsy in case of death, except where autopsy is forbidden by law.

21.13 Action at Law

The policy must provide that no action at law or in equity may be brought against the insurer until the expiration of 60 days after written proof of loss has been submitted, as required by the policy. No such action shall be brought after the expiration of three years from the time written proof of loss has been furnished. In other words, if the insured or beneficiary decides to sue the insurer, the suit cannot be brought earlier than 60 days after claim proofs have been submitted nor after the expiration of three years from that date.

21.14 The Optional Provisions

Payment of Claims. As previously noted, an individual health insurance policy may, if the insurer wishes, include any of several other provisions referred to in the law as optional provisions. Some of these are separate from the required provisions; some are optional paragraphs that may or may not be included in provisions that are required. For example, a one-paragraph payment of claims provision is required. However, the insurer has its choice of using either or both of two optional paragraphs in this policy provision. One of these optional paragraphs concerns benefits payable to the estate of the insured or to a beneficiary who is a minor or is otherwise incompetent to give a binding release. The policy may provide that amounts up to $1,000 may, in any of these situations, be made "to any relative by blood or connection by marriage of the insured or beneficiary" who is, in the opinion of the insurer, equitably entitled to the money. Generally, this means someone who has incurred any final expenses on behalf of the insured or beneficiary. It will be recalled that a provision similar to this is permitted to be included in group life insurance.

A second paragraph that may be included in the required payment of claims provision concerns the payment of benefits for hospital, nursing, medical, or surgical services. The policy may provide that benefits for such services may be paid directly to the hospital or the person rendering such services unless the insured requests otherwise in writing at the time, or before, proofs of loss are filed.

Change of Occupation. The insurer may, but is not required to, include in an individual health insurance policy, a provision relating to adjustments in benefits or premiums in the event the insured changes to a more or less hazardous occupation. These optional adjustments may be summarized as follows:

1. If the insured has an accident or becomes ill at a time when he is engaged in a more hazardous occupation than the one in which he was engaged at the time he applied for the policy, any benefit payable will be adjusted to the amount which the premium that was paid would have purchased at the more hazardous occupation. In other words, the benefit will be adjusted downward, but there will be no adjustment in the premium. Note that this is the same principle that is used in the misstatement of age adjustment in life and, as will be noted later, health insurance.

2. If the insured's occupation at the time he suffers a loss is less hazardous (according to the insurer's rating schedule) than the one in which he was engaged at the time he applied for the policy, the company will reduce the premium to be paid in the future and refund any past overpayments to the policyowner. In this event, the premium rates and classifications of risks used will be those last filed by the insurer with the commissioner of insurance in the state concerned. If such filing was not required, the rates and classifications used will be those the insurer has most recently made effective in the state prior to the occurrence of the insured's loss. This approach may be contrasted with the approach used in the misstatement of age provision. (If a policy does not contain this optional change of occupation provision, the insurer may not make any adjustment in either the benefit or the premium because of a change of occupation.)

Commission of a Felony. An individual health insurance policy may include a provision, at the option of the insurer, that exempts the insurer from any liability in the event the loss was caused by the insured's commission of a felony, or by an attempt to commit a felony.

Misstatement of Age. An individual policy of health insurance may, at the option of the insurer, include a misstatement of age provision. This provides that if the insured's age has been misstated, all amounts payable under the policy shall be such as the premiums paid would have purchased at his correct age. This, of course, is essentially the same as the counterpart provision in the individual life insurance contract.

Other Insurance. Overinsurance is recognized as a significant factor in the overutilization of health insurance, and insurers attempt to discourage it as much as possible. In any situation where an insured may receive more in disability income benefits than he would receive in take home pay while working, there is a strong temptation to submit claims in connection with borderline or, at times, nonexistent accidents or sicknesses. Guarding against such ill-founded claims is a necessary objective in the drafting of health insurance contracts.

Two optional provisions that may be included in an individual health insurance policy for this purpose concern other insurance the insured may have. One of these provisions relates to a situation where the insured may have two or more policies in the same insurer. Generally this will be possible only with policies that are not underwritten individually, such as policies sold by machine. In such situations, the policy may include a provision that any amount of insurance on the insured in excess of a stated amount shall be void, and all premiums paid for the excess shall be returned to the insured or to his estate.

Alternatively, the additional insurance with the same insurer provision may provide that insurance on the insured "under a like policy or policies" shall be limited to the one such policy the insured (or his beneficiary or estate) may elect. In that case, too, provision is made for the refund of all premiums paid for the other policies. In this situation, the insured may decide for himself which policy (of the same insurer) he wishes to retain or, in the event of his death, his beneficiary or personal representative may make the election.

There are two optional provisions concerning insurance with other insurers. One concerns policies providing benefits on a "provision of service" or expense incurred basis, and the other relates to policies providing benefits on an other than expense incurred basis. In either situation, the provision states that if the insured has other valid policies providing the specific benefits and if the insurer had no notice of such other policies, the liability under the policy containing this provision shall be limited to a specified proportion of the total loss suffered by the insured. The proportion is found by dividing the amount otherwise payable under the policy containing the "insurance with other insurers" provision plus other valid coverages of which the insurer had notice by the total amounts payable under all valid coverages.

To use an oversimplified example, assume that John J. Insured has four policies in four different companies providing essentially the same kind of benefits. Policy A is the only policy which has the insurance with other insurers provision and Insurer A has notice of policy B but not of policies C and D. Each of these policies provides benefits that, in the absence of this provision, would pay $500 for a specified loss. If the above-described provision is applied, the amount Insurer A will pay is calculated as follows: $500 (which would otherwise be payable under Policy A) plus $500 payable under Policy B (of which Insurer A had notice) divided by $2,000, or 1,000/2,000, or 1/2. Thus, Insurers B, C, and D each would pay the $500 benefit; but A, because it had no notice of the insurance with C and D, would pay only half of the specified benefit, or $250.

Insurers using one of these provisions may also include a definition of "other valid coverage," with the commissioner's approval. The definition must limit such coverage to coverage provided by organizations subject to regulation by insurance law or insurance authorities "of this or any other state of the United States or any province of Canada and by hospital or medical service organizations and any other coverage the commissioner may permit to be included." If a definition is not included, the term "other valid coverage" shall not include group insurance, automobile medical payments insurance, or coverage provided by hospital or medical service organizations or by union welfare plans or employee or employer benefit organizations.

Relation of Earnings to Insurance. Another optional provision is captioned "relation of earnings to insurance." This is also a provision that may be used to help counteract the tendency of insureds, in some instances, to acquire so much insurance that they may have more income by qualifying for disability or medical benefits than by working.

The relation of earnings to insurance provision concerns the situation where the benefits payable under all loss of time (disability income) coverages the insured has exceed his monthly earnings at the time disability commenced (or his average monthly earnings over the two years preceding the disability for which he is claiming benefits). In that event, the insurer's liability is limited to a proportionate part of the total benefits that would otherwise be payable under the policy in question. This proportion is found by dividing the insured's monthly earnings by the total benefits to which he would be entitled under all valid loss of time coverages. Excess premiums are refundable on a pro rata basis. The benefits payable under all loss of time coverages the insured has cannot be reduced below $200 per month or the total benefits specified in all such valid coverages, whichever is less.

For example, John Policyowner has a policy from Insurer A providing $200 per month income for total disability resulting from accident or sickness. It includes the relation of earnings to insurance provision. He also has another policy from Insurer B which provides $400 per month disability income coverage but does not have a relation of earnings to insurance clause. John's average monthly earnings at the time he became disabled were $500.

In this case, the benefits payable under John's policy with Insurer A may be reduced, since his total loss of time benefits ($600) exceed his average monthly income ($500). Insurer A's liability will then be reduced in the proportion John's monthly earnings bear to the total benefits he would be entitled to, or $500 divided by $600 [$200 + $400]. Thus

Insurer A will pay only 5/6 of 200, or $166.67. Insurer B will pay the full $400, since its policy did not have the relation of earnings to insurance provision.

It should be noted, however, that John will still be overinsured, since his total benefits will exceed the income he would have earned if he had continued working. In addition, his take-home pay would have been still further reduced by withholding under the federal income tax. His disability income payments, by contrast, are not subject to the federal income tax.

Assume now that both policies have this relation of earnings to insurance provision. In that instance, Insurer B would pay only 5/6 of $400, or $333.33. Together, the insurers would exactly replace the insured's earned income. Because of the federal income tax situation, however, John would still be better off financially by not working if he could collect his disability income benefits.

It seems clear, therefore, that even if all health insurers included this relation of earnings to insurance provision in their disability income policies, the problem of overinsurance would not be resolved effectively, even in this limited area. This is true also, to some extent, of the "other insurance" provisions, which predate guaranteed renewable and non-cancellable health insurance policies and are not suitable for use in them. The inadequacies of any of these provisions with respect to resolving the problem of overinsurance has been recognized for a long time, and the problem has been under serious consideration by the health insurance industry as well as regulative bodies. As yet, however, no very effective answers to the problem have been found.

Cancellation. If the insurer intends to reserve the right to cancel a policy of health insurance at any time, the policy must include a cancellation provision. This, too, is an optional provision. If included, it permits the insurer to cancel the policy at any time by written notice delivered to the insured or mailed to his last known address. The notice must state the time—not less than five days later—when the cancellation shall take effect. After the policy has been continued beyond its original term, it may be canceled by written notice to be effective upon receipt, if the insurer wishes, or on a later date as specified in the notice.

When a policy is canceled, the insurer must refund that portion of the premium that applies to any period beyond the date the cancellation is effective (the unearned premium). If the insured cancels, a special slightly higher premium rate called a short-rate may be used in computing the unearned premium refund. This table must have been filed with the insurance commissioner of the state where the insured resided when the policy was issued. If the insurer cancels, a regular pro rata refund is made. In either case, cancellation must be without prejudice to any claim which had its origin prior to the date when the cancellation took effect.

This final sentence in the cancellation provision is especially significant and means, of course, that if a claim arises during a period in which the policy is in force, the insurer cannot, by canceling the policy, reduce its liability for any covered expenses arising from that claim. The effect in a particular instance is illustrated in the case of *The Service Life Insurance Company* v. *Elizabeth E. Branscum.*[1] In that case, the company refused renewal of the policy and denied a claim for expenses incurred after the policy had been terminated.

The facts were these: The policy provided benefits for hospital confinement. Bobby Harms, a covered person because he was a member of the policyholder's family, was injured in an automobile accident on March 20, 1959. At that time the policy was in full force and effect, and the insurer paid benefits for Bobby's hospitalization from March 21, 1959, to May 11, 1959, and again from June 8, 1959, to June 23, 1959. A monthly premium was due on July 17, 1959, and the policyholder sent the insurer a check in payment of it. The insurer refunded the premium and notified the policyholder that it was electing not to renew the policy, except with certain waivers (meaning exclusions from coverage for certain conditions).

After the policy was terminated by this refusal to renew, Bobby was hospitalized again, apparently from injuries suffered in the same automobile accident; and the insurer refused to pay benefits on the basis that the policy was not in force when the hospitalization expenses were incurred. The policyholder then brought suit.

The court held that the insurer was liable for benefits arising out of the later hospital confinement because these expenses were part of the claim that arose while the policy was in force. The court referred to an earlier case in which a similar question had been presented and quoted from the court opinion as follows:

> It is provided in clause 15 of the policy that cancellation on any anniversary date is without prejudice to any pending claim. *Such, of course, would be the law even if not expressed in the clause.* [Emphasis added.]

It concluded that the insurer was liable in this instance, saying:

> We therefore conclude that the rights of the appellee accrued at the time of the injury while the terms of the policy were in full force and effect. The cause of action arose immediately at that time and the insured was entitled to recover the full amount that was due him under the policy. The appellee asked for the sum of $728.57, penalty and attorney's fees, and that amount does not appear to be contested. We find that the court was justified in making the award for those amounts.

---

[1] 234 Ark. 463, 352 S.W. (2d) 586 (1962).

It is notable that a cancellation provision cannot be used in a number of states, and the use of such a provision is limited in others. Limitations and restrictions such as these are part of a general regulatory pattern concerning continuation provisions that will be discussed more fully in a later section of this chapter.

Unpaid Premium. As previously noted, the insurer may include a provision in the policy concerning the deduction of an unpaid premium from any claim settlement. This provision, as set forth in the uniform policy provisions law, reads as follows:

> Upon the payment of a claim under this policy, any premium then due and unpaid or covered by any note or written order may be deducted therefrom.

This becomes important when a claim arises during the grace period. In that case, the claim will be paid, but the insurer has the right to deduct the premium from the amount of settlement if this optional provision is included in the policy.

B. THE BENEFIT PROVISIONS

In addition to the required and optional provisions, individual health insurance policies contain a number of policy provisions that define the benefits payable; the exclusions applicable; and such provisions as those relating to renewability, conversion rights for dependents attaining a specified age, and other provisions necessary to explain and limit the liability of the insurer.

In very broad terms, individual health insurance policies provide benefits designed to help replace income lost because the insured is unable to work as the result of sickness or accident (disability income coverages); benefits in the event he incurs expenses for hospital, surgical, and medical care; and benefits in the event of accidental death and dismemberment. Some policies (generally referred to as limited policies) provide benefits only in the event the insured suffers a loss as the result of accident. Other such limited policies provide benefits if the insured incurs expenses resulting from specified diseases, such as polio or cancer; and still others provide benefits only in the event of travel accidents which result in disability or death.

From this point of view, health insurance coverages may be divided into these broad categories:

1. Income disability coverages.
2. Medical expense coverages, including hospital policies and surgical and medical expense coverages.
3. Accident and dread disease coverages.

21.15 Disability Income Policies

Disability income policies are intended to provide an income to be paid on a periodic basis in the event the insured is unable to work at his own or any occupation; and disability is customarily defined in either or both of those forms, as discussed in section B. of Chapter 7.

Health insurance policies providing income disability benefits are generally characterized by relatively few exclusions and limits up to as high as $2,500 per month or more. The coverage is basic, intended to protect the insured from loss of income because of accident or sickness. Indeed, policies of this kind are frequently referred to as loss of income coverages.

21.16 Hospital and Surgical Coverages

Hospital and surgical coverages represent a very large segment of the health insurance policies available and generally provide specified benefits designed to reimburse the insured for the expenses of hospital confinement, up to limits specified in the policy. Usually, benefits are also provided for surgical expense and medical care while in the hospital.

Depending upon the limits established for medical expense coverages, such policies may also be classified as basic coverages, major medical, and comprehensive medical expense policies. Basic medical expense coverages provide benefits for hospital confinement, beginning with the first day of confinement, and surgical benefits beginning with the first dollar of expense incurred. In other words, there is not generally a deductible amount of expense that must be incurred before these benefits become payable.

Major medical expense coverages, by contrast, are intended to provide coverage for the major medical expenses that result from long periods of hospital confinement or expensive surgical procedures. In order to accomplish this, major medical coverages generally specify a deductible amount, which must be borne by the policyowner or paid under his basic coverage before benefits become payable under the major medical policy. Such coverages usually include also a "coinsurance" or percentage-participation provision which requires the insured to share a percentage of the medical expenses he incurs above the deductible amount. Typically, this percentage participation requirement provides for a sharing on an 80–20 percent basis, with the insured assuming 20 percent of the costs.

Comprehensive medical expense policies generally combine the basic and major medical expense coverages in one policy. Comprehensive medical expense policies are characterized by a very low deductible, often $50.

C. DEFINITIONS OF TERMS

21.17 Injury and Sickness

Although health insurance policies provide benefits under many different circumstances, they typically insure against loss resulting from injury or sickness or both. In order that the coverages may be described as clearly as possible, therefore, these terms are often defined in the policy. Illustrative definitions might read as follows:

> *Injury.* Injury means accidental bodily injury sustained by the insured while this policy is in force and shall include all injuries sustained by the insured as the result of any one accident.
>
> *Sickness.* Sickness means any sickness or disease first manifesting itself while this policy is in force and shall include all complications arising therefrom.

Note that the injury covered must be sustained while the policy is in force and the sickness or disease must first manifest itself while the policy is in force. Preexisting diseases or conditions, therefore, are not intended to be covered.

21.18 Hospital

The intent under hospital policies is to provide benefits in the event the insured incurs expense by reason of being confined in a hospital, but not to provide benefits in the event the insured needs only custodial care. For this reason, many hospital policies contain a definition of "hospital" in order to exclude claims for benefits when the insured is confined in a nursing or convalescent home. Illustrative of some of the problems involved in drafting such definitions, as well as some of the claim questions that may arise in connection with them, is the case of *Travelers Insurance Company* v. *Page*.[2] In that case, the policy included a definition of hospital that read as follows:

> . . . The term "hospital" as used herein means an institution which meets all of the following tests: (a) It is engaged primarily in providing medical care and treatment of sick and injured persons on an in-patient basis at the patient's expense and maintains diagnostic and thereapeutic facilities for surgical and medical diagnosis and treatment of such persons by or under the supervision of a staff of duly qualified physicians; (b) It continuously provides twenty-four hour a day nursing service by or under the supervision of registered graduate nurses and is operated continuously with organized facilities for operative surgery; and (c) It is not, other than incidentally, a place of rest, a place for the aged, a place for drug addicts, a place for alcoholics or a nursing home.

---

[2] 120 Ga. A. 72, 169 S.E. (2d) 682 (1969).

The insured's daughter (also a covered person) was confined in a psychiatric treatment institution where there were facilities for suturing and similar minor treatment. However, there were no facilities for major surgery—indeed, it was admitted that if any of the patients had required even a tonsillectomy they would have been transferred to a general hospital. The insurer contended, therefore, that the institution was not a hospital as that term was used in the policy. The court, however, held that the policy definition of "hospital" did not speak of major surgery, and that to impose such a requirement would be going beyond the terms of the policy, saying:

> We must, therefore, in construing the term most favorably to the insured, construe it to mean that the facilities for any "operative" surgery continuously maintained as provided in the policy is a sufficient compliance therewith. To say that operative surgery means that an institution to be a hospital under the policy must have facilities for both minor and major surgery would be equivalent to saying that it must have facilities for all surgery. The policy does not require this. If the policy had even gone so far as to specify major surgery, we could not require that the hospital have facilities for all major surgery; neither can we require that it have facilities for all types of operative surgery. The policy did not require it and neither can we.

21.19 Physician

Health insurance policies also frequently include a definition of "physician," in order to clarify the nature of the liability the company is willing to assume. The objective is to assure that the treatment for which expenses were incurred by the insured was given by a qualified practitioner. This type of definition is being regulated by statute in some of the states, however, in order to assure that the term is not defined so narrowly as to exclude the payment of benefits for treatment administered by medical practitioners whose practice is general in some areas but not, perhaps, in others. An Illinois statute,[3] for instance, provides that when benefits are payable for the expenses of any medical treatment rendered by a person licensed under the Illinois Medical Practice Act, they must be payable on an equal basis for that service when administered by any person so licensed. The following illustrative definition is believed to meet the requirements of most such statutory provisions.

> Physician means a licensed practitioner of the healing arts performing services within the scope of his license as provided by the laws of the jurisdiction in which such practitioner resides.

---

[3] Section 982b, Illinois Revised Statutes, 1973.

D. EXCLUSIONS AND LIMITATIONS

Most individual health insurance policies list some conditions for which benefits will not be paid. Generally, these conditions are listed in a special section of the policy titled "Exclusions and Limitations," and the number differs from one type of health insurance policy to another. Disability income policies for instance, typically include very few limitations. Usually, benefits under such policies are not payable in the event the disability results from war or any act of war, attempt to commit suicide or self-inflicted injury, and any injuries or illnesses for which benefits are payable under Workmen's Compensation Laws.

Hospital expense policies, by contrast, may contain more exclusions. Thus, a hospital surgical policy might exclude losses incurred as a result of:

1. Injury or sickness for which the insured is entitled to benefits under Medicare, or any Workmen's Compensation, Occupational Diseases Law or any similar law.
2. Care or treatment received while confined in facilities provided by the Veterans' Administration, unless there is a legal obligation for the insured to pay for the treatment or services provided.
3. Sickness contracted or injury sustained as a result of war, declared or undeclared, or any act or hazard of war.
4. Injury or sickness of the insured while in the military, naval, air force, or other armed services of any country, and the pro rata unearned premium for any period of such service shall be returned to the insured upon request.
5. Pregnancy, childbirth, abortion, miscarriage or any complications thereof.
6. Any attempt at suicide, whether sane or insane, or any intentionally self-inflicted injury.
7. Dental treatment of the teeth or gums, unless required by injury to natural teeth.

State legislatures and insurance departments have reduced the number of allowable exclusions in the past several years. For instance, the insurer cannot exclude treatment for tuberculosis in some states, nor for alcoholism in some states. Treatment for mental illness is also frequently required to be covered, although benefits may be limited for such treatment.

21.20 Benefits under Government Programs

Many hospital and surgical coverages terminate when the insured becomes eligible for Medicare benefits; and policies frequently exclude benefits if the insured is in the armed forces. The purpose of such exclusions is to prevent the payment of benefits for expenses that are compensable under some other plan or program. A special problem arises, however, when benefits are excluded if the insured is treated in a veterans' hospital.

Veterans are entitled to receive treatment in veterans' hospitals for nonservice-connected injuries and disabilities without charge if they are not able to pay for such treatment. Generally, inability to pay is established by signing an affidavit to that effect. The legal question arises when the veteran signs such an affidavit and yet has hospital insurance that would reimburse him for some or all of the hospital expenses he might incur elsewhere.

In one such case,[4] the veteran assigned his health insurance policy to the Veterans Administration and signed the customary papers indicating his inability to pay for the treatment. The Veterans Administration attempted to recover from the insurer and, when the claim was denied, sued the insurer. The court held that the Veterans Administration could not recover, saying:

> . . . But standing out controllingly in the situation is the fact, emphasized above, that the insured claimed, qualified himself to receive, and accepted, the care furnished him, as a veteran's beneficence under § 706, and so was, under the statute, without any obligation to pay therefor, an obligation that would make the value of the Veterans Hospital "expenses actually incurred" by him as an insured.

In other words, the person who makes an assignment cannot assign greater rights than he himself has. In this instance, the insured would not have been able to recover the benefits, since he had incurred no expenses; and the court held that the Veterans Administration was in the same position as the insured.

Similar cases have created a sufficient number of legal questions in this area that state insurance departments have sometimes required variations of such exclusions as they are used in health insurance policies. One such variation requires the insurer to provide that treatment in such institutions is excluded "unless there is an obligation on the part of the insured to pay."

E. RENEWAL PROVISIONS

21.21 Cancellable Policies

Unlike life insurance policies, health insurance contracts often include some restrictions on renewability. Some health insurance policies include

---

[4] *United States* v. *St. Paul Mercury Indemnity Co.,* 238 F. (2d) 594 (C.A. 8, Neb., 1956).

the optional cancellation provision previously mentioned and can thus be canceled by the insurer at any time. All that is necessary is to give the required notice to the policyowner and refund any premium or part of a premium the policyowner has paid for coverage beyond the date the cancellation is effective. The number of such freely cancellable policies is diminishing, however; and the practice is definitely being discouraged by legislatures and insurance departments.

21.22 Optionally Renewable Policies

A second group of individual health insurance policies is made up of policies that cannot be canceled but which the insurer may refuse to renew at its own option. In such situations, the insurer must give the policyowner notice of its intention not to renew; and many of the states are limiting the insurer's right to refuse renewal. For instance, several of the states do not permit an insurer to refuse to renew a policy except on an anniversary of the policy date. Thus, if the policy is issued on March 1, 1974, the insurer cannot refuse to renew it until March 1, 1975, even though it may be renewed by the payment of several quarterly or monthly premiums in the meanwhile. This guarantees at least one full year's coverage if the policyowner wishes to pay the intervening premiums, if any, as they fall due.

State statutes generally require that the conditions of renewability be stated on the face page of the policy; and a number of the states are limiting to certain specified situations the circumstances under which insurers may refuse to renew such policies. Illustrative of this type of statute is the law in New York[5] which applies to any policy in which one third or more of the premium is allocable to hospital, surgical, or medical expense benefits. After such policies have been in force for two years from the issue date or the date of the latest reinstatement, the insurer is forbidden to refuse renewal except for one or more of the following:

1. Fraud in the application for the policy or any benefits under it.
2. Moral hazard.
3. Overinsurance or duplication of insurance benefits "according to standards on file with the superintendent of insurance."
4. Discontinuance of a class of policies.
5. Filing of false claims.
6. Other reasons that may be approved by the superintendent of insurance.

In no event may any insurer refuse, after the expiration of the specified two-year period, to renew any hospital or medical expense policy because

---

[5] Section 164 (6), New York Insurance Laws.

of a change in the physical or mental condition or the health of any person covered by the policy. Nor may any insurer require, after the end of the two-year period, as a condition of renewal, any rider, endorsement or other attachment that would limit the nature or extent of the benefits provided by the policy.

21.23 Noncancellable Policies and Guaranteed Renewable Policies

Some health insurance policies may be continued by the policyowner on essentially the same basis as policies of whole life insurance, merely by paying the renewal premiums when they become due. (The insurer can neither cancel nor refuse to renew them.) Health insurance policies of which this is true are generally divided into two groups: (1) policies that may be referred to as "noncancellable" or "noncancellable and guaranteed renewable" policies, and (2) those that may be termed "guaranteed renewable."

Noncancellable Policies. According to a definition adopted by the National Association of Insurance Commissioners (NAIC) in 1959,[6] the terms "noncancellable" or "noncancellable and guaranteed renewable" may be used only to refer to policies "which the insured has the right to continue in force by the timely payment of premiums set forth in the policy (1) until at least age 50, or (2) in the case of a policy issued after age 44, for at least five years from its date of issue, during which period the insurer has no right to make unilaterally any change in any provision of the policy while the policy is in force."

Note first that the policyowner has the right to continue a noncancellable policy if he pays premiums "set forth in the policy" and that even so, this right does not necessarily continue beyond the insured's age 50, or five years from the issue date if the insured is more than 44 when the policy is issued.

Guaranteed Renewable Policies. The NAIC definition specified that the term "guaranteed renewable" may be used only with respect to a policy which the insured has the right to continue in force by the timely payment of premiums (1) until at least age 50, or (2) in the case of a policy issued after age 44, for at least five years from its date of issue, during which period the insurer has no right to make unilaterally any change in any provision of the policy while the policy is in force, except that the insurer may make changes in premium rates by classes.

The basic difference between a guaranteed renewable policy and one that may correctly be referred to as noncancellable is that the insurer

---

[6] See *Proceedings* of the National Association of Insurance Commissioners, Vol. I, 1960, page 153.

reserves the right, under a guaranteed renewable contract, to increase premium rates if this is done by class of policies. Exactly what constitutes a class in this sense, however, presents a problem. The most obvious approach to the question is to consider that the policies issued in a given state and on the same policy form constitute a class. After a few years, however, policyholders will have moved in and out of different states. The experience developed under the policies of policyowners who remain in the state in question, therefore, may be inapplicable to those policies held by insureds who have moved to other parts of the country where medical expenses are different. For this and similar reasons, the right to increase premiums on a class of policies is not as simple in practice as the wording might suggest.

Face Page Requirement. Several states require that the renewability provision or provisions of an individual health insurance policy appear on the first or face page of the policy. The objective is understandable. The conditions of renewability are important, and the policyowner should not have to search the policy to ascertain them. The importance of complying with such a statutory requirement is illustrated in the case of *Caswell* v. *Reserve National Insurance Co.*[7]

The Caswell case involved a policy that was renewable only at the option of the insurer. The insured had been paid benefits for expenses resulting from a heart attack, after which the insurance company offered to renew the policy only on condition that a rider be attached to the policy excluding payment of benefits for heart and circulatory system diseases. The company maintained that since it had the right to refuse renewal outright, it had the right to insert a new exclusion in the policy and refuse renewal unless the condition was accepted. The policyowner tendered the renewal premium and insisted on renewal of the policy as it was originally written. The insurer refused and the policyowner sued, claiming benefits that would have been payable under the terms of the policy as originally written.

On behalf of the policyowner, it was contended that the policy was in violation of a Louisiana statute requiring renewability provisions to appear on the face page of the policy, as follows:

> (8) In any case where the policy is subject to cancellation or renewal at the option of the insurer, there shall be prominently printed on the first page of such policy a statement so informing the policyholder.

The insurer contended that the renewability provision appeared on the first page of the policy proper, and that the outside, or cover page should not be considered as being part of the policy. The court, however, noted

---

[7] 272 So. (2d) 37 (La. App., 1973).

that the cover page included a few items of policy information and held, therefore, that the renewability provision did not appear on the front page of the policy as required, saying:

> Therefore, we hold that as a matter of law the requirements of the statute were not complied with in that the page on which the caveat was inserted was not the first page of the policy as was required.

The court, therefore, held that the policyowner could not be required to accept a new limitation as a condition of renewal and that benefits were payable as contended.

F. PREEXISTING CONDITIONS

Among the several areas that have presented serious and continuing problems in connection with claim settlement under individual health insurance policies, the general area of preexisting conditions has been one of the most persistent and troublesome. Individual health insurance policies typically provide that the insurer will pay benefits for losses resulting from accidents that occur or sicknesses that "first manifest" themselves after the effective date of the coverage.

The basic objective of such language is to insure a true risk of loss. Thus, if the insured receives treatment after the effective date of his policy but for injuries suffered in an accident that predates the policy, his claim will be properly denied, just as the automobile insurer will not be liable for the cost of repairs to one's car resulting from an accident that happened before the policy was applied for. Nevertheless, the question of preexistence is not so easily resolved in many situations. Many illnesses have had their origins in conditions of which the insured had no knowledge but which, in a strict technical sense, existed prior to the effective date of the coverage. Attempting to draw too fine a line in such situations has resulted in some questionable claim practices and serious misunderstandings. Preexisting conditions, therefore, have been the occasion of numerous misunderstandings and some inequities; and a number of approaches have been taken to establish some guidelines that will help to reduce the problems.

The Uniform Individual Policy Provisions Law, as previously noted, includes a required policy provision which, after the expiration of three (sometimes two) years, precludes the denial of a claim on the basis that the disease or condition existed prior to the date of the policy unless it has been specifically excluded by name. Thus, if an applicant has had treatment for a back injury and states this on his application, the underwriter may decide to accept the application but issue the policy with an amendment rider excluding benefits for medical treatment or hospitalization resulting from disease or injury to the lower back. Under a policy with such an exclusion amendment, the claim examiner may properly deny a claim for benefits for such treatment throughout the period in which the policy remains in force.

The insurer does not ask extensive questions on the application for some types of health insurance policies, depending instead on a policy provision that specifically states that preexisting conditions will not be covered for a specified period. In such situations the applicant's medical history is neither requested nor revealed, and the policy provision is relied upon to protect the insurer from serious antiselection. Customarily, the term preexisting disease or condition is defined as a disease or condition for which the insured has been under medical treatment or has consulted a physician within a specified period, such as six months prior to the application date. Benefits are generally payable under such policies even for such preexisting conditions, after the policy has been in force for a stated period—usually 6 to 12 months.

Acceptable underwriting and claim settlement principles with respect to preexisting conditions were adopted by the National Association of Insurance Commissioners in 1966. First, these principles restate the rule previously noted—that an insurer may exclude by rider, from the coverage provided by the policy, any disease or condition that is revealed on the application and which the insurer does not consider acceptable according to its rules and practices of underwriting. If any adverse health condition is revealed in the application but is not so excluded, the company must be considered to be on the risk and must pay any claim submitted resulting from such condition. In other words, the company had notice of the health condition. It did not exclude it from coverage under the policy. Therefore, it is considered to have waived any defense that the condition preexisted the date of the policy.

If the condition was not revealed on the application and the company, if it had known the truth, would not have accepted the application or would not have issued a policy on the same basis, it has the right to deny any claim resulting from the unrevealed condition; and it may rescind the policy on a basis of material misrepresentation or fraud.

G. GROUP HEALTH INSURANCE POLICIES

21.24 Required Provisions

The National Association of Insurance Commissioners has not developed a model bill for group health insurance contracts and, in general, such contracts are not subject to the detailed regulatory specifications that apply to individual health insurance policies in most jurisdictions. However, many of the states have statutory definitions of eligible groups for group health insurance plans, and required policy provisions are specified in some cases.

Florida, as an example, specifies three provisions that must be included in group disability (health insurance) policies, as follows:

(1) A provision that, in the absence of fraud, all statements made by applicants or the policyholder or by an insured person shall be deemed representations and not warranties, and that no statement made for the purpose of effecting insurance shall avoid such insurance or reduce benefits unless contained in a written instrument signed by the policyholder or the insured person, a copy of which has been furnished to such policyholder or to such [insured] person or his beneficiary.

(2) A provision that the insurer will furnish to the policyholder for delivery to each employee or member of the insured group, a certificate setting forth the essential features of the insurance coverage of such employee or member and to whom benefits are payable. If dependents are included in the coverage, only one certificate need be issued for each family unit.

(3) A provision that to the group originally insured may be added from time to time eligible new employees or members or dependents, as the case may be, in accordance with the terms of the policy.[8]

A final paragraph concerns provisions relating to notice or proof of loss, the time for paying benefits, or the time within which suit may be brought under the policy, and forbids the use of any such provision in a group disability policy if it is less favorable to the individual insureds than would be permitted in an individual health insurance contract.

21.25 Coordination of Benefits

Overinsurance is, if anything, more difficult to ascertain and control in group health insurance coverages than under individual policies. The results of overinsurance are essentially the same, whether the result of individual or group benefits. There is a tendency to incur medical expense that might not otherwise be incurred and to prolong disability conditions beyond a reasonable recovery period if the insured is eligible for benefits that would more than compensate him for the economic loss actually suffered. The wide coverages provided under group plans make it especially easy for the same person to have several sources from which to receive benefits, since some of such plans are the automatic result of his employment. Often the same accident will entitle the injured person to benefits from a Workmen's Compensation insurer, his employer's group medical expense coverage, perhaps his spouse's insurance in another group, and one or more individual policies of various kinds.

Overinsurance in individual health insurance can be controlled not only by appropriate policy provisions but also, to a certain extent, through underwriting requirements. If issuance of the policy applied for would

---

[8] Florida Insurance Laws, Sec. 627.657.

result in the applicant's being overinsured, the insurer will disapprove the application entirely or offer a policy for a reduced amount. In group health insurance, however, it is not practical to underwrite the individual insureds. For this reason, group insurers have made frequent use of antiduplication provisions in their group health insurance contracts. In order to reduce the misunderstanding that results from the use of such provisions, a Joint Study Group of life and health insurance associations has developed a model group antiduplication provision.

This model provision can be used in any kind of group medical expense policy, whether basic, comprehensive, or major medical expense. The various coverages to be coordinated may be defined in different ways to include many or few different types of coverages, including individual and group, Blue Cross and Blue Shield, and benefits provided under governmental programs. Total benefits are established as "allowable expenses," a term that is defined as "any necessary, reasonable, and customary item of expense at least a portion of which is covered under at least one of the plans covering the person for whom claim is made."

When a claim is submitted, the order in which the various insurers must pay is established, and the insurer primarily liable pays up to the limits of its contract. The carrier secondarily liable then pays the difference between the payments made by Insurer A and the insured's total allowable expenses. This arrangement is considered to be more easily understood than a prorata approach such as that used in the "insurance with other insurers" provisions for individual policies.

SUMMARY

Individual Health Insurance Contracts

Although the largest amount of health insurance today is written under group insurance contracts, the most extensive and detailed statutory requirements relate to individual health insurance contracts and are set forth in the Uniform Individual Policy Provisions Law. This law prescribes two types of policy provisions: required and optional. The insurer has no choice but to include the required policy provisions in its policies. Optional provisions may be used or not used, but if the subject matter of any of them is used, the provision in question must be included. It is not necessary to use the exact words in the exact order of either required or optional provisions as they appear in the law, and the insurer may use more favorable wording if it wishes.

Accident and sickness insurance is defined in this law as "insurance against loss resulting from sickness or from bodily injury or death by accident or both." The text of the policy must be presented in a type that meets minimum specifications; and each policy form, rider, and endorsement must be identified by a form number appearing in the lower left-hand corner of the first page.

An individual health insurance policy may insure one person, or more than one if the policy is applied for by an adult and the additional covered persons are members of the adult's family. Generally, children of the insured are eligible for coverage until they attain age 19 or, if they remain in school, until they attain age 23. Legislation has been enacted in several of the states requiring insurers to retain any child as an insured under the parent's individual health insurance policy beyond the usual terminating age if the child is incapable of self-support because of mental or physical impairment.

The required provisions include the following: an entire contract provision, a grace period provision, a provision permitting the policy to be reinstated, a provision relating to change of beneficiary, and a provision entitled "time limit on certain defenses." Optional policy provisions relate to the insured's change of occupation, other insurance he might have, and the relation of earnings to insurance. There are also optional provisions concerning exclusions in the event the insured is injured as the result of committing or attempting to commit a felony.

Entire Contract Provision.   The entire contract provision is similar to the provision on the same subject required to be included in life insurance contracts. It defines the documents that will be considered to comprise the contract and must provide that no change in the policy shall be valid until approved by an executive officer of the insurer and endorsed upon or attached to the policy.

Grace Period.   The grace period provision requires a grace period of 31 days unless the premium is payable weekly or monthly, in which case the grace period may be 7 or 10 days, respectively. If the policy is cancellable or renewable at the option of the insurer, special language concerning notice must be included in the grace period provision.

Reinstatement.   The reinstatement provision must provide that if a reinstatement application is not required, acceptance of the premium for a lapsed policy at a later date will automatically reinstate the policy. The provision specifies that a reinstated policy will cover only accidents that occur after the effective date of reinstatement and sickness that begins more than 10 days after the reinstatement.

Change of Beneficiary.   If the health insurance policy provides a death benefit, a change of beneficiary provision is also required.

Time Limit on Certain Defenses.   The time limit on certain defenses provision is similar to the incontestable clause required in individual life insurance contracts. The basic purpose of the provision is to limit the period of time in which an insurer will be permitted to defend the denial of a claim on the basis of material misrepresentation in the application.

Claim Provisions. An individual health insurance policy must contain a provision that the insurer shall be given notice of a claim within 20 days after the occurrence or commencement of any loss covered by the policy or as soon thereafter as is reasonably possible. The policy must also provide that the insurer will furnish claim forms within 15 days of the date it receives notice of a claim. Another provision must state that proof of loss must be given to the insurer in writing; and the policy must specify that claims will be paid immediately upon receipt of proof of loss unless periodic payments are involved. Periodic payments cannot be made less frequently than monthly.

Any sum payable as a death benefit must be paid in accordance with the beneficiary designation, if any; otherwise payment will be made to the estate of the insured. The policy must include a provision that the company at its own expense shall have the right to have the insured examined and to make an autopsy in case of death except where it is forbidden by law. The policy must provide also that no action at law or in equity may be brought against the insurer until the expiration of 60 days after written proof of loss has been submitted.

Optional Provisions. The optional provisions include a payment of claims provision. The policy may provide that amounts up to $1,000 may be paid to any relative by blood or connection by marriage of the insured or beneficiary who is, in the opinion of the insurer, equitably entitled to the money. Usually this means someone who has incurred final expenses on behalf of the insured or beneficiary.

The insurer may, if it wishes, include a provision relating to adjustments in benefits or premiums in the event the insured changes to a more or less hazardous occupation. Under this optional provision, if the insured has an accident or becomes ill while engaged in an occupation that is more hazardous than the occupation in which he was engaged at the time he applied for the policy, the benefit payable may be adjusted to the amount which the premium paid would have purchased at the more hazardous occupation. If the insured's occupation at the time of loss is less hazardous than the one in which he was engaged at the time of application, the company will reduce the premium to be paid in the future and refund any past overpayments to the policyowner.

An individual health insurance policy may include a provision exempting the insurer from liability if the loss is caused by the insured's commission of a felony or attempt to commit a felony.

A misstatement of age provision may be included in an individual policy of health insurance. This provision is very much the same as that included in the life insurance policy. It simply provides that if the insured's age has been misstated, all amounts payable under the policy shall be such as the premiums paid would have purchased at his or her correct age.

Overinsurance is recognized as a significant factor in the overutilization of health insurance, and insurers wish to discourage it whenever possible. For this reason, there are two optional provisions that may be included in individual health insurance policies that will permit the insurer to adjust the benefits payable under the policy if the insured has other insurance, either with the same insurer or another insurance company providing the same or similar benefits. The relation of earnings to insurance provision is another optional provision that may be used to help counteract the tendency of insureds to acquire more insurance than is needed to offset the losses they may experience.

Cancellation. If the insurer wishes to reserve the right to cancel the policy at any time, the policy must include a cancellation provision. Notice must be given before the policy may be canceled, and any unearned premium must be refunded. Cancellation must be without prejudice to any claim which originated prior to the effective date of cancellation.

Unpaid Premium. The insurer may include a provision that permits it to deduct any unpaid premium from a settlement.

The Benefit Provisions

Classified according to the kinds of benefits provided, health insurance contracts may be divided into the following: income disability coverages, medical expense coverages, and accident and dread disease coverages.

Disability income coverages are designed to provide an income in the event the insured is totally disabled as the result of accident or sickness. Total disability is generally defined either as inability to work at the insured's own or at any occupation, or a combination of those two definitions.

Hospital and surgical coverages are intended to help reimburse the insured for the expenses of hospital care and surgery. Medical expense coverages may be classified as: (1) basic medical expense coverage, which provides benefits beginning with the first day of hospital confinement and the first dollar of medical expense; (2) major medical coverages, which are designed to meet the larger medical expenses that result from longer hospital stays and expensive surgical procedures; and (3) comprehensive medical expense coverages, which are designed with a very low deductible and yet cover major medical expenses as well.

Definitions of Terms

Many significant terms are defined in health insurance policies in order to clarify the coverages intended. Thus injury may be defined as "accidental bodily injury sustained by the insured while the policy is in force."

Sickness may be defined as "any sickness or disease first manifesting itself while this policy is in force."

The word "hospital" is typically defined as an institution which is engaged primarily in providing medical care and treatment to sick and injured persons on an in-patient basis, and usually it is required to maintain 24-hour a day nursing service and to provide facilities for major surgery. Often, the definition specifically states that the institution shall not be a place for the aged, a place for drug addicts, or a nursing home.

The word "physician" is also frequently defined in health insurance policies. Such definitions may be subject to regulation by special statutes in some states. Usually, the purpose of the statutes is to prevent narrow definitions that do not include some medical practitioners whose practice is general in the state in question.

Exclusions and Limitations

Disability income policies do not generally include many conditions under which benefits will not be payable. Hospital expense policies may have more exclusions, such as (1) injury or sickness for which the insured is entitled to benefits under Medicare or Workmen's Compensation laws; (2) sickness contracted or injury sustained as the result of war, or while in the military, naval, or other armed services of any country; and (3) attempt at suicide. The exclusion of benefits if the insured receives treatment in a veterans' hospital has presented a special problem, since the insured may be entitled to treatment without charge in such hospitals. Exclusions are sometimes modified, therefore, to eliminate the payment of benefits in the event of treatment in such hospitals unless a charge is made for the treatment received.

Renewal Provisions

Some individual health insurance policies include a cancellation provision and thus may be canceled by the insurer at any time, if the required notice is given and the unearned premium is refunded. Other health insurance policies are renewable only at the option of the insurer, although some states forbid an insurer to refuse renewal except on an anniversary of the issue date of the policy.

A policy which the insured has the right to continue by the timely payment of premiums as they become due and which the insurer cannot modify unilaterally may be referred to as a "noncancellable" or "noncancellable and guaranteed renewable" policy.

If the insured has the right to continue the policy by the timely payment of renewal premiums as they fall due and the insurer cannot make unilateral changes except to raise premiums by class, the policy may be referred to as "guaranteed renewable."

A number of the states require that the renewal provision of the policy be printed on the first, or face, page of a health insurance policy.

Preexisting Conditions

A preexisting condition is a condition that had its inception prior to the effective date of the policy. The second paragraph of the "time limit on certain defenses" provision precludes the insurer, after three years from the effective date of the coverage, from denying a claim on the basis that the disease or condition was preexisting, unless the disease or condition was specifically excluded from the coverage of the policy.

In 1966, the NAIC adopted a set of underwriting and claim standards relating to preexisting conditions. Briefly, these standards specify that if a disease or condition was revealed in the application for a health insurance policy, and if the underwriter excluded it from coverage, a claim resulting from such disease or condition can be denied. If the condition was not so excluded, the insurer will be held to have waived any defense against a claim growing out of the preexisting condition. If the disease or condition was not revealed in the application, it will be treated on the same basis as any other misrepresentation; and if material or fraudulent it will justify the rescission of the contract.

Group Health Insurance Policies

Required Provisions. The NAIC has not adopted a model bill for group health insurance contracts. However, many of the states have statutes defining eligible groups for health insurance plans and some have statutes listing required provisions.

Coordination of Benefits. Because individual underwriting is not customary in group health insurance, overinsurance of some individuals is especially likely to occur. For this reason, various approaches have been made to prevent or reduce the duplication of payments that sometimes occurs. A model coordination of benefits provision has been adopted by the NAIC which, when used, makes it possible to establish the order in which the various insurers will be liable when coverage is provided under several policies for the same medical expenses.

ILLUSTRATIVE CASE

The insurance company in this case brought an action for a declaratory judgment declaring that it had not insured the applicants for disability income and accident policies. One of the applicants was killed and the other injured two days after the dates of the applications. The circuit court decided in favor of the insurer, and the claimants appealed. The reviewing court referred first to the case of *Simpson* v. *Prudential Insurance Company*[9] and another case that followed the *Simpson* decision, stating that those decisions were controlling. The opinion, in the words of the court, continued as follows.

CANNON v. SOUTHLAND LIFE INSURANCE COMPANY[10]

In *Simpson* the claimant was a wife who was the beneficiary under an insurance policy on the life of her husband, which she claimed the insurance company had bindingly contracted to issue. She sued after her husband was killed in a motor vehicle accident while his application for the insurance coverage was pending.

Here the claimants are a mother, Rosa Culp, the named beneficiary under a disability income, accident and sickness policy on her sixteen-year old son, William Bromley, which she claimed the insurance company had bindingly contracted to issue, and Tony Leroy Cannon, a sixteen-year old youth who had contemporaneously applied for similar insurance coverage. Bromley was killed and Cannon injured in a motor vehicle accident while their applications for the insurance coverage were pending. In *Simpson* and here a first premium was paid to the agent. We said in the third sentence of *Simpson:* "the principal question presented is the construction of the husband's application for insurance and of a 'conditional receipt' issued by the insurance company upon payment of the first annual premium." The same decisive question is presented in the present case, and, in a declaratory judgment action brought by Southland, a Texas insurer licensed in Maryland, Judge Travers declared summarily that Southland had not insured either Bromley or Cannon by accepting their applications and premiums and issuing the conditional receipts since each was too young to be insured for the coverage applied for under Southland's honest objective age standards of insurability. We think his decision correctly reflected the controlling Maryland law set forth in *Simpson* and *Medairy*.

The affidavits in the present case disclose that William Culp desired to increase the insurance coverage on three youthful employees of his, one Mc-Dorman, Cannon, and his stepson Bromley, each being sixteen years old. On May 23, 1969 J. Paul Briddell went to Culp's home and took the applications of the three youths for disability income policies with a $5,000 accidental death rider. Part of the application process was for the agent to sign, detach from the application form and deliver to each applicant a conditional receipt acknowledging payment by Mr. Culp's check dated May 26, 1969 of the first quarterly premium. The claimants say Briddell told them the insurance would be effective immediately; Briddell says he told them the insurance would be in force from the date of the check (three days later). Judge Travers held that "in [my] view of the case, this difference in testimony is immaterial." We agree.

[9] 227 Md. 393, 177 A. (2d) 417 (1962).
[10] 283 A. (2d) 404 (C.A. Md., 1971).

Southland had on file with the Insurance Commissioner of Maryland a rate book which reflected Southland's settled course of action to insure under disability insurance policies only individuals between the ages of 25 and 55 years. Some months after the date of the rate book Southland sent to all underwriters a memorandum that read:

> Disability Income Rates Below Age 25:
>
> For several weeks now we have been uncertain how to handle applications on persons under age 25. I suggest that for the future we consider anyone from age 20 through 25 at the same premium rate charged for a person age 25. From an underwriting standpoint, we will need to be very selective in issuing contracts on persons in this age group, but there are some applicants where the insurance is justified and can be issued.

Apparently Briddell and the regional manager of Southland, one Wheelbarger, either did not remember, or chose optimistically to ignore the regulation of Southland that the general minimum age for disability insureds was twenty-five, or in selected instances, twenty. Briddell quoted the sixteen-year old applicants the premium rates set out in the rate book for twenty-five year olds.

On May 25, two days after the boys had signed the applications and received the conditional receipts, there occurred the accident in which Bromley was killed and Cannon injured.

Briddell, aware of the accident, delivered the applications to his district manager, Wheelbarger, who forwarded the McDorman and Cannon applications to Southland's home office with no notations as to the accident. They were routinely declined by the underwriting department, which had no knowledge of the accident, in the regular course of business for the stated reason that the applicants were under the minimum age for this type of insurance. The Bromley application with proof of loss forms attached was sent to Dallas later, and rejected for the same stated reason as the other two.

Wheelbarger then, on Southland's order, tendered the premium paid to Cannon and Rosa Culp, who rejected the tender and demanded insurance proceeds instead. Southland then instituted the suit which is now before us.

Appellants argue that (1) Briddell knew the applicants were but sixteen years old when he accepted their applications and his knowledge is Southland's knowledge, and Southland is estopped to use age as a reason for declining to insure; (2) since Southland had insured certain applicants who were younger than twenty-five, it had waived its standard of not insuring persons under twenty-five; and (3) Southland's age standard of insurability was not an objective standard within the rule of *Simpson* and *Medairy*.

We think that these contentions are foreclosed by holdings of *Simpson* and *Medairy* and the instant facts.

❄   ❄   ❄   ❄   ❄

Much of the argument the appellants make here was made in *Simpson*. The Court said there (pp. 398–399 of 227 Md., p. 421 of 177 A. 2d):

We agree with the learned trial judge that the agent lacked authority to bind the Company by the statement as to immediate coverage attributed to him by the plaintiff. The absence of such power was clearly set forth not only in the application, but in the receipt itself, upon which the plaintiff's claim must stand or fall.

The Court then discussed at some length the various views as to conditional receipts that have been taken by the authorities and said (p. 406, 177 A. 2d p. 425):

We think that the clause [in the conditional receipt] means that the applicant must meet an objective standard of insurability, and that this standard is the company's own standard for the plan, the amount and the benefits applied for, and at the rate applied for. Honest satisfaction is the standard usually applied under contracts calling for the satisfaction of a party, in the absence of some clear indication to the contrary. . . .

The burden is, of course, on the plaintiff to show that the proposed insured met the objective test of insurability. The evidence does not make it clear whether he did or did not do so. . . . Evidence of insurability of the applicant according to the general standards of the industry would, we think, be sufficient to establish a *prima facie* case for the plaintiff. This the defendant might rebut by proof of its own objective standard (if different), or by evidence to show that the applicant did not meet this standard (whether the same as the general standard or different from it), or by evidence to support both of these contentions.

In the present case by virtue of the terms of the application and of the conditional receipt and the payment and acceptance of the premium amount, a contract in plain, simple and understandable terms was created, not of immediate insurance but of back-dated coverage of the type applied for if the applicant met Southland's good faith standards of insurability for that type of coverage. The contract of insurance would come into being only if the application was accepted. *Simpson* at p. 403 of 227 Md., 177 A. 2d 417. Southland promised to insure only if the applicant was an "acceptable risk" on the date of application "according to the underwriting rules of the Company on the plan, for the amount and at the premium rate applied for." The applicants here could not meet the company's requirements of insurability because they were too young. Age is certainly as objective a standard as a condition of health. There is nothing to the argument that because Southland had insured and would insure selected risks as young as twenty that it had abandoned or waived its age requirements. The applicants were all younger than twenty and would not have qualified even if Southland had lowered the general minimum of twenty-five to twenty before they made application. Appellants failed to meet the burden of proof which rested upon them to show that the applicants met Southland's honest objective standard of insurability and Southland proved that they did not. The judgment below properly was in favor of Southland.

Judgments affirmed, with costs.

QUESTIONS FOR REVIEW

1. List five provisions required by the Uniform Individual Accident and Sickness Policy Provisions Law to be included in an individual health insurance contract.

2. Briefly summarize the "entire contract" policy provision.

3. List two ways in which the grace period provision for health insurance policies may differ from the grace period provision in individual life insurance contracts.

4. If an individual health insurance policy is reinstated effective as of September 5 and the insured becomes ill on September 10, will benefits be payable for loss incurred as the result of such illness? Why or why not?

5. What is the purpose of the "time limit on certain defenses" provision?

6. List four optional provisions that may be, but are not required to be, included in an individual health insurance contract.

7. For what basic reason do insurers endeavor to discourage overinsurance?

8. List and briefly summarize two policy provisions that may be included in an individual health insurance policy for the purpose of reducing the benefits payable if the insured has two or more policies providing the same type of benefits.

9. Define and differentiate between a cancellable health insurance policy and one that is optionally renewable. What is the essential difference between a "noncancellable" health insurance policy and a policy that is "guaranteed renewable"?

10. What is a preexisting condition? According to the underwriting standards adopted by the NAIC in 1966, under what circumstances will preexisting conditions be covered?

Appendixes

A. Regular Life Application Form

LIFE APPLICATION—Page One ⟶ **Ajax Life Insurance Company**

1. (a) Proposed Insured *(Print name in full)*
First Name _____ Middle Name _____
Last Name _____ Social Security Number _____
— —

(b) Mail Address _____
Zip Code _____

(c) ☐ Male ☐ Female   (d) Birthdate Mo. Day Year   (e) Age Last Birthday   (f) State or Province of Birth

(g) ☐ Married ☐ Single   (h) Occupation of Proposed Insured *(Give exact duties)*

(i) Employer's name and address

2. (a) Applicant's Name *If not Proposed Insured (Print name in full)*
First Name _____ Middle Name _____
Last Name _____ Social Security or Tax Acct. Number _____

(b) Mail Address: If not same as for proposed insured, give applicant's address in explanation section.

(c) If Proposed Insured under age 16, Print name of Successor Owner.

(d) If Proposed Insured is under age 16, is ownership to pass automatically to Proposed Insured at age 21? ☐ Yes ☐ No

3. (a) Basic Amount and Plan applied for:
$ _____

(b) **Additional Benefits** applied for: *(Specify by name, amount or number of units, and years of benefit desired, where necessary.)*

	Amount				Mo. Income Amt.
☐AD		*☐ WPP		☐ 2 YR ID	
☐OAI	Amount	*☐ AI RTR	Amount	☐ LT ID	Mo. Income Amt.
☐10 YR RT	Amount	*☐ CTR	Units	☐ INCR TERM	Initial Amount
☐MTG	Yrs. Amount	*☐ AI MTG	Yrs. Amount	☐ T65	Amount
☐FI	Yrs. Units	*☐ AI FI	Yrs. Units	☐	
☐FI to 65	Units	*☐ AI FI to 65	Units	☐	

*Complete Appropriate Section on Page 2

4. (a) How shall dividends be used?
☐ Paid-Up Additions
☐ Accumulate
☐ Reduce Premium
☐ Cash Payment
☐ _____

(c) How much personal and business Life Insurance do you now have? $ _____ *(If $25,000 or more, give complete details)*

(d) How much accidental death insurance do you now have, excluding Group? $ _____

(b) If provided, is Automatic Premium Loan provision elected? ☐ Yes ☐ No

5. Beneficiary Designation Do Not Use for Family Life Plan. If Change of Plan, this designation revokes and changes any earlier designation. *(Give Full Name, Age, and Relationship)*
Primary — FULL NAME _____ AGE — RELATIONSHIP _____
☐ Interest Option with Full Right of Withdrawal or ☐ One Sum
Successor — FULL NAME _____ AGE — RELATIONSHIP _____
☐ Interest Option with Full Right of Withdrawal or ☐ One Sum
Final — FULL NAME _____ AGE — RELATIONSHIP _____

One Sum Settlement Only
Settlement to other than natural person to be **One Sum**. Any **Family Income Benefit** to be paid in accordance with policy provisions.
☐ Check here if another method of settlement is desired and complete question 40 on Page 2.

---

6. (a) Do you have any Individual or Group income benefits for accident or sickness? *(If so, and ID is applied for, complete question 33 on Page 2)* ☐ Yes ☐ No

(b) Are negotiations for any other life insurance on your life now pending? *(If so, state companies and amounts)* ☐ ☐

(c) Is this policy a replacement or change of any existing policy or policies? *(If so, explain)* ☐ ☐

*(d) Has insurance on your life ever been declined, postponed, or modified in amount, plan, or rate? *(If so, explain)* ☐ ☐

*If Yes, do not give Binding Receipt and do not collect any money.

7. (a) Are you now on active duty in a branch of military service? *(If so, complete question 39, Page 2)* ☐ Yes ☐ No

(b) If discharged from military service in past 6 months, what was your separation date? _____

(c) Were you ever exempted, rejected or discharged by the armed forces for physical or mental reasons? *(If so, explain)* ☐ Yes ☐ No

(d) Have you flown during the past 5 years in any kind of aircraft, as a pilot, crew member or student pilot, or is such flight contemplated? *(If so, complete Aviation Section on Page 2)* ☐ ☐

*(e) Do you or did you ever engage in mountain climbing, vehicle racing, SCUBA, skin or sky diving, or other similar avocation? *(If so, explain)* ☐ ☐

*If Yes, do not give Binding Receipt and do not collect any money.

8. Have you ever received treatment or joined an organization for alcoholism or drug habit? ☐ Yes ☐ No

9. To the best of your knowledge and belief are you now free from disease, in sound health, and without deformity or loss of limb, or impairment of sight, hearing, and speech? *(If not, explain)* ☐ Yes ☐ No

10. To the best of your knowledge and belief do you have, or have you ever had, or been treated for: *(Circle applicable items and give details)* ☐ Yes ☐ No

(a) Dizziness, fainting, convulsions, frequent headache; paralysis or stroke; mental or nervous disorder? ☐ ☐

(b) Shortness of breath, asthma, emphysema, tuberculosis, or other disorder of the respiratory system? ☐ ☐

*(c) Chest pain, palpitation, high blood pressure, rheumatic fever, heart murmur, heart attack or other disorder of the heart or blood vessels? ☐ ☐

*(d) Tumor, cancer or disorder of lymph glands? ☐ ☐

(e) Recurrent indigestion, jaundice, any type of ulcer, colitis, or other disorder of the stomach, intestines, liver or gall bladder? ☐ ☐

(f) Sugar, albumin, blood or pus in urine; stone or other disorder of kidney, bladder, or reproductive organs? ☐ ☐

(g) Sugar diabetes; arthritis, gout, or disorder of skin? ☐ ☐

(h) Allergies; anemia or other disorder of the blood? ☐ ☐

(i) Any other mental or physical disorder not listed above? ☐ ☐

*If Yes, do not give Binding Receipt and do not collect any money.

11. Give your exact height and weight. feet | inches | pounds

12. Give names and addresses of all doctors consulted by or for you, for any reason, including hospitalizations, during the past five years, with full details of treatment and results. *(If none, so state)*

Names and Addresses of Doctors and Hospitals	Disease or Disorder	Date, Treatment and Result

13. **Explanations:** *Show question number as reference. If space is insufficient, use reverse side or additional sheets, which shall be a part of this application.*

661

The Proposed Insured, and the Applicant if other than the Proposed Insured, each represents that all statements and answers contained herein and in any Medical History made a part hereof, are complete, true and correctly recorded and it is agreed that the company shall not be presumed to have knowledge of any information not so recorded.

It is agreed that the acceptance of the policy shall constitute an approval of the provisions therein and a ratification of the beneficiary designation and of any corrections therein except that no change shall be made by the company as to amount, classification, plan of insurance or benefits unless agreed to in writing by the policy Owner. It is also agreed that only the president, a vice-president, the secretary or an assistant secretary of the company has the authority to make or modify contracts or to waive any of the company's rights or requirements, and in writing only; and that neither the soliciting agent nor the medical examiner is authorized to pass upon insurability.

If a Conditional Receipt has been executed on the date application is signed, then the terms of such Conditional Receipt shall be effective. Otherwise there shall be no liability under the policy until it is delivered and the first premium thereon is paid while the Proposed Insured and any other person proposed for insurance are living, and then only if the statements and answers contained in all parts of this application are, without material change, true and complete as of the time of payment of such premium, in which case such policy shall be deemed to have taken effect on the Policy Date thereof.

It is further agreed that all provisions of law are hereby waived which would forbid the disclosure to the State Farm Life Insurance Company by any physician, hospital, clinic, insurance company or other person or organization of records or knowledge that has or may be acquired concerning the health, medical history, hospitalization, diagnosis or treatment of the Proposed Insured and any other person proposed for insurance.

Any life insurance policy issued on this application shall be owned by the Proposed Insured, or the Applicant if other than the Proposed Insured.

Dated on _____

Signature of
Proposed Insured _____
(Not required if Proposed Insured a Juvenile)

at _____

Signature of Agent as
Witness to all
Signatures hereon _____

Signature of
Applicant _____
(Not required unless Applicant is other than Proposed Insured)

2-31-1970.1

(If a firm or corporation is to be the Owner, give its name and signature of authorized officer other than Proposed Insured.)

Agent's Statement		
1. Are you related to the Proposed Insured? *(If so, how?)* Yes ☐ No ☐	7. What is to be the regular mode of premium payment?	13. Is this policy a replacement of any existing policy or policies? *(If so, explain fully)* Yes ☐ No ☐
	8. Amount of premium stated to the Proposed Insured?	14. Is this a business insurance case? Yes ☐ No ☐
2. How long have you known the Proposed Insured?	9. Who is to pay premiums? *(Full name and relationship, if other than Proposed Insured)*	15. Exact Location of residence Street address ....
3. What has been Proposed Insured's annual *earned* income, each of past three years? 19...... $............ ; 19...... $.............. ; 19...... $..............	10. Is a pro rata premium to arrange due date desired? *(If so, in what month is first regular premium to be due?)* Yes ☐ No ☐	City .... State.......... Co.............. (If a rural area)..........miles in.........direction from..................on...................road How long at this residence?................. What was exact previous residence address? ....
4. Is the Proposed Insured in the Medical Class? *(If so, when is the medical examination to be made, and by whom?)* Yes ☐ No ☐	11. Is Preliminary Term Insurance desired? *(If so, what is to be the Policy Date?)* Yes ☐ No ☐	
5. What settlement was made for the initial premium?	12. Is Proposed Insured now a Ajax Life policy holder? Yes ☐ No ☐	
6. Was a Binding Receipt issued? Yes ☐ No ☐		

LIFE APPLICATION—Page 2 | **Ajax Life Insurance Company** |

Application For Family Plans and Family Insurance Benefits
(Complete questions as applicable for family members to be insured)

14. (a) **Spouse of Proposed Insured** *(Print name in full)*

First Name _____ Middle Name _____

Last Name _____ Social Security Number _____ — —

(b) Birthdate | (c) Age Last Birthday | (d) State or Province of Birth | (e) Exact Height feet / inches

(f) Exact Weight pounds

(g) Occupation of Spouse *(Give exact duties)*

(h) Employer's name and address

15. To the best of your knowledge and belief is spouse now free from disease, in sound health, and without deformity or loss of limb, or impairment of sight, hearing, and speech? *(If not, explain)*   Yes ☐ No ☐
16. Has spouse ever had heart disease, rheumatic fever, high blood pressure, asthma, epilepsy, tumor, diabetes, or tuberculosis? *(If so, explain)* ☐ ☐
17. Has spouse been admitted to a hospital or similar institution within the past five years? *(If so, explain)* ☐ ☐
18. Has spouse consulted a physician for any reason within the past five years? *(If so, explain)* ☐ ☐
19. Has spouse ever received treatment or joined an organization for alcoholism or drug habit? *(If so, explain)* ☐ ☐
20. (a) Children under 18 (birthday basis) proposed for coverage:

Name (First Name, Middle Initial)	Relationship to Proposed Insured	Birthdate Mo.	Day	Year	Amount Now Insured For
					$
					$
					$
					$

(b) Does the last name of any child of the Proposed Insured differ from the last name of the Proposed Insured? *(If so, explain)*   Yes ☐ No ☐

21. To the best of your knowledge and belief are all children now free from disease, in sound health, and without deformity or loss of limb, or impairment of sight, hearing, and speech? *(If not, explain)* ☐ ☐
22. Has any child ever had a congenital defect? *(If so, explain)* ☐ ☐
23. Has any child been admitted to a hospital within the past five years? *(If so, explain)* ☐ ☐
24. Has a physician been consulted for any child within the past five years? *(If so, explain)* ☐ ☐
25. Has any child ever had rheumatic fever, heart murmur, or asthma? *(If so, explain)* ☐ ☐

Application for WPP Benefit
(Complete questions 26 through 32 on juvenile cases when WPP benefit is applied for on life of applicant)

26. (a) **Applicant's Name** *(Print name in full)*

First Name _____ Middle Name _____

Last Name _____ Social Security Number _____ — —

(b) Birthdate Mo. / Day / Year | (c) Age Last Birthday | (d) State or Province of Birth | (e) Exact Height feet / inches

(f) Exact Weight pounds

(g) Occupation of Applicant *(Give exact duties)*

(h) Employer's name and address

27. To the best of your knowledge and belief is applicant now free from disease, in sound health, and without deformity or loss of limb, or impairment of sight, hearing, and speech? *(If not, explain)*   Yes ☐ No ☐
28. Has insurance on life of applicant ever been declined, postponed, or modified in amount, plan or rate? *(If so, explain)* ☐ ☐
29. Has applicant ever had heart disease, rheumatic fever, high blood pressure, asthma, epilepsy, tumor, diabetes, or tuberculosis? *(If so, explain)* ☐ ☐
30. Has applicant consulted a physician for any reason within the past five years? *(If so, explain)* ☐ ☐
31. Has applicant ever received treatment or joined an organization for alcoholism or drug habit? *(If so, explain)* ☐ ☐
32. Has applicant flown during the past 5 years in any kind of aircraft, as a pilot, crew member or student pilot, or is such flight contemplated? *(If so, complete Aviation Section)* ☐ ☐

33. (a) Individual or Group income benefits for accident or sickness now in force

Company	Year Issued	Principal Sum	Income Benefits per Month Accident	Sickness

(b) **Maximum Period for which Benefits Payable**

(c) Describe any Restrictions by Waivers

Aviation Section

34. Do you now hold or have you ever held a pilot's certificate for aircraft?   Yes ☐ No ☐
Do you hope to qualify for a higher classification? ☐ ☐
35. Have you ever been disqualified for any type of certificate for medical reasons, or been grounded or reprimanded for violation of regulations? *(If so, explain)* ☐ ☐
36. Are you required to or do you fly planes with untried or experimental features or designs? *(If so, explain)* ☐ ☐
37. How many solo hours have you flown?

Pilot—Crew Member—Student Flying

38. (a) Give particulars of all flights you have taken, giving data for each year separately and stating *"none"* where none: *(Count each take-off as a separate flight)*

	History of Past Flights					
	Last 12 Months		1—2 Years Ago		Prior to 2 Years Ago	
	Flights	Hours	Flights	Hours	Flights	Hours
As a pilot or co-pilot, military aviation						
As a pilot or co-pilot, civilian aviation						
As a crew member, military aviation						
As a crew member, civilian aviation						
As a student						

(b) What type of plane(s)?

39. (a) If on active duty, complete the following
Branch of Service _____ Rank or Pay Grade _____
Where Assigned _____
*(b) If not now, do you expect to be assigned to a hazardous area overseas? *(If so, where and when)*   Yes ☐ No ☐
*If Yes, do not give Binding Receipt and do not collect any money.

40. If settlement specifications are desired which are contrary to those indicated in question 5 on Page 1, specify below:
(For Primary)

(For Successor)

If Primary survives the Insured, the method for Successor shall be One Sum, except that any unpaid instalments under Option 2 or 4 or any unpaid certain instalments under Option 3 may be continued to Successor if requested by check mark here: ☐

Explanations: *(If space below is insufficient, use additional sheets, which shall be a part of this application)*

Show question number as reference and name of person to whom it applies

DO NOT WRITE IN THIS SPACE

B. Specimen Policy Form

AJAX LIFE
Insurance Company

INSURED

AGE

POLICY NUMBER

AMOUNT OF
BASIC
PLAN

POLICY DATE

TOTAL
INITIAL
AMOUNT

HOME OFFICE: _____ , _____

Guide to policy provisions

The Application and Additional Benefits Provisions, if any, are found following page 16.

The Owner and the Beneficiary of this policy are as designated in the application unless changed as provided in the policy.

Ajax Life Insurance Company agrees to pay the insurance proceeds under this policy to the Beneficiary upon receipt of due proof of the Insured's death, in accordance with the provisions on the following pages.

The insurance provided by this policy, beginning on the Policy Date, is granted in consideration of the application and of the payment of the specified premiums during the lifetime of the Insured. The first premium is due on the Policy Date.

Ajax Life Insurance Company has caused this policy to be executed on the Issue Date.

SPECIMEN

John C. Smith
Secretary

Roger M. Roe
President

Registrar

PLAN DESCRIPTION
Basic Plan provides a Whole Life Benefit with Waiver of Premium for Disability. Schedules of Benefits and Premiums on page 3. Amounts of Insurance on page 5. Insurance payable on death. Annual Dividends. Premiums payable for life unless policy previously paid up or endowed by dividends.

FORM 7510   PAGE ONE   740101

Definitions of Terms

Additional Benefit. Any benefit, other than the Basic Plan and Waiver of Premium Disability, made a part of this policy and included in the Schedule of Benefits.

Amount of Basic Plan. The amount of insurance on the life of the Insured provided by the Basic Plan and exclusive of any insurance provided by any Additional Benefits.

Benefit Period Ends. The coverage for each benefit extends to, but does not include, the anniversary of the Policy Date in the calendar year shown.

Initial Amount. The amount of coverage on the effective date for each benefit.

Insurance Amount. The amounts of insurance on the indicated anniversaries of the Policy Date provided by the Basic Plan and any Additional Benefits, exclusive of Accidental Death Benefits, if any.

Non-Forfeiture Values. The values of this policy which are guaranteed and which are determined in the manner set forth within the Non-Forfeiture Provisions.

Policy Months, Years, and Anniversaries. Policy months, years, and anniversaries shall be measured from the Policy Date.

Premiums Payable. Premiums are payable from the effective date to the anniversary of the Policy Date in the calendar year shown.

Total Initial Amount. The amount of insurance on the Policy Date on the life of the Insured provided by the Basic Plan and any Additional Benefits, exclusive of Accidental Death Benefits, if any.

POLICY IDENTIFICATION

INSURED	JOHN DOE	29	AGE
POLICY NUMBER	3,047,790	$10,000	AMOUNT OF BASIC PLAN
POLICY DATE	MARCH 22, 1974	$10,000	TOTAL INITIAL AMOUNT
ISSUE DATE	MARCH 29, 1974	I	POLICY CLASS

SCHEDULES OF BENEFITS AND PREMIUMS

SCHEDULE OF BENEFITS

FORM	DESCRIPTION	INITIAL AMOUNT	BENEFIT PERIOD ENDS	ANNUAL PREMIUM	PREMIUMS PAYABLE
7000	BASIC PLAN (WHOLE LIFE)	SEE ABOVE	WITH LIFE	$187.20	FOR LIFE
	WAIVER OF PREMIUM DISABILITY		IN 2005		

SCHEDULE OF PREMIUMS

BEGINNING	FOR PERIODS OF: 12 MONTHS	6 MONTHS	3 MONTHS	1 MONTH
MARCH 22, 1974	$187.20	$95.00	$48.45	$16.60

INITIAL PAYMENT OF $16.60 WILL PROVIDE COVERAGE TO APRIL 22, 1974

SPECIMEN

POLICY NUMBER 3,047,790

SCHEDULE OF INSURANCE AND VALUES

- INSURANCE AMOUNT -		END OF POLICY YEAR	CASH OR LOAN VALUE DOLLARS	PAID UP INSURANCE DOLLARS	EXTENDED TERM INS	
ON INSURED	MAR 22,				YRS	DAYS
$10,000	1974					
10,000	1975	1	.00	0	0	0
10,000	1976	2	59.30	180	2	14
10,000	1977	3	190.50	560	6	104
10,000	1978	4	325.30	930	9	201
10,000	1979	5	463.70	1,290	11	361
10,000	1980	6	605.70	1,650	13	303
10,000	1981	7	751.20	1,990	15	89
10,000	1982	8	900.10	2,330	16	123
10,000	1983	9	1,052.20	2,650	17	72
10,000	1984	10	1,207.30	2,970	17	318
10,000	1985	11	1,365.20	3,270	18	142
10,000	1986	12	1,525.90	3,570	18	287
10,000	1987	13	1,689.30	3,860	19	30
10,000	1988	14	1,855.40	4,130	19	104
10,000	1989	15	2,024.20	4,400	19	151
10,000	1990	16	2,195.60	4,660	19	176
10,000	1991	17	2,369.50	4,920	19	180
10,000	1992	18	2,545.80	5,160	19	167
10,000	1993	19	2,724.30	5,400	19	137
10,000	1994	20	2,904.80	5,630	19	94
10,000	1995	21	3,073.90	5,820	19	14
10,000	1996	22	3,244.20	6,010	18	290
10,000	1997	23	3,415.60	6,190	18	193
10,000	1998	24	3,587.90	6,370	18	90
10,000	1999	25	3,761.00	6,540	17	345
10,000	2000	26	3,934.80	6,700	17	233
10,000	2001	27	4,108.90	6,860	17	116
10,000	2002	28	4,283.20	7,010	16	360
10,000	2003	29	4,457.40	7,150	16	241
10,000	2004	30	4,631.20	7,290	16	117
10,000	2005	31	4,804.30	7,430	15	354
10,000	2006	32	4,976.60	7,550	15	229
10,000	2007	33	5,147.80	7,680	15	99
10,000	2008	34	5,317.70	7,790	14	331
10,000	2009	35	5,485.80	7,910	14	200
10,000	2010	36	5,652.10	8,010	14	64
10,000	2011	37	5,815.90	8,120	13	294
10,000	2012	38	5,976.90	8,210	13	158
10,000	2013	39	6,134.50	8,310	13	17
10,000	2014	40	6,288.50	8,400	12	249
10,000	2005	AGE 60	4,804.30	7,430	15	354
10,000	2007	AGE 62	5,147.80	7,680	15	99
10,000	2010	AGE 65	5,652.10	8,010	14	64

SPECIMEN

NON-FORFEITURE FACTORS
FIRST 20 YEARS   147.10100
THEREAFTER   134.23240

NON-FORFEITURE VALUES AT THE END OF ANY POLICY YEAR PRESUME PAYMENT OF
ALL SPECIFIED PREMIUMS TO THE END OF SUCH POLICY YEAR.

POLICY NUMBER 3,047,790

7510   PAGE 5   740101

OWNERSHIP PROVISIONS

Owner. The Owner is as designated in the application for this policy unless otherwise provided by endorsement. The Owner shall, during the lifetime of the Insured, have the sole right to exercise every privilege and to receive every benefit under this policy, subject to the rights of any assignee of record and to the rights of any irrevocably designated Beneficiary.

The Owner, subject to the rights of any assignee of record, may designate irrevocably as Beneficiary a natural person who is to take in his or her own right, and thereafter the written consent of any irrevocably designated Beneficiary will be required for the exercise of any right available to the Owner under this policy.

Change of Ownership. During the lifetime of the Insured the ownership of this policy may be changed, subject to the rights of any assignee of record, by written request to the company accompanied by this policy for endorsement. No change of ownership will take effect until endorsed on this policy by the company, but when such endorsement is made the change will relate back to and be deemed effective as of the date the request was signed, whether or not the Insured is living at the time such endorsement is made.

Any change of ownership will be subject to any payment made or other action taken by the company before the endorsement is made. A change of ownership, of itself, shall have no effect on the interest of any Beneficiary. The rights of a deceased Owner shall pass to the executors, administrators, or assigns of the deceased Owner unless otherwise provided.

SETTLEMENT PROVISIONS

Payment of Benefits. Any sum payable upon maturity as an endowment or upon surrender for cash shall be payable to the Owner, unless otherwise provided for by endorsement hereon. Settlement of any sum payable upon the death of the Insured shall be made, as herein provided, on receipt of due proof of the death of the Insured.

Settlement of any sum payable shall be made by the company at its home office.

Beneficiary Designation. The Beneficiary Designation is as specified in the application for this policy unless otherwise provided by endorsement on the Issue Date or subsequently changed as provided for in Change of Beneficiary Designation. The Beneficiary Designation shall consist of the identification of the Beneficiary or Beneficiaries and the method of settlement of the sum payable.

If the applicable method of settlement is one sum, payment of the sum payable at the death of the Insured shall be made to the Primary Beneficiary, if living; otherwise to the Successor Beneficiary, if living; otherwise to the Final Beneficiary, if living. If no Beneficiary survives the Insured, payment of the sum payable shall be made to the Owner, if living; otherwise to the executors, administrators, or assigns of such Owner.

If the applicable method of settlement is not one sum, settlement of the sum payable shall be made to the Primary Beneficiary, if living. If at any time there is no Primary Beneficiary living, any payment due shall be made to the Successor Beneficiary, if living. If at any time there is no living Primary or Successor Beneficiary, the then present value of any remaining guaranteed payments on the basis of compound interest at the rate of three per cent per annum shall be paid in one sum to the Final Beneficiary, if any; otherwise to the Owner, if living; otherwise to the executors or administrators of the last survivor of the Owner and all Beneficiaries.

If at the death of the Insured there is more than one Beneficiary then entitled to share in any sum payable, then such sum shall be divided into equal shares, unless otherwise specified, among the persons who are then entitled to payment, and each person's share shall be separately applied under the method of settlement for his or her benefit. If any Beneficiary entitled to a share shall die after such division, the then present value of such Beneficiary's share shall be divided

SETTLEMENT PROVISIONS (CONTINUED)

equally among the other Beneficiaries then receiving payment, unless otherwise specified, and paid in one sum to such Beneficiaries.

If children of any person are named as a class as Beneficiary, the designation shall include only lawful children born to or legally adopted by that person.

The company may rely upon an affidavit by any Beneficiary relating to the date of birth, death, marriage or remarriage, names and addresses and other facts concerning all Beneficiaries, and the company is hereby released from all liability in relying and acting upon the statements contained in such affidavit.

Change of Beneficiary Designation. The Owner has the sole right to change the Beneficiary Designation of this policy during the lifetime of the Insured subject to the rights of any assignee of record and to the rights of any irrevocably designated Beneficiary. Such change shall take effect upon the receipt and recording by the company of a signed written request in form satisfactory to the company, but when so recorded, the change shall relate back to and be deemed effective as of the date the request was signed, whether or not the Insured is living at the time the request is recorded.

The company reserves the right to require the policy for endorsement of a change of Beneficiary Designation. A change of Beneficiary Designation shall be subject to any payment made or other action taken by the company before the recording of the request. A change of Beneficiary Designation shall revoke any prior Beneficiary Designation.

Optional Methods of Settlement. Settlement of any sum payable may be made in one sum or in accordance with any of the following optional methods of settlement:

1. Interest. Retained by the company as a fund with payment of interest at the end of payment intervals. Payments of interest will be made annually unless more frequent payments are elected. Interest shall be payable at an effective rate of not less than three per cent per annum ($30.00 annually, $14.88 semi-annually, $7.41 quarterly, $2.46 monthly for each $1,000 of the balance then retained by the company).

Payment of the balance retained under this optional method of settlement may be made at any time subject to any limitation of withdrawal rights provided for by the Beneficiary Designation. The amount retained by the company may be withdrawn by the person entitled to payment in sums of not less than $100, unless otherwise provided.

Regardless of the payment interval selected by the Owner or Beneficiary, if necessary to bring the amount of each guaranteed interest payment to at least $20 per person entitled to payment, the company may change the payment interval to a less frequent payment interval so that the guaranteed interest payment will be at least $20; but if the annual guaranteed interest does not equal or exceed $20 the Limitations provision shall be applicable. In the absence of an election of a method of settlement, this option shall be effective.

2. Fixed Years Instalments. Payment in equal monthly instalments at the end of monthly payment intervals for a fixed number of years according to the Fixed Years Instalments Table. A person entitled to payment shall have the right to withdraw the commuted value of the unpaid instalments on the basis of compound interest at the rate of three per cent per annum, unless otherwise provided.

3. Life Income. Payment in equal monthly instalments at the end of monthly payment intervals during the remaining lifetime of the payee, according to the Life Instalments Table for the sex and the age at last birthday of the payee on the date this method of settlement becomes effective. The company reserves the right to require satisfactory evidence of age of the payee before making any payment under this method of settlement. A payee shall not have the right to commute any instalments under this method of settlement.

4. Fixed Amount Instalments. Payment in equal annual, semi-annual, quarterly, or monthly instalments of a fixed amount at the end of the specified payment intervals until the balance of the fund retained by the company, together with compound interest at an effective rate of not less than three per cent per annum, is exhausted. The final payment shall equal the unpaid balance of the fund. The instalments must be at least $60 per annum per $1,000 of the fund retained by

SETTLEMENT PROVISIONS (CONTINUED)

the company. A person entitled to payment shall have the right to withdraw the unpaid balance of the fund retained by the company, unless otherwise provided.

5. Joint Life Income. Payment in equal monthly instalments at the end of monthly payment intervals while two payees live and, after the death of one, for the remaining lifetime of the survivor. The amount of monthly payment is to be determined according to the Joint Life Instalments Table for the sex and the age at last birthday of each of the two payees on the date this method of settlement becomes effective. The company reserves the right to require satisfactory evidence of age of the payees before making any payment under this method of settlement. A payee shall not have the right to commute any instalments under this method of settlement.

6. Other Settlement. Payment in any other manner that may be mutually agreed upon with the company.

Commencement of Payments. The first payment under methods of settlement 1, 2, 3, 4, and 5, shall be payable at the end of the first payment interval following the beginning of the first Settlement Year. The first payment under method of settlement 6 shall be payable on the first agreed upon date occurring on or after the beginning of the first Settlement Year.

Participation. Dividends or additional interest such as the company may apportion shall be payable under any settlement method.

Election of Method of Settlement by Beneficiary. After the death of the Insured and before any settlement has been made, if the Beneficiary designated has an unlimited right of withdrawal under any method of settlement or the right to a one sum settlement, such Beneficiary may elect to receive payment in accordance with any of the methods of settlement, provided the amount of any stipulated payment would be not less than $20.

Change of Successor by Beneficiary. After the death of the Insured, if a Beneficiary entitled to any sum payable has an unlimited right of withdrawal or com-

mutation, such Beneficiary may designate a successor to his interests, to the exclusion of any Successor Beneficiary named by the Owner, and may as often as desired change the successor to his interests to receive any remaining balance of the amount retained by the company at the death of the Beneficiary by filing with the company written request therefor in such form as the company may require.

Settlement Year. The first settlement year for an Optional Method of Settlement shall begin on the date of the death of the Insured, or on the date this policy is matured as an endowment or is surrendered for cash. Each successive settlement year shall begin on an anniversary of such date.

Limitations. Except as otherwise prescribed by law, no payment of interest or of principal shall, in advance of actual payment by the company, be subject to the debts, contracts, or engagements of any person entitled to payment, nor to any judicial process to levy upon or attach the same for payment thereof.

If, upon the death of the Insured or upon the maturity of this policy as an endowment or upon its surrender for cash, the amount of any guaranteed payment provided for under a method of settlement, other than the last payment, would be less than $20 per payee, immediate final settlement shall be made in one sum with the payee or payees who at the time of settlement would be entitled to the first such payment if living on the due date thereof.

If, at any time after payments or withdrawals have commenced under a method of settlement, any future guaranteed payment provided for, other than the last payment, would be less than $20 per payee, immediate final settlement shall be made in one sum with the payee or payees who are then living and who would be entitled, if living, to the next succeeding payment.

If an assignee of record, or a corporation, association, partnership, trust, or estate is the payee, whether as trustee or otherwise, the optional methods of settlement shall be available only with the consent of the company.

FIXED YEARS INSTALMENTS TABLE—Method of Settlement 2

MONTHLY INSTALMENTS THAT $1000 WILL OBTAIN FOR NUMBER OF YEARS ELECTED

No. of Years Elected	Monthly Instalments	No. of Years Elected	Monthly Instalments	No. of Years Elected	Monthly Instalments	No. of Years Elected	Monthly Instalments	No. of Years Elected	Monthly Instalments	No. of Years Elected	Monthly Instalments
1	$84.68	6	$15.18	11	$8.88	16	$6.54	21	$5.33	26	$4.60
2	42.96	7	13.20	12	8.26	17	6.24	22	5.16	27	4.49
3	29.06	8	11.71	13	7.73	18	5.98	23	5.00	28	4.38
4	22.12	9	10.56	14	7.28	19	5.74	24	4.85	29	4.28
5	17.95	10	9.64	15	6.89	20	5.53	25	4.72	30	4.19

LIFE INSTALMENTS TABLE—Method of Settlement 3

Age Last Birthday			Monthly Instalments for Life that $1000 Will Obtain				Age Last Birthday			Monthly Instalments for Life that $1000 Will Obtain			
Male	Female	Life	With 5 Years Certain	With 10 Years Certain	With 15 Years Certain	With 20 Years Certain	Male	Female	Life	With 5 Years Certain	With 10 Years Certain	With 15 Years Certain	With 20 Years Certain
10 & Under	14 & Under	$3.21	$3.20	$3.18	$3.16	$3.13	45	49	$4.30	$4.28	$4.23	$4.16	$4.06
11	15	3.22	3.21	3.19	3.17	3.14	46	50	4.36	4.35	4.29	4.22	4.11
12	16	3.23	3.23	3.21	3.18	3.15	47	51	4.44	4.42	4.36	4.28	4.16
13	17	3.25	3.24	3.22	3.20	3.17	48	52	4.51	4.49	4.43	4.34	4.22
14	18	3.26	3.25	3.24	3.21	3.18	49	53	4.59	4.57	4.50	4.40	4.27
15	19	3.28	3.27	3.25	3.23	3.19	50	54	4.68	4.65	4.58	4.47	4.33
16	20	3.29	3.29	3.27	3.24	3.21	51	55	4.77	4.74	4.66	4.54	4.39
17	21	3.31	3.30	3.28	3.26	3.22	52	56	4.86	4.83	4.75	4.62	4.44
18	22	3.33	3.32	3.30	3.27	3.24	53	57	4.96	4.93	4.84	4.69	4.51
19	23	3.35	3.34	3.32	3.29	3.26	54	58	5.07	5.03	4.93	4.77	4.57
20	24	3.37	3.36	3.34	3.31	3.28	55	59	5.18	5.14	5.03	4.86	4.63
21	25	3.39	3.38	3.36	3.33	3.29	56	60	5.30	5.26	5.14	4.94	4.69
22	26	3.41	3.40	3.38	3.35	3.31	57	61	5.43	5.39	5.25	5.03	4.75
23	27	3.43	3.42	3.40	3.37	3.33	58	62	5.57	5.52	5.36	5.12	4.82
24	28	3.45	3.44	3.42	3.39	3.35	59	63	5.72	5.66	5.48	5.22	4.88
25	29	3.47	3.47	3.44	3.41	3.38	60	64	5.88	5.81	5.61	5.31	4.94
26	30	3.50	3.49	3.47	3.44	3.40	61	65	6.04	5.97	5.74	5.41	5.00
27	31	3.53	3.52	3.49	3.46	3.42	62	66	6.22	6.13	5.88	5.51	5.06
28	32	3.55	3.54	3.52	3.49	3.45	63	67	6.41	6.31	6.03	5.61	5.11
29	33	3.58	3.57	3.55	3.51	3.47	64	68	6.62	6.50	6.18	5.71	5.17
30	34	3.61	3.60	3.58	3.54	3.50	65	69	6.84	6.71	6.34	5.81	5.22
31	35	3.64	3.63	3.61	3.57	3.53	66	70	7.07	6.92	6.50	5.91	5.26
32	36	3.68	3.67	3.64	3.60	3.56	67	71	7.33	7.15	6.67	6.00	5.30
33	37	3.71	3.70	3.67	3.63	3.59	68	72	7.60	7.39	6.84	6.10	5.34
34	38	3.75	3.74	3.71	3.67	3.62	69	73	7.89	7.65	7.02	6.19	5.38
35	39	3.79	3.77	3.75	3.70	3.65	70	74	8.21	7.93	7.20	6.28	5.41
36	40	3.83	3.81	3.78	3.74	3.68	71	75	8.55	8.22	7.38	6.36	5.43
37	41	3.87	3.86	3.82	3.78	3.72	72	76	8.92	8.53	7.56	6.44	5.45
38	42	3.91	3.90	3.87	3.82	3.76	73	77	9.32	8.85	7.75	6.51	5.47
39	43	3.96	3.95	3.91	3.86	3.80	74	78	9.75	9.20	7.93	6.58	5.49
40	44	4.01	3.99	3.96	3.90	3.84	75	79	10.22	9.56	8.11	6.63	5.50
41	45	4.06	4.05	4.01	3.95	3.88	76	80	10.72	9.94	8.29	6.69	5.51
42	46	4.11	4.10	4.06	4.00	3.92	77	81	11.27	10.34	8.46	6.73	5.51
43	47	4.17	4.16	4.11	4.05	3.97	78	82	11.87	10.76	8.62	6.77	5.52
44	48	4.23	4.22	4.17	4.10	4.01	79	83	12.52	11.19	8.77	6.80	5.52
							80 & Over	84 & Over	13.22	11.64	8.91	6.82	5.52

JOINT LIFE INSTALMENTS TABLE—Method of Settlement 5

JOINT MONTHLY INSTALMENTS FOR BOTH LIVES THAT $1000 WILL OBTAIN WITH SAME AMOUNT TO LAST SURVIVOR FOR LIFE

Age Last Birthday	Male	35	40	45	50	55	60	65	70	75	80 and Over
	Female	39	44	49	54	59	64	69	74	79	84 and Over
Male	Female										
35	39	$3.52	$3.58	$3.64	$3.68	$3.72	$3.74	$3.76	$3.77	$3.78	$3.78
40	44	3.58	3.67	3.76	3.83	3.88	3.92	3.95	3.98	3.99	4.00
45	49	3.64	3.76	3.87	3.98	4.07	4.14	4.20	4.24	4.26	4.28
50	54	3.68	3.83	3.98	4.13	4.27	4.39	4.49	4.56	4.61	4.64
55	59	3.72	3.88	4.07	4.27	4.48	4.67	4.83	4.96	5.05	5.11
60	64	3.74	3.92	4.14	4.39	4.67	4.95	5.21	5.43	5.60	5.72
65	69	3.76	3.95	4.20	4.49	4.83	5.21	5.60	5.97	6.27	6.51
70	74	3.77	3.98	4.24	4.56	4.96	5.43	5.97	6.53	7.05	7.49
75	79	3.78	3.99	4.26	4.61	5.05	5.60	6.27	7.05	7.88	8.66
80 and Over	84 and Over	3.78	4.00	4.28	4.64	5.11	5.72	6.51	7.49	8.66	9.91

This table illustrates joint instalments for specimen age combinations only. Instalments for age combinations not shown shall be determined on the same basis as those in this table and may be obtained from the company on request.

PREMIUM PROVISIONS

Payment of Premiums. All premiums after the first are payable in advance at the home office of the company, or to an authorized agent of the company upon delivery of a receipt signed by the president, a vice-president, the secretary, or an assistant secretary, and counter-signed by such agent. Premiums may be paid for twelve months, six months, three months, or one month as specified in the Schedule of Premiums on page three of this policy.

The frequency of premium payment may be changed on any premium due date except as provided in the Waiver of Premium Disability Provisions, if any. Payment to and acceptance by the company of a premium on a new frequency of payment shall constitute a change in frequency for subsequent premiums.

Grace Period. A grace period of thirty-one days shall be allowed following the due date for the payment, without interest, of any premium after the first. During such grace period this policy shall remain in force but if a premium due on such due date is not paid before the end of such grace period this policy shall lapse, except as provided in Credits to Avoid Lapse and, if applicable, Automatic Premium Loan.

If the death of the Insured occurs prior to the end of the grace period, any unpaid premium or balance thereof, which is applicable to the policy month in which death occurs shall be deducted from settlement of the sum payable.

Credits to Avoid Lapse. Any dividend credits as defined in the Dividend Provisions of this policy shall be applied toward the payment of any premium unpaid at the end of the grace period. If the total of such credits shall be less than the unpaid premium, such credits shall be applied as a pro rata premium as of the due date of the unpaid premium and on the day immediately following the last day of any pro rata premium payment period the unpaid balance of such premium shall be due and payable. A grace period

shall be allowed for the payment of such unpaid balance, as provided in Grace Period.

Notice of the application of dividend credits shall be given to the Owner and the Owner shall have a period of ninety days, from the due date of the unpaid premium, in which to elect to have an available Non-Forfeiture Provision made effective as of such due date.

Automatic Premium Loan. This provision shall be in effect only if a written election has been made by the Owner and is on file with the company prior to the expiration of the grace period for an unpaid premium or any unpaid balance thereof after application of Credits to Avoid Lapse.

If this provision is in effect, any unpaid premium or unpaid balance shall be charged as an indebtedness against this policy provided that the unpaid amount is not greater than the maximum loan value, as defined in the Policy Loan Provisions, less any existing indebtedness on this policy. The automatic premium loan shall bear interest from the due date of the unpaid premium or unpaid balance and shall be subject to the same terms and conditions as provided in the Policy Loan Provisions of this policy.

This provision shall not be effective if the maximum loan value, less any existing indebtedness on this policy, is insufficient to pay the unpaid premium or unpaid balance. The Owner may revoke the automatic premium loan election at any time by written request, but such revocation shall have no effect upon automatic premium loans made prior to receipt of the written request by the company.

Premium Refund on Death of Insured. The death benefit shall be increased by that portion of any premium which has been paid for any period beyond the end of the policy month in which the death of the Insured occurs.

DIVIDEND PROVISIONS

Annual Dividends. Annual dividends such as the company may apportion shall be payable at the end of each policy year after the first while this policy is in force other than as extended term insurance.

DIVIDEND PROVISIONS (CONTINUED)

The Owner may elect in writing that each dividend payable be applied under one of the following methods:

1. Premium Payment. Applied toward the payment of premiums.

2. Paid-Up Addition. Applied to purchase a participating paid-up life insurance addition to this policy, the net value of which shall be not less than the dividend used to purchase such addition.

3. Dividend Accumulation. Left to accumulate at compound interest at a rate not less than three per cent per annum. Dividend accumulations not applied under Credits to Avoid Lapse will be added to, and be a part of, the sum payable at the death of the Insured or upon surrender for cash; or they may be withdrawn at any time.

4. Cash. Paid in cash.

The dividend method will be changed, as to any subsequent dividends, upon receipt of the Owner's written request for such change. If no election has been made, method 3 shall apply.

Dividend Credits. Dividend credits as used in this policy means the total of any accumulated dividends under dividend method 3 and any current dividend available under dividend methods 1 or 3 as defined in Annual Dividends.

Election of Paid-Up Policy. Upon written election by the Owner and the surrender of dividend credits, this policy may be endorsed as a participating paid-up policy whenever the dividend credits, if applied as a net single premium increased by three per cent, are sufficient to purchase paid-up insurance in an amount equal to the difference between the Amount of Basic Plan insurance and the amount of reduced paid-up insurance then available under the Non-Forfeiture Provisions. Such paid-up insurance shall be payable under the same conditions as the insurance otherwise provided by the Basic Plan.

Election of Matured Endowment. This policy may be matured as an endowment whenever the sum of any dividend credits and the cash surrender value of this policy shall equal the amount of insurance then in force provided by the Basic Plan. Such endowment maturity shall be effective only upon written election by the Owner and the surrender of this policy and of any such dividend credits.

POLICY LOAN PROVISIONS

Policy Loan. At any time while this policy is in force, other than as extended term insurance, the company, on proper assignment of this policy and on its sole security, will advance to the Owner any amount which is not greater than the maximum loan value, if any, less any existing indebtedness on this policy and any unpaid premium or balance thereof. At its option, the company may defer granting a loan under this provision, other than to pay premiums on policies in this company, for a period not exceeding six months after a request for a loan has been received by the company.

All or any part of the loan may be repaid, with accrued interest on the amount so repaid, at any time while this policy is in force other than as extended term insurance. Whenever the total indebtedness to the company on this policy exceeds the maximum loan value, this policy shall terminate thirty-one days after the company has mailed notice to the last known address of the Owner and the assignee of record, if any.

Maximum Loan Value. The maximum loan value shall be that amount which, with interest at the rate of six per cent per annum to the date on which the next premium is due or, if no further premiums are payable, to the next anniversary of the Policy Date, equals, as of such date, the sum of the loan value and the present value of any existing paid-up life insurance additions. Loan values on anniversaries of the Policy Date are shown in the Schedule of Insurance and Values on page five of this policy.

Loan Interest. Interest on the loan shall accrue from day to day at the rate of six per cent per annum and shall constitute an indebtedness to the company against this policy as it accrues. Interest shall be payable on

POLICY LOAN PROVISIONS (CONTINUED)

each anniversary of the Policy Date subsequent to the date of loan until such loan is repaid. If such interest is not paid when due it shall be added to and form a part of the loan, and bear interest at the same rate.

If at any time the total indebtedness to the company on this policy including accrued interest, is equal to the maximum loan value, the accrued interest shall then be payable.

GENERAL PROVISIONS

The Contract. The policy consists of the Basic Plan, any amendments and endorsements, and any Additional Benefits included herein, together with the application, a copy of which is attached hereto and made a part hereof at issue, and this policy constitutes the entire contract. All statements made by or on behalf of the Insured in applying for this policy shall, in the absence of fraud, be deemed representations and not warranties, and no statement shall avoid this policy or be used in defense of a claim hereunder unless it is contained in the application.

Only an endorsement signed by the president, a vice-president, the secretary, or an assistant secretary of the company can waive or modify the conditions or provisions of this policy. No other person has the authority to make or modify this contract, to extend the time for paying a premium, to waive any forfeiture, or to bind the company by making any promise or representation or by giving or receiving any information.

Change of Basic Plan. The Basic Plan may be changed by mutual agreement with the company.

Reinstatement. This policy may be reinstated within five years after the date of lapse if it has not been surrendered for its cash surrender value. Reinstatement is subject to (1) the payment of all overdue premiums with compound interest at the rate of six per cent per annum on such overdue premiums; (2) the payment or re-establishment of any indebtedness existing at the date of lapse together with compound interest at the rate of six per cent per annum on such indebtedness; and (3) receipt of evidence of insurability of the Insured satisfactory to the company.

Indebtedness. Any indebtedness to the company on this policy shall be deducted from any settlement.

Assignment. The company assumes no responsibility for the validity or effect of any assignment of this policy and no assignment will be recognized until a copy of such assignment has been duly filed with the company. An assignment of this policy shall operate to the

extent thereof to transfer the interest of any Beneficiary whom the assignor has the right to change, and to render any part of the sum payable to which the assignee is entitled payable in one sum, notwithstanding any beneficiary designation in effect at the time the assignment was executed. No assignment of this policy or any interest thereunder made after the death of the Insured shall be valid unless the company consents thereto.

Age. This policy is issued at the age shown on page three, which is the Insured's age last birthday on the Policy Date according to the date of birth as given in the application. If the Policy Date coincides with a birthday of the Insured, the age shall be the Insured's age as of such birthday. If the date of birth of the Insured has been misstated in the application, every benefit accruing hereunder shall be such as the premiums paid would have purchased at the correct age.

Incontestability. The Basic Plan of this policy shall be incontestable after it has been in force during the lifetime of the Insured for a period of two years from the Issue Date, except for non-payment of premiums, and except as to provisions and conditions relating to waiver of premium benefits in the event of total disability.

Each Additional Benefit included in the Schedule of Benefits on page three and made a part of this policy contains its own provision regarding incontestability.

Suicide. The suicide of the Insured, while sane or insane, within two years from the Issue Date is a risk not assumed under the Basic Plan of this policy. In such event, however, the Beneficiary shall receive an amount equal to the premiums received hereon, without interest.

Each Additional Benefit included in the Schedule of Benefits on page three and made a part of this policy contains its own provision regarding benefits in the event of suicide.

NON-FORFEITURE PROVISIONS

Non-Forfeiture Values. A schedule of the non-forfeiture values of this policy appears on page five. Cash values shown are as of the end of the policy years indicated, and such cash values provide the amounts of paid-up insurance and the periods of extended term insurance appearing in the schedule. These values do not include allowance for any paid-up life insurance additions and are subject to adjustment on account of any credits or indebtedness on this policy. Values at any time except at the end of a policy year shall be determined on a basis consistent with that described in these provisions and with due allowance for any premiums paid for the policy year then current. Values not appearing in the schedule will be furnished on request.

Cash Value. The cash value of this policy at the end of any policy year when all premiums due have been paid shall be the then present value of the future guaranteed life insurance benefits provided by the Basic Plan and by any Additional Benefit providing for non-forfeiture values, exclusive of any existing paid-up life insurance additions, less the present value of the annual non-forfeiture factors for subsequent policy years. If any premium or balance thereof due under this policy is unpaid, and less than ninety days have elapsed since the due date of such unpaid premium or unpaid balance thereof, the cash value shall be the same as on such due date.

If this policy is being continued as extended term insurance or as reduced paid-up insurance, and more than ninety days have elapsed since the effective date of such insurance, the cash value shall be equal to the present value of the future guaranteed life insurance benefits which otherwise would have been provided if such form of insurance were continued in force, except that in the case of surrender within thirty-one days after a policy anniversary the cash value shall be determined as of such anniversary.

Cash Surrender. Upon receipt by the company at any time of written request by the Owner and the surrender of this policy, this policy shall terminate and the cash surrender value, if any, shall be payable. The cash surrender value shall be the sum of the cash value and the present value of any paid-up life insurance additions less any indebtedness on this policy. At its option, the company may defer any payment hereunder for a period

not exceeding six months after receipt of written request by the Owner and surrender of this policy.

Extended Term Insurance. This provision is available only if this policy is in Policy Class I or II.

Upon receipt by the company of this policy for endorsement and written request by the Owner prior to, or within ninety days after, the due date of any premium or balance thereof, if a cash surrender value is available, the amount of death benefit provided by the Basic Plan under this policy, increased by the amount of any paid-up life insurance additions and any accumulated dividends and less any indebtedness to the company on this policy, shall be continued in force from such due date as non-participating extended term insurance.

The period of the extended term insurance shall be such that the present value of the guaranteed benefits provided thereunder shall be equal to the cash surrender value on such due date plus any otherwise unapplied current dividend available under dividend methods 1, 2, or 3 and any accumulated dividends under dividend method 3.

This provision shall be automatically applied if any premium or balance thereof remains unpaid at the end of the grace period after application of any dividend credits in accordance with the Credits to Avoid Lapse provision and, if applicable, the Automatic Premium Loan provision.

Reduced Paid-Up Insurance. Upon receipt by the company of this policy for endorsement and written request by the Owner prior to, or within ninety days after, the due date of any premium or balance thereof, if a cash surrender value is available, a reduced amount of insurance will be continued in force from such due date as participating paid-up life insurance. The reduced amount of insurance shall be such that the present value of the guaranteed benefits provided thereunder shall be equal to the cash surrender value on such due date.

If this policy is in Policy Class III, this provision shall be applied automatically if any premium or balance

NON-FORFEITURE PROVISIONS (CONTINUED)

thereof remains unpaid at the end of the grace period after application of any dividend credits in accordance with the Credits to Avoid Lapse provision and, if applicable, the Automatic Premium Loan provision.

Actuarial Basis. The cash or loan values, extended term insurance, and reduced paid-up insurance provided by this policy are not less than the minimum values and benefits which would result from use of the Standard Non-Forfeiture Value Method, interest at the rate of three per cent per annum, age last birthday, and the assumption that deaths during any policy year occur uniformly throughout that year, nor are such values and benefits less than the minimum values and benefits required by the governing law of the territorial jurisdiction in which this policy is delivered.

All present values referred to in the Non-Forfeiture Provisions and the Policy Loan Provisions of this policy shall be computed on the basis of the Commissioners 1958 Standard Ordinary Mortality Table, except that extended term insurance shall be computed on the basis of the Commissioners 1958 Extended Term Insurance Table, interest at the rate of three per cent per annum, age last birthday, and the assumption that deaths during any policy year occur uniformly throughout that year.

All net single premiums referred to in this policy shall be computed on the basis of the Commissioners 1958 Standard Ordinary Mortality Table, interest at the rate of three per cent per annum, age last birthday, and the assumption that deaths during any policy year occur uniformly throughout that year.

WAIVER OF PREMIUM DISABILITY PROVISIONS

Benefit. Upon receipt at its home office of due proof that the Insured has become totally disabled as hereinafter defined, and subject to all the terms and conditions of these provisions, the company shall waive the payment of each premium becoming due under this policy during the continuance of such disability, commencing with the premium due on or next following the date of commencement of such disability; provided, however, that no premium shall be waived, the due date of which is more than one year prior to the date of receipt by the company at its home office of written notice of claim hereunder on account of such disability.

Such waiver of premium shall apply to the entire premium under this policy, including the additional premium for every additional benefit made a part of this policy as shown in the Schedule of Benefits on page three, and shall be in addition to all other benefits under this policy, including dividends, which benefits shall accrue as though the premiums so waived had been paid in cash.

The frequency of premium payment shall not be changed during a period of disability for which claim is made hereunder.

Disability Defined. Total disability is disability as the result of bodily injury or disease which wholly prevents

the Insured from (1) performing during the first twenty-four months following the commencement of such disability substantially all the work pertaining to the Insured's occupation or business, and (2) engaging thereafter in any occupation for which the Insured is or becomes reasonably fitted by education, training, or experience.

Independently of any other cause, the total and irrecoverable loss of the sight of both eyes, or of the use of both hands, or of both feet, or of one hand and one foot, shall be considered total disability.

Waiver of premium shall be allowed only for total disability originating after the insurance under this policy took effect and after the anniversary of the Policy Date on or next following the Insured's fifth birthday but originating prior to the anniversary of the Policy Date on or next following the Insured's sixtieth birthday and which disability has continued uninterruptedly for a period of at least six months during the lifetime of the Insured.

If any premium under this policy is due and unpaid before receipt by the company at its home office of written notice of claim hereunder, waiver of premium shall be allowed only if such notice is received within one year after the due date of the first such unpaid pre-

WAIVER OF PREMIUM DISABILITY PROVISIONS (CONTINUED)

mium and the total disability as a result of which claim is made commenced either (1) before such due date, or (2) subsequent to such due date but within the grace period allowed by this policy for the payment of such unpaid premium, in which case before waiver of premium is allowed the Owner shall pay in cash such unpaid premium with compound interest at the rate of six per cent per annum from the end of the grace period following the due date of such unpaid premium.

Risks Not Assumed. Waiver of premium shall not be allowed for disability that results directly or indirectly from (1) intentional self-inflicted injury of any kind, or (2) war or any act attributable to war, whether or not the Insured is in the military service of any country.

As used in this provision, "war" means declared or undeclared war or any conflict involving the armed forces of any country or coalition of countries or governments through an international organization or otherwise.

Notice of Claim. Written notice of claim hereunder must be received by the company at its home office during the lifetime and during the continuance of total disability of the Insured. Failure to give such notice within such times shall not invalidate or diminish any claim if it shall be shown not to have been reasonably possible to give such notice within such times and that notice was given as soon as was reasonably possible.

Any premium under this policy becoming due after notice of claim is received and prior to approval of claim shall be payable as though no notice of claim had been received, but will, if paid to the company, be refunded upon approval of such claim. Any premium paid to the company and later waived under these provisions but not refunded by the company prior to the

Insured's death shall be added to, and be a part of, the sum payable upon the death of the Insured.

Proof of Continuance of Disability. Before waiving any premium, the company may demand due proof of the continuance of total disability, but such proof will not be required more often than once a year after such disability has continued for two full years. If such proof is not furnished, or if at any time during the period of twenty-four months following the commencement of disability the Insured is able to perform the work pertaining to the Insured's occupation or business, or if at any time after such initial twenty-four month period of disability the Insured is able to engage in any occupation for which the Insured is or becomes reasonably fitted by education, training, or experience, no further premiums shall be waived. Any premium waived which was due on a date not within the period of disability shall constitute an indebtedness against this policy bearing compound interest at the rate of six per cent per annum.

Termination. These provisions shall automatically terminate if this policy matures, expires, or becomes paid-up, or on the anniversary of the Policy Date on or next following the Insured's sixtieth birthday, whichever occurs first; or if any of the Non-Forfeiture Provisions of this policy become effective; or on the due date of any unpaid premium payable under this policy, except as provided under Grace Period.

Termination of these provisions shall be without prejudice to any otherwise allowable claim for waiver of premiums under this policy on account of total disability commencing prior to such termination.

Cost. The cost of this waiver of premium disability benefit is included in the premium for this policy.

AJAX LIFE
Insurance Company

HOME OFFICE: _____, _____

PLAN DESCRIPTION

Basic Plan provides a Whole Life Benefit with Waiver of Premium for Disability. Schedules of Benefits and Premiums on page 3. Amounts of Insurance on page 5. Insurance payable on death. Annual Dividends. Premiums payable for life unless policy previously paid up or endowed by dividends.

FORM 7510

740101

C. Accidental Death Benefit

C. ACCIDENTAL DEATH BENEFIT

Policy Provisions Included. This Accidental Death Benefit constitutes an Additional Benefit attached to and made a part of this policy. The Ownership Provisions, Settlement Provisions, and Premium Provisions, together with the provisions of this policy entitled The Contract, Reinstatement, Indebtedness, and Assignment, shall be made a part of this Accidental Death Benefit. No other provision of this policy, except as named herein, shall apply to or be made a part hereof.

Benefit. The company agrees to pay as a part of the sum payable the amount of Accidental Death insurance shown in the Schedule of Benefits upon receipt of due proof that the death of the Insured:

1. Occurred while the policy and this Accidental Death Benefit were in force and after the anniversary of the Effective Date on or next following the Insured's fifth birthday but prior to the anniversary of the Effective Date on or next following the Insured's seventieth birthday, and

2. Resulted directly, and independently of all other causes, from bodily injury effected solely through external, violent, and accidental means as evidenced by a visible contusion or wound on the exterior of the body (except in case of drowning or internal injuries revealed by an autopsy), and

3. Occurred within ninety days of the date of such injury.

If any sum is otherwise payable under this Accidental Death Benefit, the company agrees to pay in addition to any other payment under this Additional Benefit the amount of Accidental Death insurance shown in the Schedule of Benefits if death results from the Insured's travel as a fare paying passenger on a licensed public conveyance operated by a common carrier for the regular transportation of passengers.

Consideration. The insurance provided by this Accidental Death Benefit is granted in consideration of the application and of the payment of premiums for this Additional Benefit. The Schedule of Premiums on page three includes the premium for this Accidental Death Benefit.

Risks Not Assumed. This Accidental Death Benefit does not insure against death resulting directly or in-
directly from (1) suicide or intentional self-inflicted injury of any kind, whether the Insured be sane or insane; (2) bodily or mental infirmity or illness or disease of any kind; (3) the commission of an assault, or an attempt to commit or the commission of a felony; (4) the use of any type of aircraft (a) while the Insured is a pilot or crew member of such aircraft or has any other duties aboard such aircraft, (b) for the purpose of descending from such aircraft while in flight, or (c) for the giving or receiving of instruction or training; (5) the descent for any reason from any type of aircraft while in flight; (6) operating or riding in any type of aircraft under the control or charter of any military service; or (7) any act of war.

As used in this Accidental Death Benefit, "war" means declared or undeclared war or any conflict involving the armed forces of any country or coalition of countries or governments through an international organization or otherwise.

Termination. This Accidental Death Benefit shall terminate on the earliest of (1) the anniversary of the Effective Date in the calendar year shown in the Schedule of Benefits on page three under *Benefit Period Ends,* (2) the anniversary of the Effective Date on or next following the Insured's seventieth birthday, (3) the date on which any Non-Forfeiture Provision becomes effective, (4) the date the Basic Plan becomes paid-up under the Election of Paid-Up Policy provision, if available, unless the Owner elects to make this Additional Benefit a paid-up benefit by payment of the required single premium on or before the date on which the Basic Plan becomes paid-up, (5) the date on which the Basic Plan matures as an endowment, or (6) the due date of any unpaid premium payable for this Additional Benefit or for the Basic Plan, except as provided in the Grace Period provision. Premiums for this Accidental Death Benefit shall not be payable beyond the termination of this Additional Benefit.

On or before a premium due date or within thirty-one days thereafter, the company will terminate this Additional Benefit as of such premium due date upon receipt at its home office of the Owner's written request and the return of the policy for endorsement.

Incontestability. This Additional Benefit shall always be contestable.

ACCIDENTAL DEATH BENEFIT (CONTINUED)

Suicide. The suicide of the Insured, while sane or insane, is a risk not assumed under this Additional Benefit.

Age. This Additional Benefit is issued at the Insured's age last birthday on the Effective Date according to the date of birth given in the application for this Additional Benefit. If the Effective Date coincides with a birthday of the Insured, the age shall be the Insured's age as of such birthday. If the date of birth of the Insured has been misstated in the application for this Additional Benefit, every benefit accruing hereunder prior to the termination of this Additional Benefit shall be such as the premiums paid would have purchased at the correct age.

Effective Date. The Effective Date of this Additional Benefit shall be the Policy Date, unless a different Effective Date is shown under Accidental Death in the Schedule of Benefits on page three of the policy.

Execution.   The **Ajax Life** Insurance Company, at its home office in Bloomington, Illinois, has caused this Accidental Death Benefit to be executed in accordance with the provisions herein.

Roger M. Roe
PRESIDENT

John C. Smith
SECRETARY

740101

D. American Bankers Association Assignment Form

FORM DESIGNED, PRINTED, AND DISTRIBUTED BY
AMERICAN BANKERS ASSOCIATION
BANK MANAGEMENT COMMISSION
(REVIEWED AND APPROVED 1950)

FORM No. 10—LIFE INSURANCE ASSIGNMENT

ASSIGNMENT OF LIFE INSURANCE POLICY AS COLLATERAL

A.　**For Value Received** the undersigned hereby assign, transfer and set over to _____

_____ of _____

its successors and assigns, (herein called the "Assignee") Policy No. _____ issued by the

_____

(herein called the "Insurer") and any supplementary contracts issued in connection therewith (said policy and contracts being

herein called the "Policy"), upon the life of _____

of _____ and all claims, options, privileges, rights, title and interest therein and thereunder (except as provided in Paragraph C hereof), subject to all the terms and conditions of the Policy and to all superior liens, if any, which the Insurer may have against the Policy. The undersigned by this instrument jointly and severally agree and the Assignee by the acceptance of this assignment agrees to the conditions and provisions herein set forth.

B.　It is expressly agreed that, without detracting from the generality of the foregoing, the following specific rights are included in this assignment and pass by virtue hereof:
1. The sole right to collect from the Insurer the net proceeds of the Policy when it becomes a claim by death or maturity;
2. The sole right to surrender the Policy and receive the surrender value thereof at any time provided by the terms of the Policy and at such other times as the Insurer may allow;
3. The sole right to obtain one or more loans or advances on the Policy, either from the Insurer or, at any time, from other persons, and to pledge or assign the Policy as security for such loans or advances;
4. The sole right to collect and receive all distributions or shares of surplus, dividend deposits or additions to the Policy now or hereafter made or apportioned thereto, and to exercise any and all options contained in the Policy with respect thereto; provided, that unless and until the Assignee shall notify the Insurer in writing to the contrary, the distributions or shares of surplus, dividend deposits and additions shall continue on the plan in force at the time of this assignment; and
5. The sole right to exercise all nonforfeiture rights permitted by the terms of the Policy or allowed by the Insurer and to receive all benefits and advantages derived therefrom.

C.　It is expressly agreed that the following specific rights, so long as the Policy has not been surrendered, are reserved and excluded from this assignment and do not pass by virtue hereof:
1. The right to collect from the Insurer any disability benefit payable in cash that does not reduce the amount of insurance;
2. The right to designate and change the beneficiary;
3. The right to elect any optional mode of settlement permitted by the Policy or allowed by the Insurer;
but the reservation of these rights shall in no way impair the right of the Assignee to surrender the Policy completely with all its incidents or impair any other right of the Assignee hereunder, and any designation or change of beneficiary or election of a mode of settlement shall be made subject to this assignment and to the rights of the Assignee hereunder.

D.　This assignment is made and the Policy is to be held as collateral security for any and all liabilities of the undersigned, or any of them, to the Assignee, either now existing or that may hereafter arise in the ordinary course of business between any of the undersigned and the Assignee (all of which liabilities secured or to become secured are herein called "Liabilities").

E.　The Assignee covenants and agrees with the undersigned as follows:
1. That any balance of sums received hereunder from the Insurer remaining after payment of the then existing Liabilities, matured or unmatured, shall be paid by the Assignee to the persons entitled thereto under the terms of the Policy had this assignment not been executed;
2. That the Assignee will not exercise either the right to surrender the Policy or (except for the purpose of paying premiums) the right to obtain policy loans from the Insurer, until there has been default in any of the Liabilities or a failure to pay any premium when due, nor until twenty days after the Assignee shall have mailed, by first-class mail, to the undersigned at the addresses last supplied in writing to the Assignee specifically referring to this assignment, notice of intention to exercise such right; and
3. That the Assignee will upon request forward without unreasonable delay to the Insurer the Policy for endorsement of any designation or change of beneficiary or any election of an optional mode of settlement.

F.　The Insurer is hereby authorized to recognize the Assignee's claims to rights hereunder without investigating the reason for any action taken by the Assignee, or the validity or the amount of the Liabilities or the existence of any default therein, or the giving of any notice under Paragraph E (2) above or otherwise, or the application to be made by the Assignee of any amounts to be paid to the Assignee. The sole signature of the Assignee shall be sufficient for the exercise of any rights under the Policy assigned hereby and the sole receipt of the Assignee for any sums received shall be a full discharge and release therefor to the Insurer. Checks for all or any part of the sums payable under the Policy and assigned herein, shall be drawn to the exclusive order of the Assignee if, when, and in such amounts as may be, requested by the Assignee.

G.　The Assignee shall be under no obligation to pay any premium, or the principal of or interest on any loans or advances on the Policy whether or not obtained by the Assignee, or any other charges on the Policy, but any such amounts so paid by the Assignee from its own funds, shall become a part of the Liabilities hereby secured, shall be due immediately, and shall draw interest at a rate fixed by the Assignee from time to time not exceeding 6% per annum.

H.　The exercise of any right, option, privilege or power given herein to the Assignee shall be at the option of the Assignee, but (except as restricted by Paragraph E (2)) the Assignee may exercise any such right, option, privilege or power without notice to, or assent by, or affecting the liability of, or releasing any interest hereby assigned by the undersigned, or any of them.

I.　The Assignee may take or release other security, may release any party primarily or secondarily liable for any of the Liabilities, may grant extensions, renewals or indulgences with respect to the Liabilities, or may apply to the Liabilities in such order as the Assignee shall determine, the proceeds of the Policy hereby assigned or any amount received on account of the Policy by the exercise of any right permitted under this assignment, without resorting or regard to other security.

J.　In the event of any conflict between the provisions of this assignment and provisions of the note or other evidence of any Liability, with respect to the Policy or rights of collateral security therein, the provisions of this assignment shall prevail.

K.　Each of the undersigned declares that no proceedings in bankruptcy are pending against him and that his property is not subject to any assignment for the benefit of creditors.

Signed and sealed this _____ day of _____, 19_____

_____	_____(L.S.)
Witness	Insured or Owner
_____	_____
	Address
_____	_____(L.S.)
Witness	Beneficiary
	_____
	Address

INDIVIDUAL ACKNOWLEDGMENT

STATE OF _____

COUNTY OF _____ }ss:

On the _____ day of _____ 19 _____, before me personally came

_____, to me known to be the individual _____ described in and who

executed the assignment on the reverse side hereof and acknowledged to me that _____ he _____ executed the same.

_____

Notary Public

My commission expires_____

CORPORATE ACKNOWLEDGMENT

STATE OF _____

COUNTY OF _____ }ss:

On the _____ day of _____ 19_____, before me personally came _____

_____, who being by me duly sworn, did depose and say that he resides in _____

that he is the _____ of _____, the corporation described in and which executed the assignment on the
reverse side hereof; that he knows the seal of said corporation; that the seal affixed to said assignment is such corporate seal; that
it was so affixed by order of the Board of Directors of said corporation, and that he signed his name thereto by like order.

_____

Notary Public

My commission expires_____

• • • • •

Duplicate received and filed at the home office of the Insurer in _____ _____, this _____ day of _____ 19_____

_____

By_____

Authorized Officer

NOTE: When executed by a corporation, the corporate seal should be affixed and there should be attached to the assignment a certified copy of the resolution of
the Board of Directors authorizing the signing officer to execute and deliver the assignment in the name and on behalf of the corporation.

BMC 136-6-1941

E. Notice of Life Insurance Lapse and Late Remittance Offer Form

AJAX LIFE INSURANCE COMPANY

NOTICE OF LIFE INSURANCE LAPSE
AND LATE REMITTANCE OFFER

POLICY NUMBER

DATE PAYMENT DUE

TOTAL AMOUNT TO REMIT $_____

To restore full protection
*mail remittance before this late remittance offer expires*_____

CONDITIONS FOR ACCEPTING LATE REMITTANCE WITHOUT PROOF OF INSURABILITY

The policy referred to above having terminated at expiration of the 31-day grace period, except as any Automatic Premium Loan or nonforfeiture provision may apply, this offer to accept a late remittance without requiring evidence of insurability is made subject to each of the following conditions:

1—OFFER IS FOR LIMITED PERIOD

The remittance must be post-marked on or before the date this Late Remittance offer expires. Checks and drafts will be accepted subject to collection only.

2—INSURED MUST BE ALIVE

Payment must be tendered BEFORE death of the Insured.

3—NOT A PRECEDENT

The voluntary offer to waive evidence of insurability is a special offer and is NOT to be considered a precedent.

4—GRACE PERIOD IS NOT EXTENDED

This offer is NOT an extension of the regular 31-day grace period, and does NOT continue the protection in force. If the payment is not made before death of the Insured occurs, the situation is the same as though the offer had not been made.

If advantage of this Late Remittance Offer cannot be taken before it expires, application for reinstatement may still be made thereafter by using the form on the other side of this Notice of Life Insurance Lapse.

Please
MAKE A QUICK CHECK
BEFORE LATE REMITTANCE OFFER EXPIRES

L 1157 3
(ADULT)

ADULT REINSTATEMENT APPLICATION

SUBMITTED IN CONNECTION WITH POLICY No._____

A written answer to each question is necessary—do not use check marks.

1. Are you now free from disease, in sound health, and without deformity, loss, or impairment of limb, sight, hearing, and speech? (*If not. explain fully*)   Yes or No

2. What is your present exact height and weight?

    ....feet .... inches .... pounds.

3. Since the date of original application applying for this policy:

    (a) Has there been any change in your weight? (*If so, give details and explain loss or gain*)   Yes or No

    (b) Are you now or have you been under any kind of treatment or on a restricted diet for any complaint or cause? (*If so, explain fully*)   Yes or No

    (c) Have you had any unusual and recurrent pain or discomfort in region of chest or abdomen which caused you to take any home remedy, patent medicine, or drug, or to seek the advice of a physician, either formally or informally? (*If so, explain fully*)   Yes or No

    (d) Has any medical examiner or physician expressed an unfavorable opinion as to your insurability or health? (*If so, explain fully*)   Yes or No

    (e) Has insurance applied for on your life been declined, postponed or modified in amount, plan or rate? (*If so, explain fully*)   Yes or No

    (f) Have you made any claim for sickness, accident, or pension benefits? (*If so, explain fully*)   Yes or No

4. To what extent do you use alcoholic beverages?

5. (a) What is your present occupation and what are the exact duties?

    (b) What is your employer's name and address?

6. Have you ever flown or do you contemplate flight in any kind of aircraft, as a pilot, crew member, or student pilot? (*If so, explain fully*)   Yes or No

7. Have you ever been exempted or discharged from service in the military, naval, or air forces of any country for physical or mental reasons? (*If so, explain fully*)   Yes or No

8. Are you now a member of the National Guard or of any other branch or reserve component of the armed forces of any country? (*If so, explain fully*)   Yes or No

9. Give names and addresses of the physicians you usually consult:

10. *To explain your answer to any question herein, give details in this space or in a separate letter.*

11. State below the particulars of ALL diseases, injuries, ailments, or surgical operations which you have had or for which you have been under treatment, observation, or diagnostic study since the date of original application applying for this policy.

Disease, Injury, Ailment, or Surgical Operation	Date—Month and Year	Complications	Duration and Date of Recovery	Remaining Effects	Medical Attendant's Name and Address

12. Has a physician, specialist or other practitioner been consulted by or for you, or have you been under medical care, since the date of original application applying for this policy, for any reason not stated above?   Yes or No (*If so, explain fully*)

Dated this_____day of_____ , 19____ at_____

_____   _____
Signature of Witness   Personal Signature of Applicant

F. Glossary of Legal Terms

A

Absolute assignment. An irrevocable transfer of all ownership rights under an insurance policy from the owner to another person.

Accidental death. Death as the result of accidental bodily injury; that is, injury that is unintended, unexpected, and unusual.

Accidental means, death by. Death resulting from a cause that is accidental, so that both the cause and the result are accidental.

Adjective law. The law concerned with the legal procedures to be followed in enforcing or defending one's rights.

Ad litem. For the suit; thus, a guardian *ad litem* is a person appointed to represent a minor or other incompetent person in prosecuting or defending a suit.

Administrative law. That area of public law that deals with the various departments of the government and prescribes the way they operate. It is especially concerned with the collection of taxes, citizenship and naturalization, police, the public safety, etc.

Administrator of one's estate. The person appointed by a court to administer the estate of a person who dies without a will.

Administratrix. Feminine of "administrator."

Adverse claimants. Persons claiming or asserting rights in opposition to each other.

Affiant. The person who makes and signs an affidavit.

Affidavit. A written or printed statement, sworn to or affirmed before an officer having authority to administer such an oath or affirmation.

Agent. A person having the power to represent and act for another in the creation or modification of contracts between the person represented and others.

Aleatory contract. A contract of which the results, in the sense of advantages and disadvantages, depend upon the happening of an uncertain event. As contrasted with a commutative contract, it is an agreement under which one party may, and often does, receive a benefit greatly in excess of the value he has parted with.

Ambulatory. Movable, revocable. Customarily used, in discussing wills, to denote the power a testator has to change his will at any time he wishes throughout his life.

Answer. A pleading in which the defendant in a suit sets forth the grounds for his defense.

Anticipatory breach. A breach of contract that becomes evident before there is a present duty to perform. It must be clear that the promisor will refuse or will not be able to perform the contract as promised, and thus it gives a present right of action.

Apparent authority. In agency law, the authority the agent is permitted by the principal to *appear* to have.

Assignee. The person to whom an assignment is made.

Assignment. The transfer of a *chose* in action from one person to another. If all ownership rights are transferred irrevocably, it is said to be an absolute assignment. If all or a part of the rights are transferred on condition that they shall return to the owner upon the repayment of a debt, it is said to be a collateral assignment.

Assignor. The person by whom an assignment is made.

Averment. A positive statement of fact in pleadings.

Avoid. To annul or cancel.

B

Bankruptcy. The status of one who has been brought within the scope of the bankruptcy law, either by his voluntary act or by reason of the actions of his creditors.

Beneficiary. The person for whose benefit a trust is created; one who receives the benefit. In insurance, the person to whom the proceeds of an insurance policy are payable. In insurance, an irrevocable beneficiary is one whose designation cannot be revoked and whose interest under the policy cannot be reduced, as by a policy loan or cash surrender, without his or her consent. A revocable beneficiary is a beneficiary whose designation can be revoked by the policyowner. A revocable beneficiary, as such, has no rights under the policy and, in most jurisdictions, is said to have a "mere expectancy."

Bequeath. To give personal property to another by will.

Bilateral contract. A contract under which obligations are assumed by both contracting parties.

Binding receipt. A premium receipt which provides life insurance from the date of the receipt, subject to the insurer's right to terminate the coverage if the proposed insured is found to be uninsurable.

Burden of proof. The necessity of affirmatively proving a disputed fact or facts by a preponderance of the evidence.

C

Case law. That area of the law that is made up of reported cases.

Cause of action. Any set of circumstances that will support an action at law.

Cestui que trust. The person for whose benefit a trust is created.

Chose in action. A right of action for the possession of personal property.

Claimant. A person who claims or asserts a right or interest.

Collateral assignee. The person to whom a collateral assignment is made.

Collateral assignment. A transfer of some or all of the rights of the owner of intangible personal property as security for the payment of an indebtedness, usually on condition that if the debt is repaid as promised the assignment will be extinguished.

Common disaster. A disaster in which more than one person loses his or her life.

Common law. In a general sense, that body of rules, principles and maxims developed and followed by courts in English speaking countries over many hundreds of years. The term is sometimes used to distinguish case law from statutory or legislative law. It is also used in a very general sense to refer to a heritage of principles and concepts concerning customs, public policy, and basic ideas of justice that are followed by courts of common-law jurisdictions.

Community property. In community property states, property of husband and wife owned in common. It consists of all property acquired by either spouse during the marriage, other than by gift or inheritance.

Commutative contract. A contract under which each of the contracting parties gives and receives relatively equivalent values.

Conditional receipt. A receipt given for money received in connection with a life insurance application, which provides for coverage prior to the date a policy is issued if specific conditions are met.

Condition. A provision in a contract which has the effect of modifying, suspending, or revoking the principal obligation if a future, uncertain event happens or fails to happen.

A condition precedent is a condition which must happen or be performed before the obligation becomes effective.

A condition subsequent is a condition which, if it happens, takes away rights already vested or established.

Conservator. A guardian.

Consideration. As used in contracts, any act or promise requested and received by the promisor in exchange for his promise. It is sometimes stated as any "benefit to the promisor or detriment to the promisee."

Contract of adhesion. A contract drafted by one party and accepted without modification by the other.

Counterclaim. A claim presented by the defendant in an action and growing out of the transaction or contract on which the plaintiff's action is based.

Counteroffer. In contracts, the counterproposal made by an offeree to an offeror whose offer he does not wish to accept in the form in which it was originally made.

D

Declaratory judgment. A judgment that declares the rights of the parties or expresses the opinion of the court on a legal question but which does not require that any action be taken.

Defendant. The person against whom an action or suit is brought.

Demurrer. A formal answer in an action at law in which the defendant, in effect, admits the truth of the facts as stated but asserts that they do not constitute an actionable wrong or otherwise justify proceeding with the action.

Devise. A gift of land or realty by the last will and testament of the donor.

Disclaimer. The refusal or renunciation of an interest, right, claim, or power. Also, the document in which the renunciation is expressed.

Domicile. That place where a person has his fixed and permanent home and to which, when he is absent, he intends to return.

Donee. The person to whom a gift is given.

Donor. The person by whom a gift is given.

Dry trust. A trust which requires no action on the part of the trustee to carry out the terms of the trust.

<h3 style="text-align:center">E</h3>

Endorsement. A writing on the back of an instrument. In the law of negotiable instruments, an act by which title to the instrument is transferred.

Equitable assignment. An assignment which, though not enforceable at law, will be given effect in equity by the application of principles of equity.

Equitable estoppel or estoppel *in pais*. That form of estoppel resulting from the conduct of a person who has knowingly misrepresented or concealed material facts or permitted such misrepresentation or concealment, with the intention that another will act in reliance upon such information, where the latter does so act and suffers damage as the result. In such cases the guilty person is precluded from asserting the truth as a defense.

Equitable remedies. Remedies such as specific performance, reformation of a contract, etc., which at one time were available in a court of equity rather than a court of law.

Estoppel *in pais*. See equitable estoppel.

Executor. The person named by a testator and appointed by the court to dispose of the testator's property in accordance with the terms of his will after his death. (Feminine form, executrix.)

Exemption statutes. State statutes having as their purpose the exemption of certain classes of property from the claims of creditors.

Exoneration statutes. Statutes, particularly in community property states, that make payment in good faith to a known claimant sufficient to discharge a life insurer's liability, if a person having an adverse claim under community property laws does not assert it before such payment is made.

<h3 style="text-align:center">F</h3>

Fiduciary. A person occupying a position of trust and confidence with respect to duties and responsibilities which he is to discharge with the highest degree of good faith for the benefit of another.

Fraud. In general terms, any misrepresentation of a material fact, made knowingly and intentionally, with the intention that another will rely upon it, when that person is entitled to rely on it, does so rely, and suffers injury as the result.

<h3 style="text-align:center">G</h3>

Gift *causa mortis*. A gift in contemplation of one's death, made when death seems imminent, and made on condition that if the donor does not die as anticipated of the illness or injury then suffered, ownership of the property reverts to the donor.

Gift *inter vivos*. A voluntary transfer of property from one living person to another without consideration.

Guardian. In common usage, one who legally has the care and management of the person or the estate, or both, of another person who, because of age or disability, is incapable of managing his own affairs.

I

Interlocutory decree. A provisional or temporary, not final, decree.

Interpleader. A court procedure under which a person or corporation holding money or property belonging to another, but which two or more persons claim, may pay the money into court and require the claimants to prove their claim and thus settle the question in one proceeding rather than several.

Intestate. Without making a will. Often used to refer to the person who died without a will.

Irrevocable beneficiary. See Beneficiary.

J

J.N.O.V. Judgment *non obstante veredicto*. Judgment notwithstanding the fact that the verdict of the jury was to the contrary.

Jurisdiction. The power and authority of a court to hear and decide controversies.

L

Legatee. A person who receives a gift of personal property by last will and testament.

Lien. A hold or claim by one person on the property of another as security for a debt or charge.

Living trust. A trust created and to take effect during the lifetime of the grantor, as contrasted with a testamentary trust, which is created by an appropriate provision in the grantor's will and, therefore, does not become effective until his death.

M

Ministerial act. An act performed in a prescribed manner, without the exercise of personal judgment or discretion.

Minor. An infant; one who is under the age of legal competence.

N

Necessaries. With reference to the contracts of infants, things that are proper and suitable to the person according to his circumstances and situation in life.

Negotiable instrument. A written promise or request for the payment of a certain sum of money to order or to bearer. A negotiable instrument is transferable without assignment, by endorsement and delivery or by delivery only.

O

Offeree. The person to whom an offer is made.

Offeror. The person by whom an offer is made.

P

Pari delicto. Equal in guilt or fault.

Parol evidence rule. The rule that if a contract has been reduced to writing it is presumed that any preceding oral contract, if there was one, was merged into the written contract, and parol or extrinsic evidence will not be admitted to vary or contradict the terms of the written instrument.

Patent ambiguity. An ambiguity that is evident on the face of an instrument without explanation or further evidence.

Per curiam. By the court; thus an opinion written by the whole court rather than by one judge.

Personal property. Movable property, as contrasted with real property, which is land and any buildings attached to it.

Plaintiff. The person who initiates an action at law.

Pleading. The procedure followed by the parties to a suit or action at law, by which they alternately present written statements, each responding to the preceding one, until they arrive at a single contention, affirmed by one and denied by the other, known as the "issue," which is the basis for the trial.

Pledge. A deposit of personal property as security for a debt or other obligation.

Power of appointment. The power given to a person who is not the owner of real or personal property to appoint or designate a person or persons who will receive it.

Precedent. A case decided by a court of law which is considered as authority for a similar decision in a later case presenting the same factual situation.

Presumption. An assumption without actual proof but reached by inference based upon facts that are known and supported by common sense and a knowledge of human nature and motives known to influence human conduct.

Prima facie case. A case which is sufficient on the face of it to justify a decision in favor of the person on whose behalf it is presented and which can be defeated only by rebutting evidence on the part of the other party.

Pro tanto. For so much; as far as it goes.

Probate estate. The estate over which a probate court has jurisdiction.

Promisee. The person to whom a promise is made.

Promisor. The person by whom a promise is made.

Proximate cause. That cause which in a natural and continuous sequence, unbroken by any intervening efficient cause, brings about the injury or death and without which the result would not have happened.

Q

Qui facit per alium, facit per se. He who acts through another acts himself—that is, the acts of the agent are the acts of the principal.

R

Ratify. To adopt or approve and confirm.

Reformation. An equitable remedy permitting an agreement which through error, mistake of fact, or inadvertence, does not express the intention of the contracting parties to be re-formed to express that intent.

Rescission. The act or legal procedures necessary to cancel, annul, or abrogate a contract.

Rescind. To cancel or annul.

Residuary legatee. The person who receives "all the rest, residue and remainder" of the personal property left by the testator after payment of debts and particular legacies.

Res nova. A new case; a question not previously decided.

Revocable beneficiary. See Beneficiary.

S

Spendthrift trust. A trust established to provide a fund for another which includes a provision intended to secure it against his improvidence and protect it for his benefit against the claims of his creditors.

Stare decisis, **doctrine of.** The practice of looking to prior court decisions as precedents in deciding later cases, so that when a decision has been made in connection with a given set of facts, that decision will be followed in later cases involving identical facts unless there are strongly compelling reasons for a different decision.

Statute of frauds. A statute originally enacted in England in 1677, which has been enacted with some modification by most of the states in the United States. It commonly provides that no action shall be maintained on certain specified kinds of contracts unless there is a note or memorandum of the agreement, signed by the person to be charged or by his authorized agent.

Substantive law. That part of the law that creates, defines, and regulates rights; as contrasted with adjective law, which sets out the procedures for enforcing rights or obtaining relief if they are violated.

Summons. A legal document issued by the court and served upon the defendant, notifying him that an action has been commenced against him and that judgment will be given against him unless he answers the complaint.

T

Tender. An offer of money or property.

Testamentary disposition. A disposition of property, without consideration, which is not to take effect until the death of the grantor.

Testamentary trust. A trust created by an appropriate provision in the grantor's will and therefore not to become effective until his death.

Testator. One who makes a will.

Testimonium clause. The clause in a legal instrument which customarily reads: "In witness whereof, the parties hereto have hereunto set their hands and seals."

Tort. A legal wrong or injury independent of contract, for which an action will lie.

Trust. An arrangement under which one person holds and administers property for the benefit of another or others.

Trustee. The person appointed or obligated by law to execute a trust.

U

Uniform Simultaneous Death Act. A law developed and enacted to govern in situations where two or more people die under such circumstances that it is not possible to say who survived the other or others.

Unilateral contract. A contract under which only one of the parties has an obligation or promises to be fulfilled.

V

Vested rights. A right is vested when it has become the property of some particular person or persons as a present interest and cannot be divested without his or their consent.

Vitiate. To impair; to destroy or annul.

W

Waive. To surrender a right or privilege.

Ward. A person, especially a minor, who is placed by law under the care of a guardian.

Warranty. In the law of insurance, a statement or condition relating to a fact or action to be taken in relation to a contract, which fact must be exactly true or which action must be taken in exactly the manner stated or the contract will be void.

Index of Cases

Index

This book has been set in 10, 11, and 9 point Caledonia, leaded 2 points. Part numbers are in 24 point Venus Medium Extended and chapter numbers are in 30 point Venus Bold Extended. Part titles are in 18 point Venus Bold Extended and chapter titles are in 18 point Venus Medium Extended. The size of the type page is 27 by 45½ picas.